Advance Praise for
How Does That Make You Feel?

"Funny, smart, frustrating, heartbreaking, but above all honest—true tales of that most private of relationships between therapist and client. Told from both sides of the couch, but always from the heart."

—Judith Sills, author of *The Comfort Trap*

"This book is as engrossing and illuminating ▯▯▯lume of good short stories. It explores the hidden, f▯▯▯▯▯▯'-s, crannies, and complications of the co▯▯▯▯▯▯▯▯▯ ▯ between therapist and patient, a subjec▯ ▯▯▯▯▯▯▯▯▯ ▯ be endlessly fascinating. One feels the pre▯▯▯▯▯▯▯▯▯ ▯in's humane, sensitive, and experienced ▯▯▯▯▯▯▯▯ n that is wide-ranging and comprehensi▯▯▯▯▯▯▯▯▯ ▯ issues. Many talented writers on view ▯▯▯▯▯▯▯▯ ▯rovoking moments. You don't have to have ▯▯▯▯▯▯▯ ▯ch to enjoy this book. All that is necessary is an intere▯▯ ▯eople and the struggles of modern life."

—George Hodgman, bestselling author of *Bettyville*

"With rapier wit and a big dose of humanity, Sherry Amatenstein and the amazing writers she has assembled ask us to look at ourselves. And I think we'll be better for it."

—Jenny Lumet, actress and award-winning screenwriter of *Rachel Getting Married*

"Reading these fascinating, no-holds-barred essays, it's sometimes hard to tell who is 'crazier'—the patients or the therapists!"

—Lee Woodruff, *New York Times* bestselling author of *Perfectly Imperfect*

"These searingly honest essays brilliantly capture the uniquely complicated relationships that therapists and patients share in the course of trying to navigate our lives. If you've ever revealed your most private hopes, dreams, fears, and longings with a stranger in a high-backed chair—or been that stranger in a high-backed chair—you'll be so engrossed by these stories that you may end up skipping your session."

—Lori Gottleib, bestselling author of *Marry Him*

"*How Does That Make You Feel* is an eye-opening look at therapy. With essays ranging from the profoundly emotional to the downright hilarious, we can all learn something about a relationship so many of us hold dear, that between a therapist and their patient. Invaluable insight that will undoubtedly foster better understanding all around."

—Mara Schiavocampo

"As a person who's been through therapy—and both loved, and hated, and then loved and hated it again—this book speaks to the experience on the couch unlike anything I've ever read, and reading it has given me not only a better understanding of the therapeutic process, but also a better understanding of myself."

—Kevin McEnroe, author of *Our Town*

How Does That Make You Feel?

How Does That Make You Feel?

TRUE CONFESSIONS FROM BOTH
SIDES OF THE THERAPY COUCH

EDITED BY Sherry Amatenstein

SEAL

"The Pregnant Therapist" by Jessica Zucker originally appeared in *The New York Times*.

An earlier version of "Changing the Story" by Jonathan Schiff originally appeared in *The New York Times*.

Note: Throughout this book, names and identifying details have been changed to protect the privacy of individuals.

ISBN 978-1580056243

Library of Congress Cataloging-in-Publication Data is available.

Published by
SEAL PRESS
An imprint of Perseus Books
A Hachette Book Group company
1700 Fourth Street, Berkeley, California
Sealpress.com

Cover and Interior design by Tabitha Lahr
Icon art © Tim McGrath

Printed in the United States of America
Distributed by Publishers Group West

This book is dedicated to my parents, whom I miss every day. Bernard and Bernice Amatenstein were supportive of my midlife decision to become a shrink as well as the reason I needed one myself.

This book is also dedicated to all those in need of and dispensing mental health treatment (the two are not mutually exclusive!). There is no shame in admitting to emotional problems, and I hope one day soon there will be no stigma attached to such an admission.

CONTENTS

Introduction: We're All Crazy

| *Sherry Amatenstein* |

*We're all crazy and the only difference between
patients and their therapists is the therapists
haven't been caught yet.*

—Max Walker

*I maintained that psychiatry, in the broadest
sense, is a dialogue between the sick psyche and
the psyche of the doctor, which is presumed to
be "normal." It is a coming to terms between the
sick personality and that of the therapist, both in
principle equally subjective.*

—Carl Gustav Jung

Of course you wonder what your therapist thinks of you.
Of course your therapist has thoughts about you that on
occasion practically leap off his or her tongue into your ears.
How could it be otherwise—flawed humanity is the shared

cloth of the healer and the one with the naked psyche twisting in the room. And with personal details about your shrink just a Google search away, it is tougher and tougher to keep Oz behind the curtain.

But Internet searches only reveal external factoids. The drive behind this book is to bring daylight to both sides of an artificial (payment is rendered) yet profound joining. Imperfect as this joining is, it is deeply intimate as well as collaborative—at times creating a connection that can feel purer than any other bond.

Yet the bond is illusory, as therapeutic boundaries serve to contain the "relationship" to the sanctioned forty-five to fifty minutes per serving. Thus:

* Sex is a no-no.
* Grabbing a few drinks together after a session, a no-no.
* Also a no-no—lending one's shrink a five spot (though I once lent a patient money).

These rules exist for a reason. Therapy is about the patient. Or it should be.

Again, that doesn't mean patients are not stark raving curious about their shrinks, and their shrinks' lives. What is this human magnet for revelations about your demons, desires, and most shameful secrets really like? And what does the human magnet really think about you?

How Does That Make You Feel will satisfy the itch for answers. The book includes thirty-four essays written by renowned writers who are or were patients, as well as by therapists.

Within these pages, patients will find a healthy way to examine their fascination with the "human" side of therapists without jeopardizing the relationship with their own shrink.

Within these pages, therapists will find a cathartic release from the pressure of pretending they can do this work without a very human cost. Therapists are not robots, and what patients think of them matters, no matter how hard we try to detach.

The whoosh of air released in these no-holds-barred essays is powerful enough to carry Dorothy back to Kansas sans shoes. In "I Really, Really Hate You," Beth Sloan (a pseudonym for obvious reasons) devotes her acid pen to recounting exactly what runs through her mind when her patient, the crown princess of narcissism, jabbers on. "Triplex" is Adam Sexton's hysterical account of the weirdness of living with his then-girlfriend and her then-therapist, while Patti Davis's "The Therapist Who Shouldn't Be One" details the havoc that ensued when the man she was dating suggested she visit his therapist to help unravel the family dysfunction that was part and parcel of growing up Reagan.

The emotional kaleidoscope dips the other way via essays including Priscilla Warner's moving ode to her beloved deceased therapist in "I'm Afraid Our Time Is Up" and Molly Peacock's "Not Even a Smidgen," revealing how her relationship with her therapist of nearly forty years morphed into friendship after the latter's career-ending stroke. And wonder no more what it feels like on our end when you terminate us. (Are you convinced your therapist either does a "happy dance" or works to keep you forever so as not to lose income?) Martha Crawford reveals all in "Back into the Wild."

Perhaps the boundary blurring began in the media with Dr.

Melfi and her six-season pas-de-disgusted with Tony Soprano, in which viewers were privy not only to her true thoughts about the gangsta patient but her personal trials. Now, in the era of Dr. Drew and mockumentary shows like Lisa Kudrow's *Web Therapy*, wherein the therapist who needs more help than her patients offers three-minute shrinking sessions, the pendulum is swinging too widely toward cheapening the sanctity of the therapeutic relationship.

This anthology will humanize "shrinks" to the millions of "shrunks" agitating to know the real deal, but will not trivialize the process. In a pinch, who knows, *How Does That Make You Feel* may serve as a worthy (and less expensive) substitute for a therapy session.

Legend of Icons

therapy-givers

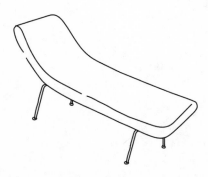

therapy-goers

I Really, Really Hate You

| *Beth Sloan* |

Marcelle (name changed for reasons that will soon become clear) throws herself into the brown leather chair in front of my well-ordered desk, Chanel and Prada shopping bags swinging from both arms.

Sweat trickling off her immaculately threaded brows and huge tears running down her cheeks, she begins to scream, "You know what, Dr. Beth. I hate his fuckin' guts." Choking on her saliva and copious tears, Marcelle is barely able to catch her breath. "He's a cheap fucking bastard. I have to live on the stupid allowance he gives me every week—$2,500 bucks." Marcelle receives a weekly allowance from her husband because she is known to spend enormous sums of money on a whim, on one occasion almost bankrupting the family.

Although I believe that diagnosing patients often pigeonholes them into a particular treatment modality, which may or may not be thoroughly effective in treating what is likely a

1

cocktail of diseases, I find it almost impossible to refrain from diagnosing Marcelle with terminal narcissism. Narcissistic Personality Disorder (NPD) is among the most difficult to treat, due to a narcissist's resistance to even gentle criticism. Narcissists believe they are the center of the universe, requiring constant admiration and accolades while treating the people in their lives like servants. They often create lies about their accomplishments in order to fulfill their fantasies of self-worth. Sadly, underneath all this hubris lies a frightened and abused little child who has built illusions of grandeur to surround and protect a fragile ego from further hurt and abuse.

Marcelle is the daughter of a businessman with ties to organized crime, who showered her with material goods and constant accolades practically from birth. A story she enjoys repeating is that her father bought her first pair of diamond earrings when she was four, followed the next year by a mink coat. She would wear them to school and pretend she was Queen Elizabeth and all the students and teachers were her subjects. Marcelle's father is a chronic adulterer, while her mother is a functioning alcoholic who, while drunk, often delivered hard, twisting pinches to her daughter's arms for trifles like not eating her broccoli rabe and making a "yuck face." Not only were Marcelle's arms almost continually black and blue, but these repeated assaults contributed to deep personality and emotional issues.

Also bruising to the little girl was her mother's constant labeling of her adored father as "a no-good bum and a liar." Marcelle stopped speaking to her mother three years ago, after the older woman insisted that Marcelle cease communication with her father because he is still cheating, even though the couple now live in an assisted living facility.

The pain Marcelle endured from that maternal breach drove her into therapy with me just under two years ago. Lately, we end up talking a lot about her marital unhappiness.

I say, "Marcelle, during your and John's last joint therapy session, you were the one who came up with the $2,500 weekly allowance figure, correct? Now you are saying it's not enough money to cover your personal expenses?"

"Barely," she screams while pounding her fists on my desk a bit too close to my face. "Fuck you, Dr. Beth, why do you always take his side?"

Alas, that's her interpretation. I am so uncomfortable with people, especially patients, who violate my personal space. I want to grab both those skinny arms and yell into her plastic surgery–altered face, "Don't you ever get that close to me again with your fists!" However, a good shrink accepts a patient's behavior toward her as long as there is no physical harm and then tries to help the patient become cognizant of and reflect on her bad behavior. But Marcelle's aggression toward me makes me sweaty, viscerally tense, and meek.

I manage to say, "Marcelle, why do you think I am taking John's side?"

"Because you always fucking do. You think I'm a cheap whore, don't you?"

"Of course not. Why do you think that's my opinion of you?"

Is that a tear I see threatening to fall down that chiseled porcelain cheekbone?

"Sometimes I pick up a vibe from you . . . the 'I hate this chick' vibe." She recovers from her moment of vulnerability: "Beth, what the fuck? Were you born yesterday? Do I have to explain every goddamn thing to you in detail?"

My reply is a soft, "Yes."

A familiar feeling rises into my chest, the nauseating feeling of anticipating humiliation. The popular girls in junior high used to look at me the way Marcelle is looking at me now. A slap or a punch in the stomach was soon to follow. I always choked back my tears and never let them see me cringe. During that time in my life, I developed asthma, certainly an emotional reaction to their bullying and a great excuse to miss a good amount of school and avoid their wrath.

I take a puff of my inhaler and continue, "Why don't you and John discuss the allowance amount at home, the way we spoke about last week? Do you remember what we detailed?" I wheeze.

"Yeah, yeah, love and compassion," she sniffs. "Forget John and my cheapo allowance. I came here today to talk about my boobs." With that, Marcelle lifts her shirt to reveal two perfect breasts.

My chest tightens again as I frantically puff at my inhaler. "Why are you showing me your breasts, Marcelle?"

"Are you a closet lezzie, Beth? Is that why you look uncomfortable?" she asks.

"No, but I am still wondering why your breasts are out if you are not nursing, Marcelle."

"I want your opinion. They are too small, right, Beth?" she asks.

"Marcelle, breasts are not my specialty. Brains are, so why you are seeking my opinion about the size of your breasts?" I ask a bit forcefully. My hands are sweaty and shaky, so I lower them to my lap. "I think the real question here is, why don't you like your breasts?"

She doesn't reply, and I don't press for an answer. I never

feel like I have given Marcelle the best of me when she leaves a session. I rarely push the envelope during our weekly visits as I do with other patients. With Marcelle, I hold back to protect myself from the inevitable wrath and insults. A good therapist should not allow herself to be affected by a patient's acting out. The person is in therapy because her life thus far has made her unwell. Yet with Marcelle I become a coward and retreat.

As Marcelle adjusts and dresses herself, I flash back to a night when I was fourteen, listening to Cousin Brucie, sitting in my big Papasan chair, eating chips, legs folded in the lotus position, and thumbing through *Seventeen* magazine . . . My mother barged into my room wearing only a T-shirt. She lifted one leg onto my chair, revealing most of her naked vagina.

I was horrified when she said, "Do you see how my lips are hanging down like cow's udders? Having you did this to me. You made me ugly down there. I hope you were worth it!" Message delivered, she left the room, slamming the door behind her.

Has my drive for success been solely about proving to my narcissistic mother that I am indeed worth her sagging labia? I've discussed this incident at length in my own therapy, but it looks like I'll be bringing it up yet again during my next session.

"Hey, Beth, you here with me, or did my boobs scare you into a coma?" Marcelle jokes with a crooked smile.

"If I recall correctly, you had your last breast augmentation less than three years ago and it was quite painful. Why do you feel so dissatisfied with your body that you would put yourself through that again?"

She snaps, "How could you possibly understand? I bet you haven't looked at your tits in years."

Never has a more untrue statement been uttered. Just this morning I stood naked in front of the mirror in my closet, saddened by how my body has evolved over the years. Post-menopause, I look like a Peruvian fertility statue—round belly, large sagging breasts, heavy thighs. I can't muster a response to Marcelle, instead saying silently, *No Marcelle, I don't live a spa lifestyle like you do . . .*

"Guess what, Beth?" Marcelle is grinning from ear to ear. She tells me that her younger sister's husband dumped her "for a much younger chick."

"You appear to be happy about this, Marcelle." I am saddened by the information. I met Juliette during a family therapy session. Even though she was often the victim of Marcelle's acting out, I was impressed by the compassion she displayed.

"It's about time something went wrong for Little Miss Goody Two Shoes, especially after what she did to me," Marcelle said.

"What did she do?"

"You know, she got married before me. That's a fucking horrible thing to do to an older sister. What's worse, she made me her maid of honor, and I had to go the whole night with everyone asking me if I had a boyfriend." She ends on a triumphant note: "Ha, now she knows what it feels like to be humiliated in front of the family."

Someone suffering such an awful disease as narcissism deserves compassion from a therapist, yet so many times in my sessions with Marcelle I can't deliver. I understand her meanness and its origins, yet she makes me cringe. I think, *Marcelle Constantino, I really can't stand you!*

My mother was a teen mean girl who became my live-in bully. I was slim most of my youth, yet she made fun of my size 4 body—measuring my food and snacks on a Weight Watchers scale and calling me "Elephant Girl" if I gained two pounds.

In the throes of morbid depression after my first husband left me for a Playboy Bunny (they met at a bachelor's party at the Playboy Club), I was unable to eat without vomiting, my weight going down to a sickly looking 102. My mother thought I looked wonderful and would often say, "Divorce becomes you. Perhaps you should do this more often."

Did she think that she was being funny? Her lack of compassion and selfishness always broke my heart. I wonder if Marcelle is adding to her sister's broken heart, or if our time together has taught her to show a microcosm of compassion toward others. In general, narcissists are too involved in their own life drama to feel empathy for another human being.

I ask, "Marcelle, aside from feeling a sense of satisfaction about what happened to Juliette, how are you treating her right now? I'm sure she is in a great deal of pain."

Marcelle begins to cry again, pointing her finger in my face. "Listen, Beth," she shouts, "I have learned a lot from my sessions with you. Juliette is staying with me with her kids and her dogs and the boys' snakes and water dragons. You know why, because I have fuckin' compassion. Yeah, I feel bad, especially when she cries. Somehow I don't have the heart to make fun of her weight or big nose right now, okay?!"

Yes, very okay. "I'm proud of you, Marcelle, go on . . ."

* * *

A few months later, Marcelle terminates therapy. Her depression has lifted and she is "cured!" I put up no resistance, rather feeling a sense of joy that I won't have to see her again.

Marcelle taught me that the best thing I can do for myself is avoid narcissists and bullies whenever possible. I no longer choose to treat people with NPD, recommending them to therapists who have stronger emotional constitutions than mine. After all the years of my personal therapy, I still am not strong enough to endure emotional beatings and belittling.

As one of my brilliant therapists told me many years ago, "Sometimes understanding is the Booby prize!" She was right—to understand the deep psychological workings of an abuser is only a small part in the journey toward a "cure." It can take a lifetime. My journey continues.

Shrinking Around

| *Susan Shapiro* |

"You depended on Dr. Winters like a father figure," said the bespectacled therapist I was auditioning to be my new head doctor. "So his moving away shook your foundation, making you feel orphaned."

"What's so confusing is that he's fine and happy, so I'm sitting Shiva here by myself, feeling like I'm crazy to be hurt. He said we can email, Skype, or do phone sessions, but it's not the same," I blurted out.

"Do you always speak so quickly?" Dr. Glasses asked.

"I have three kid brothers, so I had to rush to get a word in edgewise. Do you always speak so slowly?"

"You should consider leaving Manhattan for someplace quieter, like the suburbs."

Next.

* * *

Some people went speed dating; I went speed shrinking. It started when I'd felt devastated by the relocation of Dr. Winters, the brilliant New York therapist who'd helped fix my life over the last dozen years. Then I'd realized he charged $200 a session while possible replacements on my medical network cost only $25 co-pay. *Screw him for deserting me*, I thought. For one overpriced Winters tête-à-tête, I saw eight shrinks in eight days, looking for his clone. I lived in Greenwich Village, so thousands of potentials popped up in my Google search within a fourteen-block radius—one building with three hundred therapist offices alone. On the eighth whirlwind intake appointment, I met a nice PhD with curly hair.

"Dr. Winters helped me quit smoking, toking, and drinking," I said. "While losing weight, a miracle."

"I can't compete with the ghost of Dr. Winters. And stogies are my weakness," said the candidate I nicknamed Dr. Cigar. He was kind and humble; I made a second appointment. He worked in the same building as my literary agent, who—hearing I was speed shrinking—said, "Write that down." I was glad I did. By age forty-eight, rejections for my fiction had depressed me for decades. But the fictionalization of my crazy quest for my next analyst was my big breakthrough.

* * *

I was overjoyed when my debut comic novel *Speed Shrinking* came out a year later. To promote it, I planned a party with eight shrinks, inviting writing students and friends to speed shrink as I had. I'd offer three minutes to spill their problems, and then a timer would blow a whistle. I hoped they'd buy my book and pick up business cards and leads to pursue a real session later.

I secured an eclectic mix of healers: an Indian psycho-pharmacologist, a Middle Eastern hypnotherapist, a Jewish Jungian astrologer, a Queens-based marriage authority, an Upper East Side sex therapist, a Reikian healer, and a Greenwich Village LGBT specialist. I was psyched Dr. Winters was coming too. When he canceled at the last minute, I was bereft, now needing someone to replace him on the couch and at my book gala.

A friend recommended Kenny Light, a thirty-nine-year-old known for his cheap, short-term behavioral bent, who was often on television and radio with the slogan "Kenny Light: Media's Most Popular Psychotherapist." Since I was dying for book press, he seemed a good match. I left him a message to see if he'd fill in the empty chair for the evening.

"I'd love to be your substitute shrink," Kenny Light said, returning my call.

Interesting choice of words, since he'd be the replacement for Dr. Winters, though only for my book bash. In his TV clips, Kenny looked tall, dark, and slender like Dr. Winters, but more hip. He seemed sharp enough to be my rebound shrink for one night. At the event, two hundred people crammed inside a Soho bookstore. I lined up a long row of eight little tables, so guests could meet the eight doctors. Kenny arrived, downtown chic in blue jeans, a white shirt, and a blue blazer. He had two men in tow.

"Sven and Arno are from the largest Swiss radio station. Hope you don't mind if they record it. We can post the link on their website and Tweet it. They have seventy million followers."

Kenny came with a media entourage to plug my book—how endearing. An aspiring press whore, I was already infatuated with this guy. Yet like a recent divorcée, I compared him to Dr. Winters. Kenny was twenty years younger, less intense, more casually dressed, and with better press connections. Another big plus—he wasn't leaving Manhattan. Kenny—and the party—was a splash.

"The LGBT psychologist said if I could come out to my parents, I can also tell them I lost my job," my student Erasmo told me afterward. "He's right. I can't live in shame. I'm calling them now."

"The sex therapist said not to worry about the twenty-year age difference between me and my boyfriend and focus on how kind and passionate we are together," said my pupil Riley—who decided to say yes to her beau's proposal.

"Wait! Don't you need to talk this out further?" I asked. "This is just an *introduction* to analysis."

A serious shrinkaholic, I made it clear I wasn't providing three-minute enlightenment. This was a chance to meet a therapist to click with long term. Like speed dating, you didn't wed after 180 seconds; you merely took someone's phone number. "Make a fifty-minute appointment next," I suggested, glad some attendees scheduled actual sessions. It was hard to get a good therapist. I'd originally found Dr. Winters through my husband's ex-fiancée, Eleanor, also a shrink. (Don't ask.)

I was proud to be turning novices on to psychoanalysis in a fun way, demystifying the process, and offering an array of therapists to pick from, some working on a sliding scale, all while plugging my novel. *Publishers Weekly* ran an article. Then came *The New York Times*, *Daily News*. Radio and TV bookers clamored for interviews. So did several heads of psychoanalytic institutes looking to expand their practices, along with anxious patients eager to cheat on their regular doctors.

My husband Charlie—who hated my impatience, disdain for small talk, and penchant for psychoanalyzing everyone—said, "You've invented the exact thing that only you were put on this planet to create."

I emailed Dr. Winters an update: "My event rocked! I want to do it again! Will you be in the next one?"

"Beware all excitement. It takes you out of yourself. You always have to go back to yourself," he wrote back.

What a downer. Unsure whether Dr. Cigar could be a shrink that stuck, I sometimes paid to see Dr. Winters when he was in town. But seeing him sporadically was inconsistent and confusing. When happier Kenny wanted to meet, I fantasized he'd become my new shrink. I asked where his office was. "I'll be in your neighborhood," he said. "I'll stop by your place at nine."

That could be more of a date than a business rendezvous. "You can meet my husband," I said, though Charlie had a late meeting.

"I read your novel. It was very intelligent without losing the engaging tone or humor," he said.

He had me at *very*. "Can you help me get more ink?" I asked when he came over.

"Actually, I have a book I want to write myself," he countered. "Let's collaborate."

I already had a solo book that I was desperate to promote. But this guy specialized in getting his face on the tube daily. "Let's hear your idea." I led him to the leather couch in my living room. I took out a notebook and pen like a shrink doing an intake session.

"Quick fixes, fast recovery time. I only see a patient once every two weeks. For two months at most."

"Why such a short time frame?" I asked.

"Most shrinks out there are full of shit," he said accusingly. "They overcharge and try to manipulate patients to become dependent on a long-term basis. I want to do a book that exposes that."

Ha! I was the exact *wrong* person to sell this idea—I was a therapy-lifer.

"Speed shrinking isn't advocating three-minute therapy," I clarified. "It's a fun party to turn young people on to committing to do the real, long, hard work."

"But you must know therapists who get their patients too dependent on them for long periods," he said.

I did know one: Dr. Winters. Yet I'd saved more than the cost of our therapy from not buying any more of the cigarettes, dope, and alcohol he'd made me quit.

"Do you mean psychiatrists or psychologists?" I asked.

"All of them," Kenny said. "Psycho-pharmacologists, therapists, Freudian analysts, social workers."

This guy was provocative, like Dr. Winters. I liked provocative. "So they're all money-hungry liars?" As a journalist, I often played devil's advocate to see how much a subject might reveal.

"It's a real racket." Kenny crossed his arms.

Trashing the therapeutic process I believed in, Kenny was indicting me. Yet given the pain I still felt from losing Dr. Winters, he could be right. "You want to write a screed called *The Therapy Racket*?"

"Yes, with a better title though."

I didn't mind arrogance in seasoned professionals. Dr. Winters was arrogant. But he was a genius with a PhD and thirty years experience. Had Kenny Light earned his attitude?

"You're a psychotherapist with just a master's degree?" I asked. "Your website says licensed professional counselor."

"What's your point?" Kenny asked.

"Your bio says you earned a two-year master's degree from a tiny school. After seeing patients for $50 to $100 dollars on a short-term basis for six years, you feel qualified to trash *all* doctors and PhDs? People could say you don't have the credentials to do that."

"Being right gives me moral authority."

"Ever been in therapy yourself?"

"Don't need it," he said.

"Married? Kids?" I asked. He shook his head no. "Ever lived with a woman?"

"I was engaged once. What's this have to do with a book project?"

"For a book on non-dependent therapy, I was curious about your emotional connections."

"Hey—are you speed shrinking me?" Kenny smiled.

I nodded. "What if the kind of therapy you're preaching is motivated by fear of commitment?"

"You're good," he said. "You sure you're not a therapist in hiding?"

"Writing teachers are like shrinks, but we get paid less."

He laughed. Good sign: he had a sense of humor and could take criticism.

"Look, I teach people to change quickly," he said. "That's why I love speed shrinking."

"You do get that it's to help people find a shrink, not do therapy in three minutes," I reiterated.

"Three sessions should do it," he said. "I tell my patients 'Don't Think, Do.' Write that down."

"Dr. Winters said, 'The only way to change is to change. Understanding follows.'" Why was I quoting the head doctor Kenny was supposed to make me forget?

"Mine's better. It's faster," Kenny bragged.

I usually liked fast. But Dr. Winters' words were a haiku. Kenny's were a Nike ad. Still, that could be good. He was commercial. And tech savvy.

"I say no to needy clients who want to see me weekly to nip the dependency in the bud," he said.

Did he just call his patients needy clients? Sounded like he was in advertising. "Dr. Winters used to say, 'An addict depends on substances, not people.'"

"I tell my clients to stop clogging up their minds with beer, pot, and cigarettes," Kenny said. We were fighting the Battle of Shrink Aphorisms.

"Dr. Winters' theory is, 'Underlying every substance problem I've ever seen is a deep depression that feels unbearable. It's not unbearable; it just feels that way,'" I recited like a pathetic broken heart on a first date babbling incoherently about her ex.

"How long were you seeing Dr. Winters?" Kenny asked.

"Twice a week for ten years," I admitted. "We still email, but it hurt when he left the city."

"I'm sorry," he said. "But see? You were too dependent on him."

He was right, I was. "Tell me more about the idea for your book."

Kenny shared the chapter headings: "Go for It," "Get with It," "Don't Overthink Everything," "Don't Be Dependent," and "Live Your Dream Life." I visualized our self-help project. But each simple sentence Kenny said made me miss every word ever uttered by Dr. Winters. Even Winters' angry screeds had eloquence and complex rhythms.

Years before, Dr. Winters and I had come up with an idea for a book on substance abuse, the addiction version of Dr. Irvin Yalom's best-selling case studies, *Love's Executioner*. Yalom also published a book with a patient, fueling my fantasy of transforming from Dr. Winters' patient to his colleague, but we'd never finished ours. After Kenny left, I opened old computer files, rereading Dr. Winters' case studies of patients. I loved his stories of dangerous addicts he'd seen through relapse and recovery. When I was single and dating two guys named David, the wrong David sent roses. Now, caught between two shrinks, the wrong shrink was offering poetry.

To get over Dr. Winters' desertion, I needed a new shrink, a new book, or a new shrink to collaborate on a new book. I called my agent, Rob, mentioning I might co-author *Get Fixed Fast* with Kenny Light. Rob Googled Kenny and was impressed by his television links.

"With his platform, I bet we could get six figures from a thirty-page proposal," Rob said.

I summoned up my business acumen instead of indulging messy emotions, which had led me to the non-lucrative pursuits of poetry, teaching, freelance journalism, fiction, and expensive long-term therapy.

"I'll give Kenny your email," I told Rob that Friday. "If you like him, let's sign an agreement."

Monday Rob called. "I met with Kenny. I like him. But Kenny doesn't like *Get Fixed Fast*. He prefers *The Therapy Racket*. He said you hated that idea."

"I named it!" I said, half amused, half annoyed by Kenny's

title theft. "It could be fascinating coming from the sixty-year-old head of the American Psychiatric Association. Not a thirty-nine-year-old single childless guy with a master's degree from an unknown school, in the field only six years."

"Anyway, Kenny doesn't want to work with you anymore," Rob said. "He wants to do it himself."

"He told *you* that but not me?" I raised my voice. "And asked you to sell a solo project for him?"

"You wouldn't want me to sell it?" Rob asked.

"Go for it," I said, forgiving Rob for being an aspiring business tycoon, as we all were trying to be.

I wasn't surprised when Kenny dumped Rob for a bigger agent he'd met at my shrinking party.

Meanwhile, my next event got on NPR, BBC, CNN, and the CBS Morning Show—where the anchor interviewed me lying on a couch, a hit on YouTube. "It's the new Twitter therapy. Three minutes to fix your life!" the headlines idiotically blared.

"It's not three-minute therapy! It's just an intro!" I tweeted and posted, sending the links to Dr. Winters.

"Be careful; press is your new heroin," he warned.

"They love me," I answered. "What could go wrong?"

Then a famous screenwriter parodied the practice on his *PsychologyToday.com* blog post "Speed Shrinking, Oy, Vey!" Internet trolls chimed in with nasty comments. A Tufts newspaper trashed the "cultural phenomenon," as if anyone else had ever done it but me. The American Psychiatric Institute decreed that confessing problems to multiple psychoanalysts in public desecrated the profession's integrity since there was no patient-doctor confidentiality. A doctor at a diagnostic website labeled it "disturbing" to get counseling without being assessed long-term, as if threatened I was poaching his patients.

"It was a book party, you moron!" I emailed back.

"If you post angry responses, the blogosphere will hate you," my husband warned.

"These eggheads are ridiculous," I said. "I'm completely pro-therapy."

Indeed, Dr. Winters' astute advice and approval had mended my addictions, marriage, and food problems and unlocked my career potential. When he came to town and promised to speed shrink, I scheduled a special book event for him. He showed up—but we had a horrible fight when I got jealous of him treating my female protégée without asking me first. It turned out that sharing the concept of analysis with the world was easier than sharing my own confidant. I fired him from being a speed shrinker in the future and then paid for a session with Dr. Cigar to analyze the Oedipal triangle I'd unwittingly set up.

"I don't need Winters!" I yelled at Dr. Cigar. Alas, he wasn't so helpful with addictions. He advised me to "eat junk food whenever you feel like it." This led to late-night cupcake binges, as I became an icing addict. Fatter and high on sugar, I fielded messages from psychoanalytic institutes in Australia and Japan, asking me to run speed-shrinking parties. But I couldn't man them with quacks, nor could I screen foreign psychologists in different languages. I was afraid I'd gain too much weight to look good on the small screen.

Thanks to Kenny's connections, I got calls from Jay Leno and the Oxygen Network's hit reality TV show *Bad Girls Club*. Alas, they just wanted me to stage speed-shrinking parties for Leno and the Bad Girls to attend, offering fodder for their punch lines. But I was not a party planner! My mother was a party planner. (Let's analyze that.) Meanwhile, my shrink novel was sinking. As I stood with a stack of books ready to sign, hordes of people kept rushing past me to find a new guru gratis. They didn't even know it was a book. I'd become almost famous for the wrong thing.

So it seemed speed shrinking worked better in my plot than my life. When editors rejected my new novel, Dr. Winters was the first person I phoned. He called back immediately to talk it through (for free). We wound up finishing the addiction book we'd started, ironically called *Unhooked*. Ultimately, shrinking around for substitutes taught me the flip side of the spectacle: important people in your world are not replaceable.

My Shrink's Ultimatum

| *Laura Bogart* |

T he first call I make after leaving the hospital—where, for the last several hours, I have been tested for anything and everything that could be causing the sudden vise-tight squeezing of my chest; the dark drums of heartbeat railing, ever-quicker, in my ears; the dizziness, the nausea—is to Roberta, my therapist. I spill everything into the receiver: I was at my parents' house (for the occasional Sunday dinner, a concession with a boundary) when my heart became a piston and I thought I was dying. She murmurs with sympathy as I describe the stress tests, the MRI, the bloodwork that left my arm black and bruised. I confide that, even in my fear and pain, I wished that the matinee-idol doctor wasn't seeing me with limp, greasy hair, lunar-pale skin, and electrodes fixed to my chest—and I'm grateful when she laughs because now I can laugh. And that means I'm okay.

And I am okay, at least according to Dr. McFoxy: there are no signs of cardiac distress. He suspects I've had a panic attack, which isn't uncommon in women my age (early twenties), and it's borderline predictable in graduate students who, like me, are shouldering multiple part-time jobs as well as a full-time course load. When I tell him that I'm currently in counseling, diagnosed with PTSD and generalized anxiety, he nods and writes me a prescription for Xanax, a temporary succor until my next appointment with Roberta. A few days later, I am in her office, a white-walled room soothingly attired with Impressionist paintings and beach-style Pier One furniture, a space that has held my epiphanies and confessions, the first place where I could cry without fear.

She sits across from me with her shoes off and her legs tucked under her, displaying the kind of we're-all-just-girlfriends-here casualness that has inspired my trust. But there is something taut and sad in her eyes. Roberta says she cares about me so much (so very, very much), and that, after my hospitalization, she's realized that she hasn't cared for me in the best way. Because, in the year we've been seeing each other, she hasn't brought up "the weight"—the weight, of course, being my weight, the weight that, she says, leaves me vulnerable to "a real heart attack"—and she's scared for me. And Roberta isn't sure she can continue with me unless I'm committed to losing it.

* * *

I did not start seeing Roberta (not her real name)—a referral from my school's health office—because of anything to do with my weight. When I was a child, bearing my father's anger on my skin, enduring the hot breath and clammy hands of the neighbor boy who would pull me under a blanket patterned with Lion King characters and stick his fingers inside my vagina, my body became a rental space: a place I occupied, but did not own. I'd grown up in a hothouse of thwarted stoicism, a family where we'd eat and drink and yell and hit to quell our pain—anything and everything, really, except for talking about it.

However, when I was in my twenties, night terrors pushed me into counseling. Sometimes, my mind would come awake as my limbs locked in place and I would feel like a bird banging against a too-small cage; other times, I would wake up sweat-drenched and roaring. Then there was the night I came to in the shower, with the spray on at full blast. And I knew that my heart couldn't take another dream of drowning.

Roberta was not one of those nod-and-murmur shrinks I'd seen on TV, the patrician type who takes notes in front of you. She leaned forward in her seat and talked with her hands. Her words were unvarnished, blunt; even though she wore chic suits and heels that intimidated me, she was reminiscent of the stoop-washing women of blue-collar Baltimore, women whose brassiness and unconscious candor had always inspired me. Roberta had served as an advocate for domestic violence survivors, and when she told me, in no uncertain terms, that what went on in my house wasn't "discipline," I believed her. She was naked in her rage—at everything my father did, and everything my mother didn't do—and seeing someone be so angry on my behalf made me believe that I was worth a damn, and that I always had been.

Once a week, I watched this petite woman grow outsized with indignation, talking with a preacher's passion and thunder about all that I'd missed out on as a child, all that I deserved: a bedrock and a nest. Her tenderness for the pudgy little girl I'd roughly shoved into a back room of my mind gave me a new perspective on everything I'd been through, a fresh empathy for myself. I couldn't stand the sight of that girl waiting at the window, hands pressed against the glass, watching for someone, anyone, and taking a kiss, a fist, a cold hand invading a warm, wet place, as love. Roberta guided me through those long dark hallways of the soul and stood with her hand on my shoulder as I fit a key into each wrought-iron door. She would not let me describe my abuse in the vagaries of denial ("Well, you know, he touched me"); she made me describe it all in graphic, cathartic detail, and she wept with me until I was wrung out.

Then she told me it was time to take joy in my body, to let it serve my own pleasures and not someone else's sick curiosity. She let me borrow her personal copy of *The Hite Report* and coached me through the purchase of my first vibrator. When I confided I'd brought myself to my first orgasm—and the world clicked over from Kansas's grainy black and white to a Technicolor Oz—she jumped out of her seat and high-fived me. At times Roberta was the mother I'd wished I had, or, at least, the ball-busting auntie I needed. Which is not to say that our sessions weren't often excruciating—I would leave her office feeling as stripped and dried as winter bark. But this emptiness could be assuring: I was pulling out the memories before they could sink their stingers into my brain—wasn't I? My sleep was not immaculate, but it was longer and clearer (and accomplished on the dry land of my bed). I remember talking about Roberta with a friend, the look of awe that crossed his face as he said, "Roberta really loves you."

For months, that love seemed unconditional—and then Roberta started talking about calorie logs.

* * *

When I began my sessions with Roberta, I was (and, spoiler alert, still am) fat. Truly, objectively, tipping the scales at over 200 pounds, fat. I do not have a pillow-hipped Raphaelite build or a sweet little tummy. I am (and have almost always been) the recipient of many a side-eye, many a stop-and-stare. I didn't get this way due to any illness or injury, just calories in and calories staying put. Years of bullying and browbeating— the kids who called me Free Willy; the concerned teachers who asked if I "really needed" a cupcake at the class party; the ob-gyn who evangelized about stomach-stapling surgery while my feet were in the stirrups, chirping, "You can still have chocolate cake but in much smaller portions," as she jabbed the cold speculum inside me—had turned my body into a liminal concern, something to be dully, peripherally aware of, and cared for only when sick or bleeding. Certainly nothing that could be beautiful.

In the months after my panic attack, Roberta made my body the fulcrum of my discontent. As a child, I binged: cold pizza and Cheez-Its lightly warmed in the microwave, hand- fuls of crackers and mug after mug of ice cream. Roberta claimed—in a voice with the struck-bell brightness of revela- tion—that I was trying to get so big I'd be untouchable. Not only to men, she'd add, but also to myself—bearing this weight estranged me from my pain. She really cared about me, and she saw me denying myself all the things I deserved in life, all the things she wanted for me. I would never have a loving hus- band because of my weight. And because I would never have a loving husband, I could never have children. I would always be anxious and alone, unable to move through the world with the rightful confidence my intelligence and talent afforded me. I would sit, listening to her, hollowed with shock. Roberta had been so right about so many other things—and certainly, our culture agrees that there is only one way to look healthy. And beyond the issues of aesthetics created by the lady mags and the lad mags and the billboards and the cult of primetime TV, there is the belief that Doctor Knows Best. Questioning our caregivers, resisting treatment—that was just another way to stay sick.

Perhaps it was time to put away my skillets and my wine, even though cooking remained one of the few solitary pleasures I could squeeze in between day jobs, classes, and work on my master's thesis. Legions of my foremothers had lived on Lean Cuisines, no? And perhaps it was time to make use of the student gym, despite the ever-long lines for equipment that wasn't built to be comfortable for someone my size, and despite the co-eds who snickered as I huffed and puffed like the Big Bad Wolf.

But these good-for-me things sure didn't feel good. They made me feel smaller, and not in the way Roberta intended. My stomach shrank, hard and taut. Hunger made me into a set of wolf-jaws, always primed to snap, always tasting blood. I remembered myself as a little girl, the little girl Roberta said she loved so much, savoring a warm drizzle of caramel down my throat, licking the salt from my teeth. Those were the moments when I was nobody's daughter, nobody's good little girl. Nobody's victim. Nobody could tell me how to be, what to do. Those moments were about what I wanted, and even if it was in excess, it was mine. Those were the moments when I got to be alone with myself. The obliterating fullness felt like love.

Roberta would not consider that there had been something necessary, even sacred, in the binge because it allowed me to survive, to become the woman whose wit and intellect she praised. When I told her I wasn't sure I wanted children (I was, after all, only in my twenties), she said that would change. The woman who'd encouraged me to splurge on a magic bullet and push my body toward new constellations of pleasure shut her mind around an idea of hearth and home that might have seemed organic and healthy to her, but tasted like bad medicine to me.

When I told Roberta I enjoyed yoga far more than the treadmill (and would be more likely to stick with it), or that there could be men who might like me at a size 22 (and not just behind closed doors), a glazed, even disdainful look crossed her features. She explained that only fetishists (i.e., creeps) were into "obese women." Those two words fell out of her mouth as two hard chips of ice; they cracked on the floor and left a clear, cold reflection: in that reflection, I saw the faces of my father, my molester, my bullies—anyone who'd ever tried to bend my body to their will. Roberta may have loved me, but she didn't love all of me.

Now, every time I approached her office, my heart hammered into my throat, and I felt that noxious hiss of anxiety. She wanted me to get better, but better had a very specific dress size.

* * *

I let go of Roberta in fits and starts. My doubt was not a fist punching through the absolutism of her advice. It was a thin stalk pushing against the hard, parched ground of The Best For Me, slowly, tentatively, and then with a gathering strength. I began to bypass the sterile, freezer-burned Lean Cuisines and stand over my stove top, relishing the smell of rosemary potatoes sizzling in olive oil, swaying in place to Nina Simone as I sampled a piece. Over the course of a year, I went from weekly therapy sessions down to every other week—much to Roberta's consternation. She told me—in varying tones of anger, hurt, and genuine sorrow—that I was in denial. I would never get better if I didn't realize I had a problem.

But sitting down to dine and letting the strain of the day melt into the soft, earthy pleasure of a meal I'd prepared just for myself felt, at my core, like the self-care Roberta believed I'd only enact on a StairMaster. I stopped grinding my knees into bone dust on the machines, stopped subjecting myself to covert *oinks* as I waited for the treadmill. In the privacy of my living room, I did a gentle yoga DVD. My muscles, which so tightly held memories of the belt and breath under the hot blanket, began to yawn open. I learned to breathe into my aches. My sleep was untroubled. My heart steadied into a calmer rhythm. And that thin stalk of doubt finally pushed into the earth hard enough to let roots grow.

Roberta eventually told me she'd have to stop seeing me unless I saw a doctor and went on a formal weight-loss plan. She sat with her feet tucked under her, but now this familiar position had a kind of malevolent insouciance: what could this (naturally) thin woman ever understand what it was to lose weight—not just the blunt mechanics of calories in and calories burned, but the act of abandoning a body that had borne her through the worst moments of her life and given her some of her deepest pleasures?

Anger hissed through me like a green gas, the same anger Roberta wanted me to have for my father and my abuser, a righteous anger that told me I mattered. I started to remind her that I'd already had lab work done months ago, when I'd had my panic attack, and the doctor insisted that my "numbers looked good." Everything was fine, he'd said, physically speaking. I did not say anything then; still, that moment was the beginning of me being done, finally, unequivocally done. When I did not respond to her ultimatum, Roberta suggested that we end our sessions. She cried, and I cried, too. Her tears must have been of regret, anger, and disappointment—I know mine were. Mostly, though, I cried with relief.

Roberta may have cared about me, but she wasn't caring for me. She may have pitied the little girl who found solace in Rocky Road, but she never tried to understand her.

These days, I joke that despite her best intentions, Roberta has turned me into a self-actualized fat woman. Her stances about love and hope and health for a fat woman are the targets I load my bow against. I read books titled *Big, Big Love*, *Fat! So?* and *Hot and Heavy*. I eat steak and squash and drink whiskey, and yes, I will see the dessert menu, don't mind if I do. There are still days when I stare down my amplitude in a mirror and wish I could be thin (I do live in this culture, after all), but there are also days (more of them) when I savor the tidal roll of my hips as I walk. I have a new therapist to help me with what I call "mental upkeep," and I have told her straight up that I want to be well, but that, as God is my witness, I will never get on another StairMaster again. She goes by Eve, and, like her namesake, she's a free thinker. Eve believes that my panic attack wasn't brought on by a fear of dying from high cholesterol (or any of the other boogeymen of obesity); she thinks Roberta may have asked me to let too many demons out of too many closets far too soon.

Still, I remain grateful to Roberta for a few things—and chief among them is a photograph clipped to a refrigerator of myself as a little girl. Roberta wanted me to keep this girl in mind every time I opened the door. But I do not look at her softening cheeks and gently sagging chin, and long to change her. She has been told, too many times, that she is bad, that she deserved it, that she is wrong. I look into her green eyes, and I see something bright and beautiful: the will to survive. And I say thank you.

When the Therapist Cries

| *Juli Fraga* |

The first time I met Peter, George W. Bush was president. As a nation, we were recovering from the trauma of the terrorist attacks on September 11, 2001. People emotionally bruised from the aftershocks of this tragedy filled the community mental health clinic where I worked. Generalized anxiety, post-traumatic stress disorder, and major depression were common diagnoses among our patient population. I could tell Peter had come for another reason. In the waiting area, I noticed the walker beside him, the way his head flopped to the side, and the T-shirt, shorts, and sandals he wore even though it was nearly winter in Colorado. He shuffled as we walked into my office.

As we began our first session, I learned that two years earlier Peter's body had begun to betray him. At various times throughout the day, for no apparent reason, his hands and feet weakened, and he tripped easily. Peter had amyotrophic lateral sclerosis, also known as ALS or Lou Gehrig's disease, a neurodegenerative illness that interrupted the way his brain communicated with his muscles. He wore summer attire all year long because loose-fitting clothing allowed him to still dress himself. Since Peter could no longer tie his shoelaces, he opted for flip-flops despite the doctor's suggestion of ankle braces and sturdier shoes. In those ways, Peter was holding onto his independence, but his illness was not what brought him to therapy.

He needed help writing a letter to his daughter, a college-bound teen living in another state, whom he had not seen since she was a young girl. Lacking the dexterity to write with a pen, Peter literally needed help putting words to paper, but most important, my patient needed help finding the words to use in this most important missive of his life.

ALS was robbing Peter of his speech. As a result, he spoke very slowly; his words seeped out like the last bits of molasses at the bottom of a jar. His voice sounded like a vinyl record played at a too-slow speed. Most sessions, Peter spoke just a handful of sentences.

That year I became his therapeutic scribe, weaving his thoughts together, crafting the letter on his behalf. The first lines were the hardest. "I'm not sure how to begin," Peter confided.

I pulled my chair up close to allow him to see the words as I wrote. Peter began the letter many times, first with lines such as, "I have something to tell you," and "I am not sure how to say this," but he quickly asked me to erase those statements. We examined the origin of his writer's block. What did it mean to communicate with his daughter after nearly ten years of silence? How could he not be afraid of saying the wrong thing?

He called himself a neglectful father. A decade prior,

his wife had divorced him because of his excessive drinking. Peter's alcoholism ended a shared custody arrangement, and his wife and daughter moved out of state. Peter never pursued visitation because he felt undeserving of it.

Peter's story echoed my own: my father disappeared after my parents divorced. I was eight. The year I graduated from Central High School, I wrote my dad a letter. I told him about my upcoming graduation and that I was heading off to college. I asked why he had vanished but reassured him I was not angry, hoping to soften his reentry into my life. I sent my letter by certified mail to ensure that it reached him. It did. But he didn't reach back.

My childhood loss colored my experience with Peter, touching a tender spot inside me. I admired Peter's determination to reconnect with his only child after such a lengthy absence. I knew firsthand that composing the letter meant facing feelings of loss and grief. Writing to my father had reignited my longing for a paternal figure, and brought to life a sadness I'd buried deep inside.

Over many weeks, I learned to read Peter's cues like a traffic light. When I spoke, he nodded his lolling head in agreement or shrugged his shoulders when he was unsure of my interpretations.

I suggested that fear contributed to his writer's block, causing a case of emotional congestion that made it difficult to express himself. I knew my interpretation was risky. "Defended" patients like Peter, who have difficulty expressing their feelings, often shy away from feeling vulnerable, too. I sought to soften his resistance so that we could deepen our work.

Peter asked me to expand on my thoughts. I said he spoke

about his daughter in a distant way, as if he were report-ing the news. I asked if he felt this emotional armor kept him safe. He agreed with that analysis. I encouraged Peter to speak from his heart. What might he say if he weren't afraid?

My gaze met Peter's as he began the letter once more. "Try not to overthink it," I recommended. He looked away from me and dictated to his daughter, "I am sorry I have not loved you more."

The rawness of his words caught me off guard. My eyes welled up as I heard Peter finally express profound regret for abandoning his daughter. His apology mirrored the words I'd hoped to hear from my father. I saw more clearly how ALS was stripping away Peter's future. He had not loved his daughter enough and now, with time running out, how could he possibly repair this relationship?

My clinical training prepared me to welcome my patients' tears but taught me very little about how to acknowledge my own. A patient's tears are viewed as an opening for clin-ical exploration, but a therapist's tears may be interpreted as rare and problematic, indicating an over-identification with the patient's emotions—counter-transference on overdrive. Yet recent research by Dr. Amy Blume-Marcovici and her col-leagues states that the majority of therapists shed tears with their patients. In 2013, Blume-Marcovici surveyed 684 thera-pists in the United States and found that 72 percent had cried in session, suggesting tears are the norm rather than the exception.

"You're crying," Peter said with a hint of concern in his eyes.

I told Peter his words had touched me. The instant he spoke them, the man and father he was shone through.

Together, we explored what my tears meant to Peter. He

said they reassured him. For the first time, he'd expressed regret for abandoning his daughter, and his words were not criticized. He told me friends and family had asked, "How could you sever ties with your only child?" As a result of these questions, he rarely mentioned his daughter to anyone. Shame silenced him. I invited him to share more of his fathering story. And he did.

Slowly, he also talked more about his illness. He told me about the tears others had shed since his diagnosis. His friends cried because they felt sorry for him and were perplexed about how to offer help. They cried because they felt helpless. But Peter did not want anyone to solve his grief; he wanted a witness. I was that person. When I wept, my tears joined hands with his sorrow.

Each week in preparation for our session, I propped my door ajar before helping Peter walk from the waiting area to my office. I positioned two support pillows on the couch where he would sit and placed a glass of water on the table beside it.

We began our work in the early fall. One late spring day, Peter arrived in a wheelchair and asked if I liked his new ride.

By this time, Peter had shared the dreams he held for his daughter. He hoped she would become a veterinarian because he remembered that she loved animals. He wanted her to continue summer camping trips like the ones they took when she was a child; those were among his fondest memories. He longed to reconnect with her and schedule a visit, although the distance and his deteriorating health made that possibility unlikely.

I recognized that he viewed his college-age daughter as a child, yet I didn't touch upon the disparity between Peter's desires and her potential reality. I viewed his dreams as a pocket of his own imagination. That part of his psyche, where his daughter was held, shut down for years, had been resuscitated.

A few months later, during a sticky, hot summer afternoon, Peter arrived visibly upset. His doctor had recommended that he move into a care facility where he could receive around-the-clock assistance. The clinic where I worked was over sixty miles from Peter's new home, which meant our work would end prematurely.

We had a few weeks to say goodbye. We talked about the loss that accompanied the disease, and I empathized with how much ALS controlled Peter's life. A new insight emerged. Peter realized ALS mimicked the role alcohol once played. It, too, eclipsed his joy. Therapy morphed into a place of sanctuary where his feelings were welcomed. This haven allowed Peter to search for and find the devout words for his daughter.

Although I was saddened that Peter's therapy with me would end, I viewed our early goodbye as an opportunity to communicate my care for Peter. I felt heartsick that his disease swept him away just as we deepened our work in therapy.

On the day of our last session, we mailed the letter together. He wheeled beside me as I walked two blocks down the road to the little blue mailbox. I held the door open as he dropped the letter inside.

Back in my office, I told Peter I was honored to have shared our work together, witnessing his story and helping him bring it to life. At the end of the session, I cried as we said goodbye. No words were needed as he witnessed my tears; he simply looked at me and welled up, too.

After our sessions ended, I thought of Peter often. I wondered if his daughter contacted him, and if they reunited.

I worried about the fast progression of Peter's illness and hoped he received nurturing care in his new living facility. From time to time, I thought of calling the care center to check in on him. But Peter had a new therapist, and I didn't want to disrupt their work together.

The following year Peter's new social worker left me a message. It sounded ominous. "I have some information for you about your former patient, Peter," she said.

When we spoke that afternoon, her words conveyed my worst fear. Peter was dead. I wanted to ask if his daughter had ever reached out to him, but refrained because I didn't know if Peter had ever confided this intimate, most painful part of his life in their work together.

After the phone call, I took a quiet moment to remember Peter. I cried, recalling our walk to the little blue mailbox, and the letter that illuminated the emotional work he completed in therapy. I wished his spirit well and hoped he passed away peacefully. I also thanked Peter for the gifts he bestowed upon me: the opportunity to catch an intimate glimpse inside his life, offering me a front-row seat in a lesson of courage and love.

Over ten years later, Peter's presence lingers in my clinical work. The tears we shared gave me permission to openly express my emotion with other patients. Last year, when a woman's baby was stillborn, we cried together as she grieved. When patients who struggle with infertility finally become pregnant, we shed tears of joy. Crying has become an emotional cord between my patients and me, communicating an understanding that words cannot.

Lies I Told My Therapist

| Anna March |

The entire six years I saw my therapist, Lynn, I lied to her. Not little lies, the kinds I knew my friends told their therapists about exactly how many men they'd slept with or how much they'd had to drink at that party last weekend. I told big lies. That I'd gone to grad school, that I'd finished college. That my boyfriend—who became my husband while I was seeing Lynn—and I were happy. I lied in big ways and small, weaving a web of words to give her the person I thought she wanted, not trusting anyone, even a therapist, to care about me and my messy life.

I told her the lies I had been telling my mother since my early twenties, about ten years before I started seeing Lynn. I simply told Lynn the same story about my education and relationship I told the world so as to maintain the lies to my mother. Then I went about my business of doing the larger work with Lynn, which was, in the end, learning to feel I mattered.

Despite my lies, I came to know over the course of a summer season, our third together, that she cared about me for who I was and that made it possible for me to believe I mattered in the world. I hadn't until then. Sadly, it was too late, in my mind, to unravel my lies with Lynn by the time I felt comfortable enough to do so. But her seeing me for who I was made it possible for me, after I stopped seeing her, after everything in my life fell apart a few years later, to know somewhere in me that I had worth, something I hadn't known before her. I held on to that, and over the course of the next many years that faith in my own worth grew and I was able to rebuild my life. That's the germ of a life, after all, believing you matter. It's what Lynn gave me, despite my lies.

People remember moments and forget years, but I remember the small moments of the season when how I felt about myself changed. As well as the ethos of that time, which turned out to be love.

But first, we grieved.

JUNE 2001

On the day I realize Patty is going to die soon, I bring a bag of the season's first peaches to Lynn's office. I like therapy on Wednesday afternoons because the suite of offices Lynn shares with other therapists is uncluttered then, quiet. There's none of the early-morning or late-in-the-day hubbub I dislike.

On some level, I don't want to be Lynn's patient—just a close friend dropping over for a little chat—and the homey atmosphere of Wednesday afternoons makes this possible to imagine.

All winter and spring, my Wednesday routine was marvelous: I'd sleep late, read, have some lunch, see Lynn, then go over and visit Patty. Surreptitiously smoke a few cigarettes with her, have a snack, and then head home for a late nap.

But then, last month, Patty got sick and Lisa, Lynn's only daughter, committed suicide, and everything became confused and confusing. So I bring the peaches, perhaps to restore some sense of familiarity to Wednesday afternoons.

As if.

I'm late for the appointment, and I find Lynn in her office with another therapist, Judy, who isn't usually there on Wednesday afternoons. I sit down with them and offer peaches. Lynn shakes her head and mouths no, but Judy says, "Oh, sure."

We are several bites in before Lynn says, "Don't you need to wash those?" and then Judy and I start to laugh. "Naaaaah," says Judy. I'm relieved by her presence, and maybe Lynn senses that because I start talking.

"Patty's going to die."

It comes out before I even know it and somehow they both know we should just stay still. No one moves. I finish my first peach and then my second while telling Judy and Lynn the facts of the matter: Patty's worse; she's going to die; it's a matter of weeks.

It's hard for me to tell Lynn all of this. I'm so incredibly sad about Patty, and yet Lynn has just lost her child, so I feel awkward talking about my grief. It seems inconsequential in light of Lynn's, despite her telling me many times over the two weeks since she's come back to her practice after burying her daughter that she doesn't need her patients to take care of her. She says she is managing her own grieving and that working helps her. But still I feel ridiculous. I find myself instead wanting to ask about her daughter. What I know about Lisa has been pieced together from *The New York Times* obituary and the rare comment from Lynn.

Lisa was a Harvard-educated physician suffering from such debilitating MS that she "just couldn't go on," in Lynn's words. It was awful, that first week Lynn was back after the suicide. Just looking at her thin face, pulled tight for the first time since I had known her, was enough to make my own problems seem random, stupid even. While Patty is a central figure in my life, like a second mother, she is in fact nothing more than a close friend of the family. So I am relieved that Judy is there if only because I can pretend I'm telling her, not the grieving Lynn, all about my sadness.

It's also fitting to have two women here, one to help me access the information and emotions that I am protecting the other one from hearing. It mirrors my relationship with my mother and Patty. There are things that, for whatever reason, I can't discuss with my own mother, but I have spent hours and hours discussing them with Patty.

I'm sure I'm guilty of transference, or counter-transference, or counter-counter-transference. Freud would not approve. But that can wait until later to be sorted out. For now, I just know Patty is dying and I am feeling wrecked. Lynn is a wreck, too, having lost Lisa, and it is a relief to talk to Judy. I start dubbing her my "other therapist," just as Patty was always my "other mother."

I've always felt that I've had many mothers—my own, my grandmother, nuns, friends' mothers, boyfriends' mothers, aunts . . . There were always many women who surrounded me and carried me through my childhood, adolescence, and adulthood. I am the product of a million Eves who have mothered me in bits and pieces.

But Patty is the star of this parade. She is my Second Mother, my Wild Mother, my Cool Mother, my Sexy Mother, my Jewish Mother, my Vulgar Mother. My Other Mother.

Married, pregnant, and the victim of domestic violence by age seventeen, she left her abusive husband, gave birth in a barn, raised her son, met a "nice Jewish boy" and converted, married him, and had three more kids. In the late 1960s, when her oldest son started abusing drugs and alcohol, she founded a community-based addiction services program. She was quoted in *The Washington Post* as saying the "suburban parents" of her son's friends needed to "stop looking for some black pusher from the city and start looking at their own kids." Patty was not loved by the PTA mothers for such comments.

Later she ran for elected office. My mother ran Patty's first campaign. Patty served as a state delegate and then senator for many years. She was avidly pro-choice, a feminist who loved a good scotch with her political colleagues as much as she loved "wearing a sexy bra and panties" *under* her senatorial suits.

Hanging over the breakfast nook in her kitchen was a framed sentiment: "Yea, though I walk through the shadow of the valley of death, I am not afraid, for I am the meanest bitch in the valley." I thought it the most incredible thing I'd ever seen. In the kitchen! But it fit her—not that Patty was a bitch, but she was tough and everybody knew it. That wall hanging, over the years, came to embody her essence for me. Years later, when she exiled it to a shelf in the basement, I would journey downstairs to visit the discarded talisman. My second mother was a study in contradictions—drawing on Golda Meir, Rosalind Russell, Bella Abzug, and Betty Grable while ending up an original.

When I fell during basketball practice and my own mother was tied up with work, Patty took me to the emergency room to have an x-ray of my wrist. We stopped at Baskin Robbins on the way back, for good measure. Patty taught me to paint my fingernails, swear like a sailor, blot lipstick, make chicken soup. My mother taught me the nuts and bolts of sex, but Patty told me about the importance of orgasms and talked about how wonderful love could be. Patty tucked me into the station wagon with her own, older kids and their friends—schlepping us to the beach for long weekends.

Patty always gave me a place to turn with my emotions, always sought out my feelings. When my mother hid my biological father's identity and refused to discuss the fact that the man I had thought was my father had sexually abused me, having another mother figure to turn to talk with made all the difference in the world.

When I moved to California from the East Coast for a stint in my twenties, it was Patty who wailed for me to come home: "Your mother can't put this kind of guilt on you; it wouldn't be right. But I can." Since I moved back a couple of years ago, she and I have been closer than ever. I love to visit her, sit around and talk, hear her stories. Her emphysema is getting worse. She wheels oxygen tanks around everywhere she goes—continuing to smoke all the while.

We're both night owls. My phone routinely rings after midnight. She calls to say goodnight, discuss *Nightline*, find out how my evening went, ask what I wore, quiz me on what I'm reading, and chastise me for not reading more. "Haven't you finished that goddamn book yet? You really need to start reading that Carol Shields I gave you." Long after the rest of the world has gone to bed, she and I are up prowling around. When I finally go to bed, I smile, imagining her, still up, reading, watching the news. Keeping watch over the world.

Perhaps my relationship with Patty makes it easy to imagine myself as something of a daughter figure to Lynn—especially now. Blood and biology don't mean as much to me as roles and niches. I know I flatter myself to think my presence in Lynn's life lifts even one bit of her grief.

Here we are, Lynn, Judy, and I, pain swirling all around. Patty is dying. Lisa is dead. I'm fearful and sad; Lynn is consumed by grief. Eating peaches with Judy makes as much sense as anything else.

JULY 2001

Patty died at the end of June, and I feel orphaned. I am alone in the world with just my mother, I keep thinking. I can't do any "work" in therapy. I am grief-struck and fighting the growing knowledge that I am going to have to, at some point, confront the layered nest of pain that is the relationship with my own mother, but for now I sit on Lynn's comfortable couch and talk about books. This whole month, it is what we do. We talk about Don DeLillo, whose work she introduces me to. We talk about the blurry line between memory and fact. We read Carol Shields at the same time, as Patty and I did, and we talk about our own mothers and the way they don't read. We don't talk about having lost Lisa and Patty, people who didn't share our love of books. We don't talk about what we're doing, talking about books for $125 an hour, twice a week. We don't talk about the fact that she thinks my history is different than it is. She thinks I graduated from high school, went to college and then grad school, received a master's degree in public policy. Instead, I dropped out of high school, ran away with my boyfriend, took the

GED, and went to college intermittently over the next couple of years before dropping out altogether. I faked the last two years. I faked grad school. What I'm lying about doesn't matter. What does matter is that I'm lying about it and have been, for ten years now. I can't imagine how to unravel it, to come clean, with Lynn, with my mom, with the world.

Instead, Lynn and I talk about the formative books, the books that made us who we are. We talk about *Anne of Green Gables* and Anne Frank; we talk about Virginia Woolf; we talk about George Eliot. We talk about Balzac and Flaubert and Fitzgerald. We talk and talk and talk. We read and read and read.

This is who I am—a reader. Someone whose interior life is rich and replete with characters and voices and stories and fictions. A serious reader whose mother thinks she has spent too much time with her nose in a book. A liar who has been crafting stories to survive her life all her life. A liar who doesn't want to be one anymore. A liar who is afraid and grieving, who can't tell her own truth, but can grapple with the larger truth in fiction. A liar whose kind therapist is letting her be who she is, who seems happy to have me—a girl with her nose in a book. Who seems happy to let me explore the world in the only way I know how, at least for now.

It will be years before I realize the magnitude of what Lynn has given me this month.

AUGUST 2001

In the middle of the month, Lynn announces she is going on vacation until after Labor Day with her son and daughter-in-law and grandchildren—details she never would have shared before her daughter's death. It seems abrupt, this trip. Is she in bad shape? Does she need a break? Or does the short notice indicate she didn't want me to be anxious for a long time in advance of her departure?

At the end of our final session until September, I say, "Thank you." And she says, "No, thank *you*."

I know in an instant what she means. She is thanking me for being a big part of her grieving summer. That instant changes so much for me; in fact, it changes everything. All of a sudden, I realize, or maybe admit in my head what my heart has always felt, that I've always felt unwanted by my mother, a bit like a burden. In that moment when Lynn thanks me, it alters my self-perception; I have meant something to her this summer.

I matter.

SEPTEMBER 2001

What happens when someone dies? How do you go on amid so much sadness? What is the right way to grieve? These unanswerable queries all played out as the entire country asked the same questions.

Across the nation, newspaper opinion pages and television stations echoed my inner sadness. While I was coping with my loss and sadness, the nation was heavy with mourning the loss of so many people from the terrorist attacks on September 11, 2001, and the sense of safety we had before that day. That made me feel at once overcome and consoled. There is something intrinsically private about grief and the ways we mourn our private losses. Yet grief is universal. Usually it's just not shared so universally. But, as C. S. Lewis said, no one ever told me that grief would feel so much like fear. In the wake of 9/11 we grieved as a public while I grieved for Patty and Lynn for her daughter. We were all racked with sorrow.

For a while, I kept thinking I would soon be finished grieving. I now realize I will probably never be finished. Grief does not end so much as evolve into something else. We don't stop grieving people we've lost; rather we allow our memories and fond feelings to fill the voided crevices.

There is a quote I've always loved from the Tang Dynasty: "Here at the frontier, there are falling leaves. Although my neighbors are all barbarians, and you, you are a thousand miles away, there are always two cups on my table." It makes me think of Lynn, of our afternoons, our talks. Her caring for me.

Later, I'll be able to see how smart she was, to comfort me by reading with me, talking about books with me. Later I'll wonder if it was by design or just the way two bookish women could be together amid so much sadness. The way one patient could get what she needed, one therapist could do her work of helping her patient begin to unravel her own stories.

Wally Lamb wrote, "God exists in the roundness of things." As the present becomes the past, I know every summer ends. September is always right around the corner, yet it arrives when we least expect it and are ill-prepared for the changes it brings. We do our best. We fling ourselves into the air and hope to land on solid ground.

* * *

There is a photograph that both astonishes me and says everything I know to be true. It's Jackie Kennedy on November 25, 1963, the day of her husband's burial. She is in the black dress and pearls she wore to the funeral, leaning forward, proffering a birthday cake, candles ablaze, to her son. It is his third birthday as well as the day a nation buried his father. A clown cutout is pinned to the wall, and little children mill about. She is having a party for her son. Life goes on.

Life is for the living, and this is what the living do. We lose those we love in ways both ordinary and tragic: We lose a husband to an assassin, his brain splattered across our pink suit. We lose a daughter to the ravages of a cruel disease. We watch our guiding stars, our childhood idols, suffer and wither and die. We lose loves and friends and those who matter most. We bury our own children.

We are a people dark and cold, aching with the pain of losses so big it is a wonder we survive. But life *is* for the living. And this, too, is what the living do: We have hope when reason gives us no reason for hope. We hold out cake and have parties for our children. We keep the faith.

We tell stories; we recall the good times and allow them to fill us. At our best we incorporate the finest parts of those we have loved into ourselves. We are living; we remember. We remember to love again. Life is for the living. Even if they are liars. Life is for the living.

Therapist Without a Clue

| *Sherry Amatenstein* |

Today is my birthday.

I am "celebrating" my birthday by seeing nine patients in a row. Boom, boom, boom, boom—assuaging other people's hurt while I bury my own. It's been decades since birthdays felt like firecrackers and shooting stars. But today is my first birthday since Dad died seven months ago. A titanic heart attack four years prior carried off Mom, so I'm a newly minted, fifty-something orphan.

That's not the tipping point making me quake at the prospect of sitting in my home office in Long Island City, a block from the East River, listening to nine patients from behind my hopefully wise-and-empathetic-therapist mien. Recently, I've endured a new abandonment, this one by Janet, a friend who neglected to tell me over our eleven years of serene communing that our bond had an expiration date. Last year for my birthday she treated me to the biggest hit on Broadway. It's been weeks since Janet's responded to an email; today, she hasn't even sent a text.

I expect romantic relationships to go sour, and I've got the litany of exes, including the one I married, to prove it. But female friends are supposed to be like diamonds, congressional deadlock, and mother love: forever.

* * *

Mark slumps in, dragging his worn briefcase and wearing his typical glum expression. He fidgets on the midnight blue couch, staring down at the shining hardwood floor. Good thing I'm a therapist; otherwise I might take personally Mark's inability to look me in the eyes.

He resumes his mournful tale where it ended last session: "I still haven't heard from Tami after leaving three messages. Why do people keep leaving me?"

Oh, how I yearn to uncork a bottle of wine and commiserate. Instead, I dig the nails of my right hand into my left palm to snap myself back to therapist mode. "Mark, I know it feels awful when people seem to disappear, especially someone you thought was a close friend . . ."

"People *are* awful,' he says flatly, decapitating his Dunkin' Donuts cup by removing the lid with a vicious snap.

While pooh-poohing his apologies for the coffee spillage— "You got out some aggression. The couch can take it"—I telepathically agree: *Yeah, people can be disgusting.*

How could Janet, my new ex-friend, stop answering my phone calls without explanation? I met Janet, a fellow therapist, at a spiritual retreat where we were paired for an empowerment exercise aimed at eking out emotional closure from a hurtful relationship. I had been reeling since Sandra, a friend I'd regarded as my "sister of the soul," seemingly dropped off the face of the earth.

Janet, standing in for Sandra, had patiently listened to my plaintive questions: "Why not tell me what I've done? If not that, at least say you're done with the friendship; why just leave?" In turn, I stood in for Janet's ex-husband, who'd apparently taken advantage of her kind heart in myriad ways.

To my patient I say, "Feeling sorry for yourself may be familiar, but it's not productive. People are wrapped up in themselves, not thinking about what effect their actions are having on others. What was going on in Tami's world that might have led to her tuning out?"

"Well, her mother is sick. But I was really sympathetic . . . all I wanted to do was help." This last part is said with lifted gaze. The fear and loneliness I see mirror what I feel but rarely show.

* * *

I never showed all of me to Janet, fearing her sweeter-than-cotton-candy personality would be repelled by the inner darkness I inherited as a child of Holocaust survivors.

Indeed, my comfort with discomfort is what drew me to my profession. Most days listening to my patients evokes a sacred trust and honor, much the same as I felt listening to my parents' stories of what they endured in Poland. Growing up I'd been too cowed to share my suffering—not being included by two girls at school in their chatter didn't compare to what Mom experienced being wrenched from home and taken to a concentration camp at age fourteen.

To offset the darkness, sometimes I craved the company of someone perpetually sunny. Over the years Janet's Soho apartment had become a sanctuary. When I felt spiritually beaten down in my first career—writing and editing articles such as "How to Lose 5 Pounds a Week While Stuffing Your Face"—and, later, by the agonizing decline of my parents, Janet issued invitations for wine, foie gras, and Scrabble, often including a cooking lesson for domestically impaired me. When she was released from the hospital after undergoing chemo for thyroid cancer, I brought take-out and stayed overnight on several occasions.

Her need for quiet during that ordeal was easy for me to grant. I'd already made my midlife career switch and found the intensity of listening fifty-minute hour after fifty-minute hour to the traumas, rants, and obsessions of others fulfilling but exhausting. Occasionally friends requested free "shrinking." One-sided relationships increasingly felt like the norm, so it was a treat when nothing was expected of me in my personal life other than showing up.

And the effort not to interrupt patients' narratives with tales from Sherryland makes it even harder for me to engage in two-way conversations in my off-hours. When I have a bad cold or lose my wallet, it's easier to post on Facebook than burden a friend. Easier, but isolating.

I became a therapist to help people better understand themselves, but the one with the weaknesses pinned under the glare of the police spotlight is me. I am impatient, can be self-involved and sometimes harsh, and am oftentimes mildly depressed and guilty of self-criticism I would never tolerate in my patients. I guide them: "What do you *like* about yourself? What is *good* in your life? Let's build from there."

I'm great at helping my patients. For my own gnarled psyche—call me a therapist without a clue.

* * *

"Mark, I know you want to help Tami, but what do you think *she* wants?"

Hand limply encircling the coffee cup (eh, the couch will survive), he says, "But I had her best interests at heart. I offered to spend time with her mom so she could take a break."

"I know, but what did *she* want?"

Mark's heart is thumping so loudly I can hear it break. "She wanted to handle her problems by herself."

I am at full therapist throttle: "So one way to look at her radio silence is that it's about her needs, not a rejection of you."

As he grants me a timorous, "Maybe," my eyes well. I reached him.

* * *

More than any other friend, Sandra, my onetime sister of the soul, knew how to reach me. Sandra was a Wall Street tycoon turned naturopath. We became pals after I interviewed her for my *Cosmo* article, "Young Women Who Made a Mint." I was accustomed to feeling out of focus to people, including family, so being with someone who totally got my off-center personality was like shedding a deformity.

Soon we were having Lucy-and-Ethel-style adventures— during a trip to Los Angeles, we convinced a Beverly Hills realtor to show us Pia Zadora's home (it made Liberace's mansion look tame) and veered off from a back-lot studio tour to crash an empty *Seinfeld* set. Don't tell, but we stole an engraved mug and a VHS tape.

Sandra supervised my "fling" with an Iraqi I met at a disco, counseling me to bring him to the suite we'd wrangled at the Chateau Marmont, where she hid in her bedroom listening to loud music, ears cocked for a scream.

Five years after the start of our Technicolor twinship, I persuaded Sandra to start a naturopathic beauty business. (She'd cured a zit that covered half my face with one application of her homemade concoction.) I also persuaded her to let me invest thousands of dollars.

Two years later the business and my nine-month live-in relationship with Jim, a comic to whom I'd given what I erroneously thought was a loan, failed within the same month. Sandra cried hysterically, saying, "I can't take the guilt of losing your investment or that I encouraged you to be with Jim, who stole more of your money."

I insisted she not be upset on my behalf. "I'm a big girl. I make my own decisions. Do *not* feel guilty. If anything, I should feel guilty for talking you into starting the business."

She squeaked, "Okay, honey. You know how much I love you," and we sealed our eternal bond with a hug.

A month later she stopped returning my phone calls and I began years of self-torture, ransacking my brain to figure out what I'd done to lose her.

* * *

Mark asks, "So I should leave Tami alone?"

I tell both of us, "Yes, and don't let what she needs, does, or doesn't do rule your self-definition. *Reactivity to someone else's neurosis is a terrible way to live.*"

I repeat that line to myself intermittently over the next five hours to stitch it into my being. Therapist card trick: maintaining laser focus on a patient while retaining a corner of my brain. Okay, Sandra had a right to leave if my presence riddled her with guilt. I can let go while still missing her, along with missing the unfettered me who could frolic and have flings without weighing what there was to lose. While Janet's exit is not as emotionally potent, it triggers fresh yearnings for Sandra.

Intently listening to a litany of sadness and dysfunction— a battling couple, a bipolar teen, and an alcoholic just out of rehab—I feel anew the sting of my myriad of self-inflicted bruises.

These days I dread loss so much I rarely extend myself, except in this room. There are many patients I've come to love, several I'd want to join after a session for wine, one I'd want to date if he weren't a patient and if I weren't also treating his wife. If my patients only knew that sometimes I envy their lives . . . Many are miserable, but many are courageous enough to tear through the scar tissue, layer by layer.

I just want to finish this day, get through a birthday drink with my oldest friend Dave, and crawl home to a well-deserved coma.

* * *

Kendra, today's final patient, puts my needle on the reserve tank—making *Saturday Night Live*'s Debbie Downer character look like Pollyanna on steroids.

She hasn't even hit the chair before proclaiming, "No one's ever had a worse subway trip than I just did. It took forever!"

"I'm sure it was awful, but there's a lot of competition for worst subway trip ever," I tell her. "Once my train stopped for three hours because someone had jumped onto the track just in front of us."

A frown. "Okay, that is worse . . . but *all* my subway rides are bad. I bet most of yours are good."

"I'm sorry for your bad train karma. But, you know, even though this is just our third session, I've noticed everything you go through has to be the worst thing anyone has ever gone through. Wonder why that is?"

Kendra's face performs a variety of contortions until it lights with dawning certainty. "With six kids, my parents never listened to me unless I said something was wrong."

"Oh . . . so perhaps looking for sympathy has become a habit?"

Tears pool at the corners of her eyes. She grabs Kleenex from my ever-present box. "Wish I'd just told them I needed attention."

After Kendra leaves, her words continue to reverberate: *Wish I'd just told them.*

Impatiently I root through the oversized canvas tote that holds my life. Finding my iPhone, I go to Contacts and tap "Janet."

* * *

I've chosen a profession that doubles back to my childhood mode of being invisible while serving as the "chosen one" to listen to Mom's stories of unendurable suffering. Bearing witness made me shrink into myself. It's appropriate in my work, but in my off hours I opt to make my presence felt.

Janet, the last person left without caller ID, picks up. Her chirpy voice droops when she discovers the caller is the person she's trying to erase. "Oh, ah, happy birthday, Sherry."

"Thanks." My stomach's in knots, but my voice is wobble-free: "Look, Janet, it's obvious you don't want our friendship to continue. And that's your right. But you know what I went through, being left in the dark with Sandra about why she ended the friendship. And you and I have been in each other's lives for eleven years. That merits a closure conversation. What happened? Did I do something?"

A silence long enough to fly to the West Coast and back. Then an icicle-drenched response: "People have dropped me and I've let the friendship go without asking questions."

I've gone too far to turn back. "Look, I know we were never a perfect fit. Sorry if my pushiness upsets you, but I'd like to know, did I do something?"

"My feelings just changed. That's all. It happens. I wish you well, but I just don't love you anymore."

Cotton candy dipped in acid.

"Well, I know you don't like confrontation, Janet, but I deserved some kind of answer. It's a matter of respect. I wish you well, too."

I click off. Sometimes I miss the days you could slam the phone in someone's ear. Though that wouldn't befit a fifty-something therapist.

Good thing I have plenty of Kleenex. Uh uh, no tears. I made the effort. Nothing is ever assured, wrapped expertly with pretty ribbons and a bow on top. Life is loose ends and dangling participles. If I don't play, I lose. Janet acted distant and weird after my father died, admitting she doesn't deal well with sadness and death. (Good luck to her patients!) I forgave her, but I guess she couldn't forgive me for making her feel inadequate. That's her issue, not mine.

Just because I'm not a Holocaust survivor doesn't mean it's selfish if I reach out for sympathy, praise, celebration . . . I tap Contacts on my iPhone again. Dave's voice mail picks up. I announce, "Remember I said we didn't have to do anything fancy tonight for my birthday? I changed my mind."

Artist Shrink Confessional

| *Royal Young* |

My first word was "mask." From my earliest years, I was inspired by the papier-mâché skulls hanging all over my father's colorfully cluttered Lower East Side studio on the first floor of our renovated tenement building.

At thirty, I landed my first gallery show in Williamsburg, Brooklyn. Randall Harris, the owner of Figureworks Gallery, had decided to take a chance on the vibrant images I painted on Plexiglas inspired by vintage *Playboys*, old noir Hollywood, and Pop Art.

I couldn't wait to tell Dad I had followed his dreams, building on our family legacy. My paternal grandfather, Morris Brozgold, had disparaged Dad's artistic ambitions. Morris hated my dad for fleeing the cold Midwestern house he grew up in to pursue creative passions on the untamed streets of Soho in the 1960s. On a rare visit to New York, Grandpa Morris turned to my dad in front of his paintings and said, with an antagonizing smile, "This is nothing I couldn't draw."

I knew part of the reason my dad gravitated toward psychology and earned a degree in social work while struggling as an artist was his desire to understand the deep and complicated ties between family members. He had an urgent need to unravel his own father's harsh disapproval. Yet like father, like son: throughout my childhood, Dad disparaged my artistic ambitions. Now, with my success, I was convinced my father finally would be proud.

But when I burst into his studio, shouting, "Dad, I got it!" he barely looked up from his table.

"I should show them my own work," he replied, putting the finishing touches on a papier-mâché bunny in a smoking jacket with a protruding hot pink penis. The rabbit was an effigy representing Hugh Hefner, part of a series of sculptures my father had titled *American Men*.

"Aren't you happy for me?" I asked.

"Do you think they'd be interested in seeing my series?" my father asked.

"Sure, I guess." I shrugged, hurt. Dad seemed too focused on his own success to really care about mine.

"You don't seem comfortable with my artwork," Dad said.

"Whatever," I replied, reverting to moody adolescent mode, not able to tell him how I really felt. I was livid.

I also felt guilty. My father had given up so much to become a social worker and earn a real income to support my mom, my brother, and me. Didn't I owe him? Yet, part of me screamed in rebellion. I wanted my father to be my parent, not my rival.

As a kid, I'd been addicted to the taste of my father's artistic success, the world it allowed me to access, so different from the rough crooked streets of the Lower East Side where we lived. In the late 1980s, my parents were pioneers in the neighborhood our Jewish ancestors had long since abandoned for the suburbs, renovating the tenement building they had bought for $25,000 by cleaning out the debris from its former existence as a shooting gallery for junkies.

I loved the loud, wild streets around us with their bright pastel murals on the sides of buildings and bodega gates, corners commandeered by prostitutes in neon green spandex and gold chains, and hydrants broken open in summer when even the concrete was hot.

Yet I also felt out of place, a shy kid more comfortable reading books than playing tag, whose mom had to come to elementary school classes each year to explain to the other kids what Hanukkah was. Instead of having playdates like normal children, I enjoyed making my neuropsychologist mother administer Rorschach tests to me, hoping to impress her and win her love by deciphering the amorphous blobs of black ink she dutifully held up for my inspection. Mom thought my hobby was cute, but it held something more layered for me. Without quite understanding it, I was trying to use her psychoanalyst's tools to decipher an adult universe I often felt was scary and beyond my control.

At other times, I would retreat into my father's studio, where he supplied me with sketchbooks, markers, paints, and pencils. When I tore up creations I hated, Dad taped them back together, saying, "There are no mistakes in art." I felt most loved when my parents assured me I was normal, perhaps even especially talented. Creative freedom and being able to get inside other people's heads was a balm for the aimless depression I often felt, even as a young child. According to some distorted sense I had of Freudian theory at nine years old, I feared I had inherited sadness.

But art as salvation was also in my blood. My father's work was commissioned by the MTA, and Dad worked with kids at PS 41 in the West Village to create mosaic murals that were installed in the Christopher Street Subway Station. On a spring day in 1995 when I was ten years old, my parents let my younger brother and I take the day off school, and we went to the opening. As trains rumbled past I marveled at my father's brightly colored work depicting New York history, Emma Thompson and the Stonewall Riots, Washington Square Park as an African burial ground, and bohemian séances. I felt like Dad had decorated my city.

But my father's private persona was darker. As part of an art project he'd been working on practically since my birth, my father corresponded with people who placed sleazy ads in personal columns. Dad's endeavor was called *Hidden America*. Under a pseudonym he wrote letters to these strangers, trying to figure out their life stories. At the end of every correspondence, he painted a portrait based on the photos the person had enclosed. Dad collected a correspondent from every state in the USA. The letters themselves were deeply confessional, a form of psychosexual therapy with my father as a masked Jungian Svengali—a magician in charge of interpreting and realizing their most personal dreams. As I grew older, my first word, "mask," also began to stand for my father's separate lives. Duplicity.

Sometimes he was a balanced man, a therapist who saved people daily at FROSTED, a residence on the corner of Houston and Allen Street for ex-prostitutes and junkies who had AIDS. Sometimes my father was a secretive artist huddled in his studio on the first floor of our building—a sort of creative den filled with his sexual creations. Often my father was angry, screaming curses at cars who ran red lights or the elderly Dominican lady on our block who always tried to give us religious pamphlets, saying, "Jesus loves you."

"Jesus does not love me!" Dad yelled at her.

In my teens, attending LaGuardia High School where I majored in visual art, I rolled my eyes when my father told me, "You're a great listener. You should think about studying social work when you get to college."

"I don't want to be an artist like you, Dad," I shot back. "I'm not going to compromise," I added, ignoring his wounded expression.

At fourteen, I resented that my father had seemingly given up on his dreams of artistic success. He was teaching ceramic classes in a home for the blind, where he also ran a men's therapy group. I couldn't see that my father loved caring for people, only that he had never grabbed the glittering fame and fortune I felt sure I would.

My father had always projected most of his dreams and failures on to me, his firstborn son. But the social work degree and gentle skill he used to heal his drug-addled and disabled clients proved useless to reach his son. Dad was too close to me to see me clearly. My normal adolescent depression Dad diagnosed as failure. My disinterest in academics my father saw as laziness, but his judgment didn't delve deep enough into my real issues. Like my father, I wanted to be creative, something both my parents had always encouraged. But at eighteen, Dad declared I needed "structure and stability," a prescription I scoffed at, until I defied a midnight curfew and he bolted and chain-locked the door! I was also dealing with the aftermath of the terrorist attacks on September 11, 2001, a day that changed my city and teenage worldview forever. More and more, I felt that the adults in my world—the people who were meant to protect me, like my parents and people in power—were not actually in control.

I wanted to get as far away from New York and my overbearing father's rules as possible. So I chose Bennington, a clothing-optional liberal arts college in Vermont with no grading system. And I began drinking more and more.

At Bennington I started hiding my empty liquor bottles in the closet, but they multiplied, spilling out into my dorm room, clinking at the foot of my bed. After my parents visited for a weekend, I got wasted and hurled all my empties out my window into the frigid winter night, watching them fall past pine trees—dark marks against the snow.

The next afternoon, coming back from class, I discovered my resident adviser had picked all the empty bottles up and dumped them on my bed, bits of dirty ice melting from handles of Jim Beam onto my sheets.

I dropped out of school after that year, moving back into my childhood bedroom, where I tried to hide my growing drinking habit. My parents viewed my depression as an indication that I was imploding. They didn't know I was struggling with addiction. It didn't help that at twenty, I had grandiose fantasies of the megastar fame that had always eluded my father.

"They're hiring at Duane Reade!" Dad shouted at me, when I told him of my artistic ambitions.

After two years of burning through cocaine-fueled gallery parties, extra roles in independent films, and inappropriate relationships, I ended up going back to college. I took journalism classes at the New School and worked hard as an intern making photocopies and then as a reporter for *Interview*, the infamous magazine founded by Andy Warhol. For seven years, I interviewed authors like Martin Amis, Chuck Palahniuk, Susan Orlean, and Anne Rice, asking them personal questions. The resulting articles were more like philosophical therapy sessions. My questioning style was inspired by my dad's belief in analysis and by his revealing correspondences with strangers. I asked interviewees questions and listened deeply and without judgment to their answers.

"How well can you really know the people you love?" I asked author Shannon Moroney, who wrote a memoir about discovering her beloved husband was a violent criminal.

Moroney carefully answered my question: "The very scary thing is that all of us have free will and the capability of betraying one another's trust." She added, "People say to me, 'How could you trust again?' But I think, how could I not?"

I didn't feel that my father had betrayed my trust, but I did feel that he had never seen me clearly. I interpreted Moroney's answer to mean that I, too, should keep trying to show my father my true self and figure his out as well. So I began to be more open with my father, telling him about my struggles with alcohol and my long-distance girlfriend, as well as, disastrously, my recent small triumph: the gallery show in Williamsburg. His opportunistic response to that last confession did feel like a betrayal, a rejection of my accomplishment. I had always wanted my father's artwork to win him fame but had grown to love Dad's mellower "social worker" side, a side I saw more often since he'd renovated an old room in the back of my parents' house, where he now saw private clients. It became my favorite room when I visited, filled with Dad's books on Buddhism and meditation, lush plants he tenderly watered, and the low hum of a fish tank filled with darting goldfish and plastic shipwrecks.

The day after Dad responded so hurtfully to my news, he emailed me. I expected an apology; for years, my father had said I'd never amount to anything. Instead, he'd written about attempting to contact the owner of my new gallery. Great, now he wanted to coast on my small success!

Screw him! I was painting again and felt that I had proven both my father and my wasted younger self wrong. My biggest addiction was creativity. Even if I still couldn't afford to pay rent in the neighborhood where I grew up, I hadn't ended up like the junkies and catatonic alcoholics who once dotted the Bowery.

I decided to confront my father and headed over to my parents from my Bushwick apartment. Before I could say anything, he pulled me into his office, saying, "I need to talk to you." Dad looked serious.

He sat on the orange couch, where his patients usually perched, while I sat on the "therapist chair." I noticed one of my drawings displayed prominently on my father's old oak desk: a skull-like face surrounded by colorful flowers.

"You know my father never really encouraged my creativity," Dad said.

I nodded.

"That's not an excuse. But it's partially an explanation for how I reacted to your show," Dad continued. "My first thought was of myself. It was like I wanted to use you. I could feel it was disgusting in the moment, but I couldn't stop."

I just nodded, hypnotized by my father's words, feeling like his confidant. I was sitting in the seat of power; I could shrink and fix him. "Yes." I stood up.

Dad continued. "I've been doing art my whole life and I'm about to turn seventy-five and the truth is I haven't gotten to where I want. I still feel desperate. I'm still struggling to get recognition. I think about death."

"I want recognition for you, too," I burst out.

"You're my son," he said. "Not my agent."

Sitting in the therapist's chair, I forgave my father and understood that the same hunger drove us both. A craving for intangible successes, which we had to let go. Family was what mattered, love what had sustained us during the years my father would smash porcelain plates in blind rages or later, when I would stumble home blind drunk.

"Hug?" Dad asked.

When Dad got up from the patient's couch, I noticed he was a bit stiff at the knees. And we hugged, not therapist and patient or confidants or rivals or artists, just father and son supporting each other's weight.

Therapy Is for White People

| *Jenine Holmes* |

For a black Baptist, bred in Detroit by two God-fearing Southerners, to enter psychoanalysis required an extraordinary event. It happened when my boyfriend of three years—a healthy, anti-drug Stanford law student—was found dead in November 1990. Art was twenty-six.

A month later, the medical examiner determined pulmonary edema caused by untreated pneumonia had taken Art's life. By then the grief and guilt I'd amassed, the deepest of my twenty-seven years, was ignored because cultural presets demanded my attention.

I grew up believing blacks buried our emotions and held secrets close. Secrets helped African Americans survive enslavement. Secrets fueled the Underground Railroad. Secrets still prevail. Charles Blow hid his bisexuality for years until revealing it in his brutal 2014 memoir, *Fire Shut Up in My Bones*. It was not until *The New York Times* editor Anatole Broyard lay on his deathbed that he disclosed to his daughter, Bliss, that he'd "passed for white" after entering college up North, leaving his darker Southern clan behind.

Therapy is for white people, the rule went. "Take your burden to God" was the message delivered from pulpits. "Pray on it," my grandmothers advised. Blacks lean on God and bury the rest. And my parents followed the code. By the age of twenty-two, I'd lost three grandparents, one to a massive heart attack. My family bore through each funeral without requiring a tissue.

Art's Irish-Hungarian family was our polar opposite. He, his sister, and his father discussed everything—their past, their future, and, in particular, his dad's disapproval of Art having a black girlfriend.

As we searched my Upper West Side neighborhood for a parking spot suitable for his black Buick, Art announced, "My dad will have to accept you."

I sat silent, staring at the tightly wedged cars, marveling at the resoluteness even the simplest parts of life required.

A day later, my phone rang. Art's voice held a cheeky tone. "Hey, my dad wants to say hello." Muffled angry tones followed, and a new baritone crackled onto the line.

Our exact conversation has faded. But his father's utter disdain, his complete repulsion, is a memory that can be called up like the tangy sting from an accidental sip of sour milk.

"You're no better than anyone else, and no one is better than you," was the flag under which my parents had raised my brothers and me. To have someone not only hold a different banner but hold it high was peculiar. For reasons beyond me, Art's Dad and I had a second conversation. There wasn't a third.

While I kept my white boyfriend secret from my Arkansas-born-and-bred dad, I highlighted Art's brilliance to my mom, a talent-loving teacher.

"Art's smarter than I am." It was a big admission for a girl who'd graduated from Cass Tech, a prestigious four-year college preparatory high school.

"He's just smarter in a different way."

* * *

I'd attended Parsons School of Design in Manhattan, one of the top art colleges in the nation. But Art's brand of brilliance was dissimilar to creatively welding a paintbrush or shaping a chunk of clay. His constantly curious brain was a marvelous machine.

As we cruised along the Long Island Expressway, Art's telescope tucked in the backseat of the Buick, looking for the right place to search for Orion or the red planet, he'd turn and say, with a sly smile, "Give me two three-digit numbers."

I'd comply. Art would multiply the figures using his brain as a blackboard and then explain his airborne calculation, amusing himself and amazing me. He was unlike any guy I'd known.

I was different from Art's Queens dating pool, turning him on to Billie Holiday, Anita O'Day, and Nina Simone and taking him jogging around Manhattan parks, sharing my love of running with him. We survived his first year at Stanford Law School intact. During his second, Art moved from the dorm into an apartment and then lobbied for me to join him. I was afraid of leaving Manhattan without a ring.

"Christmas will be really great for you this year," Art hinted over the phone in October. Perhaps a ring and proposal were coming.

A month later I sobbed into the receiver, begging Art's father to say that he wasn't dead. I kept pleading and crying until he released a wail, animal and broken. Shattering.

The funeral service was held at St. Mary's in Astoria, Queens. I wasn't invited to sit with the family.

A week later, my mom shipped my brother Jeffrey to Manhattan to secure my kitchen knives and gas oven. For two weeks in our cocoon of familial denial, we savored shoot-'em-up action movies, Notre Dame football, and Sam Adams beers. Then Jeffrey left.

Numb and alone, I returned to work. Advertising, much like an operating coal mine, always has shifts available. I clocked in and spent my lunch hours in a restroom stall weeping. Once home, I'd crack open a Cabernet and polish off the bottle, my reward for making it through the day still breathing.

Mom's voice was tense during our phone calls from Michigan. But my Manhattan friend Jeri was frantic. "Please call my colleague, a therapist," she pleaded for weeks. "I'm worried about you."

"I'm fine, Jeri, really," I said in a flat monotone, my impersonation of how a woman in control expressed herself.

"You don't sound fine, honey. You sound terrible."

Relationships are like lightning strikes. You never know when a great one will appear, or how it will change the landscape of your life. And if Art's death was a bolt of the worst kind, meeting Jeri was its polar opposite.

Divorced, with two children under the age of ten, Jeri employed live-in sitters, all Parsons students, in exchange for room and board. During my junior year of college, I moved in with Jeri and her sons and remained until graduation.

I loved her "never-give-up" approach to life, her passion for a good meal and great conversation. But her chitchat had limits. "I can't discuss my cases. It's not ethical."

No matter. Her work as a psychoanalyst served as a single, bright narrative thread to my New York City tapestry. As in Woody Allen films, themes of therapy were woven into most Manhattan lives. But not mine. That is, until Art's passing. Then, Jeri's inner Sigmund Freud emerged.

"Please, honey. Call this friend of mine."

"I'm fine," I said, for nearly a month, holding to the crumbling cliff of sanity by steadfastly refusing to acknowledge where I stood.

* * *

Blacks constitute about 12 percent of the population of the United States, but according to Salman Akhtar, MD, "African Americans represent an abysmal .00007 percent of the membership of the American Psychoanalytic Association." Co-author with Jan Wright of *The African American Experience: Psychoanalytic Perspectives*, Akhtar noted, "A survey from 1995 identified only 24 African American analysts practicing in the country." Perhaps blacks couldn't fathom entering a field where the unspoken was voiced. And our culture of secrets helped maintain the dearth. "We do not share our errors, failures, and faults with white people," was the mantra many lived by. But after a month of pressure, I gave in to Jeri.

* * *

Dr. H, tall and pale-skinned with gold wire-framed glasses, perched behind a large, dark mahogany desk in his Upper East Side office. On the window ledge behind him, lush green plants flanked his shoulders. Sunlight sliced through the room. Not a Woody Allen couch in sight.

"I heard you've had a difficult time," he said.

"Someone I loved died, but I'm okay now."

"That kind of loss takes more than a few months to come to terms with."

"No, I'm fine."

"I'm sure you still have bad days, right?"

I reluctantly nodded. We agreed on his fee and twice-weekly appointments, a real challenge.

"It'll be tough getting out of the agency."

"There are always phone conferences, so we stay on track."

Out of excuses, I kept the meetings with Dr. H, a major miracle for a copywriter with colleagues who considered you weak if your lunch breaks required more than the fifteen minutes to score a salad. Or weep in the bathroom.

I found it horrendously difficult to discuss Art, so our first fifty-minute sessions contained wordless gaps, empty spaces I was supposed to fill with dialogue. Dr. H said nothing, wielding a pleasant expression and calm nature. Far from annoyed, he seemed willing to wait for me to set the tone. Soon I realized that my sessions could be spent how I wanted, discussing whatever felt comfortable. So I started with advertising. But soon talk of work produced a lightning strike.

"After my first day at the agency, that evening, I learned Art had died. My second day I had to call my boss and tell him I wouldn't be in."

"A rather difficult call to make."

Dr. H's acknowledgment of the difficulty of the call moved me toward understanding that much of my life fell under the heading of difficult.

"It's quite a loss you've experienced, at a young age."

"I feel old. I can't look at hanging out, clubbing, and

clothes the same way I did before. Now I know bad things happen."

Hearing such a truth that normally rolled around my head out in the ether leveled a shock.

Dr. H peered at me, his eyes glinting with warmth, an expression I'd later recognize as pride, pride that I'd made an important stride.

So I kept moving further into the difficult, the hard, and the horrible. I doled out the details of my relationship with Art, his death, and the guilt that my move to Palo Alto might have saved him. How I had loved him and had been loved by him. How Art's death had topped the earlier loss of my Parsons' professor who was leveled by cancer at the age of fifty. Ivan had had twenty-four more years than Art.

Sharing the thoughts rampaging through my brain freed up mental bandwidth, making their presence easier to withstand. So I kept up the appointments, but only Jeri knew. With my mom, dad, and brothers away in Michigan, keeping my secret was just a matter of keeping my mouth shut.

Having a sliver of personal time, twice weekly, contained a certain charm. But I knew our meetings had a use-by date. My commitment was for two months and only two months, to appease Jeri and Dr. H, to showcase my stability. As pleasant as it all was, I dreamed of freedom from this room and from discussing my past.

On a frosty February afternoon, Dr. H started our fifty-minute session oddly. He spoke first.

"Miss Holmes, while we've started doing important work here, I'd recommend you go into analysis. As a psychiatrist I don't delve into deeper personal histories. However, I can make a referral."

I'd had no idea that therapy came in different servings, as if it were a dim sum menu. No matter. Once the pall cleared, I said, voice cracking, "No, thanks. I'm fine."

"You've experienced a traumatic event and need more time to process it."

"Dr. H, I really don't need to take up more of your time."

He stared across the desk for a moment and then said with notable sadness, "All the best to you. If you want to discuss anything, please call me."

Three decades later, I can still recall the warm river of relief that carried me back to the ad agency, southward on Madison Avenue, on foot. I peered into shop windows, alive with possibility, believing anything they contained could be mine. I'd met the challenge of therapy. I could achieve any goal.

From March to May, I remained on the island of drinking and denial. My family back in Michigan was assured of my mental stability, simply because I continued to work. The Holmes family mantra, expressed by my Depression-era grandparents who survived floods and the segregated South, was "Just Do It" long before Nike adopted that phrase. So I worked, went home, drank, and started again. A Sisyphean game. Then the office closed for the first three-day summer weekend.

Without a physical diversion, I paced about my apartment, unmoored, clad in a floor-length, sleeveless, pale nightgown, sobbing and howling, driven by my guilt and grief, like Ophelia. Memorial Day weekend lived up to its name.

My cries cracked and broke the air; my stomach heaved and hurt. These tears were different than the silent weeping that could be contained to a bed or bathroom. This grief had a will of its own, unwieldy and relentless. And with no work to sandbag against the agony, for two days tears flooded in.

Sunday afternoon, desperate for a distraction, I clicked on the TV, spotting a title on the electronic cable guide I thought might help: *Terms of Endearment*. The experience was paramount to gulping a glass of water while drowning.

By evening, I no longer tried to respect my apartment's sheetrock walls. I wailed and shrieked in a homemade version of primal therapy. Not because I'd read about it, or because Dr. H had broached it as a treatment, but simply because it hurt too much to keep the pain inside.

* * *

Tuesday morning, before sunrise, I began dialing Dr. H's office. When the answering machine picked up, I'd hang up the phone and return to sipping my coffee. After thirty minutes I'd dial again, needing to connect to a real human being. An hour and a half later, he answered.

"I think I'm having a nervous breakdown," I whispered. Hearing the words outside my head gave them a greater gravity. Words I couldn't reveal to a mere machine.

"Come to my office now."

I threw on my clothes, jammed some cash into the pocket of my jeans, and ran for the door. I can't even say for sure that I showered. What I can say for sure is this: I no longer wanted to carry the banner of blackness. No longer would I honor the code of "we do not share our business with white people" for the protection of the black diaspora. I wanted to save my life.

Dr. H and I restarted our sessions. He became a much-needed anchor as I worked to manage the whirling grief and endless drinking that I'd come to acknowledge as self-medicating. I talked more. I shared more. Two months later, thanks to Dr. H's recommendation, I was assigned Dr. S—a curvy woman in her mid-thirties with wavy dark hair—through the Psychoanalytic Institute, a nonprofit that offers low-fee treatment services to the New York metropolitan community. Dr. S needed a reliable patient to complete her analyst coursework. I needed the sliding scale, which meant I paid $15 per session.

By now I was beginning to see the results of therapy and the help it could provide. But as my new shrink set down the rules, panic rose.

"Why do we have to meet three to four times a week?"

"It helps me see the ebb and flow of your life, so I can understand you better and help you more."

"Okay," I said weakly.

We discussed my work with Dr. H, and Dr. S shifted her questions, inquiring if I was ready for the rigors of analysis.

"It won't be a problem."

"You seem certain. Can I ask why?"

"That weekend, I felt myself coming apart. Frankly, it frightened me so, I'd do most anything to prevent experiencing that again."

She smiled.

"Will I have to lie down?" I asked, eyeing the oatmeal-colored couch across the room, where the shape of a small pillow lay under a thin, white, linen towel.

"In time. But for now, we'll talk this way, facing each other."

And so we began. I started out with the death of Art and how I was managing. It all seemed to be going well, until Dr. S broached the subject of my childhood.

"I'm not here to discuss that. Art's death will give us more than enough areas to plow through. And we haven't even covered the loss of my college professor Ivan from leukemia. Art helped me through that."

A silence flooded the room. My fingernails dug into my palms.

"You know, the loss of your college professor is linked to the loss of Art. They're not mutually exclusive."

That fresh insight zinged my brain. I made my living shaping words, seeing them in my mind's eye and placing them onto the page or computer screen. Now the words of my shrink were beginning to reshape my thinking. It would not be the last time Dr. S formed an insight of importance for me.

So I talked about my workaholic dad and worry-filled mom, about the time I decided to take a solo weekend in the Oceanside town of Greenport, a two-hour drive from Manhattan. Calling all the way from Michigan, my mom laid down her demand over the phone.

"Jenine, cancel the trip. I don't want you traveling alone."

"I need some time out of the city," I said, and changed the subject. More than a year after Art's death, I still found it difficult to be in my apartment alone, in my skin.

The next morning, as I carried my suitcase to the front door, my landline rang.

"Jenine, I'm begging you," Mom said, choking back tears. "Please don't go alone."

In my then twenty-eight years of life, my mother had never begged me to do anything. Maybe Art's death had affected her, too. I lived in the city of eight million stories. Not all of them have happy endings. But now Dr. S was encouraging me to make my own happiness. And this road trip, my first major journey since Art's death, was my stake in the ground.

"Mom, I'll call you when I get there," I promised, and then clicked off. An hour later I found the courage to get in the car.

Dr. S sighed and then said something remarkable. "Jenine, parents sometimes try to inoculate their children against the dangers of the world by using fear. But it comes from a place of love."

My brain cracked open, new cells forming and shaping from her insight.

So I opened up to Dr. S and stayed open. After a few months, I noticed that my dreams of Art had lessened, my survivor's guilt had waned. Others noticed the change, too.

"What's going on with you?" Elisabeth asked over after-work drinks. "You hardly share anything anymore. Are you even dating anyone?"

"Guess I tell my shrink all that now."

The air crackled. Elisabeth glared. My friend, a white Manhattanite, was in therapy, so her jealousy was surprising. Over time I'd learn that sharing the granular details of my life with girlfriends was gossip fodder. Confiding in Dr. S helped create lessons my mother and girlfriends couldn't match.

When a first date went horribly wrong, Dr. S put a fresh lens to the event. "When you start dating, people put their best manners forward. If that was his best, perhaps he did you a favor."

"I still feel adrift after Art's death. It's been a year and a half and I'm still unsure how to date."

"Don't let your loss define you. You still get to choose."

It had never occurred to me to return to the land of selectivity.

While I was becoming more open and honest in psychotherapy, I continued holding the secret from the majority of my friends and family. And my new agency. I kept my cards close, dashing out of the office four times a week, keeping my creative directors and co-workers in the dark. I took a taxi from Chelsea to the Upper East Side. Afterward, I worked an extra hour to make up for the extended lunchtime. After two years, Dr. S still merited that kind of hustle.

But one afternoon as I darted back to my desk with my lunch, a creative director bellowed my name. I sprinted to Nat's office at the far end of the loft and settled into a chair that faced Nat's desk. His eyes raged. Standing to the left of Nat was his partner Marty. He was broad-shouldered and stood over six feet tall. And in this moment his face was tight with worry.

"Where do you go at lunch time?" Nat said.

"Out . . . to grab lunch."

"*Grab lunch?* You're gone almost two damn hours."

I grimaced.

Nat's face reddened. "We know you're working here *and* at another ad agency!"

"No! I go to therapy. I'm in analysis!" I yelled.

"Why didn't you tell me that when I asked where you went last week?" Marty asked.

"I was ashamed."

"*Ashamed?* I go! Marty goes! We all go!" Nat got up from his chair, bolted around his desk, and hugged me.

I exhaled.

I'd outed myself at work but failed to do so with my family. I feared their fierce disapproval, even reprisal. But like Anatole Broyard, I, too, came to see every secret has a shelf life.

A few weeks later, as my mom updated me on the shenanigans of her eighth-grade students, I cut in and announced,

"I'm seeing a therapist." I used the word *therapist*, rather than the correct term, *analyst*, reasoning that it came across as lighter, less Woody Allen neurotic, more acceptable to my mother's ears than reality.

"If that's what you feel you need to do," my mom said and went back to her student stories. Sadness crouched on my chest. A piece of me had hoped she'd ask questions, hoped she'd want to know if the sessions were helping me. In time, I realized the centerpiece of my analysis was self-help, evoking a personal change, not changing my mom. I could only work to understand her better.

Over time, there were other stressors—the pressures of advertising, my father's heart attack and death, my surprising pregnancy, which led to an even more surprising miscarriage, and the end of a three-year relationship. Life provided enough coal to mine in the carpeted solitude of my shrink's Upper East Side office.

Before the miscarriage I'd flown to Minnesota to meet my boyfriend's family. Dr. S and I had begun discussing my ending treatment. Life was good until it wasn't, until the bad lightning struck again.

Afterward, I'd make my way to a park bench in Carl Schultz Park to regroup, to reapply my blush and mascara, putting on my game face before returning to the office. I needed to sit among the green leaves and the young lives at play as I put the past to rest.

* * *

Two years later, Dr. S and I agreed it was time to reduce my sessions to twice a week. In our seventh year together I laughed more during more sessions. At times, Dr. S joined me. I made my way back to the land of advertising without post-session park time.

On a warm afternoon in May, she announced, "Our work is coming to a close in a month. I wanted to get a sense of how you feel."

"I understand myself better. But we can't stop. I still have baggage," I joked from the couch.

Dr. S laughed. "Everyone has baggage. But yours is labeled. And you know what's inside."

I stared up at the cream-colored ceiling. A gaggle of girls from the neighboring private school giggled their way down the sidewalk, just beyond the window, their sneakers and shoes scuffing the cement. I would miss this space, this time.

"The goal isn't to unpack everything but to give you the skills to understand yourself better, what your triggers are," she said.

The doctor was right. I'd changed. The woman I'd become under her watchful, supportive care was better than the one I'd shed. Jenine 2.0 moved through the world with less anger, less worry, less fear; she was more comfortable with discomfort. I mourned the dead and lived my life guilt-free. I was prepared to leave the psychiatric nest, but I'd miss the partnership of patient and doctor.

I swiveled my sandaled feet from the couch and stood up. Afternoon sunlight saturated the small room. I faced Dr. S.

"Is hugging allowed in analysis?"

"Yes, of course."

She smelled of Chloe perfume and Pantene shampoo.

"Can I email you every now and then?"

"Yes, I'd be happy to hear from you."

I wanted her to know when milestones occurred, such as

the finalization of my adoption of an Ethiopian child. Dr. S was instrumental in my making the leap from single woman to single mom, in helping me manage my worry and fears about adopting a child on my own, in turning the Holmes family work mantra back on itself: "Busy people can always do more. You can handle it," she said.

Dr. S suggested I keep dating and searching for the right guy, hoping romantic lightning would strike again, as it had with Art.

"Your life isn't always lived in the order society tells you it will be. You can run a parallel path," she wrote in an email. "Look for the guy while working toward adoption."

And when I thought I'd found the guy, only to subsequently realize that I hadn't, again Dr. S was there, via the Internet, for support.

Two years after I ended treatment and three years after I began the process of international adoption, I was able to email Dr. S the photo that the Ethiopian orphanage sent to my New York social worker. A photo and report were created to help prospective parents choose whether to complete the adoption. And once I saw the image of a smiling two-month-old girl, I knew. I started the paperwork, emailed the image to my family, a few close friends, and, of course, my former shrink.

"This may seem odd to say," she emailed back. "But she has your eyes."

* * *

My black family taught me how to survive and thrive, but three white people taught me the importance of feeling the good, the bad, and what lies in between. Life happens in the in-between. It takes knowing what sets you off, rather than going with silent, sullen destructive acts. Or giving into crippling fear. Now I activate a new code. Fear still finds me at times. But when it comes, I take out my labeled luggage and peer inside.

My parents rarely spoke in terms of race. However, my mom told my brothers and me throughout our childhood, with a rare forthrightness regarding racial matters: "The Jews are like us. They've suffered, too." Perhaps that "suffering" is what helped me most. Suffering can shape a true appreciation of the good when it comes along.

* * *

I've learned the power of words is found by releasing them. As a writer, I hold and shape words on to the page, into experiences. But as a human being I've learned the importance of letting them go. If I hadn't, I firmly believe, Jenine 1.0 wouldn't have survived.

It is seven years since I ended analysis, yet I think of my former shrink almost daily. How could I not? Ours was one of the longest and most important unions of my life.

After seven years of making my way to the Upper East Side, toward connection and understanding, I find no matter the weather, I can't stay inside the office at the noon hour. I must go out and see what's happening in the world beyond the press and grind of advertising, to remember that good lightning strikes abound, to recall the value of moving my body and mind toward something more important than food.

Not Even a Smidgen

| *Molly Peacock* |

It was never an absolutely "classical" analysis. It was more like exploring a vast chambered nautilus shell, say, the size of a small planet—for thirty-eight years. Not a straight four decades, but in bits and fits and long waxes and silent wanes. Then just before our, what was it, thirteen-hundredth(?) appointment (more than a thousand lustrous chambers), I received a call from her colleague saying that my psychotherapist had suffered a debilitating stroke. Apparently it was the biggest brain bleed they'd ever seen in that frenzied New York City hospital emergency room—an AVM. (Arteriovenus malformation occurs as the brain develops in the womb, like a little time bomb. Hers went off at age seventy-seven.) When I heard, "She will never practice again," on that cold, humid March Sunday in 2012, I assumed she would die. Instead we entered a new chamber that, even in my forty years as a poet with a huge tolerance for strangeness and metaphor, devastates and inspires me. Call it a coda for that never absolutely classical analysis.

Let me say straight off that she no longer practices. And that she has asked me to name her: Joan Workman Stein, Radcliffe Class of 1954, Smith College School of Social Work, Analytic Training at the Postgraduate Center for Mental Health (now the Postgraduate Psychoanalytic Society and Institute). She was first my therapist, then my analyst, and later an interesting combination of both. Before I get into particulars, let me describe Joan to you at her most vivid. Why describe? Because when one is mystified, describing, like drawing, pins things down. She is short, about five feet, two inches. In her prime: dark haired, dark-eyed, piquant, trim, with an expressive face, intelligently alive. Her vocabulary was, and still is, full of a New Yorker's hyperbole— "marvelous," "exciting," "huge," "spectacular"—yet this energy used to be held in check by a slow walk to open the door to her apartment (I could hear those steps as I waited in the hall), and the low hello of welcome as neutral as an expressive person could muster. She was beautifully, slightly unconventionally dressed, in the way that many painters, no matter how tall, short, fat, or proportioned they are, have an innate sense of what looks perfect on them. A woman who wore red lipstick with élan.

And she was someone who, though capable of waiting hours for me to creep out of the rainforest of my own tears and silences as if she were Jane Goodall patiently waiting for a chimp, could also speak her mind in no uncertain terms. On occasion, when the years of "the worst" were long over, I sometimes, especially if we had an appointment on the phone, wrote down what she said. Here's one, word for word, at least as I scribbled it, from five years before her stroke:

If I wrote about my work, what I'd write about is how the classical Freudian psychoanalysis leads toward termination, toward cleaning up all the little issues. But in fact, many therapists now see patients for decades. Termination is no longer thought to be something that must come to an end as if it were a course of penicillin. The fear used to be that, if you hold on to patients, they will have an unhealthy dependence that reflects the therapist's own pathology. However, if you work with people who are creatively re-inventing themselves, then the therapy is inventive. You don't have to give it up like smoking or alcohol! Instead it increases the likelihood that things will work out. I have the absolute conviction that it's a creative process, that it isn't pathological, not even a smidgen.

Not even a smidgen.

I first saw her in my twenties, in face-to-face therapy in Binghamton, New York, as I left a young marriage and launched into graduate school. But our most serious labor—our analytical work—took place in my thirties and early forties as I forged my literary career in New York City. Twice, sometimes three times a week, for eight years—all that my teacher's salary at a Quaker school with a generous insurance policy allowed me. I grew up, got a grip, and slowly managed (between screaming matches and makeup sex with the artiste who greeted me at 5 p.m. still in his bathrobe) to make a true life of letters—four books of poems! President of a national poetry organization. My wild father, a violent alcoholic, had died; my wilder sister had given up heroin for methadone. My depressed mother was free and managing financially and emotionally. I'd gotten the literary existence I dreamed of by the indirect route of describing my dreams with Joan's encouragement—and note the word *courage* between the "en" and the "ment." Also notice the "rage" at the end of courage. Joan had the courage to see me deep into the journey. I supplied the rage.

Rage was the last thing I experienced after her colleague called. It was instant, unmitigated grief. I burst into tears. Unlike with my mother's, father's, or sister's deaths, I didn't have a complicated reaction. This was pure, full-out keening, basic and unalloyed. As an older woman, I hardly ever feel anything unalloyed. Layers upon layers of emotions and experiences react and reify and ricochet as things happen in my seventh decade. (I'm sixty-eight, and Joan is eighty-one.) In this latest loss I had the pleasure of purity. I pitched into childhood; I could have been Timmy losing Lassie.

* * *

In our sessions I constantly used the image of a tin pail. A white-enameled tin pail sat in the kitchen at my grandparents' very cozy, very primitive little house (it had electricity, but no running water) near the swinging wooden door that led to a pump room where you pumped well water for everything: to flush a toilet, fill a kettle, wash a body or a dinner's worth of dishes—all the ablutions. The pail was essential to the activities of living. It had a singularly important role, as I felt I did in my own family. In our house, also small but distinctly not cozy since my father in his rages had broken all the decorative objects, I cooked, cleaned, and saw to my sister's homework plus my father's beer bottles from the age of twelve to eighteen, when I blessedly left for college to re-begin my adolescence.

Crucially, my grandparents' pail stood empty until it was time to be used. Like the pail, I was fully formed but dry, a well-made, functional receptacle (a responsible girl. My college advisor said, "Molly, you were 104 the day you were born!"), beautiful in shape. But I was only formed on the outside. My inordinate adult responsibilities left no time for the inner core to coalesce, for a natural childhood and adolescent growth. Yet, I had enormous energy and a personal power I only partly recognized. Others did. Especially Joan.

In the early 1990s when, after a twenty-year gap, I re-encountered the man who had once been the boy who took me to the senior prom, we shared a fully adult kiss. It suddenly felt as if I had been filled with well water. At one point in a session, Joan reached her hand over the top of my headrest pillow from her position behind the couch and held my hand as I trembled (literally) at the prospect of that teenage attachment becoming full-fledged love. Then she cheered when I married him. Off I went into the random beauty of a totally unexpected turn: creating a bi-national life between the Canada of my maturity (and part of my ancestry) and the New York of my youth.

Almost immediately after I married that boyfriend, my mother, who'd been seriously depressed, died of lung cancer. A couple of years later my sister relapsed into addiction and then, diagnosed with throat cancer, died of an overdose. The telephone became critically important. Being on the phone—I was in Canada and Joan in New York City—was like being on the couch. I couldn't see her and spoke into the satisfying blackness. At first we kept up these regular appointments because of those crises, and later because I feared that, if I let go, I'd have to start all over again with someone else if my husband got really sick. (He is a six-time melanoma survivor, and I developed a way of living a "two-track" life, one track full of plans for life insurance and retirement, the other full of "seize it now, you might never have another chance.") So I didn't want to go to a Canadian analyst. I wanted to carry New York with me; I wanted my collaborator, my witness, my questioner, my encourager, my analyst who, unlike the other analysts who sensibly vacationed in August, *instead* took off six whole weeks in April (National Poetry Month, for heavens sake!) and May to venture to Italy without us, her patients. I wanted my infuriator.

"I assume when Freud was an analyst, there were no phones," she joked one pre-stroke day in one of our 2007 sessions, when I was writing things down:

> *I'm not generally as drawn to the phone as a lot of people are, but I'm totally comfortable on the phone with you. It comes down to the fact that you can read me on the phone, and I can read you. Otherwise, it would evaporate. On the phone, we're really dependent on language. So we have to give voice to all sorts of levels. With so many patients, it's their body language, but with you I can get it over the phone . . . I have to be very sensitive to language.*

Sensitive to language. Perhaps it was a thirty-eight-year poem we were writing.

I am drawn to the phone and am devoted to my iPhone,

with its library of audiobooks for when a person wakes up in the night. Three months after Joan's stroke I went to Dublin and, jet-lagged in a hotel bed, rolled over onto this beloved cell. When it suddenly glowed with her name (had I pressed Joan's number on my Favorites?), I canceled the call—marveling at the unconscious. I'd actually reached out to her in my sleep!

Another chamber of the dream life?

But it *wasn't* my torso that had pressed Joan's number. The call had come from *her*. Returning home, I discovered she'd left a message on our land line—reaching out to the twenty-seven-year-old young woman who had once appeared at her door and who still existed at the surviving edge of the blast-hole in her memory. It was a tentative voice on the voice mail, having recovered just enough language to leave a message: "I. Can't. Be. Your. Therapist. Anymore." Then the central core of her warmth and emotion became volubly present in the next four ringing words. "I miss you hugely."

I hightailed it to New York.

We were there in her living room, the therapy room. She sat in her chair. I sat on the couch I usually lay on. She looked surprisingly good, despite the still shaggy hospital-stay hair. She wore a long black sweater vest and a low-slung silver belt over her black pants. But now there was an attendant who slipped into the bedroom to leave us alone. Joan's face wore a new expression, a wide-eyed quizzical look. She told me that she could not read a novel, or write an email, or watch a whole hour of TV—"But I hope," she said, "I hope." There was absolutely no possibility of continuing her practice. A cadre of doctors and post-stroke therapies awaited her. But the unadorned directness of our former, therapeutic conversations was alive. I could be as forthright and presumptuous as always. "Would you rather be dead?" I asked her. "No," she answered with candor. "I check myself for signs of depression all the time." That's the therapist talking. But then I heard a new tone of voice, and a new assertion. "Since I can paint, I want to live."

You know, chambered nautili have distinct shapes. That's why their calcification is beautiful. But now the shape of this one was dissolving. We were back at sea.

For all along, in what I thought was *my* analysis, I have also been inside *her* story.

And herewith is the tale of the woman who dressed like a painter—and became a painter at last:

When Joan was a college freshman, just after her father died, the Radcliffe dean sent her, a gifted girl who had studied art with a group of adult artists in high school, off down the street to study painting with a die-hard abstractionist at Harvard. But all she wanted to do was paint images of her father. Faces were what mattered. His face. The human form as close as one could come with one's hand to draw and paint it. Figuration. Then the abstractionist delivered his blisteringly brutal critique.

The bold seeker I knew, and know, and love, did what any self-respecting student with a rebellious heart would do. She walked out of the class.

But after that she froze in stubborn rigidity. Never went back. And didn't pick up a brush for more than twenty years.

* * *

For decades in our work together (or play—the back and forth of metaphor, analogy, simile), I refused to ask anything about her. "If I know about you, I'll feel I have to take care of you,"

I said. And we guarded those boundaries as distinctly as Henri Matisse guarded his figures when he outlined them in black. But slowly, as that central core of myself filled, as I wrote a memoir, performed a one-woman show, collected my poems into further volumes, and then embarked on the huge project of writing the biography of Mrs. Mary Delany, an eighteenth-century woman who invented collage in her seventies, the biographical details of Joan's life became meaningful to me. So I began to ask some questions, and she began to answer me. In the past decade, she has in various versions confided the story of the critique and how her painting stopped, and how, when she moved to New York in her forties (the late 1970s and early 1980s), she began taking psychoanalytic training and painting again. I knew when that happened because some of those watercolors began appearing on her walls.

On this day of my first visit to our altered universe, there was a whole gallery of her work. And I, who thought I might never have the chance to see her after that, was emboldened to ask for a painting. It was almost at the end of the hour (isn't that when the best "work" gets done?) that I summoned the courage to ask. She was delighted and asked me to choose. I asked for a still life of lemons and a blue bowl that now hangs on my wall—I pass it hourly. Two yellow citrus fruits. One fruit for the devastation of the end: the end to novels, the end to reading *The New York Times*, the end, ever, to walking in the city by herself, the end to flipping out a bank card and stopping to get cash at an ATM—those machines are objects of mystery and mistakes now—and another fruit for the yield of time, the shining possibilities of the coda. Now, the brush is all. The chastised seventeen-year-old has lifted up her head, and her dark hair is gray, and her hands have arthritis, and she doesn't see nearly as well as she did before the stroke. Nevertheless, the once-stopped life of the artist now flows. Now flowers.

We walked from watercolor to watercolor discussing their patterns and light. And there I watched the woman who backed me up in every artistic decision return to the artist she'd once lost. The therapy room/living room of her one-bedroom Upper West Side apartment? Now it's a *studiolo*. Paints are permanently installed on the small dining area table. Not much to read piled up, but the classical CDs are on. Print departed. Music stayed.

From her clothes. To her walls. What a delicious sense of line and design. I have shared memories of how Joan used to dress with several of her other patients, one of whom, the novelist Janice Eidus, published a piece about her online. In our reminiscences we delighted in Joan's clothes: one coat-vest was a paisley of reds, browns, and blacks. Joan wore it over a black turtleneck and black pants. Add the belt with its silver buckle. Cap that with well-cut hair, streaked with gray. Apply the signature lipstick.

Description. It re-creates life from extinction. Analysis is all gone now.

It is hard for me to write it: the analyst I knew is dead.

But the painter is alive, and hungry.

Time for brunch—*brunch???* How we have altered. Who is she now to me? Sort of mother. Sort of sister. Sort of friend. Partner in endless levels of ambiguity.

The enthusiastic, cane-wielding Joan tucks away a whole platter of French toast. "I like being with you," she says, and I beam. Who doesn't want their analyst (excuse me, former analyst) to like being with them? "Because you're not afraid of me." She is sublime in her clarity. "Other people don't know what to do with me. They're afraid or embarrassed. They push away. They're nervous. But you get me."

And what do I get? Or is it beget? The creation of something the mind makes as it meets a description the hand makes: art. Continually the old image of Joan passes through the new. It is time for *me* to get *her*. No! I only want to be gotten . . . But that idea is misbegotten. What a model she is for continuing on with zest, and for the salutary, life-giving power of an art she gave up—helping me, and so many of her other writer-artist patients, never give up on this power in our lives. I see it rescue her, refresh her, fill a world with the vigor of her perceptions. The vigor of my own art was born in the hiatus of hers. After she stubbornly walked out of that abstraction class at Harvard, after the critique shut her down, she turned to living faces. She married, had two sons, divorced, eventually became a talented psychotherapist, moved to New York City, established her practice—and began taking art classes again. A molten life, a modern woman's life.

One thing that hasn't changed at all is her voice: it is rich, ribbony, husky, and open to laughter, to a good chortle. It comes across on a voice mail with a deep, distilled quality, for she regularly leaves me messages—another thing I can't quite get used to.

Language. Gauge. Engage.

"We work so well on the phone because we're both very engaged," I wrote down in those 2007 notes. Joan went on about our not-so-classical analysis:

> *It's got a life . . . You and I have had the leisure*
> *of going for decades . . . What it's enabled me to*

*do—well, one has a sense of one's own history
and epiphanies. I feel as though I have your life
in my head in the same way as I know myself.
To have the images and vocabulary to enter into
someone's mental study . . . It's the way one feels
when they are finally bilingual, have studied a
language so long they dream in it.*

* * *

Will I ever be bilingual in the new and old Joan, the dead and the living Joan, the artist become the listener, and again become the artist? When I hear, "Since I can paint, I want to live," I take the deepest consolation from those words. But I deeply miss the therapist I love. Images of the Joan who helped me flicker across the Joan I help into a taxi to jaunt to a museum. After three years I am still in the state of shock that is a little bit like being caught on the other side of a simile, not being able to cross back into the reality you tried to describe with that simile in the first place. "Her face was wet as a trout," Anne Sexton wrote in her book of fairy-tale poems, *Transformations*, about a girl weeping. Sometimes I feel my tears changed me into that fish—and I cannot swim back.

Yet the activity of making art—the creative process that never comes to an end "as if it were a course of penicillin," that always is "creative" and not "pathological, not even a smidgen"—is exactly what happens when a person "is creatively reinventing herself." And with that breathtaking thought I must put the nautilus that was once like a small planet but is now something small enough to hold in my hand back on the shelf. It is an artifact now. But an artifact (as anyone who has seen a photograph of Freud's room, or has been to the living room–therapy room, now *studiolo*, of Joan Stein, or to any analyst's space well knows) can provoke our deepest responses. So now, with that vast planet of a shell whorled back into its small, sturdy, redoubtable suggestion of an image:

I lie down to dream in her.

An Unexpected Healer

| *Mindy Greenstein* |

It's the summer of 2006. I'm forty-three years old and sitting on our red living room rug, sobbing so hard I can barely hold up my head. And it's not only because I have never liked that boring rug. I'm thinking about my sons, Isaac, five, and Max, ten. How long would I have to survive to make sure Isaac always remembers me? How long could I stay vibrant and fun, so that Max keeps close that version of me instead of the vulnerable, cranky person I'm quickly becoming?

When I'd trained years earlier as a clinical psychology intern on locked inpatient psychiatric units, I never worried about receiving a diagnosis of schizophrenia. And during the time I worked as a forensic psychologist for the Federal Bureau of Prisons, I never feared one day becoming an inmate myself. But from the day I started my postdoctoral fellowship in psycho-oncology at Memorial Sloan Kettering Cancer Center, I was keenly aware one day I might find myself in my patients' shoes. Rather than conquer this fear—impossible!—I learned to live with it and even to appreciate the way it forced me to think about what it meant to have a meaningful life. My patients often coped better if they turned their *Why me?* into *Why not me?* As a psycho-oncologist, I did something similar. I didn't spend my time hoping it would never happen to me. Instead, I learned to accept that it could happen and went on with my day. Or so I thought.

Cancer patients often experience their lives as bisected into the *before*, which they remember almost nostalgically, and the *after*, overwhelming everything that had come before. My job was to help patients rediscover coping skills that they had used to weather previous crises, or to discuss solutions to practical problems, like trying relaxation exercises. But one of my ultimate goals was to help them maintain a sense of continuity in their lives, to remember the ways in which they used to find meaning and how they might still, despite the fears weighing them down. If they were mothers or fathers, they still had children to tend to and laugh with. If they used to love taking photographs or fighting for a cause dear to their hearts, when the dust settled there would still be scenes to shoot and causes to champion.

Helping people cope with existential crises inspired me to realize my long-forgotten childhood dream to be a writer. I started writing personal essays about my work, whether they were about issues like denial or how it felt to sit at someone's deathbed.

When I discovered, at the end of my fellowship, that I was pregnant with Isaac, I took time off to raise my two boys and write a book about what I was learning at both ends of the life cycle. It felt like a special privilege to help others contemplate their mortality while I could appreciate and enjoy the early bloom of life. I was encouraged by a literary agent, though he felt I needed a "cohesive narrative arc" to tie my varied experiences together. I had no idea what that meant but hoped I'd figure it out along the way.

* * *

Since I received my breast cancer diagnosis, I have cried often. But this particular morning, collapsed on the rug, my sobbing reaches a new intensity, as if all the terrors are finally rushing me at once. I am terrorized not only by what I know but even more by what I don't know. I don't yet know my cancer's stage or prognosis, or whether I'll need chemotherapy or radiation. I don't know what side effects I'll have to endure, either temporarily or permanently. All I know is that tumors have popped up all over my left breast, I'll need a double mastectomy, and the best outcome I can hope for, based on the biopsy, is Stage II, the dividing line between early- and late-stage cancer. Will I die before my kids are teenagers? I don't know. How much do I trust medical science? I don't know that either. I'd had a clean mammogram and a clean bill of health from the gynecologist just a couple of weeks before I discovered my tumors while doing a breast self-exam, which doctors no longer recommend (good thing I didn't know that).

My biggest shock is how hard this is. All my work with cancer patients seems to have flown out the window, all the time spent helping men and women cope, talking about their lives, learning how to live with either total uncertainty or *the new normal*. Now, I am a civilian like everyone else, sobbing, not sleeping for nights on end, unable to focus. I force myself to do the relaxation exercises I used to teach others, which helps a bit, though not enough.

I will consider taking psychiatric medication, but not yet. Meds might take the edge off my terror, but they won't teach me how to navigate it. I consider restarting the psychotherapy I'd been in for sixteen years. It's been a couple of years since I "graduated." But for now I prefer spending hour after hour on the phone with breast cancer survivors, most of whom I've never met in person. They are friends of friends or members of email groups I belong to, and their kindness and generosity with their time floor me. As long as I'm on the phone with them, I feel less alone.

My tears erupt, this particular morning, in the silence of our apartment while my husband is at work and my sons are in school. I realize that no matter how many loving people try to comfort me, no matter how many survivors I have known in worse straits—whose surgeries left them with a crater where their cheek used to be, or who lost limbs, or who have no hope of living out the year—I still feel profoundly alone in the world. And I think, *The real fight has not even started yet. How can this psycho-oncologist already be coping so badly?*

Then something extraordinary happens. An image flashes through my head, just for a moment. But a moment is enough. My crying stops almost instantly, and I feel at peace for the first time since this whole nightmare began. It is an image of Sarah, a hospital inpatient I treated briefly years before. It is this image that creates my new *before* and *after*. It is the moment I know I will find my way.

* * *

I met Sarah during the first year of my psycho-oncology training. Officially, the medical team asked me to see Sarah to assess her ability to understand and consent to treatment. But it was more than that. She'd just been diagnosed with a digestive cancer and was already facing a make-or-break surgery in a few days; she would either be cured or die within the year. But Sarah, then in her late sixties, also had another problem: paranoid schizophrenia. Thanks to a cocktail of psychiatric medications she'd been taking for thirty years, she had been able to carve out a life for herself at her group home, and to actually thrive. But those medications had to be stopped immediately—as did all oral food and liquids—in the days leading up to her surgery. Psychologically speaking, Sarah was on her own for the first time in decades, just when she most needed help.

As soon as I walked into Sarah's hospital room, I saw the first effects of her going off medications so abruptly. The medusa-like mass of brown and gray tangles about her head was my first hint she was in the midst of a psychotic episode. Personal grooming was often the first to go: when your mind is dealing with raging delusions about people wanting to kill you, or voices commanding you to do bizarre things, who thinks of picking up a comb or toothbrush? The second hint was even more straightforward: raging delusions and hallucinations. Sarah reported hearing voices constantly. And she was sure her boyfriend at the group home had been murdered by staff and that all the home's staff and patients were covering it up.

But one aspect of Sarah's demeanor didn't fit this otherwise intense scene: she was the most serenely hopeful person I'd ever met. She spoke evenly and without fear, whether discussing the details of her diagnosis—which even in her deluded state she understood perfectly—or the voices and alleged murder. Wondering if this was the calm before the storm, I asked about the voices.

"There are three of them. Jesus, Moses, and Satan. It's like they're sitting on the bed with me and they all say different things."

"Is it upsetting to start hearing voices again, when you haven't heard them in such a long time?"

"Oh, no!" Sarah's lips curled up at the edges in a smile. "Jesus and Moses say nice things to me. They tell me everything will be all right. They say the doctors are trying very hard. Like that."

"What about Satan?" I prodded. "What does he say?"

"Oh," she shuddered, "it's too horrible. I can't repeat it."

"How does that feel, when he tells you such horrible things?"

Sarah looked at me almost maternally and laughed.

"Oh, him?" she snorted, waving her hand in the air as if shooing away a pesky insect. "I just don't pay him no mind."

Was this seeming strength for real, or a dam about to burst?

It was real. I continued to see Sarah every day, though I came to realize she didn't really need my help. Despite her wild hair, delusions, and hallucinations, she sailed through the next days, including her surgery. She kept listening to the voices that helped her stay calm and ignoring the ones that didn't. The doctors were able to remove the cancer. She would need follow-up but no further treatment. Better yet, her prognosis was excellent. Back on psych meds, Sarah happily returned to the group home, her fear of murder conspiracies a thing of the past. When I bumped into her a few months later at her follow-up appointment, her grooming now matched her demeanor: her hair was gathered up in a neat bun, and she wore a lovely beige suit with matching shoes. We greeted each other with a smile.

It is the image of Sarah cheerfully shooing away Satan that flashes through my mind while collapsed on the red rug, stopping my tears cold and filling me with warmth and hope. If she could find a way to ignore her demons, *why not me?* I don't know how, just that I'll figure it out. This faith brings with it a new serenity. It turns out it was I who needed Sarah's help, rather than the other way around.

Soon, I start integrating my *before* and *after*. To my surprise, it isn't only the people who were cured, like Sarah, who inspire me. It's everyone trying to live their life in the face of life's random cruelties. I think of a dying grandfather who treated his young grandchildren to a trip they'd remember forever, even though they might not remember him; or the man who hoped there were newspapers in heaven so he could keep up with all the latest inventions. I remember so many who tried to teach their friends and family—sometimes even from their deathbeds—the joy of being alive for as long as we've got. Rather than scaring me, my memories console, as they remind me what fine company I'm in.

* * *

It has been nine years since that day on the rug. I did have chemotherapy and, a few years later—after a second bout of cancer—radiation, too. With Max now in college and Isaac in high school, I no longer worry how well they'll remember me. I am back at Memorial Sloan Kettering as a psycho-oncology consultant, as well as for yearly follow-up checkups. I did finally publish that book, *The House on Crash Corner (and Other Unavoidable Calamities)*, about what I learned from both sides of the hospital bed. I've even softened toward the rug.

I guess I found that cohesive narrative arc.

The Tao of Apples

| *Kurt Nemes* |

At almost sixty, I was hoping to coast into retirement in a few years. For nearly half my life I'd lived in the Washington, D.C., area, working for an international bank a block from the White House. But then my organization restructured. My new boss, fifteen years younger than me, called me into his office. Originally from Nigeria, Bayo had practiced labor law in London for two decades and spoke with a crisp British accent.

"Kurt, you must learn to conduct investigations."

He meant sleuthing for staff misconduct: theft, sexual harassment, bullying, misuse of benefits, and conflicts of interests. Our reports would go to senior management, who meted out discipline. I'd heard stories that witnesses cried and the subjects were belligerent during interviews. It was hard to imagine me, a friendly extrovert, liking this new task.

After twenty-six years, I'd risen to the level of senior trainer in our Ethics office. I loved my job and was good at it.

I flew all over the world to conduct workshops on values and received top ratings from participants, who came to trust me to the point that many called with their problems well after the workshop.

Now those who trusted me might start treating me like a member of the rat squad. Worse, most of my colleagues, unlike me, had law degrees. At my age, I feared being unable to learn the new skills required to match them.

"I'm not a lawyer," I protested.

"You needn't be one," replied my new boss. "I've got retired secretaries doing this. Also, I don't want you to do workshops by yourself anymore."

"But people tell me I'm a gifted trainer."

"Unless you've handled a misconduct case, you lack credibility." This stung. My expression must have been defiant because he next let slip that our organization was downsizing.

"If you can't do the job, Kurt, I will have to advertise your position."

The injustice of his ultimatum shocked me. In the days following I stewed, the scene replaying endlessly in my head. I couldn't let this go. In fact, my anger only grew as days turned into weeks. Before long, my anger became anxiety as I realized he really might get rid of me.

When I attempted to perform the new job, it was difficult concentrating and I forgot important details of my assigned cases. I developed symptoms of depression: insomnia, racing heart, anxiety, weight loss, and hopelessness.

Around Thanksgiving my condition worsened. I hadn't slept for weeks. In despair I wound up on the floor sobbing in front of my wife, Laura. She drove me to my general practitioner, who'd been my family doctor for twenty years. After describing the stress at work, I begged her to help, suggesting an antidepressant.

"I'll prescribe Wellbutrin, but have you thought about going on disability?"

"I can't. They'll fill my position."

Looking me in the eye, she said, "Kurt. It's your right. You can always get your job back, but you can never regain your health."

The stigma attached to disability worried me, but even my doctor felt the job was ruining my health. Secretly, I felt thrilled: I had an excuse to stay home, like a note from Mom.

At work, I visited the disability nurse, who described the application process. If approved, I could take up to two years off at 70 percent of my salary. This was better than I'd imagined. Still, I debated whether to leave or just tough it out.

Laura and I went apple picking the next day, and over a cup of steaming cider I asked what she thought about my doctor's recommendation.

"I don't understand," she said. "Why can't you just do what your new boss wants?"

"I wasn't hired for that. Besides, it shows he doesn't respect me."

"So how is taking disability for two years going to help you gain his respect?"

"Whose side are you on?" I asked, immediately regretting my outburst.

"Kurt, you're a smart guy. You can beat this."

"Maybe, but it's going to take at least two weeks for the Wellbutrin to kick in. What am I supposed to do until then?"

After a moment, she said, "Why don't you call Larry?"

Larry was a Washington psychiatrist we'd met at a party.

He was maybe in his seventies, but we'd hit it off and corresponded since then.

"But I couldn't become friends with him then."

"Why not?"

"He'd know too much."

Overcoming my embarrassment, I contacted Larry as we drove home. He said he'd be happy to see me, despite my concerns that there were existing boundary issues since we knew each other socially.

"I like to think of myself as a kind of small-town doctor," he said. "In olden days, you'd see your MD at the store, at worship, or at the market. You'd be friends."

An expensive friend—Larry charged almost $300 an hour. Luckily my employer's insurance paid 80 percent. Larry also offered a twofer: talk therapy and medication monitoring.

His office resembled Freud's in London: mandalas hung on the walls, Persian carpets covered most of the parquet floor, and orchids bloomed in the bay window.

Larry even looked a little like Freud as he scratched his peppery beard, nodded, and listened to my backstory. My parents were Hungarian and Belgian immigrants who worked in factories. As Catholics, we confessed to priests, not therapists. My first marriage ended after twenty-two years and two daughters. I rebounded with a new wife, and my career thrived. Then my new boss derailed everything. It took me almost the whole session to spew this out, and I finished with: "My doctor says I should go on disability."

"That's the stupidest thing I've ever heard," Larry said.

"What?"

"Kurt, I know you. You are very competent. You work at a great place and have a good job. But you're stuck in a loop of negative thoughts. They're overwhelming you. Hearing them overwhelmed me."

"Sorry, but this is what's going on in my head constantly. I can't sleep. As soon as I close my eyes, it starts again."

"No need to be sorry. Here's what you do. Every time you get an obsessive or self-deprecating thought, take off your watch and move it to the other arm."

"That's it?" I asked. There was no way this watch thing could reverse a lifetime of overthinking.

"Trust me. It will interrupt negative thoughts. When you move the watch, notice it, and think about a time when you were happy or felt proud."

He added Prozac to my Wellbutrin and said: "Our time is up."

"What about my boss?"

"We'll tackle that next week."

On my way to the door, I tried cramming in one more bit of information to show how deep my problem went, thinking he'd respond to a Freudian angle: "When I was in high school, my mother once said to me: 'You think too much, and about the wrong things.'"

"She was right. See you next week."

At the next session, Larry coached me on strategies for dealing with my new boss. Unlike my motherly general practitioner, who had offered me an excuse to bail, Larry acted like a tough-love dad: "Kurt, your boss has the right to assign you new duties. Why fight it and sabotage your career? Instead, just throw yourself into the work and knock it out of the park. You might end up liking the job."

At another session, Larry took aim at the inferiority complex dogging me since childhood. The last of four brothers and one sister ("We were trying for another girl," my mother admitted), I constantly wore hand-me-downs. My parents idolized my oldest brother, the first child on both sides of the family to go to college. He *literally* became a rocket engineer and worked on the Mars lander. Desperate to be noticed, I became a jokester and show-off like many babies of the family. I worked my way through college but never felt as smart as my brother—or as loved. Until they passed away, whenever my parents called to chat, they'd ask, "What is it you do?"

Switching my watch helped, but it didn't always stop me from judging myself. One day I came in to Larry's office obsessed at what a failure I had been—in my marriage, as a father, as a son. Larry got a smile on his face and leaned in.

"Do you like commercials?"

"Yeah, I guess."

"I love commercials. It's amazing how in just thirty seconds, the writers and directors can convey a whole story and get you to buy their product. I wish I could write like that."

"Me, too."

"So, here's what I want you to do. Write three commercials starring Kurt that show how great you are. Take your time. Visualize directing and starring in them yourself. Then, whenever you start to think about being worthless, play one in your head."

I tried it but only came up with two scenarios. In one, I'm at the beach on a sunny day. I look up as an airplane flies by, pulling an advertising banner that reads, "The New and Improved Kurt Nemes." Women on the beach point at me and say, "Look! That's him!" In another fantasy, two women chat over coffee, thumbing through an issue of *People*. One of the women points to a story: "It's Kurt Nemes. Isn't he dreamy?"

Although these fantasies brought a smile to my face, they also caused discomfort. I'd been brought up to be humble, not boastful. Who did I think I was, a Kardashian?

Maybe not, but being a Nemes was looking brighter. During a team meeting, my boss surprised me with this report on my performance at a recent training: "Kurt is a jewel of inestimable value. That's what we say in Nigeria."

When I reported on this to Larry, he commented: "Oh, I like that. It's much better than dreamy."

"But what if he was only throwing me a bone?" I asked. "Maybe he was being condescending, and I wasn't smart enough to get it."

"Kurt, let me ask you something. Do you really want to be happy?"

Caught off guard, I fumbled with my thoughts.

Larry smiled and said in a tone of true brotherly kindness, "If you're not going to be your own champion, Kurt, no one's going to do it for you. Everybody has their own stuff. They could care less about your struggle and aren't out to try and get you. That's just way too egotistical. At some point, you've got to take responsibility for your own life. That's the only way you'll change."

Was that it? Was it just easier to feel wounded than to grow up? With this reasoning, I saw part of me might be taking advantage of my illness so I could avoid risk and change.

Between my medication and sessions with Larry, I also listened to podcasts of dharma talks, read Buddhist texts, meditated, and exercised. When an ad for a free online course on happiness from the University of California at Berkeley showed up in my inbox, I jumped on it. Professors at the university claimed that genetics determine 50 percent of a person's happiness, 10 percent derives from life circumstances, and 40 percent stems from one's daily activities. Statistics report that happy people volunteer, nurture social connections, forgive, apologize, step in when needed, and practice gratitude.

As I studied, I saw how much rage made my world shrink—I blamed others and acted like a victim. Engaging with life, not running from it, was a much better course of action.

Would I have gained the same insight following my general practitioner's suggestion to go on disability? I don't know.

I do know that what I did was effective. I started to enjoy my new duties rather than rail against them. When our unit delivered a global training program to over 1,200 managers, my boss gave me a prominent role in implementing it. I team-taught and discovered that many of my lawyer colleagues had a fear of public speaking. As I coached them, they began to mentor me in investigations.

After reporting my progress with professional self-confidence, Larry called me "the comeback kid."

I even began appreciating my boss. He could have sacked me if he had truly thought I was incapable of learning, after all. One day I poked my head in Bayo's office.

"Thank you for believing in me," I told him.

"I knew you could do it," he said.

Another tough dad, even if he was young enough to be my son.

One Sunday, at our local farmers market, I spotted Larry at a distance, buying apples while holding a cell phone to one ear. He carefully hefted and studied each one, dropping the good fruit into his bag and placing the others to one side. I smiled, appreciative of my big-city, small-town shrink. He had taught me to do the same.

My Serial Therapists

| Beverly Donofrio |

What I've learned from ten therapists over thirty years, in four states, seven towns, and one foreign country:

1. Social workers can work miracles.

At your first appointment, right after your first therapist—a chubby, middle-aged social worker—jots down a list of the thirty-seven drugs you've taken in the past year, she asks, "What brings you here? What's troubling you?" And this is what you tell her: pregnant in high school, twenty-one now with a four-year-old kid, on welfare, stuck in a dumpy public housing project, arrested for possession of your friend's marijuana with intent to sell, named the leader of a drug ring on the front page of the newspaper. You're bad news, bad luck, the town pariah, and you sleep sixteen hours a day.

Your social worker responds: "You're an intelligent young woman. You should be in college," and you burst into tears as she plots a way to make it happen.

2. If you tell your psychiatrist you hate your breasts and he suggests you take off your shirt in therapy, don't do it; you may end up sleeping with him.

You do. And you do.

It's a bad idea to sleep with your psychiatrist.

When the psychiatrist who runs the clinic announces to his staff that he's looking for an interesting, intelligent patient, the miracle-working social worker hands you over. It's flattering to be thought interesting and intelligent, and after the first session you're dizzy with love. He has a beard to his chest, a ponytail, and sandals, and recommends books by Virginia Woolf, Simone de Beauvoir, Tillie Olsen, Grace Paley. . . . You talk about those books, but mainly you talk about sex because that's what you think you do in therapy. After you tell him having a baby ruined your breasts and you're ashamed of them, he suggests you take off your shirt. It takes two months of analyzing, ruminating, and fretting, but the shirt finally comes off, and it feels the opposite of liberating; it's humiliating. You never take it off again and soon afterward you quit Dr. L, because—or so you believe—you've won a scholarship to an elite university and have too many books to read and too many miles to drive. But you think about him constantly and in the spring return for a couple of sessions. He thrills you by suggesting that instead of therapy you do co-counseling. That means you will be therapists for each other. You think: jackpot! Every Friday you drive to his house and swoon as you lie together on a hammock chatting. One night you have margaritas at a Mexican restaurant and then have sex. You think it's the fleshiness around his middle that disgusts you. A few days later you tell him you want a prescription for Valium, which he will not give you. You think if he were your friend, he'd give you the drugs; if he's going to act like your therapist he never should have slept with you. Now you have a "legitimate" reason to dump him.

3. Shrinks can be crazy but good for you.

You graduate from college, move to New York City, get hit by a car, go to graduate school for creative writing, can't write a word, work too many hours, sleep all the rest, drink too much, and show up at the hospital clinic where you've been in therapy twice a week for half a year and are told that, unfortunately, the resident-in-training you've been seeing, Dr. F, "won't be in and we don't know for certain when he will return." Your heart beats so hard you feel that your eyeballs may pop out of your head. This is worse than a betrayal of trust, this is an affirmation that you're out of your mind to count on anything or anyone, ever—and that something about you drives people, even paid therapists, away. You cry hysterically walking along Avenue A; the people you pass blur through your tears, not that you're looking at them. You, who barely let a week go by without a man in your bed, are so in love with this young man that you've been celibate since the first day of therapy. You know this is transference, but knowing it makes no difference. You are a kitten left by a garbage can on a subzero night. Dr. F calls you up, his breath trapped in his chest as he whispers conspiratorially, "My father—not the administration of Beth Israel Hospital—my father has decided I need a vacation."

"When will you be back?"

"They told me not to call my patients. But I wanted you to know."

He *does* care about you. You remain faithful, crying every

night, fearing he will never return, reciting your litany of repulsive faults and personality traits that drive people away, despairing that you will never find love, never be happy, never have energy, joy, interest, and humor. Then he returns. He helps you believe it wasn't your repulsiveness that drove him away. You stick with him, never letting him forget that you know he must be crazy; you ask him a thousand times, "How can I trust you?" It's not his being crazy (aren't we all?) that frightens you; it's his desertion.

Eventually he will graduate and go into private practice yet charge you no more money than you were paying at the clinic. At the clinic, for the first year, he barely said two words, such as, "Why are you hiding your face in your hands?" which you did every session, twice a week, for over a year. Now he not only asks but occasionally answers questions and even sometimes offers advice, which you don't always listen to but appreciate nevertheless. You are in therapy with him for five years when you get a book contract and begin your transition out, graduating before you leave New York City for a summer of writing in New Hampshire from which, for your own peace, sanity, and betterment, you never return to the city.

Years later Dr. F will write, congratulating you on your book, and enclose a check he never cashed with a note saying he thought it might make a nice memento. Years after that, when you receive a letter from his niece telling you that Dr. F died of AIDS and that "He was very proud of you," you wish you could remember what you did with the memento.

4. Trust your own intuition over your shrink's.

You're living in a place where after a year you have not made one single friend, you have to drive two hours to buy decent

Parmesan cheese, and one day the farmer's wife across the road stops by to chat as you stack wood, waves to a Volkswagen bumping down the dirt road, and then comments in a smug, singsong voice, "That's Alice. Alice used to live in your house. She's an *artist*. With her it was always, 'I wonder why. I wonder why.'" And you wonder why you're still in this backwoods, backbiting place. You tell all this to your Jungian therapist, who tells you, "Stay put; wait it out; things will change." Don't listen to him. Fly away fast.

5. Some shrinks are drunks.

If you read in the paper that your psychiatrist's car, which he'd parked by the bay, had to be retrieved by the Coast Guard after the tide came in, and then you read he got a DWI, dump him. He may sober up, but don't let it be on your dime.

6. If your therapist suggests you meditate, listen to her.

If she also tells you that some people find believing in a God that loves them unconditionally will help them heal, do not run the other way with your hands over your ears, screaming. Try to believe. You may somehow miraculously find faith, and you may heal.

7. Avoid shrinks who are not as smart as you.

If your social worker/therapist doesn't understand what you're saying because you use "big" words like "apoplectic," run the other way.

8. Sometimes they tell you to do things that you don't want to do, which are good for you, even transformative.

If your therapist keeps harping on you to confront your parents about your lousy childhood, do it, even if by then they're practically geriatric. Your mother may deny that she was a rage-aholic who slapped and pinched and pulled your hair because her fading memory has become selective to protect her from pain. But maybe she will apologize anyway, saying, "I don't remember, but if I did, I'm sorry. I'm really sorry," and hearing this, you may lose the bite of anger and take her hand. When you confront your father about hitting you, though, he may say, "You deserved it," which makes you go apoplectic and yell, "You were a brute. I was a kid. You're a bully," to which he responds, "You're craaazzzyyy." You won't speak to him for six months, but when you call him, afraid he could die and you will feel terrible, you say, "Dad?" and he says in a tone that breaks your heart, "Let it go, Bev, please, just let it go." You do let it go, and being around him begins to feel different. You let him chop the garlic when you cook and stir the pudding for the pie, marvel at how tender he can be, and one day discover that for the first time since you were four years old you actually love your father.

9. If a therapist tells you to paint mandalas and record your dreams and bring them to therapy, dedicate yourself to it.

You may learn that you long for the wilderness, that solitude feeds you and so does your family. Those sessions will plant the seed that eventually roots you back east—within two hours of your son, grandchildren, siblings, parents—up in the Catskills with your dog, and forests all around.

10. Some of the best therapists have no license or formal training.

If she does cleansings using a turkey feather to douse you with smoke, if she makes a fire in her fire pit and invites you to sit all night till sunrise with a dozen other women passing a talking stick, if she invites you to stay in her cottage on what she calls her "Holy Land," after you've been raped and are writing a book about healing from it, accept her invitation— even if it means you can eat no animal products on the Holy Land and you have to tolerate women howling at the moon and taking their shirts off the minute they step out of their cars. Howl at the moon, too, if you can make yourself, sit bare-breasted under a tree on a moonless night and wait for the owl to land overhead and talk to you. It may be the voice of God that twenty years ago a therapist suggested you believe in.

Why I Didn't Enter Therapy Sooner

| *Charlie Rubin* |

It turned out that by getting engaged to Eleanor I was also marrying her shrink, Sento. Everyone called him Sento. And I should call him Sento, Eleanor said, because that's what his patients did, not that I would ever truly be one, which was my loss.

Sento had been working miracles on Eleanor and her brother Lucas for years. After a decade-long disquisition on why it's better to keep a new shirt in its plastic wrapper forever and never wear your new shoes, Lucas was apparently ready to "open out" into an exalted place where therapy would truly, finally, free him to enjoy his clothes.

Sento wanted a crack at me as well, being predictably desolate that his star patient, Eleanor, studying to be a psychologist, was engaged to a playwright who refused to go into therapy. But when Eleanor repeated one of my dreams in her session, Sento reversed field magnificently: "How he dreams, with the images of an artist," and asked Ellie, would

I perhaps allow him to reference my vibrant dream in his Division 39 lecture in Boston?

You hear the blarney? I suspected blarney. But having recently been maimed by a *Times* review calling my work on a musical's book "the key inessential element," I was eager to imagine a gator pond of conference therapists sunning themselves in my bold images, and then all of them *re*-dreaming my dream that very night, telling *their* patients about it, and then *them* re-dreaming it, too—until my dream had fertilized the Manhattan of patients on couches and armchairs with sweat pads that I ostensibly wanted no part of.

Even today, years later, when I am propelled to the part of myself that still thinks it can befriend the bully (or yearns for a bashing—surely these things complicate over time), I am still roaming Sento's townhouse office while he curses me out unconditionally beside his display of fifteenth-century Genoese armor: Eleanor, Eleanor—oh, I do not appreciate what she is! "More brilliant than *you* will ever be, or I," he added, sounding the egalitarian note that would doubtless embody the therapy we'd never share. "You think you are brilliant. But who beside yourself ever called yourself this? Some headmaster? You don't want to marry Eleanor! She tells me you are *enthralled* by the scene in *My Antonia* when the wolves attack the wedding party. This gruesome scene *empowers* you, Charles, you *must* see why, because the bride is thrown to the wolves!"

"So is the groom," I said. "I forget who goes first."

"Wrong. Mistaken. The *bride*. Alone."

"I forget who goes first," I said. "But they both go."

* * *

Backing up, if I wasn't entirely keen to embrace therapy, it was because I blamed it for the loss, years earlier, of my best friend Les Luggman, the other summer camp intellectual. In adolescence it is useful to have a friend who hates more disturbingly than you do. That was Les, both of us thirteen in 1963 at Camp Winakawwkee, which was famous then for its futuristic water bicycles and a *Life* magazine cover photo of Les pretending to be electrocuted while bestride one on the lake. (*Life* captioned it "hijinks.") Winakawwkee was a venerable summer camp for high-end Jewish boys who would emerge from overnight sleeper trains on the first day, shaking hands with each other. "Winakawwkee campers will be your associations for life," owner Doc Sonnenblick assured us at every campfire. It was a camp where handshaking mattered and Judaism didn't; settled into our bunks, we all bragged that our families celebrated Christmas lavishly and caught up on our best gifts. (One year I went too far and said "sleigh bells." But by then I was an outcast.)

Les's weakness was that you could get to him. When the counselors punished him for smiling on the tennis court, he ran into the woods, weeping. "Nobody cares if I live or die!" He was gone for weeks, with all of us forbidden to mention him. And since we'd heard there were microphones hidden in the mess hall, nobody did.

It got worse that winter when Les's parents told my parents that Les was finished at Winakawwkee.

"Not invited back?" said my kind father. "It won't be reported to his colleges." He added, "I don't think. Shouldn't be. You never know."

But then something took Dad's breath away—Les had been sent to a psychiatrist.

"Certainly Yale," Dad said. "Forget about Yale. Right off his map. Big state school. Best he can hope for."

It seemed that Les had been spotted getting up early every morning to take a long, lush piss on the All-Around Campers Honor Roll Rock out by the arts and crafts hut in sacred Winakawwkee War Dead Field.

But it wasn't him; it was me. Loyal Les! He took the fall, knowing how I relished my sunrise power-splash twinkling paint chips off the names of immortal campers 1926 Ozzy Tubbs and 1927 Boats Donkelstein.

Alarmed, my parents now sent me to a private school full of grinds and strivers. "No-therapy-kids" was the grand scheme that went wrong with my very first pal, Roy Z., whose father was a Park Avenue therapist, and whose mother told my mother that when they wanted to control Roy they'd go into his room and hide all his clocks. *But how does he know when to get up for school?*

"He must have a secret clock somewhere that we can't find. But we will. We've got his watches."

I fell in with Teubo next: Teubo's mother was a world-renowned opera singer.

"Ohhhhh, Charlie," Teubo would say, gritting his teeth and wincing, "I *can*not, can*not* picture my father fucking my *mother*." Teubo signed my yearbook, "You, me, and my mother."

I said, "I'm honored." I said it slowly, as if you could vocalize the British spellings we were all trying out that year. Honoured. Hon-ourrred.

Best of all was Mitch: My parents beamed watching Mitch and me putzing back and forth to the public library, unaware we were compiling a list of hotels where the Gestapo liked staying in Occupied Europe. "They preferred four-star," said Mitch, "but a clean three-star was not out of the question." Meanwhile my parents heaved a sigh of relief that, not a moment too soon, I had finally befriended normal boys who controlled their urine.

* * *

The next time therapy entered my life was college. I got into an exchange program to Wellesley, an all-women's school that was quietly thinking of admitting men. Eight men— "co-eds," they thrillingly called us—living in the basement of a dorm in probationary, genderistical coexistence. The girls would come to breakfast in their nightgowns and shorty pajamas. But it was all tame; we were like their brothers (getting erections watching our sisters pour skim milk over Frosted Flakes). The girls tended to talk therapy at breakfast—though only at that meal. You were shunned for bringing it up at dinner, which was for pregnancy scares, or at lunch—I forget what lunch was. Three different women asked me to join them in "proxy" sessions with their health service counselors where I'd be introduced as an important campus co-ed while the shrinks tried to deduce a signal from me: boyfriend, last night's mistake, Svengali, gay? One woman, Bethly, wanting me to impress the doctors for whom she had named her lab animals, asked, could I recite the 5 Criteria for Rational Behavior? I got two. She said, "I'll give you the other three, but if it comes up—don't know all five. It'll smell put-up job."

Eleanor hated those Wellesley stories because, to her, as usual, my whole therapeutic context was passive. It wasn't my therapy. I was just *there*. She also loathed my story about how Gramps's parting words to me at the front door were usually, "Son, life should be lived with regrets."

I explained, "He was starting to get things backward. He meant *without regrets*! He was handing me rolled-up bread balls and saying, 'Son, put this silver dollar away and think of your old grandfather some time.'" (He should be happy. I can barely type this without losing it.)

What I couldn't tell her is that, after a while, I began to regard Gramps's advice sagely. It seemed to simplify the world. My friend Andrew, who lives in Thailand, used to say, "Every choice is probably the wrong choice." He will always be my friend for that.

In any case, I started therapy, at last, but for the wrong reason—to please someone else, Eleanor. But because she was someone I feared that I'd wronged, and might wrong again, I decided to cut myself some slack there. Larry, a psychologist who wouldn't tell me where he lived, turned out to be terrific. Theoretically, I was there to discuss why I couldn't marry Eleanor after all this time. Larry was good on that topic but vastly preferred digging into my obsession with the movie *The Great Escape*. "All war movies," he said, "are about breaking into or out of an impregnable fortress."

One day I brought in a dream that had jolted me awake. I wore soft contacts then, and in the dream I can't see. I manage to pull the lenses out—there must have been dozens caked in each eye. I start pulling them apart, crumpling and ripping them, but finally there's one good one in the center of each stack. I put them back in and see perfectly. Larry said, "What do you feel that's about?" I said, "Therapy."

He told me where he lived.

Larchmont. I was a little disappointed.

Eleanor and I have evolved the kind of relationship where we email each other with enthusiasm. But, though we live only two miles apart, we haven't seen each other in twenty years. So there's "work" to be done.

I told her once that I check the obits for Sento regularly. I think that pleased her. He'd be quite old by now. But as my brother-in-law Mike, a doctor, says he's learned in hospitals, "The monsters never die."

But this is how the story really ends:

Larry's office was in a huge medical building in the East Eighties—therapists, mainly. In the hall I could hear the thrum of wellness. I thought some of it might be mine.

But when I got a job in L.A., I figured I was done with therapy. I had waited, I had hit the ball hard when I saw my pitch, and I had come up at least on third as a middle-aged guy ever-resourceful with sports analogies.

I gave Larry a book of Barry Levinson screenplays as a thank-you and went out in the hall with that rugged feeling of doneness that is so hard to come by. Then another of the hall shrinks strolled up beside me at the elevator. She was squat, bell-shaped, sixtyish with a thick Bavarian butter-cream accent, and she watched as I punched both the UP and DOWN buttons simultaneously.

"My bad habit," I said, endearingly. "I never know which to push. The DOWN button because I want to go down. Or the UP button because the elevator wants to come up."

"Ah yes," she said, "Zzzuhhh elevator's needs are allvvvays as important as our ownnnn."

The Shrink Gets Shrunk

| Jean Kim |

Early during my second year of psychiatry residency at a major hospital in Manhattan, our outpatient clinic director announced a "very special opportunity" for the residents, thanks to our new affiliation with an esteemed psychoanalytic institute. We could meet with one of their senior members for a free consultation to get referred for our own psychotherapy. I was paired with a woman I'll call Dr. Meir, who had trained as a psychoanalytic therapist. A resonant memory from our early sessions: bemoaning that after college I'd quit playing violin, an instrument I'd been devoted to since age five. As Dr. Meir noted, "It makes me sad it's been five years since you played your violin. I imagine it just sitting in its case in your basement."

Despite mostly adhering to the idea of therapeutic neutrality and self-nondisclosure, Dr. Meir never hid the fact that she was an avid classical music fan and mourned that I had put my talent on ice. But that was the nature of our valuable relationship, which wasn't the typical doctor-patient dynamic, since I was a budding shrink myself.

The idea of psychiatrists getting their own treatment has been a long-standing tradition, reaching back to Sigmund Freud and his commonsense philosophy that in order to optimize one's own abilities as a psychoanalyst for others, it is necessary to iron out one's own set of biases, transferences, and pathologies. The idea morphed from a generational tree of apprenticeship, in which one psychiatrist could say he or she was analyzed by Freud himself, and subsequently, another could report being analyzed by that psychiatrist, and onward down to the present day, so that we were all "children" of Freud. But aside from that vaguely cultish mentality, it was a reasonable and important idea that as people who carry the responsibility for patients' deepest secrets and vulnerabilities, we, too, should be healthy. This involves availing ourselves of the self-awareness and insight-building exercises that are part of good psychotherapy.

There is a stereotype that mental health providers go into the profession to treat their own mental health problems, the unflattering stigma that crazy treats crazy. Indeed, I had quietly endured many years of my own mild but unpleasant conditions self-diagnosed as low-level chronic depression (dysthymic disorder) and social anxiety. The only prior mental health contact I'd sought out was a couple of brief therapy visits to a well-meaning but inexperienced psychiatric resident at the college student health center after I wasted a year in unrequited love, struggled to focus in school, and felt aimless with my life goals. That short treatment did help.

I felt that my situation, if anything, heightened my sense of empathy for and devotion to my patients. Psychiatry had become a calling, a way for me to ease others' suffering. Patients I treated in the hospital typically were going through much more severe and painful situations, such as major depression, suicidality, hallucinations, addiction, and mania. With my mood and anxiety issues and also my experience growing up as one of only a handful of Asian Americans in my Maryland hometown, I knew something of how it felt not to belong, to feel judged as an outsider. I could relate to feeling not quite in sync with the society around you, experiencing some of the loneliness that mental illness often brings.

For various reasons—a terribly busy schedule, fear of commitment, lack of money, shame—I kept the name and number of the psychiatrist the senior consultant referred me to, but did not go for a year. A few months after beginning my third year of residency, when we started to treat our own patients on an outpatient basis, I felt more down than usual. I couldn't figure out if it resulted from the increased intensity of one-on-one sessions with patients—the reflections and reverberations of their flood of troubles. It could have been just taking stock of my life a year after the terrorist attacks on September 11, 2001, and my completely bumbling inability to even flirt with anyone despite being in my supposed prime at age twenty-seven. Or maybe it was the combination of my personal stage-of-life troubles with the additional stress of hearing everyone else's that was too challenging to handle alone anymore. I took a deep breath and left a message at the number.

Dr. Meir quickly called back, and we set up our first appointment. I don't know if it was just the idealization and hope of a positive counter-transference, but when I saw her, honestly I felt relieved—I just liked her. Dr. Meir had a warm and delicate smile, a gentle way of tilting her head as she did so, and a lilting, elegant Old World accent. Something about her looks and voice reminded me of an older Ingrid Bergman, one of my favorite actresses when I was growing up; my father had compared my mother to Ingrid in the early days of their college romance. I also liked that the therapist was European, an immigrant who came to the United States in her early adolescence; it made me hopeful she would understand what it was like not to quite fit into American culture. Yet she would be Western enough to help me negotiate some of the cultural adjustment issues with which I still struggled. (My parents had emigrated from South Korea a few months before my birth. They clung to their traditions rather strongly, which proved difficult at times for their Americanized daughter.)

It wasn't easy to open up to Dr. Meir, especially since I remained insular with my family, unused to discussing certain topics or secrets with an outsider. It shocked me to hear my therapist ask, "Do you hear how harsh you are on yourself?" In our sessions, I kept saying that people hated me because I was socially awkward, or that I always thought I had done something wrong at work despite receiving positive feedback. I had never realized negativity was my modus operandi. Dr. Meir's explanation felt like absolution. The walls around my mind became full of holes leaking in sunlight.

Gradually, this stranger earned my trust. She seemed gentle at baseline, but appropriately direct and tough when needed. I learned I was way too fearful of independence thanks to my overprotective mother, with both of us experiencing unnecessary anxiety whenever I did anything for myself. Once I mentioned in session I was waiting for my mother to visit the city to help me with various errands. I'd mail Mom my broken shoes to drop off at a Korean shoe repair shop back home in Maryland, and ask her to bring discount toilet paper from Costco (the megastore hadn't arrived yet in Manhattan). Raising an eyebrow, Dr. Meir said, "And why can't you do those things yourself?" It was one of those mellow shakes I needed. That week I found a nice cobbler down the street and ordered a large shipment of toilet paper from Amazon. I signed up for the gym for the first time. I now consider myself independently resourceful.

I also had to confront deep-seated traumas related to a hardworking but violent and erratic father who probably suffered from an untreated mood disorder exacerbated by too many sleepless nights on call as a doctor giving anesthesia to mothers giving birth. Dad had an old-school Asian mentality that was averse to mental health treatment for himself, despite his early training as a psychiatrist. He switched to anesthesiology because he felt too self-conscious about his English skills.

But I finally thought it was important to get help even if he hadn't, to learn everything I could, even if it hurt to face my feelings or anxieties, even if the advice came from a white stranger.

I loved her natural enthusiasm when I'd share my wacky dreams: Dr. Meir would pull out pen and paper, ready to have at it with a fascinating interpretation. In one, there was a shiny, whirling airplane spinning outside a skyscraper window, shattering the glass. Within this dream, I was in an office talking to Dr. Meir, and I jumped onto my therapist to shield her from the breaking glass. In real life, Dr. Meir was actually moved as she interpreted in a quiet voice, "You were trying to save me."

My psychiatrist was also very generous about mentorship,

not hesitating to offer wisdom about the challenging cases I was treating and the career I was entering. This guidance was invaluable to a minority female with few role models in the field I was entering and with parents who didn't know how to negotiate the minefield of professional academic hospital politics. I found myself at times adopting phrases of hers, even similar gestures, when talking to my own patients. The same slow nodding, the same calls for kindness toward oneself. My mother jokingly, perhaps a touch enviously, called Dr. Meir my "Jewish American mother."

I never quite took Dr. Meir off the pedestal, perhaps my way of protecting her from my deep streak of cynicism and melancholy. It made me wonder if patients did the same thing to me sometimes, although that didn't seem to be the case when they yelled and complained and demanded things like brand-name Prozac approval or higher dosages of Klonopin or letters for Social Security disability. Sure, my shrink was still a human being; she occasionally dozed off as I babbled (although I couldn't tell anymore after I switched to lying on the couch and staring at the ceiling, old-school-Freudian style). I griped at her once over mistakenly referring to my background as Chinese instead of Korean, which opened up an important discussion about how cultural slights and invisibility had affected me throughout my life. Once, I glimpsed Dr. Meir and her spouse sitting in the front row of a chamber music concert at Lincoln Center. She was a rabid classical music fan indeed.

I felt sad when Dr. Meir had a tough year. She broke a shoulder in a skiing accident and had to wear a sling, a bad event that seemed to foreshadow her next crisis—a divorce. It wasn't my place to console her, as I would with my own patients. That it wasn't my place to console her led to guilt. Other times, I kept secrets, reluctant to confess awkward moments with mutual colleagues that might affect her relationships with people she cared about. Consequently I didn't reveal that a colleague I'd seen in Dr. Meir's waiting room was the same one I'd told her I had a crush on, and I didn't share that another supervisor who worked in her institute had been drunk and acted weird at a party.

Because I imagined that my patients also kept crucial secrets from me, I learned to gently probe, even asking them directly if I suspected there was something important they weren't sharing.

It proved interesting to negotiate our boundaries as work colleagues versus patient and doctor. When Dr. Meir was due to present at Grand Rounds (a prestigious weekly academic presentation) at my hospital, it was so anxiety provoking I stayed away. I wasn't sure what I was scared of: I knew she'd give a great presentation. I knew no one would know of our therapeutic relationship. Maybe the change in venue from her office, from personal therapist to workplace authority figure, was too much for me to process.

I continued to see Dr. Meir even after I finished my residency, into the early years of my career as an attending psychiatrist, my first serious relationship in nearly a decade, and its eventual demise. Ironically, she was fine with seeing me present a few years later at Grand Rounds at her own affiliated hospital when I ended up working there, and afterward gave me wonderfully supportive comments: "I saw someone who was calm, poised, knowledgeable, and confident." It was a blessing to hear this, given I'd had cricket-like restless legs that kept me up the night before.

My eight years of therapy helped me grow outside the walls of my own foibles and biases, to overcome serious anxieties and self-doubt. I realized how difficult it was to chip away at similar resistances in my patients, and how trust had to be earned. But my experience as a patient also gave me an inside scoop, so I could talk to them directly about what they were afraid of—therapy changing the core of who they were, being called weak . . .

Those were common fears that informed my therapeutic practice. When I'd talk to patients who had crossed the threshold into serious clinical depression, distinguished by a flatness of facial expression, helplessness, and rejection of hope, I knew I'd have to broach the sensitive subject of medication, with its specter of feeling altered artificially. I knew this fear well since it had prevented me from trying any medication for years, even with my general trust in and respect for Dr. Meir's judgment. Yet once I did go down the rabbit hole and start on an antidepressant (which really helped me), I was able to truly connect and let patients know how meds could pull them back onto safe land from their maelstrom of shifting moods. I could say exactly what it was like when the storm started clearing. They could feel my honesty, and that trust could help them.

After eight years of treading my own healing path, I realized that Dr. Meir couldn't help me overcome some situational stressors and challenges out of our control: the high cost of living in Manhattan and the cutthroat, penny-pinching work culture in New York's hospitals, so I ended up leaving the city of American ambition and dreams.

At our last session, I sobbed, and she gave me the warmest handshake. At the last moment, her free hand swung over to join her other hand and mine.

The foundations Dr. Meir helped build allowed me to flourish in the slightly softer environs of Washington, D.C., where I moved next and forged a clinically rewarding experience treating my own patients one-on-one. After that I moved to a military clinic. I listened to the painful, heart-wrenching stories of soldiers coming back from the wars in Afghanistan and Iraq and tried my best to help them. I developed deeper respect and compassion for people caught up in violence and its effects, and because of my therapy, I could keep up with the emotional toll for a while. Eventually, though, I decided to take a break from full-time clinical work and venture into teaching and writing.

My guard came down enough to let me fall in love at last with a wonderful, kind man. I transitioned to a new therapist Dr. Meir recommended, a male this time, which further challenged my ability to trust in a positive way, given my issues with my father. He doesn't ask me about my violin, which I haven't started playing again, although I think about it. It's important to keep growing and learning because no one is an island, especially a psychiatrist.

Therapy Undercover:
Satin Shirts and Sex Talk

| *Estelle Erasmus* |

"**D**o you think of me when you masturbate?" the man asked.

The lights in the room had been switched off, the shades drawn. I couldn't see him, but I could sense him licking his lips in anticipation of my answer, like some old-time villain in a film noir.

"Yuck, no. That's gross," sixteen-year-old me replied, disgusted at the thought.

His name was Ron. He was my married, forty-five-year-old child psychologist. This mode of questioning was par for the course during our weekly therapy sessions.

"Come on. Don't I turn you on?" he cajoled.

"No. You don't."

My answer never changed, though he campaigned constantly as if one day it could.

"Why not?" he whined in the hurt tone of a hormonal

teenager, which I found ironic because *I* was supposed to be the only hormonal teenager in the room.

My parents had brought me to Ron, who specialized in emotionally challenged teens, because I was in the full flush of adolescent rebellion. They found it impossible to control me, while I found it intolerable living with both of them and my sister in our Long Island home in the late 1970s.

Defying my paternalistic, professional father at every turn, I stayed out past my 11 p.m. curfew, drank beer, smoked pot, and dated nerdy college freshmen, though I managed to retain my virginity. A favorite pastime was shoplifting small items like pots of Maybelline eye shadows and Bonne Belle lip gloss from the local drugstore.

I was a mass of contradictions: smart but lacking in emotional intelligence; an equal fan of Debbie Gibson ballads and Joan Jett rock anthems; a studious bookworm who loved to dress up in Spandex and go to clubs or attend midnight screenings of the *Rocky Horror Picture Show*. My friends ranged from literary, tea-drinking goody-two-shoes who collected clothes for the homeless to stoners, one drug bust away from getting their juvenile delinquent cards.

My dad ruled our house as if he were an ancient despot. When there was a conflict between the needs of the women in the house and his, Dad's needs always dominated. When he came home from work, he would silently change the television channel I was watching to the evening news— the program *he* wanted to watch. When we had cake for dessert, he claimed the biggest slice for himself, and when our family went out to dinner, it was always his choice— Chinese. If I went out with friends, he asked me intrusive questions afterward and would sulk if I didn't want to answer or needed a moment to myself. He'd also often walk away in the middle of my answers. He insisted I help with the gardening on weekends, which I hated, and made every excuse to evade.

It was a strange dichotomy: held hostage to his whims, I was either too visible or invisible, and in equal measures he either paid me the wrong kind of attention or was dismissive. Both hurt intensely. I reacted the only way I knew: by yelling.

In contrast, I shared a close relationship with my beautiful mother. She saw me as an extension of her, since we looked alike. She also never met a boundary she couldn't or wouldn't cross.

"Your dad is cheap," Mom would complain. She resented how he'd slowly peel the dollars from his wallet to dole out her weekly allowance, and wait until appliances were on sale before buying them. My dad encouraged my companionship with Mom, as it took the burden off him. She and I spent hours together shopping, eating, and gossiping. And my mom encouraged my contemptuous attitude toward my dad—gloried in it—and in between rants she helped me stalk the guys I dated by driving past their homes multiple times and dissecting every moment I spent with them. My younger sister, who in later years confessed she'd never felt a part of our family, stayed out of the fray.

Although it's been more than thirty years since I last saw Ron (name kept the same to protect no one), I remember him as small of stature, big of ego. Though he was barely five feet, four inches tall—in contrast to my busty but gangly five feet, seven inches—Ron resembled a mini–Roman emperor, with a large, preternaturally tan face, an aquiline nose, and a head of thick, coiffed hair, moussed and blow-dried to perfection. I was a fair-skinned brunette with a heart-shaped face, sporting a Dorothy Hamill haircut that I could see reflected in his shoes, which were polished to a high sheen. He wore thick gold chains around his neck, under a strategically opened satin shirt, out from which peeped an aggressive tuft of chest hair.

During our initial sessions, as I complained about my father and his autocratic rules, Ron focused his unrelenting gaze on me, listening intently in a way I found mesmerizing.

Being heard was a new experience: my dad talked *at* me, and my mother was too self-absorbed to hear what I was saying unless it involved her.

I loved having the focus of attention squarely on me for the first time in my life.

Like a horse trainer grooming a skittish filly into a champion, Ron painstakingly built my trust step by step, week by week. First, he agreed with me that my parents were too tough. Next, he pointed out that by "yessing" them, I could satisfy their need for control yet still do what I wanted. That was a revelation: I didn't need to fight to get my way. My parents considered my new copacetic behavior a triumph of the therapy they'd insisted on. My life at home became easier.

Given this breakthrough, I was more than willing to open up to Ron the first time he broached sex talk.

"So, do you think about getting laid?" he asked in the same casual tone he'd employed when asking about my after-school activities.

"No," I said. "I'm saving my virginity."

"Well, don't tell me that you've never had a guy go down on you."

I was surprised at this line of questioning but figured he was a parent-approved doctor. My doctor.

"Just once, a few months ago," I answered him, as casually as he'd posed the question.

"How was it?"

"It was okay."

"Just okay? You didn't have an orgasm?"

"No. I was too nervous."

"You do have orgasms, don't you?" he sternly inquired.

"Yes . . ." I wondered where he was going with this.

"When? When you masturbate?"

"Of course."

"Good. Do you think of me when you masturbate?"

"Um, no."

"Okay. Anyway, the guy eating you out didn't know what he was doing," he said. "You have to make sure that the air hits the vagina—that increases the stimulation."

I was uncomfortable but riveted. Just as I had his complete attention, he now had mine.

He told me that I shouldn't tell my parents what went on in our sessions—because those were private and personal. I followed that advice. I didn't know where all this was going, but it was a new adventure. And besides, I reasoned, Ron had already helped me so much.

The following week, Ron listed several changes he said I needed to make, as if he were some sort of petite Professor Higgins molding my coarse Eliza Doolittle.

"Do you want to learn how to be a woman, not a scared little girl?" he challenged me.

"Yes," I said emphatically. "I want to be a woman."

"Then you need to listen to me," he said. "I can teach you. I can help you."

"Okay, I will."

"You have to really want it, or it won't work," he said.

"I really want it," I replied, wondering what he could possibly say.

"Good. First of all, you're too uptight. Second, you need to get in touch with your sexuality, and third, I'm going to get you to feel a lot more confident about your body. Look at your posture. You're slumping. Straighten up," he ordered. I lifted my chest and straightened my shoulders, following his directions to the word.

Eyes closed, Ron appeared to be in deep thought. Then his eyes popped open and peered directly into mine as he said, smiling, "I know where we can start."

I didn't expect his revelation to be, "Estelle, you have great tits. You should show them off, and stop wearing a bra."

I was taken aback by his vulgar description of my breasts but figured that was just his way of making a point.

"But I don't want them to sag," I told him with all the vigor of a prim librarian.

"Bullshit," he said. "Just go braless."

So I did.

I didn't realize it was a test.

My breasts bounced as I walked around the house. My mom was aghast at my display, but I sniffed that I didn't like wearing a bra. I reported my actions to Ron, who was pleased with how I'd stood my ground, and kept our secret.

It wasn't long before Ron introduced meditation to our sessions, claiming it would help me relax. He emphasized that this part of our work together was really important. "It's the key to getting in touch with your sensual nature, so you can know what it means to be a woman, ready to be fucked by a man," he told me.

I took in what he was saying, despite his surprisingly filthy word choice, hungry for knowledge. I was curious about the worlds of sex and sensuality he referenced, and my trust in him was total.

He said we would start the following week.

I looked forward to my first meditation session with Ron with great anticipation, as if I were a sun-parched desert and he a cloud about to release healing, life-affirming rain.

During our first official meditation session, I lay down on Ron's red plaid couch, and he dimmed all the lights in his office until we were surrounded by blackness, our faces and bodies invisible to one another.

Ron began speaking in his sonorous bass. His voice had a nice timbre to it, I recall.

One of the first scenarios he described—which I later learned was his favorite—was a beach fantasy scene. He asked me to imagine I was lying topless on the beach, with a wisp of a bikini bottom covering my pubic area. I would notice not one, but two guys checking me out, which would turn me on. I'd get wet as I spread my legs farther apart, inviting the horny guys to get a closer look at my pussy because they wanted to fuck me.

He asked me every few minutes if I was getting turned on. I was, by the story, the words, but not by Ron.

He loved using the words *fuck, pussy, cock, balls, clit, dick, suck, cunt* and would ask me to repeat them during the sessions. It's no small feat to get an innocent girl to use the lusty language of a would-be porn star.

During other sessions, Ron painted the picture of me going to the mall sans panties and then purposely bending down to pick up something I'd dropped and giving the lurking guys—there were always lurking guys in Ron's fantasies—a show. Or, maybe I'd undress in front of my bedroom window, letting my teenage male neighbors or their dads get an eyeful of my "wet cunt," as Ron described it. He loved the "sensual" imagery of a young girl fully lubricated and ready for intercourse and would use those images throughout our meditation sessions, as if the words could manifest the deed.

Ron encouraged me to make these fantasies a reality in the interest of exploring my sensuality, but I was too practical and spooked to follow through. Instead, I'd make up stories that I had acted like an exhibitionist, going braless or forgetting to wear panties in public, so he would feel that I listened to him, when I was really just "yessing" him, as he'd taught me to do with my parents.

At one meditation session, I heard his disembodied voice huskily asking me to touch my breasts and tell him what I was doing. I followed his orders.

"Don't you think about my dick getting hard, getting ready to fuck your pussy and stroke your clit?" he'd ask me as I lay there half-heartedly stroking my breasts, per his instruction, under my shirt in the dark.

Whatever charms Ron imagined himself possessing, I was immune to them.

"No," I replied. "I don't want to fuck you."

During another session he requested, "Stroke your clit till you come all over your hand." I refused.

A lesbian friend of mine was also going to Ron because her parents thought Ron could "fix" her. We discovered that we both saw Ron as needy and whiny. We made fun of him for driving a red Porsche, the car driven by pathetic married men with something to prove. We'd also laugh about his constant craving for filthy sex talk but agreed that we both liked him and that he was helping us learn how to deal with our parents.

One day in between small talk, sex talk, and meditation sessions with Ron, I received a fantastic bit of therapy from him. I was in the midst of regaling him with yet another story of my dad's bullying when he said, "Estelle, I'm going to tell you something that will shock you."

"What is it?" I was primed to hear anything.

"Your dad is not the main problem. Well, he's part of the problem. He can be a bully. But the real problem is your mother. She's extremely narcissistic and competitive with you and creates a division between you, your dad, and your sister. She's the one who is manipulative. And, your *mom*, not your dad, is the one you need to protect yourself from," he emphasized.

I was shocked. My mother? She was my partner in crime— my confidante—the woman I confessed all to even when there was nothing left to say.

And yet, Ron's words resonated as truth. I finally understood why I felt terrible when my mother, who usually teamed up with me against my dad, would band together with him over my bad behavior—real or imagined. Time after time she abandoned me—I was used for entertainment and then dismissed when it suited her purposes.

My self-absorbed parents constantly used me as a lightning rod for their dissatisfaction with each other, I realized in the most powerful moment with Ron I'd ever had. It was practically a religious experience.

That day changed everything. For the first time, I put boundaries around my relationship with my mother. By no longer sharing the details of my life with her or allowing her to trash my dad in my presence, I slowly took back my power. My contemptuous attitude toward my dad dissipated as we started spending more time together. The summer before I left for college, I worked for him and learned to appreciate his leadership, kindness, fair work ethic, and common sense. Building our relationship without my mother's interference was helpful. I was able to communicate my needs, and sometimes he even listened. Finally, I was strong enough to calmly say, "Sorry, Dad, I love talking to you, but I need some alone time when I get home from work," and to my delight, he understood.

My last time in Ron's office, as I was preparing to leave for college, I cried and presented him with a poem, thanking him for all he had done for me. He told me that he'd treasure it always and that he'd miss me. I think I saw the glimmer of a tear in his eye, too.

In return, I had many of his words to remember him by, though it was years before I put any of it into practice in my sex life.

Only recently did it dawn on me that Ron abused his power in our unequal relationship. I realized I could have had him thrown in jail. I figured out that he was committing a felony by sexually exploiting me. And, as the mom of a young daughter, I felt the kind of rage I should have years ago when he insidiously infiltrated himself into my life, preying on me, grooming me for his own sexual gratification.

Last year I tried to locate Ron to get his license revoked but couldn't remember his last name. Perhaps he is locked in an old-age home somewhere, or perhaps an emotionally disturbed young girl, or one of her parents, took him out. I pray he no longer has access to vulnerable young girls and cannot pervert their innocence the way he did mine.

Still, I don't believe my time with him had a negative effect on me. I've since discussed this with my gifted female therapist of many years. I believe I didn't experience a negative fallout from the "therapy" because I didn't desire Ron sexually and because I enjoyed the attention, the words, and the fantasy (I'm a writer, after all). At the time I didn't view what he was doing as a violation, although he absolutely used me. Although Ron thought he was in charge, I didn't take his ridiculous desire seriously. Also, he helped me learn how to get along with my parents and revealed to me the truth about my mom's competitive nature, which has never changed.

Just as I left for college, I learned from my sister that my mother was going to Ron for weekly therapy sessions, which Mom stopped before I came back for Thanksgiving break.

I supposed he had branched out to suburban moms. I supposed she thought that if I had benefited from him so much, she could, too.

I heard that during her time in therapy, she briefly stopped wearing a bra.

I'm sure she didn't realize it was a test.

We never talked about it.

I don't believe we ever will.

The Therapist of My Dreams

| *Janice Eidus* |

As a kid growing up in the 1960s in a Bronx housing project, I'd never met a therapist, and I didn't know anyone who would admit to seeing one. I'd read a little bit of Freud, though, and had the notion therapy might one day rescue me from my unhappy home. I was particularly enthralled with his concept of the id, ego, and superego. My dysfunctional family, I believed, was all id.

My left-wing parents taught me many wonderful things, most especially to value ethnic and racial diversity. But they were deeply unhappy people. My father, filled with rage, was often violent. My mother was clinically depressed. She didn't—or couldn't—protect my brother, sister, and me from our father's fists.

My sister, Alice, my elder by three years, was also filled with a blind, violent rage that she sometimes took out on my parents but mostly on me, as I was the littlest and weakest—and also, in her words, "the competition" for our father's love. Years later, after my sister died from a rare cancer, my mother admitted that she had known throughout Alice's childhood that Alice had desperately needed professional help for her emotional issues. "But Daddy didn't believe in therapy, and forbade it," she said.

After my mother made a serious suicide attempt when I was seventeen, she spent two weeks in the psychiatric wing of our local hospital. "The psychiatrist there was crazy," she told me, in disbelief. "He said I'm a narcissist trying to live vicariously through my children!" Even then, I knew his assessment was true, as painful as it was for me to admit. She was self-centered and uninterested in her children's emotional needs.

In college, I read Karen Horney and Carl Jung and met with my first therapist. I poured my heart out to her about my boyfriend, who was a high school dropout and heroin addict. "He treats me like dirt, but I'm obsessed with him," I admitted, shamefacedly.

"You're Jewish, right?" she asked. Her navy blue A-line skirt and crisp white shirt reminded me of a uniform.

I nodded, unsure why that mattered.

"So, go to the youth dances at B'nai B'rith." She smiled enthusiastically. "You'll meet a nice boy there. That'll give you a kick in the pants to leave this loser."

"Okay, I will," I lied. I knew that my desire for my boyfriend was beyond B'nai B'rith's powers to fix and that I would never return to her office.

"Miss Hazel," as she liked to be called, was my next therapist. I saw her for about a year. She was sweet and soft-spoken. Although she never said anything that helped me to change my behavior or thinking, I felt she cared about me, and I needed that.

Miss Hazel got married and left New York. My next

therapist bragged to me that he'd been a "C student, but smarter than all the creeps who got As." After him, I met weekly for a year with an elderly woman who wore trifocals and often fell asleep during our sessions.

The fact that I'd not yet found "the therapist of my dreams" didn't dissuade me from believing that person was out there. And that person, I was certain, would "get" me instantly, curing me both of the lack of self-esteem that led me to become involved with one man after another who treated me badly and my bouts of depression.

At times, I also fantasized about marrying a therapist. I would have one therapist to whom I confided my sorrows during daylight hours, and one with whom I shared my bed. Each would accept me as I was—psychological wounds and all—and would be equally responsible for my emotional healing.

When I was set up on a blind date with Benny, I felt excited. Marilyn, a new friend, had orchestrated the date. "Benny is a very successful psychiatrist," she told me.

Marilyn and I were both young, aspiring fiction writers. We met at a writers' conference to which we'd each won a fellowship. Sharing our literary dreams over beers, we bonded instantly.

Marilyn and Benny had briefly dated. They were now "great friends," according to Marilyn. "He's smart and funny—perfect for you."

Benny and I met up at a cozy Spanish restaurant in the West Village. He was tall and gangly in a way I didn't find appealing. Yet, I so very much *wanted* to want Benny. I'd heard it said that physical attraction could grow over time as you got to know someone's wonderful traits.

Before the waiter appeared to take our orders, Benny regaled me with stories about his fabulous apartment, thriving practice, and piano playing. "I could have been a professional pianist, but I chose to help others." His voice struck me as faux humble, and that worried me.

Still, I trusted Marilyn. "Benny is a great shrink. His patients all love him," she had said. Surely, if that were true, he would possess humility and empathy. In my fantasies, those were among the traits great therapists had in spades.

A ponytailed waiter appeared to take our orders. "I'll have the paella," I said.

"I'll have the paella, too. But no mushrooms! Not a single mushroom." Benny's voice was so loud that a few people at other tables glanced at us.

After the waiter left, Benny leaned toward me. "I can't stand the sight of mushrooms. They're so phallic. I can't bear seeing penises on my plate."

"Trust me," he added, reading my stunned expression, "I don't have a problem with gay men. In fact, I have a special rapport with my gay male patients."

I suddenly felt terribly worried for all his patients—male, female, gay, straight.

During dinner, he spoke of his athletic prowess and keen intellect. I made a classic female mistake. I felt sorry for him. How sad that he was so confused he couldn't even *look* at a mushroom because it reminded him of his own (and others') genitals. How sad that he hid his insecurity behind insufferable bravado. *Poor Benny,* I thought. But maybe his own problems were what enabled him to understand and help his patients.

After the meal, I agreed to go to his apartment to hear him play the piano. Then I would leave and never see him again. I would just have to keep searching for those two ideal shrinks—the one I would pay to help me, and the one I would marry—who must exist somewhere.

We hailed a taxi to Benny's uptown digs. His apartment had a sunken living room, wraparound windows, and a terrace.

I sat on his pristine white leather sofa and sipped a glass of wine. He sat tall at the piano, making lots of dramatic hand flourishes as he played Beethoven and Bach merely adequately.

I placed my drink on the sharply angled glass coffee table. "That was lovely." I picked up my purse, ready to go.

The next thing I knew, he was beside me on the sofa, pushing me down and slobbering all over me. He was a lot stronger than I was, but I managed to push him off.

I then made another classic female mistake: I was polite. "You must have misread my signals. I hadn't intended for you to kiss me." I couldn't imagine that Benny, a therapist, would deliberately force himself sexually on me. Sure, I had read the occasional article about male shrinks who slept with female patients. But they were the exception, not the rule. Most therapists were honest, caring people.

"Is this enough of a signal for you?" He threw me down once more, and resumed slobbering in my face.

Once again, I pushed him off. This time I stood as I grabbed my purse. I felt frightened. How crazy was he? I began walking fast toward the door. He followed me, too closely. Now I was angry. "If you come near me again, I will punch you in the face." I spoke coldly, enunciating each word.

Sneering, he lurched toward me. Using strength I didn't know I possessed, I hauled back and punched him, hard, in the face.

I caught a final glimpse of him before I flung open the

door and hurled myself through it. He looked utterly baffled and hurt. His cheek was flaming. I raced down the stairs, not wanting to wait for the elevator, in case he came after me.

Marilyn called me the next day. "Are you insane?" She sounded furious. "You hit Benny!"

Although I was still reeling from what had happened, I managed to calmly describe Benny's actions. I expected her to take my side, to tell me she was casting Benny aside as a friend.

"Well, you really hurt his feelings. Despite what you say, you must have given him some signals." Her voice was sullen.

I said an abrupt goodbye and hung up. Bile rose into my throat, and I felt nauseated. I would never speak to Marilyn or Benny again. Marilyn had betrayed our friendship, and Benny, I felt, was a monster.

But I still clung to the idea that therapy would rescue me, and that I needed rescuing, even though, in many ways, my life was fulfilling: I was writing, publishing, and teaching. I had close, loyal friends. But insomnia and nightmares plagued me, and I chose unwisely in romantic love, feared true intimacy, and often felt verbally attacked.

That night with Benny forced me to become more realistic. I ceased to look for an "ideal" therapist who didn't exist. Shrinks were human in all the good, bad, and ugly ways the rest of us were. Benny just happened to be particularly ugly.

It wasn't long after my date with Benny that I did find the therapist I needed—a middle-aged woman with a booming laugh who wore long, flowing skirts and lots of turquoise jewelry. During the twenty years I worked with her, until she was incapacitated by a stroke in her late seventies, she helped me to sift through the pain of my past in a way that allowed me to start letting go of it. She was smart, kind, and ethical.

She possessed great humility and empathy. Still, sometimes she forgot things I deemed important, and occasionally she grew snippy with me. She was human.

Also, not long after my date with Benny, I fell in love with a supportive, loving man whom I eventually married. I quickly realized that it didn't matter to me that he wasn't a therapist. He, too, was decidedly human and real—and that was just fine with me.

As for Benny and Marilyn, I've Googled them both. Marilyn published one novel, got married, and had a son. After that, her trail runs cold.

I can't find Benny because I don't remember his last name. Searching for "Benny, psychiatrist, New York" doesn't work. I fervently hope that he no longer practices. I'd like to think that somewhere, somehow, he got his comeuppance. I'd like to think that his patients grew wise and left him. And that they all found love in some form, as well as the therapists of their dreams, just as I did.

My Old Therapist

Plays on a New Team

| Kate Walter |

"**I**'m Sarah. I'm a psychotherapist," said the chatty woman I'd been talking to on the bench outside Integral Yoga near my home in the West Village. She was a stranger, but people often socialized after class. "Do you live in this neighborhood?" she asked.

"I live in Westbeth," I replied. It's a nearby artists' housing project locally infamous for its oddball characters.

"Everyone I meet who lives in this neighborhood has seen a shrink in my building," said Sarah. "It's huge and full of therapists."

When she told me the location—off Fifth Avenue—I pictured the lobby in my mind. "Oh, my former partner Slim and I saw a lesbian couples counselor there a long time ago, like in the 1990s," I said. "Michelle. Do you know her? I can't recall her last name, but she's cute and short. My regular therapist recommended her. We wanted to see a gay woman."

"Yes, I know Michelle. But she's not a lesbian," said Sarah, looking puzzled. "She's married to a man. Has been since I've known her, about ten years."

"What?" I yelped. "Are you sure we're talking about the same person?"

Sarah said Michelle's last name; she was definitely my former therapist. I almost choked on my granola bar as I tried to process this new information. I had always thought my old shrink was gay, like me. I tried to create a time line. Had Michelle been having a sexual identity crisis while Slim and I were her patients? If so, might that confusion have affected the way she practiced therapy? I'd assumed a lesbian could best understand queer couple dynamics and that's why I'd insisted on that criteria. Had Michelle's interpretations consequently been too cautious and unchallenging? Suddenly I worried her comments, helpful at the time, had been off base.

Slim and I went into couple's therapy because we'd been screaming a lot. (One night our cranky upstairs neighbor even called the police.) Getting help was my idea, but Slim agreed we needed an intervention. I was the shrinkaholic in the family, so I appreciated her making this effort.

Michelle proclaimed we had power and control issues. It was funny and complicated in a very Sapphic way. Michelle's analysis was that Slim, a fashionable femme, was acting like a stereotypical man—cutting off and refusing to explore her feelings. I was the soft butch, nurturing the relationship, acting like a typical woman. Slim wanted me—the sensitive one—to initiate sex, yet Slim, the control freak, insisted upon running the relationship. I resented doing all the emotional work, especially since I often felt powerless.

Counseling helped us learn to communicate better. Michelle taught Slim to own her feelings and use the first person: "It bothers me when I just swept and you spill crumbs on the floor when you eat," as opposed to saying: "You are such a slob with food."

During our time with Michelle, we also addressed our battles over Slim not being out in her workplace. This regression occurred after she switched careers. (I was a college adjunct and a freelance writer; she worked as a photojournalist.) I'd been angry when Slim didn't invite me to an informal party thrown by her colleagues. Slim worried she'd lose assignments from homophobic editors if they knew her truth. Slim's closeted workplace behavior did not change during counseling, but I learned to be more tolerant, even though I disagreed. Maybe Michelle should have pushed Slim to be more out on the job? Or was this hindsight twenty years later?

Slim and I left counseling after a year and slipped back into bad patterns. I'd wanted to continue, but she refused. Still, we'd ended therapy on a positive note, with Michelle saying we had done good work. I never imagined Slim would dump me horribly more than a decade later in 2006. During the years-long devastation that followed, I processed my grief through writing—in 2013 selling a memoir about being dumped after twenty-six years together, rebuilding my life through therapy, yoga, and joining a gay-accepting church. Slim did not leave me for another woman: she just felt bored and wanted to explore the unknown. I'd begged her to reconsider and talk to someone, anyone, but she refused.

The woman I'd adored for over two decades emotionally amputated me, and she screwed me financially, too, walking off with our retirement funds, which was legal since we were not married. Slim always told me not to worry that I made less money, that she'd take care of me when we were older. She would not discuss any sort of "good faith" settlement. I was left broke and brokenhearted. Luckily, I landed a full-time college teaching job a few years later. Today I have tenure and a pension.

While I am in a good place now, there is something disturbing about discovering my lesbian couples counselor is straight and married. Never mind Slim and I last saw Michelle in 1995. Almost falling off the bench in shock, I said to Sarah, "Wow, what a surprise."

This was not the relaxed feeling I normally experienced after yoga class. "I'm sure Michelle was gay when my partner and I were her patients. My shrink knew her through the lesbian therapist network."

"Michelle's a recovering alcoholic," said Sarah. "She specializes in treating addictions. She probably slept with women when she was drinking."

"What?" I said, thinking her explanation sounded homophobic and that this was one gossipy shrink. I guess rules about confidentiality didn't apply unless the subject was your patient.

Michelle had once mentioned being in Alcoholics Anonymous, but I gathered she'd been sober for years. Yes, people change when they stop using, but switching your sexual orientation from gay to straight was not something I'd expect from a therapist who (I thought) was lesbian identified.

Of course I knew sexuality could be fluid. About fif-

teen years ago, I reviewed a book for *The Advocate* by Jan
Clausen, a prominent gay female writer who described being
ostracized from the community after she moved in with a
man. Ironically, I'd found her critics narrow-minded.

Though Sarah seemed loose-lipped, there was no reason
for her to fabricate a story about Michelle switching teams.
Besides, Sarah was as surprised as me by this bombshell,
but in reverse. I gathered she had had no idea Michelle was
once a lesbian. I waved goodbye to her and immediately
Googled my old counselor when I got home. Michelle's
professional profile indicated she specialized in relationship
issues, addictions, and couples. It stated that she works with
LGBT people.

During my breakup, I'd resumed individual therapy with
Dr. R, my longtime lesbian therapist, the one who'd originally recommended Michelle. I saw her twice a week for ten
years, starting in 1985, tapered to once a week, and eventually stopped in the late 1990s. I go back as needed during a
crisis, such as my father's death and Slim's desertion.

When I shared the new information with Dr. R, my therapist confirmed she'd also heard Michelle was now straight. I
guess juicy gossip travels fast along the gay grapevine.

"You sound like you feel betrayed," my therapist said.
It was true. I felt duped, hoodwinked by someone I'd trusted
with intimate details of my sex life. Dr. R helped me understand more when she pointed out that many people, going
back to Freud, believe sexual identity can change.

I'd experienced this phenomena with Mara, my first "get
out the U-Haul" (popular lesbian expression for moving in
together) girlfriend, who I later discovered bounced back and
forth her entire life. Slim had been married to her high school

sweetheart, a gay man, before they both came out. I wondered initially after our split if she'd go back to men. She didn't.

"It makes everything seem uncertain and scary," I shared with Dr. R, "especially when I'm trying to meet someone new. How can I trust anybody if even my shrink was sexually confused?"

"You put her on a pedestal as an expert," said Dr. R, "but she is just a person."

It wasn't upsetting to hear about an actor or author or singer who switched teams, like Holly Near (a gay icon when I was younger), or even New York mayor Bill de Blasio's wife, Chirlane, who'd once identified as a dyke. But I wanted my former lesbian couples counselor to stay gay, not hop into bed with a man.

I came out after college, over forty years ago, and could not imagine going back. It never felt right when I slept with boyfriends back in the day. My astrologer said I have the gay-est chart he's ever seen, with lots of Uranus, the queer planet.

Perhaps my overreaction to the news about Michelle was generational. I came out in the 1970s, when it was important to the movement to declare yourself gay or lesbian. Bisexuals were considered in transition. Was I now being stodgy? Today, millennials embrace "pan-sexuality." Same-sex marriage is legal in all fifty states, and transgender issues are in the headlines. Due to the courage of the LGBT political pioneers, everyone has more sexual freedom, more choices.

My intuition told me the universe brought me this newsflash about Michelle for a reason. What a strange coincidence that I sat next to a therapist who knew my old shrink. Michelle was a minor character in my life, but this update got me thinking—do we ever really know anyone? I never expected my relationship with Slim to end; she promised we'd grow old together.

That weekend, as I wrote in my journal, I realized my discomfort had much less to do with Michelle than with me. I felt dissed that an authority figure, one who weighed in on the love of my life, had rejected women for a man. The shock was déjà vu, mirroring my surprise when Slim left. It felt like a double rejection, though she and I stayed together for eleven years after ending couples counseling. Slim cast me aside, just as Michelle cast aside her sexual identity. Hearing about Michelle brought back the rebuff I'd felt when Slim left. At this point, I was over Slim but still single, only occasionally feeling a sting of pain.

Once I stepped back from the shock, I recalled that Michelle had been a good therapist, gently pointing out how Slim and I repeated our parents' negative patterns in our relationship. Michelle's final gift was the belated realization that nothing she said—or didn't say—could have altered the ending between me and Slim.

You're on the Air

| *Binnie Klein* |

"**Y**ou played *Madonna*?!" My patient Shira is an expressive, wonderfully cocky, and very hip Yale sophomore. This is her opener as she strolls into my office. "Yes," I say, watching her settle into the black leather recliner across from me. She looks horrified. Shira likes to feel that she's "in the know" about trends, pop culture, and especially music. She's derisive and unimpressed that a Madonna tune has appeared on my radio show. It's too "average." It's "retro." She'd probably play obscure, indie Brooklyn bands if she were the DJ selecting music.

Shira and I are in uncharted territory. I'm a psychotherapist who hosts a weekly music and interview show on the radio. My musical tastes, the questions I ask guests, what makes me laugh, and what fascinates me—it's all out there in the ether, for anyone who is listening. My "celebrity" is quite minor, but I work in a provincial, psychoanalytically influenced New England community, and the attention I get seems to induce a frisson of anxiety in some of my colleagues. "So," they say, eyes widening, "you're on the *radio*? Do, um, do your patients know? Do they *listen* to your show (horror of horrors)? How do you handle that?"

I understand their curiosity. Therapists face new challenges to our privacy these days. Even before most patients have stepped into the office, they've consumed unfiltered information about us via the Internet. We're being Googled. This phenomenon has forced more and more therapists to recognize and cope with many aspects of ourselves already being public—privacy no longer really exists. The delicate and important balance of public versus private has preoccupied us since Freud's notion of the analyst as a blank screen onto which fantasies will be projected (a methodology most useful for psychoanalysis, but not for psychotherapy, which is what most of us practice). Throughout our careers, we calibrate how much to reveal about ourselves (or our own feelings) to each individual. The basic paradigm—for us to reveal less—remains useful. Although we ask for great revelations from the patient, if we contributed all our personal details, associations, and vulnerabilities, the therapy process would degenerate into comparisons of experience. There is a concept I learned while taking boxing lessons: "finding your range." It means that you need to be just the right distance away from your opponents—not so far away that you can't reach them when you need to and not so close that you will be overly vulnerable and swallowed up.

Clinical techniques have expanded; contemporary theorists studying the uses of therapeutic self-disclosure have gone on to explore ways that authentic, in-the-moment feedback (and in some cases, information about the therapist) can especially benefit patients who struggle in relationships in which no one has provided "mirroring," or ever questioned their own particularly distorted beliefs. We make careful decisions for each clinical pairing.

For therapists practicing in a small town, things are already claustrophobic. My colleagues talk about running into patients at the local pool, the gym, or around town. (I'd rather a patient hear me on the radio than see me in a bathing suit!)

Sometimes those "collegial" reactions to my radio activities make me feel that I've been slapped with a subtext—that I must be doing something *wrong*. I worry they think I should pack myself back into analysis to examine my own narcissism. So when my peers appear a bit shocked, it helps when I reflexively clarify that it's not a radio advice show about mental health problems. I'm not immune to bouts of anxiety, so I'm attempting to reassure myself, too. None of us just live in our office chairs. Patients begin to stitch together their quilted portraits of us as soon as they see our parked cars in the assigned spaces (old Honda Civic? Brand-new Saab?), view our décor (Paul Klee reproductions? Primitive sculptures?), experience our sense of humor (or lack thereof), and learn where on the Cape we're vacationing or that we don't like to travel. This information does not have to be considered unfortunate "leakage." It is inevitable real-world information, and we have a reliable tool for the complexity of this issue. We can explore what each detail or nuance means to someone—and we can accept that we function in a dual capacity—both symbolic and real.

With some patients who do hear me, it can be, as with Shira, an opportunity for them to directly express aggression, envy, or criticism. Shira and I had been working together for seven months, talking about her struggles in relationships. Her offhand comment about Madonna was the first time she had challenged me directly, even just a little. I admire her critique of the Madonna tune. Many college-age patients are such perpetually "good students" that they treat therapy as if it were another class. They're fearful of making a mistake and want to please any authority figure. Shira's challenge is a welcome contribution that is a healthy expression of her own tastes and individuation.

I listen for any feelings or fantasies about my "other dimensions," if and when they come up, giving room and space for anything someone needs to express. If I bring it up ("So on my radio show I interviewed so-and-so"), there's usually a dynamic in the relationship that causes me to go there, some way in which the patient makes me (and often others) feel invisible or unimportant. Occasionally I'm thinking that there needs to be *some* idealization of me for the therapy to work, and that hosting a radio show gives me some gravitas. I could swear that recently, after I casually mentioned an author interview I did on the air, a patient who had not known about my radio life began to listen to me more closely, as if my wisdom suddenly deepened. And sometimes it just slips out because I want to be . . . more real, as multidimensional as my patients, or because my own counter-transference compels me to say, "Hey, I'm cool." The gratification of occasional admiration is like a cool drink of water to a parched throat.

I give so much to my patients—I am laser-focused on every word they say, attentive, warm, compassionate, and hardworking. I quietly tune myself to patients' melodies, and each hour begins with someone else's song. As clinicians we are trained to suppress automatic reactions, modulate our responses, wait for the best moment to speak, assess potential effects and timing of interpretations, and listen. We restrain the impulse to shift the focus to us; that goes with the job. I'm not alone in sometimes wanting to burst through the confines of the psychic-midwife role, and say "Hey, over here! On the diving board! Look at me! I have some special things going on outside the office!"

Sometimes patients want to impress us with *their* creative efforts, and maybe this occurs with me a bit more often because of the radio show. Recently a new patient, an artist and musician, placed a CD of his original music on my desk as he was leaving the office. He mumbled, "Heard you like avant-garde music . . . and maybe you did radio once?" The CD, forlorn and unprotected without a sleeve or a clear reason for being there, sat unheard on my desk for the next week.

"Yes," I said at the next session. "I do radio."

"Actually, I know that. I listened to a few of your interviews. I am your biggest fan now!! I tried to find the music shows, but the computer archive of past shows wasn't working right."

A wish to help him find the shows flared briefly, like a firefly in the darkness. I suspected he would enjoy them and imagined how nice it would be to get that ego gratification. But that was not the point.

"The CD you brought in . . . I think I should give it back to you . . . because I . . . we don't know yet . . . what exactly does giving this to me mean to you?"

He thought for a moment and, with spontaneous honesty, said, "I want you to, um, like me, I think. I want to impress you."

I've worked with this issue of having a public life outside therapy for multiple decades and decided long ago that radio was too important a part of my creative life to give up—whatever the lingering biases about a therapist not having too big a personality. It stretches back to my childhood in the early 1960s, to a field trip to WGBO's studios in Newark, New Jersey. Seeing the creativity involved in producing a radio show, watching the DJ establish an on-air intimacy and using multiple aspects of the "Self" to do so, I was immediately smitten with the idea of being an on-air host.

For me, as for many kids, radio was a soundtrack to my emotional and social life. In grade school, I followed AM radio, with its Top 40 hits and fast-talking disc jockeys. My best friend and I would lie in bed, talking to each other on our princess phones, writing down the Top 10 being counted down. The Righteous Brothers, Petula Clark, and the Temptations eventually gave way to the Beatles, the Rolling Stones, and the more intimate and intense experience of FM and public radio, with its non-commercial zeitgeist. From Newark, I heard radio hosts on the New York stations WBAI and WNEW and found comfort and solace in their late-night voices. They talked. They talked a *lot*. And if Allison Steele, the "Nightbird" of WNEW, chose to play an entire album side of a Procol Harum record—so be it. Their voices were comforting. So I understood when a patient said, "Last week, when I wasn't able to come in for my session, I knew I could hear your voice on the radio, and it was very soothing."

As a wild child of the 1960s, I didn't get my career trajectory in shape until I was thirty. I had a long moratorium in my twenties after dropping out of college. In other words, I was floundering. At twenty-five, I became involved with a non-commercial radio station in Bridgeport, Connecticut. I was also back in school, doing some writing, and alternately working as a typist, editor, secretary, or whatever I could find. Hosting a show became the centerpiece of my week. This was the pre-CD era, so like a Sherpa I schlepped some of my own vinyl collection up the three flights of stairs. I always wanted something new to play, some spoken-word oddity that might create the perfect prelude to a piece of music; thus I always needed a range of choices on hand. William Butler Yeats seemed to go with Patti Smith. The French poets wanted to be punctuated by punk rock. On this station, we could be as experimental as we liked. When a segue worked, I felt powerful, excited, fulfilled! I studied hard and passed the Federal Communications Commission licensing test, which involved computations of wattage and power output and the memorization of obscure regulations I would never need. That was a happy day. I started out with shows on Tuesday and Thursday nights, from 11 p.m. until 3 a.m.

Several years after becoming a radio host, I went off to Smith College to study clinical social work. Making radio a career didn't seem feasible—I wasn't a commercial type of host, and I was clueless about how to negotiate my way toward National Public Radio. I had no mentors, which is not a complaint, more of an explanation and a disclosure—I often felt I had to blaze my own way, to my disadvantage. In contrast, life as a therapist made a remarkable amount of sense. I'd always been fascinated by psychology and human behavior. I'd had my own experiences in the patient's chair. I'd been reading Sigmund Freud and Carl Jung, and I very much wanted to do meaningful work.

During my time at Smith, I took a break from radio to focus on my studies. My internships at Clifford Beers Child

Guidance Clinic and Yale University Department of Mental Hygiene were intensive. After a second fellowship year at Yale, I started a private practice. The early years were extremely stressful. In an effort to anchor myself, I carried a collection of meaningful totems—a book by a beloved author, a special rock in my pocket, my favorite mug—as I went back and forth to the shared office I rented by the hour. I typed up my notes from the clinical sessions religiously—patient said/I said—as if they were epic novels.

I'd been in practice for around five years when I realized I missed radio. I returned to the station and pre-produced a weekly segment about the AIDS epidemic that another DJ aired on his show. It was a gentle way back in. Then I took on a weekly four-hour Saturday night music show.

Decades later, in that sly way in which how we spend our time determines the shape of our lives, I am still doing radio, and I am still in private practice. And I'm still struck by how often I evoke that curious or puzzled reaction from colleagues. Does assuming the role of therapist mean you give up your passions? Die a slow death of the spirit?

Over the years, my on-air persona has developed. Around five years ago I began interviewing authors, celebrities, musicians, and activists. The book I published in 2010 (*Blows to the Head: How Boxing Changed My Mind*) connected me to many other writers who wanted to talk about their work. The book itself is a memoir about my midlife involvement with the world of boxing and the history of Jewish boxers. During my on-air conversations with boxing writers and famous trainers, I became freer about revealing aspects of my own history. I used humor; I was self-deprecating; I could often be silly. I spoke with emotion about the music I chose and what it meant to me. I talked about films I'd seen that week and books I was reading.

I am always a bit self-conscious on the air because of my profession. A patient might be listening, so I hold back on sharing what I do on the weekends, where I walk my dog, or very personal things that have happened in my life—I try to focus on pop culture and information. I feel embarrassed if I make a mistake and a bit of profanity in music goes out over the air. If patients *are* listening, I want to do a good job and not be a sloppy DJ. When I do wander into a personal anecdote, I withhold anything that I imagine might be too wildly disturbing or disruptive to a listening patient. Of course, it's impossible to completely control what might be disruptive to different individuals!

Being a psychotherapist and radio host does involve keeping a close eye on all the balls in the air. I'm sure I drop one now and then, but most of the time the juggling does not pose unmanageable complications. I believe as therapists we can work successfully in the postmodern age with new theory-bases and approaches to the increasingly more public aspects of our identities. So I continue to lug my bag of tricks up the stairs to the studio each week and present new Icelandic rock, electronica, or poignant tunes by singer-songwriters. I can promote the works of brilliant authors, which I love to do.

Coming to the end of a music show recently, I recall Shira's dismissive reaction to my playing Madonna. This particular morning (I'm now doing two hours every Thursday), I'm not playing Madonna—I'm ending with Kate Bush's "Running Up That Hill." *What would Shira think of that choice?* I wonder, as I start packing up my radio bag full of CDs. My bag is lighter now that there are more alternatives to vinyl. I'll just have time for lunch before I go to my office and spend the afternoon seeing patients. I remember the time Kate Bush's debut album arrived in the studio, how thrilled I was by her strange, ethereal voice and complex musical arrangements. I put down my bag and leap out of my chair just as I did then, and find myself twirling around the studio. Her five-octave vocal range is transporting. I raise my arms.

At least one of the virtues of radio is that no one can see me dancing.

Triplex

| *Adam Sexton* |

The following is a New York story: it's about real estate and therapy. Not *my* real estate, God knows. Not my therapy, either. It's the story of the time my girlfriend and I lived in her shrink's apartment. The names have been changed, except for the name that should have been. Which is mine.

When I was in my early twenties—this was in the 1980s—I worked for a Famous Newsmagazine and lived in my parents' Westchester house. Humiliating. None of my friends needed roommates, though. And I couldn't afford a place of my own—a studio apartment in New York? Are you kidding me?

I met a girl named Heidi, fell in love. I want to be clear about that: I loved Heidi. Would I have insisted we move in together, though—find a place after only five months of dating—if I didn't want so badly to leave my parents? Probably not. One thing was for sure: once I got out, I wasn't going back.

Heidi was asked to take a leave of absence from graduate

school. She'd failed a course, something fundamental. So she, too, needed someplace to live. I told her we should look in Hoboken, in Jersey. Hoboken was something like Brooklyn's Williamsburg then, or Bushwick: dirty, with musicians.

We found a place on Adams Street, in the back of town, near the train tracks. Across Adams Street: a *pollería*, where they sold live chickens, then killed them and plucked them for you. In a "social club" up the street old men played *bocce*—you could hear the click of the balls, walking past on Adams. The bar where the indie rock bands played was a long, long way away.

One bedroom, one bath. Only there was no bath in the bath, not even a sink. Just a shower. When you sat on the toilet, your feet sort of went in the shower. We brushed our teeth in the kitchen, by a stove like a car from the 1950s. The heat for the whole apartment came out the side of the stove, through some vents—was that . . . legal?

For the next six months I rode the PATH train each day to the headquarters of the Newsmagazine. I'd never been phobic, but I began to fear being caught in the PATH train beneath the Hudson as water flooded into the tunnel. When I worked nights, the company paid for radio cabs to take me home (again: the 1980s), and riding through the Holland Tunnel I had the same fantasy. The drowning fantasy. Heidi told me it didn't work that way. The tunnels were under the ground that was under the water—under the riverbed.

"The guys who built the tunnels bored holes in the rock beneath the river," she explained. "Water won't come rushing in, sweetie. It *can't*."

Heidi studied some, during those months. She scrubbed the stove our heat came out of, scrubbed it inside and out. And she sewed some things for the new apartment: a duvet cover, I think. Pillowcases. Twice a week, she visited her shrink.

Her therapist, Jen, had an office in lower Manhattan. Heidi had begun seeing her when we moved together to Hoboken. Heidi liked Jen, liked taking the PATH to her office on Tuesdays and Thursdays. Unlike Heidi's former therapist, Jen gave advice. Jen was practical, Heidi said.

The Adams Street lease ran out a few months before Heidi's return to school up in New Haven. We needed to find a place to live from the end of May until the end of August.

"Why don't you two move in with us?" my mother asked. "We'll set up an apartment, in your old room on the third floor. Daddy and I won't bother you. I promise. Remember the little fridge you brought to college? We'll plug it in."

Heidi and I checked out the *Village Voice*. We asked around. It was hard because we were looking to rent short-term.

The most promising option: a room in a house in Montclair, New Jersey, a half-hour or so on the bus from Port Authority. The house was owned by two sisters, older. Spinsters, I guess you could call them.

They interviewed Heidi and me in their parlor, china figurines all around with dust on the figurines' surfaces. There was lace in abundance, also dusty. It was like a scene out of Wharton or Henry James. The parlor smelled of dust and Bengay. We sat on the edge of a sofa of horsehair; the spinsters spoke of "kitchen privileges."

"It's only four months," Heidi said, outside, on the blessedly dust-free Montclair, New Jersey, sidewalk. "By September those two will be history—*our* history. We can do it!"

The plan was to move to New Haven in September. I would find a job up there, perhaps in a bookstore or as a waiter someplace. I'd quit the Newsmagazine. I was tired of being an editor—I wanted to write.

In the end the old ladies decided not to rent. Or maybe they rented to someone else. Who knows? With three weeks left in the Hoboken lease, we faced the prospect of moving in with my parents. That's when Jen stepped in.

Jen's practice occupied one floor of a triplex south of Wall Street. A New York apartment with three stories—who knew there *was* such a thing? Jen and her husband had moved to a house in the suburbs months before, and they still couldn't sell the triplex, Heidi said.

"She wants to know if we'd like to live there," Heidi explained after one of their sessions. We sat at our Hoboken kitchen table, by an open window that faced the backyard. The backyard consisted of concrete squares like sidewalk seg- ments, all broken. "Just for the summer, and just on the first and third floors. The second floor is Jen's office. Her waiting room. In exchange for rent we'd keep the place clean, which shouldn't be hard since all the furniture's gone to their house in the 'burbs. Occasionally we'd show someone the apart- ment. Potential buyers."

"Wait," I said. "'In exchange for rent'? You mean Jen's not going to charge us . . . anything?"

"She knows we're in a bind," Heidi said to me, nodding.

From someone's apartment window, dance pop played: Lisa Lisa, I thought, or Stacey Q.

"She wants to help us out."

"I'll take it!" I said.

"Don't you think it might . . . complicate things with my therapist?" Heidi asked, her own devil's advocate. The song that was playing was "Only in My Dreams."

"We're going to live in Manhattan for free. I'll take it!" I cleared my throat. I said, "*We'll* take it."

* * *

Jen's apartment was even stranger than described. It had entrances on the twenty-first, twenty-second, and twenty-third floors. The windows on 21 ran along the floors of the rooms: the master bedroom, an additional bedroom, and two bathrooms. No windows reached higher than your knees. Not one. On 23, where the living room, dining room, and kitchen were located, the windows lurked just beneath the ceiling; to look out a window, you stood on a chair. Floor 22 lacked windows altogether. Floor 22 was where Jen saw her patients.

Her patients included Heidi, of course, who every Tuesday and Thursday morning that summer got out of bed, brushed her teeth, pulled on some clothes, and went upstairs to see her therapist. A narrow, carpeted stairway led directly from the master bedroom to the office, but Jen told Heidi to take the elevator and enter from the waiting room—to keep things professional. After her session Heidi rode the elevator back to 21, where I was usually sleeping. She wouldn't have confided details about her session, though, even if I'd been awake. Heidi was half-German and half-Danish. Her people weren't big on sharing their feelings.

The master bedroom held a queen-size bed, two nightstands, and our luggage. On the parquet floor in the otherwise empty second bedroom stood a card table and a folding chair. My portable typewriter sat on the table, and every now and again I sat on the chair.

Sometimes we ran into Jen in the kitchen, up on 23, her

hair gone frizzy in the New York City summertime humidity. She poured herself coffee she'd made while I still slept and then carried the steaming cup downstairs to her office. I wondered, when these encounters took place, just what Jen knew about me. Did Jen know I'd asked Heidi not to shave her armpits? That I'd told Heidi once that she was fat? The things we did in bed, or didn't do—did Jen know about them? I wondered, did Heidi tell Jen about the time in Hoboken I sat on the toilet and threw up in the shower? Then I thought: why would Heidi tell Jen about that?

Was Jen aware of this kind of intimate detail, though? Did she think me unkind, or even repulsive? I'd chosen to share my secrets with Heidi, my soft spots; I hadn't chosen to share them with Jen, and now I was staring her down every couple of days. Then again, I'd agreed to live inside her apartment.

The light from the windows up by the ceiling streamed in upon a dining-room table surrounded by high-backed chairs that were hard to move. The living room held nothing but a rug of forest-green. Jen's fridge was empty, too, but for bags of Zabar's coffee she'd yet to grind and multiple tubs of a butter substitute called Country Crock.

It was at this point that Esther entered the picture—reentered the picture. I had met Esther in Philadelphia, after college, at someone's off-campus apartment before an Elvis Costello concert. Esther's lips were so full and pillowy that another girl had once asked her if she'd considered a lipectomy. I liked the faint twang in Esther's sandpaper voice and the way her lashes visored her big green eyes. Her skin was smooth and the color of cream, a blank page I wanted to write all over. Esther was what my mother would have called *zaftig*—ample and curvy. I liked that, too. We had spent the night together once, in Philly post–Elvis Costello. A day or two later she dumped me. I'd never got over it.

We'd stayed in sporadic touch through mutual friends. I'd see her at parties and try not to moon and fawn. Suddenly, during the summer Heidi and I spent at Jen's, Esther started calling me regularly. At first she wanted to "get caught up." Then she started seeking advice on the guy she was dating. I listened, for the most part, asked some questions. Showed support. And Esther kept calling, a few nights a week, while the air conditioner in Jen's dining room blasted from a window near the ceiling and Heidi reviewed her grad-school notes. Heidi didn't mind my phone chats with Esther, said she was happy that I had a friend. But would I mind talking down in Jen's office? She was trying to concentrate.

"Josh said I humiliated him, at dinner the other night," Esther told me, starting to cry.

Shifting the phone from one ear to the other, I murmured sympathetically and leaned back in Jen's chair.

* * *

Esther and I never had sex on Jen's couch. We did have sex in Jen's bed, though, in the master bedroom down on 21. It was four or five in the morning, so Jen wasn't seeing a patient then, at least. Still, I cheated on my girlfriend in my girlfriend's therapist's bed.

Heidi was up in New Haven, back in grad school. Sometime in August, I think, I'd told her I no longer wanted to leave New York. (That was the big betrayal, Heidi said later—my failure to move with her, when I'd said I would. Not the sex.) Since Jen hadn't sold the apartment yet, I said, why shouldn't I stay? Heidi would be busy with schoolwork anyhow! I'd visit her on weekends. Or she could come and visit me, at Jen's.

Jen had always placed cleaning supplies here and there throughout the apartment, signaling that we should tidy one area or another. Now her hints became more explicit, with mops and buckets and bottles of Murphy's Oil Soap everywhere—in the master bathroom on 22, by the window next to the toilet bowl. Beside the fridge that was stuffed with Country Crock. Was she asking me to clean up, I wondered— or just to clean up my act? (Maybe Heidi *had* told Jill that I'd once called her fat.) Either way, with Heidi up in New Haven, no one stood between Jen and me any longer. Our relationship was one-on-one, though we rarely, if ever, encountered each other in person and never spoke.

Summer turned to fall. I brought a black-and-white TV from my parents' house and placed it on the floor beside the card table. I sat in a folding chair and watched the summer Olympics in South Korea—the Olympics in which Florence Griffith Joyner ran in a one-legged body stocking and long, painted fingernails and won. I watched the Mets play the Dodgers in the playoffs. The Mets lost. Flo Jo died from an epileptic seizure, though not 'til years later.

As leaves fell from the rare street trees in the gloomy Financial District, Jen grew more aggressive, though no less passive. The cleaning supplies seemed to multiply, and to migrate to corners they'd never appeared in before. Early in the morning I'd be awakened by a long beep from the answering machine, followed by Jen's voice saying someone wanted to see the apartment. Moments later the dark bedroom's door would swing open, and there she'd stand with a would-be buyer, while I cowered under the covers. I wonder now if she phoned from her office upstairs. She never tried to talk, though—to say, "Adam? I don't think this is working out."

I kept expecting a confrontation because, well, wasn't that what therapists did? Confront things? Maybe not.

* * *

I volunteered that I'd been sleeping with Esther, one night in December at Heidi's New Haven place. Heidi told Jen on Christmas Day, from a toolshed outside her family's country house, on a portable phone. She needed privacy, obviously, and the shed was the best place for that, in the country. The only place. I remember Heidi coming inside afterward, her face red from the cold—it was snowing lightly—the phone, its antenna extended, held tight in her mittened hand.

I didn't know what the fallout would be from this phone call. Heidi had told Jen about Esther, sure. But had she mentioned I'd cheated on her in Jen's bed? (Even I knew that was non-negotiable.) If not, maybe I could continue to live in the triplex. People cheated on people, right? And if anyone should know that, it was a shrink. Maybe, as a student of human nature—as one who was exposed, hourly, to the full spectrum of irrational behavior—Jen would understand, as she'd understand a patient. Would understand me, and would let me stay.

When I returned to New York before New Year's Eve, I found a note from Jen on the card table telling me to pack my stuff and leave. So that settled that.

For a while afterward I lived in Esther's apartment. In the basement of somebody's split-level house on a Rockland County cul-de-sac—across the Hudson from New York City, but via the Tappan Zee Bridge, not some scary tunnel. That ended when I cheated on Esther, with a journalism-school student I met at my job waiting tables. Then the student got a real job, on a paper in the rural South somewhere—Mississippi? I asked her to stay, but she left the city, left me.

I felt rejected by the J-school student—obliterated, almost, by her. I was stricken by something like grief and had no one to talk to. I got in touch with a shrink I'd seen during college and started therapy.

I also moved back into my boyhood bedroom. My parents didn't bother me, as promised. I set up the TV I'd watched at Jen's, and the little fridge I'd used in my college dorms. The room was small but functional. It was almost like an apartment in New York City.

The Therapist Who Shouldn't Be One

| *Patti Davis* |

Many years ago, in an era known as the 1980s, I was dating a man whose strained and complicated family history had turned him into a rather strained and complicated man. Which is why I was attracted to him in the first place over other (healthier) men because why go for an emotionally smooth ride when you can jump into roiling waters? But I digress. This man—who quickly became my boyfriend—religiously saw his therapist every week and was quite adamant about how helpful therapy was in coming to terms with his battle-torn family history.

Having come from a pretty battle-torn family myself, I wasn't surprised when he suggested that I, too, could benefit from therapy . . . in particular, with his therapist. I'd had some therapy before that, sporadically, but there were a number of things I didn't know.

Item number 1 on my ignorance list: Unless you are in couples therapy together, you should not be seeing the same therapist as your significant other. You will inevitably end up talking about each other, in between talking about how Mommy and Daddy messed you up. This presents a conflicting experience for the therapist and creates some suspicion between you and your partner, and therefore should be avoided.

But, not knowing this, I signed on for weekly appointments and, predictably, many of my sessions were about my boyfriend whom I knew would be sitting in that same chair at ten o'clock the following morning, probably talking about me. I decided that whatever discomfort I felt about this must be more evidence that I really needed therapy because an emotionally healthy person wouldn't think such things. I was not dissuaded of this notion by the therapist. In fact, he sounded an awful lot like my boyfriend at times: critical, patronizing, condescending. He would call my responses immature, say things like, "Someone with more experience would see it differently," and sometimes wave his hand dismissively as if I were annoying him. Frequently, when I spoke about my relationship he'd cut me off and say, "I can't comment on that. He is my patient as well." Between the two of them, I was not feeling good about myself.

Item number 2 on my ignorance list: Never ask about the wall decorations. This therapist had knotted-up towels on the wall. They were cheap towels, I noticed, and seemed to be knotted in a variety of shapes. Finally, I had to ask what they were. After several moments of stony silence, he said (voice dripping with disdain), "They're towel sculptures, made by a patient of mine." I wanted to say, "Well, I don't think they'll be hanging in LACMA any time soon." But, wisely, I didn't.

Then came the holidays. I brought a small gift (I think it

was a candle) to a mid-December session. He wouldn't take it from my outstretched hands, telling me instead to set it down on a nearby table, and then (after another stony silence) demanding to know why I was bringing him a gift. "Uh . . . because it's the holidays?"

Item number 3 on my ignorance list: You aren't supposed to bring your therapist gifts. I think this is actually written down somewhere and people know about it, although I obviously didn't. And I have no idea what the reasoning is— because it might look like a bribe? Blackmail? A come-on? Regardless, I unwittingly screwed up, and he didn't hesitate to let me know it. I took the gift with me when I left, feeling that I just couldn't get anything right.

After about eight months of this, I finally woke up to the fact that I was being bullied and torn down by both of them. My boyfriend criticized my clothes and my hair and mocked my opinions. I found myself standing in front of the mirror, frightened that he wouldn't like what I was wearing. Isn't a relationship supposed to be a positive thing? And shouldn't therapy build you up? I decided to break up with both of them. Boyfriend first, then therapist. Mr. Strained-and-Complicated had a very dramatic and unfriendly response, basically telling me no one else would want me. Happily, I was finally unaffected by his put-downs. I was feeling much better about myself.

So good, in fact, that I decided to break up with the therapist in person rather than on the phone. I went to my next appointment and told him it would be my last. Stony silence. And then he said in an ominous tone, "This is a very bad idea. Dangerous, in fact. We were just getting to some really vital issues with you." *Really?* I thought. *Because most of these sessions were spent complaining about my boyfriend, not discussing issues.* He continued in the same ominous tone: "If in six months you start having muscle twitches, or full-blown anxiety attacks, if you start feeling nauseous all the time, promise me you'll come back right away."

"Yeah, sure," I said, in the most insincere tone I could muster. "I'll mark it on my calendar. Six months. Got it."

I left there thinking that all the time I'd spent with this man had actually taught me one important lesson: even though someone has a degree in psychology and a list of patients, he can still be manipulative, toxic, and probably more ill than most of the patients he claims to treat. Just as there are lousy car mechanics, there are lousy therapists. The towel sculptures should have tipped me off.

The Knausgaard Digression

| Diane Josefowicz |

His reputation preceded him: I'd heard of my therapist long before I knew him. But then again, sometimes a reputation does arrive ahead of its owner, like a dog straining at the end of a leash. Years ago, as an undergraduate on my way to class, I saw my future therapist's name on a placard marking the entry to his office; now and then, he appeared in the newspaper, weighing in on some matter related to mental health. Once, as I browsed in a bookstore, my attention was caught by a volume bearing his name, a quasi–case study about a man estranged from his son. One scene struck me: watching his son from a distance, the man notes a detail that betrays the son's insecurity. The moment was superficially tender, and its genre—a parent recognizing a child—sweetly classic, Shakespeare crossed with a fairy tale. Yet I felt a keen aversion. The book called for a different reader, someone who didn't mind being made quietly complicit in the subtext, in the view that a father's affection was best communicated through petty criticism. I left the book in the bin, yet the image of the critical father stuck with me, a burr in the mind.

Years later I moved back to that small town, a place so close-knit and gossipy I'd rather not call it by name. By this time, I had a spouse, a young child, a mortgage—all the trappings of adulthood. Yet I was unsteady on every front: as a writer, a wife, a mother. In the chaos of relocation, I let my antidepressant prescription lapse. "You should see someone," my husband said, and surprised me by arranging an appointment with, of all people, the man whose name kept appearing on the edges of my consciousness. That I acquiesced so easily to arrangements made without my participation now seems an indication of how urgently I required help. Off I went, expecting a clinical conversation, a fresh prescription, and a brief follow-up, preferably by phone.

In person, he was peculiar. At our initial interview, he weighed my hand in his, wearing the sour expression of a person who'd expected more for his money. Ignoring my first, fleeting impression—*this will never work*—I doggedly recited my symptoms and history. He suggested restarting birth control pills, which had improved my mood but recently given me a blood clot. To offset that problem, he said, we'd supplement with a blood thinner. I'd run the risk of bleeding to death, should I happen to hit my head on a day when the level of medication in my blood happened to be high, but . . .

"You can't be serious," I said.

He inclined his head with the reticence of a child taste-testing a vegetable.

"I'm just saying," I stammered, "it's a little too *cowboy* for me."

"Maverick," he corrected, upgrading my vocabulary, and made a note on a yellow legal pad.

I left with the antidepressant prescription I came for, along with an inexplicable feeling of excitement. In retrospect, it's obvious that I was out of my mind. It was in this addled state that I agreed to weekly psychotherapy.

It was a prickly therapy shaped by innumerable petty fights. As a therapist, he was like a rearview mirror: everything I reported he reflected back in a smaller, more distanced form. Was I arguing with my husband over household chores? *Good help*, my therapist sighed, *is so hard to find*. Was I fighting with my in-laws? *A man must cleave to his wife*. Faced with these bloodless synopses, I wondered if my self-presentation was grandiose. Yet when I cast my experiences in modest terms—for instance, framing all conflicts with others as mere differences in point of view—he would complain that I was being good instead of honest. More than once I made an ass of myself—slamming out of session, canceling angrily—trying to communicate my need for a response more attuned to the distress I felt.

Eventually, we tired of our roles—his, the dull, platitudinous gentleman and mine, the walking, talking hissy fit. But, strangely, we found we had not exhausted each other or the therapy. It was a delicate moment, this laying down of arms, and the truce might have been brief indeed, had it not coincided with the English translation, starting in 2012, of *My Struggle*, the celebrated six-volume roman à clef by the Norwegian writer Karl Ove Knausgaard. This work, which chronicled the daily activities of a blocked writer named Karl Ove who felt hemmed in by domestic responsibilities, provided my therapist and me with a shareable object, something we could happily mull over together, rather than staying unhappily mired in one another's shortcomings. And the books were pleasurable, an element that should not be underestimated in the treatment of a person living miserably in an anhedonic fog.

Like many of his admirers, I devoured Knausgaard's reports from the front lines of domestic misery. He became a vivid third presence in therapy; the world of this frustrated writer's novels was enough like my own to make the sessions resonate. If I took this or that position on Karl Ove's decision, for instance, to waste time in a coffee shop pretending to write while his wife was home with their kids, I had also implicitly taken a position on the meanings of my own procrastinations in my similarly time-crunched marriage. But Karl Ove reminded me of someone else, too: the critical father of my therapist's story, the one who'd watched his son from a distance with imperfectly concealed ambivalence, whose image I'd found so aversive years before. I grew convinced that despite my therapist's avowed neutrality, he had his own reasons to sympathize with Karl Ove. My therapist, who also introduced me to the autobiographical novels of Edward St. Aubyn, did have a taste for roman à clef.

During this period, I opened sessions with my usual complaints: too much pointless teaching, too much housework, insufficient time to write. "What you're saying makes me think of . . ." and my therapist would summarize a vignette from *My Struggle*. "But I'm not *him*," I would object. "Our circumstances are different."

"They're quite similar," my therapist would counter. "Neither of you can stand to be like everyone else." As I bristled at the implicit accusation—that I was basically a brat— my therapist asked me to see things from Karl Ove's point of view: he was emasculated by child care responsibilities like taking the children to sing-alongs. Wasn't it unfair that I, as a woman, could bring my child to these activities and not feel humiliated?

At other times, my therapist seemed to regard specialness in a more benign light. When he ran into a patient at the DMV, the man had waved him through the line. "It's the only time I've ever been helped by anyone knowing me around here," he confided.

"So you're *that guy*, the one who jumps the queue while everyone else"—I meant, people like me—"waits with the meter running on the babysitter?"

"You're still having trouble with child care? Listen, that reminds me." He leaned forward conspiratorially. "Someone sent me an advance copy of the new Knausgaard."

"Well," I grouched, "aren't you special?"

* * *

The Knausgaard Digression was becoming a nuisance, but I couldn't end it. If I told the simple truth—my therapist's references to Karl Ove irritated me—I feared I would set off weeks of fresh bickering over my supposed overweening entitlement. I could note what Knausgaard's less admiring reviewers already had: as a white male with a degree of economic security unavailable to most of humanity, Knausgaard's complaints reeked of privilege. Not only had he made a huge narrative project out of his undistinguished existence as a father who, when asked to perform a role typically foisted upon the mother, resents the needs of his small children, but by appropriating the title Hitler used for his own vicious gasbaggery, Knausgaard had also clothed his project in the ambiguous power that still adheres to the name of a modern tyrant. Wasn't it all a bit much? Yet the prospect of browbeating my therapist into rejecting Knausgaard's project on moral grounds held zero appeal. I would not expend energy becoming the self-righteous feminist counterpart to my therapist's male chauvinist pig, no matter how much he wanted it.

Did he want it? Was that the dynamic?

When I asked, he nodded. "Yes," he said blandly. "It's been known to happen."

* * *

My therapist's blandness is, of course, the point. He says I can't distinguish his neutrality from simple ignoring and that my frustration with him stems from my confusion of the two. He might be right. I have plenty of experience with ignoring that takes the form of a seemingly neutral and objective attack on reality. As a child I lived with my parents in an L-shaped ranch house. My room was at one drafty end of the L. When I complained that the room was cold, my father neutrally and objectively told me that I was imagining things. I bundled myself into sweaters, knowing better than to argue with my short-fused dad. It was only when I left for college that my father examined the heating vents and discovered that, sometime in prehistory, they'd all been painted shut.

Throughout my childhood, my father played edgy games, like one he called "Gestapo."

"What's your name?" he asked, crouching so we were eye to eye.

I told him my name, and he pretended to slap me across the face. I flinched.

"You lie! What's your name?"

I made up a name.

"You lie! You lie!"

On the spectrum of my father's games, "Gestapo" was friendly. Others were not. A memory: I am small, three or four, with a tendency to engage in antic misbehavior—throwing myself off the sofa, running pell-mell down the hall. I am reprimanded, shouted at, and eventually, when the conflict reaches a pitch, spanked: lifted bodily, pressed across a knee. The spankings are accompanied by enormous emotion, my father's shouts, my screams of protest. At dusk, when his car pulls into the driveway, a pall descends: I stow my toys, and my mother pushes me toward the door: "Run to him. He needs to feel that you're happy to see him." But I'm not supposed to run, and I am definitely not happy to see him because when he is near, I feel afraid. One time, I misbehave, and my mother stays my father's hand. "Can't you see she's frightened?" My heart pounds. His face changes color. He breathes his hot sour breath into my face. He shouts: "ARE YOU AFRAID OF ME?"

I sob: "No." And wait for the blow, as I am obviously lying.

* * *

Knausgaard's father must have worked from my father's playbook. Like my father, Knausgaard *père* was an angry man whose rages so frightened his children they became preternaturally vigilant. "The speed of the car up the gentle gradient to the house, the time it took for him to switch off the engine, grab his things, and step out, the way he looked around as he locked the car, the subtle nuances of the various sounds that rose from the hall as he removed his coat—everything was a sign," Karl Ove recalls, "everything could be interpreted." In this threatening atmosphere, Karl Ove sought invisibility. I recognized his adaptations, right down to the "jerky, almost duck-like gait" he developed in order to "walk fast inside the house without making a sound." I, too, remember walking like that, how my foot would cramp at the arch.

Later, Karl Ove has trouble with his daughter who, at age four, "can be so cheeky I completely lose my head." He finds this threat to his authority so intolerable that he must "shout at her or shake her until she starts crying." Once, Vanja responds differently: "The last time I was so furious I shook her and she just laughed." Taken aback, he lays a hand on her chest. "Her heart was pounding. Oh, my, how it was pounding." I felt for Vanya, this spirited girl who knew what it was like to split the difference between fear and rage. It is only when Karl Ove hurts his younger daughter that self-awareness glimmers. "Her tears flow, and she bows her head and slinks off with slumped shoulders, and I feel it serves her right. Not until the evening when they are asleep and I am sitting wondering what I am really doing is there any room for the insight that she is only two years old."

To frighten a child, to undermine the security of someone small and dependent, grants a cheap power. The limits imposed by the parent constrain what the child can do, say, think, imagine; and any child so burdened can't help but pass those limits on. I'm only now starting to see how my father's rage shaped me—how it made me blind and, therefore, dangerous—if only to myself. For one thing, I can't identify a sadomasochistic entanglement with a charismatic man even when I'm stuck in one. Perhaps especially not then.

* * *

It's Wednesday, session time. As I'm about to begin, my therapist leaps up and cranks the heat. I hide my surging gratitude behind a pose of friendly interest, but I'm really trying to imprint the details of his specific person—his loose-jointed movements, his relaxed posture—on my memory, as if at any point I could lose him forever. Therapy has not freed me from my vigilance, but it now yields a bittersweet pleasure. I do like him.

"Did you see the review of Knausgaard's latest?" I ask. "The one praising his celebrations of ordinariness?" I am eager to please, to honor small truths achieved through painstaking neutrality, and yet he soon turns the conversation to the subject of Knausgaard's specialness, and my own.

"You want me to admit that I can't be happy if I have to live like everyone else does," I say, "that I'm stuck resenting the need to take out the trash."

"Don't you have to be special?"

My father's breath in my face.

"You're the one who brags about your advance proofs and your special treatment at the DMV."

"You can't write that essay," he says.

He means the one you're reading, in which I have a point of view—which is neither neutral nor objective, by definition. We've been talking about it, sort of: I bring it up, he winces, I fall silent—as I do today, picking at my unraveling cuff. How long have I been wearing heavy sweaters to therapy?

"Hello?"

"I can write what I want. You don't have to like it."

"Why can't this be an *ordinary* therapy?"

This used to hurt. Now I just laugh: a sharp, derisive snort.

"You mean one in which I don't write? I didn't sign a non-disclosure agreement. You knew what I was when we began."

"So did you," he says.

* * *

I'm dithering over how to end this essay. I want to make a full and honest account, but like any psychotherapy patient, I'm necessarily an unreliable narrator of my therapeutic experiences; the transference overwhelms the reality of the encounter. But as it turns out, I'm in good company: Knausgaard might be unreliable, too. As I write these words, the fifth volume of *My Struggle* is circulating in English translation. If early reports are to be believed, in this volume Knausgaard finally addresses the provocation of his title, by means of a long essay exploring Hitler's psychology during his salad days: a portrait of the tyrant as an ordinary young man. It seems that Knausgaard wants to show how sociability requires an expansion of the self, rather than its obliteration, which is what Karl Ove has been fighting all along. I see the point, but I also see another expansion—of Knausgaard's many volumes into my living room. He's clever, this Karl Ove. He's installed himself as a charismatic figure and now, after hundreds of pages of violent tedium, he has shown his readers what lemmings we are. It appears we're not finished with charisma, with our willingness to follow figures like Hitler and Gandalf and the Great and Terrible Oz. And, I suppose, my father and my therapist, not to mention Karl Ove. But what's on the horizon is just another tongue-lashing. Whatever, Karl Ove: I've had enough hectoring. I'm ready for different Gods.

The Pregnant Therapist

| *Jessica Zucker* |

Olivia sat across from me in my sunlit office, shadowed in grief. She'd been trying to get pregnant for years and had been coming to see me for nearly all of them. After three miscarriages and two unsuccessful in-vitro fertilizations, she spoke softly of her strained marriage, wringing her hands in her lap. I shifted my weight from one leg to the other, listening intently; she shifted her eyes toward the window. But no amount of diversion could hide what sat between us: my unmistakably pregnant belly.

As a psychologist who specializes in women's reproductive and maternal mental health, I hear countless heartbreaking stories from women struggling to get pregnant, coping with perinatal anxiety, grieving miscarriages, contemplating terminating pregnancies, and weathering postpartum mood and anxiety disorders. Somehow, during my pregnancy, my own anxiety didn't spike. I remained steady.

Understandably, my patients wanted to know about my pregnancy; a third entity had entered the consultation room, altering the therapeutic dynamic. They peppered our sessions with questions like "How do you feel?" (especially during the first trimester, when I glowed olive green) and "What are you having?" (I didn't know.) They wondered aloud how my impending motherhood would affect my work life.

Olivia expressed concern that I would lose the pregnancy and pressed me for details about my status and symptoms. "Thank you for checking in," I'd respond. "I feel fine." Then I'd turn the focus back to her. Together we explored the feelings my pregnant belly evoked for her: her envy of my seemingly "easy" go of it, her fear that my pregnancy would end badly, her fantasy that my being a specialist in reproductive health somehow made me "immune"—that "probably nothing bad would happen" to me.

My baby was born that fall.

Traditional psychoanalytic theories envision the therapist as a blank slate on which patients project their thoughts and fantasies, a distant expert interpreting the patient from behind an inscrutable facade. Patients' concerns are seen as problems the doctor can "fix" through psychological suturing. Contemporary psychoanalytic viewpoints, by contrast, have given rise to a very different understanding of the therapeutic alliance, one in which the relationship itself is ultimately what's curative. But the therapist's quasi-anonymity remains a central tenet. Patients might inquire about a therapist's personal life, but unless it benefits the patient's growth to answer the question directly, the therapist usually explores what the question means to the patient.

So when my body changed shape and my protruding belly filled the consulting room, the traditional therapeutic construct got turned on its head. Pregnancy asserts the therapist's presence and shatters her privacy in a way that nothing else does. My baby bump represented different things to different patients: an active sex life, a certain relationship status, a desire to raise a family. And as my patients often told me, it stimulated longings that stemmed from their own maternal lines.

Four years later, pregnant for the second time, I miscarried at sixteen weeks. After a day of bewildering bleeding and foreboding cramps, the baby emerged in the bathroom while I was home alone. I found myself in a psychological haze of despair that is still in the process of lifting from my psyche. One day obviously pregnant, the next I was a deflated, empty vessel.

I wondered how the change in my physical and mental presence would be experienced by my patients. Olivia, for one, chose not to return to therapy for a while. She said that my second-trimester miscarriage represented her "biggest nightmare" come true. "If a late pregnancy loss happened to you," she explained, "it means it could happen to me."

I speculated that my miscarriage might potentially strengthen some of my patient interactions because I now understood their grief from a corporeal, not simply a theoretical, perspective. But I also recognized that my miscarriage might accentuate my vulnerability in ways that could hinder the therapeutic process. Would my patients be inhibited from freely discussing what might now, in the face of my fresh pain, seem like mundane details of their daily lives? I feared that they might want to protect me, comfort me, run from me, or shield themselves from my anguish.

Processing this particular type of trauma was not something I had learned about en route to completing my doctorate. Even the textbooks that I'd read about pregnancy complications never mentioned the therapist—*her* pregnancy—or how to address within the therapeutic dyad her obvious loss of a pregnancy. I would have to learn this as I went.

Olivia returned to my office three months later, newly pregnant. In one session, near the end of her first trimester, she paused in thoughtful silence—and then whispered, "I'm worried that what happened to you will happen to me."

Several months later I got pregnant again. The beginning of this pregnancy coincided with Olivia's last trimester. I, like Olivia, was now angst-ridden and plagued with uncertainty, despite evidence that the baby was healthy. This time around, Olivia seemed particularly attuned to my eyes. "You look worried," she'd say tenderly.

I reassured Olivia that fear was inevitable given loss—grief knows no time line. With glassy eyes and a deep sigh, she said that hearing me talk about my residual worries eased the sense of isolation that surrounded her miscarriages, allowing her to feel less alone. She was growing less afraid of losing again. Soon thereafter, Olivia gave birth to a healthy baby boy.

I continued, while pregnant, to hear agonizing stories of pregnancy complications. Far from a pristine therapeutic dyad, my patients and I haphazardly made our way through a maze of human emotions.

In the winter I gave birth—and took a much-needed maternity leave. When I returned to my office, I wept as I entered the consultation room, tears of relief, an emotional exhale following so many anxiety-laden months. Back at work, no longer preoccupied with pregnancy, I felt a sense of renewal and a sturdiness that I hadn't substantially embodied in over a year. I was more fully there, deeply present. I had missed this.

Recently, a new patient, Maya, came to me, ten weeks

pregnant. Fifteen minutes into her first session, while describing sleepless nights filled with fear about becoming a mother, she paused, glanced at my bookcase, and then looked back at me: "Can I ask—are you a mother?"

There was a time when I would have reflexively asked Maya what my maternity might mean to her. But instead I considered revealing a small but profound piece of my life. What I hope to offer my patients now, in both subtle and demonstrative ways—shared and silent—are the arduous lessons learned through personal pain and reflection. Far from a blank slate, but no longer a focal point of the therapeutic relationship, I've landed somewhere in between, a much more ideal middle ground.

"Yes," I began my reply to Maya. "I have two children."

With Some Gratitude to

My Asshole Former Therapist

| Pamela Rafalow Grossman |

I found him on a bus.

I saw an ad for a therapist network: "Call us and you'll be matched with a counselor who meets your needs." Honestly, I liked the bus placement. This ad, I figured, was for people like me in New York City, who took mass transit and simply wanted some help getting from point A to point B, in the city and in life.

Back in college I'd gone to a few counseling sessions through the Student Life program. I had some of the typical undergrad issues: stress about my workload; dislike for one of my suitemates. But I also needed help coping with the aftermath of my mother's death from cancer when I was fifteen. Her loss made the whole world feel less solid, less navigable.

Now, a few years after graduation, I was away from the security of most of my close college friends (it was the early 1990s—I wish we'd had Skype then), living again near my still-reeling family, and trying to figure out my next steps. What would be the harm in calling?

A soft-spoken man answered the phone. He asked what I hoped to gain from therapy. I told him I needed to learn to be more assertive. I was tired of getting pulled into personal and professional situations that weren't right for me and losing opportunities because I failed to speak up or even backed away. I wanted to change these patterns before I screwed things up too badly.

What I didn't say at the time was that I especially needed help asserting myself with men. My first relationship in New York had been with a guy I'd known was wrong for me ten minutes into our initial date—though knowing that didn't prevent me from crying when we split for good after an on-again-off-again slog of about two years. I didn't know how to get my male boss to acknowledge my contributions. When men bumped into me on the street, I was the one who apologized.

This wasn't my first post-college attempt at therapy. A friend had encouraged me to see his "genius" therapist, who also treated his sister. The genius didn't advertise on public transportation: he was available only through personal referral. I'd gone to meet him with high hopes, but as we discussed working together, he revealed things that my friend *and* my friend's sister had shared with him in therapy. Genuinely confused, I asked him as gingerly as possible about confidentiality issues. His demeanor instantly grew cold. He cut our session short, telling me that if I didn't like how he did things, we were obviously not a good match. My face hot, I said goodbye as quickly and politely as possible—angry, but wondering if the mistakes made had somehow been mine.

* * *

The bus-ad therapist made a few *Mmmhmm* noises during our phone call, posed a follow-up question or two, and then asked gently if I might be interested in working with . . . him.

It struck me as remarkable that the very therapist who'd answered my call would be among the best, in the whole network, for my needs. Also, given how much I missed my mother and hoped for the kind of guidance she might offer, I was more interested in working with a woman. But this guy, hearing my situation, offered his own services. That seemed promising. Maybe the best way to work on assertiveness with men was to hire one in just this capacity—not my friend's genius but someone else, someone better.

I went for a consultation to check him out. His Park Avenue office building seemed appropriately professional and his office suitably decked out with degrees—though it was an independent office, with no evidence of a network to be seen. He answered the door himself: he had gray hair, pale skin, and what might be called a neutral face. He was in his late sixties or so. He didn't look especially insightful or deranged or handsome or unattractive or intelligent or dull. I was neither taken with nor repelled by anything he had to say. I asked a few questions, got good-enough answers, and figured, "Let's do this." I agreed to see this man—I'll call him Dr. D—once a week.

During our first official session, his office phone rang. I assumed he'd forgotten to turn off the ringer but was proven wrong when he answered the phone. *He answered the phone?* I wasn't in the middle of something especially emotional, but was that the point?

He stayed on the line just long enough to say he'd call the person back. It was a one-time fluke, right?

Wrong. During our second session, he answered the phone again and stayed on a bit longer. His part of the conversation was minimal—"*Mmmhmm*" (his favorite response to anything?), "Sure," "May I call you back in a little while?" It could have been a business call or his wife asking him to get cookies on the way home. It was clear, however, that there was no emergency happening. Just a phone call.

When he hung up, I asked if this phone thing was his general practice during sessions and was told yes, indeed. This was not a question I'd thought to pose during our meet-and-greet.

In the third session, I beat the phone to the punch. I told Dr. D I did not think his letting the phone ring (or answering the damn thing) would work for me—since this was therapy and, just maybe, I could be discussing something I considered important.

He told me we could work together to resolve this issue. Uh—no. I responded that there was no work to be done on it: I needed him not to take phone calls during our sessions. He said I could request at the beginning of each session that he turn off the ringer, and we'd go from there.

Just a few appointments in and he was already annoying the hell out of me.

Then there was the issue of the couch.

As in, there was one in the office, and Dr. D felt I should be lying on it.

I asked if he suggested that most of his patients lie on the couch, and he said yes. I wondered, but did not ask, why he had not mentioned this during our consultation. I'd taken psych classes in college; in fact, I'd minored in psychology.

I would have understood: a Freudian. Then I would have opted against seeing him.

I'd thought that lying on the couch was a nearly vanished approach to therapy, seen primarily in Woody Allen movies and, from what he's said in interviews, in the actual life of Woody Allen. It seemed incredibly outdated. And I felt sure it was wrong for me personally: I wanted conversations; I wanted visual cues; I wanted to see the faces of people I was talking to. The counselors I'd had at school looked me in the eye, laughed with me, passed tissues. In addition, I'll admit I have issues with Freud's views on women (penis envy, anyone?). Reading him for classes, I'd viewed his work as seminal, of course, and as a building block for modern therapy, but it did not speak to me in terms of my own needs.

But here we were, Dr. D and I. Even though the irritating, apparently Freudian, phone-answering therapist I had was very different from the unassuming one I'd thought I was getting, I had committed. We'd said yes to each other, and I felt determined for this to work. I reminded myself of Dr. D's initial assessment: that he'd be happy to help me and felt sure he could.

And so I'd arrive each week; ask him tersely to turn off the phone ringer; watch him do it and feel pissed, every time, that I had to ask; start talking; and then ten or fifteen minutes in, have him ask me if I was ready to consider the couch. Work issues: couch. Goals and fears: are you ready to move to the couch today? I felt that I could tell him I'd decided to join a money-laundering ring to support a brand-new coke habit, and he'd blandly suggest that all discussion of being a felon on a bender works better from the couch.

It was a leather couch, classic and seemingly well made.

It happens that I don't like leather furniture. But whatever I thought about this couch, I knew I did not want to spend my time in therapy discussing why lying on it was not for me. Dr. D wasn't letting go of the issue, so I did. About eight sessions in, he brought up the couch yet again and I said, basically, "Whatever." I stretched out on that couch, stared at the ceiling's moldings and at delicate cracks in its paint, and tried to keep talking.

This went on for three or four sessions more as I discussed work, a new boyfriend, life in New York, and whether in fact I wanted to live somewhere else. I felt I must be patient of the year—bold enough to put her own petty comforts and satisfactions aside to do things her counselor thought were best. Dr. D never spoke. From the couch, I could not see him and had no idea how, or if, he was reacting to my words. None of this felt good to me, but more important, it didn't feel helpful. Was I wrong? Was I benefiting in ways that I just couldn't see?

And then.

I was lying on the couch, talking. Dr. D seemed . . . quiet. Quite silent. Suddenly, I felt alone in the room, and it freaked me out. Screw that couch. I sat up and turned around.

Dr. D sat by the window, gazing out to the horizon. He looked serene and untroubled; how nice for him. He was about eight feet from me yet a million miles away. No longer talking, I sat and watched him. And sat and watched him, for half a minute or so, while he took in the view and apparently daydreamed.

Finally, it was his turn to notice the silence. His gaze turned sharply from the window to me, and whatever he saw in my face turned his pale skin paler. He stammered, looked at the floor, and looked back at me. And then I started to scream at Dr. D.

I demanded he tell me what I'd been talking about. He could not. I asked if he was tape-recording our sessions—which might have explained, if not excused, his absence of attention at the time. But he was not, and frankly I would have been angrier if he'd done that without my knowing. I pointed out, at a high volume, that doing things his way had led us to a point at which he had absolutely no idea of what I, his patient, was saying; and though I was not the therapist, I was pretty sure that was bullshit in the extreme.

He stammered a bit, something about the value of expressing anger within a controlled therapeutic setting, before trailing off. I gathered my things, turned on my heel, walked out, and slammed the door. I never saw Dr. D again.

I did, however, speak with him again, after he sent a bill for the appointment he'd daydreamed through. I called him; he answered; I wondered if the call was interrupting someone else's appointment. I told him what he could do with his bill, and I hung up.

Over the years, I wondered about Dr. D. I questioned everything. Was there ever a network? Did all calls responding to that bus ad lead only to him? And who was he, anyway? Was he a therapist at all? I wouldn't have known if his framed degrees were fake. Maybe he was just some guy who'd figured out that if you could get people to lie on a couch while they were talking, you could zone out for fifty minutes and then charge for your "services."

I went on with life. Slowly I got better at dating, better in general at surrounding myself with people who were good for me and keeping distance from those who were not.

I developed a writing career, worked on trusting my gut, and stopped apologizing for taking up space. I did this on my own, without further therapeutic "help." Every now and then I searched for some trace of Dr. D on Google and found none. Then, about three years ago, I came across an obituary that seemed to be his; it indicated he was in fact a psychologist with a Freudian background.

He'd had two children and a wife. He was also, I learned, a devotee of the arts. If we'd met at a party, we might have had an enjoyable chat.

The obit raised more questions than it answered. On paper, he looked like he could do his job. Why had he been such a terrible therapist? Had he always been lousy, or had he become that way over time? Had he known he was a terrible therapist? Was I the only one who'd told him so?

So this was not the therapist or the therapy I was looking for. Rather he was inept or burned out or possibly just an asshole. However, given that I expressed my disgust with him clearly and not once but twice, it's safe to say that knowing Dr. D helped me go down the path of learning to assert myself with men.

I'm Not Supposed to Love You

| *Nina Gaby* |

What's love got to do with it?
—Tina Turner

This is not about you. The "I love you" piece. It's about me as a therapist, a psychiatric nurse practitioner, *a clinician*, and how I'm not supposed to love you. I learned that rule in my education and training at a big university teaching hospital where even a handshake was considered a slippery slope to major boundary violations. I'm not supposed to have any feelings about you. But of course, I do. Ask anyone in the therapy field about what we call transference and counter-transference, that transaction of feelings between therapist and patient. How it affects what we think of you. How it might deeply affect the decisions we both make. And how to differentiate between the dangerous feelings and the safe, human feelings. I'm not your friend or your mother. You hire me to have a cold, clinical eye and to keep you safe with the right medication, the right therapy. And I need to keep me safe. Because we know how messy emotions get. Isn't that what brought us here in the first place?

We have confidentiality rules to help protect us from the truth of both of our sets of stories, so I describe "you" as a carefully constructed composite. Even if "you" want your story told, I am deconstructing you into a kind of word collage. I'm old now (somehow I've become sixty-five), and I can't deny that you have made the collage of my life richer, and never once has experiencing "love" for you created a problem.

We both may bear very similar sorrows. By protecting you, I also protect myself from the things I can't talk about with you. The way my own life was defined by depression, anxiety, alcoholism, a family suicide when I was ten. How there were hushed funeral preparations interspersed with screaming battles that could be heard throughout the neighborhood. I wondered if it was that very screaming that caused my father's cousin—more of an aunt to me, given the enmeshed dynamics in this first-generation family of ours—to kill herself. The horrible fight just before she took her life, was that the reason, or as my imaginative ten-year-old brain suggested, was it something much worse? Was it our fault?

I never knew because in those days no one talked about these things. Was it pills, the kind of thing a movie star would use? A razor? Was there a note?

What I did know was that alcohol use in my family accelerated soon after. That suddenly another aunt died and my mother careened out of control. That my parents used me as the touchstone for their deepening anger and anxieties. Can I tell you that by yelling at me, they diffused their anger but drove me to the point at which I stole a razor blade and hid it under the pink plastic jewelry tray in my dresser? Of course not, but I can tell you I know what it feels like to want to escape. Some days, for my young self, the idea of escape took the form of wanting to commit suicide; other days I thought about joining the circus. I soon learned for myself how efficient alcohol could be.

What would I say today to a suicidal ten-year-old? I would say whatever it took to put us both back in control; I would offer information that might demystify her terror and confusion. After all, isn't that what a career like this is all about? Using our own pain as a catalyst for good, or at least the illusion of control over potentially bad outcomes?

* * *

These are some of the things I remember from the course of a day, a year, a career.

I remember your kindnesses.

They are not forgotten. I remember the sun burning a small spot on the loveseat between you and your wife as you explained that your decision to end your life was carefully considered. Your son, in a chair next to you in my office, reached over and took your hand. "Well, Father." I recall you were "Father" and not "Dad." You were from another culture, full of graceful words and formal mannerisms. Your wife was swathed in luminous traditional silk. She looked at me directly and said, "We would never hold you responsible." At first I was simply present, deeply involved in the emotionality of this moment for your family. But then the thought came: *How would I document this conversation? How might I be held liable as the psychiatric professional if you killed yourself?* And then the ten-year-old me reached out from my unconscious, saying, *Do something.* I tried to focus just on your words, poetic in their cadence. "I have had so much, done so much. I have been the head of a department, taught many students, had beautiful children, grandchildren. Such success. Such happiness, yes? Now I have early dementia and I have to come here because I am drinking too much. My family is very worried." Your wife nods, adding that you never developed hobbies, always so busy with your profession. "Now he sits in the house. Forced into retirement. Losing his mind. He drinks."

It becomes more personal to me at that moment—who wouldn't drink? My family is alive again in my mind's eye. Alcohol for most, eventually; dementia for some. Unbidden, the image of my darling grandmother, her eyes cloudy with Alzheimer's, enters the room. Even though I have been sober for many years, I catch myself because I have to shut down those thoughts. I have to remain objective, but I am struggling, imperceptibly I hope, for breath. The sun has moved away and I look at the clock on my desk. I reschedule you for another appointment, without your family. You come in the next week. You have no intention of not drinking, no intention of going on an antidepressant; you have loved your life and tell me I am clearly sadder than you are. For a moment we shift roles. You, now the professional, holding a part of my heart in your eyes, promise me you will not commit suicide on my "watch." With kindness, you keep that promise. My charting on your case has been impeccable, giving me the illusion of control, and after I left that facility, your decision became someone else's problem.

Years later I think of you. Despite the rules, we cannot ignore the existence of a type of love woven into the collage that is the work we do, and this specific way we need to talk about our experiences. Carefully, we can only say so much, for your privacy and ours. While explaining HIPAA (the Health Insurance Portability and Accountability Act) and patient privacy to my students in staff meetings, we often horrify these students with our seemingly cavalier attitudes behind the closed doors of our conference rooms. "Staff meetings are the Vegas rooms of health care," we explain, laughing. "What's said here stays here." We try to be funny because sometimes that "love" just has to be funny. Otherwise, how could we keep coming back day after day? Sometimes we have our own "unique identifiers," I tell the students. Novel ways to remember who's who. What story belongs to which person. I write hints on Post-it notes: "Great teeth." "Cute purse." "Bad hair." The fluorescent lights cast shadows on the students' faces as they try to understand: "Dead baby." "Heroin overdose." "Swastika tattoo."

When they ask how we can do this work day after day, I answer that some days they won't be able to separate themselves. That some days they will carry things home in their heads they wish they could leave behind, no matter how much they care.

And I admit there are days when we just don't want you, the patient, to show up. The students gasp, surprised. Surprised that we want you to break an appointment or surprised that we would be so honest as to say it? Sometimes it's because we care too much, I tell them. We don't want to be mad at you. "We can lead a horse to water," as a supervisor once reminded me when I felt dismayed and disempowered. When I wanted to know the absolute truth about a situation and there was no absolute truth, only a set of interpretations. Only a treatment plan not followed. Or the day when I was not equipped to overlook your tattoo. Or when my own narrative is back at center stage for whatever reason. Maybe my sister's mood disorder has reemerged and I feel guilty all over again for being a lousy big sister, or my daughter calls me in the middle of my workday, in the midst of a panic attack, and I feel guilty for my very DNA. It's out of my control, and I don't like that.

So if you don't show up, I don't need to feel helpless or hopeless or absorb your intractable depression or your incessant trauma intrusions. Or maybe there's just too much paperwork. Or maybe it's your anger.

I remember your anger.

One day you yelled at me in my office. We were outlining your goals, and as I made my recommendations (which you, or at least your insurance company, pays me to make), you lost your shit. "How can I do what you are telling me to do? Go into rehab? The hospital? Who will pay the mortgage? Who will take care of my kids? Who will take care of my crazy wife/father/child? Who? Who? YOU?" My training reminds me that you aren't really angry at me. But can I admit that I was relieved when you retracted your release-of-information documents and didn't reschedule? When you left my office without throwing a chair at me?

One night in the raucous emergency department as I tightened the leather restraint around your wrist so you could not slice me again with your jagged fingernails, you screamed at me: "You are the great white devil and I am the small black nation." Ah, quite the metaphor, I sadly agreed. The alternative in this power differential would have been to return you to the cops so they could take you back to the highway overpass where you could freeze to death. Then you did to me all you had left to do. You spat. You came back later and apologized. Did you stay on your medication? I don't know; I lost track. But decades later I think of you. And unlike my family's anger, it's an anger I can manage or walk away from.

I think of you at eighteen, a child yourself, with multiple sclerosis, depression, and three toddlers. Dragging your babies and the two strollers across two city bus lines to get to my office. How my supervisor got mad at me for helping you back on the bus. How it broke certain boundaries. How it might affect my "care." And I admit that I'm still sad for you, for your impossible life, despite knowing I did my best to try to help you.

Last week, during another staff meeting, under another set of fluorescent lights, we joked some more. Another Vegas room. But my heart wasn't in it. I made some off-color remarks about the new computerized record system, how sometimes when patients show up they get in the way of me and my new laptop. But what I really wanted to say to my colleagues was, "What about love? Truthfully?" Because without it I wouldn't be able to finish out the afternoon.

* * *

Eventually I ask the kid about his tattoo, the backward swastika so prominent on his forearm. I don't say anything about why I'm asking, just ask what it means to him. He tells me it's for his uncle who killed himself; his uncle had "them things all over." The kid says he has no idea what it means. He just misses his uncle. And then this gangly, raw, tough kid hugs me as he leaves my office.

My Therapist's Mistake

| *Amy Klein* |

At thirty-five, I felt stuck: I was dating a guy I didn't love and mired in a job I was starting to hate. I couldn't quite believe how my life was turning out—I was neither the successful career woman I aspired to be, nor the young, fecund housewife my former New York Orthodox Jewish community had wanted me to become. But I felt powerless to change.

I needed help.

I was living in Los Angeles and found a psychiatrist who was warm, laid-back, and open. He didn't ascribe to one particular psychological discipline, or think there was any magical solution to problems. He was just a person to talk to and help me figure things out. Dr. X and I spent the better part of a year questioning my life choices: Why did I keep getting back together with my boyfriend Brian if I didn't love him? Why did I feel so guilty wanting to leave my workplace—after all, I'd been a manager at the company for four years! My therapist showed me I had options—to start dating others, to look for a different job—options a "stuck" person doesn't realize she has.

One typically sunny Thursday (so not conducive to therapy!), I had a breakthrough. "I feel like I'd be abandoning my boss," I said, the guilt of potentially leaving weighing on me like a wet awning. A brilliant man who'd brought me from New York, my supervisor had counted on me to remake the company. I was his wing woman. So how could I leave him?

"Is this the guy that you're sleeping with?" the doctor said.

"Wait, what?" I shot straight up in my chair. "My boss?"

"Yeah, the one with whom you had an affair."

I looked at my therapist in horror. I had no feelings for my boss—he was married. Growing up in the Orthodox Jewish community, I hadn't slept with many men, period. (I'd been waiting for my wedding night, but when that failed to materialize, I took matters into my own hands, literally. I started breaking a few other Jewish laws to boot.)

Besides, as a feminist, I'd never steal another woman's husband. So, no, I wasn't having an affair with my boss . . . or with anyone, for that matter. Perhaps my doctor was confusing me with another patient? "Do you even know who I'm talking about?" I demanded.

Dr. X shifted out of his nonchalant stance in the comfy leather chair across from me and leaned forward. "The one you admired so much, the one who moved you here from New York?"

Okay, he wasn't mixing me up with someone else. He knew *exactly* who I meant. Apparently he believed I felt bad about leaving my job not because I was letting someone down, but because all my feelings for my boss were romantic—or worse, tawdry.

Over the past year, I'd often wondered what my shrink thought of me, if I was entertaining, if he liked me. Now I knew: he thought my real stories were so boring that he'd embellished my life, made me over in his mind into someone else, someone more enticing. But no matter how secular I might ultimately become, an adulterer is not the kind of woman I wanted to be.

"I never had any sexual connection to my boss," I insisted, mortified. My therapist and I rarely talked about sex. I was still trying to figure out casual encounters—in my off periods with Brian—how you didn't have to be in love to be in lust. (Which is probably all I really felt for Brian!) That didn't mean I'd *sleep* with my superior.

"I'm sorry," he finally said. "I don't know why I thought that."

I said okay and shuffled out. "See you next week."

* * *

I wasn't really a lifer patient: I saw therapy as something you did to get help with a specific problem, like hiring an SAT tutor before the exam or a physical trainer before your wedding.

I'd only seen a shrink once before—a decade earlier. I'd recently left home, which I'd assumed would bring elation. Independence, finally! No one controlling my every move, monitoring my religiosity. Instead I felt depressed, unable to eat, sleep, or laugh. In twice-weekly sessions with a psychotherapist, I learned the suppressed sadness was my past catching up to me, and the sooner I let the emotion out, the better I would feel. After a year of talk treatment, I'd come to terms (somewhat) with my childhood—my inattentive, silently sparring parents who had just gotten divorced—and was ready to focus on my future. So I left therapy, I thought, for good.

Ten years later, when I got deadlocked at work and with the boyfriend, I again sought help.

I'd chosen Dr. X because he seemed my opposite: a secular atheist who, I learned over the past year, was a staunch individualist, unable to understand why anyone would do anything based on what other people thought. He certainly knew nothing about my Modern Orthodox Jewish community or its continuing stranglehold on me, even as I became less observant, eating non-kosher, sleeping around, but still thinking along the path on which I'd been raised.

"But where would we send our kids to school?" I asked in an early session, trying to show how it would never work with Brian. He was a blue-collar guy, traditional but not well-versed in Judaism; nothing like the intellectual doctors, lawyers, and businessmen my religious friends had married. I loved how into me he was. But was that enough?

"But you don't even have kids," Dr. X pointed out.

"No, but you have to figure these things out *now*." I tried to explain to him how my community worked: "Before you start dating someone, you have to know exactly what type of lifestyle you want, where you want to live, what type of synagogue you plan to attend, and how many kids you want, not to mention how to raise and support them."

"Can't you just figure it out as you go along?" he'd asked. "See how you feel?"

For once I was silent. Did people really live like that? Without planning everything every step of the way?

Tucking myself in the doctor's dark office each week, away from the relentless California cheer, I caught a glimpse of a world different than any I had ever known: people lived according to their hearts, not their obligations. So what if Brian was a good provider who loved me, or my job paid a good salary and my boss counted on me. True, they anchored me from the abyss. Just as religion once protected me from the nebulous secular world. But they were imprisoning me, too.

Witnessing my therapist's bewilderment, his reaction to such a constrained lifestyle, I learned I didn't have to be stuck in any of it—even my religion—if it didn't feel right. I was running away from a life but had no clue where to run *to*, until I restarted therapy.

I was so grateful to him for that.

But over the week, I kept thinking about his preposterous mistake. And I became more and more upset. I'd heard of therapists falling asleep on their patients, or not recognizing them in public, or forgetting a crucial detail in their lives, but never fabricating an event as wild as this one.

In therapy, the relationship between the patient and doctor often mirrors what transpires in the patient's other relationships: that's why many people spend time scrutinizing what goes on in the therapeutic relationship. But I usually didn't tend to overanalyze "us." After all, I was paying him to help me with others. But this time, I needed to explore what happened and call Dr. X on his error.

So, at our next session I admitted, "I'm really upset you thought I slept with my boss." I thought if we discussed how betrayed I felt, and why, I could forgive him, or at least move past it.

He looked uncomfortable. "Well, the way that you talk about your boss . . ."

"Yes?"

"You talk about him as such an intimate; you're so invested in his opinion—I thought you'd been sleeping with him."

"So it's my fault you leapt to that ridiculous conclusion?" I said, hackles rising.

"No, of course not, I'm just saying you could get why I would think that," he said.

I did not get it. And how did he not see that his ignorance about my essence saddened me, and that I felt doubly let down at his inability to acknowledge the harm he'd done?

I thought I'd found a safe place, a man who was different from me, yes, but who knew me. He'd helped me come to terms with the fact that I'd grown up in a society that held different values and beliefs than those I held deep inside, that had made me feel so alienated from my family and community. I thought that by knowing me, Dr. X could help me become *me*. But he was just like all the rest of them. He didn't know me at all.

I continued therapy for a few more weeks. But it wasn't the same. I couldn't count on him.

Maybe I couldn't count on anyone that way: completely, irrevocably, infallibly. That's what I'd been doing with my boyfriend, my boss, my therapist. I had wanted from them what I'd once gotten from the God and religion I'd left: Security. Certainty. Comfort. But it wasn't enough to stay in relationships that weren't working anymore—even if I was afraid of leaving, afraid of what was on the other side.

So I did it. I left therapy, I left my job, I left my boyfriend. All I had was me, now.

Maybe my therapist's mistake was the best lesson I could ever learn.

I'm Not the Right One for This Job

| *Megan Devine* |

I wanted to be a therapist right up until the day I became one.
My very first day on the job, listening to an addict tell
me about her abusive boyfriend, I should have quit. I went to
my supervisor in tears, overwhelmed with my client's pain,
with all the problems she brought to the room. My supervisor
comforted me: "It's going to be okay. You're going to be a
great therapist."

"What if I don't want to be? I'm not the right one for
this job."

But I stayed.

He sat on my couch, as he'd done every week for over a
year. Licking his lips, which were dry from all the medication
he was on. Fidgeting. Eyes shifting from side to side as he
listed all the things going wrong in his life.

It was a long list.

He was too scattered to get the house cleaned, but the
dirt depressed him. He couldn't afford to be more depressed.

He didn't know how to talk to his son, but he got so worried about sounding stupid, which made it harder to talk. He rarely left the house most days. All those years of electroshock therapy, plus the cocaine use—it robbed him of the ability to feel, but he knew he felt bad.

There was just so much wrong.

I sat, listening, thinking: *Man. This poor guy needs a therapist. He really needs help.*

It was several seconds before I realized: I am his therapist. I am his therapist, and it's my job to help.

* * *

I'm not the right one for this job.

"The impostor syndrome, sometimes called impostor phenomenon or fraud syndrome, is a psychological phenomenon in which people are unable to internalize their accomplishments. Despite external evidence of their competence, those with the syndrome remain convinced that they are frauds. Proof of success is dismissed as luck, timing, or as a result of deceiving others into thinking they are more intelligent and competent than they believe themselves to be. They don't believe they are right for the job, and no amount of success can convince them otherwise."

That is what Google told me. Sitting at my desk after this session with my client, I definitely felt like a fraud. I was nowhere near skilled enough to help this man.

For the millionth time, I questioned my choice of profession:

Dear man on my couch, not only am I not able to help you, but I don't want to help. I don't want to help you anymore. I'm out of my depth,

even five years into this private practice thing.
I can't guide you through this because I don't
know how and I don't want to know how. I no
longer want to try.

I'm not an impostor; I'm just not the right
one for this job.

But I stayed.

Even knowing what I knew—that I did not want to be a therapist—I moved slowly, persecuting myself with questions about my motives, doubting my plans for the future, weighing the fact that I'd still have to pay my student loans against the fact that I hated the profession they paid for.

I might not have ever quit.

And then, one ordinary, fine summer day, I stood on a riverbank while a game warden told me they had found my partner's body, six yards downstream from where I had last seen him. It took hearing the words, "I'm sorry, but he's passed," for me to say the words, "I quit."

*   *   *

I quit.

I quit at the riverbank.

*   *   *

I spent three years trying to be anything but a therapist. I worked on farms. I became a cheese-maker. I took informal vows of silence. I wrote because I couldn't stop writing. I ignored the people who suggested I turn back to my clinical work, help myself by helping others.

I resisted. I refused.

I quit at the river.

But I didn't stay quit. I couldn't stand the thought of all the widows, all the new people in pain, thrown into the wasteland that passed for grief support. I couldn't let them call out for help and find nothing but vaguely passive-aggressive platitudes. I couldn't let them bear their pain alone. I couldn't let them find what I'd found.

After three years in dairy barns, I returned to the counselor's seat.

I spend my days now inside the intense pain of others. I listen, I counsel, I teach.

I love my work. It's beautiful and useful and right.

And the truth is, I never feel the way I did that day with that client on the couch all those years ago. I never listen to the stories of the grieving and think, *Man, they need help.* I never feel incompetent, just humbled. I know I am inadequate. I can't fix this; I can't fix any of the pain they're in. I can't do anything here. I know this. Which is why I'm good at my work.

I am the right person for this job, which is why "impostor syndrome" doesn't fit me anymore. I'm the right person for the job because I question everything. Because I know that nothing helps. Because I know. Because I've been on that floor, howling in pain. I've been on that floor, dragging myself hand over hand, convincing myself to stay alive, to not kill myself right there, not because I didn't want to, but because I'd be pissed at myself if I messed it up. Because I wouldn't want to make a mess someone else would have to clean up. I've been in that place.

I'm the right one for this job because I have hated the world and everyone in it while I stood, tears streaming down my face, in love with the world and everyone in it. I know that love is not enough and that all the beautiful things in the world do not matter. Not one bit do they matter, and they never will, and still they are everything, and I can't survive without them.

I am the right one for the job because I know nothing helps. Because I lived it. Because I admit it every day. Because I show up for my clients and say, "I am not an expert in this, and I'm here, and I'm with you. I'm here."

* * *

But there is something I don't say. What I don't say is that I don't want anyone looking up to me, thinking I've got my shit together. Thinking I came through this unscathed. As if I came through this unbroken.

I'm not an impostor; you just don't know who I am.

One of my students wrote: *something broke in me when my wife died, and it has not yet been restored.*

Something broke in me the day Matt died. And if I could have stayed only that broken, I would have. Flayed alive.

But I didn't stay only that broken.

Things broke in me in the months and years after his death that have not been restored. There are parts of myself I left behind on the forced march of making this new life. There are parts of me that never stopped screaming. I have quietly closed the door to those rooms. I don't visit.

Maybe I do have a little habit of thinking nothing I do is ever good enough. I have high standards for myself, and well I should. I don't mind owning that. And I don't mind owning that I am not perfect at grief, because that is a raft of shit. No one is perfect at grief. It is what it is. You survive how you survive.

And still, I am angry at myself, at times, for being broken, for having left parts of myself behind, for having regrets about what I did and how I lived—more exactly, how I failed to live. That anger flares into outrage, railing against the universe: I DID THE BEST I COULD. I tried everything I knew to try.

And that's a lie. That's where it's hard. Because I didn't try everything. I didn't keep reading books that brought out my spiritual side. I didn't keep sitting in empty churches, feeling Matt and feeling love, right alongside the dry heaves and nightmares. I didn't. I couldn't keep trying so hard. I chose not to. I blame myself, and I rage against an allegedly benevolent universe, one that didn't make it easier for me to stay. To stay beside myself, with myself, there. Right there. In the screaming beginning of this.

Good job, but I should have done better. I survived, and I'm okay, but I could have done better. I lost something vital, and it's my fault.

I believe I failed.

I could have hung on to that self, that torn open self. I wanted to. As much as it hurt, it had incredible light. Incredible love. But I am not that person anymore.

She was better. Softer, trusting, more aware. My life is more beautiful now than it has ever been, but that earlier me was better.

I left myself. In my darker, harder moments, that's what I believe. I could've done more. I could've done better. I should have.

I should have stayed only that broken.

So I don't think you should look at me as if I'm some model to look up to. I'm the right one for the job, but I'm not right. There are things that no one knows, ways I have let myself down, choices I don't want anyone to emulate.

In all of it, in everything I do now, I'm speaking from that spot. That place, the one where I'm embarrassed at the ways I left myself behind, the rooms that are passed by, the doors I closed. I don't want that for you. I don't want you to look back and think you lost yourself somewhere. I'm telling you in tenderness because I want that for myself.

I am who you think I am, but I am not who I was. Don't look up to me.

And I'm the right one for the job.

The Grief Group

| *Barbara Schoichet* |

Six months before I turned fifty, I was laid off from my job at Paramount Pictures. A week later my girlfriend of six years left me for her hairdresser. I dove into an emotional free-fall, and then came that third and most devastating blow. My mother called to tell me she had pancreatic cancer . . . and died four days later. No longer tumbling through a black hole, I landed in a place absent of color.

Everyone was worried. Friends stopped by to coax me out of my bedroom. One gave me a massage, another a crystal to keep away bad juju. I'm not sure which was worse, having my grief disrupted by their visits or finding myself longing for the next person to drop by. But dealing with my three sisters, who insisted that I still celebrate my birthday, was most disturbing, especially when they ganged up on me during a conference call.

"Pack your bags. We're taking you to Las Vegas this weekend," Naomi in Chicago said. "And you can't say no. We've already bought the tickets."

"No," I said. "No, no, and no."

"Oh, come on," Sandra in San Jose chimed in. "We've booked two suites in Caesar's Palace and gotten front-row seats to Elton John. I've heard that sometimes he invites people on stage to sit around his piano."

"Have fun," I said. "I'm not celebrating anything. I've already picked out the spot on my couch where I'm going to sit and cry."

"Stop it, Barbara," said Harriet in El Paso, where just a month ago we had buried our mother. "You're going to have a fun birthday with us in Las Vegas if we have to fly to Los Angeles and drag you onto the plane."

I went to Las Vegas, managed to convince my sisters I was fine, and then came home only to fall back into a depression so cavernous I felt it had no bottom. It was definitely time to go to therapy, time to deal with what was *really* bothering me. I wasn't just harboring a deep sadness, I was experiencing an unbelievable anger I couldn't discuss with anyone. Sure I wanted the studio to go bankrupt, and yes, I wanted my ex's house to slide into a sinkhole, but it was my mom who really drew my rage. The doctors had given her at least six months, but she died in less than a week. For God's sake, the woman was late for every carpool, piano recital, and school play, but given the possibility of dying early, she was all over that.

My father, who had died nine years before, battled heart attacks, a stroke, and pneumonia to keep living. Why hadn't mom fought for at least a month so I could get to El Paso to see her? She had an eternity to be dead but instead raced off into the cosmos to be with my dad, taking with her whatever it was I so frantically felt I should know.

I despised myself for these feelings. What kind of person longed for a therapeutic breakthrough to the extent that she wanted her mother to suffer through the horrors of pancreatic cancer just so she could clear up a few things? My stomach turned thinking of my selfishness. *I* was that kind of person. I wanted my mother to be there for me during this terrible time, to encourage every move I made, and most of all, I wanted her to help me deal with her death.

I was no stranger to depression, and I'd seen a number of wonderful therapists who pulled me back from the abyss of lost love and guided me through the tunnel of loneliness that follows. I'd even beaten a pillow with a rubber bat that a psychiatrist in Marin County insisted would help me release the inhibitions planted in me in high school. I knew when I was falling back into childish behaviors or adolescent angst, so before I regressed any further I joined a therapy group at a center for healing in Santa Monica with options for a variety of losses, including parents, children, and siblings.

There, in a room full of pillows and Kleenex, I met sixty-something Emily. She'd just retired to spend more time with her husband, who was dying of cancer, and suddenly her mother broke her hip and died. Like me, she was instantly an adult orphan. Like me, she was furious.

"My mother and I had a complicated relationship," she said, hugging the life out of a pillow. "Of course I loved her, but sometimes I go in my garage to yell at her for abandoning me."

The facilitator smiled. "Anger after a death is really quite normal. Many times it's God we're railing against."

"Yeah, right." Emily rolled her eyes. "I need my mother to help me get through this, not some figment of my imagination in the sky."

"The essence of your mother is with you," the facilitator said. "You must know that in your heart."

"Essence my ass!" Emily snapped. "If my mother is anywhere, she's sitting on a cloud knocking back highballs with my dad."

More buoyant than I'd been in months, I decided to leave the group early just in case one of the real weepers brought me down. But there, standing inside the elevator, was the epitome of depression—a skinny teenager with stringy hair and a disconnected gaze. She took a step back when I walked in and quickly studied her shoes. It felt as if we were convicts in a holding cell, and if I'd been my normal smartass self, I'd have asked her what she was in for. Instead I said, "I haven't seen you before. Do you work here?"

She shook her head. "No, I go to a special group for multiples."

I must have looked confused. We were in a grief support center, not the psychiatric ward of a hospital.

"Don't worry, I'm not Sybil or anything." Her face reddened. "I'm in a group mourning multiple deaths. My whole family died in a fire. I was the only survivor."

I put my hand over my gaping mouth. "I'm so sorry."

She offered me a comforting smile, one I should have given her. "I haven't been able to talk about it," she said. "But I'm getting there."

When the elevator opened I walked out, careful not to look back. There weren't any words for this girl. But then I did turn around, hoping to absorb some of her sorrow. Surely I could let go of some of my anger to make room for a bit of her pain.

Once outside, when I was sure I was out of her eyesight, I broke into a sprint, the kind of effortless gallop I had as a child. The despair and confusion I'd been carrying around fell away, and I decided I would call the healing center the next day to tell them I was okay, that I could get through this grief stuff on my own. Truth be told, I didn't like how perky our group facilitator was and how she always seemed to be whispering. I didn't like the dimly lit room where we met, the obligatory hugs, and all the crying. I probably would have a lot more success just getting Emily's number so I could ask her out for a few drinks and some private ranting.

"I'm all right," I chanted with each footfall as I ran away from the center and that poor girl's horror story. "I'm okay," I said, gripping the steering wheel on the way home. "I'm just fine," I said, staring at my bedroom ceiling as I tried to fall asleep.

But I wasn't all right, okay, or just fine. The next morning my persistent despair draped over me like a familiar black shawl. Just because someone else's losses were more tragic than mine didn't make my grief any less debilitating. I still had no work to go to, no lover to comfort me, no mother to call for consoling wisdom, and worst of all, my arthritic knees were throbbing after that little sprint.

I trudged into the bathroom and looked in the mirror, expecting to see another layer of wrinkles etched on my rapidly aging, unemployed, unlovable self, certainly not the face of someone I thought I'd never see again—my mother.

"Go back to therapy." I heard her voice in my head as I watched my lips move in the mirror. "And for God's sake, brush your hair."

For a long time I couldn't stop staring at my reflection. How had I not noticed how much I looked like my mother? I studied my jaw . . . By God, it was *hers*. I watched it wobble in the same way hers had trembled forty, maybe forty-five years ago when she sat at the foot of my bed to apologize for yelling at me.

"Mommy had a bad day," she had explained, shrugging. "Sometimes we have bad days. But we're going to be all right, aren't we?"

"Yeah," I said to my reflection. "Sometimes we have a *lot* of bad days. But we're going to be all right."

* * *

It's been over ten years since I attended that grief support group, and yes, I took my mother's advice and went back the following week and for several weeks thereafter. I remember when I was allowed entry into the group we were all asked to commit to a certain number of sessions—twelve, I think—and I didn't understand why this commitment (which I'd nearly broken several times) was so important until some people didn't show up.

To be honest, I can't remember the names or faces of any of them now, except maybe Emily, but I'll never forget how I felt when I walked into a session and a group member wasn't there. I was confused, concerned, and unsettled. I felt forgotten, even abandoned—all the feelings I'd experienced when my mother died . . . even anger. Were they healing faster than I was? What was wrong with me that they didn't want to help me anymore?

Looking back, I still remember how I mocked almost everything about the group, how weepy some people were, how these virtual strangers somehow believed it was okay to touch me. And yet it was startling when any one of them was suddenly gone. I guess I didn't want the consistency, familiarity, and trust developing among us to be disturbed. There had been so much disruption in our lives that this petri dish of people, all here to find a "cure" for our common ailment, needed to remain stable for us to regain our stability. We were unwilling members of a club no one wanted to join, an association with one single requirement—we had to have recently lost a parent—and damn it, there was no way out of that club . . . or was there?

The word "recently" is key, and I learned the importance of that word while in my grief group. It was more than merely understanding that the adage "Time heals all wounds" would eventually apply to my suffering, more than realizing there are various stages of grief and I was slowly working my way toward acceptance. *Recently* means you're still feeling tremors from the shock of your loss, but in therapy you are reminded your world will eventually stop shuddering even after the most devastating of quakes rocks your world. Our perky little facilitator drove this concept home on the last day our group met.

"Everything must come to an end," she said, passing around a basket full of rocks. "And so must this group. Please take a rock as a reminder of your time here. Notice that each rock is hard, yet smooth." She shrugged. "Difficult and easy—that's life, isn't it?" She smiled. "I promise you that you're all going to forget that fact—especially during times of great loss—but it's one of the few constants we can all count on."

I put the rock in a safe place, though I have no idea where that place is. But the hard truth represented by that rock remains. We all lose jobs; relationships fall apart; loved ones die. The thing to remember is that a smooth patch is coming in which you might find a better job, sell a book, meet someone who excites you, and best of all . . . you might see a long-lost loved one show up in your mirror.

I'm Afraid Our Time Is Up

| *Priscilla Warner* |

I used to joke about the fact that I didn't want to know anything personal about my psychiatrist. I'd never use her first
name—Roberta. Sometimes I referred to her simply as *Jaeger*.
That's how she answered the phone when I couldn't make
it into Manhattan for an appointment and called her office
instead: "Jaeger here!"

I had no idea how old my therapist was. Sixty-ish? Pretty
and chic, she wore her dark brown hair in a sleek bob, setting off her high cheekbones and bright brown eyes. She
was petite and wore her elegant clothes beautifully. And she
dressed up for me! In tailored skirts and tops, stylish pumps,
perfectly appropriate scarves, and jewelry.

Although her office was on Park Avenue, I managed to
overlook the formality of Dr. Jaeger's doormen and lobby. I
considered myself an Upper West Side or Greenwich Village
sort of girl.

Of course I was hardly a girl. At forty-eight, I was a
long-married suburbanite, the mother of two sons then fif-

teen and eleven. I'd suffered from debilitating panic attacks for decades and seen two other therapists—one in my twenties, another in my thirties.

I had specific goals in mind for this round of therapy, I told Dr. Jaeger at our first session. I wanted to keep things professional. There'd be no transference between us. I'd make sure of that. I was going to treat her more like a business colleague than a friend.

Or mother substitute.

"My boys are going to grow up and leave home," I explained to her. "Raising them with my husband has been the best experience of my life. I know I'll need some help heading into the empty nest years."

I wanted to finally accomplish something personally fulfilling and creative. I'd been an advertising art director for many years, but thought I had a novel or memoir waiting to be written. "Not art," I warned Dr. Jaeger. My mother was an artist whose intense imagery haunted me.

I was hoping to find ways to weather the roller coaster of menopause with fortitude. I knew my shifting hormones were setting off more panic attacks.

For years, I'd been adept at minimizing my troubled background with clever conversational shtick. At our first session, however, Dr. Jaeger saw through my colorful banter, as I recalled my manic depressive father's struggles, his twin brother's nervous breakdowns, my mother's depression, and the fact that my namesake, my father's favorite cousin, became a homeless schizophrenic. Add my father's infidelity and bankruptcy to the mix, and I had quite a story to tell.

"What was your safety net?" Dr. Jaeger asked me at the

end of our first session. "It sounds like you didn't have a lot of adults you could rely on as a child."

"I cobbled together my own safety net," I realized, recalling the roles that friends and their parents had played in my life. My mother and father had married young. In many ways, they'd seemed more like people trying to find their way in life than parents. My father confided in me about his marriage and business problems. My mother was often lonely and frustrated, creatively and in her marriage.

Over time, Dr. Jaeger gave me the confidence to believe I could break the cycle of unhappiness and dysfunction in my old family by building a new one with my husband. My panic attacks had started when I was fifteen; I wanted to be a grounded and supportive mother to my two sons during their adolescence.

Dr. Jaeger became a huge part of my safety net as I built my new life.

She was unfailingly warm and kind. When the last minute of our session approached, Dr. Jaeger would glance at the clock on her desk and say, with an apologetic smile, "I'm afraid our time is up." Then she'd stand, walk me to the door, and blow a kiss goodbye as I left, ushering me back out into the world with love.

Although I took breaks from therapy during the decade that I was Dr. Jaeger's patient, I returned whenever I needed help. My therapist guided me through the grief that erupted when my mother was diagnosed with Alzheimer's. "You're experiencing a double loss," she explained to me. "Of the mother you had, and the mother you wish you could have had all these years."

She dispensed pithy words of wisdom to me, such as, "You had a mother. She just wasn't very maternal." Or, "Your parents didn't raise you, but they did let you grow up."

My own children thrived, thanks in large part to the fact that Dr. Jaeger helped me manage my own anxiety. She took delight in their accomplishments, remembered their endearing quirks, and loved seeing photos of their evolving, handsome faces.

My confidence grew, and my writing career took off. I co-authored a best-selling book with two other women and toured the country speaking publicly. My panic attacks were controlled with the help of the Klonopin Dr. Jaeger prescribed.

Inspired by Tibetan monks who meditated so effectively that neuroscientists studied their brains, I vowed to learn how to meditate. I wrote a book about my adventures with Buddhist teachers, Kabbalistic rabbis, therapists, and healers.

I was eager to try something besides talk therapy and to cut back on Klonopin, which often made me tired. Dr. Jaeger researched and approved of two therapies I ended up loving—Somatic Experiencing and EMDR. Anxiety had produced very specific, frightening physical symptoms in my body, which these therapies helped me process and discharge.

The first draft of my book included a description of my long relationship with Dr. Jaeger. I had much to celebrate, I told her when we met to discuss what I'd written. We weren't seeing each other regularly, but I still relied on her wisdom and support occasionally. And I was honored when she complimented my writing.

A week later, I emailed my beloved therapist to set up another appointment. Quickly, I received a terse response from her account, saying she had suffered an accident and would not be available for several weeks.

I thought that was odd.

Nothing about Dr. Jaeger had ever been odd.

I assumed someone had hacked into her email account. Careful not to cross the boundaries I thought were so important, I emailed her back: "I don't mean to be inappropriate, or invasive, but I am concerned. I wonder if you could share with me anything about what is going on."

A day later I received a response from Dr. Jaeger's son. His mother had suffered an accident, he wrote, and it would take some time for her to recover. He was optimistic she would be able to share the details with me soon. "She is loved and we are all hoping for a speedy recovery," he wrote. "There will be an update on her voice mail by Christmas."

Could I wait until Christmas? That was a month away.

A friend invited me to a class at Columbia Teacher's College the next week, called "The Psychology of Loss and Trauma." She thought I'd appreciate hearing her professor lecture, since I'd explored a childhood trauma in my memoir. When I was sixteen months old, I'd almost died from an acute infection in my windpipe. My parents had recounted the story to me often: "Your fever soared to 106. We rushed you to the hospital. That night, while you were alone in your room, your throat closed up and you stopped breathing. A resident found you in distress and performed an emergency tracheotomy."

* * *

My tiny throat had been slit open, probably with no anesthesia. No wonder I'd had trouble breathing all my life and hyperventilated with every panic attack.

But when I sat in a classroom listening to stories of people who'd endured horrific life experiences—rape, childhood

238   How Does That Make You Feel?

cancer, and incest—I thought about how lucky I was, despite the hundreds of panic attacks I'd experienced. When the lecture ended, I stepped out into the hallway to check my voice mail. Then I decided to place a call to Dr. Jaeger to see how she was doing.

A man's taped message had replaced my beloved therapist's familiar voice.

"This is for the patients of Dr. Jaeger," he said. "We are sorry to say that she passed away . . . ."

I burst into tears. My heart skipped beats, flopping around in my chest. I couldn't catch my breath.

My friend appeared and put her arm around me. She guided me out of the building as I walked unsteadily, making my way to my car, slowly.

On the sidewalk, my lungs began to convulse. I shivered as I felt a panic attack coming on. My throat began to tighten. "Breathe in and breathe out," I told myself again and again.

* * *

We made it to my car, and my friend opened the door for me. Then she had to return to speak to her professor for a few minutes.

I sat in the driver's seat of my SUV, stunned.

Sounds came out of me that I didn't recognize.

Alone in my vehicle, I wailed, with the windows rolled up and the rest of the world unaware of my pain.

Gradually I began to pull myself together. My jagged, uneven breaths became more regular. I summoned every ounce of strength I'd developed over the last few years.

My safety net was gone.

I would have to construct a new one for myself.

I channeled every morsel of wisdom and kindness Dr. Jaeger had ever bestowed upon me. I also practiced the grounding exercises I'd learned from EMDR and Somatic Experiencing.

My friend returned, and I drove her back to her apartment, slowly. We said goodbye, and I drove home to the suburbs, carefully.

My house was dark and empty when I arrived and sat down in my front hallway, in a big red velvet chair that had been my mother's. I lit a candle and placed it on a table beside me.

* * *

And I meditated.

I tried to summon Dr. Jaeger, to remember what we'd talked about the last time I saw her.

But I couldn't.

A few days later, Dr. Jaeger's memorial service took place at a packed funeral home on the Upper East Side of Manhattan. I brought my husband with me for support. He'd never met my therapist, and I wanted him to learn about the woman who'd helped me so much. We sat in the last row so I could cry without self-consciousness.

But I ended up laughing and smiling a lot during the service. I learned so much about the woman who knew so much about me.

Hundreds of colleagues, friends, and patients mourned and celebrated Dr. Jaeger's life. Speakers referred to her wide circle of friends, professional integrity, and wonderful sense of humor.

Her daughter described their ritual weekly outing—a cocktail apiece at a swank hotel every Friday after work.

They'd hold hands as they walked back to Dr. Jaeger's apartment afterward.

Where I'd sat with her for so many hours.

* * *

Dr. Jaeger was loved by her children, grandchildren, colleagues, and friends. At the end of the service, they gathered in groups, talking quietly.

I recognized a fellow patient who'd spoken at the service, and approached her to exchange email addresses. A week later, we met at a diner halfway between our two suburban towns. Sitting in a booth, we picked at our eggs, crying and reminiscing about our wonderful therapist. We'd both grown up with complicated mothers. Dr. Jaeger had filled a hole in our lives, with kindness.

Then we went our separate ways. I didn't feel like sharing more of my most intimate memories of Dr. Jaeger with this patient. I felt that would diminish them somehow. And what could this woman do for my pain? She wasn't a therapist.

I remembered the name of a psychiatrist Dr. Jaeger had once given me for a friend and made an appointment. Late afternoon light filtered through the blinds of this woman's modern office. I missed Dr. Jaeger's cozy, dark study. I missed the glass paperweight on my therapist's desk, and her plump, blue enamel pen. I began to cry. "I don't know how to mourn Dr. Jaeger," I told the stranger sitting across from me.

"Talk to people who knew her," she suggested.

"That's just the point," I said. "I don't know anyone who knew her."

There was no such thing as a mourners' support group

for patients who loved Dr. Jaeger. I was counting on this woman to tell me exactly what to do with my pain.

But she seemed locked in her own private mourning process, which didn't seem right to share with me. At the end of our session, she rose and walked me to the door.

There would be no goodbye smile or blown kiss. Suddenly this woman's eyes filled with tears. "I could never be half the therapist that Dr. Jaeger was," she told me. "Dr. Jaeger was irreplaceable."

Great, I thought, as I waited for the elevator outside her office.

I had lost an irreplaceable therapist.

Fortunately, while I was writing my book I'd met a wonderful psychologist, who'd treated me very effectively with EMDR. I reconnected with her and began processing Dr. Jaeger's sudden death with the technique that so many people find effective for treating trauma.

Still, I developed heart palpitations, and my internist prescribed a beta-blocker. My heart was broken, and Dr. Jaeger wasn't around to fix it.

* * *

Slowly, I made progress healing from my therapist's death. One night I searched my messy nightstand drawer and found a cassette of one of our sessions, which I'd taped in order to write my book. When I pushed play, my therapist's distinctive voice, with its slight Brooklyn twang, filled my dark bedroom.

Instantly, I was back in Dr. Jaeger's office. I remembered the way she'd smile as she opened her door, ushering me in to my appointment. She'd tilt her head slightly, taking my emotional temperature. One look and Dr. Jaeger would know just how to proceed. She could see instantly if I was tired and weak, happy and confident, elated or sad. She'd lead me to a chair by her desk, sit down across from me, and straighten one of her chic skirts. Then we'd begin.

But we will never begin again.

No one will ever know me the way Dr. Jaeger did.

Not even my husband, the love of my life, has seen me broken down sobbing, mourning, and recognizing the pain of my past the way she did.

In the next three years, I'd lose my mother, my father-in-law, a friend, and my sister-in-law.

* * *

The pain and shock of Dr. Jaeger's death has been softened by subsequent loss and grief. She gave me tools to process traumatic life events, including her own death. But when I walk by her building now, I recognize my naïveté during those years when I tried to pretend that my therapist wasn't someone I loved deeply . . . that ours was a strictly professional relationship.

And I smile.

"My shrink isn't a mother substitute," I'd always tell friends, proud that I was able to keep things on a professional level. "She's not a friend or a family member," I'd say.

It turned out, however, that chic, petite Dr. Jaeger was all of the above.

A Long, Strange Trip

| *Dennis Palumbo* |

Despite myself, I kept looking at my watch.

I was sitting across from a well-known Hollywood producer at a tony restaurant on Sunset Boulevard. We were just finishing lunch—the usual mix of overpriced food and lurid showbiz gossip—and now it was time to get down to business. I was a screenwriter, there to hear the guy's pitch for a movie he wanted me to write. The year was 1986.

But I barely listened as he enthusiastically laid out the story. Not out of boredom or lack of interest in the idea. Rather, I was afraid I going to be late for something else.

Which turned out to be the case. So, lunch finally over, and not five minutes after shaking hands goodbye, I was in my car, barreling down Sepulveda Boulevard, on my way to join a roomful of crazy people.

Because, unlikely as it seemed, I was their therapist.

* * *

To paraphrase an old saying, show business was very, very good to me.

After arriving from my hometown of Pittsburgh in 1975, determined to break into the entertainment industry as a writer, I went through the usual *Sturm und Drang* of every other poor soul with similar dreams. In my early twenties, married and broke, I sold school supplies over the phone (on commission) and spent nights standing at the rear door of a nightclub called the Comedy Store, selling jokes to stand-up comics. I also wrote. Feverishly. Relentlessly. Spec screenplays and TV scripts. Comedy sketches that I submitted, unsolicited and unsuccessfully, to the then-popular variety shows on network television: *Sonny and Cher. The Jacksons. The Carol Burnett Show.*

Finally, I got both smart and lucky. Smart in that I teamed up with a wonderful writer named Mark Evanier. Lucky, because a spec script we wrote for the TV series *M*A*S*H* landed us an agent, who got us an episode of the series *The Love Boat*. (A lame story about a trio of friends trying to help a nerdy fourth guy lose his virginity. Yes, very classy. Real Noël Coward stuff. But don't laugh—I still get residuals from that episode, the most recent a check for 13 cents from a broadcast somewhere in the Balkans.) From there, we ended up on the writing staff at *Welcome Back, Kotter.*

After a few years as a team, Mark and I parted amicably. I wanted to try my hand at writing feature films. More struggle (the above-mentioned *Sturm und Drang*, 2.0), and then fortune smiled on me again. I ended up co-writing a film called *My Favorite Year*, starring one of my favorite actors, Peter O'Toole. Other assignments followed, and I embarked upon the usual ups and downs of the screenwriter's life. Some good years; some lean ones.

All's well so far, right? Not exactly. Although I'd ostensibly "made it" in Hollywood, the atmosphere of the industry felt toxic. At least for me. I apparently didn't have—nor did I want to learn—the killer instincts my agents kept urging me to display. Moreover, the narcissist in me resented the insipid, audience-pandering script notes that writers routinely get from producers, studios, and network executives.

I wanted to write films, comedic or not, about how people actually behaved: how they loved, fought, lost heart—but perhaps found enough inside themselves to persist, if not prevail. Hollywood wanted to make *Jaws* and *Star Wars*. Films I loved, but didn't want to write.

Then my personal life went to hell. My marriage ended, and I struggled with prolonged bouts of depression and anxiety. Isolation. Sleepless nights filled with disturbing dreams. Yet occasionally, within that emotional chaos, I felt something else stirring. The notion that maybe I didn't really belong in show business. That there was something else I should be doing.

Some other path I should be following.

Unless this was just more egoistic self-absorption, I worried. A search for a life raft to cling to as I drifted through an unsatisfying personal and professional life. Or maybe I was just going crazy.

In the midst of this confusion, in the mid-1980s, I was offered a deal to write a screenplay based on the life of famed mountain climber Willi Unsoeld. He and his best friend Tom Hornbein had been the first climbers to make the summit of Mount Everest via the dangerous West Ridge. Telling Willi's personal tale, encompassing true courage and profound heartbreak, would require both extensive research and considerable travel. Which I happily undertook, feeling the year-long project would be just the distraction I needed to get out of my own head for a while. Truth is, I hadn't liked it in there for a long time.

Part of the research involved interviewing Unsoeld's colleagues and friends in the mountaineering community. I even went to mountain-climbing school in Jackson Hole, Wyoming, after which I managed to survive a climb to the top of the Grand Teton. During that same trip, I met Mike, a climber then working as a river-raft guide. But his true love was the Himalayan range. And his true home was Kathmandu, Nepal. When he learned of the film project, he suggested I visit him there and head up into the Himalayas. In the footsteps of Willi Unsoeld himself.

In those years, Nepal was a very different land than it is today. A Hindu kingdom, with the king himself considered an avatar of Vishnu, one of the trinity of supreme gods in that venerable religion. Failure to have Vishnu's photo up on the wall of your house was a crime punishable by death. But the modern world was steadily encroaching. The country had its first radio broadcast during my time there, though kids wearing Michael Jackson T-shirts had been playing pirated music videos endlessly for months. And pockets of leftists met in cafés and marketplaces plotting the overthrow of the ancient rule. All of which led to the crisis-fueled parliamentary government Nepal has today, with its inevitable bureaucracy—and corruption.

But all this was in the future. I arrived in Kathmandu in the final days of the "old" Nepal. After weeks exploring the fabled city and environs, Mike and I geared up and went into the mountains. I ended up living and trekking in the Himalayas for nearly two months, most of which were spent at ever-increasing altitudes, sleeping in tents or renting a one-night stay at a village inn. Endless days of steady movement up and up, through vistas of pristine mountains, green terraced hills, and scalloped valleys. Hours of silence on the trails, interrupted only by slight nods to the Nepalese farmers and tradesmen traversing in the other direction. Evenings by the fire, talking quietly with our Sherpa guides, gazing up at a sweep of stars unlike any I'd ever seen. Until, at 18,000 feet, I stood, exhausted and exhilarated, looking down at the clouds, through which rose the proud, timeless peaks of the lower mountains.

There's a lot of time to think in those long spates of silence on the upper trails, moving one measured footstep at a time, breath coming in gasps in the thinning air. Reflecting on my life up to that point. On my failed marriage, my successful though curiously unsatisfying career. I thought about how much I loved writing—I was always selling short stories to mystery magazines or doing essays for the *Los Angeles Times*—but felt estranged from the film business. How, in ways I couldn't define, being a writer in Hollywood was souring my love of writing.

There's one other thing about being on the top of a mountain. Sooner or later, you have to come down. So, finally and reluctantly, I came home to Los Angeles. I still had a movie to write, meetings to attend, phone calls to make.

But I also knew something else.

I knew I had to change my life.

* * *

Two weeks after returning from Nepal, still aglow from the experience I'd had there, I waited for a sign. An omen. Some flicker of enlightenment that would shine a light on this new path I needed to take.

While laboring by day on the Unsoeld screenplay, I read

books by night about Eastern philosophy, biographies of Buddhist teachers like Shunryo Suzuki and Thich Nhat Hanh. As well as those about noted Western seekers, from Carl Jung to Thomas Merton to Alan Watts.

And waited for that sign.

Until, to my chagrin, I was visited by something else instead. The return of crippling anxiety and numbing depression. Add in a number of disastrous short-term relationships with women, all with the good sense, ultimately, to "get outta Dodge."

Meanwhile, though my finished Unsoeld screenplay went nowhere (and in fact was handed off to another screenwriter), I still won writing jobs. A rewrite here, a TV pilot there. Given my emotional turmoil, it's no shock my work wasn't up to my usual standards. At one point, even my agent said to me, "What's happened to you?"

What about my Nepal experience? I wondered. Hadn't it been transformative? Shouldn't I be more "centered," at peace, more certain about my next steps? After all, I'd read Maugham's *The Razor's Edge*. I'd even seen the movie adaptations (first one with Tyrone Power, then Bill Murray). Shouldn't I, divorced and nearing forty but healthy and reasonably successful, be less of a fucking mess? Instead of some poster child for "Spoiled, Entitled White Guy Who Still Feels Sorry for Himself?"

Finally, unable to cope with my debilitating feelings or to tolerate my own shameful self-absorption, I asked a good friend what he thought. His advice: therapy.

A word I'd dreaded for years. Since the last years of my marriage. Since the advent of my depression and anxiety. Even though by now I'd read dozens of books about psychological theory, clinical treatment, the lives of famous, ground-breaking analysts . . .

"Therapy" was a word I'd dreaded since the first time I read Alice Miller's *The Drama of the Gifted Child*, whose description of early childhood dynamics hit so close to home I couldn't get out of bed for two days. Afterward, I told myself I must've had a touch of the flu.

But my friend insisted, and so, at the end of my rope, I made an appointment with a well-known therapist. The first time I sat down opposite him, I announced, "Don't get too attached to me, I'm only gonna be here for a couple of sessions."

I stayed eight years.

* * *

For me, therapy was (and occasionally still is) painful, difficult, embarrassing, infuriating, enlightening, surprising, disheartening, thrilling and—did I mention?—painful.

Exploring the depths of my own narcissism, my willingness to rationalize, and my frequent denial of the obvious was a deep source of shame for me. Yet I slogged on, enduring twice-weekly sessions that often left me more bewildered and heartsick than when I started.

When that same good friend asked me, sometime later, what I thought of therapy, I said without a moment's hesitation, "I hate it."

Which I did.

The problem was, I also loved it.

I found the process itself exhilarating, as though—similar to my experience in Nepal—I'd ventured into a new, uncharted, profoundly beautiful but mysterious realm. I continued my voracious reading in psychology, both clinical material and books for the general reader. Histories, biographies. I was transfixed. I wanted to swim in it.

I started taking classes in the field at Pepperdine University's Graduate School of Education and Psychology. Though I'd only a vague feeling about what it was I was doing, what my actual plans were, I kept signing up for more, semester after semester. I told myself that even if nothing "official" ever came of all the classwork, I'd at least end up with a master's degree in psychology. Something any writer could benefit from, right?

During this time, I also began volunteering at A Touch of Care, a private psychiatric hospital. At the suggestion of one of my professors, I joined him in leading a group of schizophrenics doing psychodrama. Throughout my schooling, even when I started interning at a low-fee family clinic, I kept working with these hospital patients, using guided psychodrama exercises and role-play to help them explore, understand, and contain their inchoate thoughts and feelings. Over the years, I began thinking of them as *my* patients, too. They were also the source of a joke I often repeated, to the effect that I had little trouble working with schizophrenics—not after years of dealing with Hollywood producers and studio execs. (Okay, I didn't say it was a *good* joke.)

In retrospect, I realize one of the oddly exciting things about being in grad school and working with therapy patients was the secrecy. I'd remarried by then, and other than my wife and a few close friends, nobody knew what I was up to. Certainly nobody in the entertainment industry. Screenwriter by day, grad student in clinical psychology by night. And on weekends. When I started my internship at the family clinic, which sometimes required seeing individual patients and couples during daytime hours, my life became more complicated. I was constantly rescheduling pitch meetings with studios and script notes sessions with producers. Like Bruce Wayne, nobody—not even my agent—knew my secret identity.

Not that being a grad student didn't present other challenges as well. Like many of my fellow students, I had a day job while pursuing my degree. But mine was a bit different than theirs. They worked as secretaries, lawyers, real estate brokers, or high school teachers. When they found out what I did, many made it clear they thought I was crazy to consider abandoning a successful screenwriting career to become a therapist. Even though I insisted that I hadn't made up my mind yet. That I didn't really know what I was going to do with my degree—or even whether I'd stay in school long enough to get one.

That indecision wasn't always appreciated by my instructors. A number expressed concern I was being a dilettante. One professor spent a whole semester calling me "Mr. Hollywood" in class. *That* was fun-and-a-half.

Though I, too, was often suspicious of my motives. *Was* I a dilettante? Was my interest in clinical work just grandiosity, mere self-importance masquerading as some seemingly altruistic desire to "help people," whatever the hell that means?

Which brings us back to that lunch with the producer. Ironically, he'd asked to meet with me because my Hollywood career was on another "up" swing: I'd done a production rewrite on a hit movie and just signed to write a pilot script for the ABC network. All while fighting off a rising panic that my career—my life—no longer seemed to reflect who I felt I really was. Or at least was becoming.

So there I was, racing down Sepulveda, anxious to get

to the psych hospital and those waiting patients. And it hit me. My own lightweight version of the "Road to Damascus" conversion story. Though my road was paved, clogged with traffic, and led to Culver City.

I realized I wasn't just anxious to finish lunch because I was running late. *I was anxious because I couldn't wait to leave*. Because I'd rather be working with the patients at the hospital than discussing a potential movie idea.

That, in fact, I wanted to leave screenwriting and become a therapist.

That night, I told the few people who knew of my graduate studies what I was planning: a total career change. Most said I'd lost my mind. They used more polite language, but that was the gist. Which only made things harder for me, since I pretty much thought the same thing. Only my wife and my best friend were totally supportive, for which I've always been grateful.

After six more long years, including thousands of supervised intern hours after graduation, I took the tests and became a licensed psychotherapist. Then I quietly retired from screenwriting. I've been in private practice almost twenty-seven years now, primarily treating people in the entertainment business.

Funnily enough, being a full-time therapist re-energized my love of writing. Now I provide essays for a variety of publications and websites. I also write a series of mystery novels whose protagonist is—what else?—a therapist.

To quote the late Jerry Garcia: "What a long, strange trip it's been."

What Being Wrongly
Committed Taught Me

| *Eve Tate* |

In evangelical culture, it's often thought that people who are experiencing hardship are suffering for one of two reasons: they have either sinned against God and are thus experiencing the consequences of that sin, or God is using hardship to teach them a lesson that will help them mature as Christians.

When I found out my mother had called local police to have me involuntarily committed to a psych ward in Mt. Gretna, Pennsylvania, I felt pretty sure I was guilty of the first.

God was clearly punishing me. I had disobeyed my mother's wishes for me to go to a state school near her home in Lebanon County, Pennsylvania, instead attending expensive and secular NYU in New York City. I didn't know my dad's wishes. He and mom divorced when I was a baby, and I'd stopped visiting him in sixth grade.

For much of my visit to Pennsylvania over winter break, I retreated to my childhood bedroom because I felt sad about my mother's disapproval of my college choice. During meals,

I'd sat mute. On Christmas Day, I didn't even bother to apply makeup for our family dinner.

A few days later, during a fraught conversation about her signing loans for my next semester at NYU, she'd said: "It's not biblical to go into so much debt for a degree." I threw my cell phone across the room, not looking where it landed while yelling: "NYU has a program that no other school offers!" The phone accidentally hit my mother, who wailed, "Jesus, help me!"

I had no idea I would wake the next morning on New Year's Day to the sound of a social worker calling my name from outside my childhood bedroom door.

* * *

"Eve? This is social services. Are you awake?"

I bolted upright in bed. I'd been sleeping in my underpants. Quickly, I donned a pair of green leggings and a silk Ann Taylor blazer that were lying on the floor. I left my bedroom. A woman with stringy brown hair and glasses stood at the top of the staircase.

The social worker said, "Your mother called because she's concerned you might be in danger. You need to come with us." A male police officer stood near the bottom of the stairwell. When we got outside, I saw two police cars and an ambulance parked in the street, blocking my silver '97 Ford Taurus in the driveway. My mother's dark blue Toyota sat parked on the curb. She emerged from it and walked over to me, hands in pockets.

"Why are you doing this?" I begged.

"You need some help and medication. You need to go to the hospital for a few days and get some treatment. You weren't listening to me about NYU."

Once I arrived at the psychiatric hospital, I watched help-lessly as a nurse packed my purse and electronics neatly into a plastic container resembling the type first grade teachers use to pass out pencils on the first day of school. She asked me to remove my clothes and don a gown, which she then lifted to my shoulders to check for hidden weapons and drugs. My clothes were returned to me after the nurse confirmed they held no illegal objects.

That night, wearing my leggings and blazer, I lay still on the bed I'd been assigned. It felt like my life was over.

A doctor came to see me the next afternoon. He had a dark beard and wore a button-down shirt with a tie. He asked if I knew why I was there. My mother had gotten upset when I'd thrown a cell phone, I explained. His question: "Any thoughts of harming yourself or others?"

"No."

"How are you feeling now?"

"I'm fine."

"You really want to get out, don't you?" he deduced. Seeming unnerved, he edged his chair as far from me as pos-sible and wrote some notes.

I nodded. I was shaking. "Well, yeah, of course I do."

"Okay. That's all we need from you for now."

After a lunch of bread, cheese, milk, and broccoli, I was herded into a group therapy session. A large man wearing jeans passed out sheets of paper with questions printed on them like: "How am I feeling?" and "What are some coping skills I can use to handle these feelings?" and "What are some qualities I like about myself?"

I felt like I was in remedial school. I had only recently started discovering qualities I liked about myself: I was smart, charming, attractive, and possessed a gifted imagination. I didn't need to be reminded all over again that there was no use for such qualities here.

Growing up, I'd felt like I didn't belong, and shied away from people, both at my mother's church and in school. It wasn't until Pennsylvania had been in my rearview mirror for nearly two years that my confidence had started growing. I'd been exposed to new people from a variety of backgrounds, even called "a scholar" by a teacher. I had also begun spending time with a boy I'd met at orientation. Although we weren't physically intimate, he'd made me dinner and called me beautiful.

I hadn't gotten the impression that I was pretty from my father. When I'd visit my dad, much of the time was spent at his church, where he was a pastor. Many of his sermons focused on sin and suffering.

As did the messages I heard from pastors at my mother's church. Consequently, fear and suffering seemed normal, even healthy. I got the impression God thought my heart was evil. The King James Version of verse nine of the seventeenth chapter of the Old Testament Book of Jeremiah stuck in my mind: "The heart is more deceitful than all else. And is desperately sick."

Sitting in group therapy, instead of answering the questions on the printout, I thought back to age ten when I had felt compelled to count to seventy-seven—a number of biblical prosperity—as I brushed my teeth and washed my hair. I'd count to seven when touching the doorknob of my bedroom at my dad's—to eviscerate fear that something bad would happen to a family member or me if I didn't do things to perfection.

The feeling of compulsion I felt at that age intensified, and I became scared to dress myself in the morning or go to school. My mother took me to the hospital, where a doctor diagnosed me with OCD. She consulted more pastors, looking for other answers to explain my suffering. "It's rebellion," the wife of a pastor in Hershey had decreed, adding, "There's some demonic spirit of rebellion at work here." My mother went to "deliverance" seminars, hoping to cure me. Nothing worked.

Things were worse when I stayed at Dad's house. I had felt scared and alone there, exhibiting such severe signs of social withdrawal that he'd decided to stop the visits. I heard him say to my mother one day as she waited in his sunroom for me: "If she doesn't want to be here anymore, she shouldn't come. We don't need to deal with lawyers. She should just stop coming."

And that was that.

Mysteriously, the summer after I stopped seeing my father, the OCD symptoms disappeared. Fear and intense anxiety remained. I still felt inadequate and self-conscious, but I no longer performed counting rituals before going to school in the morning.

It took me years to realize that my father had instilled dread and doubt in me with his sermons about the sinfulness of the heart. One of his mantras was: "God will punish reprobates who follow their selfish desires!"

It was true my father was an aggressive person. But as a toddler I'd sensed and taken on my mother's fear of him—by then her ex-husband—before I even got to know him as his daughter. From a young age, my father represented darkness. No wonder I felt trapped when I went to see him.

After the group session ended, another social worker asked me a few questions, clarifying that I was a student at NYU in New York City. "Are you looking for a job up there?"

"I have a part-time paid position waiting for me at Al Jazeera."

"Al Jazeera. Maybe that's part of the problem too. Al Jazeera is an Arab thing. That's probably not good or safe. Don't you think so?"

She finished questioning me, and I returned to a central room where other patients were making puzzles or staring at the wall.

In the morning—two endless days after I'd arrived—a doctor informed me my case was about to be evaluated. I was led downstairs into a big room with lots of windows along one side. My gaze was drawn outside to a group of pine trees glistening in the sunlight, their branches covered by melting snow.

The room seemed more stylish than one would expect for a rural behavioral health center. The walls were dark wood, decorated with framed pictures, and a shiny wooden table took up most of the space.

Doctors and lawyers sat around the table—eight total. My parents—who had not to my knowledge been in the same room since that day in the sunroom—sat beside each other at one end. I took the seat set aside for me, in between two lawyers. "Eve was sleeping on the floor of this woman's apartment in New York City who was smoking weed last fall," my mother stated. "And last summer, she slept in her car. We're trying to show her she doesn't have the money for school right now and that she should work steadily at a job and save money by living at home until she does."

My father, whom I'd recently started having phone conversations with, out of a desire to reconnect and build a healthy relationship, added: "She's obsessed with writing some science fiction novel. And the places she's been sleeping—as her mother just stated—are not safe."

When it was my turn to speak I confirmed my parents' statements about my living conditions, trying to seem calm.

The doctor who'd spent three minutes with me over the last two days offered his diagnosis, rattling off a list of disorders including depression and OCD.

My heart pounded so hard I was sure everyone in the room could hear it. I'd never get out of this prison. Suddenly, a lawyer to my far right declared, "The patient does not need to be here. We are satisfied she is safe for release." Apparently, he and his team were able to sense this was really a matter of anger and miscommunication between my parents and myself.

I guess God had been looking out for me. I was being delivered! Getting confined here indefinitely would cause the same feelings of sadness and entrapment I'd experienced visiting my father at a young and confused age. I'd likely attempt to perform my way to perfection with counting rituals. Here, there would be no way out.

Taking deep breaths, I sat motionless in my chair, feeling the release of tension. The lawyer sitting next to me leaned over and whispered in my ear: "I urge you to work this out with your parents or else you're going to have a big problem. Resolve the dispute as soon as possible."

My parents dashed out of the room. Trailing close behind, I saw them talking to a social worker in the hall, demanding a hearing override. "I'm sorry," was the response.

"There's nothing more we can do except recommend outpatient therapy."

My belongings—including a dead cell phone—were returned. My parents went to their jobs.

* * *

In evangelical culture, therapy is neither discouraged nor encouraged. In the Christian communities where I grew up, it was believed God could heal all maladies with his spirit. However, it was also thought that God places man-made solutions—like therapeutic counseling—in our lives when life becomes really difficult.

It was with the latter concept in mind that my mother found the confidence to take me to monthly sessions with an outpatient therapist for the OCD symptoms I had in middle school. I'd been angry about the sessions, which felt like punishment for misbehaving.

It wasn't until I turned seventeen that I met a counselor who helped me become more open-minded about therapy. She was from one of my mother's churches in Pennsylvania, called Life Center. "God can't work in us in the same way if we're not open to his gifts," she had said, adding, "Look at therapy as something that can help you until your heart has been fully healed by God."

This statement helped me to re-envision who God is. And because I had been conditioned as a child to seek God's approval in all things, I was able to consider therapy as a temporary solution. I interpreted that statement to mean God approved of me seeking extra help when I really, really needed it.

* * *

The therapist I have now—whom I've been seeing since the fall of 2014, right before I returned to NYU—questions the religious dogma I was fed from birth. He points me to Maslow's hierarchy of needs. He reminds me to not put too much pressure on myself. For me, having a stable place to live in Manhattan is a feat.

It's not necessary to condition myself to suffer through life. It's not good to be controlled by other people, even my parents. That's what he tells me. He says I have trouble trusting him, and that I'm holding back in more than one area of my life. I tell him there are times I feel that therapy is a waste.

I'd rather not talk about my past relationship with my difficult father—although the therapist insists it has a lot to do with how I have viewed men. I'd prefer not to talk about my disapproving mother's influence on my life—although he insists her influence is part of the reason I have trouble allowing myself to feel good when I accomplish something.

He reminds me that I have good things in my life now. I'm with a man who shows me love and approval. I am able to perform well in school, and can deal with excess feelings of anxiety in healthy ways, like going to the gym or having dinner with a friend.

Still, my relationship with my therapist is distant because I withhold details from my past. I'm not a fan of the way mental health is treated in the United States; seeing a well-meaning therapist who is part of the same system that held me against my will, and that posits mental illnesses as incurable imbalances, scares me. If I had thoughts of hurting myself, how could I express my feelings of despair without being considered suicidal? How can I feel safe talking to a man that is part of a system that wrongly held me against my will?

I can't. I have been traumatized by a group of people who see the world in shades of black and white, of good and evil. And I have been labeled dangerous and mentally unstable by people deemed medically qualified by the state, for having shown emotion and sadness toward my parents' treatment of me and my educational goals.

Something is wrong with the way Americans understand depression and other mental disorders. Feelings of sadness are not things you can categorize under labels of depression and OCD. Feelings of sadness cannot be explained solely by chemical imbalances. It's necessary to look at the circumstances of an individual's life. Everyone goes through dark times. We are all disordered and dysfunctional in one way or another. People who are brave enough to talk about their dysfunctions shouldn't be reduced to cases.

My refusal to accept doctors' labels of me as mentally unbalanced gave me the strength to return to New York and break away from religion, where I was able to find a therapist who is patient with my disinterest in talking, and has been patient with my financial difficulties. The therapist doesn't force me to talk about the emotional trauma I experienced if I'm not ready. Nevertheless, he consistently reminds me that talking about it will allow him to help me.

Yet my abandonment of the social construction of religion doesn't mean I have abandoned the idea of a God who is able to repair the psychological damage caused by trauma. That God is still very much a part of my life, although he doesn't manifest in the same way that he does for other evangelicals I know. For me, a relationship with God is not equivalent to going to church many times each week or looking for someone to preach to on the subway about the importance of loving Christ.

My relationship with God is more internal, found in the small things. I now find God through the sense of satisfaction that comes from doing my schoolwork well, through the love I receive from my significant other, and even through the insight and coping skills I am learning in therapy.

Talking to a therapist won't solve my problems. But talking to him has helped me learn to make thoughtful decisions instead of fear-based ones. I am now aware that for much of my life I condemned healthy feelings of self-confidence as sin and hubris.

Perhaps, over time, I will become more trustful. Many people who've been diagnosed with a mental disorder may still be living with the belief that they're permanently disabled, feeling hopeless, as if there is no way out of the darkness.

I'm blessed to realize that such problems are often only deep childhood wounds, in need of healing.

The Never-Ending Therapy Session

| *Linda Yellin* |

Tuesday, October 13
4:00–4:45
Upper East Side, Manhattan

Therapist: So, Linda, how was your week?
Linda: Terrible. The weatherman said it would rain, I carried my umbrella all day, and then not a drop. It's stirred up a lot of trust issues for me.
Therapist: About your father?
Linda: No. About Al Roker.
Therapist: I'm sure it wasn't personal. Give Al another chance. He can't control the weather.
Linda: Can we talk about my control issues?
Therapist: We've already talked about them.
Linda: I'm worried I'm on the spectrum.
Therapist: Which spectrum?
Linda: All the spectrums.

Therapist: You're fine. Trust me.

Linda: With my trust issues?

Therapist: I'm your therapist. Of course you trust me. We spent a lot of time on that.

Linda: Oh, no! Is that a spider?

Therapist: Where?

Linda: Under your desk. You know I go crazy around spiders. We should discuss my phobias. Snakes! The sight of blood! I freak out every time I shave my legs.

Therapist: That's not a phobia. That's a dull razor. I think you're fine, Linda. We've covered all the men who've rejected you, your imaginary gluten intolerance, your trauma over being the tallest girl in grade school, your getting fired from every ad agency you ever worked at, that small budgeting issue—and by the way, thank you for finally paying me—the sugar addiction, the Facebook addiction, the misunderstanding with the Greyhound bus driver, and why you never had children. You're ready to graduate from therapy. Other people need this time slot.

Linda: You're replacing me?

Therapist: No. I'm congratulating you. On being emotionally healthy.

Linda: You're tapping into my separation issues. It took me three years to change hairdressers. I still can't walk down Lexington Avenue without feeling guilty.

Therapist: I'm sure he's over it. He probably doesn't even remember you.

Linda: Really? I lie awake at night scared to death nobody will remember me, that no one will come to my funeral.

Therapist: I promise, I'll attend.

Linda: But you're older than me. What do you know? Am I going to die young?

Therapist: You're too old to die young.

Linda: What about my aging issues? I can't remember the last time a construction worker said, "Nice ass."

Therapist: And that's something you miss?

Linda: Not the construction workers. The ass.

Therapist: We covered your body issues for over six years. If anything pops up you can call me. We'll do a phone session.

Linda: Are those cheaper?

Therapist: No.

Linda: Why not? We should discuss that at my next session.

Therapist: You don't need a session to discuss a session. You're done. Stop looking for trouble. Don't create drama. That might be the most important coping skill you can learn.

Linda: Then we should work on it. Next Tuesday? Same time?

Therapist: Okay, Linda. One more session.

Linda: I feel so much better now. Thank you. I'm looking forward to next week.

Therapist: Don't forget your umbrella.

Changing the Story

| *Jonathan Schiff* |

> *But what physician has not had patients who don't make sense at all? To tell the truth, they're our stock-in-trade. We talk and write about the ones we can make sense of.*
>
> —Walker Percy, *The Thanatos Syndrome*

An old *New Yorker* cartoon features a man suspended upside-down from the ceiling, like a stalactite. A psychiatrist explains to the wife that the first objective is to convince the man that he is a stalag*mite*.

Funny—but it invites a serious question: is a clinician ever justified in helping a client to believe in a fiction?

Bruce was a genius. I know that because he told me. In every session. He was a parolee who had twice served prison time for raping children. But he was innocent. He told me that, too. He had been framed. Both times. By different people.

He told me that he was so smart that he could get people to do anything he wanted them to do. He said he felt guilty because he had played "mind games" with a prison psychologist who eventually killed himself. I asked if the psychologist could possibly have killed himself for any other reason. Bruce knew that wasn't possible because of the catastrophic potential of his mind games. And it was quite a burden to live with the consequences of his power, he confessed. To make matters worse, people did not see his genius, while they did see him, wrongly, as a sex offender. That's why he was depressed.

Bruce came to me for depression treatment at an out-patient mental health agency and did not want to discuss recidivism. He already attended court-mandated sex offender treatment elsewhere, and he had, of course, committed no crimes. But how was I to help him with depression? I had a hard time focusing on the problem because I kept getting distracted by my fear for the kids living in his neighborhood. In addition, I discovered that a part of me didn't want him to feel better. I lacked the "unconditional positive regard" that the psychologist Carl Rogers felt was necessary for fostering healing. You try to like every one of your clients, but there is no clinician who has succeeded in doing so.

I have had empathy for clients who committed sexual crimes, but after three meetings, I concluded that I couldn't develop empathy for Bruce. I resolved to tell my supervisor that I couldn't in good conscience continue to work on the case. I would ask if Bruce could be transferred to another therapist.

But before I could find out, my next session with Bruce ended up solving the problem for me. He told me that his depression had vanished. He felt great because he had decided to move to a small, isolated cabin.

I wondered. The cabin lacked heat, electricity, and hot

water, and Bruce did not own a car to take him to the nearest store, miles away. He had spent his life in cities or prisons, and he weighed about a buck twenty, so he didn't strike me as a frontiersman.

He said he had gotten the okay from Parole; the Parole officer would check on him at his new address. He said he would walk to his mandated sex offender counseling.

Social workers are supposed to ask questions that help clients to rethink questionable decisions. But so many questions were going through my own mind.

Was there really a cabin? Had anything he told me been true? Had he been trying to induce a sense of confusion in me to make himself feel more powerful?

I told myself the cabin would be farther away from children. But my first ethical obligation was to the client, not the children, since they were not at imminent risk as far as I knew. My client might be better off in isolation. Alcoholics stay away from liquor stores and bars, after all. Maybe on some level, I thought hopefully, Bruce knew that he had a problem and wanted to move away from temptation.

Or maybe I wanted him to be unhappy?

Then again, how did I know for sure that he wouldn't be happy in the country? I didn't have any experience living there.

Was it possible that he wanted to go on the lam?

If so, a warrant for his arrest would be issued as soon as he missed sex offender counseling or failed any other parole requirement. And even if someone in the law enforcement community was asleep at the switch, I could not legally notify anyone, since Bruce had refused to sign the consent allowing me to contact others.

Could I convince him to stay in the city? How? Did he

listen to anyone? Did what I said make a difference?

I needed to hurry up and decide. He would be out of the office before I knew it.

Sure, he would have a rough time in the winter, but he had survived prison, and what could be worse than that, particularly for someone convicted of sexual crimes against children? If things did become too difficult in the country, he could always move back.

If he stayed, I might have to keep working with him. But could anyone really help him with depression when he refused to deal with the clash between his predatory inclinations and what society permitted?

What if he was making the wrong choice, but nothing I said would change his mind? In that case, was it better to instill confidence in him by praising him?

What if I showed doubt in his decision? Would he then get angry and storm out? But if we ended on good terms now, he would feel free to come back if he needed therapy. Could he really be helped by a therapist who didn't like him? Would any therapist have positive regard for him?

These and other thoughts came quickly and discursively. Meanwhile, I didn't know what to say. I asked some questions to assess if he was manic or suicidal (no and no). But I had to say something else, so I praised him as a crafty thinker.

And he ended our final session declaring his love of living in nature. That was the last I heard from him.

There is scarcely a session on which a therapist cannot look back and wonder what could have been done better. I certainly spent much time discussing this case with my supervisor afterward. But ten years later, the case defies full explication. Because I did not twist any facts, I would be showing

Bruce-like grandiosity if I claimed that I gaslighted Bruce—made him believe something that wasn't true. However, I did not help dispel his illusion. And by praising his intelligence, did I help foster that illusion? And if I did, did I do that to help or hurt him?

I wonder if I would have acted differently if I had had more time—if Bruce had broached the issue before he had already made up his mind, or if I had known him better after working with him for a longer time.

Maybe it would be nice if we could decide on one story and stick with it. But I don't think anyone can be sure of the right story. Sometimes you can't tell a stalactite from a stalagmite.

How About a Hug?

| *Allison McCarthy* |

I f there's an etiquette book titled *How to Behave at the End of Therapy*, I haven't read it. I certainly wouldn't have read anything like that when I was sixteen, the year my sessions with Suzanne—a thirty-year-old licensed social worker with a master's degree in counseling—came to a halt. The county that funded the local sexual assault center didn't think victims were entitled to such an *extended* period of therapy (two years, in my case) on their dime. Their new policy: six months of counseling and then out the door, into the world, case files stamped RECOVERED.

Patients could, of course, continue sessions through the therapist's private practice (if it existed), but many of us were unable to afford the higher co-pays or travel longer distances to see a therapist who was now operating outside the hospital. This decision, made by the county to cut costs on long-term therapy, effectively stranded dozens of the sexual assault center's patients. Including me. The center granted us two sessions to wrap up our work.

The news shocked the adolescent patients and their parents, but in Suzanne's eyes, I saw everything: her frustration with the bureaucracy, how the two of us weren't anywhere near "finished." Still, it was out of our hands. Together, we would have to arrive at something like a stopping point.

I hadn't even wanted to go to therapy when our sessions began, right on the cusp of back-to-school season in the fall of 2000. The visits to the county hospital and its sexual assault center were my mother's idea. On a Sunday night, my mom handed me the pack of Marlboro Lights she found in my dresser drawer and said, "Do you want to talk about this?" She might have assumed I stole them from my father's apartment when I saw him during his visitation over the summer; he smoked, after all, and kept the sort of emotional distance that might have prevented him from noticing a missing pack of his cigarettes. But the gentle, nonjudgmental tone of her voice drew me in, made me trust her with the whole truth. I told her about the family friend who gave me the cigarettes—what he led me to do in his apartment and in his car and on the phone and in AOL chats for nine months. Now that she knew the truth, I begged her only to keep me away from him because he wanted more and more from me—intercourse, something I could not fathom doing with this thirty-year-old man who had a wife, a baby, a stepdaughter my age.

"It'll ruin his life if you tell anyone," I said. "I was drunk, Mom. I should have said '*Stop*' that night. Or after. It's my fault. I'm the one to blame." I was better than a defense attorney, pleading my case for her to let this go and cut their family out of our lives so I never had to see him again. I didn't tell her that he gave me Kentucky Gentleman Bourbon, encouraged me to drink to the point of blackout, and directed me to watch the *Gangbangers 3* porn he rented from the neighborhood video store. Before that first night with him, I was an honor roll student, a teenager who had never tasted more than two sips of beer or smoked a cigarette. I thought of his hand on my thigh—how it felt like something I'd let happen, how it made me just as guilty as him.

My mom hadn't known about the night I got drunk—when she'd asked the next morning about what happened at the sleepover with his stepdaughter, I told her that we stayed up to watch movies. I wrote the real story in my journal, buried deep inside my backpack so it couldn't be found.

For almost a year after the first assault and all the ones that followed, I carried the things this family friend and I had done under an impenetrable shroud of silence, my thick paperbacks and baggy clothes meant to keep the world at bay. I felt certain these stolen moments with a grown and married man giving me French kisses and jerking off when we were alone and pushing my head to his crotch and fumbling between my legs were wrong, but not criminal—to me, these were instances of wrong I had done, stories I would have no choice but to take to my grave.

My mom had asked, over and over, if I was okay, and I never said, "No, not really." I knew she would listen if I told her what was going on, but the fear of what could happen to him if I told anyone had trapped me. I smoked the cigarettes he sometimes bought me and rolled the filters between my fingers as if they were rosary beads of worry, guilt, sorrow. I walked home from the school bus stop with headphones on and rewrote my favorite Tonic lyrics, changing "I don't know when I got bitter, but love is surely better when it's gone" to "love is surely better when it's *wrong*."

I didn't know why I did that, changing the words.

But deep down, I knew.

My mother, of course, saw the story differently. The next day, she called social services and filed charges.

At the sexual assault center, I sat in an office with beige walls and a floor covered in art supplies and brightly colored toys intended for younger patients. I sat on a faded brown couch made from material that wasn't quite leather and waited until I could hear the click of high heels coming down the hall. The woman who opened the door stood only an inch or two taller than me, but her shoulders were twin steel blades slicing air. She nodded at me and then took a seat in an overstuffed chair to my left. Wisps of brown hair fell to her shoulders and she brushed them out of her face so that our eyes could meet. Her gaze was kind and curious.

I wasn't ready to talk.

In movies, the reluctant patient sits in a corner without saying a word as the therapist pries the cringing raw meat from the clamshell. But in real life, it's hard not to answer a question from someone who looks at you with such intention and empathy. Suzanne's tone wasn't quite as soft as my mother's, but I could hear the same refrain: *It's not your fault. It's not your fault.*

"Allison, in your own words, what happened?"

My halting declarations were more like questions: "My mom thinks . . . that I'm a victim? I don't think I am? He didn't do anything wrong?"

My new therapist seemed patient, acted as if we had all the time in the world to work through this nightmare. Suzanne helped me navigate the eighteen months of victim statements to the police, conferences with the county prosecutor, court dates, assignment to a social worker, the plea bargain. She helped me to see what I couldn't, how my rapist manipulated me over and over. Suzanne blinked and nodded when I said, "He told me I couldn't tell anyone. I felt just as responsible for what happened." Suzanne, who coaxed the word *rape* from my reluctant teenage sulk of a mouth. The hardened stance of my shoulders—body hunched over in a shell of defensive posturing—needed time to shift into something else: limber, louder, forthcoming.

The prosecutor's plea bargain made my discovery of truth in therapy seem almost pointless, the reduction of charges from second-degree rape (a charge filed "if the victim is under the age of 14, and the person performing the act is at least four years older than the victim") to fourth degree sexual offense, an insulting dismissal of his actions. But over time, Suzanne helped me understand how the law's murkiness and cowardice in punishing my rapist was not a reflection on the real truth of what he had done to me. By speaking out in therapy, I came to realize who was responsible, what it meant for a grown man to impose that wrongful sense of responsibility on a teenager, how he warped my ability to open up to my mother and tell her the truth all those months earlier, when it first started. The limitations of the legal system would not stop me from growing into a person who was no longer a victim, but a survivor. In Suzanne's office, I found what the justice system could not give me—a sense of being heard and believed.

We talked about other things as I recovered. We talked about my home life, my parents' divorce, the guy I'd started dating who never quite committed to being my boyfriend, yet knew how to push every button to keep me hanging on for his affection. Suzanne listened. She told me that love was an action, love was my choice: I didn't have to choose this self-centered pseudo-boyfriend, this neglectful and absent father. I didn't have to give either of them my love. I started to draw the parallel lines between my father and the pseudo-boyfriend. My past and present began to make a strange kind of sense. Suzanne told me that when the time came to explore consensual sex, I would know that it was right because it would feel right—and I would know the difference between being desired and being coercively compelled.

I owed Suzanne so much. She cleared the path for the woman I was going to be.

And just like that, the county decided it was time to give me the proverbial boot. There was a huge skein of emotion between Suzanne and me, one thousand ends that could never be wrapped up neatly in two sessions. But my gratitude for this woman moved me to action. I wanted to give her a hug.

We had never touched in our sessions, except perhaps a slight brush of hands when she passed me a box of Kleenex. Could I hug my therapist? Was it even appropriate to ask?

A certain degree of tension arises when these questions are posed by a patient. In her 2013 interview with *Psych Central*, clinical psychologist Deborah Serani argues that boundaries help her clients "have the most meaningful and healthy therapy experience." Serani is clear that she never hugs clients: "if someone feels the need to hug me hello or goodbye or needs to shake my hand every session, I generally ask what these physical exchanges mean for them. In therapy, expressing words is always better than acting out actions."

Of course, sixteen is already an awkward age—clumsy touches and tenuous grasps at intimacy were a lot more common than requests for a hug. I certainly wasn't a charter member of the school's Hug Club, an organization that touted its mission as "spreading love, happiness, and positive vibes through a warm embrace." Unlike the kids in that club, my friends and I passed notes in journalism class and traded lunches. We didn't hug unless someone asked for one in tears amid the high drama of a high school breakup.

Hugs were the kind of social gestures that I accepted rather than initiated because I was quiet, bookish, shy, terrified of rejection. I thought of my first love, the pseudo-boyfriend I told Suzanne about in those hour-long sessions, how he was the one to broach the topic of holding hands, the one who said we ought to kiss and then took the lead. I couldn't bear the thought of someone like Suzanne—wise, thoughtful, sincere— shaking her head "no" at my nervous request.

Over the two years of our sessions, Suzanne served as a cross between victim's advocate and life coach, the confidante who pushed me beyond my comfort zone and into places that were sometimes scary, but also honest and real. With her encouragement, I ventured into extracurricular activities that required risk and rejection, but also gave me a sense of community among my peers: writing and directing student plays, drafting articles for the school newspaper, working as fiction editor for the literary magazine. Suzanne's therapy also informed my political framework of social justice. Without Suzanne's guidance, I would not be the feminist who understands that a teenager's confused response to a rapist's attention is not "yes," a drunk yes is not "yes," and that anyone who tells you to keep rape and sexual assault secret is only protecting him- or herself.

In those last two sessions, Suzanne and I came to a resolution: I could take care of myself through better life habits, like quitting smoking *and* the pseudo-boyfriend. I could go forward and be a person who recognized love, who could receive it. I went from hiding in baggy clothes to basking in the summer sunshine while wearing shorts and tank tops. I wanted physical contact on my own terms, touch that did not violate me.

Then, it was time.

Her smile—warm, a little sad—gave me the confidence to ask: "Is it okay if we hug?" She could say no. It would sting, for sure. The hug felt loaded with the full force of her approval, as if it had the power to convey her truest feelings: *You're a good person, Allison. You are better than what was done to you.*

"What do you think?" she asked. "Is it okay?"

"I think it's okay," I said.

In the movie version, our embrace would be the stuff of teary drama, the sobs of Will Hunting and the soothing repetition of his shrink Sean Maguire's "It's not your fault, it's not your fault, it's not your fault." In real life, I didn't cry and neither did Suzanne. When we hugged, I felt the sharp bones of her shoulders. We were no longer the same height. I had grown and was now a little taller. But I leaned in to the hold. I felt a surge of pride in myself for asking, a surge of gratitude for Suzanne in accepting. And then, as if by predetermined decision, we let go.

From time to time, I faced temptation to stray from the upward path Suzanne showed me, yet I've always found my way back to a better place. I found other therapists who helped me through grief and bad breakups. The hug of Suzanne's acceptance and my everlasting gratitude could never fully heal all that was broken in my teenage self. But through my work with Suzanne, I found ways to ask, to touch, to reach.

Back into the Wild

| *Martha Crawford* |

Psychotherapists call it the "termination process."

I prefer to think of it as being released back into the wild.

There are quite lovable clients whom I have been glad to see go, as they twist in the wind—stuck, sticky, and untangleable, by me at least. Some begin, and remain, perhaps with good cause, suspicious about therapy and its usefulness in their life. Some may need other therapists, other modalities, or entirely different paths than the ones I know how to travel. I try to think about what or who might serve them well and refer them to therapies that will suit them better than mine.

And there are a rare few who, after a good start, settle into a sour, toxic relationship—clients who merely and consistently refuse or are unable to match my energies in the office, or in their lives, who demand that a therapist-magician "fix" their lives—and I am no magician. These relationships challenge me to protect myself from being drained, used, and drawn into a masochistic space . . .

There have been times, usually when someone needs to move away after a long stretch of work, when the final brave-faced goodbyes have left me alone in the office, that I have set my head down in my hands and wept for a good bit, closing the arc of the entire emotional journey. Following years of investment of my energies, attention, and nurturance, I sometimes need to grieve the empty nest that will not be filled ever again, by the same person, in the same way. These clients have driven me forward, made me face my deficiencies, nipped at my heels—making me a healthier, wiser human being.

Most leavings are slow, almost imperceptible: Sessions are reduced from weekly to monthly, and eventually dwindle to occasional returns for quick tune-ups. My function as a safety net simply, slowly fades away.

Eventually I will open my email to find a wedding photo, graduation announcement, thank-you note, baby pictures, or an obituary. A note about what happened or didn't happen next. I am always grateful for the news and the chance to rejoice or grieve.

These relationships stop taking place in the office, but the sense of each other is retained—so the relationship itself continues to exist, internally, for both of us, without regular external contact.

* * *

For several years, I worked as a clinical consultant with girls in foster care and group homes across New York City—sometimes we would only meet for a month or two before they were transferred. Many years later (and more than once) I'd find myself on the subway, suddenly embraced by a grown woman exclaiming my name: *"Martha!! I remember you!!! You were nice to me!! I never forgot you! Do you remember me?"* I did. I do. I always will. And I gladly missed my stop to gaze at photos of their kids, to hear about work or school and learn about how they took our brief connection and built a life on top of it. We changed each other, became a part of each other's lives; we wrote our names on the other's neuro-pathways. We committed acts of permanence upon one another.

Authentic connections, even brief ones, are stored forever inside us in the place where nothing is ever really lost.

Some departures are abrupt, startling, confusing. An alliance, taken for granted or illusory, suddenly disappears without my understanding why. Sometimes the client simply never returns, never responds to outreach. Other times the "breakup" comes by text or email. Sometimes I feel in my gut that this is good news: the client's expectations have been met and his or her belly is full. Other disappearances leave distress and disturbance behind them, often for a long time: I wonder what injury I inflicted, what I forgot that needed to be remembered, what question I asked that was too probing, what failure or oversight drove them to take flight.

The lack of closure can be extremely hard to tolerate: why couldn't they just come back for a final session or two? Just to discuss my error, to allow me to take responsibility for my part, to tell them what our work together meant to me—and to release them if they still need to go.

Then there are the Lifers.

There are those with unimaginable wounds, who are absolutely entitled to a lifetime of support and admiration for having survived the unsurvivable, scars and all. For others with sufficient disposable income, therapy becomes an integral part of their wellness in the world, like a gym membership—a part of their preventive care.

There are the types, like myself and most of my colleagues, who have attached to the process of psychotherapy itself as part of their ongoing spiritual hygiene. Those who see therapy as a path, a sacred practice, are often artists, writers, creatives, other therapists, people who court the unconscious, who work with their intuition, whose calling in the world requires vigilant self-awareness, who need a close, well-maintained relationship with their inner life.

* * *

Becoming a therapist is one of the easiest ways to never leave therapy, and many of my clients have done just that—joining the ranks of psychotherapists who never really left: Once upon a time we staggered into treatment as patients, and just stayed there. We moved into the office. We made the consultation room a template for our own practice and now spend our days creating the healing space that someone offered us.

There is a special bird that lives in a wonderful healing space I visit often: a wildlife rescue center in the Hudson Highlands. His name is Edgar Allen Crow. He lives surrounded by wounded snakes, owls with injured wings, abandoned blind litters in need of bottle feeding. Most are expected to return to freedom once they have grown sufficient strength or maturity.

Edgar will never leave. A crow, found as a lost hatchling, he imprinted on an older woman who fed him. He has learned to speak the language of his rescuers: "Hello! HELLO! HELLO!!" His communications alternate between the wild guttural avian cry of his own kind and the American English equivalent learned from humans who tried to speak crow language: a perfectly articulated "Caw." He is a translator living in the same transitional space that therapists do—the crack between the worlds—mastering both the language of civilization and the primal cries of wild instinct. Preserving the calls of the wild for those that are in danger of forgetting. Allowing those who know little of their own animal instinct to listen in a language that they can tolerate.

I wonder about the other creatures—the ones that were healed and released: Some seem to remember the transformative and transitional energies of the center, and visit regularly, circling overhead, marking their scent-trail, reminding themselves of the path back to help and rehabilitation should they, or their offspring, ever again need assistance. Perhaps some stay nearby after their release, hoping to catch a glimpse of a hand they licked; or even waiting to help escort others, disoriented by their own sudden wellness, back to the culture of freedom and wilderness. But most, I'm sure, ultimately take flight or race for the thickets—and rarely, if ever, look back.

As it should be.

Some people are reluctant to engage in the psychotherapeutic process at all, for fear they will never be set free: the traditional psychoanalytic models still reign in their imaginations. There is a fear of dependency, a fear that the therapist won't let them go, or that they will be held hostage, infantilized, exploited by the therapist's never-ending hunger for the weekly check written at the end of each session.

* * *

Oftentimes during their first consultation, clients, like anxious airline passengers, want to know if they can find the clearly designated exit before settling into their seat. "How long do you usually see people for?" or "I think I will only need to come for five or six sessions. Is that okay?"

To give their fears some credence, there probably are some clinicians who are reluctant to let clients leave.

Traditional analytical models may deem client's attempts at leaving "premature termination" and as mere resistance. And many people do take flight from treatment at the moment when it gets difficult or when they sense that psychotherapy could reorganize life as they know it, changing relationships, work, or long-held beliefs about themselves.

I let them go. I trust my clients to make their own choices and assess their own readiness. I also trust life itself to put any essential lesson they are fleeing in front of them again and again—until it is digested and assimilated, or returns in an unavoidable form.

* * *

By the way, if the conflict does resurface, I'm not going anywhere and I won't lock the door after you leave. I'll be right here, same cell number, same email—happy to roll up my sleeves and get back to work if and when you return.

Many do.

The first time I left therapy I told my therapist that after six years of meeting with him twice a week, when being a patient had practically been my primary vocation—that I had to stop. I could see no way on my limited income to cover full-time graduate school expenses, rent, *and* psychotherapy.

What came next startled me.

He said, "Okay."

He didn't fight for me, protest, or appear to feel rejected.

He also didn't seem particularly upset or happy to see me go, or insist on over-processing the how and why and unconscious muck beneath my decision. He just said, "Okay," and wished me luck.

I felt stunned, unmoored. Maybe a little abandoned. I hadn't expected him to drop his end of the rope when I released mine. I'd thought I owed him something for all that he had seen me through. I thought he would need something back from me, something more than my fees and heartfelt gratitude.

I assumed my leaving would disappoint him. I thought I should feel guilt about disrupting his income stream. But, here he was: kind enough, but essentially unaffected. He hadn't been dependent on me just because I had been dependent on him? It was confusing and liberating. I understood for the first time that I really did not have to take care of him at all. I did not have to worry about harming him. I did not owe him anything emotionally. We were even. I was not in debt or indebted. Fresh oxygen filled my lungs.

When I was able to afford it and return to therapy, I felt a new freedom and a deeper sense of safety knowing that I was not under any pressure from him to stay. He accepted my departure and return without demand or recrimination. I try to offer my clients the same gift.

It is not always easy to let people go when we are invested in them: In my first year out of social work school, I joined a supervision group led by a woman who taught at a group therapy institute. I learned a great deal from the supervisor and found her practice methods provocative and intellectually fascinating. But after six months the group started wearing on me; I knew I would never be able to embrace their methods as my own.

As I began the process of trying to extricate myself from the group, my fellow therapists/group members began trying, in earnest, to "solve" whatever problem they suspected was causing me to leave. The discussion became increasingly frustrating as the group clung to me. I wanted to leave gently, respectfully, and with gratitude—not be pressured into pushing away colleagues I respected or devaluing anyone's practice model.

Just as the tension began to peak, the supervisor said: "Do you need the group to help you to leave? Or to help you to stay?"

Help me to leave?

Help me to leave.

Help me to leave you.

What a sacred, generous idea.

I could think of so many people that I wished could have helped me to leave, in so many ways.

It was the most important gift I received from that group, a gift I still cherish. It is also one of my favorite gifts to pass on. I enjoy watching the surprised, relieved expression on a new client's face when I promise I will help him or her to leave, if ever that is needed.

And I've learned to appreciate the bittersweet pleasure of watching them take flight.

About the Contributors

Laura Bogart's work has appeared in various journals, and she is a regular contributor to *DAME*. She has completed a novel titled *Don't You Know That I Love You?*

Martha Crawford, LCSW, is a writer, psychotherapist, and clinical supervisor in private practice in New York City. She is the author of the blog *What a Shrink Thinks*. She also provides writing support through Subtext Consultations, an online writers clinic for those experiencing blocks or challenges in their creative processes.

Patti Davis is the author of eleven books, both nonfiction and fiction, including *The Long Goodbye*, *Till Human Voices Wake Us*, and *The Blue Hour*. Her most recent novel is *The Earth Breaks in Colors*. She also wrote the screenplay for the Hallmark movie *Sacrifices of the Heart* and has contributed to magazines and newspapers.

Megan Devine, LPC, is the author of *Everything Is Not Okay: An Audio Program for Grief*. She is a licensed clinical counselor, writer, and grief advocate. You can find her at RefugeInGrief.com.

Beverly Donofrio, named a master memoirist by the *Daily Beast*, has published three memoirs: the *New York Times* bestseller *Riding in Cars with Boys*, which was made into a popular movie; *Looking for Mary*; and *Astonished*, called "astonishing" by more than one reviewer. Her three children's books are much praised: *Where's Mommy?* (the latest) was chosen by the *New York Times* as a Best Children's Book of 2014. Her NPR documentaries are perennially re-broadcast, and her personal essays have appeared in the *New York Times*, *Washington Post*, *Los Angeles Times*, *O: The Oprah Magazine*, *Marie Claire*, *More*, *Allure*, *Spirituality and Health*, *Village Voice*, *Huffington Post*, and *Slate*, as well as many anthologies. She is an instructor at Wilkes University's Low Residency MFA program and currently lives in Woodstock, New York, where she is working on a collection of essays.

Janice Eidus is a novelist, essayist, and short story writer. She has twice won the O. Henry Prize for her short stories. Her novels include *The War of the Rosens*, *The Last Jewish Virgin*, and *Urban Bliss*. Her short story collections are *Vito Loves Geraldine* and *The Celibacy Club*. Her work has appeared in such magazines as the *New York Times*, *Arts & Letters*, *Lilith*, *Jewish Currents*, and *Purple Clover* and is widely anthologized in collections including *The Oxford Book of Jewish Stories*, *Desire: Women Write About Wanting*, and

Dirt: The Quirks, Habits, and Passions of Keeping House. She lives in New York City with her husband and daughter.

Estelle Erasmus is an award-winning journalist, writing coach, and former magazine editor-in-chief. Her writing has been published in *Redbook, Brain, Child, Yahoo!*, the *Washington Post, Marie Claire, Good Housekeeping,* and more. She is a contributor to eight anthologies, including *Mothering Through the Darkness: Women Open Up About the Postpartum Experience* and *Love Her, Love Her Not: The Hillary Paradox* (both by She Writes Press). Her Twitter handle is @EstelleSErasmus, and she blogs at musingsonmotherhoodmidlife.com.

Juli Fraga, PsyD, is a psychologist and writer in San Francisco who specializes in relationship concerns, maternal wellness, and women's health. Her Twitter handle is @dr_fraga, and her website is DrJuliFraga.com.

Nina Gaby is an advanced practice nurse in psychiatry, a writer, and a visual artist. Her work has been shown widely, and her sculptural porcelain is in the permanent collection of the Renwick Gallery of the Smithsonian. Gaby has been a psychotherapist for twenty-five years and on the faculty at a number of universities, has contributed to numerous anthologies, and has just published her own collection, *Dumped: Stories of Women Unfriending Women* (She Writes Press, 2015). Gaby is a member of several Vermont-based professional organizations, including the Psychiatric Nurse Practitioner Interest Group, the Burlington Writer's Workshop, and the Vermont Book Arts Guild, as well as the national Association of Writers and Writing Programs. She blogs at ninagaby.com.

Mindy Greenstein, PhD, is a clinical psychologist and psycho-oncologist who serves as a consultant to the Department of Psychiatry and Behavioral Sciences at Memorial Sloan Kettering Cancer Center. In addition to her academic papers and personal essays, she has written two books: *The House on Crash Corner* (Greenpoint Press, 2011) and *Lighter as We Go: Virtues, Character Strengths, and Aging* (Oxford University Press, 2014). Dr. Greenstein lives in New York City with her husband and two teenage sons.

Jenine Holmes received her BA from Parsons School of Design and her MFA from Spalding University. Her essays have appeared in the *Detroit News, New York Press,* and the *New York Times* and on *Forbes.com* and *LearnVest.com*. She lives in New York City with her daughter.

Diane Josefowicz's fiction, essays, and reviews have appeared recently in *Conjunctions, DAME,* and *Fence*. A regular contributor to the *Saint Ann's Review* and *Necessary Fiction*, she holds an MFA in fiction from Columbia University, where she served as a writing instructor in the English department, and a PhD in the history of science from MIT. With Jed Z. Buchwald, she is co-author of *The Zodiac of Paris* (Princeton University Press, 2010), about an ancient temple ceiling that, in 1821, was looted from Egypt and brought to Paris, where it caused a crisis of religious authority. She is at work on a novel and a second nonfiction book about nineteenth-century Egyptology.

Jean Kim, MD, is a psychiatrist and writer working in Washington, D.C. She is a clinical assistant professor of psychiatry at George Washington University and received her MA in writing from Johns Hopkins, where she won an Outstanding Graduate Award in 2015. She is a blogger for *Psychology Today* and has written for the *Washington Post, The Daily Beast, In These Times, The Rumpus, Salon,* the *New York Post,* and other publications. She was formerly on the psychiatry faculty at Mount Sinai and Weill Cornell Medical College in New York City, and received her BA in English from Yale and MD from Virginia Commonwealth University's Medical College of Virginia.

Amy Klein has been a journalist for the past fifteen years. She writes about health and fertility for the *New York Times* and other publications. She lives in New York City with her husband and daughter. She has never returned to therapy after the experience described here. Her website is KleinsLines.com.

Binnie Klein, LCSW, is a psychotherapist in private practice in New Haven, Connecticut, and a lecturer in the Department of Psychiatry at Yale University. She is the author of *Blows to the Head: How Boxing Changed My Mind* (SUNY Press, 2010). She hosts a popular weekly music and interview show (*A Miniature World*) on WPKN-FM radio.

Anna March's writing has appeared in a wide variety of publications, including the *New York Times*'s "Modern Love" column, *New York Magazine, Tin House, VQR, Hip Mama,* and *Bustle,* and she writes regularly for *The Rumpus* and *Salon.* She frequently writes on topics at the intersection of political and popular culture related to inclusive feminism, sexuality, and gender. She is co-founder of the Lulu Fund: Supporting

Racial, Gender & Class Justice in Literature. She is founder of LITFOLKS, a literary hosting organization in L.A. and D.C., and on the Advisory Board for *Angels Flight Literary West* and *Literary Orphans*. Her novel, *The Diary of Suzanne Frank*, and essay collection, *We Can Do It: Notes from a Feminist Killjoy*, are forthcoming. She is finishing a memoir, *Happy People Live Here*, and is at work on a new novel. Learn more at annamarch.com or follow her on twitter @annamarch.

Allison McCarthy is a writer who focuses on personal essays, intersectional feminism, and social justice. Her work has been featured in print and online publications such as *DAME, xoJane, The Frisky,* the *Washington Post,* the *Guardian* (U.K.), *AlterNet, Time.com, Autostraddle, Medium.com* ("Human Parts" series), *Bitch, make/shift, Ms.* (blog), *Girlistic, YourTango, Hip Mama, Global Comment, Role Reboot, Shameless, The Feminist Wire, ColorsNW, The Baltimore Review,* and *Hoax,* as well as in several anthologies. She currently lives in Maryland.

Kurt Nemes is a D.C.-based ethics and training professional. His work has appeared in the *Washington Post* and other publications. He lives in Washington, D.C., and blogs about leadership, classical music and self-healing. His Twitter handle is @kurtnemes.

Dennis Palumbo, MA, MFT, once a Hollywood screenwriter (*My Favorite Year, Welcome Back, Kotter,* etc.), is now a licensed psychotherapist and author of *Writing from the Inside Out* (John Wiley). In addition to blogging for the *Huffington Post* and *Psychology Today*, he writes the acclaimed series of Daniel Rinaldi mystery novels (Poisoned Pen Press). For more info, visit DennisPalumbo.com.

Molly Peacock, a poet and a biographer, lives in Toronto, Canada. Her latest nonfiction is *The Paper Garden: Mrs. Delany Begins Her Life's Work at 72* (Bloomsbury USA, UK/ McClelland & Stewart/Random House Canada), and her most recent book of poems is *The Second Blush* (W. W. Norton and Company/McClelland & Stewart/Random House Canada). She serves as series editor of *The Best Canadian Poetry in English* (Tightrope Books) and was one of the creators of Poetry in Motion on New York City's buses and subways.

Pamela Rafalow Grossman's journalism has been published in outlets such as the *Village Voice, Ms.,* and *Real Simple* magazine; her essays in *Time.com, Essence.com,* and elsewhere; and her poems in journals across the country. She is currently working on a documentary. All this came to pass with no help at all from the therapist she writes about here.

Charlie Rubin has been a comedy writer for three decades. He wrote for *Seinfeld, In Living Color,* and *The Jon Stewart Show* and then moved from comedy to drama on *Law & Order: Criminal Intent* from 2004 to 2009, where he wrote ten episodes. He's worked with and for Norman Lear, Larry David, the Wayans Brothers, Lorne Michaels, Carol Burnett, and Dave Attell, as well as with William Finn in musical theater, and wrote for *Spy* and *National Lampoon.* He's currently writing a feature about urban surfing for Robert Chartoff Productions (of *Rocky* fame) based on his *New York Times Magazine* article. He's a tenured professor who created, developed, and runs the TV writing concentration at New York University's Tisch School of the Arts and has taught in Singapore and Chiang Mai, Thailand, and at Columbia University. He occasionally reviews thrillers and espionage for *The New York Times Book Review*. He hopes to write about therapy for the rest of his life.

Jonathan Schiff, LCSW, has a PhD in English and a master's degree in social work. He is a psychotherapist in private practice in Brookline, Massachusetts.

Barbara Schoichet has a PhD in creative writing from Lancaster University in England and an MFA in creative writing from Sarah Lawrence College in New York. She has taught creative writing at Stephens College, Santa Fe Community College, and Denver University, and for one year abroad in England. Barbara's memoir is titled *Don't Think Twice: Adventure and Healing at 100 Miles Per Hour* (G. P. Putnam's Sons, 2016). Her previous publications include a nonfiction book titled *The New Single Woman: Discovering a Life of Her Own* (Contemporary Books) and two children's books for Price, Stern, Sloan's *Amazing Maze* series. Her short stories have appeared in *Westword, Permafrost*, the *Sarah Lawrence Literary Review*, and *MSS*, a literary magazine founded by John Gardner.

Adam Sexton is the author of *Master Class in Fiction Writing: Techniques from Austen, Hemingway, and Other Greats*. His essays and short stories have appeared in the *Bellevue Literary Review*, the *Mississippi Review*, and *Post Road* and on Babble.com, SmithMag.net, and other websites. He teaches creative writing at Columbia and Yale.

Susan Shapiro, an award-winning writing professor at the New School and New York University, freelances for the *New York Times*, the *Los Angeles Times*, the *Washington Post, Newsweek,* the *Wall Street Journal, Salon,* and *Psychology Today.* She's the bestselling author of ten books, including, including the novels *What's Never Said, Overexposed,* and *Speed Shrinking*; the co-authored nonfiction books *Unhooked* and *The Bosnia List*; and the acclaimed memoirs *Lighting Up, Five Men Who Broke My Heart,* and *Only as Good as Your Word.* You can find out more about her popular "Instant Gratification Takes Too Long" classes and seminars on her website SusanShapiro.net or follow her on Twitter at @susanshapiro.net. This is the first project she's ever done with her husband Charlie Rubin, whose last shrink she stole to get him to propose.

Beth Sloan is a pseudonym for a psychologist with a PhD who lives and practices in northern New Jersey.

Eve Tate is a writer living in New York City, where she studies at New York University.

Kate Walter is the author of *Looking for a Kiss: A Chronicle of Downtown Heartbreak and Healing* (Heliotrope Books, 2015).

Priscilla Warner co-authored the *New York Times* bestseller *The Faith Club*, a memoir about her interfaith relationship with two New York mothers in the aftermath of the terrorist attacks on September 11, 2001. After an extended book tour across the country, Warner vowed to heal from the panic attacks that had plagued her for decades. She learned how to meditate and wrote about her adventures with Buddhist teachers, therapists, and healers in another best-selling memoir, *Learning to Breathe*. Warner lives outside New York City, where she teaches writing and is working on her next book as well as art inspired by her childhood drawings.

Linda Yellin's novel *Such a Lovely Couple* is about her first husband. Her memoir *The Last Blind Date* is about her second husband. After running out of husbands, she wrote *What Nora Knew*, a novel about Nora Ephron and romantic movies. All of the books are published by Simon & Schuster.

Royal Young is an author and visual artist born and bred in downtown New York City. His debut memoir *Fame Shark* is a cult classic, and his writing has appeared in the *New York Times, New York Post*, and *Interview Magazine*, among others.

Jessica Zucker, PhD, is a psychologist based in Los Angeles. She is the creator of a line of pregnancy loss cards and the #IHadAMiscarriage campaign. Her writing has appeared in the *New York Times, The Washington Post, BuzzFeed*, anthologies, and elsewhere. Dr. Zucker has been featured on Good Morning America, CNN, and NPR. Her website is DrJessicaZucker.com.

About the Editor

Sherry Amatenstein, LCSW, is a NYC-based therapist and author of *The Q&A Dating Book, Love Lessons from Bad Breakups*, and *The Complete Marriage Counselor*. She contributed to Seal's anthology, *Shades of Blue: Writers on Depression, Suicide, and Feeling Blue*.

Before becoming a therapist, she spent two years volunteering at a suicide hotline. She was also an interviewer for Steven Spielberg's USC Shoah, a foundation dedicated to taking audio-visual testimony from Holocaust survivors.

Amatenstein is a former editor at Hearst and ivillage .com. Currently an adjunct writing professor at New York University, she freelances for numerous publications, including *Hemispheres* and *vox.com*. She runs relationship seminars nationwide and has offered relationship advice on *Today, Early Show, HuffPost Live, Inside Edition*, and *NPR*. When pressed, she admits to having conducted a pre-marriage counseling session on an episode of *My Big Redneck Wedding*. Visit her at howdoesthatmakeyoufeelbook.com or tweet her at @sherapynyc.

Acknowledgments

I gratefully acknowledge:

My fabulous contributors. I so appreciate your talent, your commitment to the project and your willingness to bear with me through endless rewrites. If any of you need therapy as a result of the experience, I can make a great recommendation.

Liza Fleissig and Ginger Harris-Dontzin, my indomitable agents-cum-cheerleaders. You are the best!

Laura Mazer. There are no words to express my awe at your passion, talent, and belief in this project. I hope every book author is lucky enough to come across an editor as devoted as you.

Krista Lyons, thank you for allowing this book to come to life!

Amy Ferris. My angel, my Seal sister, thank you for your support and for telling the Seal Team: "This is a woman and a book you need to run with!"

Paul Kelly. I so appreciate your unswerving love as well as tech support. I finally have mastered the art of the zip file.

Sloan Smiloff. I'm so grateful you were with me on this journey, and so many others.

Amy B. My marketing genius friend. Your creativity has enriched my life for years.

David LaBarca. I'm so lucky to have someone as honest and loyal as you to witness the ups and downs of these past many decades. You've always made me laugh through the tears.

Barbara Egenthal. God blessed me when (s)he gave me such an amazing sister. You always have my back, and hopefully vice versa.

Selected Titles from Seal Press

Shades of Blue: Writers on Depression, Suicide, and Feeling Blue, edited by Amy Ferris. $16, 978-1-58005-595-6. The writers in *Shades of Blue* share real and unforgettable stories of their personal battles with depression, grief, and suicide, offering solidarity, and hope for all those who feel as if they're struggling alone.

Riding Fury Home: A Memoir, by Chana Wilson. $17, 978-1-58005-432-4. Exquisitely written and devastatingly honest, *Riding Fury Home* is a shattering account of one family's struggle against homophobia and mental illness—from the suffocating intolerance of the 50's through the liberation made possible by the women's movement in the 70's—and a powerful story of healing, forgiveness, and redemption.

All the Things We Never Knew: Chasing the Chaos of Mental Illness, by Sheila Hamilton, $24, 978-1-58005-584-0. *All the Things We Never Knew* takes readers on a breathtaking journey from David and Sheila's romance through the last three months of their life together as David's bipolar disorder pulled their lives apart and into the year after his death. It details their unsettling spiral from their lives before his illness and reveals the true power of love and forgiveness.

Beautiful You: A Daily Guide to Radical Self-Acceptance, by Rosie Molinary. $16.95, 978-1-58005-331-0. Drawing on self-awareness, creativity, and mind-body connections, Molinary incorporates practical techniques into a 365-day action plan that empowers women to regain a healthy self-image, reframe and break undermining habits of self-criticism, and champion their own emotional and physical well-being.

What You Can When You Can: Healthy Living On Your Terms, by Carla Birberb and Roni Noone, $16, 978-1-58005-573-4. *What You Can When You Can* (#wycwyc) is a book, a movement, a mindset, and a lifestyle—one that harnesses the power of small steps to let you achieve your health and fitness goals on YOUR terms. The #wycwyc (pronounced "wickwick") philosophy applies to anything that contributes to a healthy, happy life.

Yogalosophy for Inner Strength: 12 Weeks to Heal Your Heart and Embrace Joy, by Mandy Ingber, $24, 978-1-58005-593-2. Building on the concepts in her *New York Times* best-selling book *Yogalosophy*, Mandy Ingber, fitness and wellness instructor to the stars, now gives us a revolutionary and inspiring self-care program to uplift and strengthen the alignment of mind, body, heart, and spirit during times of adversity like loss, transition, grief, or heartbreak.

Find Seal Press Online
www.SealPress.com | www.Facebook.com/SealPress | Twitter: @SealPress

More Great Resources
from Focus on the Family®

Beyond the Masquerade
By Dr. Julianna Slattery

Many Christian women wear masks in an attempt to look the part of the "good" wife, mother, and church-goer. But those masks separate us from God, plaguing women in the form of depression, eating disorders, shame . . . and on and on. But there is hope! *Beyond the Masquerade* reveals how Christ can heal and transform our lives, freeing us from bondage. Includes discussion questions for small groups.

Dreams of a Woman
By Sharon Jaynes

Most women grow up dreaming of becoming a bride and mother, being beautiful, and longing to have a best friend. *Dreams of a Woman* brings insight into these deep desires by exploring the lives of women whose dreams were shattered, restored, and answered.

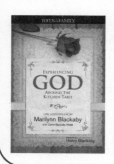

Experiencing God Around the Kitchen Table
By Marilynn Blackaby and Carrie Blackaby Webb

Pull up a chair and have a seat at the kitchen table of someone who has faced life's blessings as well as its trials. Marilynn Blackaby weaves in lessons she's learned over the years as she shares her personal stories. Her experiences and wisdom will bring hope and encouragement to women's hearts.

FOR MORE INFORMATION

Online:
Log on to FocusOnTheFamily.com
In Canada, log on to focusonthefamily.ca.

Phone:
Call toll free: 800-A-FAMILY
In Canada, call toll free: 800-661-9800.

BPZZXP1

FOCUS ON THE FAMILY®

Welcome to the Family

Whether you purchased this book, borrowed it, or received it as a gift, we're glad you're reading it. It's just one of the many helpful, encouraging, and biblically based resources produced by Focus on the Family® for people in all stages of life.

Focus began in 1977 with the vision of one man, Dr. James Dobson, a licensed psychologist and author of numerous best-selling books on marriage, parenting, and family. Alarmed by the societal, political, and economic pressures that were threatening the existence of the American family, Dr. Dobson founded Focus on the Family with one employee and a once-a-week radio broadcast aired on 36 stations.

Now an international organization reaching millions of people daily, Focus on the Family is dedicated to preserving values and strengthening and encouraging families through the life-changing message of Jesus Christ.

Focus on the Family MAGAZINES

These faith-building, character-developing publications address the interests, issues, concerns, and challenges faced by every member of your family from preschool through the senior years.

| FOCUS ON THE FAMILY® MAGAZINE | FOCUS ON THE FAMILY CLUBHOUSE JR.® Ages 4 to 8 | FOCUS ON THE FAMILY CLUBHOUSE® Ages 8 to 12 | FOCUS ON THE FAMILY CITIZEN® U.S. news issues |

For More INFORMATION

 ONLINE:
Log on to
FocusOnTheFamily.com
In Canada, log on to
FocusOnTheFamily.ca

 PHONE:
Call toll-free:
800-A-FAMILY
(232-6459)
In Canada, call toll-free:
800-661-9800

Rev. 12/08

one

You Got
Me What?

I was sitting in my parents' living room when my boyfriend, Mike, said he had a surprise for me. He pulled from behind his back a little box. You know what I mean when I say that the box was just the right size. Mike and I had been dating for more than three years, and the "M" word had begun springing up quite regularly in conversation. I opened the box with great anticipation, only to find . . . a key chain.

Reading my expression, Mike realized that he had made a huge blunder. He meant the key chain as a little gesture, never thinking that I would assume it was a ring. (Yeah, 25-year-old guys can be a little clueless.) I was embarrassed by my assumption, and Mike felt awful about the mistake. We both began tripping over our words, trying to get past the awkwardness of the moment.

Have you ever had an experience like mine—expecting a gift that didn't quite turn out to be what you thought it would? Trying to show some gratitude through your disappointment, eking out a "thank you" for the electric drill you thought was a KitchenAid or the fluffy socks you hoped would be a necklace?

When Mike finally did pop the question (with a real ring!) a few months later, we began to look toward marriage. As part of our

preparation, we skimmed through books about sexual intimacy, including *Intended for Pleasure* by Dr. Ed Wheat and *The Gift of Sex* by Cliff and Joyce Penner. The titles of those two books by themselves appropriately summarized what I had hoped and dreamed our sex life would be like—a gift given by God for the purpose of pleasure. Fourteen years later, I feel like I'm still trying to figure out the gift!

The gift of sex can sometimes seem like the key chain in the ring box—we got our hopes up for nothing. When married women share honestly about their frustrations and dashed hopes, sex often tops the list. Instead of creating the oneness referred to in the Bible, sex seems to provoke conflict and division. Couples steam and fight over issues ranging from the frequency of sex to pornography. More than one bride has wondered if she could exchange this "gift" for something at the local department store!

Sex, the Gift That Keeps on Taking

Over the past several years, I have been speaking to women's groups on the issue of sexual intimacy in marriage. The first time I spoke on the topic, my face was beet red, I had hives on my neck, and sweat trickled down my arms. To make matters worse, the audience was absolutely silent. I was going out on a huge limb, feeling like I was making a complete fool of myself. Surely these silent women were judging me. From the looks on their faces, no one could relate to the "headaches" I was sharing.

Lord, why am I here, humiliating myself by talking about this topic? They all probably think I'm a freak. Then and there I determined never to publicly tackle the topic again, if only I could get through the next 45 minutes.

It didn't take long before I realized that the silence in the room had nothing to do with judgment. When I finished speaking, women flocked to me, many with tears in their eyes. Secrets, frustrations, and

questions came pouring out as I spoke with each one. Finally they had found a safe environment to address the deep concerns they had harbored for so long.

Some confessed that they hated sex. Others felt guilty for going months, even years without having sex with their husbands. A few had questions about what the Bible says about role-playing, oral sex, vibrators, or sexual videos. Still others wondered how they could ever get past the loss of trust resulting from a husband's infidelity. A few secretly confided that they wanted sex but their husbands didn't.

Now I no longer fret about speaking to women about sex. Experience after experience has taught me that practically all wives struggle in this area in one way or another. Rarely have I met a woman who consistently embraces sex with her husband as a gift. Most women view it as a chore, a burden, or a heartache; it's a source of conflict, rejection, and perhaps shame. In even the healthiest of marriages, couples struggle with issues such as how often to have sex, finding time for sex, what is appropriate, and how to combat the constant temptations in our sexually explicit culture.

I remember speaking one day to a group of women on this topic. I joked that many women prefer a good book and a piece of chocolate to sex. A woman from the audience yelled out, "I'd take an accounting textbook and a plate of broccoli over sex any day of the week!"

How about you? Can you relate to these feelings? Do you see sex as a blessing or a curse in your marriage? Or maybe it depends on your season of life. How do you make sense of the idea that sex is God's gift to you?

A Different Kind of Gift

Have you ever gotten a gift that was wrapped in several boxes? First you open a big box, only to find one slightly smaller. You open that one and find yet another wrapped box. The exercise continues until finally you

get to the real gift. By this time you're thinking, "This had better be good, like car keys or jewelry."

In many ways, the gift of sex is more like this kind of gift. Throughout the course of your marriage, you'll continue to unwrap layers of the gift. The sexual relationship between a husband and wife is a long journey with many seasons. Each season potentially presents new joys and unique challenges. Unfortunately, many women (and men) give up when the first few legs of the journey disappoint. After a few years of frustration, fighting, and disappointment, they presume that this is their lot; sex just isn't going to be that great. These words are seldom audibly spoken, but both husband and wife settle into a ho-hum routine. They look forward to the infrequent times when sex is actually pleasurable, and they bear with the dry spells. Every now and then their disappointment bubbles to the surface and the accusations fly.

God's gift of sex to a married couple is a mysterious gift indeed. On the surface, it promises two things: pleasure and intimacy. There are times in most marriages when these two promises are fulfilled. Sex can be very pleasurable, and it can also heighten emotional intimacy between husband and wife. However, the time comes in all marriages when the "gift" brings neither pleasure nor intimacy. Then what?

Shelly and Jack were in exactly that spot. Looking over the 15 years of their marriage, they could pinpoint only a few stretches when sex was a blessing. Far more often, it had become a source of conflict and pain. Jack complained that Shelly was never interested.

"Why do I always have to be the one to initiate and pursue you?" he asked.

Shelly retorted, "Jack, we have four children, and I'm exhausted! Besides, when was the last time we actually went on a date? I'm not a vending machine that can meet your needs whenever you want!"

When I talked with Shelly alone, she explained further how the issue of sex was tearing her apart. "I feel like a terrible wife, but I just

don't like sex right now. I feel like it's just one more need I have to meet. I have nothing left to give. When we have sex, I just lay there, and I hate it. But I know that Jack faces all kinds of temptation. I suspect that he's into stuff on the Internet, and I feel like it's my fault."

Not all couples experience the stereotypical problems represented by Shelly and Jack. Sometimes the headaches come in other forms.

For Alyssa and Brad, sex has created tension almost since day one of their marriage. Early on, Alyssa experienced tremendous pain during intercourse. In fact, the couple didn't fully consummate their marriage until almost a month after their wedding. This early setback wreaked havoc. Brad was not only frustrated but felt like a failure as a lover. He began avoiding sex. Now, several years later, Alyssa can't figure out how to get her husband interested. She wonders, "Am I not attractive? What's wrong with me?" Although neither gives voice to their feelings, both are overwhelmed with rejection and insecurity.

Still other couples fight through issues of infertility, impotency, depression, infidelity, and spells where they can barely stand to be in the same room. "This is *not* what I signed up for," each partner internally concludes.

Are We Normal?

Underlying much of the frustration and disappointment in your sexual relationship may be the question about what is normal. Based on everything you see in the media, read in books, and observe around you, you may conclude that the setbacks you and your husband may be experiencing in the bedroom are unusual, that somehow you're missing out on the gift so many others seem to be enjoying. Because sex is a private and intimate topic, you may not often hear about the struggles and doubts that other women face. Even if you talk to your friends about sex, the conversation never gets to your underlying fears and disappointments.

Almost everyone wants to know whether they're normal. Is it normal to go months without wanting sex? Is it normal to never have an orgasm? Is it normal to need something risqué or forbidden to become excited? Is it normal for a woman to be drawn to porn? Is it normal for a guy to have no sex drive? How often does the normal couple have sex? Is it normal for sex to be boring?

Every sexual relationship is unique. Research can help us understand the basics of how marital sex works and how men and women tend to function sexually, but it can't define what is normal or, more important, what a healthy sex life look likes. What research can tell us is that it is very, very normal for a couple to struggle with various "headaches" throughout the journey of sex. Although the obstacles vary, every couple has a series of them to overcome. The fact that the obstacles exist is less important than how a couple deals with them.

The Lies We Believe

One of the biggest mistakes we make in marriage is to embrace a superficial understanding of the gift of sex. After unwrapping the first box, we assume that's all there is to the gift. Once the promises of pleasure and intimacy wane, we store the gift with the boxes of unused china and crystal we once took so much care to select. Oh, but there is so much more to the gift—so many layers yet to discover!

I believe that most women struggle with three lies that keep us from embracing the gift of sexuality. These lies are so subtle that we don't even know we've bought into them. Yet they generate most of the questions and frustrations that keep us from "unwrapping" the deeper levels of God's gift. As with every other good gift, the Enemy and the effects of sin have tainted married sexuality. Satan is a deceiver, twisting the meaning of God's intent for sex and blinding us from the truth that brings freedom. Throughout our time exploring the "normal" headaches of

sexual intimacy, be aware of the following lies and the extent to which you have bought into them.

Lie No. 1: God Created Sex Primarily for a Man's Pleasure

One of the facts we'll explore in this book is that female sexuality is far more complicated than male sexuality. For one thing, a man's sexuality is generally more compartmentalized, while a woman's sexuality tends to be more intertwined with emotions and relationship. Authors like Bill and Pam Farrel use the analogy that men are like waffles (with boxes) and women are like spaghetti (everything connects). Eastern cultures liken men to wood and women to water.

Physically, men are also easier to understand. It's obvious when a man is sexually aroused and when he has an orgasm; it's an all-or-nothing equation. A woman might not be able to tell if she's aroused and might not even know if she's had an orgasm. Unlike her husband, she may not be able to identify when she wants or needs sex. Her sexuality seems like a moving target.

Because women are more complicated sexually, the sexual relationship often revolves around the man's needs—when he wants sex and what arouses him. Many "good wives" have sex primarily because of their husbands' needs. A woman may or may not end up enjoying sex, but the primary motivation is all about her husband.

Later in this book, we'll talk at length about the importance of sex to your husband. As you read this information, keep in mind that sex is also God's gift to you. Male-oriented sex is not the best of what God intended for marriage. In fact, it represents an immature sexual relationship. I believe that God designed female sexuality in all its complexity not to frustrate you but to add incredible richness to the challenge of sexual intimacy. Unfortunately, most couples assume that when things don't "happen" naturally for her, the focus must just be on his needs.

God created women with a clitoris for *her* pleasure. Her body is

capable of achieving multiple and different types of orgasm. But she is a complicated creature who isn't easily understood. While he's a paint-by-the-numbers kit, she's a blank canvas with unlimited artistic potential. He's a banjo; she's a finely tuned Stradivarius that only a great musician can play. Her sexuality will naturally take more time and effort to figure out. Interestingly, a man reaches his sexual prime in the late teens, while a woman reaches hers closer to age 30.

Beyond the potential for physical pleasure and emotional bonding, regular marital sexuality actually has a host of other benefits for women. Studies have found that women who engage in regular intercourse have lower blood pressure and have a better physiological reaction to stressful events. Those who have sex once or twice a week also produce more antibodies that help fight infection. The release of the hormone oxytocin during sex increases feelings of closeness and intimacy, acts as a pain reliever for everyday aches and pains, and helps you sleep better. Many experts believe that the release of hormones during sex slows the aging process, strengthening muscles and even delaying wrinkles. An added bonus: Having sex three times a week for a year burns the same number of calories as running 75 miles!

Perhaps you find yourself in a place in your marriage where sex seems to be all about your husband. That's okay, but don't stay there. Despite what the world portrays, God did not design sex to be a yoke of slavery for wives. Don't give up, and don't settle for a sex life that centers on his pleasure alone. In fact, most men find the greatest sexual fulfillment in learning how to be a great lover for their wives.

Lie No. 2: Eroticism = Sexual Immorality

One of the challenges of writing this book has been addressing women from different generations. Even within the past 20 years, the sexual climate of our culture has changed drastically. If you were born in the 1960s or earlier, you probably grew up believing that good Christian

girls are not sexual. You may associate hot sex with guilt and have difficulty believing that God wants you to experience erotic sex with your
husband. The sexual images and lyrics on MTV were pushing the limit
in your day. Because sex was basically a taboo topic of conversation when
you were younger, you may still feel uncomfortable talking about sex
even with your husband.

If you were born after 1980, you likely found the topic of sex much
more comfortable to talk about. When you were in junior high, your
parents may have had to explain why the president was having oral sex
in the Oval Office. You grew up with sexually laden chat rooms, texting,
Facebook, YouTube, and *Sex and the City.* Through adolescence it was
normal for you to talk to friends, even of the opposite gender, about
sexual things. Psychologist Jean Twenge describes this contrast as "generation prude meets generation crude."[1]

In some ways the problems of a younger generation of women seem
to be the opposite of women born just a decade earlier. While women
from one generation may feel guilty about erotic pleasures, women from
another generation may not know where to draw the line. Younger
Christian women tend to be far more comfortable with their sexuality
but struggle with what is off-limits and to what extent it is okay to pursue their own pleasure. The commonality between the two groups is
confusion about the place of eroticism in a God-honoring marriage.

The truth is that God created erotic love. Nothing the world offers
can be more erotic than what God intended for a married couple to experience. He designed the most intense pleasure, the most satisfying
intimacy, and the most fulfilling sex. The world can't top His creation.
The Old Testament book Song of Songs attests to the fact that God
wants married couples to pursue the highest erotic pleasures together.
However, the greatest eroticism is meant to take place within the context of marriage and is guarded by the intimacy of a trusting relationship. The world sells the lie that sexual fulfillment results from looking

outside the marriage relationship . . . that pure marital sex is boring. Christian married couples believe this lie when they rely on pornographic images, extramarital flirtations, fantasies, and other outside influences to heighten their erotic pleasure.

Many of the sexual headaches women deal with revolve around this question: How do we pursue erotic love without crossing the line into sexual immorality? By default, most married couples either give up on eroticism or plunge into the world's version of it.

If you can relate to this struggle, hang in there. Whether you feel guilty about being sexual or you wonder where to draw the line in marital sexual intimacy, we'll address these issues head-on in the chapters that follow.

Lie No. 3: The Greatest Pleasures of Sex Are Immediate

Almost every married couple I've talked to has some disaster story to tell about their honeymoon, especially if they waited for marriage to have sex. Honeymoons are full of rookie mistakes; ours was no exception. Our disaster started with the fact that we had a honeymoon without a bed. Mike's parents own a log cabin vacation home in the Tennessee mountains. Since we didn't have any money, Mike asked them if we could use the cabin for our honeymoon. Not only did they say yes, but they had also just ordered a beautiful four-poster bedroom set for the cabin. But lo and behold, the furniture company delivered the furniture to their home in Florida instead of Tennessee.

Hearing about the mix-up, Mike packed a king-size air mattress for our honeymoon. We arrived at the cabin and unloaded the car only to discover that he had forgotten to pack the cap for the air mattress. Trying to salvage the situation, Mike stuffed a towel into the air hole and covered it with duct tape. Needless to say, it didn't exactly hold up. We became very familiar with the hardwood floor.

From a sexual perspective, the first year of our marriage was quite a

disappointment. It took a long time for us to figure out what we were doing. Even though I knew not to expect too much in the beginning, I was still pretty bummed. I seemed to have constant bladder infections; sex was uncomfortable at best, and painful at worst. The setbacks caused tension and frustration between Mike and me. We had looked forward to this for so long, but it seemed to cause more problems than pleasure. Eventually we graduated from those headaches only to run into new ones.

Perhaps the greatest lie women fall for is that sex is all about immediate pleasure. We naturally assume that a great sex life is one in which the couple always has fun, communicates perfectly, and experiences ecstasy together. But there is so much more to sex than what is happening in the moment. Even through the worst stretches of a couple's sex life, God can still be working on uniting a husband and wife in more subtle ways.

By God's design, sex can be fun, pleasurable, and immensely fulfilling. There are seasons in marriage when sexual intimacy and fulfillment come easily. There are other seasons, however, that are fraught with stress, resentment, and disappointment. I firmly believe that the frustrations we experience in sex aren't simply the consequences of living in a fallen world but are actually part of the gift itself. Even when sex isn't great, God is doing something in your heart and in your marriage, perhaps forging an intimacy beyond the physical.

We Are Creating Something New

As a Christian woman, it has been difficult for me at times to understand sexuality within the context of my relationship with God. Several years ago I was sitting in a Christian psychology conference when something the speaker said caught my ear. I don't even remember the context of his comment, but I vividly recall my confusion when he said, "We were all created as sexual creatures." This sounded so odd to me. Even though I

was married at the time, I certainly didn't see myself as a sexual creature. Sex to me was something separate—something I did, not something I was.

As I've struggled with this topic, I'm learning more and more that my sexuality and what I do with it is as much of an expression of me as what I say. The Bible says that our words are an expression of the overflow of our hearts (Luke 6:45). Follow me around long enough, listen to what I say, and you'll see what is in my heart. The same is true with sexuality. Not only has God created me as a sexual being, but my thoughts, actions, and attitudes ultimately reveal the desires and state of my heart as well.

God's greatest goal for me is to teach me how to love. In my own life, I have found no more practical testing ground for my heart than sexual intimacy. On the average day, I'm eager to serve my children, cook dinner, do laundry, and teach Bible studies, all with a pretty good attitude. Yet for some reason, I can't seem to muster the same positive attitude regarding sex. *Tonight? He can't be serious. Surely there's a toilet in this house that needs cleaning just so I can stall for a few minutes!*

My typical routine is to have my devotions in the evening after the kids are in bed. More than once I've been reading the Bible, praying, and praising the Lord when God has impressed on my heart that I should go upstairs and initiate sex with my husband. "Are You sure, Lord?" I ask. "I'm so into Leviticus, I just can't put it down." But the prompting is confirmed.

One evening I shared this with my husband. He responded, "That's the weirdest thing. I was just praying about that!"

Beyond my husband's prayer requests, I believe that God's prompting during my time with Him is no coincidence. As I seek to be more like my Savior, He is showing me how to love my husband. Love isn't a self-centered pursuit but a challenge to serve another person as completely as I serve myself.

Sure, God wants my husband and me to enjoy each other sexually.

He wants us to work toward learning how to please one another and to make the most of the gift He has granted us. However, He also wants to use the frustrations and headaches to challenge and stretch our understanding of what "making love" actually means.

Marital sexuality is designed for more than just pleasure. It is the Refiner's fire that reveals the deepest attitudes of our hearts. There may be no place in your life where it is more difficult to express love than in your marriage. You may be more eager to pack your bags and become a missionary in Africa than you are to show the love of Christ in your bedroom.

More than learning a new technique or strategy to spice up our love lives, we need God to challenge and change our thoughts and attitudes. Like everything else in life, sex is truly a matter of the heart. This isn't to discount the legitimate emotional, relational, and physical roadblocks in sex but to reframe how we approach them. An intimacy without conflict, understanding, compromise, sacrifice, and heartfelt communication is cheap and cannot stand the test of time. It is through the struggle that our hearts are forged together and that our attitudes are challenged to be like Christ's.

Okay, one more gift analogy. Because I have three boys, I'm very familiar with LEGOs. Without fail, Mike and I spend at least a couple of hours every Christmas morning helping our boys put together intricate LEGO sets. Whereas many kids' toys have labels that say "some assembly required," the whole purpose of LEGOs is to assemble them. Kids have much more fun building the LEGO creations than they ever have playing with the completed projects. In fact, as soon as they build them, they take them apart to create something new.

I challenge you to think of the gift of sex through this lens. Maybe you expected to open a gift that was already assembled. You naively thought, as I did, that you and your husband were destined for a lifetime of pleasure and intimacy. Instead, you found that your bedroom is metaphorically scattered with thousands of LEGOs and no directions.

Consider the fact that God's greatest gift to your marriage may not be the assembled product but what happens as you strive to put it together.

The Journey Is More Important than the Destination

Less than a year ago, Mike and I moved from the Midwest to Colorado Springs. Because we are both outdoorsy, active people, it didn't take long before we decided to tackle Pikes Peak. If you aren't familiar with Colorado Springs, the 14,000-foot peak dwarfs the city. The climb up is a 13-mile hike, gaining about 7,000 feet in elevation.

We started the journey before sunrise and hiked steadily, reaching the summit at around two o'clock. There were parts of the hike that were absolutely miserable, where we could barely take another step. My muscles ached, and I was dizzy from the lack of oxygen at that elevation. Yet there were other times during the journey that were absolutely breathtaking (in a good way). We would look out at these gorgeous views of the trees and mountains, God's beauty surrounding us. Sometimes we would stop to evaluate how far we'd already come. At other times we were overwhelmed as we looked upward at the treacherous terrain ahead. Most of the journey was just hiking—no elation and no misery but just working together and encouraging each other toward a goal. Now I take great pleasure in looking at Pikes Peak and saying to Mike, "We climbed that!"

In a similar way, you shouldn't be so focused on the destination of sex that you forget the beauty of the journey. The greatest memories aren't of reaching the peak, but of the moments you tarried together to get there. The obstacles and trials are as important in the journey as the pleasures.

During our time together in this book, we'll look at the most common sexual-intimacy headaches that crop up for women. As we explore

problems like body image, the impact of the past, pornography, and differences in desire, we'll hit some of the highlights of research and other information about sex. However, the answer to these headaches is not simply more information or even greater understanding. Although information and understanding are helpful, our relationships can be transformed only as God reveals and changes our hearts. Beyond just seeking the cure for common intimacy headaches, let's endeavor to see marital sexuality within the context of the larger journey of marriage and spiritual growth.

God is doing something in your life and in your marriage. He desires to transform your heart, to teach you how to love and how to be loved. Might the gift of sex be one area in which He is working? Are you willing to surrender this part of your life to Him?

Would you be so bold as to journey with me, inviting God to teach us to see the gift of sex as He sees it?

SOMETHING TO THINK ABOUT • • • • •

1. What "headaches" have you experienced in your marriage?

2. Which of these three lies have most impacted your sex life:
   • God created sex primarily for a man's pleasure.
   • Eroticism = sexual immorality.
   • The greatest pleasures of sex are immediate.
   How have these lies played out in your sexual relationship with your husband?

3. Choose an analogy that represents the "gift" sex is in your marriage. Write a prayer about your desire for God to redeem this gift.

two

My Bedroom Ceiling Hasn't Changed in the Past Five Years

A married guy went out for a night on the town with his buddies. While his single friends partied late into the night, the man faithfully returned home to his wife, hoping for a nightcap. He was disappointed to find her sleeping soundly, snoring softly with her mouth wide open. He went into the bathroom, grabbed a bottle of aspirin, and dropped two of them into Sleeping Beauty's mouth. The woman woke up coughing and choking on the aspirin. Once she caught her breath, she noticed her husband standing beside the bed with a coy smile, holding the aspirin bottle.

She said, "What are you doing?"

He responded, "I thought you might need a couple of aspirin."

"Why? I don't have a headache" was her confused answer.

"That's all I needed to hear!"

• • •

Why is it that in the sexual stereotypes and seemingly in most marriages, it's the woman who has the headache? Why can't wives be as eager for physical intimacy as their husbands seem to be? Why do they feign

headaches, look for excuses, or even begin to dread their husbands' sexual advances? Why is it that even women with robust sex drives often find themselves disappointed with the reality of marital sex?

I've never met a woman who didn't want to like sex. However, I've met many women who don't know *how* to like sex. Maggie's comments summarize what many women experience: "We have been married for almost 20 years now. There have been good times and bad times in our physical relationship, but mostly it's just boring. I have such a hard time getting into it. After so many years of being married, I've just accepted that it's not going to be as great as people say it is."

The next time you check out of the grocery store, notice the teaser articles advertised on the covers of women's magazines. You'll probably read article headings like "Kama Sutra for Beginners," "Five Steps to Becoming a Love Goddess in the Bedroom," or "How to Make Him Beg for More." Women like Maggie simply roll their eyes at such headlines, knowing that the reality of married sex is a far cry from such tantalizing promises.

Great Sex Doesn't Just Happen

Having sex is a natural physiological practice. People have figured out how to do it on their own since the beginning of time. Without how-to books or online instructional courses, people from every tribe and nation manage to procreate. Because sex is a natural physical act, we tend to put it in the category of other natural physical acts like eating, sleeping, and going to the bathroom. You don't have to focus on learning how to master these things—they just naturally happen.

Although sex "just happens," a dynamic sex life does not. Without effort, time, and attention, sex can easily and quickly become mundane and predictable and can even turn into a dreaded necessity to place on the to-do list.

When couples run into difficulties they tend to give up, concluding, "We're just not that great together." Ironically, they don't expect anything else in marriage to just happen. They understand that being financially healthy depends on budgets, planning, and communication. Certainly, raising good kids doesn't just happen either. Even staying healthy requires a proactive approach to food and exercise. Why should sex be any different?

What's the right response to the age-old dilemma of boring sex? Should wives like Maggie simply settle into a less-than-fulfilling complacency? Should they buy the magazines and sex toys that promise the toe-curling sex everyone else seems to be enjoying?

As a couple, have you ever set aside significant time and energy specifically to improve your sex life? Instead of approaching sex as a natural, necessary, physical act, consider approaching it as a gift, an interest, and an ability that can be cultivated. You will never be a great cook unless you experiment with new recipes, read cookbooks, and practice cooking. You will never be a great tennis player unless you take lessons and play regularly. You will never learn to play the trumpet without hours and hours of practice and instruction. Don't assume that sex is any different. You and your husband won't have a great sex life unless you make it a priority to actually work on intimacy together.

Common Barriers to Working on Your Sex Life

No doubt both you and your husband would love for your sex life to be better than it is. You'd love to enjoy sex more than you do. So what is keeping you from working toward that goal? Why do you settle for an unsatisfying sex life when you don't settle in other areas of your life? Believe it or not, you're not alone if you struggle in this area. There are several common barriers couples come up against when they think about working toward a more satisfying sex life.

Barrier No. 1: "Being Sexual Seems Contradictory to Being a Godly Woman"

With the onslaught of sexual temptation, the early onset of puberty, and the tremendous freedom teens are given in our society, adults are understandably paranoid about kids having sex. Fear and guilt are the age-old tools adults use to ward off the likelihood of teens becoming sexually active. As a result, from a very young age, kids consistently get messages that sex (talking about it, thinking about it, and certainly engaging in it) is a forbidden, mysterious pleasure.

With three boys approaching the teenage years, I certainly understand the emphasis placed on restraining teenage sexual urges and the strategies parents employ. That being said, the message that sex outside of marriage is wrong too often gets translated "sex is wrong." Both young boys and young girls grow up with conscious and unconscious messages that their sexuality is tainted. They have been taught since before puberty that the pleasure they feel associated with touching themselves or fantasizing is wrong. Most people going into marriage don't know how to have a sexual desire or feeling that isn't somehow attached to shame and guilt. Instinctively they believe that God and great sex just can't go together.

After years of training that touching, fantasizing, masturbating, and foreplay are wrong, how does a wedding ceremony erase all of that conditioning? How can a woman who has taken great care to guard her purity or a woman who has harbored the shame of a promiscuous past suddenly celebrate her sexuality?

As many times as you may hear that God created sex to be enjoyed, the message just doesn't seem strong enough to reverse years of conditioning. Think about it this way: Have you ever prayed before, during, or after sex? Have you ever asked God to help you improve your sex life? Have you ever thanked Him for the gift of sex in your marriage? Can you imagine that He is happy to see you and your husband thoroughly enjoying each other?

Often, married couples have trouble believing that God wants them to enjoy sex. Here's a fairy tale that drives home this idea:

Once upon a time there was a little girl named Kate. Kate and her siblings were born into a loving family. Their parents showered the kids with gifts, but they also set and maintained reasonable boundaries of behavior. The children were given free rein in the family's basement, which was filled with toys. Barbies, trucks, building toys, board games, electronic games, a slide, a play castle, and a playhouse filled the expanse of the room.

Curiously, Kate refused to play with any of the toys. Whenever she went to the basement, she sat in a corner staring at the toys with a forlorn look on her face. She complained whenever her parents told the kids to play in the basement. On the rare occasion that she picked up a toy, she played halfheartedly, wishing instead to be upstairs. Kate also refused to play with toys in the church nursery, at other people's homes, or at school.

Kate's parents were puzzled about her seeming inability to play. In their concern, they sat Kate down and explained, "Kate, we love you so much that we provided you and your brothers and sisters a basement full of toys. We want you to enjoy them. In fact, one of your primary jobs as a little girl is to have fun and play."

Kate responded, "I don't know how to play. I'm afraid of breaking the toys. What if I play with them wrong or break them? What if I play with a toy that I'm not supposed to play with?"

"Honey," her father responded, "that's why we built the basement for you. Anything in the basement is for your enjoyment. There are things in this house that aren't safe for you to play with, but anything in the basement is yours to enjoy. There's no wrong way to play. We want you to have fun!"

Kate's fear of playing is much like the way many women respond to their sexuality. They just can't accept that God created and designed it

for their pleasure and enjoyment. They are caught in the trap of fear and shame that keeps them from rejoicing in a great gift that God has provided.

Not only is God okay with your having great sex with your husband, He wants you to. He created your body so that sex could be incredibly pleasurable and satisfying. He designed sexual hormones to promote emotional intimacy and bonding between you and your husband. There is nothing sacred about being reserved or sexually inhibited in marriage.

Some Christian couples believe that their sexual expression should be repressed or limited. In this line of thinking, marital intimacy is almost a necessary evil that should be restrained. Christian couples above all should experience the most freedom to celebrate the oneness that God has designed for them. If you doubt this, read Song of Songs. The poetry contained in this inspired book of the Bible is not restrained or limited but driven by great passion, pleasure, and love. How tragic that God's children have bought into the lie that great sex is somehow a compromise of purity. Christian married couples, especially, should experience the greatest guilt-free pleasures from sex. Although the Bible teaches sexual restriction outside of marriage, husbands and wives have great freedom to please each other. Married sex should be a great celebration without restraint!

Barrier No. 2: "I Just Can't Get into It"
"Karen, what are you thinking about?"

Karen froze as she heard Jack's question. They were in the middle of a physically intimate moment, and Karen's mind couldn't have been less engaged. She certainly wasn't going to admit that she had been trying to figure out how to arrange a ride to youth group for their 14-year-old daughter. Not exactly romantic.

Have you ever found yourself in this type of situation? Perhaps

your mind is so prone to wander during sex that your husband knows not to ask.

This is one aspect of female sexuality that men have great difficulty understanding. When guys are into sex, they're into it. They don't think about work, the mold growing in the shower, what tie to wear with the gray suit, or how interesting that PBS documentary was yesterday. Women, on the other hand, can be physically engaged in sex and yet be mentally checked out. This is one occasion when multitasking isn't desirable. The average husband isn't thrilled to find out that his wife can have sex while mentally doing the taxes!

As a woman, you need to engage your body *and* mind to enjoy sex. In fact, Christian sex experts Cliff and Joyce Penner teach that the brain is the most important sex organ. For many women, sex becomes blah because keeping the mind engaged is such a monumental task. One woman described it as "sexual attention deficit disorder." Even women who have an extraordinary ability to focus on any other task may be prone to zone out during sex.

There are a couple of reasons why sexual ADD is so common for women. First of all, most guys don't understand the importance of capturing their wife's attention before and during sex. Emotional and physical foreplay engage her mind in the process of anticipating, experiencing, and enjoying intimacy. Without it, her body may be available, but her mind will be miles away.

Second, women sometimes don't give themselves permission to check out of life and check into sex. Many busy wives approach sex as something else to get done, not as a sanctuary for rest and fulfillment. Enjoying sex is impossible without leaving the problems and worries of the day at the door. Unlike the laundry, carpooling, or running errands, sexual fulfillment can't be accomplished through absent-minded efficiency. Ironically, it takes incredible focus for women to stay relaxed and sexually engaged.

Third, women learn to mentally disengage during sex as a way of protecting themselves emotionally. This is very common among women who have experienced ongoing sexual trauma. To numb the physical and emotional pain of unwanted sex, a woman learns to mentally check out or disengage. Through checking out, she can perform adequately while avoiding the intimacy and vulnerability of sex. Some women report being so emotionally detached that they experience sex as an outside observer or from an out-of-body vantage point. In addition to sexual trauma, this coping mechanism can also be used in marriages that are less than fulfilling. A woman can go through the motions of sex while protecting herself from the risks associated with emotionally connecting to her husband.

For whatever reason it occurs, mental disengagement is a pleasure killer. The greater the engagement, the more profound the pleasure. The ultimate goal of sex is to be fully present, enjoying the sensuality of intimacy to its fullest. As I suggested earlier, read Solomon's Song of Songs and notice the explicit descriptions of all of the senses—tasting, smelling, touching, hearing, and seeing. Sexual intimacy is a feast for the whole body.

If you struggle with "getting into it," begin by asking yourself what you may be trying to avoid. Do memories from the past keep you from the full experience of sex? Are you responding to the lack of emotional safety in your marriage? If fear is keeping you from engaging your mind, body, and soul in the sexual experience, you may need the help of a counselor to work through those barriers. Self-protection is a powerful motivation to disengage, but it comes with a price.

If you find that busyness or sexual ADD is the culprit, explore with your husband what helps you become both emotionally and physically engaged: a bubble bath, a back rub, 20 minutes to yourself, talking through an issue, or just emotionally checking in with your husband every day.

Barrier No. 3: "I Don't Know How to Enjoy Sex"

For a woman, when sex is great it provides incredible physical pleasure, a release of stress, and unparalleled feelings of closeness with her husband. But when sex is bad, it's messy, frustrating, time consuming, humiliating, and even painful. Of course, there are many times in marriage when sex falls somewhere in between these two extremes: It's not great, but it's not terrible. The million-dollar question for many women is how to go from bad or mediocre sex to actually looking forward to it.

Physiologically, a woman's body is designed to derive as much pleasure from sex as a man's body. Her clitoris is packed with nerve endings wired right to the pleasure center of her brain. The problem with enjoying sex is twofold. First of all, her sexual organs are internal and less accessible. Because of this, many women are unfamiliar with their own sexuality. Second, a woman's sexual pleasure gradually builds through foreplay, emotional bonding, and both sexual and nonsexual touch. Her husband is typically "ready for action" way before she is. Most of the time, couples do what is natural, meaning they follow his timetable instead of hers. When they have sex before she is adequately stimulated, sex may be painful and even feels emotionally exploitive.

Most likely, this isn't new information for you. In fact, you and your husband may have spent hours trying to get you going to no avail. Maybe you have begun to dread the long ordeal of foreplay, only to end up still frustrated and unfulfilled. The more he wants to fulfill you, the more pressure you feel to experience pleasure. The most obvious scenario related to this problem is orgasm. About 10 percent of women never experience orgasm, and more than 50 percent of women have trouble having one.[1]

If you fall within this group, you may have settled into the belief that female orgasm just isn't that important. Although some women most enjoy the emotional and physical closeness of sex, the sexual release of orgasm is an important element. Sexual excitement is designed to build

tension with the purpose of release. In fact, many of the physical and emotional benefits of sex are the result of the hormones released after orgasm. When a woman consistently has sex without orgasm, tension in her body builds with no release. Not only is female orgasm important, for most women it's possible.

Some experts believe that barring an untreated medical or psychological condition, all women can have an orgasm (although about two-thirds of women cannot have orgasm through intercourse alone). For those women who can't have an orgasm, there may be an underlying medical cause, such as an injury to the back, the autonomic nervous system, or the central nervous system, or some disjunction between the sex organ, spine, and brain. The roadblock may also be emotional, resulting from a past history of sexual abuse or an emotionally distant relationship with a spouse.

There are other physical, emotional, and psychological factors that may prevent a woman from achieving orgasm. These include painful intercourse; illnesses such as diabetes, hysterectomy, or cancer surgery; medications such as blood pressure meds, antihistamines, antidepressants; alcohol and drugs; hormonal changes such as those accompanying menopause; psychological causes such as anxiety or depression, stress, cultural and religious beliefs, or guilt; relationship issues such as unresolved conflict or infidelity.[2]

Both sexual pleasure and orgasm require the ability to relax and enjoy. Unfortunately, the more stressed you become about not getting aroused, the less relaxed you are. When pleasure and orgasm are elusive in sex, therapists inevitably recommend a technique originated by Masters and Johnson called sensate focus. Essentially, the goal is to let go of the pressure of orgasm and return to the basic building blocks of experiencing pleasure. Sensate focus can help you and your husband learn how to touch each other and feel pleasure without the pressure of per-

formance. At the beginning of sensate-focus exercises, the couple is en-couraged not to have intercourse but to relearn how to touch each other without performance demands. Sensate focus typically involves four progressive stages. In the first stage, the husband and wife spend one hour touching and caressing each other all over the body, but avoiding the genitals and breasts. Both take turns being the giver and recipient of the exercise. The goal is for each to experience positive nonsexual touch. The couple progresses to a second stage in which the receiver guides the other's hand, teaching what kind of touch is most pleasurable. In stage three, the husband and wife give and receive touch similar to stage two, but also incorporate the erogenous zones (breasts and genitals). Finally in stage four, the couple progresses to sexual touching that leads to intercourse and/or orgasm.[3]

As you can imagine, the assignment to caress and enjoy each other without intercourse can be in itself instructive and erotic! You can find out more about exercises like sensate focus in Cliff and Joyce Penner's book *Restoring the Pleasure: Complete Step-by-Step Programs to Help Couples Overcome the Most Common Sexual Barriers*, or Dr. Douglas Rosenau's book *A Celebration of Sex: A Guide to Enjoying God's Gift of Sexual Intimacy*.

Dr. Louanne Cole Weston, WebMD expert in the area of sexual-ity, offers additional advice on the balance of tension and relaxation re-quired for a woman to have an orgasm. She explains that both tension and relaxation, seemingly opposite goals, are imperative. A woman needs to tense up her leg, abdominal, buttocks, and pelvic muscles to reach climax. By contracting these muscles, a woman increases blood flow to the genital region, promoting both arousal and orgasm. While her muscles are tense, her brain must be relaxed so that she can focus on the sensation of stimulation. Weston recommends that women who have difficulty relaxing repeat a mantra like "I can take as long as I

want" or "This really feels great" to occupy the mind with positive, focused thoughts.[4]

Although the physical and mental tips help, the most important variable contributing to how much you enjoy sex is the quality of your marriage. Interestingly, many of the physical and emotional benefits of sex and orgasm are negated when sex occurs outside of a committed, monogamous relationship. In fact, casual intercourse and orgasm can lead to depression.[5]

Barrier No. 4: "We Don't Have the Time or the Energy"

Kissing passionately for 15 minutes . . . 18 calories.

Having sexual intercourse for 30 minutes . . . 46 calories.

Having an orgasm . . . 27 calories.

Actually having the energy to initiate and enjoy sex with your husband . . . priceless.

Dr. Archibald Hart and his colleagues conducted a survey of 2,000 Christian women related to sexuality. One of the most obvious results of his findings is that fatigue is an enormous sexual barrier for women, particularly during the parenting years. In fact, Dr. Hart found that not having the energy was the number-one reason that women don't want to have sex.[6]

Women aren't the only ones too tired to have sex. Many men also suffer from the constant stress and exhaustion of our fast-paced, wired culture. Although stress and fatigue affect both men and women, the impact is typically more detrimental to female sexuality. Some men, in fact, seek sex to help them relax and unwind at the end of an exhausting and stressful day. For most women, it simply doesn't work that way.

Women are far more likely to be shortchanged by the energy crisis. Because of the lack of time and energy, too many married couples settle for a steady diet of quickies largely focused on the husband's needs.

More than a few times I've said to Mike, "We can do it if you don't wake me up!" As mentioned earlier, female sexual enjoyment takes far more time to nurture, both emotionally and physically. When a couple doesn't have time to talk, have fun together, and enjoy each other's bodies, she's the one who ends up feeling unsatisfied.

Not having the energy for sex also becomes a marital problem when it puts a woman in the position of always fending off her husband's advances. Men are very sensitive to sexual rejection. Even though his wife may say "Not tonight" because she's incredibly tired, her husband may still take this as a personal rejection, particularly if this response has become a pattern.

Not only do men want their wives to be sexually available, but they also want them to be sexually alive. "Just get it over with" sex is, for many men, worse than no sex. Giving your husband your body as you lie there like a dead fish is little consolation. A man most enjoys sex when he pleases his wife.

Enjoying, engaging in, and initiating sex for most tired wives is a fantasy for the cover of *Cosmopolitan*. After all, you can't fake having energy.

Barrier No. 5: "I Just Don't See Myself as Sexual"

I was walking down the stairs in my parents' house with my firstborn son in my arms. As I glanced to my right, I caught my image in the mirror hanging on the wall. And then it struck me: *I am a mom*. Even though my son was a few months old, this was the first time I had seen myself holding him. Catching the mental image of myself as a mother was a significant event. Although I had been acting like a mom, it took seeing myself holding my son to embrace my new role.

You carry all kinds of mental images about yourself. You may easily picture yourself as a mom, a daughter, a teacher, or in many other roles you fulfill in your life. But do you picture yourself as a sexual woman?

Can you embrace the fact that you have sexual needs and desires? Do you accept that you are equipped, by God's design, to arouse and fulfill your husband's sexual desires?

Perhaps this is a stretch for you. Maybe your picture of a sexual woman includes a busty figure, long legs, and a flawless face. "Sexy" women walk with that swing in their hips and talk with a bedroom voice. They don't make peanut-butter-and-jelly sandwiches, sleep in flannel nightgowns, wake up with bed head, or have to wear support panty hose. As you think about heating up your love life, you may snicker at the idea of donning a negligee or initiating a night of wild passion. You simply can't see yourself as sexual.

What is it that keeps you from getting that glimpse in the mirror that confirms your sexuality? Is it your figure? Your personality? Your past? Your dignity? As long as you resist the mental image and acceptance of your God-given sexuality, intimacy with your husband will continually be restrained.

Working Toward a Great Sex Life

If you really want to learn how to bring back the passion that you once experienced with your husband or hoped that you would experience after marriage, you're going to have to make some adjustments. If you change nothing, you can be certain that nothing will change. Don't fall for the lie that sex has to be a bore, a chore, or a headache. Although these kinds of problems are normal, don't just accept them as permanent. Following are a few places to start.

Give Yourself Permission to Be Sexual
Working on your sex life may begin with giving yourself permission to care about your sexuality. Sometimes you may get into the martyr syndrome, falling for the lie that sex is all about denying self and serving

your husband. Indeed, there are times and aspects of sexuality that require sacrifice and putting his needs above your own (we'll get to those later in the book). But your sex life will never be great if you stay stuck in that belief.

Sex is one area in which you need to learn to have some healthy self-focus. By God's design, great sex only happens when you allow yourself to experience and even pursue your own pleasure with your husband. Ironically, and as I've pointed out before, he won't be sexually fulfilled unless you give yourself permission to be.

Especially for women, sex gets good when you make the conscious decision to make it a priority. While men are prompted by sexual desire, women typically experience sexual arousal and desire *after* they have made the choice to focus on sex. Even if your husband is the one to initiate sex, make the conscious decision to work on making it good and pleasurable for you. God designed sex in such a way that your husband will be all for this. Sharing in your sexuality will heighten his pleasure.

Think About Sex and Romance

There is a direct correlation between how often you think about sex and your readiness to enjoy it with your husband. Naturally, I'm not suggesting that you read raunchy romance novels or think about sex in any inappropriate format. What you *can* do is think about being intimate with your husband. During the day, think about what you love about him, how you want him to touch you, and the intimacy you long to share with him. Pull out a few pictures or love letters from when you were dating or earlier in your marriage. Remember times that were particularly sweet or lover's secrets that you've shared with him.

Part of thinking about sex means continuing to build romantic experiences together. Remembering the night 20 years ago when he swept you off your feet will only go so far. There are many nonsexual aspects

of your relationship that you can build into a great sexual relationship. The feelings of affection and romance often fade in marriage because husband and wife forget to enjoy time together; every encounter seems to revolve around the basic necessities of running a household, solving problems, managing money, and raising kids. Discover things you really like doing together, such as running, traveling, going to musical performances, learning a foreign language, serving in short-term missions, camping, cooking, or even playing video games. Men, in particular, really connect through shared activities rather than conversation. Laughter is also a powerful way to promote bonding and affection in your relationship.

Another key aspect of romance and intimacy is discovery. Think about the passion you felt while dating your husband. A lot of it was related to the curiosity and discovery of a new relationship. Everything was fresh and exciting. But after a couple of years of marriage, everything seems to settle into a rut. Even when you go on a date, you tend to go to the same restaurants. Once you stop exploring and discovering life together, your sexual relationship is likely to reflect this. Make a habit of trying new things together (sexual and otherwise).

A couple of years ago, I bought Mike a bottle of Dakar. This was the cologne he often wore while we were dating. Even this little change brought back memories and helped recharge romance and intimacy in our relationship.

Finally, try a little flirting. Couples who have great sex still flirt with each other. When we think of flirting, we typically put it in the context of singles trying to get a date. The primary purpose of flirting is to entice and heighten anticipation. Showing a little bit of flesh or teasing with a veiled sexual comment is a huge turn-on for guys. So why do we assume that flirting is for single people? If sexuality is reserved for marriage, then flirting is for husband and wife. In fact, if you want to have

a sex life with a pulse in it, flirting is critical. It's your secret language of anticipating sexual love and enticing each other.

Solve the Energy Crisis

In high school, I drank coffee to feel like a grown-up. In college, I drank it because I actually started to like the taste. Now I drink it for survival. Just recently, Starbucks put in a drive-through shop right on the road where my kids go to school. When I first saw it, I whooped and hollered in the van. My kids thought I had gone crazy. "Look, guys! Salvation is at hand!" I exclaimed.

Yes, coffee is my vice. I have never had the stamina to complete all of the activities my mind wants to, but having children seems to have drained my energy resources even more. Close friends and family members will attest to the fact that I've never physically recovered the energy I once had pre-kids. Just the other day, my nine-year-old son looked at me when I picked him up from school and said, "Mom, you look really tired. I think you need a cup of coffee."

Apart from becoming a coffee addict, consider a couple of ways you can recover your lost energy and channel it into greater sexual intimacy with your husband.

1. Take naps. Naps are one of the ways I'm learning to save time and energy for sex (especially for nighttime rendezvous). When Mike and I first were married, I typically got home from school before he returned from work in the evening. When I was really tired, I would sneak a quick nap before he got home. As soon as I heard the key jingle in the door, I would jump out of bed and straighten the covers so he wouldn't know I was napping. The few times he caught me, I was embarrassed to have needed a nap. My philosophy has totally changed.

Whenever I can manage it, I try to take a catnap in the afternoon right before the kids get home from school. When I say naps, I don't

mean the two-hour I-feel-like-I-got-hit-by-a-truck nap. All it takes is 15 minutes of quasi-sleep to give me the energy boost I need to make it through the evening. That short nap may be the difference between a sweet night of love and an argument over the fact that "you never want to do it."

2. Exercise. Although you're probably sick of hearing this from every doctor, television program, and women's magazine on the planet, exercise really is good for you. What you might not know is that it's great for your sex life, too. Even if the occasional power walk won't give you flat abs, it will help you have the energy you need for intimacy.

The primary hormone that increases libido is testosterone. This is true for both men and women. Yes, you do have some testosterone coursing through your blood right now. Exercise increases healthy testosterone levels in women, improving both energy and sexual desire. Moderate exercise also increases blood flow (and therefore the amount of oxygen available) to the brain, heart, lungs, and every other part of the body. Instead of making you tired, regular exercise gives you more energy.

If you're feeling too tired to tango, ask your husband to take a 15-minute walk around the neighborhood with you or play a game of Ping-Pong together (clothing is optional—for the Ping-Pong game, not the walk).

Adding a regular exercise routine doesn't mean you have to train for a marathon, set up free weights in the bedroom, or join an expensive gym. A brisk 30- to 45-minute walk four times a week will do the trick.

3. Identify energy zappers. In addition to finding ways to boost your energy reserves for sex, you may also need to look at your schedule. Your energy problem may be rooted not in the fact that you have too little energy but in the fact that you have too many commitments. You have 24 hours in a day and a limited supply of energy. Where is it all going? What can you cut to make time for rest, exercise, relationship, and intimacy?

In 2004, the U.S. Department of Energy began educating the pub-

lic about "vampire power." Vampire power refers to the energy that electronic devices draw even when they aren't in use. For example, when you turn a television set off, it continues to use electricity in sleep mode, ready to be reactivated by the remote control. Power adapters, portable phones and their bases, LED displays, and internal clocks and sensors are other examples of devices you probably have around your home or workplace that drain power when they're not in use. Obviously, the Department of Energy discourages the use of these vampire-power products because they waste energy. Some studies indicate that 10 percent of all household electricity is spent on vampire power.[7]

Chances are there are energy vampires in your life, things that suck energy out of you without your awareness. A huge energy vampire is emotional stress. Worrying is absolutely exhausting. You don't have to be actively thinking through a problem for it to be sapping energy from you. Most likely, you have a couple of "pots" simmering on the back burner that silently suck the energy right out of you as you go about your day. A few common energy vampires include resentment or bitterness toward someone, worrying about how other people see you, conflicts or trauma that you desperately try not to think about, and looming decisions or fears. These energy leeches float beneath your consciousness but still consume an enormous amount of strength.

How to deal with the energy vampires in our lives could be the topic of another whole book. They are often deeply rooted in issues that aren't so easy to extinguish. Running the risk of simplifying the solution, let me suggest that you deal with them head-on. It takes far less energy in the long run to resolve a conflict, confront a fear, or pour out your heart to God than it does to carry around pounds of psychological baggage.

Make Time for Sex
If awakening your sexual desire and fostering the right kind of intimacy in your life takes a lot of time, where is that going to come from? Perhaps

the best tip I can give you concerning the headache of fatigue is to schedule time for sex. Although scheduling sex might sound incredibly unromantic and lame, as I've said before, sex doesn't just happen. It has to be planned, anticipated, and budgeted.

Couples schedule sex in different ways. Some naturally fall into a pattern or understanding that they have sex so many times a week. If it has been a few days since they were intimate, both partners intuitively know that it's time to "go to bed a little early tonight." Although this works well for some couples, most need a more concrete understanding of when and how often sex will happen.

I recently heard about a unique agreement that one couple reached. After a decade of "not tonight" discussions, they came up with this solution: He initiates sex once on Monday, Tuesday, or Wednesday, and she initiates once on Friday, Saturday, or Sunday; they take Thursdays off. Instead of taking the romance out of sex, a schedule like this actually reduces tension and increases the chances of great sex.

In this case, the woman (let's call her Jess) wanted to have sex on average about once a week, while her husband (let's call him Seth) wanted sex three or four times per week. It seemed like every night Seth was initiating and Jess was avoiding.

Once they started scheduling sex, Seth could relax knowing that he would have sex at least twice a week and that his wife would actually be initiating one of those times. Jess could relax knowing that she wouldn't be hounded every time she changed her clothes. She also began to anticipate sex, thinking about it and resting up for the night she planned to initiate.

Another way of scheduling without the use of a PalmPilot or a color-coded calendar is what Mike and I call a "requisition order." A requisition order is a shot across the bow giving the not-so-subtle hint that you're ready for some action in the near future. For example, instead of

expecting you to read his body language as he kisses you on his way out the door in the morning, your husband communicates a requisition order for later in the evening. Again, this gives you time to anticipate, change your expectations of what you wanted to get done that evening, or even slip in a catnap before dinner.

Normal but Great

As you read about heating up your sex life, you may have terrifying images of swinging from chandeliers, joining the Mile High Club, taking flexibility classes, or wearing thong underwear to work every day. Relax. None of these things are necessary. In fact, great married sex can be absolutely normal.

One of the secrets to having a passionate sex life is accepting that great sex doesn't have to be wild or perverse. The greatest lovers aren't those who feel pressure to perform or the need to come up with something new and exciting for every encounter. Lovers understand and accept that much of their relationship consists of "normal" lovemaking. There are times when the passion is naturally stronger, and other times when sex seems to take a back burner. What makes the difference is the commitment to work toward becoming better lovers for each other through all of the ups and downs of your relationship.

As Ecclesiastes 3:1 states, "There is a . . . season for every activity under heaven." There are seasons of marriage where parenting, health concerns, and dealing with significant stress overshadow sex. But there must also be prolonged seasons when you and your husband make a concerted effort to learn to love each other and to celebrate that love through the gift of sex.

God in His goodness has given you and your husband the gift of physical intimacy. It's not the wrong size, the wrong color, or out of style.

It is perfect for you, but there is some assembly required. To thoroughly enjoy the gift God has given you over a lifetime, make the effort to invest in it.

The velveteen rabbit that is missing an eye, the worn Bible that has ripped pages and a broken binding, the tattered blanket that a child can't bear to part with—these are the gifts that mean the most to us. The givers of such gifts are thrilled to know that they have picked out something so perfect that it bears the scars of constant use.

Don't allow the gift of your sexuality to be the pristine antique that sits on a shelf. Thoroughly enjoy, explore, and use it. Make your sex life with your husband so fulfilling that the Giver of this great gift will smile with satisfaction over how His offering has blessed you.

SOMETHING TO THINK ABOUT • • • • •

1. Which barrier(s) mentioned in this chapter most interfere(s) with your pleasure in sexuality?
   - Being sexual seems contradictory to being a godly woman.
   - I just can't get into it.
   - I don't know how to enjoy it.
   - We don't have the time and energy.
   - I don't see myself as sexual.

   Consider talking to your husband about changes you can make together to address this barrier and work toward a great sex life.

2. What do you think about your sex life becoming "normal, but great"?

three

Is It Good to Be a Bad Girl?

Some friends of ours (we'll call them George and Liz) recently told us about something that happened to them several years ago during a romantic getaway. Because their trip was during the hottest part of the summer, they got a bargain on a room in a beautiful hotel in Miami.

One evening while they were swimming in the hotel pool, George started making moves on Liz. She suggested that they take the party to their room. George, being the adventurous guy he is, pointed out that the pool was deserted. No one would know or care if they went skinny-dipping together and fooled around in the pool. Liz protested but eventually gave in. She kept a close eye on the pool area and made sure that their towels and bathing suits were readily available.

Later in the evening, George and Liz went into the dining area for dinner. To their horror, they noticed that the bar sported a front-seat view right into the pool. The entire wall was a window! Liz ran upstairs to their room in tears. George actually got a kick out of the whole situation.

Not only is this a true story, but it represents a classic struggle that every married couple has to deal with: Within the context of marital love, are there boundaries for what is acceptable? What are the limits to the freedom a husband and wife have to enjoy each other sexually? It

seems impossible to have an honest discussion about sex without stumbling on this issue.

In many cases, a husband and wife will disagree on the answers to these questions. Often, like George and Liz, the husband is more prone to pushing the envelope with suggestions of risky behavior or crude language. However, as a younger generation of women are becoming more comfortable with their sexuality and are increasingly exposed to sensual content, they may also desire "taboo" sexual activity.

It is critical that a husband and wife come to an agreement on issues that border on sexual immorality or inappropriate behavior. Unfortunately, there is very little help in sorting through how to make these judgments. What makes matters worse is that many Christian leaders and experts don't always agree on what sexual behavior is okay and what is not. For example, is it okay for a guy to take sexual pictures of his wife and masturbate looking at those pictures when he is away from her? Solid Christian men and women have a variety of responses to this question. There is no easy right or wrong answer.

Why Fences Are Important

I first heard the story of Adam and Eve as a little girl. Since that time, I've heard and read the drama countless times, so all of the details are familiar to me. Throughout my education, I've debated and argued about what the Fall says about human nature, our sinfulness, and our relationship to God. Only recently has a new angle to this narrative occurred to me. Why was Eve engaged in a discussion about the forbidden tree in the first place? Was she lingering by it when the serpent approached her?

Genesis doesn't give us too many details about the garden of Eden, but I can imagine that it was a pretty impressive place. While there was one tree the couple couldn't eat from, there were probably thousands of plants and other trees they were encouraged to enjoy. The garden had

everything the couple could want. Whatever it contained could have occupied and fulfilled them for many lifetimes. So why focus on the forbidden object? Why do we, like the first couple, have the proclivity to flirt with danger and with the prohibited?

Many married couples spend far more time and energy ruminating about and flirting with the "forbidden" aspects of sex than they do thoroughly enjoying the multitude of pure pleasures God designed for them to experience. Some don't know how to enjoy sex without tasting forbidden fruit. Excitement is often automatically linked with doing or imagining something off-limits. Just think about terms used to describe exciting sex, such as "bad girl" or "naughty." The sexual response in a man or woman eventually becomes dependent on the adrenaline rush of doing something new, exciting, and taboo. This is a legitimate concern related to trying new things or turning up the bedroom "heat." Although enjoying, exploring, and experimenting as a married couple is wonderful, the paths such activities take can be both morally wrong and destructive to your marriage.

Perhaps in your marriage, you have felt the guilt and shame of going outside of the perimeter of what you believe is right before God. The sting of those experiences may have made you more leery and reserved sexually. Like Eve, you hide behind a tree, no longer free to roam and enjoy the garden. Afraid of the temptation represented by the forbidden tree, you feel safer huddled behind a bush.

It is impossible to freely enjoy God's gift of sex without a firm understanding of the dangerous trees in the garden. God, in His love and wisdom, gives us guidelines to keep us safe from the dangers that can attach themselves to the gift of sex. Sex beyond the boundaries of God's intention ends up creating distance, hostility, and anxiety rather than unity and love.

From my days in graduate school, I vaguely remember hearing about an experiment conducted to observe the effect of boundaries on

anxiety levels. Psychologists studied the impact on children when fences were installed around a playground on a busy city block. Without fences, the children were anxious and tended to play huddled in the middle of the play area, avoiding the dangerous perimeter. When fences were installed all around the playground, the kids played freely and used the entire fenced-in area. The clear boundaries and protection of the fence allowed the kids to feel safe enough to have fun even in a dangerous neighborhood.

Apply this truth to your sex life. Without "fences" to protect your relationship from perversion, you may be restrained from enjoying all of what God has given you to share with your husband. Or you may be so fascinated with testing the unseen boundaries that you completely ignore superior pleasures granted by God.

Finding the Fences

Inevitably, women want to know where these fences are as they enjoy sex within marriage. They wonder about sex toys, fantasy, role-playing, mutual masturbation, having sex in a public place, the use of foul words during sex, and many other "Is it okay?" questions. We could go through a list like this, and I could give you my opinion on what's okay and what crosses the line. But I'm not going to do that for a few reasons. First of all, my opinion is just that. There are many godly, wise people who would disagree with my opinion. Second, whenever we make clear moral statements where the Bible is silent, we become legalistic. In some cases, God has given us clear moral guidelines such as prohibitions against fornication and adultery. Yet in many other cases, we simply have biblical principles to pray through and apply to everyday life. There are many gray areas that require discernment and wise judgment when it comes to understanding God's best for us sexually in marriage.

Instead of going through a host of "what's okay?" discussions, I think

it's more helpful to look at basic principles that help us determine the fences that God has set up for us in the playground of marital sexuality. Within these fences, we're free to play and enjoy sex without guilt and condemnation.

The Old Testament records the spiritual history of the nation of Israel. If you've ever endeavored to read through the entire Bible, you probably recall struggling through Leviticus, Numbers, and Deuteronomy. This portion of the Bible spells out the meticulous laws the nation of Israel was bound to keep in their covenant with God. The Law left very little to question. Along with expected sexual prohibitions such as don't have sex with animals or with your father-in-law, a married couple was also not allowed to have sexual intercourse during the woman's menstruation. After having sex, a couple had to bathe and was considered "unclean" until the next day. I'm sure this brought up a few awkward discussions with the in-laws when the couple didn't show up for evening events.

Thank God, since the death of Christ on the cross, the Old Testament Law no longer condemns us. Jesus has fully satisfied the demands of the Law, freeing us from its cultural and ceremonial aspects, which were only images and shadows of the reality that was to come in Christ (see Hebrews 8:5 and 10:1, and Acts 15:22–29—and note that commandments concerning sexual immorality do *not* fall into this category!). Jesus has embodied the righteous requirements of the Law in Himself, and He calls us to do the same by living according to the Royal Law of Love (Romans 13:8-10; James 2:8).

All questions about what is right and wrong require that we wrestle through the principles of what it means to honor God in our sexuality and in our love for one another. Fortunately, the apostle Paul's letters help us navigate the difficult questions of Christian living. In his letter to the church at Corinth, Paul instructed Christians concerning how to respond to sexual temptation and also how to make decisions about the gray areas of honoring God on this earth. I encourage you to read 1 Corinthians to

understand the context of the guidelines God has given us.

In this chapter, we'll explore specific and relevant fences based on Paul's letter to the Corinthians. Although these principles were written 2,000 years ago, they can still help us determine how to glorify God through sexual intimacy.

Fence No. 1: Sex Must Involve Only You and Your Husband

> *It is said, "The two will become one flesh." But he who unites himself with the Lord is one with him in spirit. Flee from sexual immorality. All other sins a man commits are outside his body, but he who sins sexually sins against his own body.*
> —1 CORINTHIANS 6:16B–18

This passage, along with others throughout the Bible, clearly teaches that the primary purpose of sexual intimacy is to bond two people together in the formation of a new family. Sex is more than simply experiencing physical pleasure; it is an outward expression of the permanent fusion of two lives through marriage.

Paul's teaching on sexual purity emphasizes that sexual sins are destructive not only to marriage but also to our communion with God. If you are a follower of Christ, the Holy Spirit resides in you. You are a living, breathing, moving temple. Adultery and fornication invite sin to be unified with God's holy presence. Our culture marginalizes sexual sin, justifying it with excuses like "It's okay if two people really love each other," or "God wants us to experience love and feel good." The apostle Paul's stern reminder in essence says, "Don't you dare minimize the importance of sexual purity for marriage! Respect the presence of the Holy Spirit within you."

All of us are prone to temptation and falling into an immoral relationship. If King David, the apple of God's eye, could fall, certainly so can we. Justifying an inappropriate relationship is very easy to do. Even

so, most Christian couples readily accept the fact that sexual expression should just involve husband and wife. What is more often disputed is using the mental image of another person to enhance a couple's sexual experience. For example, is it okay to role-play, imagining that another person (real or fictional) is present during sex? How about watching sexually explicit movies together as husband and wife? In a graduate course in human sexuality at a secular university, my professor suggested this very thing as an effective way to sexually stimulate each other.

Jesus addressed this question in the Sermon on the Mount. He taught, "You have heard that it was said, 'Do not commit adultery.' But I tell you that anyone who looks at a woman lustfully has already committed adultery with her in his heart" (Matthew 5:27–28). Jesus' words teach us that mental and emotional boundaries are just as important as physical boundaries. Even the fictional presence of someone else in the bedroom is a violation of the intimacy designed for husband and wife alone.

The implications of this fence are clear as they relate to pornography, sexually explicit romance novels, and other material that promote thinking sexually about people other than your spouse. Anytime another person is physically or emotionally introduced into sexual intimacy (even in your imagination), you are flirting with fruit that compromises the purity of marital intimacy. This is a high standard! Yet it's ultimately for your protection and enjoyment. (We'll spend more time looking at the implications of this fence in chapters 9 and 10.)

Fence No. 2: Sex Must Be Beneficial to Both of You

> "Everything is permissible"—but not everything is beneficial.
> —1 CORINTHIANS 10:23

How do you determine if some gray area of sexuality is beneficial for your marriage? This fence can seem so fuzzy that it hardly seems helpful. When would sex between a husband and wife not be beneficial?

The fields of biology and psychology clearly demonstrate the great benefits of a healthy sex life to both the body and the mind. As we discussed earlier, sex produces hormones that literally make both the man and the woman feel closer to each other. Sex also improves your immune system, helps prevent heart disease and cancer, improves your memory, and even releases hormones that can slow the aging process.

Yet in spite of all of its benefits, sex can become a very destructive force, even between husband and wife. Satan loves to take what God created and twist it into a tool of discord and pain. While sex was designed to display love and unselfishness, it can become a tool of oppression, humiliation, guilt, and shame.

Steve and Debbie were in their early 20s and had been married a couple of years. Steve had an extremely strong sex drive. In fact, he confessed that one of his primary motivations for marrying Debbie right out of high school was that he didn't believe he could tame his sexual urges as a single man. Every day Steve expected, and sometimes demanded, sex from Debbie. Whether she was tired, sick, or emotionally distant, Debbie was clearly expected to be sexually available to her husband. Beyond having sex every day, Steve also pushed the boundaries of what Debbie was comfortable doing and saying. At times Debbie resisted. But eventually she would be so eager for the ordeal to be over that she would say or do anything to help Steve achieve orgasm.

Given these dynamics, it's no surprise that Debbie started to hate sex. She couldn't think of a time when she had actually enjoyed it. Yet every time she brought up her pain and concerns, Steve was armed with the "biblical mandate" for her to meet his sexual needs. He threatened to act out sexually if she was unwilling to fulfill his desires.

The problems in Steve and Debbie's sex life reflected a number of dysfunctional patterns that were playing out in other aspects of their

marriage. Sex was very one-sided and ultimately destructive to both of them. Whereas their sexual relationship caused Debbie to feel violated and used, it enabled Steve to become more and more selfish and demanding. This is just one example of how married sexuality can fail to be beneficial.

While you and your husband are free to enjoy each other sexually, love demands that you limit your expressions to what is beneficial and not destructive. In evaluating the whole nature of your sex life or a specific gray area, ask each other, "Does it bring us closer together as a couple or separate us? Is it painful or harmful to either of us physically, spiritually, or emotionally?"

Fence No. 3: Sex Must Not Be Enslaving

*"Everything is permissible for me"—but I will
not be mastered by anything.*
—1 CORINTHIANS 6:12B

Although God created and blesses our sexuality, sexual desire can quickly become a mastering force that enslaves us. Just because a person gets married doesn't mean that he or she won't struggle with the addictive aspects of sexuality.

Healthy sexuality is a natural, reoccurring need, not an obsession. Food is a good parallel. Your body needs food regularly. When you don't eat for an extended period of time, a growling stomach, hunger pangs, and a mild headache compel you to seek nourishment. But for some, the natural desire for food becomes an obsessive drive in their lives. Beyond the basic need for nourishment, food becomes an avenue to quiet anxiety, escape loneliness, extinguish boredom, or temporarily comfort depression. Emotional rather than physiological needs become the primary triggers to eat. The urge to eat and/or the compulsion to restrict food

intake can become a dominant force in a person's life, absorbing all of one's attention.

The same is true of sexuality. In your marriage, sex should be a regular occurrence. When you abstain for a period of time, your bodies and your relationship should begin to groan for intimacy, indicating that your marriage needs the nourishment of oneness. Yet even within the context of marriage, sexual urges can stem from unhealthy needs such as loneliness, anger, depression, and anxiety. Having sex or avoiding sex can become a mastering force in a person's life.

Going back to Steve and Debbie's marriage, you might not be surprised to learn that Steve had a longstanding addiction to pornography. Instead of dealing with his addiction, he used Debbie as an outlet. In fact, sometimes he would see a pornographic image at work and race home to have sex with his wife. Their sexual relationship became nothing more than a vehicle through which he could act out his addiction. No wonder she felt used!

Sexuality, for both men and women, can be a ravenous beast that always demands more. What aroused you last year may no longer be arousing today, so you look for new and more exciting ways to satisfy your sexual desires. Married couples can fall into the trap of constantly seeking more erotic stimuli so that their sexual experience can be more fully satisfying. For example, a couple begins with mild sexual fantasies. For a few months, this is exciting and arousing. Over time, to keep their sex life going, the fantasies begin involving other people. The thrill of pushing the limit is intoxicating. When that becomes mundane, they begin renting sexually explicit R-rated movies or soft porn to watch together. That moves into viewing more explicit pornography, and so on.

An important question to ask is, "Could this possibly begin to master one or both of us?" Don't be deceived into thinking that marriage in-

sulates you from the enslaving power of sexual desire. As Jesus warned, "I tell you the truth, everyone who sins is a slave to sin" (John 8:34).

Fence No. 4: Sex Must Not Violate Your Conscience

Since their conscience is weak, it is defiled.
—1 CORINTHIANS 8:7B

As the apostle Paul continued to teach the early church about gray areas in life, he stated that our consciences are very important in determining how to behave. If we do something we don't feel right about, our consciences become "defiled." Paul's answer to the question of which behaviors are okay and which aren't, in essence, was "It's okay, if your conscience doesn't condemn you."

This implies that for some Christians, a particular sexual behavior may be right, while for others it may be wrong. For example, some Christian couples believe that it is okay for them to individually masturbate while they are physically separated from each other. Others believe that this is a violation of their marital covenant. Based on Paul's teaching, perhaps they are both right.

The Holy Spirit actively and individually convicts us of sin. Based on our past, our weaknesses, the culture we live in, and our spiritual maturity, we may have different standards of conscience that serve as the benchmarks of what is right and wrong.

Conscience is a tricky thing. While Paul teaches that the conviction of the Holy Spirit and our gut feelings of right and wrong (determined by conscience) are important guides, he also warns that our consciences can mislead us (1 Corinthians 4). Our consciences can convict us when we're innocent, or they can fail to condemn us when we're guilty.

False guilt: the case of an overactive conscience. A group of married women got together for their biweekly prayer and gab session. One

particular afternoon, the topic turned to sex. Along with the typical complaints about the lack of energy or romance, the group started to share about ways to infuse some excitement into marriage. Most of the women had given birth within the last few years and felt like old housewives. One of the women suggested going to the underwear store and mixing in some "sexy undies" with the standard "granny panties." Holly was embarrassed and disgusted that her Christian friends would suggest wearing lacy underwear and thongs. Although she couldn't voice a logical or biblical reason why she was offended, she simply couldn't accept that God would be okay with this.

The underwear incident wasn't an isolated event. Holly held very strict guidelines for what was and wasn't sexually appropriate for a married couple. Oral sex, explicit talk, and even extravagant expressions of pleasure were sinful for her and for others. She viewed sex as necessary for procreation. She felt guilty whenever she allowed her mind to wander sexually, even if her fantasies involved her husband. During the few occasions she had an orgasm, she was embarrassed and even angry with her husband for awakening a desire that she felt was sinful.

Holly's conscience isn't a clear guide for her or for her marriage. In her case, legalistic and destructive teaching has misguided her, resulting in a guilty conscience and dirty feelings about sex. She uses her rigid standard of purity to condemn her husband and others who feel free to enjoy the gift of marital sex.

Ironically, the apostle Paul wrote about an overly strict conscience as a sign of an immature Christian. Most of us, when we come to Christ, don't know how to please God beyond following a list of rules. We evaluate each other based on how carefully and dutifully we conform to the dos and don'ts of Christian living. As we grow in Christ and become more sensitive to the prompting of the Holy Spirit, the list falls away. Our primary goal becomes not to cause God grief. Like a sensitive child, we're in tune with what our Father desires for us. Legalistic rules of right

and wrong become obsolete as love for God's righteousness and intimacy with Him become a consuming fire.

Faith that never moves beyond a list of rules is unhealthy faith based on the fear of punishment. Paul rebuked many members of the early church for their lack of growth and spiritual maturity because they still clung to legalism. As your relationship with God grows and your marriage matures, your conscience should continue to reflect God's standards. Yet within those standards, you should experience greater freedom sexually, not more restriction.

No standards: a case of a seared conscience. Rachel claimed to be a sincere follower of Christ. Because of her profession of faith, I was floored by what she said to me in counseling. She was in an unfulfilling marriage that lacked any sense of romance. She and her husband rarely talked and never touched. According to Rachel, because God knew her needs for intimacy and love, He provided another man for her. David was a godly man she met at a Bible study. As the attraction between Rachel and David grew, they shared how empty they felt in their respective marriages. Both felt neglected, unloved, unappreciated, and unhappy. Within a few months, Rachel and David were talking daily, sharing their dreams and heartaches. They even began meeting to pray together. Nature eventually took its course, and their emotional intimacy led to physical intimacy.

By the time Rachel came to counseling, she was convinced that David was her soul mate. She emphatically declared that he was the spiritual leader God wanted her to have. She believed that he understood her like her husband never had.

Beyond the cloud of romance and hormones, Rachel and David's relationship was from the pit of hell. Regardless of how fulfilling it felt, it was adulterous and sinful. Yet they had both allowed their own hearts to deceive them into believing that their sin was a gift from God.

Before we pick up stones to throw at Rachel and David, we must

acknowledge that we all are prone to justify our own sin. We watch inappropriate movies, listen to off-color jokes, gossip, slander, covet, and judge others, all under the guise of Christian concern, tolerance, and freedom.

Several years ago, Mike had an early morning job interview. The day before, he picked out his clothes for the meeting and even went for a dry run to make sure he wouldn't get lost on the big day. The interview was scheduled for 7:30 in the morning. As I took care of the baby and prepared breakfast, I yelled to Mike, "Aren't you going to be late?"

Mike replied calmly, "I'm fine. It's not even 6:30. I've got plenty of time."

I looked at the kitchen clock, which said 7:10, and then relayed the bad news to my husband. He was horrified to realize that his watch had stopped.

Your conscience is an external indicator, like a watch, that should reflect the truth. However, there are times when your conscience can be broken. You can be going through life making decisions based on inaccurate information. The prophet Jeremiah profoundly stated, "The heart is deceitful above all things and beyond cure. Who can understand it?" (Jeremiah 17:9).

While your conscience is an external dial, the Word of the Lord is a mirror. Clocks, fuel gauges, speedometers, and thermometers can be wrong, but mirrors do not lie. The New Testament writer James encourages us to consistently evaluate our hearts and behaviors in light of the mirror of God's law and grace (see James 1:25).

The Word of God can help you distinguish between conscience and comfort. Just because you may not be comfortable doing something doesn't necessarily mean that you should feel guilty doing it. While you never want to push past your conscience, growing sexually might mean that you need to push beyond your comfort level. In the same vein, just because you're comfortable with something doesn't mean it's right. As a

follower of Christ, you may be called to give up what feels comfortable for the sake of doing what is right.

Fence No. 5: Sex Must Not Be a Stumbling Block

"Everything is permissible"—but not everything is constructive. Nobody should seek his own good, but the good of others. . . . Do not cause anyone to stumble.
—1 CORINTHIANS 10:23B–24, 32A

As if wrestling with our own consciences isn't difficult enough, we also have to be sensitive to the impact of our behavior on others. The most important and natural application of this to marriage is how husband and wife impact each other.

Jamie came to counseling with her new husband, Brad, to address a host of issues. When Jamie was a young child, a distant relative had repeatedly molested her. Throughout her teen years, she had repressed the memories of this abuse. When she and her husband were married and began their sexual relationship, the memories came flooding back. Jamie couldn't separate sex from feeling dirty and violated. Brad's flirtations and sexual advances made her freeze up and respond with anger toward him. Jamie felt like a failure as a wife because she couldn't enjoy intimacy with her husband.

Although counseling helped Jamie work through her painful memories and much of the shame associated with her past, she still needed her husband to approach her with great tenderness and sensitivity. Certain words or sexual positions were triggers for the feelings of disgust and violation linked to the abuse. Although Jamie and Brad are free to experience the full range of their sexuality together, they choose to limit their expressions based on Jamie's weakness. Out of love for God and for his wife, Brad limits his own freedom to avoid causing his wife pain.

The stumbling-block principle is also applicable to temptation.

What causes you to stumble sexually may be very different from what is tempting for your husband. For example, one day during lovemaking, Mandy told her husband, John, that she was planning to surprise him at work. She instructed him to picture her walking into his office wearing an overcoat with nothing on underneath. Although Mandy didn't realize it, John faces a lot of sexual temptation working closely with a few attractive, flirtatious women at his office. The fantasy Mandy suggested is a stumbling block to him, bringing eroticism into work as he is struggling to separate the two.

Withholding sex can also be a significant stumbling block. Turning again to Paul's teaching, we read that neither husband nor wife has permission to withhold sex from the other. Going long periods of time without sexual intimacy, even for good reasons, puts you at risk to give in to temptation (see 1 Corinthians 7:4–5).

Beyond causing each other to stumble, you must also be conscious of how your speech and behavior impact the cause of Christ in general. Several years ago, I attended a marriage seminar at a local church. Although the husband and wife who taught the seminar were older Christians and very effective communicators, one of their examples ruined the whole seminar for me. They shared that in an effort to spice things up, they would sometimes drive around town together at night with little or nothing on. They told one story about trying to cover up a bit as they ordered food at a drive-through.

This married couple was certainly free to be naked together and enjoy each other's bodies; however, the way they exercised this freedom (especially as Christian leaders) is questionable. I was creeped out by the thought of them driving around together naked. I kept wondering what the result would have been if a policeman had pulled them over or their car had broken down. And worse, what effect would their actions have had on a teenager working the window at the drive-through? I attended this seminar almost 20 years ago, and this example is the only thing I re-

member from it! The most important question for this couple to wrestle with is this: "Is exercising our freedom possibly a stumbling block to younger Christians or even to unbelievers?"

Wherever you go, people watch you. You are a representative of Christ if you go by the name "Christian." Your marriage, ideally, should say to the world that marriage based on the principles of God is amazing. Followers of Christ should have a love for each other and a freedom in marriage that puts the world to shame. Yet how we express that freedom should be above reproach, never causing others to stumble morally.

The Ultimate Fence: Honor God with Your Body

You are not your own; you were bought at a price.
Therefore honor God with your body.
—1 Corinthians 6:19b–20

My nine-year-old son was invited to spend a few days at his friend's house. As I packed his bags and kissed him good-bye, I wondered how to communicate to him my expectations for his behavior. I could have said something like "Make sure you say please and thank you, eat whatever is put in front of you without complaining, help with chores, chew with your mouth closed, don't fight or argue, obey Brady's parents, be respectful, go straight to bed when they tell you to, brush your teeth every night, and oh yeah, close the door when you go to the bathroom" (yes, you have to remind nine-year-old boys to do this!).

Instead, what I said was, "Do the right thing. I want to hear a good report about your behavior."

Although a list of rules is more burdensome, the admonishment to "do the right thing" is far more comprehensive. It requires my son to think through situations that I couldn't even anticipate for him. Instead of a list of rules about our sexual behavior, the apostle Paul summed it

up by reminding us to honor God with our bodies. His instruction isn't burdensome, but it is still heavy. It means that whenever we wonder whether something is right or wrong, we must ultimately answer the question, "Am I honoring God with my body?"

Remember that God is honored when we love each other, laying down our own needs to serve our husbands. He is honored when we enjoy the pure gift of sex that He has created for married couples to experience. He is honored when we turn our eyes from offensive material and when we forgive someone who has offended us.

Although it may be difficult to talk with your husband about fences in your sexual relationship, setting and agreeing upon boundaries to keep your marital intimacy pure will ultimately give you the freedom to enjoy the full buffet that God has ordained for you and your husband.

So, What *Can* We Do?

Recently I had a spirited conversation with a friend about the principles in this chapter. "Where do you draw the line between healthy romantic input and immorality?" she asked.

"Well," I said, "when the sexual stimulation is focused on things and people outside the marriage, it becomes immoral."

"There are all kinds of outside things that can create healthy sexual feelings," she countered. "For example, seeing an older couple walking down the street, hand in hand and still in love. That inspires romantic and passionate feelings."

I had to admit that she had a point. A love song, a romantic story, or the ambiance of a dinner for two are all outside events that can prompt sexual feelings. So how do we define right and wrong in romance? Where does the line of immorality fall? Surely, God doesn't want us to cloister ourselves behind the closed doors of the bedroom with no imagination or inspiration for love. How boring would that be!

While the majority of this chapter focused on fences we need to build around our marital relationship as a protection against perversion, I'd like to talk for a moment about the healthy aspects of sexuality in marriage that we can chase after passionately, without fear of crossing the line into perversion. Many portions of Scripture provide guidelines and prohibitions regarding how to live our lives. However, the overarching theme of the Bible paints a picture of the wonderful things we can pursue wholeheartedly. In his letter to the Philippian church, Paul told believers what to focus on: "Finally, brothers, whatever is true, whatever is noble, whatever is right, whatever is pure, whatever is lovely, whatever is admirable—if anything is excellent or praiseworthy—think about such things" (Philippians 4:8).

Paul's teaching is applicable to your sexual relationship. While a sexually explicit film is neither true nor lovely, there is much in your environment that is. Think sexually about things that edify each other, that represent the pure passion that God designed for marriage. Use your imagination in ways that heighten the love you feel for your husband, not fantasies that keep you dissatisfied. For example, create a sensual atmosphere in your bedroom with candles, music, massage oil, and your favorite treats. Pull out love letters you wrote to each other earlier in your relationship. Share together about times where you felt especially intimate, physically and emotionally.

Most theologians agree that underlying Satan's temptation in the garden (and every temptation since) was the question of God's goodness. Satan planted the idea in Eve's mind that sin would be more profitable than God's plan. Every human has since wrestled with that thought. Will my way (or the world's way) ultimately bring more pleasure than what God prescribes? Does He really have my best in mind or is He out to spoil my pleasure?

Nowhere is this struggle more evident than in sex. Do you truly believe that God's design for sex is better, more exciting, and more

fulfilling than the world's? Do you trust His goodness in this area of your marriage? Do you believe that if you honor the fences He has designed, you will experience goodness and fulfillment? If so, embrace the freedom God has given you within those boundaries and explore the vast array of communion and pleasure that God has prepared for you in the garden of your marriage.

SOMETHING TO THINK ABOUT • • • • •

1. This might be a great chapter to go over with your husband. Talk with him about the "fences" and how they play out in your marriage.

2. How do you feel about having "fences" rather than specific rules regarding your sexuality?

four

Is "Sexy Mom" an Oxymoron?

Having sex greatly increases your chances of having children. However, having children does not increase your chances of having sex!

At virtually every stage, children find a way to interfere with their parents' enjoyment of physical intimacy. Both the fatigue of having an infant crying all night and the anxiety of having a teen who is an hour late returning from a date will effectively sabotage your love life.

Although parenthood is made up of many different challenging stages, don't fall into the fallacy of thinking that "this is just a passing phase." Once you have children, the parenting stage will be with you for the better part of your life. By the time this stage is over, you may have sagging breasts, you may have wrinkles everywhere, and you might be plucking hair out of your husband's ears. When the nest is finally empty, you very well may need an oxygen tank and a host of prescription medications to engage in sex with your husband. Though I'm exaggerating just a bit, the point is, don't squander the gift of sex while you wait for parenthood to end!

Sex and the Stages of Parenting

Each stage of parenting presents its own challenges to protecting the time, energy, and desire for sex. Maintaining a healthy and fulfilling sex

life throughout the parenting years requires both creativity and planning. So let's talk a bit about the obstacles each stage presents to sustaining your sex life.

Stage 1: Welcome to Our Factory

"My husband and I have been trying to conceive a baby for the past two years. It's taken all the fun out of sex. We plan to have intercourse based on when I'm ovulating and try to do everything a certain way to increase our chances of conceiving. My husband doesn't even want to do it anymore. The romance, the spontaneity, and the passion—it's all gone. All I can think about while we're having sex is 'please conceive!' "

This woman's statement reflects how many wives feel when they're trying to conceive. Fortunately for most couples, the "factory" stage of parenthood is relatively short. Within six months or so of trying, they conceive and graduate to other, noisier barriers to sex. However, for those couples who try for years to conceive, sex becomes a scientific performance and even a reminder of their disappointment or failure. They can begin to point fingers at each other and become easily frustrated when yet another month goes by without a positive pregnancy test.

If you're in this stage, you probably get one of two responses from everyone you talk to. Some people give you their (sometimes very ridiculous) formulas. "Well, we heard that if you drink a whole bottle of A1 Steak Sauce before having sex, and then do it with the wife standing on her head, you're sure to conceive a boy. We tried it, and it worked the first time for us." The second piece of advice you probably get most of the time is, "Relax and have fun! We tried to conceive for four years. As soon as we relaxed and just enjoyed sex again—whammo!—we got pregnant!"

As well meaning as these folks may be, their advice just stings. They may not have gotten you any closer to pregnancy, but they did give you

a foretaste of what morning sickness feels like. So, I hesitate to give any advice, quick fixes, or midwives' suggestions at this stage.

I will say that this is a very difficult barrier for couples to face. Make sure you're facing it together. Because you and your husband probably have very different ways of handling this challenge, you may be tempted to go into your respective corners and stop communicating. Typically, a husband doesn't understand the strong emotions his wife may experience with infertility. "There's always next month," he tries to reassure his wife. Likewise, wives don't understand the underlying performance demands that guys sometimes feel during infertility.

When one of our good friends told us that he and his wife were pregnant for the first time, the new father proudly exclaimed, "My boys can swim!" It sounds silly from a woman's perspective, but much of a man's feelings of masculinity can be tied up in his ability to get his wife pregnant. While you may be pining away, dreaming about a nursery filled with cute little clothes, he may be battling fears of inadequacy. He may feel even more inept about his inability to comfort you. Just think of the story of Hannah in 1 Samuel 1. In the midst of her despair over not having children, Hannah's husband tried to comfort her out of his own inadequacy: "Hannah, why are you weeping? Why don't you eat? Why are you downhearted? Don't I mean more to you than ten sons?" (verse 8). Now that's a clueless husband!

If you're struggling with infertility, keep in mind that someday your struggle will end. One day you will resolve it in one of three ways: by giving birth, by choosing to adopt, or by choosing to remain childless. What will outlast the struggle is how you and your husband deal with it together. Will you allow seeds of bitterness, selfishness, and division to be sown? Or will you choose to believe that God can use this struggle to forge your hearts together? If you choose the latter, you just may find great love and passion refined in the "factory."

Stage 2: Three's a Crowd

The hand that rocks the cradle wants nothing to do with sex.

Nothing can put a crimp in your sex life like a newborn. An infant can absorb seemingly endless amounts of attention and energy, especially from the mother. The relationship between mother and child is symbiotic. Symbiosis is defined in Webster's as "the intimate living together of two dissimilar organisms in a mutually beneficial relationship."

Motherhood is an amazing thing. Please understand that I have never regretted having children. *But* mothers can feel like they're joined at the hip with their offspring, especially during pregnancy and infancy.

My body changed a lot during pregnancy. Although I didn't like the extra weight, the stretch marks, or hemorrhoids, I was under the illusion that they were all temporary. I'm one of the rookies who took a pair of size 6 jeans to the hospital to change into after having my first baby. (I also brought a Nerf basketball hoop to the hospital so that Mike and I could play some one-on-one during labor. No kidding!) I still remember my horror when I saw the brown, crumpled paper bag that was now my stomach a few days after delivery.

If you're either pregnant or recently had a baby, you know that your body is not your own. As much as you love your little appendage, you will never be the same emotionally or physically. This requires a significant shift in your approach to sex.

The most obvious barriers to sex during this stage are physical. The "missionary position" doesn't work very well during the seventh month of pregnancy. The romance evaporates when your husband fondles your breasts only to be squirted by breast milk (creative guys just bring cookies to bed). Although the physical effects of pregnancy and nursing are time limited, they pose a significant barrier to sexual intimacy. You have to be a little creative and bring your sense of humor into the bedroom.

When you were first married, if you told someone that you and your husband were up all night, certain assumptions would follow. "Oh,

it sounds like you had fun!" But when you have a newborn, pulling an all-nighter has a completely different implication. Night runs into day, and clocks become irrelevant. If someone were to ask you the time, you might respond by trying to figure out how many times you've fed the baby in the last 24 hours.

To add to the physical challenges of new parents, having a baby can be very stressful. Women usually worry about their ability to care for their newborn, while men stress about providing financially. Having a baby is, in fact, one of the most stressful events of your life. It requires tremendous adjustments.

Some women also have a mental block about engaging in sex during pregnancy or for a time after giving birth. They can't reconcile the contrast between carrying an innocent, fragile baby and engaging in passionate sex with their husbands. It almost feels like watching an R-rated movie in church. Again, this reveals the underlying attitude that sex is somehow tainted or dirty. These apprehensions gradually pass as a woman realizes that sex isn't so dirty and that babies aren't so innocent.

Sex isn't the only thing that gets squeezed out of marriage during the symbiotic stage. Many couples feel as though they begin emotionally drifting apart after the birth of a baby. While the new mom is consumed with caring for her baby, the dad can feel left out.

Give yourself about four months to be completely consumed with motherhood. I suggest reserving the last two months of pregnancy and the first two months after the baby is born. Your body is wired to be completely focused on nurturing, nesting, and healing. Your husband will likely feel as though he has lost a piece of his wife. During this period, explain to your husband that this is a unique time that won't last forever. Although you may not be available for sex the way you usually are, be creative in trying to meet his needs. Your body has changed, but his has not.

When your baby is about two months old, things should begin to settle into a new "normal." Your body has likely recovered from giving birth, the baby is probably getting into more of a routine and sleeping longer at night, and a bit of your sanity should be returning. At this point, make a concerted effort to work toward intimacy. As difficult as it may be, reserve some time and energy for talking and renewing your bond with your husband.

Also, involve your husband in parenting. He probably won't hold or dress the baby the same way you do, but that's okay. If you don't share the experience of parenting with him, it will become a divisive rather than a unifying force in your marriage.

Stage 3: The Energizer Bunny Stage

We're chasing someone around the house, but not each other!

There are few things on this earth cuter than a toddler. Their sweet little voices, their absolute fascination with everything around them, their chubby hands and feet, and their rosy cheeks. Their cuteness is compensation for the incredible amount of work and attention they require. I remember thanking God that He made my boys so cute during the toddler stage. Otherwise I might have been tempted to submit my resignation as their mother.

Having toddlers is, in my opinion, the most tiring stage of being a mom. Sure, they sleep through the night, but they never stop during the day. Every second they're awake, you have to know where they are and what they're doing. Turn your back for a minute, and the little stinker might be swallowing a marble, coloring on the walls, sticking a fork in the electrical outlet, or flushing the cat down the toilet.

Toddlers have a constant need for boundaries, attention, and connection. By design, they explore the world for a few minutes and then need to be emotionally "refueled" by Mommy. They tug on your leg or crawl into your lap for a three-second hug, and then they're off again.

After a day of caring for these little Energizer Bunnies, Mom just wants to be left alone. She doesn't want to be needed or touched by anyone. Even strolling alone through Wal-Mart can feel like paradise. So when the mister starts making his moves, she wants to say, "You have got to be kidding!" It's during this stage of parenthood that women begin to systematically replace silk and lace with sweats and flannel pj's that effectively communicate, "Don't you *dare* come near me tonight." I can remember intentionally changing into my pj's in the privacy of the bathroom at times. I didn't want to take any chance that Mike might see some flesh and get the wrong idea.

Remember that the toddler stage can last a long time, particularly if you have a couple of kids in a row. As much as you may want to, you can't just delay working on sex until the youngest goes to kindergarten. Because I've felt your pain in a big way, I'd like to offer some practical suggestions to get through this demanding period of motherhood with your husband still at your side.

1. Protect the bed. Don't fall into the habit of letting your kids sleep with you. There are two primary reasons, in this modern day, that parents share their beds with their children. The first reason is to get them to sleep. It may be easier in the moment to bring them into the bed than to listen to them cry for three hours at night. Second, some women secretly confess bringing their children into the bed to eliminate the possibility of intimacy with their husbands.

In both of these situations, the family bed is covering up and exacerbating a problem rather than addressing it. Toddlers need to be comforted by a bedtime routine and transitional objects (like a blanket or "stuffy"), and then learn to put themselves to sleep. Likewise, instead of using your child to shield you from intimacy with your husband, address the problem. Why don't you feel safe or comfortable alone in bed with him?

2. Protect the bedroom. During the late toddler and early preschool years, you need to begin to teach your children to respect your privacy.

Teach them to knock on the door before barging into your bedroom. Toddlers by nature like to test the boundaries and they hate being separated from Mom. This means that teaching appropriate boundaries may be a struggle. Mothers of toddlers often can't even go to the bathroom without hearing their children scream for them or seeing chubby little fingers pry their way under the door. Be consistent while also aware of their needs for comfort during separation.

3. *Protect bedtime (and nap time).* I'm capable of being patient with my kids on most days. I meet their emotional and physical needs, give them hugs, referee their arguments, and wipe their noses. But once they go to bed, I don't want to see them again. Bedtime is the finish line. I get really, really upset when the finish line gets moved. One time when my son got out of bed first for a drink of water and then for a tissue, I scolded him in frustration, "Andrew, you are not Jesus. You are not to rise again! I do not want to see your face until morning!"

Kids respond to boundaries when they are clearly set and reinforced. Make it very clear to them that when you put them to bed, they stay in bed (unless there's an emergency—and define emergency). This is critical to protecting your time alone and your time with your husband.

4. *Protect your femininity.* During the Energizer Bunny stage, women can feel as if their whole being has morphed into "Mom." Their interests, hobbies, abilities, bodies, and brains have all been sucked into the vacuum of peanut butter sandwiches and the Wiggles. Whatever it takes for you, make the effort to maintain some of who you are through this stage. Keep at least one interest or hobby *unrelated to motherhood.* At least one day a week, dress like a woman, not a mom. Wear makeup and *real* clothes.

5. *Step into the decompression chamber.* It's impossible to go from changing diapers to doing a striptease for your husband in five minutes. Yet this is what many moms in this stage of parenting feel is expected of them. More than one mom has experienced the confusion of

having sex with the theme for *Blues Clues* going through her head. This is the one stage of motherhood when you absolutely need a decompression chamber.

Even Wonder Woman needed a private place to morph from a normal person into a superhero. Why should you be any different?

Your decompression chamber can be a personal space you escape to for a few precious moments, or it can be an activity you enjoy alone without demands or interruptions. Maybe decompressing for you is enjoying a cup of tea and a good book, relaxing in a luxurious bubble bath, renewing your heart during your devotional time, watching *American Idol*, or walking around the neighborhood. Whatever it takes, you need time to change from Mom to woman before even thinking about intimacy. Ask your husband to help you build this into your regular routine.

Stage 4: The Taxi Stage

All of the action is in the backseat of my minivan.

Psychologists often call the ages between 5 and 12 the latency stage of childhood. Moms might call it the taxi stage since they typically spend so much time in the car. Whatever we call it, it is, in fact, probably the least demanding of all the stages of parenthood. Kids in the latency stage are busy tackling the challenges of school, sports, music, and friendship. They are pretty independent and generally compliant. School-aged kids are less demanding physically than toddlers and less taxing emotionally than teens. This is a great phase for parents to reconnect and work on their relationship. (It's no mistake that I'm writing a book about sex when all three of my children are in the latency stage!) Having said that, the "taxi" or latency stage of parenting isn't without some obstacles to romance.

The first obstacle is that older latency kids start to understand what Mom and Dad might be doing behind closed doors. They may ask questions about sex and anatomy that make you feel quite uncomfortable.

Because of their increasing awareness, you may be more paranoid about what little ears are hearing at your bedroom door.

While some kids are grossed out by the idea of kissing, or more, others are insatiably curious. I was the latter. I vividly remember one experience I had when I was about seven. I was shopping with my mom in a department store. While she was busy sorting through clothing racks, I went up to a male mannequin and ran my hand over his crotch area just to see what was under there. My mom scolded me, probably mortified. She was lucky I had the sense to check out a mannequin instead of a real person!

The second obstacle is that during this stage you and your spouse can become more "Mom and Dad" than you are "husband and wife." Embracing both identities is a difficult but imperative balance. Make sure you regularly have time to be husband and wife. Go on dates, and *do not talk about the kids*. Once a year, get away *by yourselves*. Go out with other couples and have fun together. I've met many awesome parents who are very comfortable parenting together but have completely lost the sense of being married. They regularly hug and encourage their children, but they can't seem to show affection or appreciation to each other. Make sure that there is more to your marriage than parenting.

Finally, don't forget about the obstacle inherent in the words *taxi stage*. We can get our kids involved in so many wonderful activities—dance, piano, Awana, soccer, baseball, archery, scouting, chess, martial arts, guitar, swimming, tennis, volunteer work, choir, school, and of course, about 15 birthday parties a year. You can literally feel as if you live in your minivan. You and your husband can quickly become ships passing in the night. He's with Sam at his soccer game, and you're with Amanda at her dance recital. Where's the romance?

Resist, resist, resist! When you focus all your attention on the kids' activities, you have little energy or time left to develop your relationship as husband and wife. Besides, latency-age kids need much more time at

home than they do being carted around creation. They need to do chores, rest, and even experience boredom. Protect your family's time! Limit kids this age to no more than one outside activity at a time. In other words, they can do scouting or soccer this season, not both. As kids enter adolescence, increased commitments are normal and helpful, but latency-age kids need to be home, for their sake and for the sake of your marriage.

Stage 5: The Twilight Zone
Our kids are more interested in sex than we are.

Thousands of books and articles have been written about the tumultuous teen years. Any armchair parenting expert can tell you about the hormones raging in the bodies of adolescents, the mood swings, the acne, and the body-image issues. Far less frequently talked about are the concurrent changes that are evolving in the parents of teens.

Just as teens are budding sexually, their parents' bodies are beginning to wither. While a young girl is frightened by her first menstruation, her mother is dreading the first signs of menopause. While a young boy battles the embarrassment of uncontrollable erections, his father may be mortified to be researching Viagra.

Parents can experience a lot of conflicting feelings as they watch their teens mature physically and sexually. For some it triggers a midlife crisis, fueled by the need to prove that "I still have sex appeal." Others vicariously live out their sexuality through their teenagers, unconsciously fueling flirtatious and romantic behaviors in their teenage children. Still others refuse to acknowledge their children's sexual maturation and their own sexual decline.

Remember that all of these feelings are normal, based on natural physical and emotional development. It helps to have friends who are also experiencing this twilight zone, who can identify with the loss, fear, and confusion. Having these feelings isn't dangerous, but reacting to

them can be. Celebrate the mature love that you and your husband share, recalling some of the barriers you have worked through together. Affirm each other often as parents and lovers, as this phase of parenthood (and adult development) can be discouraging.

Although teens don't demand the physical attention of infants or toddlers, they do demand your constant availability. In fact, many parenting experts believe that the most important stage of parenting is during the teenage years. Parents must be constantly emotionally available to their teens. Often this support is demonstrated by attending sporting events and band performances or checking up on homework progress. It also includes teaching responsibility, making important decisions about boundaries and limits, and preparing teens to fly away in just a few years. In short, the teenage years can be very demanding.

I recently met with a woman whose children were just entering the teen years. Like many women, she had assumed that she would have far more freedom and time to herself once her kids hit junior high and high school. She explained that although she had more free time during the day, her evenings were consumed with her children: driving from one place to another, allowing them to debrief from the drama of high-school relationships, monitoring their homework and social activities, and constantly being available for those moments when they need to talk.

"Worst of all," she reported, "teenagers don't go to bed! It's not like a 10-year-old who is asleep by nine o'clock so you have some 'couple time.' They stay up later than we do! We never have time to be alone. And they don't fall for the 'Mom and Dad are tickling each other' line anymore!"

This couple is learning to be creative through their children's teenage years. Sometimes they arrange rendezvous right after the kids leave for school in the morning or meet each other for coffee or lunch. They understand that if they don't make intimacy a priority, it won't happen.

Making Necessary Changes

To make it through the land mines of parenting with a healthy, vibrant sex life, you need to consciously change a few things. Kurt knew that his wife, Allison, was exhausted. Between work, the kids, and the housework, she didn't have a moment to herself all day. Kurt graciously offered to give Allison a back rub, hoping that this attention and physical touch would lead to sex. Unfortunately for Kurt, Allison was fast asleep 10 minutes into the back rub.

Although each stage of motherhood presents different challenges, they all tax a woman's emotional and physical resources. Whether you have toddlers or teens, incorporating some of the following suggestions into your life just might save your marriage.

Learn to Say No to Other Things So You Can Say Yes to Sex

I've met many women who couldn't say no to anyone—except their husbands. The church calls and needs another Sunday school teacher. The school needs a room mom. The ailing neighbor needs a meal. Someone else needs a ride to the doctor. "Yes, sure, I'm your lady." But when the mister initiates intimacy, she says, "Not tonight" without a second thought.

Why is this? Why is it so easy to say no to someone you love while you can't reject requests from people who are practically strangers? Perhaps it's because you take for granted the love and acceptance your husband offers, while you still feel compelled to earn the love of everyone else in your life. More likely, you just have nothing left after saying yes all day long. Your husband will need to learn to move to the front of the line and ask for a little romance in the morning!

My mom has constantly reminded me of this bit of wisdom: "Whenever you say yes to one thing, you are saying no to something else." You can't possibly say yes to everyone else in your life and still have

the time and energy to be fully present for your husband. In order to say yes to him, you must learn to say no to other worthy things.

Psychologists blame a common lack of sexual desire on something called the "sunset effect." By sunset, both husband and wife are exhausted. Everyone and everything else has gotten their best efforts and energy. They leave the leftovers for each other. No surprise, the leftovers are less than wonderful. Do you remember the last time you and your husband went on a weekend getaway? Sex was probably a lot better than normal because you actually had the time and energy to talk, to play, and to linger. Making time for great sex not only includes the actual time in the bedroom but also making sure that you have something left when you get there. It means taking care of yourself physically, emotionally, and spiritually, and nurturing your relationship.

You will only carve out significant time for each other if you're convinced that this is more important than anything else you could be doing. You will have to say no to a lot of worthy causes (not to mention time wasters like watching television and surfing the Net) to say yes to each other.

Tank Up

Every married woman has experienced days, weeks, and even months with literally no energy for sex. These periods of time shouldn't be the norm. If they are for you, it's definitely time to reevaluate the energy budget. Imagine going months without brushing your teeth or taking a shower or paying your bills. It would quickly catch up with you. Intimacy with your husband is that important. You cannot survive on leftovers. However, even with careful planning and putting a high priority on sex, there will still be those times when you're just too tired to spend a full hour making love.

Your husband may not pick up on how tired you are, even though

you've been yawning all day. He may not realize that when you asked for a back rub, you really *just* wanted a back rub. So, what do you do in these situations?

Learn to say "not now" graciously. It bears repeating: Your husband is sensitive to sexual rejection. This doesn't mean that you can never say no without driving him into therapy. It does mean that you need to be careful how (and how often) you say no.

First, make sure he knows you're interested in him, but you're just too tired (or stressed) to have sex right now. Second, give him a time in the very near future when you will be interested. I'm not one to put words in women's mouths, but here are some suggestions:

- "I wish I had the energy to really focus on us right now, but I don't. Could we take a rain check for tomorrow evening?"
- "If you'll watch the kids for 45 minutes so I can take a quick nap, I'll have the energy to . . ."
- "I'm so stressed right now. I just need to talk through some things and get organized before my mind is clear enough to enjoy being with you."
- "Can we talk tonight and do it tomorrow?"
- "How about we set the alarm clock 30 minutes earlier and do it in the morning?"

Visit the convenience store. Convenient stores exist for a purpose. Even though the selection is limited and the items are typically overpriced, these stores stay in business because they are, well, convenient. No one in their right mind would regularly do their grocery shopping at a convenience store. They exist for that occasional time when you just need a gallon of milk or have a craving for a Snickers bar.

Like convenience stores, there is a time and place for "quickies," especially when you're too tired for sex with all the bells and whistles. Not every sexual encounter needs to be a 90-minute romantic event complete

with foreplay and fireworks. During busy and stressful times, sex may simply be meeting a physical need for the other person. Although it's not romantic, it is loving.

Initiate Sex When YOU Are Ready

When you find yourself in stretches of busyness and stress when the energy for sex seems to be a rare commodity, take advantage of the times when you *are* in the mood. Most guys won't protest when their wives initiate lunch-hour rendezvous, greet them at the door with bedroom eyes, or even wake them up at two o'clock in the morning for some nonverbal communication.

For a variety of reasons, you may feel strange initiating sex. Instead, you hang back and wait for your husband to choose exactly the right time to initiate, as if he can supernaturally find that tiny window of time when you have the energy, your hormones are raging, the kids are asleep, and you have nothing else to do. No wonder great sex is so rare! Since guys are by nature easier to arouse and get into the mood, it makes sense for you to initiate when you are ready.

Redefine Foreplay

One winter morning a few years ago, I woke up to light streaming into our bedroom. The sunlight alerted me to the fact that I had overslept. Sure enough, the clock read 8:15. I panicked . . . the kids had missed the bus! I ran downstairs to find Mike reading a book to Christian, our youngest.

"I knew you were exhausted, so I got the boys up and put them on the bus. I wanted to let you sleep," Mike said when he saw the puzzled expression on my face.

Mike had fed the boys breakfast, packed their lunches and backpacks, loaded them on the school bus, and even washed the morning dishes. And it wasn't even my birthday or Mother's Day! That was the

most romantic thing he had done in years. A diamond bracelet or a week in Paris couldn't have done more to get me in the mood. As author Kevin Leman says, sex really does begin in the kitchen.

During the parenting years, a woman's love language becomes the acts of service her husband does for her. Nothing is sexier than a man doing dishes or putting the kids to bed. Your husband isn't likely to figure out this aphrodisiac on his own; you need to tell him. Instead of nagging him endlessly about helping with housework, help him understand how romantic it is.

Being a Great Mom Begins with Having a Great Marriage

A few years ago, I sat across the counseling room from Dana. She was sobbing, devastated from the recent revelation that her husband had been deeply steeped in pornography for the past decade. She had been so sure her marriage was solid; she couldn't grasp what had gone wrong. Was it all a big lie?

Dana and her husband had been married for 25 years. Together they had raised their four children and served in their church and community. As Dana tore back the covers of their relationship, searching for some indication of how they could have avoided this snare, she concluded that by trying to save her children, she had lost her husband.

Dana was supermom. Hers was the house where the youth group and all of the neighborhood kids came to hang out. She was at every school performance and athletic event. She and her husband chaperoned school and church trips for their children during the teen years. In the busyness of being there for their kids, they had allowed emotional and physical intimacy to take a back burner.

Dana looked me square in the eyes and pleaded, "Juli, tell those moms not to make the mistake I made. I was so into protecting my

teens that I didn't protect my own marriage. It all happened right under my nose, but I was too busy to notice. I literally wasn't available to my husband, emotionally or sexually, for over ten years!"

Dana's experience and her advice echo what many women feel. They wonder whether being a great wife must come at the expense of being a great mom, and vice versa. Do you have to choose to cater to either your children or your husband? Must one suffer at the expense of the other?

While one *may* suffer at the expense of the other, it doesn't have to be that way. God's calling on your life is for you to be both a faithful wife and a faithful mom concurrently!

Don't get caught in the trap of choosing a role—either the role of supermom or the role of superwife. God hasn't called you to any role; He has called you to faithfulness. Your job is to consistently seek the Lord's strength and wisdom throughout your lifetime. You don't have to choose between your husband and your children when you choose to simply be obedient to the Lord in each moment.

Don't be afraid to show appropriate affection for your husband in front of your kids or take time away from them to be together as husband and wife. It's good for them to see their mom and dad hold hands, flirt, and kiss. Enthusiastically share with your kids that you are going on a "date" with Dad or that the two of you need time to be together. Fortunately, God gave kids a natural "yuk" barrier when they think about their parents having sex. Do you remember first hearing about the "birds and the bees" and how horrified you were to even consider the fact that your parents did *that*?

One of the greatest gifts you can give your children is a home in which Mom and Dad are still in love. Great parenting begins with a solid marriage. Although single moms and women in tough marriages can do many things right for their children, the presence of love between Mom and Dad is an irreplaceable aspect of a secure home. When

you work on romance, you are naturally working on parenting. The best foundation for a child's self-esteem and sex education is witnessing physical affection within the context of a mom and dad who love each other. The roles of mom and wife shouldn't compete; they should complement each other.

So, go for it . . . you sexy mom!

SOMETHING TO THINK ABOUT • • • • •

1. Do you feel like your role as a mom competes with your role as a "lover"? How does this play out in your marriage?

2. Are there things you need to say no to so you can say yes to sex? What are they?

3. Are you willing to make sex more of a priority? What are three changes you can make so that can happen?

five

A Different Kind of Headache

News flash: Men and women are different, especially when it comes to sex.

Well, duh! Of course men and women are different. I don't believe I've ever read a marriage book that hasn't highlighted this fact. Most of them devote at least a chapter to exploring and explaining how different the sexes actually are.

Most likely you could rattle off a list of sexual differences between the average woman and man. Guys are visual; gals are emotional and sensual. Guys separate the physical act from their emotions, while for gals the two are inseparable. Guys like to get to the main event; women like foreplay.

In spite of our wealth of information, the fundamental differences between men and women continue to plague marriage—specifically in the bedroom. No doubt this ranks among the most debilitating of headaches. What wife hasn't longed to be more understood by her husband? Or wished she'd married a man with a sexual appetite more similar to her own?

How can we get past the apparent sexual "incompatibility" of men and women? Let's take a quick look at this.

Not only do men and women differ in their appetites, their preferences can be worlds apart. Although these preferences aren't universal and don't apply to all people (maybe not even to you and your husband), the following generally apply:

- While women most enjoy the physical and emotional closeness of sex, the highlight for men is the pleasure and release of orgasm.
- Men tend to prefer morning sex, while women prefer late-night rendezvous.
- Men prefer quantity over quality. For women, it's just the opposite.
- Women like subdued lighting, soft music, and candles. Men prefer bright lights and spontaneity.
- Men tend to be adventurous. They like to explore and experiment. Women settle into a comfortable routine and like to stick with it.
- The average man thinks about sex several times a day, while the average woman thinks about sex once a week.[1]

Don't Get Hung Up on Stereotypes

As you think about these descriptions of men and women in the bedroom, your response to some of them might be, "Well, that's not like my husband and me. We don't fall into the normal stereotypes!" While examining the general trends, tendencies, and differences of male and female sexuality can be very helpful, it can also cause confusion when you don't line up with those descriptions. Men and women are fundamentally different. However, there is even more variation within a group of males or a group of females. In your marriage, maybe you're the one who likes adventurous sex, and your husband is straitlaced. Perhaps you initiate more often than he does.

In many ways, Mike and I don't fit into the stereotypical model of husband and wife. I can't tell you how many times I've heard statements like "Men are logical, and women are emotional," or "Women are more talkative than men." Both of those stereotypes fly in the face of our marriage. I am the logical, quiet one; Mike is talkative, relational, and intuitive. So as you read about general differences between husbands and wives, expect that your relationship will fall outside of the stereotypes in one way or another. Every person and every marriage is unique. While we share some common headaches and experiences, we also walk a personal and distinctive road.

For this reason, we will spend less time talking about actual differences (I'll give you some recommended resources that do this effectively) and more time exploring how to bridge your differences—whatever they may be. Regardless of whether you and your husband fit the stereotypes, you're still different from each other. Those differences may or may not be typical, but they still present a barrier for you to overcome. Don't get hung up on why or how you are different; instead, focus on using those differences to create oneness in your marriage rather than division.

Why Differences Cause Headaches

Imagine your love life if you and your husband were exactly alike sexually. What if you had the same desire, wanted sex at the same time, and were aroused the same way? Perhaps you think that eliminating your differences would create sexual nirvana. Think again. How boring would that be? You would never try something new, you would never need to communicate about or during sex, and most likely, you would have sex far less frequently.

Sexual differences in and of themselves don't cause the headaches. In fact, the beauty, pleasure, and intimacy of sex are intertwined in the mystery of a man and woman, so different, sharing one experience. The

headaches come from the way we deal with (or fail to deal with) our differences.

As basic as it may sound, most men and women approach each other sexually without taking gender and personal differences into account. Take Lisa and Dave as an example:

It's eight o'clock in the evening. Lisa is doing dishes after a long day of work, helping the kids with homework, and cleaning up after the family. As she stands at the sink, her mind is lost in tomorrow's agenda: *I need to pick up the dry cleaning; Sara has a dentist appointment at two o'clock; I need to get someone to cover for me at the office. Jesse's science project is due Friday—he'd better get working on it. Oh, I forgot to RSVP for that baby shower.*

Her thoughts are interrupted by Dave's hands caressing her. He kisses her neck, hinting not so subtly that he would love some action with his sexy wife tonight. Lisa rolls her eyes and communicates indifference while thinking, *That's the last thing I want to do tonight. If you really want my attention, help me finish the dishes, get the kids to bed, and let me have an hour of peace to take a hot bath.*

Sensing her body stiffen at his touch, Dave retreats from the kitchen, stung. He walks into the den, turns on the television loud enough for the whole neighborhood to hear, and proceeds to flip channels for the next hour.

This is a pretty typical event in the average American home. It represents some of the classic differences between husbands and wives. What is astounding is that both Lisa and Dave will look back on this event with frustration and confusion. If asked about this scenario, Lisa would probably say something like this: "Why would Dave assume that I want sex when I'm in the middle of doing dishes? Can't he see that I'm exhausted and stressed? I haven't had a moment to myself all day! We haven't had a real conversation in over a week. I love Dave, but I really don't feel close to him. If he wants sex, he could start by helping me

around the house, so I'm not so tired, and by actually asking me how I feel once in a while!"

Dave, on the other hand, might say something like this: "I did all the right things. I hugged her, kissed her, and told her how sexy she is. I deal with stress and temptation all day. Then when I try to focus on my wife, she turns into an ice statue. I just can't win. Lisa is great at taking care of the kids and the house, but I seem to be the low man on the totem pole. Everything takes priority over us."

If Lisa and Dave know that they have very different emotional and physiological approaches to sex, why are they confused? Why does Dave assume that his advances would turn Lisa on? Why is Lisa surprised that Dave wants sex even though they haven't talked all week? This scenario should be predictable based on the gender differences they already know about.

When a couple reaches a chasm of misunderstanding, like Lisa and Dave, they often turn their hurt and confusion into incorrect assumptions. What begins as basic differences in design gets translated into moral and personal judgments. For example, the disinterested wife is perceived as "frigid, selfish, and withholding" while the husband is considered "insensitive and uncaring, with a self-centered need for sex."

It's human nature to take the facts we have and try to make sense of them through the filter of our own experiences. This is exactly what we do when it comes to sex. We may be loaded with facts about how men and women are different, but we conform those facts to our own perception or understanding without considering that men and women are working from an entirely different paradigm!

A few months ago, I made an effort to befriend a woman (let's call her Carol) who had just joined our church. She was new in town, we had kids the same age, and I thought she might need a friend. However, it seemed the more I reached out to her, the more reserved she became. Her smile and conversation were forced, as if she was going through the

motions but had no desire to build a friendship. When I invited her and her kids over to play, Carol politely refused. Frankly, I was stung by her reaction to me. She seemed to be giving me the cold shoulder, and I felt rejected. I wondered if I had offended her, or if perhaps she thought that she was above being my friend. (I'm just being honest about my insecurity here!)

I interpreted Carol's actions in the context of my own experience. Based on my assumptions, Carol was obviously being rude and rejecting. I would never respond that way to someone who had gone out of her way to make me feel welcomed!

Over the course of a month or two, I got to know Carol a little better. I discovered that she struggled with extreme anxiety. It took all of her nerve just to get out of the house without having a panic attack. Her forced smile and standoffish demeanor had nothing to do with me or her lack of desire for friendship. My assumptions about Carol were completely wrong because I failed to take into account that her experience might be different from mine.

People fall into this trap all the time. Your 5-year-old spills his milk, and you scold him for being clumsy. You can't understand why your 13-year-old thinks a nose ring is cool. You're shocked that your boss can be so two-faced and not feel guilty about it, or that your neighbor could enthusiastically endorse a political candidate who stands for everything you think is wrong in the world.

This is the classic danger of the differences between men and women. A husband assumes that his wife's lack of interest is personal. He subconsciously assumes that she must be thinking about sex throughout the day (just like he does), but that her interest simply isn't directed toward him. Likewise, a wife discovers that her husband is tempted by pornography. Since this isn't remotely a temptation for her, she assumes that his obsession with sexual images is a direct rejection of her. She must not be enough to satisfy him.

You'll never effectively work through the differences in your marriage until you resolve to break free from the confines of your own experiences and your assumptions about your husband's sexuality!

Going Back to School

When I first decided to address the topic of sex and marriage, I read several Christian books on the topic. One night I was sitting in bed reading a book written to men, by a man, on the topic of male sexuality. What I read practically made my eyes pop out of their sockets.

I had a doctorate in clinical psychology, had taken a couple of graduate level courses on human sexuality, and had at the time been married for about 10 years. Yet I was floored by the research presented in the book. Just to make sure the author wasn't off his rocker, I read a portion to my husband. Mike confirmed that the information in the book was consistent with his own experience.

How can this be? I thought. *Why didn't I know this?*

I share this experience to challenge you. Regardless of how long you've been married or how educated you are, you still have a lot to learn about how God created your body and your husband's body. Sexuality is extremely complex, from both a physiological and psychological perspective.

For example, it has been reported that

- two-thirds of women cannot reach orgasm through intercourse alone;
- more men than women say that they have felt forced into unwanted sexual experiences;
- women experience the greatest level of sexual satisfaction when sex lasts more than 30 minutes;
- men often use sex as a way to relax;
- more than 50 percent of married men regularly masturbate;

- some women experience an increase in sexual desire during PMS;
- alcohol can inhibit orgasm; and
- a woman can be unaware of whether she has had an orgasm.[2]

Although the average woman knows a fair amount about male and female sexuality, there are still a *lot* of missing pieces. Think of the ancient fable about the blind men and the elephant. Several blind men were asked to describe an elephant, but each was led to a different part of the animal. One described the trunk, another a tusk, still another a leg. As they compared notes, each accurately describing his experience, they completely disagreed about what the animal actually looked like. The moral of the story is that facts standing alone can be confusing and misleading.

Most couples simply possess facts about how husbands and wives differ from one another. Armed with pieces of accurate information, they assume an understanding that they actually don't have. There is a huge difference between *possessing information* about your husband's sexuality and actually *understanding* his sexuality. Facts can be deceptive because they can create a false sense of mastery. Knowledge is only one building block toward understanding.

Let's go back to Lisa and Dave in the kitchen. Lisa knows that Dave has a stronger sex drive than she does. But does she know why? Does she understand why the prospect of sex at the end of a long day is attractive to him, how it helps him relieve stress and recover emotionally from a trying day?

On the other hand, Dave knows that Lisa often pulls away when he initiates sex with her. Somewhere in the recesses of his brain, he acknowledges the importance of foreplay for his wife. But he doesn't know the complex interplay of hormones and thought processes that must be

present to arouse Lisa. He also doesn't understand that his wife must be relaxed *before* enjoying intimacy.

Take advantage of some of the incredible resources that teach about both male and female sexuality from a Christian perspective. If you want to become an expert in something, you study about that topic. Most likely, you've read books on parenting, your Christian faith, cooking, and a host of other topics pertaining to your career and interests. Why should sex be any different? (See the list of recommended resources in the back of the book.)

Translating Knowledge into Understanding

Beyond what you learn about gender differences, you must resolve to translate that knowledge into understanding. Just knowing the differences between genders isn't the same as understanding. True understanding implies experience.

Imagine that you're sitting across from a friend who is in crisis. Through tears, she describes the devastation of taking care of her mother who is suffering from Alzheimer's disease. As you listen to your friend's pain, your own eyes well up with tears. Without much effort, you picture your own mother, integrating the facts of your friend's story into your own experience. You can imagine the grief of watching your mom steadily losing her independence and personality. Your heart feels as if it's in a vise as you ponder a day when she doesn't even recognize you.

The deepest level of understanding your friend is empathy. Your tears for her are real because you can identify with how treacherous her road is. You may even make statements like "I can only imagine what you're going through," or "I don't know how you're making it. I couldn't be as strong as you are."

But what if you'd never had a mother? Or what if you hadn't spoken with your mom for the past 30 years? As much as you might try to

connect with your friend's pain, at some level you would conclude that you just couldn't relate. You might offer encouragement and prayer, but you would be limited in your ability to walk alongside her. You certainly could never say, "I understand your pain."

Apply this to sexuality. You could read every sex book ever written and still lack understanding of the differences between your sexuality and your husband's for this reason: *Males and females have a completely different experience of sexuality.*

As women, we don't know what it feels like to have testosterone coursing through our bodies (thank goodness!). We don't understand how walking past a Victoria's Secret store may trigger a tremendous mental and moral battle for a man. We can't identify with the shame of frequent intrusive sexual thoughts. We don't know the humiliation of not being able to perform sexually. So naturally we take the facts we know, incorporate them into our own experiences, and usually come to the wrong conclusions. We'll never be able to fully relate to our husbands' sexuality, but we can learn to better understand their experiences by keeping in mind the following points:

1. Just because you don't understand it, doesn't mean it's not real. When we fail to understand someone's experience, we tend to disregard or marginalize it. PMS is a great example. Since guys can't relate to PMS, some suspect it's just an exaggerated feminine excuse for being grumpy. But their inability to experience it doesn't make it any less real. The same is true with your husband's sexuality. Be careful not to invalidate his feelings or needs simply because you can't relate to them.

2. Just because you don't understand it, doesn't mean it's wrong. Human nature is to believe that "my way" is the right way. As a woman, you might be tempted to assume that the female approach to sex is the right one. Perhaps you've heard women make comments about male sexuality being animalistic or base (or maybe you've thought this yourself). Both male and female sexual appetites were created by God; one is cer-

tainly not superior to the other. Nor is your approach to sex necessarily right and your husband's wrong.

3. *Just because you don't understand it, doesn't mean you can't accept it.* As simple as it sounds, a tremendous weight is lifted from a marriage when both the husband and wife simply accept their differences. There is certainly a time for explanation and conversation, but couples must also get to the point where they relax in the reality that they have fundamental sexual differences that may never be fully understood or explained.

Becoming a Teacher

In *The Way to Love Your Wife*, Cliff and Joyce Penner write, "Your wife is a very complicated creature—emotionally, hormonally, spiritually, relationally, and sexually. Her variety and intensity may appear in the sexual realm as unpredictability and strong reactions—both of which can intimidate and confuse you."[3]

If understanding your husband's sexuality is difficult, explaining yours to him may seem next to impossible. As I've noted before, women are sexually far more complex than men. Whereas a man's sexual arousal and response are largely determined by testosterone, a woman's is also impacted by the constantly changing levels of progesterone and estrogen. To make matters even more complicated, a woman must be ready both emotionally *and* physically for sex. Not only are your needs far more complex, but they are constantly changing. What got you going a week ago probably won't work tonight. Trying to understand you can seem to your husband like aiming at a moving target. Even the above-average guy has his work cut out for him!

This is why Cliff and Joyce Penner teach that a primary key to great sex is the husband learning to follow his wife's lead. They encourage the wife to be in touch with her physical and emotional needs during sex and to lead her husband based on those needs. Here are two exercises they suggest to that end:

In the first one, she teaches you by placing her hands over yours and using your hands to pleasure the front of her body. In the second, she talks constantly as you pleasure her; she's giving you a play-by-play account of what she's feeling and thinking.[4]

Your husband could read volumes of books on female sexuality (not that you'd want him to) and still fail to meet your needs. He needs to learn from you! Although this might sound strange, you need to become the expert on your own sexuality and gently teach him about what you need in the moment. He can't become a great lover for you without your help. Sex experts (how would you like that to be your job title?) also teach that men need to be *continually reminded* about their wives' sexual needs. As many times as you may have told him that you like to make out before sex, he's destined to forget once his blood begins flowing away from his brain into another part of his body.

A natural way to teach your husband about your sexuality is through shaping. Remember playing the childhood game Hot or Cold? When the person was getting closer to finding a hidden object, you would say, "You're getting warmer!" Help your husband know when he's getting "warmer" through verbal responses like moans or saying something like "That feels really good." You also need to send messages that he's "really cold" with statements like "I'm not quite ready for that" or "You're losing me." Remember, your husband wants to learn how to please you and get you into it. You're the only one who can teach him!

If you're like most women, your sexuality may still be a mystery to you. You may have trouble answering questions like, What arouses you? What time of day or month are you the most interested in sex? What can your husband do or say to help get you in the mood? What keeps you from experiencing pleasure in sex?

Again, God created your body to be sexually complex not to put a damper on your sex life but to make it a rich, exciting journey for you

and your husband. If you could achieve the best sex of your marriage on your honeymoon, what would there be to look forward to? Instead, God created sex to be more like a journey or a treasure hunt. Much of that mystery surrounds female sexuality. The first step in teaching your husband is learning about how God designed you.

Learning to Really Talk About Sex

Translating all of this information into a great sex life requires one thing: communication. You and your husband obviously can't temporarily change bodies. You can't experience what sex is like for him, and he can't imagine what it's like for you. The only bridge we have is words.

I just finished reading the novel *A Thousand Splendid Suns* by Khaled Hosseini.[5] This novel tells the story of two Afghan women. I've never been to Afghanistan and possess little knowledge of Muslim culture and history. However, through skillfully written words, I was temporarily transported into another reality. In just a few short hours, I felt a shadow of the pain these fictional women experienced. Hosseini's story gave me empathy for the plight of the Afghan women I will never meet face-to-face. That's the power of a story.

My guess is that you've had this experience as well. Novels or Hallmark specials have the ability to sweep you up into a story, characters, and settings completely different from your own. Like me, you've probably laughed and cried at the plight of fictional characters. Differences of gender, race, time, and culture fade into the background as you become immersed in the experiences of the heroes. The power of a story demonstrates that through words you're able to connect with experiences that radically differ from your own.

Unfortunately, most of us aren't so articulate in communicating our own stories and experiences, particularly related to sexuality. Perhaps no topic makes us more vulnerable. Do you really want to know what your husband thinks about sex? Do you want to understand his drive, his

pleasure, and his fantasies? How do you feel about sharing your most intimate feelings, experiences, and temptations? Most likely, past conversations on the topic haven't gone well. Tears, accusations, frustration . . . Why bring it up?

Sex is extremely personal, emotional, and even spiritual. Unlike anything else we do with our bodies, sex is intricately tied to our self-esteem, emotions, and femininity (or masculinity). Communicating about sex can seem like a land mine. Say the wrong thing, or even say the right thing the wrong way, and a tsunami of conflict ensues. So how in the world do two people who are so different understand each other without the benefit of honest and open communication? How can you possibly understand your husband's experience (and he, yours) unless he vividly explains it?

Anne and Bill are enjoying a date night out at their favorite restaurant. What better time to start working on their sexual relationship. So Anne decides to take the plunge.

"Bill, we need to talk about our sexual relationship. I really want to understand what it's like to be you. I mean, what kind of sexual temptations do you deal with every day?"

The blood drains from Bill's face. In an effort to stay composed and act normal, he swallows a barely chewed meatball that becomes lodged in his throat. Choking, the Heimlich maneuver, paramedics on their way . . . You get the picture.

There's no easy way to broach a topic that has been primarily off-limits for most of your marriage. What words do you use? How do you express your feelings without offending your husband? How will you feel if he admits to what you suspect—an involvement with pornography? What if you're confronted with a problem that feels too big for you to solve? What if you go out on a limb, and he swats you down?

All of these are legitimate questions and fears. In fact, many couples literally don't know how to talk to each other about sex. This is where

we may run into a generation gap again. While talking about sex feels comfortable and normal for a generation who grew up watching *Friends*, it's probably awkward and intimidating for those who grew up watching *The Brady Bunch*. Even if you feel pretty comfortable talking about sex in general, it may be difficult for you to talk openly about sex with your husband. You don't want to reject him by sharing complaints; you don't want to be too vulnerable by sharing your history or temptations. There's just too much at stake to wade into those waters.

Lori and Craig came to counseling specifically to address the issue of sex in their marriage. For the most part, it was nonexistent. Having married later in life, they were both in their late 40s. Lori felt hurt and rejected by the fact that Craig was rarely interested in sex. He was a loving, caring man, but he didn't like physical touch. In fact, he felt very awkward talking to his wife about sex.

As a homework assignment, I gave the couple a list of 10 questions to discuss together during the week. They included questions such as "What do you like most about sexual intimacy?" and "What do I say or do that turns you on?"

When I met with Lori and Craig two weeks later, they reported that they were too uncomfortable to talk through any of these questions even in the privacy of their own home. So for the next assignment, I gave Lori and Craig a Christian sex book and asked them to read two chapters aloud together, taking turns reading. This exercise went a long way to open up the lines of communication in their marriage.

The safest way to begin talking about the deeper issues of sex is to employ a third-party resource to guide you. In essence, let someone else tell the story first. It's far less threatening to identify with someone else's experience before telling your own.

Spend time together reading aloud some of the recommended resources mentioned in the back of the book. Chances are that it won't take you and your husband long before you begin feeling more

comfortable talking about sex. Even saying words like orgasm, pornography, foreplay, penis, and vagina becomes easier once you've read them to one another.

The next step is ensuring that your conversations about sex remain edifying rather than destructive to your marriage. The type of conversations that must occur for a husband and wife to bridge the gap in understanding are impossible without a foundation of trust. Most marriages have a battered history of attempting such conversations. Here's an example:

Heather and Todd are in the middle of a frustrating sexual encounter that seemed doomed from the beginning. Heather is never really "into it" but feels obliged because it has been over a week since she and Todd have been intimate. She approaches the ordeal as the dutiful and loving wife, assuming that Todd will be grateful for her willingness.

Todd can tell from the beginning that this isn't going to be a top-10 night. Heather obviously wants him to get the whole thing over with. Her lack of interest adds to the pressure Todd feels to get Heather into it or to get his needs met quickly. Although his sexual need is strong, the whole episode feels tainted. Todd battles through conflicting emotions of rejection and desire, anger and guilt. He tries to push away his reservations and focus on the task at hand.

Moment by moment, Todd and Heather's frustration with each other is building. Finally, Todd withdraws from Heather, practically yelling, "Forget it. It's just not worth it."

Heather is stung by Todd's comment, which seems to come from nowhere. It's 11:30 P.M.; both are tired and frustrated and feel misunderstood.

The vast majority of the average couple's sexual conversations take place in this type of environment. Frustrations and feelings are high; time and tempers are short. Judgments and accusations fly, as neither

even knows how to make a gesture toward understanding the other. And then we wonder why it's so difficult for married couples to talk about sex.

More than any other topic of conversation, you must put in place parameters to ensure that your marriage is a safe place to talk about sex. Here are a few to consider:

- Be proactive. Instead of waiting for a failed midnight experience to vent frustration, plan time to talk through issues when you're both rested and engaged.
- When you find yourself in that highly charged, late-night conversation, put it on hold. You're far more likely to reach understanding and unity if you suspend the conversation until you're both rested and out of an emotionally laden situation.
- Express the desire to understand. Ask each other open-ended questions with the goal of wanting to really know. "What is your favorite thing about sex?" "What do I do that really turns you on?" "When do you feel pressure to perform?"
- Suspend judgment. Because sex is both a moral and an intensely personal topic, open conversations can quickly become judgmental and shameful.
- Talking about sex will never be safe unless both husband and wife commit to humbly working together toward purity without finger-pointing. (We'll get more into this in later chapters.)
- Acknowledge limits to understanding. Be open with your inability to understand what your husband experiences. Recognize that he can't quite understand your feelings. That admission alone validates deep feelings that may seem impossible to communicate.
- Consider seeking help from a professional counselor or psychologist when you confront roadblocks in your conversation.

The Gift of Differences

A primary theme of this book (reflected in the first chapter) is the idea that the very things that cause frustration in sexual intimacy can also be reframed as God's gift to us. As we unwrap this curious aspect of gender differences, might we find a valuable treasure?

I've had my share of days banging my head against the wall, lamenting the sexual differences between Mike and me. In fact, there was a period of a couple years when I believed my first questions to God would someday be, "Why did You create men and women so different sexually? If You wanted us to really enjoy it, why didn't You make us more compatible?" Yeah, I felt that passionate about it.

Maybe God heard those prayers and has begun to answer my questions before I see Him face-to-face. Over the past few years, the Lord has been showing me the beauty and genius in His design. Because we're so different, it's absolutely impossible for Mike and me (or any other man and woman) to experience regular awesome sex without both of us being unselfish. In effect, God's design practically guarantees that prolonged great sex *cannot exist* without genuine love. Do you see the brilliance in that?

Sure, couples can "hook up" and experience the ecstasy of an evening. Perhaps the flame of pure passion can last a few months. But sooner or later the excitement will wear off, and the couple will be stuck in the blahs of the routine. As long as he pursues his pleasure and she hers, they will remain sexually incompatible. Only through the risk of sharing the most vulnerable feelings, and the unselfish commitment to respect the fragility and desire of the other, can man and woman sexually thrive together.

As you stare across the bedroom at the curious creature who seems so familiar yet so different, remember that God's intention to unify you goes far beyond the physical compatibility to which the world aspires.

Ironically, only by working through the puzzle of our differences can God take two souls and forge them into one.

SOMETHING TO THINK ABOUT • • • • •

1. What differences between your husband's and your sexuality cause you the most frustration?

2. If you have never done so, express to your husband your desire to understand his sexuality and teach him about yours.

3. Choose a book from the list of recommended resources that you and your husband can read and discuss together.

six

What Is This Creature Called "Man"?

Author Robert Byrne once quipped, "Anyone who believes that the way to a man's heart is through his stomach flunked geography." This humorous statement hits home with what any adult with a brain knows: Sex is very, very important to men. Research consistently shows that between 80 and 90 percent of men view sex as the most important aspect of their marriage. When asked what one thing they would like to change in their marriages, they wish that their wives would be more interested in sex and more willing to initiate physical intimacy.[1] Marriage experts Gary and Barbara Rosberg surveyed men about their sexual needs. The vast majority of men indicated that mutual pleasure and female initiation of sex were among their primary sexual needs.[2]

No doubt, our sexually explicit culture plays into the prominence of sex on a man's mind. He can't open the newspaper, turn on the television, surf the Net, or walk into a mall without being reminded of sexual desire. Yet long before the Internet or bikinis were invented, sexuality was an extremely powerful force in men's lives. History teaches us as much.

David and Bathsheba. Samson and Delilah. Reuben and Bilhah. Scripture is filled with references to and examples of men falling into

sexual temptation. Archaeological discoveries reveal that civilizations thousands of years ago had houses of prostitution. Solomon's warnings in Proverbs and the exaltations in Song of Songs written 3,000 years ago are completely relevant today. Time and culture have changed the venues of expression, yet the power of a man's sex drive has remained a constant force of both intimacy and destruction.

Before we go too much further, let me acknowledge that you may be married to a man who falls into the 10 to 20 percent of men for whom sex isn't all-consuming. Although sex may not be as dominant a factor in your husband's life, it doesn't discount the fact that it's important. In fact, many men who avoid or minimize the impact of sex in their lives do so because of past painful experiences or because of the fear of future failure. Regardless of how often your husband thinks or talks about sex, make no mistake, it is a vital aspect of who he is as a man. I'll be addressing your situation in chapter 7.

Understanding His Sexuality

Although the average wife acknowledges that her husband's sex drive is stronger than hers, she still tends to underestimate the impact this one aspect has on their relationship. According to a poll of 150 Christian married men, 83 percent stated that they don't believe that women understand a man's sex drive.[3] Husbands feel alone with their secrets and desires; they are at a loss about how to communicate this to their wives. For many men, their attempts to bridge the gap have been met with disinterest or even disdain.

From the female perspective, male sexuality is often viewed as a sordid desire. It seems to represent the worst of masculinity—passion without love, drive without self-control, sensuality without sensitivity. I've talked to more than one wife who would rather pretend that her husband's sexuality just didn't exist. At best, women tend to compart-

mentalize their husbands' sexuality. Sex represents Mr. Hyde, tainting an otherwise moral and approachable Dr. Jekyll. Here's how one woman put it:

> Although we have a pretty good marriage, sex feels like another chore on my list. I hate that my husband thinks about it so much and that he always wants it. I dread going to bed, fearing that he'll ask me for sex. Sometimes I find things to do around the house, hoping that he'll fall asleep before I'm ready for bed. I just wish I could shut him off somehow.

Truth be told, many wives can identify with this sentiment. Over time, their sex life has become a burden. They feel guilty for withholding and responsible to keep their husbands pure, but mostly they wish the whole ordeal could just be put on hold for a couple of years.

When we think about the relationship between sex and guilt, the natural link is feeling guilty about sexually immoral behavior, a flirtation at work, or a checkered past. Although these aspects of sexual sin often result in tremendous guilt, I believe even more women struggle with the "guilties" of not meeting their husbands' sexual needs.

Practically everything a Christian wife hears or reads about sex revolves around the message "Your husband needs sex, so give it up." After a hefty dose of guilt, she resolves to make sex more of a priority in her marriage. Her resolve lasts a while, but eventually she becomes resentful. She and her husband may be having sex more often, but it's not getting any better.

Although feeling guilty can cause you to examine your heart and actions, it isn't a good long-term motivator for change. Your sex life won't significantly improve because you feel bad about not meeting your husband's needs or because you're afraid he will cheat on you otherwise. Feelings of guilt are simply an indication that something is wrong. If

you don't take the time to examine the underlying problem, you'll continue in the cycle of reacting to your guilt temporarily, only to fall into the same pattern of resentment. Besides, your husband doesn't want you to have sex with him because you feel guilty; he wants you to *want* to be with him!

This chapter is all about understanding your husband's sexuality and why sex is so important to your marriage, from his perspective. Please understand, this information isn't intended to add to your guilt. Instead, I pray that this chapter will challenge your heart. As you more fully understand the place of sex in your husband's life, my hope is that you will catch a glimpse of the bigger picture of sex in your marriage. Guilt won't last, but a change based on love will.

Sex Is a Physical Need

One of the biggest differences between you and your husband is the fact that he experiences sex as a legitimate physical need. Just as your body tells you when you're hungry, thirsty, or tired, your husband's body tells him when he needs a sexual release. Your husband's sexual desire is impacted by what's around him but is determined by biological factors, specifically the presence of testosterone in his body.

Immediately after sexual release, men are physically satisfied. But as their sexual clock ticks on, sexual thoughts become more prevalent, and they are more easily aroused. The physical need for sexual release intensifies as sperm builds in the testicles. The body continues to produce and store sperm, although sperm production fluctuates based on levels of testosterone and the frequency of sexual release.

The best way for a woman to understand this dynamic is to relate it to another physiological need. If you've had a baby, you may relate to the experience of milk building up in your breasts a few days after giving birth. The buildup of breast milk becomes annoying (and even painful) until the milk is expressed. You may have even had the embar-

rassing experience of leaking breast milk when it was not expressed. A male's semen buildup is sometimes released through nocturnal emissions if it is not otherwise relieved. Just as with breast milk, sperm production tends to "keep up with demand." The more often a man has sex, the more semen his body is likely to produce.

As women, we don't experience the physiological drive for sex in this same way. There is no buildup that demands release. Instead, hormonal fluctuations drive our sexuality. Female sexual hormones are largely determined by two factors: the female reproductive cycle (menstruation, ovulation, pregnancy, menopause, etc.) and a part of the brain called the hypothalamus.

A woman's sexual desire is far more connected to emotions than her husband's sex drive is. A man can experience sexual arousal apart from any emotional attachment. He can look at a naked woman and feel intense physical desire for her, while *at the same time* he may be completely devoted to and in love with his wife. For most women, this just doesn't compute. A fundamental difference in the wiring of male and female sexuality is that men can separate sex from a relationship while for a woman, the two are usually intertwined.

In today's culture, girls and young women are becoming more involved in casual sex. Terms like *hooking up* and *friends with benefits* are code words for guys and girls engaging in sex outside the context of a romantic relationship. Women are also becoming more involved with Internet porn, obviously seeking a sexual experience outside the boundaries of relationship. Even in these scenarios, a woman's desire for sex is still linked to an emotional or relational need. For example, porn geared toward a female audience has an intentional relational component that doesn't exist in male-oriented porn. A young girl who engages in oral sex with a stranger may still be motivated by a desire for love and acceptance.

Although the physical need for sex can be compartmentalized in a man's life, his sexual behavior still has ramifications for every other part

of his life. Many women make the assumption that because sex is a physical need for their husbands, it doesn't have an emotional or relational impact. Nothing could be further from the truth. A man's sexuality has a tremendous impact on his emotional, marital, and spiritual well-being.

Sex Is an Emotional Need

Shaunti Feldhahn's best-selling book *For Women Only* underscores the fact that sex has a deep emotional impact on men. Feldhahn interviewed several hundred married men about different aspects of marriage. Not surprisingly, sex dominated their expressed needs and desires. Perhaps the unexpected twist to Feldhahn's findings was the men's *feelings* behind their sexuality. The vast majority of men indicated that being sexually fulfilled in marriage significantly impacted their confidence and their masculinity. Seventy-seven percent agreed with this statement: "If my wife was an interested and motivated sex partner, it would give me a greater sense of well-being and satisfaction with life."[4]

A man's ability to perform sexually, to arouse and please his wife, is central to his confidence as a man. The impact ripples into practically every other area of his life.

Think of the word *impotent*. Although we use it as a term to describe the inability of a man to achieve an erection, the broader meaning speaks volumes. *Impotent* literally means "unable to take effective action; helpless or powerless." A man who feels like a failure sexually, feels impotent—helpless and powerless—in all areas of his life.

Dr. Archibald Hart, in his extensive work regarding male sexuality, has concluded that a man's sexual prowess and the need to perform sexually is a fundamental emotional need. While some men become obsessed with proving their masculinity through sexual conquests, others avoid sexual interactions because they fear failure.[5]

As I mentioned earlier, men are extremely sensitive to sexual rejection and take it very personally. In Feldhahn's research, men confided

that when their wives say, "Not tonight," men really hear, "I'm not interested in you."[6]

A man can have sex with his wife every day of the week and still feel emotionally rejected by her. Having his wife just go through the motions isn't enough. Again, he longs to know that he is pleasing her and that she is sexually interested in him.

This partly explains the lure of sexual outlets like porn and fantasy. Think (briefly!) about sexual images you've seen of provocative women. While their body parts are exposed (and airbrushed!), the most sexual thing about them is their availability. Their eyes and pose scream, "I want you, and I won't reject you!" Read Solomon's description of a woman trying to entice a man into adultery:

> She threw her arms around him and kissed him, boldly took his arm and said, "I've got all the makings for a feast—today I made my offerings, my vows are all paid, so now I've come to find you, hoping to catch sight of your face—and here you are! I've spread fresh, clean sheets on my bed, colorful imported linens. My bed is aromatic with spices and exotic fragrances. Come, let's make love all night, spend the night in ecstatic lovemaking! My husband's not home; he's away on business, and he won't be back for a month. (Proverbs 7:13–20, MSG)

Notice that Solomon doesn't mention anything about the physical attributes of the woman. She is attractive because she wants him. She is taking advantage not only of his physical desire but of his emotional need to be desired.

Translation: You cannot compartmentalize your husband's sexuality. You cannot love him as a husband but reject him sexually. From his perspective, his sexuality is a central part of who he is as both a man and a husband.

Sex Is a Spiritual Need

Read what the apostle Paul wrote to the Corinthian church:

> It is good for a man not to marry. But since there is so much immorality, each man should have his own wife, and each woman her own husband. The husband should fulfill his marital duty to his wife, and likewise the wife to her husband. . . . I wish that all men were as I am. But each man has his own gift from God; one has this gift, another has that.
>
> Now to the unmarried and the widows I say: It is good for them to stay unmarried, as I am. But if they cannot control themselves, they should marry, for it is better to marry than to burn with passion. (1 Corinthians 7:1B–3, 7–9)

Paul commanded husbands and wives to be sexually available to each other to avoid temptation. He then encouraged Christians to remain unmarried, unless they have a strong sexual desire. According to Paul, battling sexual temptation is a significant reason for Christians to marry! So, what happens to the man who marries because he "burns" only to find that his wife doesn't "burn"?

Dr. Archibald Hart writes, "Most men face a lifelong struggle to control their sexuality. The struggle is between their hormones and their higher aspirations. It is a battle between their seemingly uncontrollable urges and the fear of succumbing to these urges. Ultimately, it is a struggle over integrity, right and wrong, uprightness and wholeness."[7]

Hart's statement explains why sex is a spiritual need for a married man. He likely battles daily to stay pure. His walk with the Lord and his integrity are largely determined by how he handles sexual temptations and impulses. When he gives in to lust, pornography, or inappropriate sexual relationships, he carries a tremendous burden of guilt. He may doubt his salvation and feel disqualified from the body of Christ. Be-

cause he feels so ashamed about his struggle or failure, he may feel that he can't share his burden with anyone else.

Initially, Sheila and Mark really enjoyed their sexual relationship. The first couple of years of their marriage was the honeymoon stage that most couples hope for. As time wore on, though, their sexual desires changed. Sheila was busy and exhausted taking care of their young children, and she lost interest in sex. While Sheila seemed content to put their sexual relationship on hold for the time being, Mark responded by initiating more frequently. If he was a deer panting for water, she was a camel who seemed capable of walking through the desert for months at a time without a water break.

When Mark got the message that his advances were likely to be thwarted, he stopped asking for intimacy. He had no idea how to express his frustration and despair to Sheila. Her loud sighs and condescending expression at the mention of sex communicated that she could never understand how critical their sexual relationship was to him.

Over time, Mark began to direct his sexual needs through masturbation and light pornography. A few nights a week, he would stay up late, surfing channels, hoping to catch a glimpse of something sexual. The guilt and shame he felt only intensified the rift of intimacy in their marriage. Although he rationalized his actions, Mark knew that Sheila would be devastated to discover what he was doing. More than anything else, he longed to be pure, to share his sexuality only with Sheila. But life was too busy, his desire too strong, his will too weak, and the gulf between them too great.

Like Mark, your husband depends on you to be his partner in his battle against sexual temptation. Although you aren't responsible for his actions, you are a key component in his victory. You're the only woman in the world whom your husband can look at sexually without compromising his integrity!

Again, please understand: You aren't responsible for your husband's

sexual behavior. Don't be motivated out of fear that he will act out if you don't meet his needs; rather be motivated out of love and a desire to share his spiritual journey with him.

Sex Is a Relational Need

Research indicates that sexual satisfaction and marriage go hand in hand.[8] Surprised? Probably not. From a woman's perspective, it makes perfect sense that people are much more sexually satisfied when they have a good relationship. Before drawing too many conclusions from this fact, let's take another look at it.

In graduate school, I took several classes to learn how to conduct and understand psychological research. (Not my favorite classes by any stretch of the imagination!) One of the most important principles that stuck with me was "correlation does not mean causation." Correlation means that two events tend to coincide. For our purposes, sexual and marital satisfaction are correlated. Our assumption that a good relationship leads to good sex is making the leap from correlation to causation. It's just as possible (especially from the male perspective) that great sex *causes* a satisfying marriage, not the other way around. In fact, some biological research supports this theory.

Just like sexual drive, the warm feelings of connectedness, trust, and bonding that we associate with good relationships are also impacted by brain chemistry. Oxytocin is often called the "cuddle hormone." The presence of this hormone causes people to feel bonded to each other and experience relationships as emotionally gratifying and positive. Both men and women have oxytocin in their bodies. However, the presence of estrogen in a woman's body makes the impact of oxytocin much more powerful. This partly explains why women are far more likely than men to seek emotional intimacy in their relationships.

In women, levels of oxytocin skyrocket during labor and breast-feeding, encouraging the maternal behaviors and bonding so powerfully

experienced in new moms. The only time levels of oxytocin and another hormone called vasopressin significantly increase in men is right after orgasm. (Women's oxytocin levels spike after orgasm as well.)

Have you ever noticed that your husband seems to treat you differently after sex? He's more attentive (perhaps after a brief nap), more affectionate, and more appreciative? This isn't just your imagination. He is biologically wired to bond with you after sex. He literally feels emotionally closer to you after orgasm—and that's not just a line!

The lack of regular sex is a *significant* barrier to emotional connectedness and intimacy for men. Likewise, sex is perhaps the most powerful force bonding a man emotionally and relationally to his wife.

Beyond just the act of having sex, sharing and embracing your husband's sexuality is perhaps the most powerful way to build the intimacy you so desire in your marriage. How can you truly be connected with him if you ignore or minimize the one aspect of his life that dominates him physically, emotionally, spiritually, and relationally?

So, What's the Holdup?

Typically when I meet with a couple for marriage counseling, I ask both the husband and the wife the question, "What would you like to see changed in your marriage through our time together?" Most of the time, the wife is the first to respond. She doesn't have to think too hard about the question because she usually is the one who initiated counseling. Her answer often sounds something like this: "I hope we communicate more. I want him to understand my needs. I want to feel closer and more appreciated by him."

She might also include specific requests, such as help with housework, more involvement in parenting, or a more active role in spiritual leadership.

Nine times out of ten, the husband's response has something to do

with sex. His request is usually short and straightforward. And 9 times out of 10, the husband gets some kind of disgusted or dismissive look from his wife. Her body language screams, "You have got to be kidding. That is so superficial!"

Sometimes she gives me one of those woman-to-woman looks that say, "See what I have to deal with! How are you going to fix *this*?"

Take a step back from this situation and look at the facts. The wife has made at least three or four demands on her husband. He makes only one from her . . . and she dismisses it as petty and superficial. As a wife I understand the woman's reaction. As a psychologist, I recognize that her response is illogical. Why is this such a roadblock? If sex is the one thing that would make the difference for him, the one thing that really makes him feel loved, why not make it a priority? Why is it so much easier to make his favorite meal or buy him an elaborate birthday gift than it is to meet his sexual needs?

As you read about the importance of sex to your husband, you may feel as if 50-pound bags of sand have been heaped upon your shoulders. As much as you want to be a good wife, it just feels like he's asking too much. But why? Although we have addressed and will continue to address aspects of this question throughout the book, let's look at a few reasons why sex may be unappealing to you:

- You have a physical or emotional illness that interferes with the desire or ability to engage in intimacy. Really investing in sex requires a tremendous amount of emotional and physical energy—energy that you probably don't feel you have.
- You have your own issues with sex—perhaps related to body image or scars from the past. Focusing on sex will likely bring up painful feelings and experiences.
- Sex makes you feel vulnerable. Perhaps you don't feel safe enough in your relationship to expose yourself physically and emotionally to your husband.

- He doesn't deserve it. Walls of hostility and bitterness can keep you from even thinking about sex. Why should you be the one to take the first step toward intimacy?
- Everything within you may be screaming that the relationship must be fixed before you can even think about sex.

Although these are valid barriers and concerns, remember this: *Your lack of interest in your husband's sexuality is a significant barrier to intimacy.* You may have legitimate reasons for minimizing sex in your marriage. In fact, your marriage may need a lot of work before a healthy sex life can even be considered.

I also want to emphasize that I am *not* saying, "Just do it." Your needs are just as important as his. A great sex life means taking into account *both persons'* needs and desires. I don't agree with well-meaning counselors who suggest that a wife promise to have sex three times a week with her husband. That approach is one-sided and defeats the whole purpose of sex: oneness and love.

More important than giving your husband frequent sex is a commitment to explore and embrace sexual intimacy within your marriage. There is a huge difference between the two!

Your Husband's Sex Drive Is God's Gift to You

For the most part, this chapter builds the case that sex is the greatest gift that you can give to your husband. Let's switch gears for a moment and explore how your husband's sex drive is a gift to you. (No, you didn't read that wrong, and it's *not* a typo!)

You can spend so much time fretting about and avoiding sex that you miss the obvious. While acknowledging that sex is a huge force in your husband's life, don't neglect the fact that God created that force for your use as well. In fact, you should become jealous and possessive of the power inherent in your husband's sexuality. It was intended for you!

The story of Samson has always intrigued me (Judges 13–16). What he had in brawn, he must have lacked in brains. When Sunday-school teachers tell the story of Samson, they usually skip past the fact that Samson had lady problems long before sexy Delilah entered the scene.

Samson was a strapping young man whose attention was seized by a beautiful Philistine woman. He told his parents, "Go get her for me," which they did. (I guess they never read *The Strong-Willed Child*!) During the wedding feast, Samson taunted the Philistine guests with a riddle, betting them that they couldn't solve it. Samson's brand new wife told her kinsmen the answer to the riddle and ended up marrying Samson's friend. The next time we see Samson with a woman, he is sleeping with a prostitute.

Fast-forward several years to Delilah, another beautiful woman. Three times, Samson lied to Delilah about the source of his strength. Three times Delilah betrayed her lover. Yet Samson stayed with her and eventually confided the true secret of his prowess. As strong as Samson's muscles were, his sex drive appears to have been stronger.

We often look at a man's sexual desire as a weak link or an Achilles' heel. As with Samson or David, the promise of fleeting pleasure has the power to strip him of all that he values in life. However, what can be a source of evil can also be a force of great good. Just as twisted women are able to pull men into sin, virtuous women can use the influence of sex to call men to morality, love, and godliness.

Like many wives, you may be desperate to work on your marriage. You may long for your husband to read relationship books with you or attend marriage seminars (and actually take notes). If you really want his attention, work with the way God designed him. A great sex life won't solve the problems in your marriage; however, it will fortify your husband's desire and commitment to work toward intimacy. Your sexual relationship may be the "on-ramp" to communication, conflict resolution, and building the emotional intimacy you are longing for.

Like any married couple, Mike and I have our disagreements. In fact, we even have a full-out argument every now and then. He retreats to his corner, and I retreat to mine. Each wonders when the other will extend the olive branch with a hug, an apology, or a kind word. During these tense times in our marriage, I pay more attention than ever to how I look. I'm conscious to put on makeup and wear something relatively attractive. Why? Because I desperately need my husband's attention. I want him to desire emotional and physical connection with me. It's a potent force for encouraging reconciliation.

No amount of nagging, pleading, talking, or counseling can grab your husband's attention the way his sexual desire for you can. Just look at advertising. No approach is used more frequently or more successfully than sex appeal. Why aren't you using it in your marriage? As a good friend of mine says, "If you want to improve your marriage, invest in your underwear."

Look at it this way: How is your husband likely to respond to these two statements—"Honey, I really think we need to talk about our marriage. I feel like we are drifting apart." Versus . . . "Babe, I want to work on our sexual relationship. I want to know how to please you and how to make our sex life awesome."

Which book do you think your husband would be more interested in reading: *The Seven Keys to a Great Marriage* or *Red-Hot Monogamy*?

Please understand—I am *not* suggesting that you use sexuality to manipulate your husband! Withholding sex when you don't get your way or lavishing him with it when you do is manipulation. I am suggesting that you embrace this fact: There are many forces in your husband's environment that use sex to garner his attention. They are stealing the power that God intended for you. Instead of sitting passively by, claim it.

Satan consistently twists into evil *what God designed for good*. By God's good design, a man's sex drive is strong. If it is harnessed and intensified

within marriage, it can be an incredible force fastening a man's affections and passions to his wife. I believe that it is right and godly to claim your husband's sexual desire as a potent source of influence in your marriage. This power was intended for you and for no one else. Unfortunately, if you don't claim it, someone or something else will.

"Do not worship any other god, for the LORD, whose name is Jealous, is a jealous God" (Exodus 34:14). Notice that in this verse, God tells the Israelites that His name is "Jealous." We often think about jealousy as a bad quality, so why would God define Himself as jealous? The obvious answer is that there are some things that we *should* be jealous about. God's jealousy for the hearts of His people is holy and righteous. They belong to Him and were created for His pleasure.

The same applies to your sexual relationship with your husband. You should be jealous of your husband's sexuality! It was designed for your pleasure and intimacy. The power of his sexuality was also designed for your *influence* in his life. Through his sexuality, you have a powerful place in your husband's life that should belong to *only you*. It sets apart your relationship as distinctive from every other person in his life. No one can share with him as you can. Instead of lamenting the compelling sexual appeal of pornography and co-workers in your husband's life, focus your energy on reclaiming the influence that is rightly yours.

It's Your Gift. Unwrap It!

As you digest this information, you may feel defeated by your perceived inability to meet your husband's sexual needs. Perhaps emotional or physical limitations convince you that the gift in this chapter is impossible for you to unwrap. No, you cannot compete with the raw sensuality dangled at men in our culture. You have neither the energy nor the physical attributes to look like a cover girl or a *Playboy* centerfold. Yet what you do have to offer your husband is far more profound.

Fulfilling your husband sexually encompasses so much more than the physical act. It means inviting his sexuality into your marriage, embracing all that he is, hopes, and desires. It includes wanting to fully understand him and welcoming the sexual appetite that expresses his masculinity. It involves striving with him through weakness and temptation and covering his fears and failures. No magazine, no coworker, no porn site can be this teammate and confidante for your husband. This is your place; this is your power; this is your gift. Unwrap it.

SOMETHING TO THINK ABOUT • • • • •

1. Was there anything in this chapter that caught you off guard related to your husband's sexuality? What was it and why?

2. Do you feel guilty about not meeting your husband's sexual needs? Have you ever shared those feelings with your husband?

3. Why is guilt a poor motivation to improve your sex life? What is a better motivation for you?

seven

"Try the Oysters, Dear"

Throughout their eight years of marriage, Becky and Matt had enjoyed being part of a close-knit group through their church. Most of the couples had known one another during their college years, had attended each other's weddings, and had celebrated each announcement of newborn arrivals. Because of the longevity of their relationships and how they had together experienced each stage of young-adult life, the couples in Becky and Mike's small group shared openly with one another.

Whenever the women got together for social time, they compared notes on in-laws, labor and delivery, and the common joys and frustrations of married life. Becky was happy to join in on the conversations, except when her friends alluded to sex. All of them griped about how their husbands constantly wanted sex. They joked about creative ways to say, "Not now, honey."

Although Becky chuckled and pretended to share their experiences, these conversations created a deep sense of inadequacy and shame. She could never tell her friends that she longed for the day when Matt would sexually pursue her or even respond to her requests for sexual intimacy. Surely, there must be something repulsive about her.

A Painful Reality

Of all the hidden sexual secrets that couples carry, one of the most painful is this reversal of sexual stereotypes. Without fail, every single time I have spoken on sexual intimacy and mentioned this problem, women have approached me, relieved to know that they aren't alone. Like Becky, most of them have been silent for years, listening to friends rant and rave about their amorous husbands.

Almost all marriages go through periods when the man has a lower sex drive than his wife. Stress at work, depression, grieving, a physical illness, or extreme tension in your marriage can each radically decrease your husband's interest in sex. While these periods are disconcerting or frustrating, they pale in comparison to the pain and conflict caused when this is a couple's consistent pattern of sexual intimacy.

Although it doesn't alleviate all of the pain and conflict, it helps couples to know that around 20 percent of marriages fall within this category. Both men and women are reluctant to share this struggle with others because it is so private and potentially humiliating. Because people don't talk about it, couples in the "20 Percent Club" can begin to believe that they're alone in the universe—that no one else could possibly relate to their struggle.

A primary challenge for you if you fall within this group is the shame and blame that's often attached to your sex life. As a wife, you may struggle deeply with feelings of inadequacy. You may wonder what's wrong with you and why your husband seems to not be attracted to you. You may even question your femininity and sexuality. Along with those feelings and doubts, you may also wonder if your sex drive is abnormal. If the average wife seems bent on avoiding sex, is there something wrong with you if you actually crave it?

Other days, you probably shift from shame to blame, feeling angry with your husband for his seeming inability or unwillingness to meet

your needs for love, affirmation, and sexual fulfillment. Your situation may cut to the very core of who you are as a woman. You desperately want to be cherished and embraced by your husband. His disinterest feels like a total rejection of who you are as a wife and a woman.

To make matters worse, your husband may be dealing with wounds just as deep as yours. While you long for affection and affirmation, he yearns to be a competent husband. Your husband's sense of well-being and confidence is tied to his ability to perform in all areas, including his sexuality. From the time he was a young adolescent, he has been programmed to believe that masculinity equals sexual conquest and that real men can perform in bed. Although he may not be able to articulate it, he likely feels deep shame and inadequacy rooted in his inability to perform on demand.

So, here you are, both feeling incredible shame and inadequacy. How can you reassure him when you are the one reeling from rejection? Likewise, how can he comfort you when your pain is rooted in something apparently "wrong" with him?

Understand Why Your Marriage Works the Way It Does

There are a few primary reasons why couples find themselves outside the norm in their sexual relationship. Sometimes it's simply a matter of individual differences, and other times it can be attributed to a dysfunction that you may be able to address. Unfortunately, in some cases there are more menacing reasons couples struggle with this issue. Let's look first at normal differences between individuals before we address dysfunctions and other issues.

The Short End of the Bell Curve

The next time you're in a large group of families, pay attention to the height of men and women who are married to each other. You'll notice

that in most cases, the man is taller than his wife. The average height for an American man is five feet, nine inches, while the average American woman is five feet, four inches. However, you'll find a few couples that defy the odds, with the wife being taller than her husband. Does this mean that there is something wrong with this couple? *Average* means that many will be taller and many will be shorter. So, what if a five-foot-eight-inch-tall woman falls in love with a five-foot-seven-inch-tall man? Are they weird or abnormal? Certainly not. They both fall within the normal ranges of height, but they don't represent the average coupling.

The same principle applies to sexuality. If the average married man desires sex every three days, there will be normal men who have both higher and lower sex drives. Likewise, if the average woman desires sex once a week, the bell curve will include women with both higher and lower natural sexual desire.

The first step on the journey to communication and healing is to re-visit this concept of normal sexuality. Both research and society's representations help form our perceptions of what's normal. Based on what you see on television, hear people talk about, and read in women's magazines, you may conclude that you and your husband are sexually abnormal because you don't fit the stereotypes. But don't confuse what is "average" with what is "normal." Although in the average marriage, men desire sex more often than their wives, there are very normal marriages in which the opposite is true. Be careful not to get hung up on what everyone else seems to be doing in their bedrooms. The only thing that matters is assuring that you and your husband work toward intimacy and fulfillment in your own bedroom. Standards such as how often the average man or woman wants sex are really irrelevant and may become a destructive measuring stick. Your relationship with your husband is what it is. What your friend, your neighbor, or the rest of the country is doing should have little bearing on how your marriage works.

If this explanation describes you and your husband, healing begins

when you embrace the fact that there is nothing wrong with your marriage. Like the woman married to a shorter man, although you don't reflect the average couple, you are perfectly normal. Resist the urge to blame your husband or entertain feelings of inadequacy. Every couple has a unique sexual relationship. Accept yours for what it is and enjoy working toward wholeness as a couple. You can have a very fulfilling sex life even though you may not be functioning like the average married couple.

Normal Aging

As your husband ages, his body will steadily produce less and less testosterone. He may struggle with arousal, maintaining an erection, or ejaculation. In addition to these differences in sexual functioning, men also experience a decrease in muscle tissue, more difficulty concentrating, and less energy resulting from this hormonal change. Naturally, as a man ages, he's also at greater risk for the illnesses I'll address in the next section that further complicate sexuality.

Although a diminishing sex life may be disappointing for you as a wife, it's potentially devastating for your husband. His sexuality represents his youth, vitality, and masculinity. Be very sensitive to how you respond as you notice these changes taking place in your husband. This is a tremendous loss for him, likely coinciding with other losses, such as retirement or illness. More than ever, he will need your reassurance and love.

On the bright side, the decrease of testosterone that results from aging may have some positive effects on your marriage relationship. Your husband may become more sensitive, nurturing, and relational as his sex drive diminishes. Elevated levels of testosterone in men are linked with aggressive and competitive behaviors, while lower levels correlate with nurturing and attachment behaviors.[1] Many women report with delight that their husbands are becoming more interested in talking,

bonding, and relating as they age. Their husbands' decrease in testosterone and libido has opened up new avenues of relationship.

The effects of aging on sexual desire and functioning also impact a woman's sexuality. After natural or surgical menopause, a woman's level of estrogen decreases. She's likely to experience such symptoms as vaginal dryness, decreased sensitivity to touch, and decreased blood flow to the vaginal area. These typically translate into a lower sexual desire, difficulty becoming aroused, and even pain during intercourse.

Modern medicine has provided some remedies for low sex drive related to aging for both men and women. The most common are hormone therapy and medication to increase blood circulation.

Physical Dysfunction

In many of the marriages represented in the 20 percent, the dynamic of their sexual relationship is simply a function of the bell curve, as described above. These couples don't fit the typical stereotypes, but their differences are completely normal. However, some couples experience an atypical sexual relationship because of some form of physical dysfunction.

A man's sex drive is determined largely by the presence of testosterone levels in his body. Although a man's level of testosterone naturally fluctuates throughout his lifetime, some men have unusually low levels, resulting in a very low sex drive.

An unusually low production of testosterone is medically referred to as hypogonadism. Testosterone in the male body is produced in the testicles. When a problem with the testicles results in low testosterone levels, it is called "primary hypogonadism." This condition can be caused by chromosomal abnormalities, complications with mumps during adolescence or adulthood, too much iron in the bloodstream, injury to the testicles, cancer treatment, and normal aging.

Hormones produced by the pituitary gland and regulated by the hypothalamus signal testosterone production in the testicles. When

something goes awry in this stage of the process, the problem is referred to as "secondary hypogonadism." Hypothalamic and pituitary disorders, therefore, can cause a lack of testosterone. Inflammatory diseases, HIV, depression, thyroid disease, obesity, and certain pain and hormone medications can also contribute to secondary hypogonadism.

As if your husband's system weren't complicated enough, low sexual desire and sexual dysfunction can also result from problems with blood circulation. Just about any systemic illness can impact this aspect of sexual function, including diseases of the kidneys, lungs, liver, heart, nerves, arteries, or veins. Medications such as antihistamines, antidepressants, and high blood pressure treatments may also be culprits. Lifestyle issues such as substance abuse, smoking, and obesity, as well as the effects of stress and even prolonged bicycling, can cause erectile dysfunction.

If you feel overwhelmed by all these possibilities, remember the importance of adequate and regular medical care. Your husband may be hesitant to ask his physician about his sexual functioning. However, your encouragement, your doctor's advice, and medical intervention when necessary could make all the difference in your sex life.

Emotional Barriers

A purely physiological problem can quickly snowball into an emotional roadblock. You cannot underestimate how injurious it can be for your husband to find himself unable to perform sexually or to become the victim of a nonexistent libido. Although he may appear nonchalant, more than likely he's devastated and deeply wounded. In fact, he may avoid sexual encounters because of his tremendous fear of failure.

If your husband has experienced impotency or low sexual desire, the possibility of sex can immediately invoke anxiety and fear. Rather than face possible humiliation, he may make excuses to avoid sex, perhaps even blaming you for his disinterest.

Dr. Archibald Hart makes the astounding statement that more men have experienced unwanted sex than have women. His findings are based on the fact that men feel the need to prove their masculinity through always being ready for sex:

> Men feel tremendous pressure to prove that they are adequate as men. They do this through succeeding in business and sports and through talking tough and boasting. They also do it through sex—especially through sex. Sex has long been a major arena in which to assert one's manhood. . . . Men also equate sexual frequency with masculinity. They imagine that other men are more active than they are, and may have gathered their information from that great source of all wisdom on sexual matters, the movies. Film stars always seem to be ready, willing, and able.[2]

Remember back to Viagra commercials you may have seen within the past few years. A man walks into work with a smile on his face. Everyone tries to guess what's different about him. A haircut? Is he working out? Did he get a promotion? No. Thanks to Viagra, he's able to perform sexually. The message is clear: Sexual adequacy is linked to a man's confidence, well-being, and overall sense of power in all areas of his life.

What may have begun as a physical dysfunction can quickly turn into a devastating lack of confidence, depression, or anxiety disorder, which complicates the solution.

Past sexual trauma often plays into sexual dysfunction as well. In some marriages, the wife is hypersexual because of a traumatic past, unconsciously acting out feelings of shame or compulsively using sex as a way of gaining acceptance or affection from her husband. Alternatively, in other marriages, the husband's lack of interest is due to emotional traumas he has suppressed. For example, he may fear intimacy or losing

control. These fears will naturally inhibit his desire for healthy sexual expression. He may harbor shame related to past sexual indiscretions, sexual addictions, or childhood sexual abuse. We'll address these dynamics thoroughly in chapter 9.

If your sexual role reversal is potentially rooted in either physical or emotional dysfunction, it is *not* normal. The dysfunction represents a roadblock that you and your husband must accept but also work toward resolving. As difficult and embarrassing as it may be to seek help, you may need to reach out to a medical doctor or psychologist to address the issue that is interfering with your sexual fulfillment as a couple.

Who Wears the Pants in the Family?

Another reason you may find yourself identifying with this chapter is that the bedroom mirrors the rest of your relationship. Take Annie and Dale, for example. By nature, Annie is a type A personality. She is a go-getter who has strong opinions about everything. Dale, by contrast, is an easygoing, laid-back guy. Although Annie was initially attracted to Dale's carefree approach to life, she has quickly become irritated when Dale forgets to pay bills, leaves his dirty clothes all over the house, and approaches his job with a minimal amount of effort.

As Annie's aggravation with her husband builds, she begins nagging and criticizing. She, in no uncertain terms, lets Dale know that he isn't living up to her standards. Whether Dale is cooking in the kitchen, picking out Christmas presents, or "babysitting" their children, he can't seem to do anything right, according to Annie. Being a laid-back individual, Dale allows Annie to nag and take over. Ten years into their marriage, their pattern is definitely established. Although Dale and Annie rarely fight, their relationship seems to reflect a mother-son dynamic. Annie orders the household, and Dale halfheartedly participates.

True to form, Annie drags Dale to my office for counseling. She does most of the talking as she pleads with me to fix her husband.

Through tears of frustration, she recounts how passionately Dale had pursued her when they were dating, but how his interest in her has evaporated with time. She confesses that Dale hasn't responded to her sexually for several months. She is devastated by the fact that Dale avoids sex with her but is flirtatious with other women. Dale remains quiet but also seems puzzled by his sexual disinterest.

Dale and Annie have no idea that their problems in the bedroom might be linked to the dysfunction in their overall relationship. However, as we talk, Dale begins to express how inadequate he feels around his wife. Although he presents an unfazed exterior, Annie's nagging and criticism chip away at him. If he feels defeated and incompetent in all other areas, how could he be competent as a lover? He's destined to fail Annie in that area as well.

Annie never intended to dominate her husband. Their respective personalities just pulled them into this dynamic. On the surface, their marriage seems to work. The main reason they rarely argue is because Annie is content to be in charge, and Dale is okay taking a backseat. However, the dynamic of their relationship has created underlying tension, unmet needs, and resentments that play out in their sexual relationship. Annie blames Dale for his failure to initiate and perform sexually. Dale blames Annie for emasculating him.

This pattern of marital dysfunction is certainly not new, but it's becoming more commonplace. If this relationship dynamic seems to reflect your relationship with your husband, there is hope. No matter how long you've been married, you can learn how to reverse the pattern that ultimately discourages your husband's confidence and masculinity. I feel so passionately about this topic that I wrote a book about it. The book is called *Finding the Hero in Your Husband,* and the content stems from my struggle as a young wife to learn how to use my strengths and abilities without stepping on my husband's need to lead our family.

When Normal Sex Just Doesn't Cut It

The final, and perhaps most damaging, reason couples fall into the 20 Percent Club is involvement in pornography on the part of one or both partners. One of the devastating effects of pornography and other sexually explicit material is that it sabotages the ability to enjoy normal sex. In many marriages, the husband isn't interested in sex with his wife because he has been programmed to respond to a much higher level of erotic stimulation. After viewing material filled with perfectly shaped women doing wild and perverse acts, a man naturally may have difficulty becoming stimulated by his 40-year-old average-looking, reserved wife. In his clinical research, Dr. Victor Cline described this progression as "escalation":

> With the passage of time, the addicted person required rougher, more explicit, more deviant, and "kinky" kinds of sexual material to get their "highs" and "sexual turn-ons." It was reminiscent of individuals afflicted with drug addictions. Over time there is nearly always an increasing need for more of the stimulant to get the same initial effect.
>
> Being married or in a relationship with a willing sexual partner did not solve their problem. Their addiction and escalation were mainly due to the powerful sexual imagery in their minds, implanted there by the exposure to pornography.
>
> I have had a number of couple-clients where the wife tearfully reported that her husband preferred to masturbate to pornography than to make love to her.[3]

Not only does porn present a higher level of sexual excitement than married sex, it also allows a man to have sex on his terms. Porn is always available, never too busy, and always inviting. It doesn't criticize, doesn't require foreplay or patience, isn't dependent on "feeling close," and never has a headache. When a guy is engaged in this type of sexual outlet, his

sexuality becomes centered on his immediate needs and demands. The prospect of working through the messy issues of marital intimacy is pretty unattractive.

If you suspect that this dynamic is present in your marriage, hang on. We'll take an in-depth look at porn use in chapter 10.

• • •

While reading through the possible reasons for your membership in the 20 Percent Club, you may find that your marriage fits into more than one of the categories. In fact, one cause for sexual role reversal may even feed into the others. For example, Brent naturally has a lower sex drive than the average man. He never compared himself with other men or thought anything of it until his new wife, Amy, began complaining about wanting sex more often. As a young husband, Brent has been thrown off balance by Amy's lack of sexual fulfillment. He feels like a failure as a husband. If he can't effectively meet his wife's sexual needs, he must be a loser. Because of his fear of inadequacy, he begins withdrawing from Amy, failing to assert himself in all areas of their marriage. What began as a bell-curve difference has snowballed into a serious marital issue.

As you seek to address these multiple issues in your relationship, define them without blame. Regardless of how you got where you are, assigning blame to each other will only hamper your efforts to heal. Neither you nor your husband consciously *chose* to have a low sex drive, go through depression, experience childhood trauma, or any of the other maladies that compromise your intimate life. Every couple has roadblocks to address, and this is yours.

Make Sex, Sex

Regardless of why you and your husband are in the 20 Percent Club, the most helpful route to take is to bring sex back to the purpose for

which it was designed. While a primary message in this book is that you can underestimate the importance of sex in your marriage, be aware that you can also overestimate its importance. Couples in their 70s and 80s are often asexual as one or both have medical conditions that prevent intercourse. However, their friendship, seasoned love, and shared history are often enough to maintain a marriage in which sex is no longer possible.

Being part of the 20 Percent Club often results in a couple allowing this one issue to dominate their entire relationship. Sex begins to take on an overwhelming meaning and magnitude. Both husband and wife harbor the deep fear that "something must be wrong with me." As these emotions fester, they overtake the sexual relationship and possibly even the marriage. An invitation for sex carries the weight of the deepest emotional needs of both husband and wife: Will I be accepted or rejected? Will I be competent or a failure? Sex becomes a testing ground for each partner's love, worthiness, or competence. The sexual environment is laden with expectations that reach far beyond the bedroom. In this context, no wonder both husband and wife routinely end up feeling as though they have failed and been failed.

As I mentioned earlier, your husband's level of sexual desire is based on a number of complex psychological, biological, and relational issues, many of which may have absolutely nothing to do with you. His sexuality doesn't define him, nor does it necessarily reflect how he feels about you. He can be absolutely in love with you and think you're very attractive, yet still lack the interest or ability to perform sexually. Don't allow this one aspect of your marriage to color and dominate your perception of your husband, your marriage, or yourself.

To put sex back into the appropriate context, you need to remember that it's simply one expression of how you relate to your husband. You also share childrearing, hobbies, hardships, friends, spiritual

interests, vocational trials and successes, ministry, mentors, and countless other aspects of the marital journey.

Taking the pressure off your sexual relationship may allow you to enjoy what you have instead of carrying the burden to create what you lack. Although you may experience frustration in the sexual arena, most likely there are many other aspects of your relationship that are thriving and can unify you. Build upon those aspects, even as you strive to address the roadblocks you experience in sexual intimacy.

But How Do I Address My Unmet Needs?

Hopefully this chapter has given you reassurance that you aren't alone in your struggle and has equipped you with some understanding of the variables that may be interfering with healthy sexual functioning in your marriage. But however helpful this information might be, you are likely still left with unmet needs for affection and sexual fulfillment. Following are a couple of suggestions that may be of help.

Accept What He Offers

One of the keys to growing beyond the frustration you now feel is learning to accept the many ways your husband is likely showing you love. Many of the women I've met with who identify themselves with the 20 Percent Club describe their husbands as very loving and attentive in ways other than their sexuality. These husbands may be generous with words of affirmation or acts of service. Yet their wives discount these expressions because of what is lacking. If your husband tells you you're beautiful or that he's crazy about you, believe him. As you recognize the ways that he serves and affirms you, encourage him. Additionally, encourage forms of physical affection that don't involve the pressure of sexual intercourse, such as back rubs, holding hands, playful touching, and hugging.

Learn to Compromise

Whenever one person wants sex more often than the other, the obvious answer is to compromise. The person with a higher sex drive may have sex less often than he would like, and the person with the lower sex drive may have sex more often than she feels the need to. The compromise is based on mutual love and care. Although this compromise typically works when the man is more interested in sex, it's not quite as effective when the roles are reversed. Here's why: A woman can have sex even if she's not into it. A man can't. He can't feign excitement or have a quickie just to meet her needs if he's not aroused.

One way around this is to broaden your definition of sex. If you desire intimacy with your husband and he isn't able to meet that need, be creative. How can you experience a sexual release with him outside of intercourse? Remember that you're still engaged in marital intimacy even if it doesn't involve what you typically think of as sex. There is no shame in wanting intimacy with your husband more often. And there is no shame in encouraging him to seek other ways to please you.

Growing Closer Through the Challenges

In almost every marriage, either the husband or the wife feels sexually unfulfilled, at least at some level. What probably makes your situation more difficult are your expectations. Based on what everyone else seems to be doing, as well as the cultural stereotypes, you may expect that your husband should be pursuing you. This expectation is likely a huge barrier to accepting your sexual relationship for what it is and growing closer to your husband through this challenge.

Remember that sex isn't love, but it is designed to be an expression of love. The most mature expression of love in your marriage is embracing your husband simply for who he is without demands and expectations. In fact, it is through your disappointment and lingering

needs that your love is stretched to encompass more than self-fulfill-
ment. Perhaps God desires to use your lack of fulfillment to foster a
deeper love in your heart for your husband.

SOMETHING TO THINK ABOUT • • • • •

1. If your marriage is (or has ever been) in the 20 Percent Club,
how has this impacted your relationship with your husband?
Together, try to identify why your marriage works the way it
does.

2. Which of these practical suggestions could you (and your
husband) put into play?
   - Stop comparing your marriage with other marriages.
   - Stop blaming yourself or your spouse for the way your
   sex life has unfolded.
   - Seek a medical consultation for underlying biological
   causes.
   - Seek marital counseling for the lack of interest in sex
   and/or the negative impact it has had on your relationship.

eight

I Can't Compete with That

One of my pet peeves is listening to skinny women talk about weight issues. So I'm going to lay it out for you right away. I'm not overweight, yet I've struggled with body image practically my whole life. Counting calories, promising to get in shape, hating myself because of physical imperfections, dreading the thought of wearing a swimsuit in public, judging myself and others by purely physical standards—been there, done that. Throughout adolescence and young adulthood, I probably bordered on a weight obsession. I was terrified of becoming fat.

These feelings and fears certainly played a part in my anticipation of and apprehension about sexual intimacy. What would my husband think of my body? Would he view me as beautiful? Would he consider me sexy? Throughout our marriage, would he be critical of my physical appearance or encouraging?

No matter your size or shape, you can probably relate to these sentiments. We all can find something to feel insecure about. Even Solomon's beautiful bride was self-conscious before her lover. She fretted about her tanned skin. In her time, "beautiful" women were pale, indicating that they were wealthy enough to avoid outside labor.

Every marriage deals with body issues at some level. Some marriages

have to battle through significant illness or handicaps, while other couples are hampered by everyday details involving weight or hygiene. Perhaps just as important as what the physical body looks like is a person's body image. In other words, a woman may actually be physically attractive but be haunted by insecurity and self-consciousness. Likewise, another woman may be relatively unattractive but be at peace with her physical appearance and feel sexually affirmed by her husband. A woman's weight or physical appearance often has very little to do with whether or not she's comfortable in her own skin.

There's no getting around it, marital intimacy requires your body. Arousal, sensations of giving and receiving pleasure, and the vulnerability of oneness all begin with the physical body. Naturally, if there are problems with the body, there will be problems with sex. Your physical appearance and how you feel about it *will* impact your sex life, for better or for worse.

Sex and Your Body Image

As we pursue God's design for sex, it's tough to know how to deal with this headache. On the one hand, we know that the Bible teaches us not to be too invested in the physical realm. We're supposed to store up treasures in heaven (Matthew 6:20) and focus on spiritual beauty instead of physical beauty (1 Peter 3). But we can't get around the fact that we live in a physical world and that our bodies are important here on earth. Every day, we have to engage with body stuff like showers, makeup, food, clothes, and sex. Husbands are visual creatures who care about their wives' physical appearance. So, is the body important or not?

This headache of sex shows up in very practical situations like the following:

- "I feel self-conscious about being overweight. My husband doesn't complain, but I can't get into sex looking the way I do. Do I need to lose weight to be sexy?"
- "My husband is extremely critical and cutting regarding my appearance. I feel like he's constantly comparing me to other women."
- "I've never told him, but my husband's body turns me off. He's gained a lot of weight over the years and seems to have let himself go. How do I tell him that I avoid sex because he disgusts me?"
- "Because of some physical limitations, my husband and I can't engage in certain sexual acts. I think we both feel like our sex life is less than whole because of this, even though we've never talked about it."

The solution to these and other practical questions about sex is rooted in how we think. Before we get into the day-to-day suggestions that can help you with the body-image headache, we need to take a close look at the assumptions and thinking that often underlie the problem.

How God Looks at Your Body

Don't you wish that the Bible read like a self-help book? Or better yet, what if it were a self-help hotline or Web site? Wouldn't it be great if you could type in a topic like "How to feel great about your body" and find a three-step process straight from the mouth of God that would solve your problem?

Although the Bible isn't as "user friendly" as this, it still contains relevant principles that apply to real-life dilemmas like the one we're addressing in this chapter. Granted, the early church didn't have the need for Weight Watchers, nor did the women in the early church have to

compete with the airbrushed images in the *Sports Illustrated* swimsuit edition. However, God's truth, inspired and written thousands of years ago, can lay the foundation for how God wants us to think about our bodies. Consider the following truths about your body from God's Word.

Your Body Is a Temporary Tent That Will Deteriorate

Although this truth seems pretty obvious, it isn't one we regularly apply to our lives. In fact, it flies in the face of the way our culture views the body. For those who don't place their trust in the hope of eternity, these bodies are all they have. The body isn't seen as a "temporary tent" but as a palatial residence that must be maintained at all costs. When the body deteriorates and dies, there's nothing else. So our culture fights against the concept that aging and eventual death are natural processes. We feel the pressure to look younger and healthier than we actually are. Just think about the prominence of hair dye to cover the gray, anti-aging creams and serums, control-top pantyhose, makeup to hide wrinkles and blemishes, and plastic surgery. It's actually pretty pathetic when you step back to see all of these deteriorating people trying desperately to preserve the illusion of beauty and youth.

Why do you think God designed the aging process to proceed the way it does? As humans, we reach our physical prime in our mid-20s and then start to decline. Why didn't God design our bodies to keep getting better and better as we age, until we die peacefully, beautiful and robust?

I believe God's design of fleeting beauty and strength is an undeniable reminder to look beyond the physical reality. Time and again, Scripture highlights this principle. The beauty and strength of people are compared to the fading beauty of a flower that is here one day but wilted the next (see Isaiah 28:1–4 and James 1:10–11). The writer of Ecclesiastes, once so strong, handsome, and wise, implored young men and women to remember God while they are young, knowing that the

beauty and strength of their human bodies will soon be gone. Read his description of what he was probably experiencing, even as he wrote:

> Honor and enjoy your Creator while you're still young,
> Before the years take their toll and your vigor wanes,
> Before your vision dims and the world blurs
> And the winter years keep you close to the fire.
>
> In old age, your body no longer serves you so well.
> Muscles slacken, grip weakens, joints stiffen.
> The shades are pulled down on the world.
> You can't come and go at will. Things grind to a halt.
> The hum of the household fades away.
> You are wakened now by bird-song.
> Hikes to the mountains are a thing of the past.
> Even a stroll down the road has its terrors.
> Your hair turns apple-blossom white,
> Adorning a fragile and impotent matchstick body.
> Yes, you're well on your way to eternal rest,
> While your friends make plans for your funeral.
>
> Life, lovely while it lasts, is soon over.
> Life as we know it, precious and beautiful, ends.
> The body is put back in the same ground it came from.
> The spirit returns to God, who first breathed it.
>   (Ecclesiastes 12:1–7, MSG)

For a modern-day example of this, look up beautiful movie stars from the 1940s. What do they look like now? What did they look like right before they died? No one escapes the deterioration of the body. If your sex life and confidence are based on physical beauty, you're

fighting a losing battle! All the plastic surgery and Viagra in the world won't sustain your love.

God Cares About Your Body as a Means to an End

Although our bodies won't last, that doesn't mean they're not important on this earth. But the importance of our bodies isn't in how they look, it's in how we use them. Take a look at what the Bible says about our bodies:

> Just as you used to offer the parts of your body in slavery to impurity and to ever-increasing wickedness, so now offer them in slavery to righteousness leading to holiness. (Romans 6:19B)

> Therefore, I urge you, brothers, in view of God's mercy, to offer your bodies as living sacrifices, holy and pleasing to God—this is your spiritual act of worship. (Romans 12:1)

> Do you not know that your body is a temple of the Holy Spirit, who is in you, whom you have received from God? You are not your own; you were bought at a price. Therefore honor God with your body. (1 Corinthians 6:19–20)

> So whether you eat or drink or whatever you do, do it all for the glory of God. (1 Corinthians 10:31)

God cares more about how you're using your body than what you look like. Your body is a tool to glorify Him and to love others. Often we attack body-image issues by focusing on the body as the end result, not as a means to an end. We believe the lie that if only we could fit into a size 4 or have a bigger cup size, the world would be a better place.

Before you begin to address the concerns you have with your body,

you must ask the question "Why?" Do you want to resolve these issues simply so you can feel better about yourself? Or have you taken to heart the teaching of Scripture? Your body is important not because of what it looks like but because of how you are using it.

The Gospels record many times when Jesus interacted with people on the basis of their physical needs. He healed the sick, the lame, and the blind. But remember that their physical healing was always for the purpose of highlighting something in the spiritual realm. Perhaps the clearest example was when Jesus healed a blind man in John 9:1–7. Those watching the miracle asked Jesus, "Rabbi, who sinned, this man or his parents, that he was born blind?" Jesus told them that the sole purpose the man was born blind was so that God might be glorified through him.

How are you using your body? In your marriage, does your body promote intimacy or prohibit it? The most beautiful body can be used to glorify self, to arouse the interest of other men, or to promote pride and jealousy. How about the other end of the beauty spectrum? Many times, gaining weight or disregarding your physical appearance is motivated by a fear of intimacy. The extra 80 pounds or an unkempt appearance keeps you safe from the attention of men, including your husband. To be desired by him is too threatening.

If you've placed your trust in Christ, who died to reconcile you to God, your body isn't your own. You've been bought with a great price. What you look like and how you care for yourself should no longer be motivated by the lust of the world, the pride of life, or a fear of intimacy, but by a love for God and for others. You have been called to one purpose: to glorify God with your body.

Your Body Is a Gift

The obvious application of glorifying God with your body is that your body is God's gift to you and your gift back to Him. However, Scripture also highlights the fact that your body is your gift to your husband:

"The wife's body does not belong to her alone but also to her husband" (1 Corinthians 7:4).

Solomon's erotic poetry in Song of Songs goes into great detail, describing how marital love is the exchange of the gift of the body. It's a primary way in which husbands and wives love and honor each other, particularly in a young marriage.

The day you got married, you gave yourself as a gift to your husband. Every time you have sex, you renew that commitment, giving yourself to him again. Your body and how you view it determine how you go about giving that gift.

Every year at Christmas, there are some gifts you just can't wait to give. It may be the one gift you stumbled upon that was just perfect for the person you had in mind. Or it might be that item your child has been wanting for months, and you decided to splurge. You can't wait to see the expression on your loved ones' faces when they open up what you know they've always wanted.

Contrast that feeling with the mandatory gifts we give because it's Christmas or someone's birthday, and gifts are required. You can't find anything just right, so you settle for a tie, a picture frame, or a boxed fruitcake. You might even preface the gift exchange with "It's just something little." In other words, "You probably won't like this too much, so don't get your hopes up, but I had to get you something." After they open the gift and politely thank you, you might even apologize: "I'm sorry it wasn't something more, but . . ."

If your body is a gift you give to your husband, which gift do you feel like you're giving him? Do you give it with great confidence that "You're gonna love this!" or with a lukewarm "You're gonna have to settle"?

If you don't like your body, it will be difficult to present it with confidence as a gift to your husband. You may want to make love with the lights off or prefer that your husband not touch you in certain places.

Or perhaps you fantasize about being more physically attractive during intimacy.

Please understand that how you view your body may be far more important than what it actually looks like. A beautiful woman riddled with insecurities won't be a satisfying lover. She will likely be so wrapped up in her imperfections that she won't be able to freely please her husband or enjoy the pleasure he gives her. By contrast, an average looking woman who gives her beauty confidently to her husband can knock his socks off.

Changing How You View Your Body—and His

The world's emphasis on the body is all about self-improvement, not gift improvement. You're encouraged to lose weight, get a tummy tuck, or spend thousands of dollars on clothing so that you feel good about yourself. When you begin viewing your body as a gift to your husband, your focus should shift from what is important to you to what is important to him. Most women are far more concerned about their insecurities than they are about how their husbands feel about them. Do you even know what's important to your husband?

Practically Speaking

Someone once said, "The problem with Christians is that they can be so heavenly minded that they are no earthly good." While biblical principles challenge your thinking, being "earthly good" means applying those truths to the everyday life of your marriage. You can do this in three ways.

1. Take care of your body, but don't become obsessed with it. Have you ever been inside an absolutely gorgeous home, only to find yourself counting the minutes until you could leave? The most beautiful homes

often aren't the kind you want to live in, especially if you have young children. Instead of enjoying the beauty of the home, you're terrified of getting the white carpet dirty or breaking a priceless figurine. You may even talk more quietly than normal or sit on the edge of the couch instead of making yourself comfortable.

Compare your experience in a model home with what it feels like to be in your favorite home. Whose house do you most love to visit? What home makes you feel welcomed, like you could just hang out all day? Most likely, it's clean enough to be comfortable, but not perfectly immaculate. The home probably has furniture, curtains, and pictures that are pleasing, but nothing is so pristine that it makes you hesitant to relax. The beauty of the home is a pleasant and inviting backdrop to the fellowship that really matters.

When you wrestle with how much attention to pay to your body, think of the metaphor of the two homes. Physical perfection is much less important than the overall ambience of your sexual relationship. The average husband (there are exceptions) is happy and content when his wife takes reasonable steps to care for her body. Just like a pleasant home is modestly clean and tastefully decorated, a truly beautiful wife is one who makes an effort but isn't obsessed with perfection.

If you have let yourself go and ignored your outward appearance, this likely has impacted your husband and your sex life. Just think of walking into a home that has been totally neglected. Dishes are piled in the sink, mold is growing in the toilets, the stench of dirty laundry is in the air, and cockroaches are running across the floor. No matter how much you may love the people you came to visit, you just want to get home and take a shower. Their failure to prepare for your visit is a serious obstacle to enjoying your time together.

Likewise, when a man or woman stops caring about weight, health, hygiene, and so on, it often creates resentment in his or her spouse. Just

like an obviously unkempt house, it communicates, "I don't care about how you feel."

Your appearance is important to your husband. Not only does he want to be physically attracted to you, he also wants to feel proud of the way you look. You represent him. He wants to walk into the room with you and say to the world, "This is my wife." Physical appearance isn't all-important, but it does play a part.

On the other side of the spectrum, caring about your physical appearance doesn't mean striving toward perfection. No matter what you look like, becoming obsessed with your body or weight will ultimately defeat the purpose of intimacy. Your husband, your kids, your friends, and even those who barely know you will feel ill at ease, hesitant to relax in your presence. While taking care of your body is important to intimacy, obsessing about it will kill intimacy.

I've met women who religiously diet and work out to maintain their beauty and youth. They may spend hours a day and thousands of dollars a year to ensure that their makeup, hair, and clothing are just right. All of these efforts do little to build intimacy in their marriages. This pursuit of perfection is more about an obsession with self than about creating oneness with their husbands.

2. Accept your husband's affirmations. You don't have to be an expert in sex to know that men are stimulated primarily through visual channels. This may heighten the pressure you feel to look good. Despite media portrayals, you don't have to be a beauty queen to be sexually attractive to your husband. Sometimes, we resist this truth as women, insisting that anything short of cover-girl looks disqualifies us from beauty.

I remember working with one couple who was really battling through intimacy issues, largely rooted in the wife's poor body image. Both the husband and wife were moderately overweight, but the wife, Keisha, just couldn't get past the weight she had gained by having

children. When her husband, Tyrone, approached her for sex, Keisha resisted because she didn't feel sexy. She continually promised him, "I'll get into it again when I can be attractive for you. I need to lose this weight first." Every time Keisha said this, Tyrone reminded her, "You don't need to lose weight for me. I'm very attracted to you just like you are." As often as he repeated this message, Keisha refused to accept it.

Just because you don't like your body, don't assume your husband feels the same way. God designed your husband to be attracted to the female body, even in its less-than-perfect condition. If your husband thinks you're sexy, why argue with him? Thank God that He has given your husband eyes for you, just as you are. If you're blessed to have married a guy who compliments you about your physical appearance, accept his words instead of resisting them. Your husband's most awesome gift to you is his love and encouraging words.

After giving birth to three nine-pound boys, my stomach isn't what it used to be. I'm not exaggerating when I say that it looks like a rumpled paper bag. Just the other day, one of my boys saw my stomach and pulled back as if he had just seen Gollum from *The Lord of the Rings*. My husband used to love my stomach. Once upon a time, he praised me like Solomon for how flat and flawless it was. Naturally, my post-childbirth midsection became a source of insecurity for me. I didn't want Mike to see or touch my stomach during intimacy. Once I shared this with him, he kissed my wrinkly stomach and said, "I love your stomach, marks and all. It's what carried our three little boys." I could either accept his affirmation or hang on to my insecurity. If it didn't bother him, why should it bother me?

3. *Let go of preconceived ideas about what is sexy.* A poor body image typically interferes with sexual fulfillment because we accept the world's view of what is sexy. Without a doubt, our society has a standard for what is sexy and what isn't. (Wrinkly stomachs are definitely out!) However, in the reality of your marriage, what Universal Studios, NBC, or

People magazine thinks is irrelevant. It's between you and your husband to define *sexy*. That means letting go of preconceived ideas of what defines sexy. You don't have to have long, flowing hair, a perfect figure, and a siren's voice to be sexy to your husband. Who granted the bigwigs in Hollywood or the magazine editors in New York City the role of defining sexy? Certainly not the Author and Creator of sex. God designed you and your husband to be sexual together. He created you in such a way that you inherently arouse your husband. Whether you suppress it or embrace it, you are sexual by God's design.

Unfortunately, both men and women are so inundated with air-brushed and Photoshopped images of perfection and sexually oriented material that the average husband and wife seem dumpy, lumpy, and frumpy. As much as possible, get rid of the magazines and other visual channels that make both you and your husband feel unattractive. You can be extremely attractive to your husband just the way you are and appeal to his visual preferences with the body God has given you. Ask your husband what he likes to see you in or how he likes you to wear your hair. Perhaps even take him shopping with you (if he's one of those rare men who will actually go). After all, he's the only person on earth for whom it really matters whether or not you're "hot."

The Danger of Unrealistic Expectations

Another obstacle to changing the way you view your body is your expectations. Perhaps the most difficult aspect of the body-image headache is determining just what are realistic expectations. Is it fair for your husband to expect you to stay in shape? Is it realistic for him to expect you to still fit into your wedding dress 25 years later?

Every once in a while, I'll come across a marriage in which the man holds unreasonable expectations for his wife's physical appearance. He's critical of her if she gains a few pounds, or he demands that she dress to the nines. He may suggest that she diet, work out, or consider plas-

tic surgery to keep up her appearance. (Wives can have this attitude toward their husbands as well!)

This behavior is rooted not in sexual attraction but in pride and control. The husband is really saying to his wife, "You represent me. You'd better look the part." Subtle threats of rejection are tied into this dynamic. The unspoken message is, "If you don't stay attractive, I'll be justified in cheating on you."

I can't underscore enough how destructive this dynamic is to a marriage. If you harbor these feelings toward your husband or believe that he feels this way toward you, *address the problem now!* Critical or threatening attitudes will destroy the atmosphere of safety and trust required for intimacy to flourish. Remember that a trusting, accepting relationship is far more important to intimacy than having beautiful bodies.

If we could look into the bedrooms of even the most beautiful couples, we'd likely find that they still battle sexual headaches. Our physical bodies aren't the end-all in the sexual relationship. How a husband and wife respond to each other, love each other, and embrace each other, in light of imperfection, are much more important factors in a great sex life. Even if you and your husband had perfect bodies, a critical or threatening spirit would kill the intimacy in your marriage.

Body-image problems can go both ways. Although physical appearance may not be *as* important for women, it can still be a barrier to sexual intimacy. In addition to physical appearance, poor hygiene is a common "wet blanket." Even if he says all of the right words and makes all of the right moves, who wants to kiss a guy with horrible breath or have sex when he has terrible BO?

If something about your husband's body turns you off, ask yourself, "Are my expectations realistic?" I've talked to women who complain about very normal bodily changes in their husbands. Yes, his hairline is receding, and he's not as buff as he was when he was 25. That's just part of the aging process. On the other hand, some women have legitimate

complaints and concerns, such as a husband who is significantly over-weight or pays no attention to personal hygiene. If your disappointment is based on unrealistic expectations, you need to revisit some of your as-sumptions. What are you watching, looking at, or reading that keeps you discontented with your very normal husband?

It's okay to address realistic concerns. However, addressing legiti-mate body issues with your husband can be tricky. Guys can be just as sensitive about their bodies as we are about ours. Besides, I've never heard of a man who decided to lose weight or change his appearance be-cause of a spouse's complaints. It has to be his idea. In fact, he's more likely to work on his body within the context of love and encouragement than he is if your attitude is rejecting and critical.

Instead of criticizing or complaining, there may be a time to share concern. For example, it's legitimate to bring up health concerns to a spouse who is overweight. Focusing on health is far more constructive than striving for physical attractiveness. Additionally, you're much more likely to influence your husband through encouragement than you are through criticism. When he dresses up, works on getting in shape, or puts on your favorite cologne, tell him how much it means to you.

Finally, focus on what's attractive about your husband. We've all had the experience of developing great affection for someone in spite of what he or she looked like. While physical appearance is important in the beginning of the relationship, it can be superseded by other attrac-tive qualities like kindness, a genuine smile, a sense of humor, or a sharp intellect. What qualities do you love about your husband? What quirky habits can you delight in that make him unique?

For Mature Audiences Only

A few weeks ago, Mike and I went out to dinner with a couple who were in their 70s. Somehow, we started discussing the topic of this book:

overcoming the problems that plague married couples in the bedroom. As the waiter approached our table, the gentleman we were dining with announced, as if on cue, "My wife and I are now having the best sex of our marriage!" With a twinkle in his eye, he added, "You young people don't know what you're missing."

I could just imagine what was going through the mind of that young waiter. I'm certain he retold the story many times: "I was serving a table with this couple who looked like my great-grandparents, when the old guy said . . ."

In our culture, it's inconceivable to think of great sex outside of physical attractiveness. Sex is for the young and beautiful.

To get past the dissatisfaction you have about your body (or perhaps your husband's body), you must confront the lie that sexuality is dependent on appearance. Physical attributes actually have very little to do with sexual fulfillment in a long-term committed relationship. God's design is amazing. The love He weaves into two hearts that are committed to each other represents a beauty that overshadows physical flaws and decline.

Practically all sex portrayed in our society focuses on the body. Two teenagers or young adults with flawless bodies portray hot, sweaty, passionate sex for the camera. With a few exceptions, seldom do movies feature unattractive, old, or overweight actors engaged physically. We've been conditioned to believe that sexual enjoyment and passion are totally dependent on physical fitness and attractiveness. Beautiful people have great sex. Ugly people have sex thinking about the beautiful people.

In reality, physical attraction is only the very first step to sex. In mature relationships, physical appearance fades away and is replaced by something far more significant and lasting.

Don't let the media make you feel like you're missing out because you and your husband don't look like the hottest actors and actresses.

The greatest sex is an outpouring of mature love, communication, security, and trust. I truly believe that the gentleman we dined with was right. He and his wife have been married for more than 40 years, learning to love and trust each other fully. They've experienced joy, sorrow, sickness, loss, and triumph. Their wrinkled and declining bodies can't get in the way of that kind of intimacy.

God's design for sex is so much more than enjoying a beautiful body! He longs to teach us a beauty beyond the physical. Read what Dave Burchett, Emmy Award–winning television sports director, author, and speaker, wrote about his journey of discovering true beauty after 29 years of marriage:

A Husband's Honest Reflections on Feminine Beauty
By Dave Burchett

One of my smart aleck remarks that I use periodically is that "I am not burdened by that whole maturity thing." There are many times when I go about demonstrating that in real life. But the unwelcome intrusion of "life" into my happy little routine has caused me to evaluate a lot of things. God is teaching and revealing a lot of things to me during our cancer journey.

1. I am clearly a work in progress as a follower of Jesus.

2. He has done a lot of work over the years that I was not aware of until this cancer trial came along.

Last night I had the weird privilege of helping clip off the rest of my bride's hair that was falling out from the chemotherapy. As I reflected on that moment later I realized that nearly everything I knew about beauty when I was 25 years old was wrong. Like most men I looked for appearance first and then tried to find some good qualities. Joni was a stunningly beautiful woman when I fell in love with her over thirty years ago. I have often said that I married my trophy wife first and got it over with. I also joke that I married her

to deepen my gene pool. And she has done that admirably. One of the ironies of this cancer journey is remembering how much I loved Joni's long hair in the early years of our relationship. In fact I got upset when she cut it a few years into our marriage without my consent. Her hair was a real part of her beauty in my stunted male view of what beauty in a woman means.

To be completely honest, I wondered how I would react when the chemotherapy had its inevitable effect and she would be bald. Oh, I knew I would say the right things. I am not that stupid. But how would I react inside? Would it matter more than I cared to admit? And that is when I realized how much God has been working over the years. He has been retooling my thinking and my heart. Patiently. Quietly. Lovingly.

Joni's hair began to give up while I was on a recent trip. She decided to get the buzz cut while I was gone (again without my consent). So I walked in the door and she, in typical Joni fashion asked, "Want to see my head?" When I did I realized what God has been doing over the years to a shallow and selfish guy. He has been changing me and what I perceive to be beautiful. Because the truth is that Joni is as beautiful to me today as she was with that long, shining hair thirty years ago. That is because I am learning what beauty in a woman really looks like.

Some days are better than others. I am grateful for the days when the sparkle returns to her beautiful blue eyes. Those eyes are the windows to a soul that has more depth than I could ever achieve. She is remarkable. She is my hero. Her faith inspires me. Her smile still lights up the room. I treasure each moment that I can make her laugh. The sound of her laughing is like a symphony to me. I have learned that beauty is so much more than what the world and testosterone ridden young men (or older men) think it is. Beauty is a package. One part physical to be sure. But beauty in the

covenant of marriage is also emotional and spiritual. When I fell in love with Joni I just thought I was marrying a foxy lady. I was really too stupid to know I was marrying a gift from God. The classic description of a Godly woman from Proverbs 31 fits her pretty well.

Who can find a virtuous and capable wife? She is worth more than precious rubies. Her husband can trust her, and she will greatly enrich his life...

She is clothed with strength and dignity, and she laughs with no fear of the future. When she speaks, her words are wise, and kindness is the rule when she gives instructions. She carefully watches all that goes on in her household and does not have to bear the consequences of laziness. Her children stand and bless her. Her husband praises her: There are many virtuous and capable women in the world, but you surpass them all! Charm is deceptive, and beauty does not last; but a woman who fears the LORD will be greatly praised. Reward her for all she has done. Let her deeds publicly declare her praise.

I married an amazing woman. Right now she happens to be bald . . . and so very beautiful.[1]

Through the maturing of Dave's love, his concept of beauty changed from the external to the internal. By his own admission, he was initially attracted to his wife's outward appearance and dreaded the fading of her external beauty. Yet through the process of watching that physical loveliness be stripped away, Dave found a stronger appreciation for a beauty that could never fade.

The apostle Peter wrote, "Your beauty should not come from outward adornment, such as braided hair and the wearing of gold jewelry and fine clothes. Instead, it should be that of your inner self, the unfading beauty of a gentle and quiet spirit, which is of great worth in God's sight" (1 Peter 3:3–4).

As your relationship with your husband matures, remember that your body is simply a tool to express and to learn how to love. It is the means to an end, not an end in itself. God desires to teach each of us to look beyond the physical, to use the body—beautiful or not—to develop a love that transcends this world that is passing away. Where are you in this journey?

SOMETHING TO THINK ABOUT • • • • •

1. How has the culture's definition of a sexy, beautiful couple impacted your sex life?

2. Do you agree with this statement: "God cares about your body as a means to an end"? How might that challenge your view of your body as well as your husband's body?

3. If your body were a house, how would you describe it?

4. Based on what you've read in this chapter, how might you desire to change your approach to your body (or your husband's body)?

nine

Check Your Baggage
at the Gate

I'm old enough to remember when checking baggage on an airline was absolutely free, as long as you only checked two bags per person. Then, just a few years ago, all airlines invoked the 50-pound rule. As long as you packed two moderate-sized bags, you were golden. Just recently, the airlines cut down the regulation to one free bag per passenger weighing 50 pounds or less. But that wasn't the final word. We barely had time to get used to that rule when they changed their minds once again. Now, every bag checked will cost you when you fly on most major airlines. I'm not sure what's next—perhaps they'll start charging a no-bag fee.

Checking baggage on an airline may have once been free, yet bringing baggage into a marriage has always been costly. Perhaps the price of the baggage isn't apparent to a couple up front, but in time it will exact a toll. This is particularly true of the impact of sexual baggage in the bedroom.

The trends of our culture all but ensure that a newly married couple will be loading many suitcases on the plane of matrimony. With the rise of porn use and addiction, sexual exploitation, and casual sex throughout the teen and young-adult years, almost every couple lugs some baggage into the bedroom.

Perhaps the price tag of sexual baggage explains many of the ironic findings reflecting sex in modern culture. Societal norms have granted everyone a free ride to sexually experiment as boldly and wildly as they choose. The message is, have sex with anyone, any time, any gender, in any way, and don't feel guilty about it. It's all part of personal expression and discovering yourself. Yet in a culture without shame or restraint, married men and women complain of a lack of satisfying sex. According to a survey conducted by Insight Express and *Parade* magazine, 31 percent of married couples surveyed have sex less than once a month, and 25 percent describe sex as either tolerable or terrible.[1] If you think those numbers are dismal, research suggests that monogamous married people experience higher levels of sexual satisfaction than anyone else.[2] Go figure. Could it be that lowering the morality of sexuality actually decreases the pleasure it brings?

There's a good chance that you and/or your husband stepped on the plane of marital intimacy with baggage in tow. Some luggage perhaps was the result of your own foolish choices, while other bags may have been thrust upon you without your knowledge or consent. Either way, ignoring their presence won't eliminate the cost to your marriage.

Understanding the Influence of Sexual Baggage

As a psychologist, I've run into more than a few skeptics regarding the impact of the past on the present. Many people share the belief that you should just move on. You can't change the past, so why talk about it?

Regardless of your opinion of psychology as a field, you cannot deny the fact that your past plays a significant role in how you see the world and interact with others. Think about your religious convictions, your hobbies, and your passions. They are all probably linked in some way to your childhood, your teen years, or your relationship with your mom or

dad. The past is the lens through which we naturally view the present and the future.

Your attitude and reaction to sex has been greatly influenced by your past, whether your experience was positive or negative. Did your parents display healthy affection in their marriage? Did they take the time to teach you about sex from a biblical perspective? Were you protected from sexually exploitive material, comments, or contact? How about your dating experiences through the teen years? Were you sexually active? How did the boys you dated treat you? And what about your relationship with your sweetheart before and throughout your marriage?

The impact of sexual baggage isn't consistent across the board. One woman can be wracked with guilt and shame 30 years after giving away her virginity in the backseat of a car, while another woman with a prolific history of sexual partners seems to move past it with no apparent consequences to her marriage. Every person is different, and every piece of baggage a husband or wife carries is unique.

Although there is no tried-and-true formula for how certain events will impact a person, there are cause-and-effect principles that tend to play out with some consistency. For example, a history of sexual abuse in adolescence has a different impact than childhood sexual abuse. A young woman or man who was sexually exploited as an adolescent is more likely to struggle with identity confusion and guilt than a victim of childhood sexual abuse. Why? A teen is in the middle of development, struggling with questions about her beauty, identity, and sexuality. Date rape or other unwanted sexual contact during the teen years wreaks havoc with the normal developmental process. A teen may have experienced physiological arousal during the sexual abuse, heaping on even more guilt and confusion. "Did I cause it? Did I really want it? What's wrong with me?"

As you reflect on the baggage you and your husband have brought

into your bedroom, remember that there's no formula for how you should feel. However, the following points can help you make sense of how sexual baggage may be compromising your intimate life.

Sexual Baggage Promotes Untrue Assumptions

If you want to know the difference between the work of God and the work of Satan, just look for the contrast between the truth and a lie. Jesus said that He is the truth, while Satan is the father of lies. The work of the Enemy in your sexuality will always result in you believing lies. Whatever your sexual baggage may be, it has planted seeds of untruth in your mind and heart.

As a child, Kendra was repeatedly sexually violated by her grandfather. She never told her parents about the abuse because of her grandfather's threats. Kendra also doubted that her parents would believe her because her grandfather was a highly respected pastor. To make matters even more confusing, Kendra's grandfather treated her with great affection, praising her and showering gifts on her that made her siblings jealous. Her parents couldn't understand why Kendra resisted going to Grandma and Grandpa's house.

Once Kendra reached the age of 12 or 13, her grandfather's attitude toward her changed dramatically. Instead of showering her with affection, he barely spoke to her. Although Kendra was relieved to have escaped Grandpa's touch, she wondered what she had done to earn his disdain.

As a young married woman, Kendra began confronting the lies that were planted in her mind many years before as a consequence of her grandfather's abuse. Here are a few of them:

- I'm only valuable to a man if I give to him sexually.
- My adult body and sexuality are repulsive.
- All men are perverted—especially religious men.

• Sex is something shameful that should be kept a secret.
• Love and sex have nothing to do with each other.

Although Kendra wasn't aware of believing these lies, they played out as she became sexually active with her new husband. She resisted her husband's touch and often became angry with him when he asked for intimacy. Without knowing it, she associated her husband's healthy sexual desires with her grandfather's perversion.

All baggage, not just sexual abuse, results in lies. A woman who was sexually promiscuous as a teen may believe, "I'm damaged goods. God can't fully bless my marriage." A wife who has been cheated on may have fallen for the lie that "I can never be good enough." The little girl whose father left for another family may grow up believing, "Men always leave. I'm destined for rejection." The woman who was involved in porn believes that "sex is just about the body."

Until you voice the lies, you cannot confront them with the truth.

Sexual Baggage Links Unhealthy Emotions with Sexual Response

Sometimes when I jog, I listen to audio books on my iPod. A good novel helps me forget how badly I want to stop running. The next time I run the same trail, I instantly remember exciting parts of the book I was listening to when I passed those same parts of the trail on my previous run. My experience of the trail is linked with the emotions the book evoked.

Cognitive psychologists tell us that the most powerful learning is associated with strong physical sensations. A theory called "state-specific memory recall" or "state-dependent learning" explains this phenomenon. "Learning that takes place in one situation or 'state' is generally better remembered later in a similar situation or state."[3] That's why an exciting or emotional part of an audio book will come back to mind when I run past the place on the trail where I was listening to it. It also

explains why you can recall a forgotten childhood memory by smelling a unique scent or driving past a familiar site that takes you right back to that moment in time.

Nowhere is this truer than in sexuality. Sexual response is highly impacted by the physical sensations and emotions that accompany it. Sensations, smells, words, positions, or images can evoke powerful memories and feelings from long ago.

Now apply this to how sexual baggage may be affecting your marriage. Whether or not by choice, you may have experienced sexual contact or thoughts that were linked with feelings of anxiety, guilt, anger, or shame. Perhaps these negative feelings coexisted with a powerful rush of sexual pleasure and excitement. Even years later, sexual stimuli, such as being touched a certain way or smelling a certain scent, may bring back the negative emotions that were originally linked with your sexuality.

Some women struggle with the sexual baggage of growing up in a home environment where sex was viewed as a necessary evil. A woman with this background may not have the baggage of promiscuity, but her sexual response in marriage may still be linked with feelings of guilt.

Regardless of the nature of your sexual baggage, healing may require intentionally retraining your body and mind to associate healthy and appropriate emotions with your sexuality.

Sexual Baggage Creates an Atmosphere of Distrust

I was recently talking with a woman in her mid-20s who is in a serious dating relationship. Her boyfriend shared with her that he had been pretty rebellious through his teen years, experimenting with drugs, sex, and porn. Since then, he had become a follower of Christ and had drastically changed his lifestyle. Together, they had made the commitment to abstain from sex based on their desire to honor God in their rela-

tionship. This young woman wanted to talk to me about the effect that her boyfriend's baggage might have on their relationship if they were to someday marry.

"Will he compare me to other women he's been with?" she asked. "Do you think he'll be more prone to fall sexually because of his past?"

Even though her boyfriend had demonstrated character and purity in their relationship, her trust in him had been tainted by his past behavior.

Because sexual baggage always involves sex outside of God's intended plan (even if unwanted), it always brings up trust issues. "Will he be faithful to me?" "Can I be vulnerable with him?" or even "Can I trust my own sexuality?"

Trust issues are most prominent in baggage that involves pre- or post-marriage infidelity. "If you cheated on me once, what's to keep you from cheating on me again?" Sexual baggage also erodes trust because of the element of secrecy. Think about it: Extramarital affairs, porn addiction, sexual abuse, teen pregnancy, and abortion are almost always hidden. It's not uncommon for a man or woman to hide a secret like this for decades. When the secret is finally discovered or revealed, the other person naturally wonders, "If she hid this from me, what else might she be hiding?" The kind of trust necessary in marital intimacy means no secrets (except for what you got him for Christmas). This does not mean that husband and wife should give a moment-by-moment account of every indiscretion. In fact, raking through the details of an infidelity can create more wounds. However, a foundation of trust means no skeletons hiding in the closet.

The distinction between having sex and actually having sexual intimacy is the level of trust that exists in the relationship. A couple can have sex when trust is fractured, but they won't have sexual intimacy. There is a huge difference between the two!

What Baggage Area Is Your Luggage In?

Most baggage will impact a marriage to at least some degree in the ways described above. However, there's a big difference between recovering from sexual abuse and recovering from marital infidelity. These topics are complicated and sensitive, and there are several good books that specifically address healing for these individual issues. Although this discussion is in no way exhaustive, I want to briefly address three types of baggage that many marriages are lugging around the bedroom.

Baggage Area No. 1: A History of Sexual Exploitation or Abuse

It's difficult to know exactly what percentage of people have experienced sexual abuse. Most research indicates that around 25 percent of women and 16 percent of men report that they experienced sexual abuse in the first 18 years of life.[4] However, these numbers are likely a grave underestimate, largely because many people would rather not admit to such an unpleasant experience in their past.

The numbers and percentages are really meaningless if you fall within them. Regardless of how many others can identify with your experience, you still deal with the same questions, shame, and fears.

I've met many women who say something like "I don't know if I was sexually abused." Sexual exploitation isn't always a black-and-white event. For example, is it sexual abuse when a father makes inappropriate comments about his daughter's breasts without touching them? What if he watches his 14-year-old take a shower? Was a young woman raped when her boyfriend pushed further than she was comfortable going? How about if she willingly engaged in everything up to intercourse, but he forced the final step? Was a young boy sexually exploited when an uncle showed him an issue of *Playboy* and taught him what to do with it?

In each of these situations, the answer is yes. Granted, some abuse

is more extreme and destructive than others. Sexual abuse or exploitation includes the "forcing of undesired sexual acts by one person upon another."[5] The Centers for Disease Control and Prevention defines childhood sexual abuse as "an adult or person . . . touched or fondled you in a sexual way, and/or had you touch their body in a sexual way, and/or attempted oral, anal, or vaginal intercourse with you and/or actually had oral, anal, or vaginal intercourse with you."[6]

Counselor Steven Earll defines sexual abuse more broadly:

> Sexual abuse includes emotional, verbal, and physical actions, although it is often thought of only in terms of molestation or incest. As a result, the most common types of sexual abuse are not recognized by society as problematic.
>
> Sexual abuse includes being exposed to inappropriate sexual messages or sexual situations. . . .
>
> Families can be involved in emotional and verbal sexual abuse through the use of inappropriate sexual talk. . . .
>
> Much of what is so-called "routine" teenage sexual behavior is actually sexual abuse. Sexual involvement at young ages is abuse, more so if an adult or much older teen is involved with a minor. . . . Pressured sexual involvement and date rape is also common with teen and young adults.[7]

If you were ever sexually abused, the experience may have been horrific, regardless of the nature of the exploitation or how old you were when it happened. You likely felt completely out of control and helpless. The abuse was emotionally, and perhaps physically, painful. In order to stay sane and survive such a horrendous episode, you probably employed coping mechanisms. One of the most common of these, called "dissociation," involves emotionally separating from what is happening in reality. We use this coping mechanism all of the time to escape from

boring or unpleasant tasks. When you're getting a root canal at the dentist, you try not to notice the drill, the smell of the smoke, or the searing pain. You may try listening to music, dreaming about something you're looking forward to, or reciting the Pledge of Allegiance—anything to lessen your discomfort.

Because of your past experience, sex may bring up unpleasant thoughts or feelings. To avoid the physical or emotional pain of sex, you may continue to use the coping mechanism of dissociation within your marriage. As a result, you may find it difficult to connect emotionally with your husband, even while engaging in the most intimate physical acts.

Understandably, if you have a history of sexual abuse, you may have a lot of barriers to enjoying sex with your husband. It may be difficult for you to see sex as an expression of love rather than a tool of domination. Even the thought or mention of sex may cause anxiety, making sexual enjoyment impossible.

Please don't neglect your healing in this area! If you feel tainted by what happened in your past, if you're confused about sex, or if you can't fully enjoy the gift of intimacy with your husband, seek healing. Don't allow the Enemy to keep you trapped by secrets or shadows of the past. Many who have been abused have walked the road of healing and restoration, which has freed them to fully embrace the gift of sexual intimacy in marriage.

Baggage Area No. 2: A History of Premarital Promiscuity

Premarital sexual activity in today's society is almost a given. In fact, it's often portrayed as a necessary step for "knowing yourself" and developing sexually. Despite all of the cheers for sexual freedom, research indicates that premarital sex has a negative impact on the quality of sex in marriage.[8] In fact, sexual pleasure and fulfillment in marriage are negatively correlated with how many partners a person had before marriage!

In other words, the more a person sleeps around, the less likely that person is to be sexually satisfied once she is married. Rather than ensuring that you're experienced on your wedding night, premarital sex makes you *less* prepared for fulfilling sexual intimacy.

This research can be explained by a number of commonsense consequences of premarital sex. First of all, it sets the groundwork for comparison and performance demands. Some married couples complain about not being sexually compatible. What is that statement based on? Unless they have been with other sexual partners, how do they determine what sexual compatibility is?

God designed sex to be something that cannot be compared. The exclusive intimacy between one man and one woman is one of a kind. Sex becomes great not in comparison to sex with someone else but because of the intimacy you enjoy that belongs only to you and your husband. Once another person, even from the past, enters that picture, sex is measured and evaluated by an external standard. Even if it's never spoken, there are shadows of doubt: "Are we as good together as he was with *her*?" Such insecurity is a difficult way to begin building intimacy.

Men and women with a history of promiscuity also learn to compartmentalize sex from the rest of their lives. I've met with young women who recount their sexual experiences as if they're recalling what they had for breakfast. No guilt, no excitement, no joy, no emotion. To emotionally survive frequent sexual connection followed by rejection or loss, a woman learns to view sex as an outlet for recreation and pleasure. She dumbs down the meaning and mutes the emotional impact of sexual intimacy. That compartmentalization and minimization follows her into marriage, leading to a flat sex life. If sex is an outlet for pleasure and recreation before marriage, how does it translate into this awesome expression of unity within marriage?

In an earlier chapter, we looked at the incredible bonding power that sex has on a guy physiologically. Right after intercourse, the hormone

oxytocin is released into his bloodstream. The oxytocin promotes feelings of affection and bonding. Interestingly enough, the more sexual partners a man or woman has, the less oxytocin is released after sex. In other words, sex physiologically and emotionally has a diminished bonding effect in relationships that aren't monogamous!

God designed sex to be the glue that emotionally, spiritually, relationally, and physiologically bonds you and your husband together. The presence of sexual activity in your past may have diluted that bonding as a result of residual feelings of guilt, shame, anger, or insecurity. As irrelevant as it may seem today, don't discount the impact this baggage may have on your marriage. You don't have to get into the nitty-gritty details of what happened in your (or his) past. However, you need to address unresolved issues to the extent that they compromise your sexual relationship.

Baggage Area No. 3: A History of Marital Infidelity
God considers marital infidelity so egregious that the Bible cites it as grounds for the dissolution of a marriage. I've known many couples who have recovered from the devastation of an affair, but not without great heartbreak, God's grace, and a lot of work.

Gary and Mona Shriver had been happily married for many years and were the parents of three boys when their marriage was rocked by infidelity. By their own account, neither imagined it would ever happen to them. Gary worked in ministry and became attracted to a coworker. Because Mona was busy caring for their children, Gary was particularly vulnerable to intimacy with a woman who shared his passion for work. Emotional intimacy led to physical intimacy. As often as Gary repented and tried to end the affair, he couldn't. The wake-up call came when he found himself sexually involved with yet another woman.

Gary confessed to his wife with tears and remorse, pleading with her to work on the marriage. Mona understandably went through pro-

longed stages of anger, grief, and confusion. Yet through clinging to God, difficult work with counselors and pastors, and years of overcoming shattered trust to rebuild the relationship, Gary and Mona were able to restore their marriage. In fact, they began a ministry called Hope and Healing Ministries to help couples recover from infidelity. The title of their book, *Unfaithful: Rebuilding Trust After Infidelity*, attests to what the Shrivers personally experienced and have walked countless couples through. The key to healing is rebuilding the trust that was shattered through unfaithfulness.

If you're lugging around the baggage of infidelity, I recommend that you read the Shrivers' book as well as *Love Must Be Tough* by Dr. James Dobson, *Yes, Your Marriage Can Be Saved* by Joe and Michelle Williams, and the booklet *Nothing to Hide* (see Recommended Resources on page 215 for full information). These helpful resources will guide you through the process of rebuilding the trust that has been destroyed.

The long road of forgiveness, baby steps of relearning trust, and believing that God can restore your relationship in spite of the ugliest of offenses will require humility and brokenness on the part of both you and your husband. If you identify with the baggage of infidelity, my heart breaks for you and the pain you're going through. The Lord's heart breaks too. But His sorrow in the wake of sin doesn't limit His power to make all things new.

Can Someone Help Me with These Bags?

If you ever share your sexual baggage with a trusted friend, she will likely listen empathetically, maybe cry with you, and offer a few generic suggestions. But when she realizes that your pain and confusion are "above her pay grade," she will likely ask, "Have you considered going to counseling?"

I've noticed that people who don't even believe in counseling suggest

it for friends who are suffering. It's kind of a catch-all suggestion when you don't know how else to help. To be perfectly honest, there have been times when I've been in the middle of counseling someone and wanted to suggest, "Maybe you should go to counseling." A split second later, I realize that they *are* in counseling—WITH ME! What do I do if I get in over my head? Well, then I recommend that they talk to their pastor!

Why Counseling Can Help

I actually do believe that counseling is a really important piece of handling most sexual baggage (and not just because I want job security). But before you seek counseling or recommend it to a friend, it might help to understand why counseling can actually make a difference.

First, counseling should provide a safe relationship where you can share past experiences, feelings, and thoughts that may not be appropriate to talk about in other contexts. In a counseling relationship, your counselor is legally bound to keep your secrets. In addition, she has experience dealing with all kinds of sexual baggage and won't be offended or shocked by what you share. Her job is not to judge you but to provide an affirming relationship based on truth.

Because this relationship is a "safe place," you can voice fears, secrets, or feelings that you've never before been able to express. There's incredible power in sharing a secret you've felt compelled to hang on to for years. One of the most sacred moments in counseling is when a woman confesses baggage for the first time. An abortion she had as a teen, a homosexual attraction from the past, an experience of past sexual abuse, or a current extramarital temptation. Voicing a secret to another person who won't recoil in shock or condemn you can help shatter the cage of lies that the Enemy has constructed in the darkness.

Second, counseling can help you make sense of your baggage and how it impacts your marriage. Over the past few years, I've been dealing with a very personal and painful loss. In the midst of it, I haven't been able

to tell up from down. My emotions, pain, and fear seem to cloud everything. A few times, my husband has asked me, "What would you tell a client who was struggling with this?" I'm dumbfounded and can't answer him. I just can't get out of my own emotions long enough to make logical sense of the situation. Even the most obvious connections are unclear to me.

As intuitive and logical as you may be in other situations, you can't always see your baggage objectively. You may still feel like that little girl afraid of her grandfather, or that rebellious teen shamed by her choices. You can't seem to get past the powerful barriers of anger, guilt, or fear that haunt your bedroom. You can't quite connect how an event in the past impacts your relationships today. A wise godly counselor can help tremendously by giving you an objective understanding of what you're experiencing.

Third, counseling is also very helpful in facilitating difficult conversations with your husband. The sensitive nature of sexual baggage keeps married couples from ever talking it through. They don't know where to even begin or how to keep the conversation from drifting into the danger zone. A good counselor can guide those conversations toward a healing truth.

Finally, counseling can help put the sexual baggage in context with the rest of your life and relationship. Because you don't know how to handle it, sexual baggage is typically stored in its own little locked "room." You don't want it to be a part of you or your marriage, so it's a horrific secret to be hidden away. By compartmentalizing it, you believe you can limit the impact it has on you and your marriage.

As a human being, you're hardwired to understand and integrate the events in your life into a meaningful whole. The most painful events to deal with are those that fail to make sense. You unconsciously want to understand why the abuse or affair happened and what it means. Like a puzzle missing a couple of pieces, compartmentalized baggage will leave

you feeling a lack of peace. In fact, you may find yourself dreaming about the event or thinking about it at random times. The more you try to push it out of your life or your marriage, the more intrusive it can become.

Working through baggage in counseling can take the intrusive power of sexual secrets away. The dreaded topic is no longer something you're afraid will randomly explode out of some box, but an unpleasant circumstance that you now understand and have talked through. Although the experience has impacted your life, it no longer defines you.

Finding the Right Baggage Handler

If you needed open-heart surgery, chances are you wouldn't simply look in the phone book for a doctor. You would take great care to choose the surgeon who would hold your life in his or her hands. Take no less care in choosing a counselor, because counseling can be, in a sense, open-heart surgery. Not all counselors provide a safe place and respond to your history appropriately. Counselors are people too, with their own sets of biases and history. I've heard many stories over the years of counselors who have done more harm than good. For this reason, start with a referral from a trusted source. Then have a consumer mind-set. Spend some time ensuring that the counselor is capable of helping you. Here are a few guidelines to help you choose wisely.

First, be certain that the counselor shares your moral and biblical convictions. Many of the issues you discuss with a counselor will involve moral choices and their consequences. A counselor's advice on topics like divorce, forgiveness, and sexual boundaries will all be dramatically impacted by his or her values and faith. Don't be afraid to ask questions about what a counselor believes before you begin counseling.

Second, be sure that the counselor is qualified to help you. The nicest person with the best of intentions may still give you terrible advice. What are the counselor's training, certification, and credentials? What does she specialize in? Do you know anyone who has met with her

and benefited from her counsel? These are all important considerations. Meeting with an unqualified counselor can actually add to your trauma and pain rather than helping you work through it.

Finally, make sure a counselor is a good fit. Because counseling is a relationship, the quality of the interpersonal connection matters. Based on gender, age, personality, and theoretical approach, you'll really click with some counselors and really clash with others. You may be able to determine the "goodness of fit" after one or two meetings. In other cases, you may notice that you are not making any progress after months of meeting. Or you may have a nagging sense of distrust that interferes with building a healing relationship. These are indications that perhaps that counselor is not the right fit. People come in so many different personalities, ages, and approaches. Don't be discouraged if it takes you a while to find someone who can truly be helpful. Pray that the Lord brings that individual across your path. He typically heals through the gifts represented in His body.

A Gift Through the Pain

I want you to picture yourself and your husband strolling through the streets of Venice. All around you are beautiful buildings, the smell of authentic Italian cuisine, and the sound of gondoliers singing as they paddle through the canals. Now picture the baggage you're towing with you. Are you so weighed down that you can't enjoy the beauty of your surroundings? Do your hands burn with blisters? Are you limping under the weight of bags far too heavy for you?

The Lord has designed a beautiful journey for you to experience with your husband. Since the fall of man in the garden, some baggage on the journey is a given. God desires not only to help you with your baggage but also to teach you and bond you and your husband together through it. Stop ignoring the obvious deterrents to your intimacy as you journey.

True healing occurs when sexual baggage is no longer ignored but is understood and integrated into the larger truths of who you are and who God is. Just think about all of the characters in the Bible. Why did God lay out all of their baggage in His book of history? Why do we need to know that Rahab was a prostitute and that David was an adulterer? Why did God choose to include stories of rape, murder, and infidelity with the stories of His heroes?

Your life and your marriage tell a story. Your baggage is part of that story. Although it may have begun as a shameful chapter that you'd rather burn, God desires to show His love and forgiveness through the worst of it.

The strongest marriages aren't those without baggage, but those that have integrated their baggage into a larger story of love and grace. Remember that the Lord's ultimate goal for your sexuality is to teach you about love. What might He desire to teach you and your husband through your baggage?

SOMETHING TO THINK ABOUT • • • • •

1. In which of the "baggage areas" do you (and/or your husband) have some luggage (history of sexual exploitation or abuse, premarital promiscuity, marital infidelity)?

2. Talk to your husband about how various pieces of "baggage" may be impacting intimacy in your marriage.

3. Is there any "unfinished business" (such as forgiveness, confession, or counseling) that you need to address individually or as a couple?

ten

Reclaiming Our Secret Garden

Author's note: This was the most difficult chapter for me to write because the topic represents so much anguish in so many marriages. Scripture warns us that the Devil roams around like a roaring lion, seeking someone to devour (see 1 Peter 5:8). He has devoured many with the lure of pornography and other illicit sexual material. There are no cute stories or lighthearted metaphors in this chapter. Even while writing, I was aware of the spiritual battle. This is the Enemy's turf; yet our Savior is ready and able to restore what the Enemy has stolen.

• • •

My favorite genre of movies reflects the true story of someone overcoming incredible odds. Who can resist cheering as a hero perseveres and wins when no one thought victory was possible? God's Word is filled with such true, inspiring stories—David and Goliath, Gideon, and Joseph, to name a few.

Whether you're aware of it or not, the purity of your sex life is facing seemingly impossible odds. If you want a dose of depression, take a look at these stats:

- In 2005, 77 percent of prime-time programming featured sexual content.[1]
- A study conducted in 2007 concluded that 87 percent of men aged 18 to 26 viewed pornography "in the past year" with nearly half viewing "in the past week."[2]
- According to a source in 1994, 91 percent of men raised in Christian homes reported having been exposed to porn.[3]
- 40 percent of adolescent boys aged 15 to 17 have received oral sex, and 28 percent have given it.[4]

The picture looks bleak. Hardly a marriage exists in the Western world that hasn't been tainted to some extent by our sexually open culture. Each number in the stats represents tremendous pain, anger, and disappointment. The couple fighting for purity seems to face overwhelming odds, promising almost certain defeat. The stage is set for a Savior who is able to conquer sin. Scripture points to the mystery that God's strength is perfected in our weakness. To the extent that this chapter reveals the broken places in your marriage, remember that Jesus is the Hero who beats the odds. In your weakness, you can experience His perfect grace and power.

In this chapter, we'll look at the grave danger of having loose sexual boundaries in your marriage. Please remember that this information not only applies to obvious sexual intrusions like pornography, but it also applies to more subtle threats like fantasy, romance novels, emotional affairs, explicit chat rooms, and sexually charged movies and television programs.

Understanding the Harm of Our Sexually Explicit World

There's a good chance you aren't all that surprised by the prevalence of sexually stimulating material in our culture. In fact, you may be very

aware of how it exists in your own marriage. However, what you probably underestimate is how incredibly toxic it is to your sex life and your marriage relationship.

Undoubtedly, you've heard the metaphor about boiling a frog. Place the frog in cold water. Then slowly, imperceptibly turn up the heat. The frog will stay in the water, content but unaware that his environment will soon be lethal. We're so accustomed to seeing *Hustler* on the magazine rack, *Sex and the City* advertised on television, the *Sports Illustrated* swimsuit edition at the checkout counter, and spam e-mails advertising penis enlargements that we no longer bat an eye at the dangerous waters in which we're swimming.

I've found myself surrounded by "boiling water" without even realizing it. It's so easy to explain the presence of sexually explicit commercials, magazines, movies, and novels as just a part of our culture. After all, we live in America. Like it or not, Hooters and Internet porn are here to stay. No matter how prevalent sexual material is in our culture, its overwhelming presence doesn't make it normal, healthy, or justified.

The Consequences of Engaging with Sexually Explicit Material

Over time and with exposure, you may begin to believe the lie that mild forms of sexual material, such as R-rated movies or "soft" porn, are harmless. I've spoken with many married couples who justify even hard-core porn by saying, "It's not like infidelity. We can even enjoy it together."

Your sexual relationship is designed to include only two people: you and your husband. Regardless of the culture we live in, violating this principle in action or in spirit will undoubtedly have severe consequences in your marriage. God's laws and guidelines aren't arbitrary. Time and

time again, you'll find that violating biblical principles has real consequences in the natural world.

To the extent that you and/or your husband expose yourselves to sexual material or engage in high-risk sexual behaviors, you'll likely encounter the following headaches in your marriage.

Alienation

Sex is the most intimate behavior possible between two people. God designed sex to be the act of ultimate oneness, even mysteriously foreshadowing our unity someday with Him (Ephesians 5:25–33). Ultimate unity requires ultimate trust. Getting naked with your husband, losing control as you experience pleasure, sharing your most intimate secrets and moments—these are the greatest pleasures of marriage and, at the same time, the most threatening. At no time are you more physically and emotionally vulnerable.

The real or imagined presence of someone else in the sexual relationship shatters the trust required for ultimate intimacy. How would you feel to know that your husband is fantasizing about a porn site while having sex with you? How would he feel to know that you are thinking about another man during intimacy with him?

As a couple, you're either drawing closer to each other or are drifting further apart. Many sex experts recommend sharing together in sexual fantasy or pornography to spice up your sex life. Although this may temporarily heighten your sexual excitement, the thrill comes at the expense of the awesome intimacy God designed for you. Instead of two becoming one, you're using each other for a physical release as your hearts and minds become sealed off from one another.

Seeking sexual arousal through nonpersonal sources (like porn) reinforces the idea that sex is all about you getting your needs fulfilled. It's selfish, immature sex that views others as objects that are there for the sole purpose of serving you. Obviously, this attitude is the exact oppo-

site of the way God desires for you to grow and love. Sex is intended to teach unselfish love, finding fulfillment while serving each other. Great sex is all about relationship.

The Need for Increased Stimulation

Dr. Archibald Hart has spent a good portion of his professional career studying the pleasure centers of the brain. Dr. Hart's research emphasizes how destructive extraordinary pleasure is to normal pleasure, particularly in the sexual arena. The cheap forms of sexual pleasure spoil a person's ability to enjoy true forms of sexual pleasure. For example, when a man views pornography, he experiences a high degree of sexual excitement. Not only is he sexually aroused, but he also experiences the thrill of an adrenaline rush.

The most powerful sexual response is one that is linked with adrenaline. In order to match that level of excitement the next time, the images must be more visually stimulating and more exciting. Because normal marital sex has become boring and uninteresting, he might ask his wife to engage in high-risk sexual behaviors with him, such as fantasy, having sex in a public place, role playing, and bondage. This is a never-ending game that will always demand something new and more exciting.

Feelings of Rejection and Inadequacy

If you've ever looked at *Sports Illustrated*'s swimsuit edition or Victoria's Secret models, you've likely asked yourself the question, "How can I compete with that?" As I said in chapter 8, you can't. Not only are these women in the prime of their lives, starving themselves and extremely naturally attractive, they are also surgically and digitally modified to present the illusion of perfection. No amount of time in the gym, dieting, custom clothing, or even plastic surgery can equip you to match the level of desirability presented in pornographic material, or even the

images presented everywhere else in our culture. The deck is stacked against you.

The same dynamic is true when a woman fantasizes about another man. Whether the competitor is a real or fictional character, she has made him out to be someone her husband stands no chance against. As women, we have fantasies that often have less to do with physical attributes and more to do with a man's personality or his ability to provide. The man of your dreams may be a multimillionaire who is sensitive enough to care about his wife, or even a pastor who takes the time to play with his kids and teach them about God. Just like the airbrushed models, any Mr. Right makes a real-life husband look and feel like a loser.

By entertaining images or fantasies, you exterminate the possibility of being content with the spouse God has given you. Feelings of resentment and insecurity will far outweigh gratitude and appreciation.

Although we live in a culture filled with sexual images and innuendo, be very wary of accepting this as the norm in your marriage. Many men and women don't consider fantasy, pornography, or sexual acting out to be an ethical breach as long as it doesn't involve an affair or an addiction. Jesus clearly dispelled this lie when He said, "But I tell you that anyone who looks at a woman lustfully has already committed adultery with her in his heart" (Matthew 5:28).

We must realize that flirting with sexuality and fantasy not only violates biblical teaching but will also result in a significant roadblock to the intimacy God designed for your marriage bed. God isn't a killjoy who wants to make sex boring; He's a guardian of the purity of your oneness and pleasure.

Confronting "His" Problem

As we delve into the temptations that often entangle guys, let's do so with humility and hesitation. It would be easy for us as women to jump

all over our husbands for their stereotypical weakness in matters of sexual purity. Remember the example of Jesus ministering to the woman caught in adultery. A crowd of men gathered to stone her, which was her due punishment based on Hebrew law. Jesus challenged the men, even as they were poised to throw the stones: "If any one of you is without sin, let him be the first to throw a stone at her." From the oldest to the youngest, all of her accusers left, for they all knew what it was to fall into sin.

Jesus said to the woman, "Where are they? Has no one condemned you?"

When she acknowledged that they had all gone, Jesus replied, "Then neither do I condemn you. . . . Go now and leave your life of sin" (John 8:3–11).

Although Jesus didn't condemn her clearly sinful behavior, He also called her with love out of sin. Let His example guide this discussion.

The most traumatic day of Sabrina's life was discovering her husband's involvement with porn. Sabrina knew that Andre had dabbled in porn before they were married, but she assumed it was no longer an issue now that he had a regular sexual outlet. She never thought twice about the unfiltered computer that sat in their home or the sexually explicit channels available on their television. One night Sabrina woke up to find that Andre wasn't in their bed. She moseyed into the office, expecting to find her husband busy with work. Instead, she was greeted by sexually explicit images on the computer screen. Sabrina was understandably sickened and horrified. A contrite Andre tried to comfort his wife, assuring her that this was an isolated incident. She felt so rejected and defiled that she couldn't even look at Andre. What did this mean for their marriage? Wasn't she enough to satisfy him? What else might he be involved in?

Andre and Sabrina were cold and cordial to each other for a while, neither wanting to address the elephant in the room. Eventually, the

tension faded into the background, and the couple got on with life without addressing the incident any further.

Several months later, Sabrina was browsing the Internet on the family's computer. As she began typing something into the address bar on the Internet browser, options of previously visited Web sites popped up. The salacious names left little doubt as to their content. Tears streaming down her face, her heart racing, Sabrina began searching the computer's history to find dozens, even hundreds, of pornographic Web sites that Andre had been visiting.

Perhaps you know exactly what it feels like to be in Sabrina's shoes. You understand her rage, disgust, insecurity, and confusion about not knowing what to do next. Some research suggests that discovering a spouse's infidelity (including porn use) can result in symptoms similar to those commonly ascribed to post-traumatic stress disorder, because it shatters the foundation of trust and safety in a marriage.[5] It *is* a big deal!

Understanding the Shock

The most devastating aspect of a situation like Sabrina's is the experience of having been deceived. The average man is very private about the sexual temptation he faces. He is embarrassed to admit that he struggles with sexual thoughts and feels deeply ashamed whenever he engages in acting out. To make matters worse, he intuitively knows that his wife won't understand the inherent temptations in his sexuality. So instead of sharing the struggle, he battles alone, walling off this part of himself from his wife. When his wife discovers his struggles and failures, she feels betrayed, as if she has been living with someone she doesn't even know.

I recently met with a woman who discovered her husband's porn use after almost 40 years of marriage. The revelation made her doubt everything in their marriage. Had it all been a sham? Was her husband really the man she had always thought he was? All of the years they had prayed together, served together, and made love together—what was she to

make of it? If he had kept this part of himself a secret for 38 years, what else had been a lie?

We need look no further than the life of King David to know that very godly, committed men can struggle with sexual temptation. David's story reveals that a godly man may also go to great lengths to hide the shame of his sin. His moral failure existed alongside his passion to serve the Lord and to be a faithful king.

For your husband, sexual temptation may be the daily thorn that taunts him. Feelings of shame and failure in this area may run so deep that he separates it from every other part of his existence. Although his behavior is a breach of trust that must be addressed, lean on what you know to be right and true about him as a bridge. Your husband is neither all good nor all bad. He's a fallen man who battles with sin and the desire for integrity.

Empathizing with the Temptation Without Enabling the Sin
The practical epistle of James encourages us all to be "quick to listen, slow to speak and slow to become angry" (1:19). This counsel is certainly appropriate in addressing your husband's sexual sin.

It's likely that as a woman you can't understand the effect sexual images and temptations have on your husband. If you're repulsed by pornographic images, you can't understand how he could be drawn to them. As important as it is to confront the sin, it's equally important for you to understand the temptation.

I'm no longer surprised when a woman shares with me her husband's struggle with pornography. In fact, I've learned to almost anticipate it. The Internet, cell phones, and satellite television have brought into our homes and offices what we once had to travel to a seedy neighborhood to purchase. A man doesn't have to be looking for sex; it's looking for him. The innocent husband going about his business is often, without warning, confronted with ads for phone sex, chat rooms, porn

sites, and "adult" films, not to mention women dressed seductively at the office and even at church. Although your husband is responsible for his choices, his sexuality is a target for the Enemy.

Take Scott for example. He is a devoted husband and father. Although Scott is active in his church and desperately desires to please the Lord with his life, his struggle with sexual temptation plagues him. When he was a young teenager, he discovered a stack of magazines in his father's closet. The photos of naked women and sexual acts mesmerized him.

As he matured and his relationship with the Lord grew, he became desperate to stop fantasizing and masturbating. Although he experienced periods of victory, another weak moment seemed just around the corner. He looked forward to marriage, hoping that having regular sex with his wife would solve the problem. Weeks into their marriage, he still found himself drawn to the Internet, even mentally retrieving sexually explicit images while having sex with his beautiful new wife, Erin.

Years later, Erin discovered Scott's secret. He was relieved to come clean, yet torn apart by the pain and humiliation. His heart's desire is to be pure for his wife, yet he still battles to push aside intrusive images from the past and the strong urges to view pornographic Web sites.

Many experts believe that like Scott, most boys are exposed to pornographic images by the age of 13. With the increased use of computers and the Internet, the average age of first exposure may actually be around 11! During that tender age of puberty, insecurity, and raging hormones, the seductive images prove irresistible. Exposure to porn stimulates the part of the brain that produces an extraordinary sensation of pleasure, similar to opiates like crack cocaine or heroin. Read the testimony of Dr. Jeffrey Satinover to the Senate Subcommittee on Science, Technology, and Space:

> It may seem surprising that, at this juncture, I should speak of "chemicals," when one might be thinking instead of "sex." But,

in fact, modern science allows us to understand that the underlying nature of an addiction to pornography is chemically nearly identical to a heroin addiction: Only the delivery system is different, and the sequence of steps.[6]

Naturally, Scott was drawn to repeat his first experience with pornography. His sexual response has repeatedly been paired with increasingly brazen sexual imagery. Those images were stored in his brain when he was a teen and have shaped how he views women, other men, and his own sexuality.

You can't effectively call your husband to purity until you empathize with his struggle. Jesus modeled this, as the writer of Hebrews pointed out:

> For we do not have a high priest who is unable to sympathize with our weaknesses, but we have one who has been tempted in every way, just as we are—yet was without sin. Let us then approach the throne of grace with confidence, so that we may receive mercy and find grace to help us in our time of need. (Hebrews 4:15–16)

You may not know what it's like to struggle with sexual temptation, but you do know what it's like to struggle daily with other temptations. Maybe your thorn in the flesh is gossip, dishonesty, bitterness, pride, gluttony, or coveting. Identify with your husband in this. As Jesus taught, you cannot help your "brother" with the speck in his eye until you've dealt with the log in your own (see Matthew 7:3–5). Confront your husband with the awareness and humility of your own weakness, not with the self-righteous spirit of judgment.

Understanding the temptation *does not* mean disregarding the sin, however. Many couples consider fantasy and pornography acceptable because they're so difficult to defend against. As the saying goes, "If you

can't beat 'em, join 'em." Yes, pornography is extremely common among married men. Yes, the temptation is intense for the average husband. But Jesus still calls us to a standard of purity regardless of the culture we live in. The apostle Paul reminds us, "Do not conform any longer to the pattern of this world, but be transformed by the renewing of your mind" (Romans 12:2).

While empathizing with and understanding your husband's struggle is a great help to him, excusing immoral behavior enables his demise. For your sake and his, insist on purity.

Helping Him Connect the Dots

If your husband is involved with pornography or any other outside form of sexual involvement, it's crucial that you help him understand how his actions have damaged your relationship. As explained in earlier chapters, male sexuality is much easier to compartmentalize than female sexuality. People or images for which he has no emotional connection can sexually arouse your husband. For this reason, he can engage in sexual fantasy and behaviors, believing that his actions aren't a violation of his love for you. He may view his struggle with porn as a personal battle that has nothing to do with your relationship. The rampant messages of our culture help him rationalize that he can be a loving husband while still seeking an illicit sexual release. Only when confronted with your feelings of hurt and rejection will he realize how he has fractured the trust in your marriage.

I believe a wife shouldn't continue having sex with her husband while he is *actively* engaging in other forms of sexual fulfillment and is *unwilling* to address the problem. Withholding sex in this way shouldn't be a punishment or expression of anger, but rather a loving plea to seek restoration. This clearly communicates two things to him: (1) Your behavior has fractured the trust in our relationship, and (2) I will not sexually share you with anything or anyone else. This is a loving stance that creates a crisis in the relationship for the ultimate purpose of building intimacy.

Determining What's Your Responsibility for His Struggle—
and What's Not

As I've seen wives work through their husbands' sexual failures, I've witnessed two extremes: wives taking full responsibility for the problem, and wives taking no responsibility. Neither approach is biblical or loving.

Sandy is an example of a woman who took too much responsibility for her husband's involvement with pornography. She concluded that Sam sought other sexual outlets because she wasn't attractive or available enough. In response, Sandy invested in lingerie and vowed to never say no to Sam's sexual advances. Although Sandy's willingness to help her husband is admirable, in the long run it wasn't helpful. Instead of dealing with his sinful behavior and temptations, Sam simply directed every sexual urge toward his wife. Although Sandy can help Sam, his involvement with porn isn't her problem to solve. By taking responsibility for his sin, Sandy is enabling Sam to remain immature in his approach to sexual temptation. In fact, when he falls again, he's likely to blame Sandy for not being attractive or seductive enough.

At the other extreme is Renee. Given the fact that she and her husband, Doug, have five young children, it's no wonder that they have little time and energy for sex. They frequently go weeks without having intercourse. Doug has repeatedly told Renee that their lack of sexual intimacy makes temptation more difficult for him to resist. As a sales representative, he's on the road several days a month, working with attractive women and sleeping in lonely hotel rooms with adult options on the television.

Through the course of counseling, Doug shared with Renee the temptations he faces and how difficult Renee's lack of interest is for him. Renee responded by saying, "Doug, that's your problem that you have to deal with. Just remember that while you're on the road, I'm home taking care of *your* children."

Although Renee isn't responsible for Doug's problem, she is responsible for neglecting her part of the solution.

Obviously, there's a delicate balance between the extremes that Sandy and Renee represent. God has given you the role of helping your husband, including in the sexual area. There's never an *excuse* for him to sexually act out, even if there is a *reason*. While not enabling him to cling to an excuse, do your best not to contribute to a reason for engaging in pornography. He is responsible for his own behavior, and you are responsible for yours. Just as it's a sin for him to lust after another woman, it's also a sin for you to withhold sex from your husband, except for the purpose of seeking the Lord's intervention (see 1 Corinthians 7:5).

Confronting My Problem

Stereotypically, we think of sexual temptation as a man's problem. In many marriages, this is the case. However, women aren't immune to the lure of pornography, fantasy, and emotional entanglements with other men.

Research indicates that more and more women are being lured into sexual outlets. According to a 2008 study of emerging adults (aged 18–26), about one-third of young women reported using some pornography in the previous 12 months. The actual percentages are probably higher than reported because women typically consider porn to be a guy's problem and may be less likely to admit their own struggles with it. As embarrassing as it may be for a man to admit that he views sexual images, it's even more humiliating for a woman. It's worth noting that although only 31 percent of women said they used pornography, almost half believed pornography to be an acceptable sexual outlet.[7]

Having saturated the male-dominated porn market, creators of pornography are turning their attention toward female audiences.

Female-oriented pornography tends to involve relationships and emotions. Unlike most men, women are generally not stimulated simply by viewing male and female genitalia. Sexual images are most exciting for women if they are placed in the context of a relationship or seduction. Perhaps because of the link with relationships and emotions, women involved with pornography act out their fantasies in the real world more often than their male counterparts. The statistic cited in the previous paragraph indicates that women who use porn do so less often than men involved with porn. Only 3 percent of women reported a pattern of weekly or more frequent use.[8]

Women may be more likely to engage with pornographic material as a secondary issue rather than as sex for the sake of sex. Seeking sexual stimulation and arousal is a means to an end, not an end in itself. Women often use sexual outlets to combat feelings of loneliness, boredom, depression, or pain, or to express anger. Like spending sprees, bingeing and purging, and cutting, the intense arousal and release linked with porn use helps distract some women from numb or painful emotions. Unfortunately, guilt and shame are typically soon to follow in the wake of temporary pleasure.

If you struggle with porn, you may be frustrated to learn that there are very few resources that specifically help women overcome sexual addiction. A young woman struggling with this issue recently shared that she and a friend scoured Christian bookstores in the hope of finding help. They found several helpful resources for men but failed to find one specifically for Christian women. Women simply aren't talking about their struggles with pornography. If you're struggling in this area and have found it difficult to find the help you need, don't give up. The Lord understands your struggles and wants to bring wholeness and healing in your life as you turn to Him. Following are some additional steps you can take to address this issue in your life.

Seek Accountability

Any sin, including pornography use, becomes much more powerful when it remains a secret. You were created to be part of a community and a body. By keeping your struggle a secret, you not only prevent yourself from getting help and seeking accountability, but you also intensify your feelings of loneliness and shame. The Lord most often uses relationships to heal brokenness. The Enemy would love to keep you quarantined with your computer, believing the lies that you're unlovable and ultimately alone.

As I mentioned earlier, one of the most amazing experiences I have as a psychologist is the moment when someone lets go of a secret for the first time. Whatever the secret may be, as long as she holds on to it, the Enemy convinces her of any number of lies:

"God could never forgive that."

"You are stained for life—used goods."

"No one would love you if they only knew . . ."

"God can never use you."

"You will never overcome the shadow of this."

But when a woman shares the secret places of her heart and is met with love, she takes a huge step toward wholeness. The lies are exposed for what they are—contradictions of the Word and the love of Jesus. Remember what the apostle John wrote:

> This is the message we have heard from him and declare to you: God is light; in him there is no darkness at all. If we claim to have fellowship with him yet walk in the darkness, we lie and do not live by the truth. But if we walk in the light, as he is in the light, we have fellowship with one another, and the blood of Jesus, his Son, purifies us from all sin.
>
> If we claim to be without sin, we deceive ourselves and the

truth is not in us. If we confess our sins, he is faithful and just and will forgive us our sins and purify us from all unrighteousness. If we claim we have not sinned, we make him out to be a liar and his word has no place in our lives. (1 John 1:5–10)

As difficult as it may be, please share your struggle with another woman and/or with your husband. It's the first step out of bondage and into accountability. You can't conquer your "besetting sins" (those patterns we each fall back on when stressed, depressed, or disappointed) without the power of the Holy Spirit and the accountability of the body of Christ.

Recognize When You Need Help

Although they may seem the same, accountability and help are two different things. We all need accountability because we all battle sin. Regardless of whether your struggle is with porn, pride, gossip, an eating disorder, or something else, you need to be in one or two relationships where people love and know you well enough to ask you the tough questions. Seeking professional help is much different.

By way of analogy, think of physical health. I need some teaching and accountability to do the right things to take care of my body. Left to my own devices (without the influence of my husband), I tend to work too hard and get too little rest. You may need a friend to go walking with or to meet you at the gym to help you stay in shape. Perhaps you can ask your husband or a friend to go on a diet with you. It's much easier to stay healthy when you share the journey with someone else. Sometimes, though, your workout partner isn't enough. When you've had a temperature of 104 for three days, it's time to see a doctor. When you're battling cancer, a bottle of vitamins from a caring friend will only go so far.

The same applies to your struggle with porn. The accountability,

encouragement, acceptance, and prayers of your friends are necessary but not usually sufficient. Seeking the help of a Christian psychologist or counselor is imperative if your interest in porn has become an addiction or if it is symptomatic of underlying issues, such as past sexual abuse, depression, dysfunction in your marriage, or intense emotional pain. (Refer to chapter 9 for suggestions for finding a counselor. In this case, ask if the counselor specializes in sexual addiction.)

Call Sin What It Is

In addition to Internet sites and adult films, women are also vulnerable to chat rooms and steamy romance novels. Danielle Steel and other romance novelists make their living off of this.

As a woman, I find it easy to classify an interest in a romance novel as much less threatening than a man's obsession with pornography on the Internet. But is it? They both present a fantasy that makes reality seem dull and even cruel. They both stimulate sexual feelings and interests through images and ideas that are outside of marriage.

I distinctly remember when Mike hit me square between the eyes with this in our marriage. We had rented the movie *The Bridges of Madison County*. In the movie, Meryl Streep plays a housewife in a loveless marriage. Clint Eastwood is a photographer who comes through town while her husband is away. Eastwood represents the opposite of Streep's boring, small-town life. He is adventurous, romantic, and mysterious.

After a weekend of steamy sex, Eastwood prepares to leave town. Streep must decide whether to go with him or stay in her disappointing life. The story did a great job of pulling me in. I was disappointed that Streep's character decided to stay and raise her children with her husband. I was cheering for her to leave the bum and live life to the fullest! When I shared these sentiments with Mike, he reminded me, "Juli, this is glorified adultery." Oops!

Whether your struggle is with erotic images on the computer screen, emotionally charged conversations with a caring male friend, or cheering for adultery in a movie, call it what it is: sin. I've heard more than one woman in counseling share with me how God brought a godly man into her life . . . who wasn't her husband. I've seen couples in adulterous relationships pray and read the Bible together, justifying their actions. Don't be fooled by the sentimental and romantic wrappings. It is ugly, it is destructive, and it is from the pit of hell.

Making It "Our" Problem

Regardless of whether it's your problem, his problem, or a combination that plagues the purity of your marriage, you must begin to see it as your problem *as a couple*. I do *not* mean that a wife should take responsibility for her husband's sin or vice versa. What I mean is that when sexual sin and temptation hits one of you, it affects both of you. Marriage is the ultimate team concept. One can't win while the other loses. You win and lose together.

Most experts caution against a husband or wife serving as the spouse's primary accountability partner. A trusted friend of the same gender should fill that role. However, it's vital that couples learn how to talk with each other about their struggles. Together, they can begin to build hedges that protect against temptation. For example, Mitch's job as a pastor requires him at times to meet with female members of his congregation for counseling. He also travels out of town a few times a month to speak at retreats and attend denominational meetings. After many years of struggling alone, Mitch mustered the courage to share with his wife, Deanna, that he has been sexually tempted to cross the line when women share with him about intimate issues. He also confessed, with difficulty, that he sometimes views pornography while on

the road or when Deanna and their children travel, leaving him at home alone.

Mitch's confession of temptation opened up the door for Deanna to share about her own struggles. Over the past few months, Deanna reconnected with an old boyfriend through Facebook. Their first few e-mails were just normal catching up. Then they began talking on the phone, sharing more in-depth about their lives. Although Deanna hadn't met in person with her old beau, she knew she was wading into dangerous territory.

Mitch and Deanna initially had to work through issues of trust, hurt, and rejection that their confessions brought up. They had to learn how to talk tenderly about such sensitive subjects. However, they now work as a team to combat the temptations that threaten the purity of their relationship. They plan time for intimacy before either of them travels, and they keep in touch while they're separated. They even gave each other permission to ask, "How are you doing? How have you been struggling? How can I pray for you?" Together, they also discussed parameters for appropriate conversations and contact with friends, colleagues, and counseling clients of the opposite gender.

Very seldom is temptation with anything, including sexuality, overcome in a day. Most likely, you and/or your husband will have a long battle before you. Battle as one, striving toward maturity in your love for each other and your passion for the Lord.

Killing the Giant

What Satan means for evil, the Lord means for our good. This is one of the most encouraging messages of the gospel. God has the power to take the most destructive force of the Enemy and turn it into a catalyst for righteousness. The topic of this chapter is no exception.

Millions of couples are crippled by the effects of pornography. It is believed that a majority of divorces are at least partially caused by it. In the wake of this devastation, thousands of couples have discovered a new level of intimacy because of their willingness to seek the Lord through tragedy.

Involvement with porn and other sexually explicit material can either destroy intimacy or be a call toward seeking the Lord together at a whole new level. The grace of God is bestowed not on those who have it all together but on the broken who humbly cry out for help. Time and again in the Gospels, we read that Jesus came to heal the sick and forgive the worst of sinners.

When a couple moves past their pride, selfishness, blame, and shame to cry out together for God's grace and healing, the Lord will answer.

If you and/or your husband struggle with sexual sin, be encouraged that the very thing Satan uses to destroy, God can use to redeem. If you're willing to listen, forgive, confess, love, and strive for purity, your journey together toward wholeness can forge you together unlike anything else.

Remember little David standing before the towering Goliath with a stone and a slingshot? No one gave him a prayer of survival. Yet David confidently shouted at the giant, "You come against me with sword and spear and javelin, but I come against you in the name of the LORD Almighty, the God of the armies of Israel, whom you have defied. This day the LORD will hand you over to me, and I'll strike you down and cut off your head. Today I will give the carcasses of the Philistine army to the birds of the air and the beasts of the earth, and the whole world will know that there is a God in Israel. All those gathered here will know that it is not by sword or spear that the LORD saves; for the battle is the LORD's, and he will give all of you into our hands" (1 Samuel 17:45–47).

Plead with the Lord to begin writing your victory story today!

SOMETHING TO THINK ABOUT • • • • •

1. Talk to your husband about what sources threaten the purity of your secret garden.

2. In what ways are you tempted by porn or fantasy outlets (including novels, TV, movies)?

3. What practical steps can you take to guard your marriage?

4. Consider committing with your husband to schedule a "checkup" once a month simply to assess and pray about the temptations that threaten the sanctity of your marriage.

eleven

How's Your Love Life?

"How's your love life?" The way men and women understand this question goes a long way toward explaining the differences in the way the average husband and wife approach sex. Most women interpret their "love life" as the quality of romance in their marriage. Does she feel close to her husband? Do they still date each other? Can he still make her smile simply by walking into the room?

The average guy, on the other hand, understands his love life in the context of sex. How often . . . how passionate . . . how fulfilling is the sexual intimacy in his marriage?

As women, we tend to feel a little superior in our interpretation of love. After all, our understanding of love includes feelings, communication, and relationship, a much more multidimensional and "mature" approach than simply having sex. I'm learning that both a man's and woman's understandings of love are naturally immature, centered in what makes us "feel" loved.

Based on everything I read in Scripture, I believe that God is very interested in your love life. Yet when He asks you, "How's your love life?" the question has a very different implication.

It's All About the Love

If the Bible has one theme, it's love. Throughout both the Old and New Testaments, the centerpiece of the story of God's relationship with humanity is the endless pursuit of teaching us about love—how to receive it and how to give it back to Him. So, were Jesus to ask you the question, "How's your love life?" the underlying question would be, "How are you loving?"

What Kind of Love Are You "Making"?

Throughout the Bible, God uses illustrations from our world to teach us about things beyond our experience. For example, He teaches us to refer to Him as "our Father." The parallel between God and an earthly father can be helpful. It's the closest thing we know to God's compassion, protection, and strength. However, even the best earthly father is just a shadow of God's character; God is so much more than a Father. If we limit Him to our experience with our own dads, we will substantially minimize how we understand His power, holiness, righteousness, and goodness. We'll project onto Him what the word *dad* means in our limited knowledge. Some dads are weak, abusive, or controlling. Certainly these traits are contrary to the character of God.

The word pictures and analogies of Scripture give us only a starting place, pointing to a reality far beyond what we understand. Jesus is more than a Bridegroom. The Holy Spirit is more mysterious than the wind. The power of the gospel reaches far beyond the growth of a mustard seed. And love, as we know it here on earth, pales in comparison to the supernatural love Jesus desires to see flourish in our hearts.

The kind of love we naturally understand contradicts in some ways the love Scripture teaches. Our natural love is demanding, is selfish, and takes the easy road. It revolves around what we desire, think, and feel.

We naturally love our husbands when they make us feel good, when they measure up to our expectations, and when they meet our emotional and physical needs. We receive their love only on our terms. They must approach us when we are rested and ready. They must speak our "love language."

When we first open the gift of sex, we do so with a limited and immature understanding of what it means to make love. We assume the gift is somehow broken when it isn't fulfilling or pleasurable. The true gift of sex isn't what it feels like when we open it but *who we are becoming as we wrestle with it.*

The gift of sex shows us how limited our understanding of love is, even in our most intimate relationships. It illuminates how desperately we need God to teach us how to "make love."

Learning About Love

Just like equating God with our fathers, as long as we think we understand love, we won't strive for what is beyond us. God doesn't give love—He *is* love. This is a mystery to us. What exactly does that mean? Love is something we do or feel, certainly not something we are. In fact, love often requires that we deny what we are and what our nature craves. The first step of learning about love is acknowledging that it's beyond us; it's something that we can't quite grasp.

First Corinthians 13, the famous Love Chapter, was written not just to teach us how to love but also to show us how limited our love actually is. Take a look at it again and evaluate your love life by this standard:

> Love is patient, love is kind. It does not envy, it does not boast, it is not proud. It is not rude, it is not self-seeking, it is not easily angered, it keeps no record of wrongs. Love does not delight in evil but rejoices with the truth. It always protects, always trusts, always hopes, always perseveres. Love never fails. (verses 4–8A)

Apply this to the gift of sex. Are you patient and kind? Do you envy the intimacy of another couple? Do you boast, or are you self-righteous with your husband? Have you ever been rude regarding intimacy? Are you self-seeking? Are you easily angered when your husband doesn't meet your needs or expectations? Do you keep a record of wrongs when he has fallen into temptation? Do you delight in evil or sit idly by as evil infiltrates your marriage? Or do you strive toward holiness? Have you rejoiced in the truth, even when it has been painful? Do you protect, trust, hope, and persevere even when the world tells you to give up?

The purpose of impossible standards (like this one) is to show us how inadequate we are in our own strength to meet them. They create an awareness of our weakness, fallenness, and need for God's grace and power. Not only do we fall short of God's standard of holiness for salvation, we're incapable of loving the way God wants us to. The great news is that through our knowing God and seeking Him, we allow Him to love this way through us.

You Can't Give What You Haven't Received

Have you ever re-gifted something? You received a sweater or picture frame that you couldn't really use, so you saved it as an emergency gift. Or maybe you received a gift and immediately thought of someone else who would appreciate it far more than you could.

I'm not sure what Emily Post would say about the etiquette of re-gifting. When you really think about it, every gift we give is really a re-gift in some ways. The money used to buy the gift or the materials used to create it were first a gift from God. It's impossible for us to create a gift out of nothing.

Real love is only possible through re-gifting it. Without truly experiencing and knowing the love of Jesus, your sex life is limited to the natural feelings of affection you may have for your husband. The apostle John wrote, "God is love. Whoever lives in love lives in God, and

God in him. . . . We love because he first loved us" (1 John 4:16b, 19).

Dear sister, if you haven't experienced the forgiveness and grace of God, you won't be able to extend these same gifts to your husband. If you haven't embraced the truth that God loves you in spite of your sinful heart, you won't be able to love your husband in his imperfection. If you don't understand the humility and unselfishness Jesus modeled on the cross, you won't be able to extend this kind of love in the bedroom. Jesus taught that whoever has been forgiven much, loves much. But she "who has been forgiven little loves little" (Luke 7:47). Please understand that your sexual relationship with your husband is intricately intertwined with the intimacy you have with Jesus. What barriers are keeping you from knowing His love?

Jesus' Prayer for Your Marriage

Imagine that you're sitting in a coffee shop, sipping a latte or chai, and Jesus walks in. After ordering a Caffè Americano (I'm sure that's His drink), He sits right next to you and begins asking about your marriage. You talk for a while, sharing your disappointments, your triumphs, and the intimacy you desperately long for from your husband. His eyes are gentle, yet they seem to look right into your heart. You can't explain the wonder of being known. Beyond the words you say, He knows your every thought, fear, doubt, and hope.

At one point, Jesus takes your hand. Peering into your eyes with love and compassion, He says, "Let's talk to my Father about all of this." Then it dawns on you—Jesus is going to pray for you and your marriage! What do you think He'll ask His Father? What do you hope He'll request on your account? To straighten out your husband? To take away your anger? To erase the consequences of the past? Do you think He might pray for your sex life?

To my knowledge, Jesus doesn't regularly make appearances at the local Starbucks, but He does know your every thought, fear, doubt, and

hope. Someday He will look into your eyes, and you'll understand how fully loved and known you are. And He does pray for you. Romans 8 says that Jesus sits at the right hand of the Father interceding for you, and the Holy Spirit intercedes for us too, asking for what we don't even know we need. What do you think Jesus and the Holy Spirit ask the Father for concerning you?

Amazingly, you don't have to guess. John recorded in his gospel exactly how Jesus prays for you. Right before His arrest and crucifixion, Jesus prayed for His disciples and then for all "those who will believe in me." Here is what He prayed:

> I pray . . . that all of them may be one, Father, just as you are in me and I am in you. May they also be in us so that the world may believe that you have sent me. I have given them the glory that you gave me, that they may be one as we are one: I in them and you in me. May they be brought to complete unity to let the world know that you sent me and have loved them even as you have loved me.
>
> Father, I want those you have given me to be with me where I am, and to see my glory, the glory you have given me because you loved me before the creation of the world.
>
> Righteous Father, though the world does not know you, I know you, and they know that you have sent me. I have made you known to them, and will continue to make you known in order that the love you have for me may be in them and that I myself may be in them. (John 17:20–26)

Notice that His one prayer for you was unity. Above all else, God wants you to be transformed by His love and to be unified with each other and with Him. Even now I believe that He sits at the right hand of the Father, asking that you may know the fullness of His love and be unified with the body of Christ and primarily unified with your husband.

The gift of sex is more than just an outward sign of that unity; it's a fire designed to test and to forge oneness between you and your husband. Satan will use every headache as a stumbling block to keep you immature and divided in your love. As he did so long ago in the garden, he will try to convince you that God's plan for you is broken beyond repair:

- The headache of differences . . . a curse to keep you from fulfillment.
- The headache of a man's sex drive . . . a burden to make you a sex object.
- The headache of fatigue . . . yet another demand on you.
- The headache of children . . . to ensure that your own needs are never met.
- The headache of boredom . . . a reminder that fidelity is lame compared to the world's offerings.
- The headache of the past . . . a reminder that you are condemned.
- The headache of body image . . . there's nothing desirable about you.
- The headache of pornography . . . you will never be enough for him.

While Satan's every attempt is to twist the gift of sex into a curse, Jesus longs to turn each challenge into a chance to deepen your ability to truly unify through His love. God tells us that we'll be tested for the purpose of developing character, maturity, and faith (James 1:2–4). Each headache in your marriage is an opportunity to refine the quality of your love:

- The headache of differences . . . love is not self-seeking.
- The headache of a man's sex drive . . . love is not easily angered and does not boast.
- The headache of fatigue . . . love always perseveres.
- The headache of children . . . love is patient.
- The headache of boredom . . . love always hopes and is not rude.

- The headache of the past . . . love rejoices with the truth and always protects. Love does not keep a record of wrongs.
- The headache of body image . . . love is kind and is not proud. Love never fails.
- The headache of pornography . . . love does not delight in evil and does not keep a record of wrongs.

As the apostle Paul wrote, "If you have any encouragement from being united with Christ, if any comfort from his love, if any fellowship with the Spirit, if any tenderness and compassion, then make my joy complete by being like-minded, having the same love, being one in spirit and purpose. Do nothing out of selfish ambition or vain conceit, but in humility consider others better than yourselves. Each of you should look not only to your own interests, but also to the interests of others" (Philippians 2:1–4).

He also instructs us to "get rid of all bitterness, rage and anger, brawling and slander, along with every form of malice. Be kind and compassionate to one another, forgiving each other, just as in Christ God forgave you" (Ephesians 4:31–32).

Sexuality isn't a separate compartment of your life but an expression of your heart. The headaches, disappointments, and challenges test whether Jesus' prayer and Paul's writings reflect your life.

Your sex life will either be the greatest deterrent or the most powerful conduit of love in your marriage. The difference between the two lies not in how many headaches you have but in how you approach them. Are they curses that defy God's goodness or avenues through which you learn about His love?

Open the Imperishable Gift

One day the Sadducees (religious leaders) were testing Jesus and asked Him, "Teacher . . . Moses wrote for us that if a man's brother dies and

leaves a wife but no children, the man must marry the widow and have children for his brother. Now there were seven brothers. The first one married a woman and died childless. The second and then the third married her, and in the same way the seven died, leaving no children. Finally, the woman died too. Now then, at the resurrection whose wife will she be, since the seven were married to her?" (Luke 20:28–33).

If I were asking the question, I'd want to know what was wrong with the woman. Surviving seven husbands? Sounds a little fishy to me!

Jesus answered by saying, "The people of this age marry and are given in marriage. But those who are considered worthy of taking part in that age and in the resurrection from the dead will neither marry nor be given in marriage" (verses 34–35).

News flash! There will be no marriage in heaven. I assume this means there will also be no sex. (Half of you are thinking, *How can it be heaven with no sex?* while the other half are thinking, *Obviously it would be heaven with no sex!*) God's purpose for you in sex and marriage isn't for you to perfect it for heaven. It won't even exist in heaven! Just like your money and all of your stuff, you can't take your marriage with you. Marriage and sex are simply tools through which God refines what will last eternally.

"For everything in the world—the cravings of sinful man, the lust of his eyes and the boasting of what he has and does—comes not from the Father but from the world. The world and its desires pass away, but the man who does the will of God lives forever" (1 John 2:16–17).

First Corinthians tells us that gifts of prophecy, tongues, and knowledge will be irrelevant in heaven. But what will remain are faith, hope, and love. "But the greatest of these is love" (13:13).

Remember the movie *Charlie and the Chocolate Factory*? Five lucky children found a golden ticket in a candy bar that allowed them a day at the famous chocolate factory. During their tour, they learned many of Willy Wonka's secrets and were treated to an endless delight of exotic

treats. What the children didn't know was that the "gift" was really a test, a refiner's fire to determine the one worthy of the greatest gift: inheriting the factory.

Four of the children failed along the way. Greed, impulsivity, and a lust to indulge in the pleasures of the factory disqualified them one by one. The temptations of the temporary gift tested their fitness for the greatest gift. Humble Charlie emerged through the testing.

Your sexuality is much like this children's story. You entered the factory dreaming of temporary pleasure and were disappointed by its limitations. Look beyond the gift to a more substantial eternal gift. Your marriage is like one day in a chocolate factory. The only thing that will survive the visit is the character that emerges through the journey.

Could God wave a magic wand and make sex in your marriage perfect? Sure. He could even do it without the magic wand. Yet He is far more concerned with forging your character and teaching you about the eternal than He is about your pleasure for a season. He most wants to give you a gift that will last into eternity. Now that's a gift worth unwrapping!

SOMETHING TO THINK ABOUT • • • • •

1. How is the Lord using your sex life to teach you about love?

2. What lesson of "love" are you most resistant to learning?

3. Name one thing you can start doing now to show love to your husband.

Q & A
Ask Dr. Juli

Q. *I usually feel a need for intimacy with my husband, but not really a desire for sex. Before we were married it was so hard not to have sex. Getting married seemed to make that disappear. What happened to that feeling?*

A. In making the transition from dating to marriage, three things that help increase your desire for sex have likely disappeared. First of all, time. When you and your husband were dating, you spent time together with no demands. On dates, you had hours just to talk, cuddle, and have fun. Most likely, you no longer carve out time to date. Instead, your time together is filled with running errands, cleaning the house, and negotiating life. Second, the fun has likely gone out of your relationship. You probably don't dress up for each other or plan playtime like you did when you were dating. Third, sex is no longer a taboo. The adrenaline of taking that "next step" was a powerful drive while you were dating. Instead of doing something wrong, now sex is about fulfilling an obligation. Which sounds like more fun to you?

Although you cannot re-create the atmosphere of when you were dating, there are many elements of dating that you can work to incorporate into your marriage. Set aside time, money, and energy to date, just like you did before marriage. Give your best to that time, not just the leftovers. Another key element is foreplay. Because sex was taboo, you probably spent a lot of time kissing, hugging, touching, and staring into each other's eyes. These are key elements of female arousal. Don't start intimacy in bed. Start it in the car or on the couch in front of the fireplace and see what happens. Finally, remember that as a young married

couple, you are just beginning this journey of sex with your husband. It *will* get better if you work together on it!

Q. *My husband and I have been married for almost two years and most of the time I have no sex drive. I really struggle with it emotionally. When I do feel like having sex I start to feel embarrassed and ashamed. Is this because we had sex before marriage? My husband struggles with pornography. Could that have something to do with it? I just don't know what to think or feel and am afraid of what this is doing to my marriage.*

A. It sounds like you are conflicted about whether or not enjoying sex is a pure thing. Because of the history of premarital sex and pornography, this is understandable. Your first experiences with sex and arousal were associated with feelings of guilt and shame. To get past this, it's critical that you separate sexual sin and sex. If you have not done so, confess your past before the Lord. Ask for His cleansing and forgiveness, and then accept it. If your husband is still involved with pornography, you need to address that issue. When your sexual relationship is compromised by outside sensuality, it may continue to foster your confusion about enjoying sex. Embrace the fact that God wants you to have sex with your husband and He wants you to enjoy it. You may also need to look into other causes for your low sex drive, such as your health and the level of emotional intimacy in your marriage.

Q. *Because of my husband's job we are apart a LOT. I'm wondering if phone sex between a husband and wife is okay? Also, is it okay to masturbate when you are apart for long periods of time?*

A. I shy away from answering these kinds of questions. Maybe it's because I don't want to go on record with my opinion on such controversial issues. I think it's also because it's not a matter of right and wrong, but of individual conscience. It sounds like your purpose in phone sex

and masturbation during long absences is to avert temptation and creatively experience intimacy with your husband. These are honoring motivations. However, in weighing the issue, you and your husband need to make a personal decision perhaps using the criteria listed in chapter 3: Does it involve only you and your husband? Is it beneficial? Does it enslave you? Does it violate your conscience? Is it a stumbling block for someone? If you get the green light on all of these questions, go for it and enjoy it, guilt-free!

Q. *I recently found out my husband has been looking at pornography. I thought it would help to see what he sees so we watched a porn movie together. The sex afterward was exciting but now I feel guilty and dirty. Is it okay to watch movies like this as husband and wife? If so why do I feel so bad? Help!*
A. There are two problems with the strategy of sharing in porn. First of all, it will create guilt and taint your sex life. Take a look at Ephesians chapter 5. Paul charges a husband to love his wife and present her as a radiant bride without stain or blemish. Your husband is told to protect your purity. By inviting you into a sexually compromising situation, he is failing in this duty. If you are sensitive, you will not only feel the guilt of violating a standard of purity, but will become angry with your husband for inviting you into such a compromise. Second, the excitement of watching a porn movie together will steal away the natural joy of savoring each other sexually. After eating cotton candy, an apple seems bland. The same is true with sex. God designed you and your husband to find great fulfillment and joy in experiencing sex together. That natural sweetness between you will become dull and won't even stimulate you if you feed your sexuality on the world's cheap thrills. Don't take the easy way out. Draw a line, not just for yourself, but also for your husband. It may mean a year of conflict and pain, but in the long run, your marriage will benefit (and so will your sex life!).

Q. *My husband came to me last week and asked if he could take nude pictures of me. I don't want him to because I'm afraid someone else could get hold of them. Am I being a prude? Our sex life has gotten a little stale lately so this may help spice things up a bit. Any advice?*

A. I understand your reservations about your husband's suggestion. I've heard more than one story of pictures and videos that accidentally fell into the wrong hands. If your husband's request makes you feel uncomfortable, stick to your guns. However, take note of his underlying message: sex is getting stale. By all means, work on spicing things up. Communicate to him that you also want to have a more exciting sex life. Then explore ways with which you are both comfortable to turn up the heat. As noted in chapter 2, making sex exciting isn't *always* about finding something new and kinky. It also includes working on your relationship, communication, dating each other, and protecting your sex life from the busyness of your daily life.

Q. *My husband and I got pregnant on our honeymoon. When I was pregnant we went months with no sex. After the baby was born I thought things would get better but they didn't. When we do have sex I don't have an orgasm and he says he feels guilty about that. Could that have anything to do with his rarely wanting sex? Too, his job is stressful, so I wonder if that could also be the problem. I've lost all my baby weight but it doesn't seem to have helped.*

A. First of all, your baby weight, whether you lost it or not, probably has nothing to do with your husband's lack of desire for sex. Don't take it personally. His lack of interest may very likely be due to one of the other two reasons you mentioned: your not having an orgasm and stress at work. When your husband says he feels "guilty" that you don't orgasm, he may really be saying that he feels inadequate—like he can't please you. A sensitive husband cares as much about your pleasure as he

cares about his. He may avoid sex because he doesn't believe he is good at it. Reassure him and also read a book or two together. (I recommend *The Way to Love Your Wife*, by Clifford and Joyce Penner.) The second culprit, stress, can also be a libido killer. In addition to work stress, having children right out of the gate is stressful. You never really had time to work on sex and build romance in your marriage. As difficult as it might be, it's *critical* that you take time to get away together and work on romance. If grandparents live close by, take advantage of their willingness to baby-sit. Go on dates at least twice a month. Try to get away for a weekend twice a year. It's an investment that you won't regret. In the long run, it will even make you better parents.

Q. *I know that men are wired physiologically different from women and that sex is important to them for several reasons. Here's my question: Do they really need sex? In other words, is it harmful (not just emotionally) for them not to have sex? I want to know if it's really a desire for sex versus a physical need.*

A. To my knowledge, a man never died because he didn't have sex. Sex is not a physical need like air or food. However, semen does build up in a man's testicles, creating physical tension that needs a release. If a man doesn't have sex, the semen may be released through nocturnal emissions. It's interesting to note that the more often a man has sex, the more semen his body will produce. The desire to have sex is also heightened by sexual stimuli in his environment. Instead of thinking of it as a physical need that your husband will die without, think of it as a physical, emotional, and relational need that your husband will have a difficult time feeling complete without.

Q. *I have been married for almost 30 years. I work hard to keep my weight down, but while my husband has always been overweight, he is now 50 pounds heavier than when we got married. I have*

tried everything to motivate him, including lots of prayer. I have even told him that physically I'm not attracted to him, but nothing changes. He's hurt because I struggle to view him passionately or as a lover. How can I do this when at times I'm repulsed?

A. You're not alone in this situation. I'm sure a lot of men and women resonate with your feelings. Let's dissect the problem by looking at some facts: (1) You will never convince your husband to lose weight. In fact, the more you push and plead, the less likely he is to do it. It has to be his idea. (2) Your husband is God's provision for you sexually. He's the man. You either work on it with him, or you shut down your sex life. (3) God calls you to show love toward your husband, regardless of what he looks like or how you feel about him. So, from the world's perspective, you are up a creek without a paddle . . . in a disheartening situation that's not likely to get any better. I believe there is another perspective, albeit harder to accept. What does God want to teach or show you through your situation? Unconditional love? Humility? Grace? Your situation is disappointing and frustrating, but you have a choice to either stay stuck in it or to ask God how He wants to transform you through it.

Q. *Ever since the birth of our first child my husband constantly ridicules me about my body. He's always telling me I'm too fat. I'm 5' 7" and weigh 145. That is 15 pounds more than when we got married. He often humiliates me in public and puts me down in front of other people. Because of all this I never want to have sex with him and that makes him angry. I am emotionally drained all the time. Please help!*

A. Regardless of how much you weigh, your husband has no excuse for humiliating you or putting you down, publically or privately. It's simply unloving. If your husband is treating you this way regarding your body, chances are he's emotionally cruel or controlling in other ways as well. Although it will initially be difficult, you have to call him on his behavior. I recommend meeting (by yourself) with a counselor who can

help you set some appropriate boundaries regarding what you will and will not tolerate. I would also recommend the book *Boundaries* by Henry Cloud and John Townsend. Your lack of desire for sex stems from the fact that you don't feel emotionally safe with your husband. Until you address that issue, you can't work on your sex life. And from one woman to another, you're not fat!

Q. *My husband and I have already crossed a lot of boundaries regarding the purity of our sexual relationship. We are definitely in the cycle of trying to find more and more stimulating material to make things exciting. How do we "turn the clock back" and learn to enjoy "normal" sex?*

A. First I would start with prayer, setting apart your sex life and asking God to bless your desire to please Him through it. Second, you have to expect that sex might seem dull for a while. You may have to fight the desire to think about or act out things outside the "fences." Instead of simply trying not to do something, pour your energy into healthy eroticism. Set apart time to spoil each other with a bubble bath, massage oil, creative uses of food, candles, and music. Focus on each other, at the deepest levels of intimacy. Do you believe that sin is pleasurable for a season but in the end brings death? If you do, have faith that a pure sex life may at first seem to lack pleasure, but that it will ultimately lead to abundance.

Q. *My husband has an ongoing struggle with pornography. I had no idea until we were newly married and I tried to initiate making love one night and he declined. I went to bed and later on got up and found him looking at porn on the computer. He stops and starts so many times, and I am finding it hard to trust him anymore. What do I do?*

A. Most likely, your husband really is repentant when he stops using pornography. He may sincerely feel terrible and ask your forgiveness. However, the pull toward porn is so strong that he can't seem to fight it.

He has seasons of victory and then falls right back into the struggle. He may have an addiction to pornography that he can't eliminate without professional help. For you to be able to trust him, you need to understand that he may *always* battle porn. You both need to agree on that. His struggle to watch porn may have very little or nothing to do with how he feels about you; it's simply a "thorn in the flesh." As Paul explained in Romans 7, we may find ourselves doing things we don't want to do because our flesh fights against our heart. While you need to understand this and show grace toward your husband, you also need to insist that he set up ways to combat the temptation. Obviously, the strategy he's using now isn't very effective. Together, talk and pray about what needs to change. Here are some suggestions: place filters on computers, locate the computers in the public rooms of your house, get rid of cable or satellite television, check in weekly or monthly with a "how are you doing" conversation, and find a counselor or pastor who can help with accountability and wise counsel.

Q. *I don't have any reason to think my husband struggles with porn, but after reading about how common an issue this is, even amongst Christian men, I wonder if I should discuss the issue with my husband to see if it's something he's struggling with. I never realized how significant a temptation this is for men. Do you have any suggestions for how I should broach the subject?*

A. Just because many men struggle with porn does not mean that all men do. Don't approach your husband with the assumption that he's struggling. However, I do think it would be helpful to talk to him about it. You can mention what you have read (perhaps even read a section of the book to him). Ask him if he can relate. Be prepared to hear both a yes and a no answer. If he says yes, respect the fact that he's being vulnerable with you. You may want to respond with something like, "I never knew that. I'd like to understand how porn affects you and how I can help with the struggle." On the other hand, if he says no, believe him.

Notes

Chapter 1

1. Jean Twenge, *Generation Me* (New York: Free Press, 2006), 159.

Chapter 2

1. Archibald D. Hart, Catherine Hart Weber, and Debra L. Taylor, *Secrets of Eve* (Nashville: Thomas Nelson, 2004), 94–95; and Julia R. Heiman, "Evaluating Sexual Dysfunctions," in *Current Care of Women: Diagnosis and Treatment*, ed. Dawn P. Lemcke, et al. (New York: McGraw-Hill Medical, 2008), 111.

2. Mayo Clinic staff, anorgasmia. http://www.mayoclinic.com/ health/anorgasmia/DS01051/DSECTION=causes.

3. Faculty of the Harvard Medical School, "Sensate Focus: The Foundation of Sex Therapy," *Harvard Health Publications* (2007), quoted in AOL Health, "Sensate Focus: The Foundation of Sex Therapy— The Role of Sex Therapy: Women's Health," http://www.aolhealth .com/womens-sexual-health/learn-about-it/the-role-of-sex-therapy/sensate-focus-the-foundation-of-sex-therapy.

4. Louanne Cole Weston, "Can't Orgasm? Here's Help for Women," WebMD, March/April 2008, http://www.webmd.com/ sex-relationships/features/cant-orgasm-heres-help-for-women.

5. From a 1997 study published in the *British Medical Journal*, cited in Natasha Turner, "Good Sex Is Good for Your Health," Truestar Health, http://www.truestarhealth.com/members/cm_archives 10ML3P1A33.html (accessed February 18, 2009).

6. Hart, Weber, and Taylor, *Secrets of Eve*, 71–72.

7. Wikipedia, s.v. "standby power," http://en.Wikipedia.org/wiki/ standby_power.

Chapter 5

1. Adapted from Archibald D. Hart, *The Sexual Man* (Nashville: W Publishing Group, 1994), 32–33, 68.
2. Ibid., 32, 136; and Archibald D. Hart, Catherine Hart Weber, and Debra L. Taylor, *Secrets of Eve* (Nashville: Thomas Nelson, 2004), 8, 93, 102–103, 134.
3. Clifford L. Penner and Joyce J. Penner, *The Way to Love Your Wife: Creating Greater Love and Passion in the Bedroom* (Carol Stream, IL: Focus on the Family/Tyndale House, 2007), 34.
4. Ibid., 41.
5. Khaled Hosseini, *A Thousand Splendid Suns* (New York: Riverhead Books, 2008).

Chapter 6

1. Patrick Morley, *Understanding Your Man in the Mirror* (Grand Rapids, MI: Zondervan, 2001), 137.
2. Gary Rosberg and Barbara Rosberg, with Ginger Kolbaba, *The 5 Sex Needs of Men and Women* (Carol Stream, IL: Tyndale House, 2006), 81.
3. Archibald D. Hart, *The Sexual Man* (Nashville: W Publishing Group, 1994), 79.
4. Shaunti Feldhahn, *For Women Only: What You Need to Know About the Inner Lives of Men* (Sisters, OR: Multnomah, 2004), 98.
5. Hart, *The Sexual Man*, 72–73.
6. Feldhahn, *For Women Only*, 100.
7. Hart, *The Sexual Man*, 70.
8. Archibald D. Hart, Catherine Hart Weber, and Debra L. Taylor, *Secrets of Eve* (Nashville: Thomas Nelson, 2004), 162–63.

Chapter 7

1. Study conducted by Dr. Steve Gangestad and colleagues at the University of New Mexico, published in the *Journal of Personality and Social Psychology* 91, no. 4 (October 2006); cited in S. Dingfelder,

"Men Who Cheat Show Elevated Testosterone Levels," *Monitor on Psychology* 37, no. 11 (December 2006), http://www.apa.org/monitor/dec06/testosterone.html.

2. Archibald D. Hart, *The Sexual Man* (Nashville: W Publishing Group, 1994), 72–73.

3. Victor B. Cline, "Pornography's Effects on Adults and Children," Morality in Media, 2001, http://www.moralityinmedia.org; http://www.obscenitycrimes.org/clineart.cfm (accessed February 26, 2009).

Chapter 8

1. Dave Burchett, "A Husband's Honest Reflections on Feminine Beauty," Crosswalk.com, http://www.crosswalk.com/1421547/ (accessed February 27, 2009). Used by permission.

Chapter 9

1. Survey conducted May/June 2008 by Insight Express, cited in "The Truth About American Marriage," Parade.com, September 15, 2008, http://www.parade.com/hot-topics/2008/09/truth-about-american-marriage-poll-results (accessed February 27, 2009).

2. F. Scott Christopher and Susan Sprecher, "Sexuality in Marriage, Dating, and Other Relationships: A Decade Review," *Journal of Marriage and Family* 62, no. 4 (November 4, 2000): 999–1017.

3. Catherine E. Myers, Memory Disorders Project, *Memory Loss and the Brain*, 2006 glossary entry, s.v. "state-dependent memory," http://www.memorylossonline.com/glossary/statedependent memory.html.

4. Adverse Childhood Experiences Study, 1995–1997, cited in Department of Health and Human Services, Centers for Disease Control and Prevention, "Prevalence of Individual Adverse Childhood Experiences," http://www.cdc.gov/nccdphp/ace/prevalence.htm.

5. Wikipedia, s.v. "sexual abuse," http://en.wikipedia.org/wiki/Sexual_abuse.

6. Centers for Disease Control, "Adverse Childhood Experiences," http://www.cdc.gov/nccdphp/ace/prevalence.htm.

7. Steven Earll, "How Do People Become Addicts, Part 4," 2004, quoted in Pure Intimacy, Focus on the Family, http://www .pureintimacy.org/piArticles/A000000578.cfm.

8. Robert E. Rector et al., *The Harmful Effects of Early Sexual Activity and Multiple Sexual Partners Among Women: A Book of Charts* (Washington: The Heritage Foundation, 2003), 2, 10, http://www .heritage.org/research/abstinence/abstinence_charts.cfm.

Chapter 10

1. Dale Kunkel et al., *Sex on TV 2005* (Menlo Park, CA: Kaiser Family Foundation: 2005), 46, http://www.kff.org/entmedia/upload/ Sex-on-TV-4-Executive -Summary.pdf.

2. Jason S. Carroll et al., "Generation XXX: Pornography Acceptance and Use Among Emerging Adults," *Journal of Adolescent Research* 23, no. 1 (January 2008): 16.

3. Mark D. Regnerus, *Forbidden Fruit: Sex and Religion in the Lives of American Teenagers* (New York: Oxford University Press, 2007), 165.

4. Archibald D. Hart, *The Sexual Man* (Nashville: W Publishing Group, 1994), 89.

5. Shirley P. Glass, Ph.D., AAMFT Consumer Update: Infidelity, American Association for Marriage and Family Therapy, http:// www.therapistlocator.net/families/Consumer_Updates/Infidelity.asp.

6. Testimony of Dr. Jeffrey Satinover on November 17, 2004, cited in transcripts from Senate Subcommittee on Science, Technology, and Space, November 18, 2004, http://www.obscenitycrimes.org/ Senate-Reisman-Layden-Etc.pdf.

7. Jason Carroll et al., "Generation XXX," 17.

8. Ibid.

Recommended Resources

Books

Dobson, James. *Love Must Be Tough: New Hope for Marriages in Crisis.* Carol Stream, IL: Tyndale, 2007.

Feldhahn, Shaunti. *For Women Only: What You Need to Know About the Inner Lives of Men.* Colorado Springs: Multnomah, 2004.

Hart, Archibald. *The Sexual Man.* Nashville: Thomas Nelson, 1995.

———. *Thrilled to Death: How the Endless Pursuit of Pleasure Is Leaving Us Numb.* Nashville: Thomas Nelson, 2007.

Hart, Archibald D., Catherine Hart Weber, and Debra L. Taylor. *Secrets of Eve.* Nashville: Thomas Nelson, 2004.

Leman, Kevin. *Sex Begins in the Kitchen: Creating Intimacy to Make Your Marriage Sizzle.* Grand Rapids: Revell, 2006.

Nelson, Tommy. *The Book of Romance: What Soloman Says About Love, Sex, and Intimacy.* Nashville: Thomas Nelson, 2007.

Penner, Clifford L., and Joyce J. Penner. *Getting Your Sex Life Off to a Great Start: A Guide for Engaged and Newlywed Couples.* Nashville: Thomas Nelson, 1994.

———. *The Gift of Sex: A Guide to Sexual Fulfillment.* Nashville: Thomas Nelson, 2003.

———. *The Way to Love Your Wife.* Colorado Springs: Focus on the Family, 2004.

———. *Restoring the Pleasure: Complete Step-by-Step Programs to Help Couples Overcome the Most Common Sexual Barriers.* Nashville: Word Publishing Group, 1993.

———. *Sex Facts for the Family.* Nashville: Word Publishing Group, 1992.

Rosberg, Gary, and Barbara Rosberg. *The 5 Sex Needs of Men and Women*. With Ginger Kolbaba. Carol Stream, IL: Tyndale House, 2007.

Shriver, Gary, and Mona Shriver. *Unfaithful: Rebuilding Trust After Infidelity*. Colorado Springs: Life Journey, 2005.

Slattery, Julianna. *Finding the Hero in Your Husband: Surrendering the Way God Intended*. Deerfield Beach, FL: Faith Communications, 2004.

Thomas, Gary. *Sacred Influence: How God Uses Wives to Shape the Souls of Their Husbands*. Grand Rapids: Zondervan, 2007.

Williams, Joe, and Michelle Williams. *Yes, Your Marriage Can Be Saved: 12 Truths for Rescuing Your Relationship*. Colorado Springs: Focus on the Family, 2007.

Booklet

Focus on the Family staff. *Nothing to Hide: Hope for Marriages Hurt by Pornography and Infidelity*. Colorado Springs: Focus on the Family.

Web-site

http://www.pureintimacy.org

Counseling

To speak to a counselor or for a referral to a counselor in your area, call 1-800-AFAMILY.

Contents

A Focus on the Family book published by Tyndale House Publishers, Inc., Carol Stream, Illinois 60188

Focus on the Family and the accompanying logo and design are federally registered trademarks of Focus on the Family, Colorado Springs, CO 80995.

TYNDALE and Tyndale's quill logo are registered trademarks of Tyndale House Publishers, Inc.

All Scripture quotations, unless otherwise indicated, are taken from the *Holy Bible, New International Version*®. NIV®. Copyright © 1973, 1978, 1984 by International Bible Society. Used by permission of Zondervan Publishing House. All rights reserved. Scripture quotations marked (MSG) are taken from *The Message* (paraphrase). Copyright © by Eugene H. Peterson 1993, 1994, 1995. Used by permission of NavPress Publishing Group.

The case examples presented in this book are fictional composites based on the author's clinical experience with hundreds of clients through the years. Any resemblance between these fictional characters and actual persons is coincidental.

The use of material from or references to various Web sites does not imply endorsement of those sites in their entirety.

Editor: Kathy Davis
Cover design by Dean H. Renninger
Cover photograph copyright © by Corbis Photography/Veer. All rights reserved.

Author photograph by Efrain Garcia. Copyright © Focus on the Family.

Library of Congress Cataloging-in-Publication Data
Slattery, Julianna, 1969-
  No more headaches : enjoying sex and intimacy in marriage / Julianna
Slattery.
     p. cm.
  "A Focus on the Family book."
  ISBN 978-1-58997-538-5
  1. Sex—Religious aspects—Christianity. 2. Marriage—Religious aspects—Christianity. I. Title.
  BT708.S54 2009
  248.8'44—dc22
                            2009007832

Printed in the United States of America
1 2 3 4 5 6 7 8 9 / 15 14 13 12 11 10 09

DR. JULI SLATTERY

NO MORE HEADACHES

ENJOYING SEX & INTIMACY IN MARRIAGE

Tyndale House Publishers, Inc., Carol Stream, Illinois

Juli Slattery answers the questions women are afraid to ask. I couldn't put the book down; I kept reading with disbelief at the next difficult topic she was about to tackle. Pick it up and be amazed when you start reading sentences out loud to your husband. I did!

—Dannah Gresh, author of *And the Bride Wore White*

As a researcher, I have a dilemma. I can investigate and explain the starting points that women need to know about their husbands (for example, how sexual affirmation transforms a man and his marriage), but then others must help each woman go further. Yet it is hard to find good and trustworthy resources. Juli Slattery's excellent book *No More Headaches* hits the mark in a big way regarding a sensitive subject that affects every single marriage. I highly recommend it to anyone who needs real-world yet compassionate answers about how to handle the confusion, hurt, disappointments, and just old-fashioned *differences* between husbands and wives.

—Shaunti Feldhahn, author of *For Women Only*

8/11/09

Dr. Juli Slattery "gets," understands, and empathizes with men and their sexuality better than any female author I've ever read. Her resulting advice for wives is practical, helpful, and biblically sound. Wives who read this book will be blessed by its wisdom, and husbands whose wives read this book will be blessed by its application.

—Gary Thomas, author of *Sacred Marriage* and *Sacred Influence*

Great book! I couldn't put it down. *No More Headaches* is practical, candid, hopeful, and seasoned with a splash of humor and compassion. There are not enough words to describe how really helpful this book is for women longing to reclaim the gift of sexuality as God intended. Every woman needs a copy of Dr. Slattery's book on her bedside nightstand— she and her husband will be glad it's there!

—Pam Farrel, best-selling author of *Red-Hot Monogamy* and *Men Are Like Waffles, Women Are Like Spaghetti*

I am certain that God intended sex to be a natural, sublime, and trouble-free experience. It is far from that in today's complex world. The distorting influences of pornography are rampant, and sexual anhedonia is prevalent in men. What a thrill it was, therefore, for me to see that Dr. Slattery's new book, *No More Headaches*, addresses head-on our modern confusion and frustration surrounding sex. With warmth and compassion, and deep professional and personal insight into how both women and men struggle to develop a healthy sexuality, she offers sound practical and biblical advice on how women can strengthen the sexual bond every couple should have. Though written primarily to women, it isn't just a book for them alone. I believe men can _____ into the sexual makeup of both sexes b _____ rec-ommend it to them as well.

—Archibald D. Hart, Ph.
Senior Professor of Psyc _____
Graduate School of Psychology, Fuller Theological Seminary

"Plan your enterprises cautiously . . . carry them out boldly."

SIR GEOFFROY DE CHARNY
FROM *A KNIGHT'S OWN BOOK OF CHIVALRY* (C. 1350)

CHAPTER 1

"Goddammit!" said the vice president, hanging up the phone and sinking back into bed.

"What is it, love?" asked his wife, still wearing pink eye shades.

"That was the White House. They want me to attend the prayer breakfast."

Silence.

"Apparently," he continued, "the president is 'sick.'"

"Again?"

"Yeah."

"God help him," she said, rolling over to check the time. "We only have an hour."

"Actually, less. The Secret Service said we need to leave in twenty minutes."

She pulled the covers over her head. "Well, I'm sick, too! You're going to have to pray solo, mister."

Henry Strickland smiled. They had been playing this game for forty years, she trying to lure him back into bed to play. He trying not to be late for work. He was late a lot.

"Martha, you know you have to join me, and we can't be late," he said, lumbering out of bed.

"Not on your life," said a voice under the covers.

"Duty before pleasure, and country before politics."

"Oh God, you're serious. You're really going to make me go."

"Amen," he said, walking into a closet of monochromatic blue suits and white shirts. "Now, what should I wear?"

. . .

The motorcade left the vice president's front door precisely twenty minutes later. The 1890s white-brick mansion sat in the middle of the U.S. Naval Observatory, ten acres of premium land in the middle of Washington, DC, but you would never know it. Somehow the designers had hidden it among a thistle of buildings, trees, and asphalt that constituted the nation's capital.

"Honey, you're crowding me," said Martha, as she applied makeup with one hand while holding a compact mirror in the other. Across from the vice president sat an attractive woman, half their age.

"Sir, your speech," said the young aide, handing him a folder. "I've taken the liberty of modifying the president's speech to fit your style."

"Thank you," he said, flipping open the file. His lips moved as he read, and he scribbled in the margins. Every year the National Prayer Breakfast was held at the Washington Hilton Hotel on Connecticut Avenue. The Secret Service nicknamed it the "Hinckley Hilton" because it was where a mentally disturbed John Hinckley shot Ronald Reagan in 1981. His reason? To impress actress Jodie Foster, with whom he had an obsession. Threats lurk everywhere.

Martha sat next to him, brushing rouge on her cheeks. Both ignored the sirens and flashing blue lights surrounding them. A logistical symphony, the thirty vehicles wound through the grounds of the U.S. Naval Observatory.

"Mongoose, this is Pilot," a voice crackled over the motorcade's radio network. "Mongoose" was the convoy commander and "Pilot" was the lead vehicle, each in an armored Chevy Suburban.

"Copy," replied Mongoose.

"Linking up with the Route car." A Washington, DC, police cruiser awaited the motorcade at the front gate, its lights blazing. Once it spotted the black SUVs, it flipped on its siren and sped up Thirty-Fourth Street, toward the National Cathedral, clearing rush hour traffic for the motorcade.

"Approaching Cleveland Avenue, now," said Pilot over the radio. Other black SUVs followed, while four Harley-Davidson police motorcycles, or "sweepers," zoomed ahead to block intersections and get cars out of the way. Normally the police would have closed the streets, but today's motorcade was last-minute and the morning rush hour particularly stubborn. The motorcade slithered through the traffic like a black snake.

The man called Mongoose looked like a college wrestler who had abandoned his weight class long ago but still moved like a champion. He checked his watch: 0736. On time.

"Mongoose, Stagecoach has cleared the gate," radioed the driver of the vice president's limousine, code-named Stagecoach. If a Cadillac STS and an up-armored Hummer mated, they would produce a presidential limo. The Secret Service dubbed it "the Beast," and it was battle proof. The windows could withstand armor-piercing bullets, and the body was made of a steel and titanium composite, like a tank. Each door was eight inches thick and weighed more than the fuselage door of a Boeing 757 jet. A reinforced five-inch steel plate ran under the car, shielding it from roadside bombs. The tires were a specially woven Kevlar, allowing the Beast to drive over spikes. If the tires were blasted away, it could escape at speed on steel rims. The fuel tank was encased in foam that prevented it from exploding, even if it suffered a direct hit. The limo was equipped with night vision cameras so it could drive in the dark, and the cabin was sealed with its own air supply in the event of a gas attack or the vehicle plunged into water. It even had a supply of the vice president's blood type on board. The Beast was a mobile bunker with a leather interior and a shiny black paint job.

The Beast wasn't alone. The convoy had three of them, and they weaved in and out of traffic together, playing a game of three-car monte to conceal the vice president.

"Jesus!" said Martha as the limo hit a pothole, causing a mascara smudge.

"Honey, you look fine," said Henry, without lifting his eyes from the speech.

The motorcade sped through red lights and intersections without stopping, the sweepers keeping traffic at bay.

"Mongoose, this is Pilot. We're approaching the Calvert Street bridge, but there's heavy congestion."

"Where, exactly?" asked Mongoose.

"A block before the bridge, at the intersection of Calvert and Connecticut Avenue."

"How heavy?"

"We're rolling to a stop."

Not good, thought Mongoose. Seconds later, the entire convoy eased to a standstill in a narrow two-lane street. The first law of motorcade operations: Never Stop. He picked up the radio handset, "Sweepers, clear the traffic."

Police motorcycles sped around them, their riders waving furiously at stopped cars. Cars nosed closer to the curb, but not enough to let the motorcade pass. It was no use. Traffic was backed up for blocks, and the motorcade was engulfed. Behind Mongoose sat the three presidential limos, wedged in between more black SUVs and civilian cars. Cars honked, being late for work.

"We've stopped. Is something wrong?" asked Martha.

"It's just a little traffic," said Henry, still fixated on his speech. The aide sat attentively across from him, an open laptop on her knees.

Unconvinced, Martha looked out the window. Upscale apartments lined the streets, sandwiched between big hotels, the kind that hold enormous conventions.

Mongoose furled his brow.

"There's gridlock in every direction," said Pilot.

"What's going on?" asked Mongoose.

"There's a three-car accident in the intersection, and it's obstructing traffic in all travel lanes." One car's trunk was crumpled, another car's right front smashed in, and a third was squashed in between them. Crushed glass and liquid covered the road; deflated air bags stuck out of car doors. The occupants sat on opposite curbs, glowering at each other as an angry fire truck, also stuck in the traffic, blasted its horn in the distance.

"Are emergency vehicles on-site? Tow trucks?"

"Negative. It looked like it just happened, but no one is seriously hurt."

"Shit," Mongoose muttered, startling the driver next to him.

"Everything OK, boss?" asked his driver, a former Marine still sporting a military high-and-tight haircut.

No, Mongoose thought. *Something isn't right.* He knew the area well, having driven these blocks and this bridge more times than he cared to admit while serving three presidents in twenty years. Gridlock was common during Washington rush hour, as were accidents. But they didn't happen on this stretch of road. Not at this time of day, and not just as a motorcade was passing through. There were no coincidences in this line of work.

It could be an ambush, thought Mongoose, scanning the tree-lined sidewalks. The last time his instincts pinged this hard was just before his platoon was attacked by the Taliban in Wanat, an armpit of a place in far eastern Afghanistan. He lost two friends that day. His thinking was the same then as now: *Get out of the kill zone! Get off the X!*

"Can we take the Connecticut Avenue bridge?" he asked.

"Negative. Accident traffic has backed it up, too," said Pilot.

Mongoose turned to his driver. "Can we make a U-turn here?"

"*We* could, sir, but the Beast would never clear it."

Mongoose leaned forward on the dashboard, gauging the lane to their left. The accident had blocked opposing traffic, so it was clear, but his driver was right. The limo's length was longer than the lane's width, making a U-turn difficult but not impossible.

"Stagecoach, can you execute a U-turn?" he asked over the radio.

There was a pause. "It would take a twenty-point turn. Maybe a few minutes."

Too long, Mongoose thought, *and too exposed.* The only thing worse than being stuck in traffic was having the limo perpendicular to it, with no easy escape. It would make a perfect target for a broadside, something a clever ambush team could engineer using a fake traffic accident. There was only one way out—forward.

"Pilot, Sweepers," Mongoose said. "We need to get the Package moving. Make a hole." The "Package" was the vice president.

"Copy," voices crackled over the network. Two black SUVs darted into the left lane and sped toward the accident. The sweepers directed surrounding traffic to inch away from the travel lane. A fire truck, an ambulance, and a tow truck arrived simultaneously.

"Tow truck on-site," said Pilot.

"Clear the intersection!" said Mongoose. Firemen helped connect the tow truck cable to one of the wrecked vehicles.

"Clear!" yelled one of the firemen, and the tow truck driver pulled a lever. The tow cable went instantly taught, and dragged one of the wrecks out of the intersection. Metal screeched on pavement, adding to the din of distant sirens and honks.

"Sir, ten o'clock," said Mongoose's driver, still sitting in front of the stationary limos. Two burly men moved briskly down the sidewalk opposite them. Each man was wearing a bulky overcoat and carrying a briefcase. It was February, so outerwear was normal. However, they walked like soldiers, not lawyers.

"Eyes on ten o'clock," said Mongoose over the radio, alerting the convoy to the possible threat.

"Seven o'clock," someone said on the radio. Behind them, walking in the opposite direction, were two women in running clothes and pushing baby strollers. Each stroller's bassinet was covered to keep the baby warm. Or conceal enough Semtex explosives to breach the Beast. The limo's top was its least armored area. The blast could kill the occupants, and maybe that was their mission.

"All vehicles, cover down on the Package," said Mongoose. Multiple black SUVs lurched through the traffic and surrounded the three limos, encasing them behind a wall of armored Chevies.

"Finished!" Martha exclaimed. "At least the traffic gave me a chance to look good."

"You look spectacular, dear," said Henry without looking up.

"Sir, perhaps this would be a good opportunity to mention the trade tariffs the president is pushing," said the young aide.

"At a prayer breakfast? Don't you think that's a little inappropriate?"

"No."

"OK, let's see if I can work it in."

The two men with briefcases continued to walk toward the baby strollers. Mongoose zoomed his binoculars on the men's overcoats. Did they have bulges under the armpits, concealing weapons? What was in those briefcases? Did they look heavy?

"Sir, above," said the driver, nodding in the direction of a second-story open window directly across from them. "It just opened."

"Unusual to open windows in winter," said Mongoose, training his binoculars on the windows, but saw nothing inside. "It's a perfect overwatch position for heavy weapons."

"Affirmative," said the driver, tenseness in his voice.

"Honey, how long are we going to sit here?" asked Martha. "We should be there by now. We're going to be late."

Henry looked up, as if lifted from a spell. "Tony, what's the matter? Why can't we get around this traffic?" Secret Service Agent Tony Russo sat in the front seat and was a combat vet, like Mongoose.

"There's an accident ahead, sir. Traffic is blocked in every direction, but we should be moving shortly," he said unpersuasively.

Mongoose saw a shadow move behind the open window. Below, the businessmen were approaching the women pushing baby strollers, about to converge across from the Beast. The timing was too perfect.

The life of a Secret Service agent is like a cop's. Duty is years of routine boredom, interspersed by seconds of absolute terror, when everything can go wrong. Poor judgment or slow reaction time is the difference between the quick and the dead. Now was such a moment for Mongoose.

"Dismount, but do not draw," Mongoose ordered. SUV doors opened, and Secret Service agents exited and stood behind their vehicle for cover, hands on holsters.

Martha leaned forward with concern. "Tony, what's going on?"

"It's probably nothing, ma'am," he said. "Just doing our job."

"I hate being late. How long will we be stuck here?"

"I'm sure we'll be moving soon. Once we cross the bridge, it's just five minutes to the Hilton."

Martha sat back and unconsciously chewed on a knuckle while looking out the window at the agents, hunched behind the

SUVs. The doors facing the limo were open and she could see stacks of M4 carbines and smoke grenades lying on the passenger seats. She had never seen this before.

"Henry, take a look," she whispered to her husband, gesturing at the weapons.

"It's a good time for prayer," mused Henry. "Maybe I can work this into my speech, too."

She thwacked him with her hand. "This is no time for jokes!"

Mongoose sat in the vehicle in front of them, binoculars shifting between the men, the strollers, and the open window. *Steady,* he thought. *Just keep walking, everyone.*

"Sir, should we apprehend them?" asked the driver.

"Negative. Just let them pass," Mongoose said. He had to be sure. This wasn't Afghanistan; it was Washington, DC.

"Sweepers, status?" asked Mongoose.

"We've almost cleared a hole," said Pilot. The tow truck was dragging the carcass of the last vehicle out of the travel lane, leaving a trail of green shattered glass and radiator fluid.

"ETA, Pilot?"

"One minute."

Too long, thought Mongoose. The two men slowed slightly as they approached the women. If there was an ambush, it would happen now.

"Get ready," said Mongoose over the radio. The agents tensed up, hands still on weapons and ready for a quick draw.

One man nodded to the women, who ignored him. All kept walking. No movement in the window.

Mongoose exhaled loudly. "Stand down. Stand down. All teams, stand down."

"Sir, look," said his driver. Traffic was creeping forward.

"Mongoose, we've cleared a hole," said Pilot.

"Move out!" Mongoose ordered. Agents scurried back into

vehicles, and the motorcade accelerated around the traffic, sirens blaring.

Thank God, thought Mongoose, heart still pounding inside his rib cage. *Now to cross the bridge and get to the Hinckley Hilton. Five minutes, tops.*

"See, honey, I told you it was nothing to worry about," said Henry.

"We're going to be late."

"No, we're not. They're just early," he said with a grin, handing the speech back to the aide.

Henry felt the blast wave through the Beast and saw the traffic ahead of them geyser upward, toward the heavens. A millisecond later, the *BOOM* of a colossal explosion threw him backward as the monstrous limo lifted off the ground and pointed into the blue sky. All the bulletproof windows spider-cracked as debris flailed the vehicle. Then the sickening fall. Henry felt weightless as they descended through the hole where the road should have been. Dozens of vehicles and pedestrians fell 130 feet to the gorge floor, crushing everyone below. The massive 1930s bridge imploded on top of them. Several tons of stone and steel buried the survivors alive.

CHAPTER 2

Halfway around the world, I was finishing my daily run on the white beach of Tel Aviv.

Maximum effort! I thought, breaking into a mad sprint. *One hundred meters to go!* Seagulls flew out of my way as I splashed down the sand.

Warp speed! I commanded, lungs burning. I shot past my personal finish line: a cartoonish nine-foot statue of David Ben-Gurion doing a headstand on the sand. Slowing to a trot, I checked my time. Five miles in thirty-five minutes. Not bad. I walked for another ten minutes, cooling down. Tel Aviv has one of the nicest beaches in the world, if you don't mind the Apache helicopters buzzing overhead.

"Shalom," I said, ambling into Lala Land, my favorite beach-side bar. I was a regular, and my tahini-fruit shake awaited me.

"Shalom, Tom," said the bartender.

I had been on the run for a year now, ever since I got sucked into a Saudi palace coup d'état and ten stolen nukes. The coup was foiled, but the nukes were never found. Since then, the Kingdom had placed a million-dollar bounty on me, and no place was safe. Except maybe Israel. Doomed to spend the rest of my life on the run made me angry, and it was all because of one man.

Brad Winters, I thought, and shivered despite the Mediterranean heat. He was my former mentor at Apollo Outcomes, a powerful private military corporation. Apollo was a covert world power unto itself, and Winters was its sovereign. He betrayed me and left my team for dead, so I returned the courtesy. Last I knew, he was beheaded in Riyadh for his role in the failed coup. I wish I could have been there. He was dead, but somehow I wasn't free of what he'd done.

"Can you turn on the news?" I asked the bartender. Everyone spoke English in Tel Aviv. They also spoke Russian, French, Arabic, and, of course, Hebrew. The place made me feel like an underachiever.

"Sure thing," he said, and flicked on the TV above the bar. The news was in Hebrew and showed Palestinians throwing Molotov cocktails at Israeli troops, who fired back tear gas and then live ammunition. People died. It looked like a foreign warzone, but it was only forty-five miles away.

"English, please," I said, slurping my smoothie, and he found an American cable news channel.

"Another?" asked the bartender, pointing to my empty mug.

"Sure," I said. "Throw in more tahini and mint this time."

"Tom!" said a voice behind me. "I thought I'd find you here."

"Ari!" I replied.

"Goldstar, please," he said, and the bartender slid him a beer.

Colonel Ari Roth was a gaunt man of average height. Drinking while in uniform was normal in Israel, but Roth's uniform was not. He wore a standard infantry officer's insignia with lackluster ribbons. In reality, he was a commando in the Sayeret Matkal, the Israel Defense Forces' most elite unit. It was comparable to the U.S.'s Delta Force or SEAL Team Six. Like Israel's nuclear weapons program, Sayeret Matkal didn't officially exist (hence Ari's misleading uniform) but everyone knew about it, and called it "the Unit."

"You're off early," I joked. "What's the matter? Run out of terrorists to kill in Syria?"

"I wish," he said, taking a long swig from the bottle. "It's shabbat and even we sometimes get time off." Shabbat was the weekly holy day, or sabbath, and Israel shuts down.

"If they're giving you time off, it means they've got a nasty suicide mission waiting for you," I said with a smirk. "Bartender, get this man drunk. He dines in hell tomorrow!"

Ari waved off the bartender with a smile. "No, seriously. It's just time off."

Members of the Unit don't get time off, I thought.

"Yeah, we get time off," he said, as if reading my mind. "You have a horrible poker face, Locke."

"Dammit! Bartender, give me a double scotch, no ice. Enough of the fruit shakes. They're making me soft."

"To time off," he said, grinning and holding up his beer.

"To being on the run," I said, clinking my tumbler.

"Not the same thing."

I had been sleeping on Ari's couch for the past year. We met as captains in early 1998, when the U.S. Army deployed my Green Beret team to Haifa. Saddam Hussein was threatening to attack Israel with SCUD missiles, and the U.S. secretly sent a Patriot missile unit to blow the SCUDs out of the sky. My mission was to keep the Patriots safe, and so was Ari's.

Now I was a mercenary on the lam, and he was a colonel behind a desk. We had both seen finer days. He spent most of his waking hours at Mossad's headquarters, which was nicknamed the "cinema complex" because it was oddly adjacent to a megamovie theater in north Tel Aviv. Not exactly a secret location.

The TV cut to breaking news. A bridge had collapsed in central Washington, DC, and black smoke plumed into the sky. Vehicles lay lifeless on a valley floor, surrounded by dozens of fire trucks. Rescue workers were pulling bodies out of the rubble, and sniffer dogs worked the site.

"Hey, bartender, can you please turn it up?"

"... bigger than just a terrorist attack. It's also the most significant political assassination since JFK," said a TV talking head wearing a bow tie.

The beach bar went silent and all heads turned to the multiple TV displays. Many Israelis had family in the United States. The news helicopter zoomed in on several black SUVs, burning in the wreckage. The rear end of a black limo stuck out of the debris upright, like a sinking ship frozen in its descent. Firemen were struggling to cut it open but couldn't because of its armored skin.

"That's a presidential motorcade," I said to Ari.

"Was," he corrected me. "That *was* a presidential motorcade."

"... it's the work of radical Islamic terrorists," said another pundit, who looked too young to shave. The screen showed people chanting "DEATH TO AMERICA!" outside U.S. embassies across the Middle East and Pakistan.

"Looks like Washington is undergoing its own intifada," said Ari.

"Now joining us is our all-star panel of experts," said the woman news anchor. Three pundits appeared on-screen looking a mixture of despondent and pompous. One was a retired general with a stone face, another a professor wearing a bow tie, and the third was a think tank expert who looked twelve. They began bickering immediately.

"... it seems that the terrorists had been planning this for a long time," said the bow tie. The news showed more live shots of the destroyed bridge.

"Terrorists didn't do that," I whispered.

"What?" said Ari.

"Terrorists didn't blow that bridge."

"Then who did?"

"Apollo Outcomes. They blew it, and made it look like terrorists did it."

"Mercenaries? You must be joking." He chuckled, then went silent in thought. "A false flag operation. It's possible, if they are very, *very* good. Why do you think so?"

"Because I conducted these same ops for Apollo for years. In other countries, of course. I would recognize their operational signature anywhere. We would blow bridges, crash planes, stage deadly car accidents, and arrange heart attacks. We made it look natural or framed another party, otherwise it wouldn't be covert."

Ari paused, then downed his beer with a shrug. When he was done, he let out a belch. "I'm always shocked how much that stuff is outsourced now."

"More than you know."

Ari screwed up his face in puzzlement. "I thought Apollo Outcomes was an American company that carried out the U.S. government's dirty work. I thought it was an exclusive relationship. Why would Apollo assassinate the vice president of the United States?"

I stared at the bridge carcass and the crushed cars, and was angry. "I don't know, but I intend to find out."

CHAPTER 3

Jennifer Lin stared at the TV screen, hand over her gaping mouth, and watched the live news coverage. The daughter of poor Chinese immigrants, she broke her father's heart when she insisted on joining the FBI instead of going to law school. That was five years ago, and the last time they spoke.

Lin was not alone. Other FBI special agents crowded around the large-screen TV in the breakroom, coffee breath close. Their collective shock was thick in the air.

LIVE BREAKING NEWS, read a glitzy graphic before it swooshed offscreen, replaced by a young, blond anchorwoman.

"Authorities are calling it the worst terrorist attack on U.S. soil since 9/11. At approximately eight o'clock this morning, the vice president's motorcade was on its way to the National Prayer Breakfast at the Washington Hilton. As it crossed a bridge, the bridge exploded and the entire motorcade fell to the ravine floor, hundreds of feet below. The vice president was pronounced dead at the scene, as was his wife."

"This can't be happening," muttered someone.

"Because it was rush hour, the bridge was crowded," continued the anchorwoman. "Other victims include multiple commuter cars, two crowded buses, and families with children on their way to school."

"Radical Islamic terrorists," said an agent behind Lin, almost spitting. "Gotta be."

"So far, there are around one hundred estimated casualties," continued the news anchor, "but authorities expect the death toll to rise into the hundreds. Let's go live to the bridge."

The screen faded to an aerial view of the carnage, taken from a news helicopter.

"That's the Duke Ellington Bridge over Rock Creek," exclaimed one of the agents. "I took it to work this morning," he added, but no one was listening.

The scene was grisly. Below the chopper lay the remnants of a massive neoclassical bridge, a sickening gap between its two ends. Fire billowed from its ruins, and flashing lights of emergency vehicles lit up the bridge carcass, its graceful aqueduct-like arches broken on the valley floor below. Dozens of cars lay entwined with the bridge wreckage. Trucks were flattened under armored Secret Service SUVs, themselves crushed by massive slabs of concrete and limestone. A DC street bus was shorn in half as rescue workers searched for survivors, carrying the "jaws of life" rescue tool. Worse, the 750-foot bridge collapsed atop another crowded commuter road on the ravine floor below, pulverizing twenty more cars. Then there were the bodies shrouded in plastic sheets.

The news switched to a reporter on the ground, who was sneaking around the fire trucks and moving toward the bridge. The camera jiggled as it followed him. Sirens wailed in the background. He was clearly not supposed to be there.

"Police have cordoned off all traffic around the area, so I am going to try to approach on foot," wheezed the TV reporter, probably thinking of an Emmy Award. Three survivors sat on the ground, wrapped in Red Cross blankets. One woman gently swayed back and forth, holding herself while crying. Perhaps she had lost a loved one. Maybe a child.

"Hello, we're from News Channel Eight," said the journalist while the bright camera light shone in the woman's face. "Could you tell us what you're feeling right now?"

The camera zoomed in. Her eyes were red, and her anguish turned into bafflement, then rage, as the reporter violated her grief.

"Hey you! You're not supposed to be here. Get outta here!" someone yelled offscreen. The camera pivoted to show a policeman moving toward the lens. His meaty hand reached out and violently jerked the camera down. The pavement and the cameraman's foot were the last image shown before the picture went black. The TV control room quickly switched back to the anchorwoman, who looked shaken.

"Now joining us is our all-star panel of experts," she said after a moment, turning to the pundits: a young think tank expert, a professor wearing a bow tie, and a retired general. All were men.

What bullshit, Lin thought. In her five years as an FBI agent, including a year working on an interagency task force, she had learned one thing: national security was a man's game, all the way around.

Last summer she blew a big case in Brooklyn by "accidentally" pummeling a Russian mob boss who had groped her during a sting operation. To be fair, she was posing as a high-end escort, and she had the body for it. But he didn't have permission to touch her. So she broke his arm, a tooth, and two ribs, then put him in an anaconda chokehold before the FBI assault team crashed through the hotel room door and pulled her off. However, they never caught the mobster committing crimes on tape, and they blamed Lin for screwing up the operation. Now she was exiled to a desk job in Washington.

"This is bigger than just a terrorist attack. It's also the most significant political assassination since JFK," said the academic, leaping in before the news anchor could even ask a question.

"Who's behind it?" asked the news anchor.

"Clearly it's the work of radical Islamic terrorists," said the young think tanker, then rattled off a list of possible terrorist groups that few had ever heard of.

"Concur," interrupted the retired general, gruffly. "We've been picking up chatter for the last few years about plans for a big attack on U.S. soil. ISIS and cousin groups have expressed a desire for a 9/11-type attack to rally the extremist world. This was it."

"Told ya," said one FBI agent. Others nodded. A few had done tours in the Middle East, where the FBI had offices in U.S. embassies.

"Do you think there will be more attacks?" asked the news anchor.

"We must assume so," replied the general.

The pundits sat in silence for a second, as did the break room, absorbing the gravity of the statement. All knew it to be true, but somehow hearing it aloud made it real.

"What is scarier," said the academic pundit, hijacking the conversation again, "is this was an attempted presidential assassination. The president was scheduled to speak at today's prayer breakfast, not the vice president. The only reason it failed was because the president canceled at the last minute, sending his VP instead."

"Indeed," said the think tanker, as if it was his idea. "Think of the propaganda victory it would have been for the terrorists, if they had actually assassinated the president."

The news anchor kept trying to get a word in but was edged out by the dueling pundits.

"In the nation's capital! It would have been a rallying cry for every terrorist organization in the world. It shows the world that we are vulnerable," said the academic.

"It already *is* a rally cry," concluded the think tanker, a little smug. "We should expect more attacks."

"I would not jump to any conclusions. Nothing followed the

9/11 attacks. Plus, our law enforcement has been training for this moment for years and is on high alert. If there is another planned attack, I have high confidence our law enforcement will foil it."

The think tanker frowned, checkmated by the academic. He disagreed but didn't want to declare U.S. law enforcement incapable on national news during a moment of crisis. Few would welcome such a line, and, like all pundits, he lived for applause.

"General, this seemed like a fairly sophisticated attack," said the anchorwoman, finally breaking into the conversation. "Are terrorists really capable of such things? Could it not be a foreign power like Russia, China, or Iran?"

"Certainly, those powers could have done so, but I doubt it," answered the retired general.

"Why is that?" asked the anchorwoman.

"Because they know we'd eventually figure it out and there would be reprisals. But terrorists don't care about such things," said the retired general.

"Yes, but—" interrupted the bow tie.

"That may be—" added the think tanker, leaning in. Both were ignored.

"Still, are terrorists really capable of this level of attack?" the anchorwoman asked. "It's far more sophisticated than anything we have seen before, at least in this country."

"Yes, it is possible and even likely," said the general, also ignoring the academic and think tanker. "Terrorist groups have been growing in sophistication ever since 9/11. They no longer need to weaponize commercial airliners, as their capabilities and organizations mature despite our best efforts. For every leader we kill or network we disrupt, three more pop up to replace them. We can't kill our way out of the problem."

"It's definitely al Qaeda or one of their franchise groups," said one of the FBI agents. Others nodded in agreement, but Jen Lin knew better. While her colleagues spent most of their careers chasing terrorists, she had spent her time hunting other things in the complicated shadows. Bad things.

"Wrong. Terrorists didn't do this," she said. "Russia did."

Two men laughed under their breath while another scoffed, "That's crazy, Lin. Russia would never do it because it would be an act of war. Even they're not that stupid. Besides, it profiles as terrorism."

Lin stood her ground. "Don't be so sure. Strategic deception is the Russian way of war. They even have a name for it: *maskirovka.*"

The man chuckled as the group dissipated, leaving her alone in the room. *Idiots,* she thought.

CHAPTER 4

National Security Advisor George Jackson sat at the head of the table, hands clasped together under his nose, concealing a frown. Jackson was a gaunt man of average height, with wisps of white hair and wire-rimmed glasses. He looked more like a history professor than a history maker, and he dressed the part, too, eschewing power suits in favor of tweed sport coats with elbow patches and a bow tie. Jackson could think in whole paragraphs, and he spoke with a slight Boston Brahmin accent that revealed an Ivy League pedigree. Yet he was tough, and those who mistook his genteel mannerisms for weakness were soon checkmated. White House staff nicknamed him Yoda.

The White House Situation Room was standing room only. Movies depict it as a space of nobility and decision, but actually it looks like a townhouse basement converted into a recreation room, complete with low-hung ceiling and big-screen TVs. At the back of the room, staring directly at Jackson, was a wall-size monitor showing the head of the president of the United States.

President Hugh Anderson had double bags under his eyes and a scowl that would intimidate a drug lord. His temper was legendary, even by Washington standards. A full head of gray hair and incremental plastic surgery over the years made him look early fifties rather than seventy-three. The man was obsessed with winning a second term. In school, he was the kid who always ran for class president because he craved the approval of strangers. Six decades later, he was no different. Some thought him the Captain Ahab of polls, chasing good numbers and throwing tirades when they were low. They were down a lot in recent weeks, and now this. He was pissed.

"George, why don't you know who's behind this yet?" he demanded. "It's been an hour and you still don't have any answers."

"Sir, we're doing the best we can," Jackson said, frustrated.

"Your best is disappointing. Men are made or broken in a crisis, and I refuse to be broken. This is my legacy moment. You, on the other hand, are disappointing."

Jackson sat motionless, while other people in the room looked away in nervousness.

"Find me some facts, George," said President Anderson. "I've gotten more answers out of congressional hearings compared to this farce. Twelve years a senator, only to be bamboozled by my own National Security Council!"

"Sir, if I can explain—"

"Call me when you know more," said President Anderson, cutting Jackson off. "And it better be in ten minutes. I have a call with Moscow now. Proof of life. No telling what those maniacs might do if they thought I was dead."

Jackson's shoulders slumped.

"Answers, people. Answers!" scolded President Anderson as he reached for a button and killed the connection. His mammoth face was replaced by the presidential seal, the White House's screen saver. The room sat frozen, still absorbing the barrage. Then everyone turned to Jackson and waited for him to say something.

What am I going to say? thought Jackson. The president wanted to be on the news networks giving Churchillian speeches, but instead he was cooped up at a secret bunker in West Virginia. There could be no legacy speech until he had something to say, such as who killed the vice president. And that was Jackson's job.

Except Jackson had no idea who was behind the bridge bombing. They had no leads and were in the dark.

"All right team, let's start over," he said, and the room sighed. People were angry and tempers were rising. "Homeland, you go first."

"Here's what we know so far," said the secretary of Homeland Security. "The bridge was blown from inside. The bridge is hollow, built in 1935 with interior space for a trolley car propulsion system. The terrorists packed it with explosives and waited for a motorcade to cross."

"How much explosives?"

"About five thousand pounds of dynamite," she said, and someone whistled in amazement. "The suspects placed it at critical structural connections in the old trolley car workings, crawlspaces, and cross girders, and triggered it as the VP's—" she paused "—uh, Henry's limo approached the median point of the bridge. The explosion induced a progressive collapse by weakening critical supports, allowing gravity to bring the bridge down."

"Whoever did this sure knew what they were doing," added the secretary of defense, almost in admiration.

"So the terrorists—or whoever did this," corrected Jackson, "wired the bridge and simply waited for a presidential convoy?"

"We believe so. It was inevitable that a convoy would travel this bridge, owing to its centrality, whether the convoy departed from the White House or the VP's residence. All the perpetrators had to do was wait."

"Are the other bridges wired too?" asked Jackson.

"No. We've inspected all other major bridges and tunnels in the metropolitan area and they're clean."

The others in the room sat in silence, pondering it. How

many other U.S. bridges and tunnels were vulnerable to this kind of planned attack? Too many.

"We're tracking down leads on the explosive material," said FBI director Carlos Romero, a broad-shouldered man with the bearing of a boxer rather than a bureaucrat. He built a fearsome reputation locking away MS-13 gang members as the United States attorney for the Central District of California.

"And?" asked Jackson impatiently.

"And initial forensic analysis tells us it's a commercial dynamite with a high percentage of nitroglycerin and traces of RDX, a military explosive. Not easy to procure, but procurable. Whoever did this covered their tracks well, and took their time doing it."

"How much time?" asked Jackson.

"Hard to say. Probably up to a year because that's the shelf life of commercial dynamite."

"How the hell does someone buy two and half tons of dynamite in a year, and no one knows?" interjected the secretary of state in an undiplomatic tone. Jan Novak was a known hothead and a difficult choice for America's lead diplomat. They had reviewed the same stale facts five times already and he was losing patience. So were others. "I mean, don't you need a license or something? Isn't that what you law enforcement people do?"

"Yes, you need a license," replied Romero slowly as if speaking to a child. "They probably sourced small quantities from multiple vendors and/or smuggled it in from abroad. The U.S. has lots of enemies abroad. Isn't that what the State Department does?"

Novak glared at Romero, who didn't back down.

"Gentlemen, please," said Jackson, holding up both hands as if stopping a truck. "Henry was a friend to all of us, and we're upset. Let's keep it civil."

The temperature was hot, in every way. The National Security Council's principals crowded around the oblong table in executive office chairs. Behind them stood or sat their deputies, shoulder to shoulder. It was a bit undignified, given their professional station. White House staffers wriggled around them delivering messages on small scraps of yellow paper as new intelligence arrived. The small windowless room was not intended for this many, and they had a long day ahead of them.

Jackson leaned forward, cradling his head in his hands and his elbows on the table. "DNI, do you have anything new for us?"

"Not since ten minutes ago, George," answered Michael Taylor, tossing his pen on the legal pad in front of him. He was the DNI, or director of national intelligence. Behind him sat Nancy Holt, director of the CIA. In her midfifties, she had a runner's physique and silver hair that draped around her shoulders. Her sun-weathered face revealed that she spent most of her career outside the wire, and her eyes scanned the room like an operator rather than a politico.

"Tell us again anyway."

A staffer handed the DNI a folded piece of paper. He opened and read it, eyebrows raised, before passing it to Holt. Both had inscrutable faces, which irritated Jackson.

"What's it say?" asked General Jim Butler in an annoyed Southern drawl. A third generation West Pointer, he hailed from Georgia. Now he was the chairman of the Joint Chiefs of Staff, the highest-ranking soldier in the nation.

"Sir, we just learned that a body pulled from the wreckage is a known radical Islamic terrorist," said Holt, steel in her voice. "An autopsy will be performed within the hour."

"Finally, a lead!" said Jackson, smacking the table with his right hand and smiling. The room exhaled. Holt walked to the front of the room and stuck her CAC identification card into the Situation Room's laptop. A few keystrokes later, terrorist mug shots adorned the main screen for all to see. She scrolled through several pages with lightning dexterity and then singled out one man. A fulsome beard and receding hairline did not mask a bullet hole in the forehead. The picture was dark and grainy, as if taken at night.

"No, that's not him. We killed him months ago," she said, scrolling further. "Ah, here he is." Another young man with a heavy black beard. He was smiling and carrying an RPG but looked like he was going to prayers. The photo was rasterized, having been overmagnified.

"So this is the bastard who killed the VP," hissed the secretary of state. Everyone around the table leaned in for a better look.

"Who is he?" asked Jackson.

"Facial recognition software estimates he is Abu Muhammad al-Masri, with a 90 percent confidence interval," said Holt. "He was a member of the Emni, a secretive branch of ISIS that built a global network of killers. They staged the Paris attacks and others across Europe. They tried to hit the World Cup in 2018, but we foiled it. A real nasty lot, with skills. Think of them as ISIS special forces."

"ISIS special forces, huh?" said Butler cynically. "Never seemed that 'special' to me. Just thugs."

"It's conceivable they executed today's terrorist attack, if they were resourced by a wealthy patron," said Romero.

"FinCENs has been picking up a surge of hawala activity out of Riyadh over the past six months," said Declan Hill, the treasury secretary, referring to FinCENs, or the Financial Crimes Enforcement Network. It is Treasury's lead task force for tracking illicit money around the globe.

"And we're just now connecting the dots?" asked Jackson.

"You retasked us to focus on Russia and China," responded the treasury secretary protectively.

Jackson ignored it and turned back to Holt. "Is Saudi Arabia involved?"

"We don't know enough yet," said Holt.

"Best guess then," said Jackson, but Holt shook her head.

"We're looking into it right now, George," answered the DNI. "I doubt their government has anything to do with it, but we can't rule it out. Their king is erratic."

"We also know there are several elite families in the Kingdom who secretly support the Islamic State," added the treasury secretary.

Holt stepped away from the laptop podium. "Here's a theory. A wealthy ISIS patron extracted the remnants of the Emni during the last days of the Islamic State and reconstituted the unit somewhere in the Kingdom. Then they deployed it here. Its mission: stage a spectacular terrorist attack, like 9/11, to rally the extremist world and take back the caliphate."

Jackson paused, considering Holt's scenario. The more he thought about it, the more it made sense. Still, he had to be careful. "Any other theories?"

"We're also working a Russia angle," said the DNI. "They have the capability and will to accomplish this, but we have nothing solid to report."

"How about China?" asked the general. "They're the rising threat."

"We're looking into Beijing too," added the DNI. "Same with Iran and North Korea."

"But here's what I don't understand," said the secretary of defense. "Why would any of those countries undertake such extreme measures? They know we would eventually discover who was behind today's attack, and it would be an act of war."

"Concur. It could lead to nuclear war, and all these adversaries have safer ways to disrupt us," said Jackson. "But terrorists don't give a damn."

Heads nodded.

"Anything else?" asked Jackson. "Our ten minutes are up, and I need to call back the president."

Heads shook.

"It's settled then. We're going with the terrorist theory until we find contrary evidence," said Jackson as he reached for the phone.

Holt smiled.

What a miserable day, I thought as I cleaned my 7.62 mm SCAR assault rifle in the dark. Sometimes repetitive tasks like cleaning weapons helped me think, and I needed to think. It was past midnight and I could not sleep, angry over Apollo Outcomes' assassination of the vice president and the world's failure to see it. After reassembling the SCAR, I sat back in my bed, which also doubled as Ari's couch.

"Think!" I whispered to myself, and plugged my phone into the stereo, selected Mahler's Seventh Symphony, and blasted the volume. Its dark, menacing opening echoed around my mind at high decibel, and I inhaled deeply.

"Hey, everything OK in there?" yelled Ari from down the hall. "I know your country is under attack and all, but some of us have to sleep so we can deal with the terrorist threats to our own country."

"Sorry, Ari!" I said, turning down the music. *Sorry, Ari* had become my household refrain over the past six months.

"Bravo to Mahler, though!" said Ari, padding out in a bathrobe. "Could you spin the Ninth? Last movement?"

"Sure thing," I said, switching to Mahler's Ninth Symphony. I carried an entire classical music library on my phone; it was my lifeline to sanity. Ari and I shared a passion for classical music, scotch, cigars, and war. Coincidentally, we were both single.

"Today's terrorist attack in Washington still on your mind?" said Ari as he sat down on the couch.

"I'm telling you, Ari, that was no terrorist attack. It was committed by Apollo Outcomes and made to look like a terrorist attack."

Ari shook his head in skepticism as he turned on the TV and muted the sound.

I'm the only one who sees what's really happening and no one believes me, I thought bitterly as I watched the news blame radical Islamic terrorists. The day's headlines were a nonstop drumbeat: AMERICAN VICE PRESIDENT ASSASSINATED BY TERRORISTS. AMERICAN PRESIDENT ACTUAL TARGET. 230 KILLED. The world was rocked. Several terrorist groups claimed responsibility, some I had never heard of, and I've heard of most. TV pundits ranted all day, and all were wrong.

"Well, what did you expect?" said Ari, as if reading my mind.

"Fools!" I said. "I spent the day on my satellite phone calling every friend I have left in the U.S. national security establishment. Most of them didn't take my call."

"And who could blame them? Tom, you're an internationally wanted man."

I nodded. What I didn't tell Ari was those who picked up the phone laughed and hung up, saying never call again.

"Did you try the American embassy here?" asked Ari, pouring a midnight scotch.

"Of course I did, using a fake identity. I got a meeting with the DAT," the defense attaché, "and told him the facts, but he yelled at me for wasting his time, then ordered the marines to throw me out."

Ari let out an involuntarily chuckle. "Well, I got similar treatment from higher."

"You ran this up the Mossad flagpole?" I said, surprised. You don't go to the Mossad with half-baked speculations; they are a no-bullshit organization.

"Yeah. No joy."

"As a last-ditch effort, I met with James. You know, MI6. He laughed for five minutes then demanded another pint for wasting his time. Wanker."

"Sounds like the day was a total shutout."

I closed my eyes and shook my head in frustration. "I have to stop this before it gets worse, Ari. And it *will* get worse."

"O-o-o-o-r," began Ari with caution, "maybe they are right, and Apollo was not involved." I turned to him in anger, but the thought had nagged at me all day. The more I puzzled it, the less I liked it.

"Ari, the operation was signature Apollo Outcomes. I know because I used to do these things for them overseas."

"But was it really Apollo? Think about it, Tom. Blowing a bridge and framing terrorists is classic Apollo, but assassinating the vice president? Targeting the president? Killing Americans? Operating in the middle of Washington, DC? No. They would not do that. Admit it."

I sat back and pondered it. "No, you're right. It's not Apollo's style."

"Nor is it in their business interest," added Ari.

I cradled my head in my hand as I thought. "Then who did it?"

We sat in silence because no answer made sense. Finally, Ari spoke: "What is Apollo's motto, again?"

"Its unofficial motto is 'Figure It Out.'"

"Then figure it out, Tom Locke. If what you say is true, then the U.S. and the world is in graver danger than everyone realizes. I'll take on a terrorist group any day before going muzzle to muzzle with Apollo Outcomes. Hell, I'd sooner go to war against Iran than Apollo. They fight dirty compared to Tehran."

The comment jarred me upright, owing to my many years working for the company, but Ari was probably correct. Apollo was a mercenary corporation, and that was no metaphor. They did Washington's dirty work: political assassinations, illegal renditions, experimental interrogations, black-on-black hits, covert coups d'etat, color revolutions, and domestic military operations. They recruited from SEALs, Delta, British SAS, Israeli special forces, Polish GROM, others. But they were more than for-profit warriors; they also hired MIT hackers, Harvard MBA savants, and criminal geniuses. Apollo was a cross between Delta Force, the NSA, and Goldman Sachs, and they executed the missions the CIA and military wouldn't or couldn't. Apollo Outcomes was lethality without the red tape.

God, I miss it, I thought. Now Apollo and I stood apart. My sin? I was associated with Brad Winters, its ex-CEO gone rogue and my old mentor. Winters even tried to kill me, twice. For that, I sent the man to his doom, damned to a Riyadh torture cell and then beheaded. However, none of that mattered to Apollo and its primary customer, the U.S. government. They just saw me as a threat.

It's why I can never go home, I thought wistfully, sipping my scotch. *And why no one will believe me now.*

"Could Apollo assassinate the VP in the middle of Washington DC?" asked Ari.

"Of course, but why? They would never betray their primary customer. Winters always told me that money imbues its own honesty, and that profit motive is the most reliable motivation of all."

"It's a conundrum. Yet the facts all point to one thing: Apollo blew that bridge. But it makes no sense."

"Indeed," I whispered as I swished my scotch unconsciously. *Why would Apollo take such extreme measures?*

Then I understood.

"It's all about the money," I muttered. Apollo worked for

Washington the way the old British East India Company ser-
viced the Crown—it was difficult to know who served whom.
"Perhaps Washington finally grew savvy to Apollo's game and
threatened to pull significant contracts."

"It would threaten Apollo's existence," said Ari, crossing his
arms and legs with unease.

"A desperate Apollo would take radical steps to ensure sol-
vency."

Ari nodded deep in thought. "But here's what I don't get;
Why doesn't Apollo just get a new ten-digit retainer from Moscow, Beijing, the Fortune 500, or the global 0.1 percent? That's
what mercenaries do: auction their loyalty."

It hurt to hear him say it, but it was often the truth. I knew
ex-SEALs who once draped themselves in the American flag and
now work for China in Africa. However, I only took missions
that were in the U.S.'s interest and not the company's bottom
line. Or at least so I thought; Winters lied to me about that, too,
in Ukraine.

"I don't think so because Apollo needs the U.S. as its super-
client. Think about it. No other rich country has more security
needs than the U.S., and that's what Apollo sells: security in an
insecure world. Apollo must keep America as a client, at all costs."

"Even if it means holding the government hostage to terrorism?" said Ari, again shaking his head in disbelief. "How does
that work, exactly?"

"Isn't it obvious? Apollo assassinates POTUS or the VP, frames
terrorists, the nation panics, and it guarantees another quarter
century of lucrative counterterrorism contracts for Apollo. More
attacks will follow until the company gets what it wants."

"Disgusting but plausible. Even likely. Washington created a
real Frankenstein in Apollo, the result of outsourcing too much
wet work to the private sector," said Ari, nose upturned as if he

had just smelled something disgusting. "What are you going to do now?"

"I don't know," I said, slumping into the couch. The more I thought about it, the less I liked.

"Locke, let it go. You did your best, but everyone thinks you're crazy. You're like Noah and the flood. It's not your fight anymore, and Apollo will not get away with it. The CIA, FBI—everyone—will figure it out, and when they do, they will end Apollo." Ari leaned in and whispered: "Trust me."

But Ari was wrong. He didn't know Apollo like I did. Few did, and especially not the CIA or FBI. Apollo easily manipulates them for more contracts.

"Let it go," coaxed Ari.

No, I can't, I thought. I knew that I should not have cared, but I did. Both the U.S. and Apollo had left me for dead. If I wasn't a corpse, they would both finish the job because I knew too much and was deemed a renegade.

"You've done all you can do," said Ari in a gentle voice. But I knew that was wrong, too. There was still one more thing I could do, but I shuddered at the idea. *Still, I am a patriot,* I thought, *and I always was.* Perhaps I got lost along the way, but I never forfeited my soul. I never worked for an enemy of America. My grandfather, who was shot and left for dead at the Battle of the Bulge, always told me as a young boy: "Tom, you will serve. No matter what you do in life, you will serve your country in uniform." And so I did. I found other ways to serve too, leading me to Apollo. Not everyone there was a mercenary.

"Let it go," soothed Ari, sensing my mounting rage. The American people had no idea what was about to slam them. Worse, the government did not comprehend the insider threat. Eventually they would, as Ari insisted, but too late. By then, the nation would be panicked, and Apollo could dictate terms to make the "terrorist attacks" stop. It was racketeering. Extortion. A shakedown.

"You've done everything you can," continued Ari.

"No, I have not."

"Tom . . ."

"There is *exactly* one more thing I can do."

Ari's tone switched from calming to commanding. "Locke, don't do anything stupid."

"Only I can stop Apollo. I'm the only one who could get to the bottom of this quickly and put the fire out before it got worse. And it *will* get worse."

Ari let out a loud sigh of anxiety.

"We must all take a side, Ari. You know that most of all." It is the one rule that binds all warriors, no matter what allegiance, and affords honor in the killing of enemies. Ari nodded grimly.

"Then you're going to need this," he said after a moment and walked to the closet. After rummaging around the top shelf, he pulled down a black ballistic case. "I was saving it for your birthday."

"I didn't think you knew my birthday," I joked.

"I don't," he said with a smile, handing me the case. It was heavy. I popped open the two latches and lifted the lid.

"They're beautiful," I said, and they were. Nestled in gray sponge-foam were two Heckler & Koch Mark 23 handguns with screw-on sound suppressors, laser aiming modules, and four extra magazines, fully loaded. The Mark 23 was the pistol of choice for U.S. Special Operations Forces, which listed it officially as: Offensive Handgun Weapons System—Special Operations Peculiar. *Peculiar* was a euphemism for "assassin's tool." But what made it particularly lethal was its stopping power. It shot a .45-caliber slug that blew holes in targets that dinky nine-millimeter rounds would only dent.

"I was saving them to mark your six-month anniversary with my couch," said Ari with a smirk.

"So thoughtful," I said deadpan while pulling out the Mark 23s. I held one in each hand. They felt good.

"You're going to need them."

"Screw Apollo," I uttered in agreement.

"Find evidence. Then people will listen to you," counseled Ari. "And then the government will shut down Apollo for good."

"Apollo must be stopped," I agreed. *And only I can stop it.* If not me, then who? The world was blind, and no one knew Apollo's moves better than me, given my background. More important, I had surprise. They thought me dead or, worse, drunk in some shithole country.

Fuck them all, I thought as I downed the last of my scotch and reached for my satellite phone.

That night a black Chevy Suburban sat alone near the edge of a runway. Commercial airliners flew less than fifty feet overhead as they touched down at Washington National Airport, but they took no notice of the Suburban, camouflaged in the moonless night. A narrow channel of water separated the airport's main landing strip from the small parking lot on Gravelly Point. A few disused picnic tables and rows of approach lights were the only things on this spit of land, which was invisible from nearby roads despite its centrality.

Across the river was Washington, a small city surrounded by heaps of suburbs and traffic. However, the heart of the city was beautiful, especially at night. The Capitol Dome shimmered in the distance, and the obelisk of the Washington Monument was lit up in glory. Lights from surrounding monuments, bridges, and highways reflected off the Potomac River, giving a Monet-esque impression of the nation's capital.

Another black Suburban crept down the single access road with its lights off. The driver was careful not to tap the brakes and give away their position. The Suburban glided into a spot ten feet from the first Suburban and bounced gently off the parking bumper.

Men in dark suits leapt out of both vehicles and opened op-posing passenger doors. At first nothing happened. Then an older man stepped out of the first SUV, his loafered foot gin-gerly making contact with the asphalt. The darkness obscured his features as he walked the few paces to the other vehicle and climbed inside. All doors shut.

Five minutes passed. Multiple jets roared overhead. The river continued to twinkle with city lights. Then the dark-suited men jumped out of the vehicles and opened up the opposing passenger doors again. The older man gently returned to his vehicle. Doors closed. Both black Suburbans drove into the night, traveling in opposite directions.

The next morning, the FBI headquarters was buzzing. The J. Edgar Hoover Building was a brutalist concoction of office building meets underpass. Today, the place was angry. The terrorist attack had occurred two miles from headquarters, a galling fact.

Lin had shared her theory about Russia's responsibility for the terrorist attack with a few senior colleagues. Their response was universal. First, it was laughter. Then it was: "The Russians wouldn't dare." Followed by: "You're a junior analyst. Watch and learn." Ending with: "Stay out of trouble."

She wanted to strangle them.

Maybe they're right, she thought, leaning back in her desk chair and closing her eyes. She had learned to be humble about most things since her demotion to the desk.

"Tough day at work?" joked Jason, at the desk next to her. He was her age, and had been that kid in high school who was All-American everything. Unlike Lin, he saw working at FBI headquarters as an opportunity, and he had ambition. Working a desk did not bother him. Only the boss had his own office; the rest of her division worked in an open bay. Management claimed it was for improved 'situational awareness' during collaborative investigations, but Lin was convinced it was to ruin everyone's personal life. Open offices are an eavesdropper's paradise.

"Jason, not now," she said, eyes shut and rubbing her temples. Jason had been hitting on her for six months, and it was getting old. He was a nice guy, but it would never happen. She often wondered how such a talented detective could be so oblivious.

"They got me chasing smugglers," he whispered, followed by a pirate "*Yaaaaargh!!*"

"Great, Jason," she said flatly.

"What do you call a terrorist who swallowed dynamite? Abominable," he chuckled.

"Jason. Shut up."

"I'm following a hot lead right now," he continued. "I might even get out of the office on this one."

The room's air smelled stale, and the windows were sealed. It was like working in a submarine with natural light. Lin got up and stretched. Her long, black hair spilled onto the floor as she touched her toes. Stretching always helped clear her mind. People in the office were used to it and took no notice of her occasional tai chi movements.

". . . turns out you can still smuggle just about anything in a container ship . . ."

Lin dialed him out and let her thoughts find her happy place. She learned the technique in army survival training as a way of withstanding torture. Occasionally, the FBI got slots in the Survival, Evasion, Resistance, and Escape, or SERE, School at Fort Bragg. It was three days of hell, but she fought for the opportunity to prove to the boys that she was tough.

". . . did you know there's a whole community of implosion watchers? There are hundreds of videos on the internet. I'm surprised no one got the bridge on video . . ."

Concentrate, she thought, and Jason's voice faded away. She was back at her father's second-story martial arts studio on Geary Boulevard in San Francisco. It smelled of sweat and rubber mats. The steady drone of large standing fans was punctuated by someone yelling "Aye!" followed by the slam of another's body on the mats.

She was nine but already the equivalent of a black belt, and she trained with kids twice her age and weight. She won because she was faster and more clever, taking down opponents with grace rather than brutality. Those who underestimated her because of her size and sex lay at her feet, rubbing aching body parts.

"Those too stupid to learn are made to feel!" she would declare to her victims. It was something her father told his students. Her mother died young and she had no siblings. The rest of the family remained in China, making her father the only family she had. In between practice sets, they would study the *Tao Te Ching* and consult the *I Ching* together. He taught her that power without judgment is tyranny, and that was why she joined the FBI: to stop tyrants. Why couldn't he see that?

". . . Antwerp . . . Newark . . ."

One night, when she was twelve, a homeless man in the Tenderloin jumped her, demanding her money and virginity. With a rapid-knife hand strike, she crushed his larynx and then threw him hard into a wall. Lin still remembered the distinctive *smack* of his skull hitting the brick. The creep lay motionless in the alley as she walked away. Maybe he was dead; she didn't care. *One less scumbag,* she thought then and now.

". . . Russian mob . . ."

Lin's happy place was sucked back into the Hoover Building.

"Wait, what?" she said.

"Haven't you been listening, Jen? Sometimes I think your mind wanders when we talk," said Jason.

So-o-o-o oblivious, she thought. "Just repeat what you said."

"The Newark field office got an anonymous tip last night from a dock worker. Said he felt it his patriotic duty after the bridge attack."

"What was the tip?"

"Something about a container ship last week from Antwerp with an unregistered container being offloaded before the ship went through Customs."

"How is that possible?" she asked.

"Dunno. Also, most people smuggle things *inside* containers, and not the whole container itself."

"Weird. Why would anyone do that? It seems a lot harder."

"It is, and that's the big mystery. It's why they called HQ this morning for backup."

Lin sat down and thought about the anonymous tip. New York City was her old hunting ground, but the quarry didn't leave much of a trail. "A ghost container isn't a lot to go on."

"If it was easy, it wouldn't be an FBI case," said Jason absent-mindedly as he worked.

"What about the Russian mob?"

"The informant said the *bratva* did it." *Bratva* meant "brotherhood" in Russian and referred to mobsters.

"Anything else?" said Lin, sitting upright.

"He said it happened once before, sometime last year, but didn't say more. That's all we have, and now the Russian Organized Crime Task Force is working the case."

Lin looked sullen. It was her old unit.

"Don't worry, Jen. If there's a Russia angle, they will find it. But so far, they're rolling snake eyes."

"They must be desperate if they're turning to you," she joked, but her humor failed and Jason grimaced at the swipe. "No offense. But seriously, Jason, you don't even speak Russian. I spent two years on that task force. I know the players, the lay of the land, the threat. I should be doing this, not you." Her expression turned to anger. "Why didn't Mr. Prick assign me to the case?"

"Mr. Prick" was what she called their boss, a spasmatic jerk and one of the biggest in the building. She was sentenced to his division as punishment for blowing the New York sting operation. At least that was what he told her, with a disturbing measure of pride. Things went downhill from there, mostly because he was a bully and she always stood up to them.

"You know why," said Jason, turning back to his computer screen. "Anyway, I think Newark is a dead end."

"Why do you say that?" she said, surprised.

"Because they can't find the mystery container, and don't even know if it exists. All they have is an anonymous guy's tip. Even if true, there's probably no link to radical Islamic terrorists. It's not the mafia's style." Jason sighed and looked up. "Also, Manhattan is being deluged with new counterterrorism leads by the hour and there's a shortage of agents. I think the ADIC will shut down the ghost container investigation before lunch." The assistant director in charge, whose acronym was pronounced "ay-dick," ran the show.

Lin frowned, but it made sense. Yet something gnawed at her. Tips like this were not random and the FBI knew it, which was why they were investigating. The informant was probably from a rival mafia with credible knowledge, or was trying to set up their competitor. Either way, smuggling in an entire container was new and alarming.

Who would do that? Why? Lin twirled a pen between her fingers. *Because the sender did not want the mafia knowing what was inside the container.* Only a few "senders" had that kind of power over the Russian mafia. It didn't smell like organized crime; it stank of the Federal Security Service, or FSB, the KGB's successor. It would explain how five tons of extremely regulated explosives were sourced. The container would also be an expedient way to smuggle in the expertise needed to conduct the assassination plot.

Lin smiled. It was starting to make sense, except for one glaring fact: the FSB did not work with radical Islamic terrorists. If the anonymous tip was accurate, then there were only two conclusions. First, the mystery container was simply crime related:

drugs, weapons, or women. This was the prevailing theory, according to Jason.

Or, thought Lin, *the container is linked to the bridge attack, as the informant implies.* If true, it led to dark places. The Russian mob worked only for itself and occasionally the Kremlin. The mob has no reason to kill the American president or VP because it would rain down agents upon them, putting them out of business. *But Moscow has reasons,* she thought. *Many.*

She looked around and saw everyone was hustling: working the phones, tapping away at keyboards, waiting over a printer, or huddled in impromptu meetings. *No one is thinking. They're just working,* thought Lin. An hour ago, her boss stood on a desk and told the team it was an "all hands on deck" moment, and "we need to catch these terrorists before they strike again."

Maybe they're wrong? she mused. What if it wasn't terrorists but someone framing them? Terrorists were too crude to orchestrate such a sophisticated attack, but not the Kremlin. Making it look like a terrorist attack would be the perfect decoy to dodge America's law enforcement and divert the FBI's attention, as the true bad guys staged their next attack. The FBI was like a bull to the cape when it came to counterterrorism, and all the bad guys had to do was act the matador. *And the FBI is falling for it,* she thought, involuntarily crossing her arms and legs. *We're charging the cape.*

"Jason," she said, leaning closer. "Where did you say that ship originated?"

"Antwerp," he said absently while typing.

"That doesn't make sense," she said.

Jason stopped typing. "What do you mean?"

"I learned a thing or two about international smuggling while working the Russian mob." She explained that Antwerp and Rotterdam had some of the best port security in the world.

"Only an inside job could get an unregistered container on a ship at Antwerp, and terrorists aren't that good. But the Kremlin is."

"Look, Jen. Drop the Russia thing. Please," he said in a whisper. "The boss already warned you, and you're on unofficial probation as it is."

"He may be too dim to get it, but it doesn't make me wrong. I have to try," she said, standing up.

"No Lin, don't even think about it!"

She ignored him and walked into the boss's office, shutting the door behind her.

CHAPTER 8

"We have a problem," said Holt.

No one ever likes hearing the head of the CIA utter those four words. Jackson frowned and waved her into his office. He was midconversation with the secretary of state, Jan Novak, who turned around in his chair to greet her with a fake smile. "Please have a seat, Nancy. Jan just left the Oval and is back-briefing me on his conversation with POTUS. We're in a tough dialogue with Saudi Arabia over the terrorist attack. They're being especially recalcitrant, even refusing to support our investigation." Jackson sighed. "Anyway, I hope you don't mind if Jan sits in."

"No, I don't mind," she said, clearly minding.

"It must be serious if you came from Langley to deliver the bad news in person," said Novak.

Holt winced. The man had a gift for the velvet put-down. It was how he got ahead.

"It . . . is," she said, chagrined. She carried a briefcase and set it down beside her chair. They waited for an aide to shut the office door before talking.

"What kind of problem?" asked Jackson in a measured tone. He was paid to be a problem solver and not a blame shifter.

"The terrorist theory. It's falling apart."

"Falling apart?" responded Jackson, startled.

"What do you mean, 'falling apart'?" added Novak. "I just spent the last twelve hours on the phone yelling at Riyadh, and now you are telling me I was wrong? It was *you* who put forward the terrorist theory to begin with, and the FBI keeps finding corroborating evidence pointing to the Islamic State, or whatever they call themselves now. The FBI even found a dead terrorist on-site. Foreign terrorists are clearly responsible. It's a slam dunk!"

"Yes, but there are problems."

Novak was about to reply when Jackson held up a hand for silence. Jan Novak got to his station in life by sucking up and spitting down. By contrast, Holt was no pole-climbing political appointee. She had spent a career in the CIA's Directorate of Operations, mostly as a targeter. Some thought her methods extreme, but Jackson liked her because she got stuff done, bureaucracy be damned. That was why he'd urged the president to appoint her the CIA director, even though she initially turned down the honor.

"Explain," said Jackson.

"It's TS/SCI. It can't leave the room," she said, meaning the intelligence was highly classified, and if leaked, it could compromise sources and methods.

"Go ahead, Nancy. We're all cleared here. You know that."

"The terrorist we found in the bridge wreckage—" said Nancy.

"Abu . . . something or other," interrupted Jackson.

"Abu Muhammad al-Masri. I don't think he was involved."

"What?!" said Novak in disbelief.

"I knew when I first saw his body something was off," she said.

"How so?" asked Jackson.

"I've been hunting jihadis most of my career and I ran the targeted assassination program that decimated Emni. I know them the way a magician knows a deck of cards."

"But wasn't al-Masri a part of Emni? I think you said so earlier," asked Jackson.

"Correct, he was. When we identified his body, my gut told me something was wrong. At first, I dismissed it. Then it hit me," she said, reaching into her briefcase and pulling out a thick red folder marked TOP SECRET in bold, followed by code letters. She handed it to Jackson.

"What's this?" asked Jackson as he opened the folder.

"The problem," she said.

Jackson carefully removed files from the folder and laid them out on his desk. Each was about thirty pages thick and clipped together, with a photo and cover sheet on top. Novak stood up and walked around Jackson's chair to get a better view. There were five files in all.

"Who are they?" asked Jackson as Novak fumbled for his reading glasses.

"This is al-Masri's terrorist cell in Emni. He wasn't the leader but a member," she said. "They were tight, and always worked as a unit. Always."

"That's unusual. They not trust other jihadis?" said Jackson.

"Hard to say. Perhaps that's what made them so effective. They staged the Istanbul airport attack in 2016 that killed forty-eight and injured 230. They also acted as enforcers inside the caliphate and liked to crucify non-Sunni men and gang-rape unwilling women."

"A combination of cunning and cruel," said Jackson softly as he flipped through a file.

"Sounds like pure evil to me," muttered Novak, hovering over Jackson's shoulder so he could read the CIA action reports.

"They are," said Holt, and let them riffle through the files. Jackson's face betrayed no emotion, but Novak's was a picture book of horror. He let out a low whistle at one point.

"So, what's the problem?" asked Jackson, looking up and putting down a file. "They seem to fit the threat profile perfectly."

"True. But here's the problem," she said, stabbing one of the files with an index finger. "That's the leader. He's dead." The two men looked surprised and Jackson picked up the file.

"When?" asked Jackson.

"Ten months ago. An Agency direct action team from Ground Division took him out vicinity Raqqa, Syria. Bullet in the chest and head." She gently grabbed the file from the National Security Advisor's hands and flipped to a page showing his corpse. The photo was dark and grainy, as if taken through night-vision goggles.

"What did they do with the body?" asked Novak.

"They left it. The CIA doesn't offer hearse services."

Novak scowled at Holt's jab.

"Go on," said Jackson.

Holt pointed to another file. "This guy is dead too. We hired a contract kill team to assassinate him, under Title 50 authorities. That was six months ago, in September."

"Where did you find him?" asked Jackson.

"FATA region, Pakistan, under ISI protection," she said, referring to Pakistan's notorious Inter-Services Intelligence, which also sheltered Osama bin Laden. "That's why we used Apollo Outcomes rather than our own guys, to avoid escalating tensions between our countries should they become compromised. Contractors offer good plausible deniability."

"Makes sense," said Jackson.

"Wait a minute. You hired a private-sector hit team? Mercenaries?" asked Novak in a pitched tone. He had been a high-paid Washington lawyer before being appointed as the secretary of state. He had scant background in international affairs but rendered legal services to the president during the campaign, and many thought the appointment was a quid pro quo. No one knew what those services entailed. "Is that even legal?"

"Sir, with all due respect," she said in a tone suggesting none, "there's a lot you don't understand about modern war."

Novak was about to retort, when Jackson cut him off again. "Continue, Nancy."

"These next two guys were killed by the Wagner Group in North Syria in October. Our sources inside the GRU confirmed it."

"You mean Russian mercenaries killed them," said Novak.

"Not just any mercenaries, but elite ones. The Wagner Group is Russia's version of Apollo Outcomes," said Holt.

"Just not as good," added Jackson.

"Not by a long shot," said Holt, grinning.

"Tell me about the last guy. Is he dead too?" said Jackson with unease on his face.

"Yes. He's the guy we pulled from the rubble, but a different photo of him."

Both men leaned in and stared at the picture. The terrorist looked ten years younger than the body they found in the wreckage, even though the photo was less than a year old. However, it was clearly the same individual.

"And it gets worse," said Holt. Both men's mouths hung open.

"Worse?" said Novak.

"What does that mean?" said Jackson, sitting upright.

"He didn't die here. The first autopsy was done in the field and didn't show much. However, the second one revealed he died weeks ago, and his body was preserved through refrigeration, around forty below Celsius. We found cold damage and slight body decay. Apparently, he was not immediately frozen after death but ripened along the way."

"Where did he die?" asked Novak, sitting back down and stowing his reading glasses in his breast pocket.

"We don't know, but it wasn't two days ago and it wasn't here. Someone placed his body inside the bridge, probably in a crawl-space to protect him from the initial blast and collapse."

"You mean somebody wanted us to find his body," said Novak.

"Correct. And make erroneous deductions about who was behind the terrorist attack."

"A false flag operation. I don't like where this is heading," said Jackson in a dark tone. "Nancy, do you have a new theory? Be careful and be precise."

"Yes. These men did not do it," she said, gesturing to the files on the desk. "This terrorist cell was dead months before the bridge attack, making it impossible for them to be behind the VP's assassination. Rather, the actual perpetrator is framing them. Meanwhile, we're burning precious time and resources chasing down fake leads and alienating allies like Saudi Arabia."

"You're saying this whole thing is a setup?" said Novak, sinking deeper into his chair. "The political fallout with Riyadh could be significant."

"Affirmative," said Holt.

"Well, shit," said Novak.

Jackson sat in thought, and finally asked, "Then who did it?"

"We don't know," replied Holt.

"No theories?" asked Novak.

"None," she said in a grave manner. "No country would do it because it risks war, and they know we would eventually figure it out and retaliate. No terrorist group could do it, other than the Islamic State, and we just ruled them out. I doubt organized crime could pull it off. Even if they could, why would they? It would risk much yet gain little. I'm not sure who is left." She tapped a foot as she thought. "I don't know who did this, or why."

They sat motionless in information shell shock as they pondered the implications. Jackson broke the silence. "Whoever did this is very, very good."

"And very, very dangerous," added Novak.

"Now you understand why I came to you in person," she said, and he nodded.

"But surely someone this good would know that we'd eventually connect the dots and realize the dead guy was a setup. It doesn't buy them much time," said Novak.

"Jan, the deception wasn't for us," replied Holt. "It was for the press. 'Fool the media and fool America' is what the terrorists say. But it's what the Russians do."

"Nancy, who else knows about this?" asked Jackson.

"Some of my staff, but it's code-word classified and the information won't go anywhere. Among the principals, no one knows. Just us three."

"Good," he said, staring at the files on the desk. Holt and Novak sat quietly, awaiting Jackson's decision. After a few minutes, he leaned forward and picked up the phone. "Convene a principals meeting of the National Security Council. Immediately."

CHAPTER 9

Deep in the bowels of the Hoover Building, Lin sat across from her boss. The conversation was not going well.

"Radical Islamic terrorists are not behind the bridge attack because they're simply not that good. Everyone knows it but no one wants to say it," said Lin.

"Say what exactly?" asked her boss, exasperated. He had slept in his office last night and the lack of rest was showing. His eyes were beset within dark circles and what little hair remained on his head stuck out as if attacked by static electricity.

"That it's not terrorists! It's a false flag operation. It's Russia. Moscow killed all those people and framed terrorists to get us off their scent. Deceit is their way of war. They manufacture the fog of war and then step through it. It's how they stole the Crimea, interfered with our elections, and now assassinated the VP—who they thought was POTUS. The Kremlin is framing terrorists to get away with murder. Literally."

He sighed, wanting to scream at her but too exhausted to do so. It was the third time she had pushed her Russia conspiracy theory, and he was determined it would be the last. The FBI had terrorists to catch and had no time to waste on unsubstantiated hunches by a junior analyst.

Correction. Failing junior analyst, he thought. His own boss had formally counseled him about anger management issues and told him to become a better mentor to young agents. *But they're so stupid these days,* he thought. Still, he had to make the effort, something his boss had made excruciatingly clear. *Lordy, give me patience,* he thought.

"Lin, listen to me. Carefully. The entire interagency is throwing its full weight into finding these terrorists. People with clearances and pay grades way above yours know things you do not. For example, the terrorists have grown more sophisticated in the past year, and they have the means, motive, and opportunity to execute the bridge attack. We are confirming leads everywhere. We even found a dead terrorist at the scene of the crime—"

"The Russian's could have arranged it," interrupted Lin. "Easily."

Her boss grimaced and looked up at the ceiling while clenching fists. *Perhaps he's looking for divine patience,* she thought, and could see a vein pulsating on his right temple. He was about to blow.

"No. The Russians could not," he said finally, combating his temper. "Anyway, why would they? Why risk World War III? They have better ways to attack us than assassinating the vice president. Admit it."

Lin folded her arms, trying to think of a good response. None came.

"There is *no* Russia angle. Got it? No more bullshit about Moscow out of you."

"But—"

"There is no 'but'!" he interrupted, pounding the desk with a hammy fist. "We have fourteen thousand agents looking for terrorists, everyone except you. Fall in line, Lin, or forfeit your badge and gun. Final warning!" he said, thinking, *Screw my boss.*

Lin left his office fuming and sank back into her desk chair. Jason gave her the I-told-you-so look, but she held up a hand in protest. "I don't want to hear it, Jason. Not now."

"So-o-o-o-o, how'd it go?" he asked with a sardonic smile.

"Not well."

Jason shot the I-told-you-so look again and she turned away. "Lin, everyone is pretty convinced it's terrorists. Especially the director. So are the CIA and the other fifteen intelligence agencies. Maybe you should think so too."

"A bad idea embraced by millions of people is still a bad idea."

"Lin, there was a terrorist's body on-site. It's conclusive."

"No, it's deceptive. The Kremlin staged it."

"You've got to be kidding me."

"Think about it, Jason," she said, swiveling her chair to face him. "Russia has been killing terrorists in Syria for years. Putting a dead one on ice and then planting him inside the bridge would be easy for the FSB," she said.

"It would be damned hard for the FSB or GRU or anyone to import a frozen terrorist," he said, laughing at the idea.

"Don't underestimate the Russians."

Jason groaned, equal parts pity and incredulity. "You know you would be a rising star in the Bureau if you just had patience for the rules."

"Jason, don't give me that bureaucratic bullshit. We have a country to save, and we're losing precious time. We should be tracking leads on Russia, before they evaporate." Lin's voice turned angry, tired of being ignored.

"Jen . . ." said Jason in a soothing tone, trying to calm her.

"The Kremlin sometimes uses Russian organized crime as a fifth column. I know because I worked on the Russian Organized Crime Task Force before I was exiled here. The *bratva* can procure tons of dynamite, no problem. Import a dead terrorist?" She let out a "Ha!" that startled a nearby agent. "Too easy. They can smuggle in anything from anywhere and bribe anyone. Terrorists can't do that."

Jason leaned back, closing his eyes. "Jen, do one for the team and stop thinking. Last time you did, we *both* got in big trouble. The boss reamed you for . . . how did he put it? . . . 'Girl gone rogue!' Then *I* got chewed out for letting you go. As if I was your babysitter!"

Silence.

"Jen. Jen?"

More silence. He cautiously opened one eye.

She was gone.

CHAPTER 10

I was entranced by the mystical chords of Hovhaness's symphony "Mysterious Mountain" when my spell was broken by turbulence. The Gulfstream IV jet bucked through the wind shear as we initiated our descent. I looked out the large oval window but saw little. The moonlight only revealed light and dark splotches below us, indicating trees and farmland. Small clusters of amber lights indicated the occasional human settlement.

I had spent the last twelve hours in the air, and all my money, too. The charter jet business was run by air pirates, as far as I was concerned, but discretion is expensive. Plus, my itinerary involved heaps of "transaction fees" or bribes to bypass normal formalities. I had to empty out my black bank account in Cyprus, a holdover from my days at Apollo Outcomes. Program managers like myself received dark money for random operational expenses, and I had squirreled some away in several offshore accounts.

Now we were on final approach to a small country airstrip somewhere in Shenandoah Valley, Virginia. The rural airport closed at dusk, making it an ideal point of entry for anyone wishing to avoid customs. Dulles was not possible for me, at least not now. We flew over the polar cap and down though Canada, avoiding Homeland Security's gazing eyes. They looked southward, at the Latin American smuggler routes. Not many smugglers came from Canada, especially by air.

"Pilot, what's our ETA?" I asked over the intercom.

"Twenty minutes," said a voice in a thick Bulgarian accent.

I picked up the phone and made a call, then switched back to the intercom. "The runway lights will be on in fifteen minutes."

"Affirmative," replied the pilot.

One-fifty grand bought me a fixer on the ground, local transportation, and a temporary safe house in Washington. It also got me an amnesiac airport employee to throw the light switch and flee.

The plane's cabin attendant fumed quietly in a forward seat, eyeing me. It had been this way for nine hours. Over the course of the flight, I had turned the corporate jet's posh interior into a *Guns and Ammo* centerfold. Black duffel bags were seat belted to leather seats, and the polished wooden tables were overloaded with tactical gear and things that go boom. Now it was all packed into a small ballistic chest, two duffel bags, and a weapons case. Only the M32 revolver–type grenade launcher lay on the couch, snug in its tactical bag. It was too big to pack. We made a quick stop in Beirut to pick up some choice items from an arms dealer who owed me a solid. Then we stopped in Cyprus, a hub for oligarchs and people like me.

The flaps extended with a whir of hydraulics, and the landing gear released with a clunk. I could feel the plane slow down in my gut, and I peered out the window. Farmland, patches of trees, some houses, a ridgeline in the distance. It looked lush compared to my two years in the Middle East. I never thought I would come home again, especially this way.

The plane nosed up as the ground drew closer. Power lines passed uncomfortably close to our landing gear, and the dark horizon and sky merged into one color. The plane wobbled in midair as the pilots brought it to near stall speed before there was any runway beneath our wheels. The turbines throttled up and down in rapid succession, and the ground came up fast. The attendant was gripping the ends of his armrests, staring straight ahead.

"Short runway," said the flight attendant, fear in his voice. "Not made for this size aircraft."

"I know."

We touched down hard at 2250 and the pilots slammed the brakes, causing spare ammo magazines, loose rounds, and cocktail napkins to hurtle forward. The reverse thrusters kicked in, and I felt my body weight strain against my seat belt. Things behind me crashed to the floor and one of the galley cabinet doors flung open with a crack. The plane edged left and right as we rapidly decelerated. Out the window, I saw the small terminal building zoom by; it marked the halfway point on the runway.

"Too fast," said the flight attendant, shouting over the blast of the reverse thrusters. "We're running out of runway!"

The brakes squealed, and the plane shimmied until we skidded to an unnatural stop on the grass, just past the runway's edge. The pilots throttled the starboard reverse thruster and port engine simultaneously, causing a violent U-turn back onto the runway.

"I hope we didn't wake up the entire countryside," I said.

"If the police show up, you're doing the talking," said the attendant. I had asked our fixer about this contingency, and he said it's the one thing he could not fix. Getting caught in an unregistered jet flying from the Middle East full of smuggled weapons and cash and landing in the dark of night in rural America is hard to explain to local juries.

"I need to ghost in ten minutes," I said, and the flight attendant nodded in vigorous agreement.

The Gulfstream taxied back up the runway to the small terminal, where the pilots cut the engines. I opened the fuselage door and aluminum stairs unfolded gracefully to the tarmac. The air smelled sweet and cold.

"It's good to be home," I said, walking down the stairs in a tailored suit and carrying a SCAR assault rifle with sound suppressor at the ready. I would have preferred nonlethal weapons, but they had no range. Plus, Middle East smugglers rarely stock such items. Turning around, I saw the Gulfstream dwarfed the small, single-engine planes near it. The small airport's frequent flyers were recreational pilots, and I wondered if a jet had ever landed here before.

No time for a security sweep. I need to find my ride, I thought. There were a few small hangars, some Cessna 150s, and a glorified snack bar that passed as the terminal. No one was here but us.

I saw the black BMW M5 competition sedan tucked in between hangars, waiting for me, right where the fixer promised. I felt under one of the wheel wells and peeled off the keys taped inside. Seconds later I was in the driver's seat, and the twin-turbo V-8 came to life with a throaty roar.

"Magic," I said, a phrase I had picked up in South Africa. The Beemer looked like a standard Washington lobbyist's ride but had the soul of a track car. The fixer had it enhanced, too, adding horsepower and removing the antitheft tracking device. There was no GPS or anything else that could talk to the internet. A road atlas and street maps of Washington, DC, sat in the front seat. Perfect for my needs.

I spun around to the G-IV and backed up to the plane's stairs. The attendant stood at the top, arms crossed, glowering down at me. It took us a few minutes to unload the aircraft.

"That's it," I said, walking down the stairs with the M32 grenade launcher and throwing it in the trunk. The BMW sagged slightly in the back under the weight of the weapons and ammo. It would affect evasive maneuvering at speed, causing the car to fishtail around corners. Once I reached Washington, I would make a weapons cache separate from my safe house.

I checked my watch again. Nine minutes. *Pretty good.*

"Time to pop smoke," I said, nodding to the attendant who grinned and waved as he retracted the stairs and sealed the door. The jet engines whirred to life.

I got behind the wheel and strapped in. The Gulfstream's turbines crescendoed, and the plane began rolling forward. I accelerated out of the way and toward the airport's exit, a chain-link gate conveniently left wide open by the fixer. The Gulfstream took off and thundered over my head, its landing gear retracting, as I sped down the country road.

It's good to be home, I thought.

CHAPTER 11

Of all the prestigious private-member clubs in Washington, DC, the Cosmos Club was the most elite. Like all clubs of its genus and species, it was unassuming to the casual eye. No sign announced its existence. Only those who "mattered" in vanity-obsessed Washington recognized the belle époque mansion on Embassy Row, flying its own flag.

A black Mercedes sedan sat in a line of luxury cars waiting to be valet parked. Membership was highly curated, and an invitation to dine at the Club was rarely refused.

"Good afternoon, sir," said one of the valets as he opened the Benz's passenger door. An antique cane stuck out, followed by a leg. The man grunted as he maneuvered a second, stiffer leg onto the brick pavement. With focus, he rose to his feet.

"Welcome back to the Cosmos Club, sir," said another staff member with a smile. The tall man ignored him and hobbled into the mansion. Despite his age and limp, he bore an impressive physique, like a retired linebacker. People moved out of his way as he lumbered forward and made his way through the club. The ballroom looked like Versailles and the library like Oxford.

He passed through a corridor covered in pictures of members who had won a Nobel, Pulitzer, Presidential Medal of Freedom, or other prestigious recognition, including the Cosmos Club Award. There were hundreds. Then there was an alcove of framed postage stamps with members' faces on them. The tall man ignored it all.

"Sir, your guest is already seated," said the maître d' as the man shuffled past him and into the dining room. White table-cloths with complex settings lined the room, but none too close together. The scent of grilled steak and truffle potatoes filled the air, as did the *glug-glug* of wine being poured into glasses. The Cosmos Club's seal was subtly ubiquitous: a winged earth flying over clouds but under stars, with a Masonic-looking eye beaming light down upon the cosmos.

"Please follow me."

They passed senators, diplomats, generals, judges, clergy, CEOs, lawyers, foreign dignitaries, and others locked in quiet conversation. The Club was a safe haven for privacy and a neutral ground for meetings, away from the hoi polloi of the press and public. The Club prohibited electronics, business cards, and notetaking. It was a back room where deals were cut in the DC swamp.

"Here you are, sir," said the maître d', opening the door to a private dining room lined with bottles of wine behind glass and a crystal chandelier that filled the small space. Inside sat a man wearing a bespoke suit who was only slightly younger. The average age of Club members was seventy. The man with the cane moved forward without acknowledging the maître d', who rushed to seat his guest and then slipped out. Once they were alone, the two men regarded each another.

"Good to see you, old friend," said the man with the cane.

"And you too."

"What shall we talk about?"

"You know exactly why I called you here. We have a problem."

The other man nodded.

CHAPTER 12

My safe house near Capitol Hill was underwhelming. A real estate agent would describe it as: "lots of living space," "great potential," "unique design," and "lots of possibilities." Translation: a dump. The place was a dilapidated taxi warehouse abandoned to pigeons in the industrial part of the city. Neighborhood features included an eight-lane highway overpass, railroad tracks, a coal power plant, abandoned cars, and trash. Lots of trash.

But it was home. For now.

A garage door opener was clipped to the BMW's sun visor, and now I knew why. After pressing it, the mammoth garage door opened and I drove in, headlights on. The interior was a concrete cave, and the dank air assaulted my nostrils. It smelled of axle grease and rotting rubber. I donned my night vision and SCAR and conducted my security sweeps. Ten minutes later, I discovered the biggest threat was tetanus.

At the center of the warehouse sat an RV trailer, arranged by the fixer, that would serve as my tactical operations center. The front door creaked open, and I flipped on the interior lights. HOME SWEET HOME, read a sign on the fridge in fake needlepoint. I opened the fridge door and found a six-pack of cheap beer and a cold pizza.

"Thoughtful," I said, grabbing a slice of pie. I hadn't realized how hungry I was. Four laptops sat on the table, across from a large monitor on the wall. These laptops were special because they could probe the internet anonymously. I opened one. A few clicks later, the wall monitor came alive with feeds of low-light cameras around the warehouse. Rats were the only thing moving outside.

"Now to find some friends," I said, working the keyboard.

Hours later, I sat in the corner of a coffee shop, sipping a triple espresso. Morning commuters were rotating through, when two men walked through the door. They were not like the others. The first was colossal. He wore sideburns and dressed like a lumberjack; all he needed was an ax. The second was wiry and shopped out of mountain-climbing catalogs. Sun had engraved lines into his face, making him look older than he was. Both moved like athletes.

"Tom!" said the lumberjack in a gravelly baritone.

"Lava, Tye!" I said, standing up. We shook hands, firm grips all around, and took seats around the café table.

"I couldn't believe it when you said you were back," the big guy said, smiling. No one knows where he got the nickname Lava. He was a West Point quarterback turned special forces legend, eventually commanding the U.S. Army's most elite unit: the Combat Applications Group, aka Delta Force. After retirement, he was scooped up by Apollo Outcomes, taking a lot of guys with him, including Tye. When I first joined Apollo, I was lucky enough to be an operator on Lava's team.

"Hi Tom," the wiry guy said, in a faint Southern accent. He grew up in the green hills of Tennessee and enlisted in the army at seventeen. A few years later, he was selected for Delta and spent a career fighting America's secret wars. Tye was a patriot to a fault; he only saw the good versus evil in his missions, and never the ocean of in-betweens. I never understood why a guy like him joined Apollo, and owing to this, I didn't fully trust him. But Lava did.

"Heard you was dead," said Tye.

"Turns out I'm hard to kill. It takes more than Russians and ISIS to eliminate me," I said, and gave them a quick update of my missions involving Ukraine and the Islamic State.

"Sounds like you've been in some sticky places," said Lava, not fully convinced that I was relaying everything.

"Lost my team, Lava. Outside of Donetsk. We were ghosts, and there's no way the Russians could have tracked us. No way."

"Sorry about your team, Tom. What do you think happened?"

"Someone inside gave away our position."

"Inside Apollo?" asked Tye.

"Possibly," I said with caution. *The CEO, Brad Winters, sold us out, the double-dealing opportunist!* I wanted to scream but couldn't. Up to this point, I had left Winters's name out of it. Winters and Lava got along, and I needed to know where Lava's loyalties stood. If I wanted help, I needed to win over Lava. Tye and others would follow.

Lava looked away, and Tye to the ground. *That's weird*, I thought.

"You been flying nap of the earth for a year now?" asked Lava, referring to when military aircraft fly under the radar. It was a soldier metaphor for operating undetected. "You landed five hours ago, and no one knows you're here? You're sure about that?"

"Yes," I said, puzzled by his suspicions.

"Well, your timing's shit," said Tye.

"What do you mean?"

"Follow me," said Lava, and we got up and left the coffee shop. Outside was a black up-armored Chevy Suburban. They were ubiquitous in Washington.

"Get in," said Tye, holding open a backseat door. I clambered in and reached for a seat belt. I didn't like where this was going. Tye got behind the wheel and Lava in the front passenger seat. Seconds later we swerved into traffic, and Lava turned to face me.

"Who else knows you are back?" asked Lava.

"No one, I swear. I called you first. You told me long ago that if I was ever in trouble, call you first."

Lava starred at me. Judging me. I took it.

"No one?" repeated Tye, looking at me in the rearview mirror.

"No. One."

Lava turned around, facing forward as we crossed the National Mall and turned onto Constitution Avenue. Patches of frozen snow lay on the ground and there were a few geese.

"The situation is worse than you realize, Tom," said Lava. "Do you know what we were doing last night? Hunting. For the past six months we've been hunting splinter cells across the metro area."

"Terrorists? Foreign nationals? Russians? The Chinese?"

"Worse."

"Worse? Who's worse?"

"Apollo Outcomes," said Lava, turning to me. Tye eyed me through the rearview mirror, gauging my reaction. My head exploded. *Did I just walk into a trap?*

"I don't understand," I stuttered. "I thought you still worked for Apollo."

"We do," said Tye.

"Then who is Apollo working—"

"Apollo is secretly at war with itself," interrupted Lava. Silence followed as I absorbed the implications.

"You're telling me an Apollo team has gone rogue? Here, in DC?" I said, not believing it. I just couldn't see how this was possible.

"Not just a team," said Tye. "A whole squadron."

"And they're working for a foreign client. No one knows who," said Lava.

"And Tom, you are listed as one of the rogue operatives," said Tye. "KIA last year, along with two others."

"Boon and Wildman," I said quietly. I hadn't heard from them in months and assumed they were in hiding. Perhaps they were dead.

"Affirmative," said Tye, then added sympathetically, "Wildman was a friend."

I slumped in my seat, daring to trust them. Lava had never lied to me before, why would he now? He was no Brad Winters.

"There's a kill list," said Lava. "You're still on it, even though you're listed as KIA. I never understood why, but now I know. It's because someone got sloppy. They thought you were dead but had no confirmation."

"It's why we were shocked to get your call," said Tye, "and why it's good you haven't contacted anyone else."

I sat stunned.

"You really didn't know, Tom?" asked Tye, in amazement.

"No."

We turned around at the gate of Arlington Cemetery and headed back toward the Lincoln Memorial and the Mall.

"Well, I guess I should not be surprised," I said. The time had come for the whole truth. "After all, it was Brad Winters who sold out my position to the Russians in Ukraine. He also issued a kill contract on me, when I was in Syria and Iraq. But he got what he deserved."

"What do you mean?" asked Lava.

"Winters backed a failed coup d'etat in Saudi Arabia, and I exposed him to the Kingdom's security services. They captured, tortured, and beheaded him. Wish I was there to see it," I said with satisfaction.

Tye started laughing, and so did Lava. Their laughing grew louder.

"What's so funny?" I asked.

"Winters is alive," said Tye, once he caught his breath.

"And he's leading the renegade squadron," said Lava.

CHAPTER 13

Rush hour on K Street was normally a throng of angry cars, double-parked trucks, rude bike messengers, and rushing pedestrians in suits. People outside the beltway think Capitol Hill is the epicenter of American power, but DC denizens know better: it's K Street. The intersection of K and Connecticut, and the blocks surrounding it, are home to crisis communication companies that manipulate the news cycle, law firms that have partners without law degrees, and boutique political-risk consultancies that practice the dark arts of subterfuge. Together, they formed the troika of Washington's seedy underbelly.

Today K Street was empty, even though it was a weekday morning. The threat of another terrorist attack kept even the soulless home, leaving Lin the wide boulevard to herself. She took her time walking and thinking.

Be a good soldier and just do it, she thought grimly. She knew she had to return to the Hoover Building and play the game. But it wasn't her style.

If you don't, you are just a civilian, she thought. When she left the building an hour ago, she wanted to solve the case on her own. However, going AWOL during a national crisis was guaranteed job termination. Now she just wanted to save her career.

I need to make repair, before it's too late. The FBI had given her third, fourth, and even fifth chances. She was a born badass but was marooned to a desk for her sins. However, the desk was her last chance.

How did it all go sideways? Lin stopped and felt her eyes tear up. *It wasn't supposed to be this way. Not for me!*

A year ago, she was taking down Russian mobsters as part of a FBI assault team, its only woman. In a single night, the FBI's Joint Eurasian Organized Crime Task Force arrested more than two dozen members of the Shulaya gang in Brooklyn, although the word "gang" didn't go far enough. This bloody group trafficked drugs, women, weapons, and even children—anything to turn a profit, they didn't care.

Lin cared, though. She still remembered the moment. The raid was like any other, and something they trained for in the shoot house for hours. But training cannot prepare you for everything.

"Breach!" the team leader had shouted, and she heard the battering ram crash through the shabby apartment's door. She was third in the stack and shuffled in, covering her sector with her Colt M4 carbine. No movement, no threats.

"Clear!" she shouted. They snaked through the living room, pizza crusts on the floor. Lin moved smoothly, despite being turtled up in black body armor. The room was empty.

"Clear!" they each shouted, and the four-person stack moved on. Somewhere, a young woman was sobbing. A closed door ahead. The stack advanced.

Automatic gunfire tore through the wood door, splintering it, and caught the team leader in the chest. He went down, saved by body armor, but he struggled to breathe, as if someone had taken a sledgehammer to his solar plexus.

"Man down! Man down!" someone shouted.

"Laying down suppressive fire," said Lin, taking a knee, flipping to full auto, and firing back through the shredded door. The other two members of the stack reached for the team leader's equipment vest and pulled him back through the living room and out the front door.

Click. Lin's magazine ran dry. Time slowed as her heart rate spiked and adrenaline panicked through her veins. She rolled right as automatic gunfire from the other side of the door blew it apart and exploded the cheap chandelier overhead. Her Kevlar helmet took a bullet and fell off, while her weapon slipped from her grip as she rolled. She was alone in the room.

A mammoth, shirtless man emerged through the door frame, sweeping the room with his AK-47 and screaming in Russian like the possessed. His torso was covered in tattoos: a large Eastern Orthodox crucifix over his heart surrounded by winged skulls and Cyrillic encircling it all. Saints in chains were on his shoulders and upper arms.

The man stopped and smiled at her. Russian mobsters are all men, the worst kind.

"Get out of there!" shouted one of the FBI agents from the hallway, but Lin knew better. The gangster would mow her down the moment she sprinted. Instead, she stood up, chin high and facing him, unarmed. He smiled, not because she was a sexy woman but because she was a challenge.

"You are mine, bitch," hissed the man in Russian.

"I'm nobody's bitch, bitch," replied Lin in Russian.

"What are you doing?! Get out of there!" yelled her partners from the outside hallway. One peeked around the corner with his M4 but the Russian was quick and shot the door frame around the agent's head. The man slunk back around the corner.

Simultaneously, Lin kicked the kitchen table toward the Russian. As he spun around to block it, she bounded toward him: the first step on the floor, the second step off the sliding table, the third step her legs around his neck. She twisted her hips and they both crashed to the floor. The man pointed his Kalashnikov at her head as he gasped for breath and flailed. Lin's legs tightened around his throat while she yanked the AK-47 barrel upward, causing it to fire on automatic into the wall. She ignored the pain of the hot barrel.

Click. The AK-47 was dry.

The FBI agents ran forward but not before the mobster flipped Lin on her back and put a knife to her throat, its point under her chin. She could feel warm blood trickle down her neck. One thrust and the knife would go through her nasal cavity and into her brain.

"Stop or I kill her!" shouted the Russian in a heavy accent. The two agents froze, weapons trained at his head. One called for backup.

"You do that, we blow you away," said the other FBI agent.

"I do not fear death. I am death."

Fuck this, she thought. In a rapid motion, her hands swept inward and caught the Russian's knife hand; her right connected at his inside wrist while her left walloped the back of his hand. The knife went flying across the room. She incapacitated him with a knuckle strike to his throat, leaving his grasping his Adam's apple as she rolled him off.

"Are you all right?" asked one of the agents as the other handcuffed the Russian, who was still straining to breathe.

"Yeah, no problem," she replied. Her father had taught her well in Chinese martial arts, and the most important lesson was no fear. Fear is hesitation, and hesitation is death.

As Lin stood up, she heard crying from the next room. She entered and felt the air get sucked from her lungs. Two naked thirteen-year-old girls were tied to the bed. One was crying and the other was unconscious or dead. The Russian had had his fun, for days. It was a mess.

Lin spun around and drew on the Russian. The man's eyes bulged out in comprehension. The other agents screamed at her, but too late. The top half of the Russian's head exploded as she pulled the Glock's trigger. Bits of brain and skull splattered the rear wall.

There was an internal investigation, but her teammates covered for her. They reported it as self-defense, and she was exonerated. But people knew. No one wanted to work with her after that, and her corridor reputation was set: loose cannon. It is a curse inside the Bureau. No assault team leader wanted her after that, despite her abilities, and the task force director saw her as a public relations catastrophe in the making. He exiled her to the Hoover Building for "your own safety," he had told her.

That was a year ago. She had been a top agent whom others envied, and now she just wanted to remain in the Bureau.

"They will fire you," she whispered aloud, anxiety in her voice. She could not imagine life outside the Bureau. It's all she ever wanted to do. But the notion of appeasing her boss and working a dumb desk to find nonexistent terrorists was odious. Especially when the real bad guys—the Russians—were getting away. She could almost hear them laughing inside the Kremlin, toasting vodka and slamming down shots at America's expense.

I hate the Russians, thought Lin as she stared at the black smoke in the sky a mile to the north. It was the remnants of the blown-up bridge, an act of war invisible to the government.

Morons, she thought, and picked up her pace. *I need to get back on the task force. I'll make the Russians pay. Maybe not now, but later, when I'm a senior agent. I shall not forget!* "I SWEAR IT!" she shouted at the plume of smoke. A lone passerby eyed her nervously and crossed to the other side of the street.

Lin made her plan. She would march back into headquarters, make up with the boss, become the model desk agent, get transferred back to her old task force, and then kick ass. It would take time, but she was committed.

Bzzzzz. Bzzzzz. Lin pulled out her work phone and read the text. It was from her boss.

"RETURN TO BUILDING ASAP. SURRENDER BADGE AND GUN AT

SECURITY OFFICE. YOU ARE ON ADMINISTRATIVE LEAVE W/O PAY
PENDING MISCONDUCT INVESTIGATION."

"Crap," uttered Lin as her hands trembled. She had just been
fired, by text.

Lin stood still for minutes, lost in cognitive dissonance. Then
walked aimlessly. She paused at a metro subway station, its escalators running but with no people. Downtown looked like the
zombie apocalypse had ravaged the city of its population, yet
all the escalators, traffic lights, and other automated machines
toiled on without purpose. She felt like the escalator.

Then Lin smiled with a glint in her eye. She bounded down
the escalator to the subway below. She discovered her purpose
after all.

Banging on my front door.

I was lost in a dreamless sleep.

More banging.

My hand reflexively reached for my SCAR assault rifle before my brain registered the fact that someone was inside my ultra-secret safehouse and standing at my trailer's front door. And knocking. Banging, actually.

"Locke, get your ass up!"

It was Lava. I lowered my weapon and sat up in my cot, checking my watch. Almost midnight.

"Let yourself in!" I shouted back.

"It's locked."

I shuffled to the door and opened it. Lava's burly frame and stern expression awaited me. I felt like a scrub at Ranger School again.

"Daylight's burning, Locke. You need to suit up," he said, brushing past me and entered the trailer. "Real shithole of a place you got here. Know that?"

"What are you doing here? How did you know where I was, and get past my defenses?"

"Don't insult me. Here, drink this," he said, pulling out a small metal thermos.

"What is it?"

"Energy drink. Special stuff. You're going to need it," said Lava. Before I could protest, he opened it and shoved it into my hand. "Drink it." Normally I wouldn't, but Lava was my last, best commander. He took care of his people, and I wanted to be his people again, so I drank it against my better judgment.

"Tastes like fruit punch," I said, handing back the empty thermos.

"And take this," he said, handing me a kit bag. I opened it; inside was exotic Apollo tech and weapons. During my exile, I would have killed for such equipment, but not today. Not under these enigmatic circumstances.

"What's this?" I asked.

"We don't got all day, cupcake," said Lava, tossing me a tactical cuff. It was among Apollo's most coveted proprietary tech items, and far more advanced than anything governments issue. Looks were deceiving; it was a black Velcro cuff that attached to one's inner forearm. Simple enough. But opening the inner flap revealed a touch screen that was beyond next-generation technology. It connected with the wearer's tactical suit and linkable weapons; monitored vitals; interconnected with all Apollo team members and command nodes; and delivered ultrasecure global communications, limited artificial intelligence assistance, collective targeting, and near-perfect situational awareness in a firefight. It was the envy-lust of every special operator in the world, for those who knew of it, but only Apollo had them.

"Why are you giving me this?" I said, cradling it in my hand. It was unlocked and in setup mode, awaiting my biometric confirmation.

"Because I need to know if I can trust you."

"And so you give me Apollo tech? I'm flattered but don't understand."

Lava shook his sideburned head. "If you're gonna be on my team again, Locke, then I need to trust you. And it's been a long time, Locke. You went rogue, remember?"

"It's more complicated—"

Lava cut me off. "You don't know someone until you fight with them, or against them. I need to know if I can trust you again. Suit up. We're going on a mission."

"Mission?" I stammered. "What, now?"

"Now."

Lava's missions were usually infamously impossible but never impromptu. Like SEALs, Delta, and other elites, they were meticulously planned by Tier One operators who worked exclusively on a team for months, even years. They never took along war tourists.

Unless I was the mission, I realized. Was Lava trying to eliminate me? Yes, if he didn't trust me. But would he? I doubted it, but times change. I was caught up in a secret civil war, and I had gone rogue with Winters, the enemy. Lava had reason to doubt me.

"Where are we going? What's the mission?" I said as I suited up. The body armor was exquisite. It looked like black carbon-fiber plate mail, but it could flex with the body and it was light. I felt I could pole-vault in the stuff.

"Need-to-know only," said Lava, thumping me on the chest as he passed me and disappeared into the dark warehouse. "And you don't need to know."

I still held my SCAR. If I was going to end this, now would be my best chance. The sooner you make a break from your captors, the better your chance of survival. Those who wait for later opportunities usually find themselves in a hopeless prison cell, or dead. Sooner is always better. It's basic escape and evasion.

"Locke?"

But would Lava really kill me? Somehow I doubted it. He was my former commander, and we had endured things together that bond men. Or perhaps that was just hope for an old friend. Who was a survivor. And a killer.

You must decide, I thought. *Either you kill him, or he kills you. Or he saves you. Or I kill my only friend and ally.* Or perhaps his rifle was already aimed at my head. Whatever I did, it would be consequential, and I had only seconds to decide.

"Hey, how did you get in here anyway?" I yelled into the darkness, buying time as I weighed my options. They all sucked.

"Stop stalling, Locke," came Lava's voice from the shadowy recesses. "Hurry up. Let's bounce."

OK, let's see where this goes, I thought as I strapped on the cuff and exited the safehouse.

"Good man," whispered Lava.

Half an hour later, around 0030, we pulled into a corporate airfield in Maryland, just outside the Capital Beltway. Lava drove the black Suburban down the tarmac, past rows of private jets, and into the last hangar. Inside was a lone plane. It looked like a military transport, with twin turbo-props on a high wing and a T-tail. Its back ramp was down, and men in combat gear were hauling weapon cases and parachutes from a van. I counted ten men, and they were preparing for a high-altitude low-opening, or HALO, jump mission.

"Your new team?" I asked Lava as we parked in the hangar.

"Old team," Lava said. "You're the FNG." Fucking New Guy. Also, bottom of the food chain.

It's gonna be a long night, I thought.

"Hey guys, I brought a new recruit," said Lava.

"Locke, good of you to join us!" said Tye with sarcasm and a smirk. He introduced me to the rest of the team. They were all ex–Tier One special operators: six Americans, one Aussie, a Brit, a Canadian, a German, and an Israeli. All looked combat weathered, and none seemed pleased to see me. But I was the FNG, and I knew the deal. I used to be one of them. Hell, I led my own team under Lava's command in the early days.

"Body armor, grenades, and ammo in the van," said Tye. "Grab your pleasure and get on the iron bird. Wheels up in five."

"Thanks. Where are we—" I began before Tye cut me off.

"Just get your shit, Locke."

I stared at him and he stared back, giving no quarter. In the van, I grabbed the armor, a few boxes of 7.62 mm for my SCAR, .45 rounds for my twin HK Mark 23 handguns, and four frag grenades.

"Where's my parachute?" I asked.

"We already got one waiting for you," said Tye, his smirk disappeared. "On the plane."

I didn't like it.

"Thanks, Tye, but I see one here, toward the front of the van." I clambered over the ammo crates, and felt Tye's firm grip on my calf, stopping me.

"Stop wasting time. Like I said, your chute is already on the plane," he said. We locked gazes.

"Locke, move your ass! We're moving out," yelled Lava from the plane's tailgate, his assault rifle dangling at his side. A tug began pulling the aircraft from the hangar while the ground team got in the vehicles and started the engines.

"Leave it, Locke. Let's go," said Tye.

If I were to bail now, Lava could have capped me: one in the back and the other in the skull. He had a gift with bullets. So I followed Tye and leapt onto the plane's back ramp as it began to lift. The turboprops whirred to life once we cleared the hangar, and the van and Chevy Suburban drove away into the darkness. Lava's team sat on benches facing each other, looking slightly like cyborgs in their battle suits. Meanwhile, I was struggling to put mine on as we taxied to the runway. Seat belts were ignored as we took off.

"Are you going to tell me where we're going now?" I shouted over the din of the turboprops.

"You will know it when you see it," said Lava.

"What's the mission?"

"Need to know."

"I *need* to know," I said, gesturing at the aircraft and heavily armed team of strangers. We were about to parachute into a fight, and I had the right to know why I was risking my life.

"Need to know," repeated Lava as he leaned back and closed his eyes for a nap. So did the rest of the team.

Holy hell, I thought. But being an old soldier, so did I. Pulling a weapon would be suicide because I had nowhere to run. Better to get some shut-eye. Rest was the only preparation for an imminent fight, for those strong enough to sleep before battle.

I awoke to Tye shaking me.

"Wake up. It's time," he said. The rest of the team was donning parachutes and doing functions checks on weapons. I checked the time: 0146.

"Here, for you," said Tye, pushing a parachute into my chest. I starred at it. Was this Lava's weapon of choice? If he wanted me gone, a malfunctioning chute at thirty thousand feet would be a clean erase.

"Who packed it?" I said involuntarily.

"I did," said Tye with his smirk. "Put it on."

I yanked it from him and inspected it. I was a former HALO jumpmaster with 221 jumps and a static line jumpmaster with 144 jumps. However, there's only so much you can tell about a packed chute. You only know if it works when it opens, or doesn't.

"Hey, soldier," said Lava, witnessing my doubt. "Take mine." He took my chute and shoved his into my hands.

"No, it's fine, Lava. I'm good to go with that chute."

"No, take it. I insist," he said with faux politeness as he strapped on my chute. I stared at my new parachute.

"No time, Locke. We're over the DZ in four mikes. Chute up!" cried Tye, referring to the drop zone.

Everyone was ready to go, except me. Whatever was about to happen, I knew the aircraft's tailgate would soon open and we would all tumble out, with or without a parachute. I quickly strapped it on and adjusted my combat load. My oxygen bottle pressure and flow were good, and I could breathe.

"Omega, this is Valhalla. Radio check, over," said Lava over the command net. Apollo's tactical command in northern Virginia was call sign "Omega" and Lava was "Valhalla."

"Valhalla, this is Omega. Lima charlie. Warno: possible two bogies and hot DZ," came a voice over my earpiece. Translation: We read you loud and clear, but there may be two enemy aircraft and ground enemy on the drop zone.

"Roger," replied Lava, and turned to face us. "Sound off."

"One OK," said the first guy.

"Two OK," said the second.

"Three OK."

When it got to me, I said, "Twelve OK."

"All OK," said Lava. The interior lights switched from white to red, and my night vision adjusted instantly. Through my heads-up display, or HUD, I could see the identities of each team member in green, as well as their vitals, and what was behind me. Tye.

"Get ready!" said Lava. The aircraft's tailgate lowered, and we felt the blast of freezing air rip through us. Below, the terrain was unmistakable.

Manhattan! I thought. What the hell were we doing thirty-five thousand feet over New York City? Probably imitating the flight path of a commercial airliner as cover for action.

A long minute passed as we stood ready. The jump light was still red. Should I jump or not? Lava and Tye could have given me a dud parachute deliberately. I had worked for Brad Winters too long and mysteriously showed up in the middle of Apollo's civil war, and that was reason enough.

"Five, four, three," counted the pilot through our ear pieces.

I can't risk it, I thought. *I can't jump.*

"Two."

Do not budge! I grabbed a strap dangling from the ceiling and planted my feet.

"One."

The light above the tailgate went from red to green.

"Go! Go! Go!" shouted Lava. The twelve-man team pushed forward as a unit. I held on to the strap, but Tye plowed into me, rugby style, and knocked me off my feet. We all rolled off the tailgate as a scrum, and dropped into the sky.

CHAPTER 15

Lin sat on her bar stool wearing a slinky black dress and tried to look interested in what he was saying. It was difficult. The big man on the stool next to her looked like a washed-up boxer who drank too much beer. Or, in his case, vodka.

"You know what Stalin once said during a speech?" said the man, in drunken Russian. He went by Dmitri, which was undoubtedly not his real name.

"No, what?" Lin replied in fluent Russian.

The man feigned seriousness, waving his fists as if he were Stalin. "'I am prepared to give my blood for the cause of the working class, drop by drop.'"

She made herself chuckle. He continued.

"Then someone passed a note up to the podium, and do you know what it said?"

"No," she said.

"'Dear Comrade Stalin, why drag things out? Give it all now.'" He let out a huge snort-laugh, smacking the bar with a hairy hand.

"Oh, that's funny!" she lied, as he ordered more shots of rail vodka.

The Baltimore dive bar's dim lighting and few patrons made it an ideal place to meet an informant. Actually, she had never met Dmitri before, but he came highly recommended from one of her old FBI informants in Brooklyn. Dmitri helped manage Russian mob transactions at the Port of Baltimore and was networked into the *bratva*, even though he wasn't a mobster himself. She also learned Dmitri was her Brooklyn informant's cousin.

"How is your cousin doing?" she asked, sipping her shot as he downed his.

"Vasily? He's a cocksucker, but you already knew that!" he said, laughing hard. "Vasily told me you were luscious, and he was right." Dmitri placed his hand on her inner thigh and slid it upward. She swatted it away and crossed her legs. They had been at this for half an hour: her asking questions, and him laying his paws on her.

"Vasily said you knew of a ship that came from Europe to Newark about a week or two ago. He said it was registered in Liberia and had a Russian crew. True owner unknown," she said nonchalantly, and then looked up at him with an inviting gaze. "Vasily said you could help me."

"Did he, now?" Dimitri laughed and downed another vodka. "Ships like that show up every day in Newark."

"Yes, but this one is special."

"How so?" asked Dimitri, flagging the bartender for another round.

What Lin said next wasn't strictly true. "Vasily told me it was hauling contraband. People, drugs, or . . ." She stopped mid-sentence and hoped he would finish it. She learned this technique in the FBI's interrogation course. People abhor silence in friendly conversations and will fill it, sometimes with the truth. But all Dmitri did was belch.

"Vasily said you were a connected man. I'm disappointed," she continued, with firmness in her voice. *You know something. If I can't trick it out of you, then I'll shame it out. Or worse.*

"Vasily is an asshole," he said, laughing and gulping another vodka.

"So, you're not a man in the know?" she said in a silkier tone. "Not a man worth *knowing*?"

He smiled, and gave her a refilled shot glass, which she downed. "I am a man worth knowing."

"I thought so, and I look forward to knowing you. For a long time. Tell me what I want to know."

"Maybe."

"Maybe what?"

"Maybe I know something, maybe I don't."

"Maybe you tell me?" she said, leaning forward with a coy smile.

He eyed her chest and then her face, gauging her smile. "Maybe I do know a little something about that ship."

"Like what, Dmitri?" she coaxed, her index finger slowly tracing the rim of his empty shot glass. He watched her finger and swallowed.

"Something about a container ship that came into Newark, not long ago," he said in a low voice.

"What made the container ship so special?"

"How about I tell you at my place? It's close."

"How about you tell me now?"

"Nothing is free," he said.

"Tell me first. And then we go to your place."

They stared at each other, a standoff of sorts. Finally, he looked away. "I have to take a piss," he said, sliding off the bar stool. "Don't go anywhere, little lady."

She watched him lumber off to find the men's room. He was heavy but moved like a man who could handle himself.

He knows something and I'm running out of time, she thought. Over the past two days, she had called in every favor, reached out to every contact, and broken almost every FBI rule to find out how the Russians killed the vice president—if they had—and what their next move would be. Drunk Dmitri was her last lead.

Frustrated, she checked the time. It was almost midnight. *Crap,* she thought. The bar shut down in minutes, and then she would have to go to his place to continue the conversation. Lin frowned at the thought. *Better to get it over with now.*

Her phone buzzed with yet another text message from Jason, still at FBI headquarters despite the late hour. "WHERE R U?!" it read. There were dozens more like it. "BOSS ASKING 4 U"; "CAN'T COVER YOU MUCH LONGER"; "GET IN HERE!!!"; "CALL ME!!!!!!" She ignored them all.

Lin sighed and put the phone away in her purse, nestling it beside her Glock 19M. She hated her desk job, and it wasn't why she joined the Bureau. Jason was the only one who took her seriously, and that was only because he had a crush on her. But tonight wasn't proving any better. She didn't relish the idea of more cheap vodka, Dmitri's terrible jokes, and his hands ambushing places they ought not go. Especially on his couch. Yet her only hope of walking into the Hoover Building again, without being fired, was showing up with a tangible lead. And Dmitri was her last chance.

She was getting desperate.

"It's for a good cause," Lin reassured herself, kicking off her stilettos and slipping on flats from her purse. Then she bent over so that her long black hair touched the floor, and then wrangled it into a ponytail. She hated it when hair got in the way.

"Want anything, miss?" asked the bartender. "Last call."

"No. I'll be back in a jiffy," she said, walking toward the men's room, clutching her purse. The bathrooms were down narrow stairs, in the basement, which smelled of bleach. She tried not to touch the walls. The basement corridor was even dimmer than the bar—the management wouldn't splurge for a few light bulbs. The only sounds were the steady thump of eighties rock music above and the flushing of toilets. An old pay phone was at the end of the hallway, its handset torn off long ago. Vintage rock concert posters behind Plexiglas were drilled into the walls.

Lin cracked the door to the men's room and peered inside. It was small and disgusting. Two urinals, two stalls, sinks. Another man was rinsing his hands and wiped them on his jeans. She closed the door and stood in front of the lady's room, as if she were waiting in line to enter. The guy with wet pants exited and brushed past her, taking no notice.

Dmitri is alone, she thought. *I'll surprise him.* She opened the men's room door again and slipped in, bolting it behind her. Dmitri was in a stall. *Perfect,* she thought, putting her purse down on a sink and straightening out her short cocktail dress, adjusting its spaghetti straps in the mirror. The toilet flushed. Moments later he emerged, and Lin stood before him. Her sleek body and long legs startled him as he took her in. She smiled, and he smiled back.

"I agree," he said, undoing his belt buckle and then his fly. "Let's fuck right here. Why waste time?"

"Yes. Why waste time?" She delivered a perfect side kick to his solar plexus, sending the 240-pound man through the bathroom stall and onto the toilet seat. Dmitri sputtered on the grimy floor, gasping for air. His face was red and eyes bulged out; her strike paralyzed his diaphragm, starving his body of oxygen. Lin waited for him to recover, arms crossed.

"Tell me what I want to know!" yelled Lin. "What's the name of that ship?"

"You bitch!" he growled, lunging for her.

Using an aikido move, she sidestepped out of his path, grabbed his wrist and nape of the neck, and aimed him for a sink. His head connected with enameled steel, producing a sickening thud, and Dmitri ricocheted onto the floor, dazed.

"What's the name of the ship?"

Dmitri lay motionless, as if dead.

Crap, Lin thought. *Not again.*

Then he began writhing around on the floor, holding his concussed head and gasping for air again.

"When was it in Newark?" she continued. "Who in the mob handled it? Tell me what I want to know!" She grabbed his wrist and twisted it backward and up, causing him to scream.

"Enough! Enough!" he pleaded, holding up the other hand in surrender.

"Then tell me what I need to know," commanded Lin. In her experience, informants always broke under pressure. They were the weakest animals in the criminal jungle, and that was what made them squeal. The trick was knowing how to apply pressure, and Lin preferred joint locks. Unfortunately for her, the FBI disagreed.

"A sh-sh-ship called *Lena,*" he said, stuttering from the concussion, and rubbing his head. "A container ship. It did two trips from Novorossiysk to Newark."

"Wait, what? Novorossiysk?" said Lin in disbelief and struggling to roll the name off her tongue. It sounded like *novo-roh-SEEEESK.* "You mean Antwerp, right? Antwerp."

"Antwerp?!" Now Dmitri looked surprised. "No! I thought you were talking about the *Lena* out of Novorossiysk."

"Where the crap is that?"

Dmitri looked like a kid who had accidentally told burglars where the family safe was. The *bratva* would kill him if they found out.

Lin looked sympathetic. "Don't worry, Dmitri. Just tell me about the ship and no one has to know my source. I won't even tell the FBI." A promise she would try to keep. Try.

"Novorossiysk is a Black Sea port, and where *Lena* originated."

"When?"

"Ten days ago. Six months ago."

"And what did the *Lena* deliver?"

Dmitri shook his head and looked down. "I don't know."

"You're lying. Don't piss me off!" she said, and Dmitri looked up at her in terror.

"A container in August," he blurted out, "and another last week. They were unregistered and no one knows what was inside."

"Who handled them?"

Dmitri paused. He wasn't prepared for this level of confession.

"Who offloaded the containers, Dmitri? You either tell me now or I tell the *bratva* you're hitting on an FBI woman. What's the punishment for that, I wonder? Probably involves a razor blade."

Dmitri cringed and closed his legs.

"Dmitri, last chance. Who smuggled in those containers in Newark?"

"The Shulaya," he said, head down.

Lin looked astonished. "The Shulaya? Impossible. We busted them a year ago. They're gone."

"Apparently not all of them," he said, sitting up and holding his head. "Word is they secretly offloaded each container and moved them to a distribution warehouse in Secaucus. From there, no one knows what happened. Presumably the containers were unpacked and loaded onto trucks, but no one knows for sure. Not even the Shulaya."

"What does that mean, not even the Shulaya knows?"

"That's all I know, I swear! It's supersecret mafia shit. Only the bosses know, not people like me. We get paid to mind our business and ask nothing."

"Don't give me that bullshit," she said, grabbing his wrist and twisting backward, causing him to yelp. "I'm an FBI agent and I know when you're lying. What else have you heard?"

Someone was knocking on the bathroom door. Lin ignored it.

"Only rumors," Dmitri said in a whimper, his free hand clutching his skull in pain. The door knocking turned into pounding.

"Go away!" Lin shouted at the locked door.

"Is that a chick in there?" shouted a man on the other side. "Open up!"

"Hold it or use the women's room!" she yelled, then turned back to Dmitri. "What else have you heard?"

"Are you speaking Russian in there?!" asked the man outside the door. "Look you stupid Slavic whore, turn tricks in your home. Or, better for you, the dumpster. I gotta pee!" Lin's fists clenched at *whore,* and Dmitri reflexively put his hands over his head.

"What did you call me?" asked Lin in a calm voice.

"Whore," said the man, with satisfaction. "Stupid. Russian. *Whore.*"

Lin walked to the door, unbolted it, palm-heeled the guy's nose, and bolted the door again while the man gripped his throat in pain. Dmitri winced as he heard the man's body thump to the ground through the door, followed by screams of pain.

"*You bwoke my nose! You bwoke my nose!*" the man yelled in a nasally voice, but the bar's loud music upstairs drowned out his cries. Or no one cared.

Lin turned back to Dmitri. "I know the Russian mafia occasionally works for the Kremlin here. Don't lie to me. Why did the ship come from the Black Sea? What was it carrying?"

"Just ru-ru-rumors," stuttered Dmitri, still staring at the bathroom door. "Russian intelligence has been running a major operation in the capital region for months. Double agents, hackers, a tech team—"

"Why?"

"I don't know," he said.

Her hand formed a palm heel.

"I don't know!! I swear I don't know!"

Lin relaxed, and Dmitri sat back up, rubbing his nose unconsciously. "Also, I heard a heavy team arrived in town last week."

"What kind of team?" she asked.

"A black-on-black hit team. Spetsnaz, I think."

Russian special forces. Lin paused.

This is my big lead, she thought, masking her elation from Dmitri. It was possible they came in on the container, along with a whole lot of Spetsnaz firepower. More urgent, they represented a clear and present danger. If she could verify their presence, it could reorient the FBI toward the true threat: Russia. But obtaining proof would be difficult; she would have to survive.

"I don't suppose you know where I could find them?" she asked casually, pulling out a lipstick from her purse and applying it in the bathroom mirror. She mashed her lips together so it spread evenly, and then looked down at the big man, still sitting in a fetal position at her feet.

"No," he gulped for air. "But the FSB has safe houses in suburban Virginia."

"Where?" she asked in a matter-of-fact tone while putting the lipstick away.

"McLean, near the CIA. That's all I heard. Rumors. You have to believe me!" he pleaded.

She shook out her ponytail, combing her hair with her fingers. "I do, for now. Anything else I should know?"

Dmitri shook his head. Satisfied, Lin grabbed her purse, unbolted the door, stepped over the other man's squirming body, and turned back to Dmitri.

"And one more thing. Don't leave town. We might need to talk again," she said, and proceeded upstairs.

Dmitri looked horrified.

CHAPTER 16

Hell's bells! I screamed in my head. I was in a flat spin thirty-four thousand feet above Manhattan and out of control. The city lights, the plane, and the moon spun ever faster around me, and I was getting dizzy. Soon I would black out.

The whole team was out of control. We bounced off the tailgate like tokens spilling from a slot machine, falling everywhere, rather than a coordinated group exit. Now we were in trouble, hurtling to the earth at 120 mph.

"Locke, control your descent!" I heard Lava shout over my earpiece. "It will get worse unless you correct now."

The spin accelerated, and soon the moon and Manhattan were one. My altimeter read thirty-two thousand feet on my HUD, giving me two minutes to rectify the situation. I arched my back and stuck out my leg wing to regain control, but little happened. If this were a training exercise, I would pull my rip cord now and deploy the parachute. But it was a combat jump and I had to assume there were hostile drones in the air. Also, I wasn't sure if Lava sabotaged my parachute.

"Ball up!" said an Aussie accent. The lateral Gs were pushing blood to my brain, and I felt the blackout coming.

Focus! I commanded, and breathed deeply to calm my pulse.

"Dive out of it!" shouted Tye.

Diving won't work, I knew. I was spinning too fast. Instead, I dug my right knee into my elbow, catching air against the direction of the spin with my arm wing. The spin began to slow, and Manhattan and the moon were once more recognizable.

"Keep it up," said Lava.

The spin stopped and I spread my arms and legs, deploying my wingsuit like a flying squirrel. Wingsuits gave jumpers range and control, for those who could master them. The dizziness lingered and I felt I might throw up in my oxygen mask.

"Super-duper paratrooper," said Lava. "Your vitals were spiking. You're rusty."

"I blame the equipment," I joked, and scanned for the team, but all I saw were moonlight clouds below.

"AI, find the team," I commanded my onboard artificial intelligence, embedded in the tactical cuff.

"Team located 1,200 feet below tracking 245 degrees. Shall I plot a course?" said my AI in a tranquil woman's voice.

"Affirmative," I replied. A pale blue trajectory line lit up in my HUD, pointing me toward the team, far below. Zooming in my optics, I could see they were traveling in a V formation westward, toward Manhattan. The pilot green-lighted us well past the city to match the flight profile of a commercial airliner, and now we had to "fly" back via wingsuit several miles to downtown. The Atlantic was directly below us.

Gotta catch up or get left behind, I thought. I assumed a flat track position, tucking my arms tight to my sides, palms down, legs together, and toes out. My body became an arrow, descending rapidly until I caught up with the V and changed into a delta position.

"Good of you to join the flock," said Tye.

"Silence," said Lava. In the distance, I could see the grid lights of the city and the dark rectangle in the middle—Central Park.

"Switching to tactical," said Lava, and my HUD transformed into a polychromatic dazzle of friends, foes, and obstacles. Beneath us, a 747 was on approach to JFK airport, illuminated in yellow, as was an Airbus taking off. The new trajectory line led to a red blinking dot on the west side of midtown, off the Hudson.

"That's our objective," said Lava.

"Where's our DZ?" I asked, seeing only a concrete rain forest of skyscrapers.

"You're looking at it."

I saw nothing. Just tall buildings. Maybe there was something wrong with my system. Or it was sabotaged. "I'm not seeing it. The flight path leads downtown, and there's no place to land."

"We're not landing in downtown. We're landing *above* it," said Lava, and my heart jumped with alarm. I zoomed in my optics for a closer look at the DZ. It was one of the tallest and newest skyscrapers in the city, rivaling the Empire State Building. And it shimmered. It looked like it was made of mirrored glass that reflected the darkness around it, making it hard to see. Then I spotted the DZ, marked in pale blue by my HUD.

Holy shit, I thought. The DZ was a narrow sixty-five-foot tri-angular observation deck 101 stories up, almost at the very top of the building. Successfully landing there would be like hitting a hole in one, if the hole were on top of a flagpole and you were teeing off a flying Lear Jet.

"That's impossible," I muttered, and heard Tye snickering over the comms.

"Don't blow my mission, Locke," said Lava. "We don't want your body splattered in the middle of Thirtieth Street. It might tip off security."

I zoomed in more, although it was difficult given the bumpy ride. The observation deck faced us, and above it was several sto-ries of superstructure. But it was no roof; it was a huge pinnacle in the sky with enormous triangular holes that artfully concealed machinery and water tanks. If we touched down there, we would either slip through one of the holes and crush our bodies on the machinery below, or bounce off the forty-five-degree incline and fall to the asphalt 120 stories down. There would be no recovery time, just certain death.

"Lava, that's no DZ!"

"Ten thousand feet," said Lava, ignoring me. We were zooming over Brooklyn and would be at the DZ in seconds. Quickly, I glanced around for alternative DZs. Better to piss off Lava and walk away than risk gory death, but there were no good DZs because it was New York City.

"Nine thousand."

Hell, I didn't even know if my chute would open.

"Eight thousand."

We all banked slightly right to line up the approach to the skyscraper's small observation deck.

"Seven thousand."

This is insane! I thought.

"Valhalla, this is Omega. Building is hacked. DZ is secure," said Apollo command.

"Six thousand. Copy, Omega."

I could see the small balcony clearly now. It looked like a shelf at the top of a Saturn rocket.

"Five thousand. Pull at two."

EEEEEEEE! An alarm screeched in my earpiece. "Tango," shouted Lava. My HUD illuminated a rotary wing drone in red, flying random patterns around the building in stealth mode, although I could not see it with my naked eye. My AI listed it as potentially heavily armed, an extreme measure for Manhattan. Whatever was inside the building was important enough to risk an aerial firefight above New York City.

Who would take such a risk, and what's in that building? I thought, realizing I might soon find out.

"Four thousand. Watch the crosswind."

We whooshed by the Empire State Building's antenna tower.

"Three thousand."

My AI had me pulling my rip cord high and right of the building, compensating for the crosswinds. Would the parachute deploy when I pulled the rip cord? Almost reading my mind, Tye asked: "Locke, do you trust us?"

"Do you trust me?" I retorted. He did not respond.

"Three, two, one, deploy!" shouted Lava, and I pulled the rip cord. The opening G shock tore through my body, knocking my breath out, as the canopy deployed. My boots kicked up in the air, and the crosswind caught my wingsuit, sending me away from the observation deck, three hundred feet away. Lava and three other team members touched down. Four more were on approach. However, I was off azimuth and would miss the DZ.

"Locke, you're wide," yelled Lava. I yanked on my right riser, which steered the parachute, and I swung hard right toward the sixty-five-foot isosceles triangle in the sky. Under my boots was 1,500 feet of air then traffic then asphalt.

Three others touched down on the roof deck, and Lava was already at the glass doors, working the security system. Meanwhile, I was still flapping in the wind.

EEEEEEEEEEE! The alarm sounded off. "*Warning.* Enemy drone detected seven hundred thirty feet below and rising," said my AI in her unnervingly calm voice. I looked down through my boots and could see the armed drone's blades slice the air. It looked like a quarter-size black helicopter with no lights, probably used only at night to avoid day gawkers.

"Locke, evade!" said Tye. I yanked the toggles on both risers and swung up. The drone remained motionless, but didn't spot me. Drones often have a blind spot: they cannot see above them, which might have been a reason Lava chose this crazy ingress route.

"Locke, you're about to be blown off DZ!" said Tye, meaning I would soon cross a line of no return and have to land somewhere on the street below. Although, I doubted I would get that far. The drones would spot me and shoot up my canopy, if it was armed. I would fall to my death.

"*Warning. Enemy drone rising,*" said the AI. I had only seconds. Far down, I could see the Thirty-Fourth Street subway
yard. I could try to make it.

"Locke, the drone!" said Tye, strain in his voice. Lava and the
rest of the team already disappeared inside the building. Apparently, Tye was my assigned battle buddy after all.

Just get back over the balcony, I thought as I strained on the
risers and did a sharp 180-degree turn, catching an updraft. Fifty
feet beneath me was the tip of the triangle, and two hundred feet
below that was the ascending drone.

"Locke!" cried Tye as I drifted away from the balcony and
over the street. In one second, I would be below the DZ.

Now or never, I thought, I pulled hard on the left riser, and
violently swung toward the balcony, twenty-five feet away. At the
same time, I yanked the quick-release on both risers and hurtled
weightless through the air, with 1,100 feet of space between me
and the ground. Glancing down, I saw the drone's blades rising
as I bicycle-kicked to maximize my forward momentum. But
I came up short. I bounced off the outside of the observation
deck's glass wall, just managing to grab the top with my left hand.

"Locke, hang on!" said Tye, rushing over to help me, but the
glass walls surrounding the observation deck were fifteen feet
high. I was dangling in space.

"Locke, the drone!" said Tye, as the *chop chop chop* got louder.
With a grunt, I did a pull up in full combat gear and threw a leg
over the glass wall. I rolled over the rim and slid down the safe
side, hitting hard. Meaty hands pulled me to my feet.

"Move! Move!" cried Tye, and we sprinted for the observation
deck's door. Apollo command had already hacked the building's
security as we HALOed in, but it could not control the armed
drone.

"Inside!" he said as we dove behind large planters. We could hear the thing hover above the observation deck, scanning, but the planters concealed our body heat from the drone's thermal cameras. Off a side-window reflection, I could see the machine's silhouette. It had weapons pods on its flanks. No guns or missiles protruded, but their purpose was unmistakable. After a moment, it buzzed away.

"Gutsy move, Locke, jumping like that. I thought you were a goner."

"Victory to the bold," I said, still catching my breath. "Is that thing actually armed?"

"Yeah, but don't worry. Apollo shut down the internal defenses, so we should be good to go now."

I paused, digesting what he just said. "Defenses? Like, *armed* defenses?"

"Roger."

"What kind of skyscraper is this?" I whispered.

"A fortress. The first ninety floors are normal. The top ten are the enemy's North American headquarters. They own the whole block too, through a front company, of course."

"Who is the enemy? Who flies armed drones in New York?"

"I'll let Lava fill you in. But they're like us. Dangerous. Watch your six."

"Tye, sitrep?" said Lava in his command voice.

"Operative recovered, area secure. Moving to your location now," said Tye, standing up. He looked like a black cyborg in his head-to-toe armor but moved like a gymnast. "Stay quick, Locke. Follow me close. Trust nothing in here. Nothing."

I nodded as I removed my wingsuit and oxygen bottle, but was alarmed by Tye's cryptic warning. I had no idea what we were walking into, other than it was lethal. Tye ran into the darkness and I followed, weapon at the ready.

CHAPTER 17

Rock Creek Parkway is a secret highway that runs through Washington that only locals know. There are few, if any, signs that note the entrances in order to keep the tourists out. Trucks are illegal, and those who sneak on get their tops chopped off by the low stone bridges.

The winding road snakes up the center of the city, but it looks like a bucolic valley in Connecticut rather than the urban hubbub surrounding it. During rush hour, parts of Rock Creek convert to one-way, terrifying lost tourists who mistakenly wander into its corridor.

Picnic tables with stone grills line Rock Creek for Washingtonians to have family outings. Some even have weddings there. More than a few picnic areas are set back from the road, and a few are hidden. After midnight, it was a place for teens to hook up or conspirators to meet.

The two black convoys arrived almost simultaneously. Three armored Chevy Suburbans from the south and three more from the north pulled into a parking lot side by side but facing opposite directions.

After a moment, armed men from the middle vehicles stepped out and opened the passenger doors. A tall man with a cane stepped from one backseat to the other, the door shutting behind him.

"Thank you for meeting me at this hour."

"We are allies, if not friends," said the man with the cane in a raspy voice.

"We have a new problem."

"Oh?"

"More of a complication than a problem. But left to fester, it will become a problem."

"What is it?" said the hobbled man with displeasure.

"The president. He's not following along with the script."

Silence. Finally, the man with the cane broke it. "But isn't that your job?"

More silence. "It's *our* job."

The man with the cane squeezed the ivory handle in rage but his weathered face revealed no emotion. "And what do you want me to do about it?"

"The CIA. They're the source of the problem. You can reach them in ways I cannot. Can I count on your—" the man paused, choosing his words carefully "—oblique approach to steer their analysis?"

The man with the cane could not help but chuckle. "It's the oldest joke in Washington: research agenda. You want me to provide the agenda and they perform the research? Seems like something you could easily manage yourself."

"Not this time. It has to come from outside government. It has to come from your organization. Understand that I'm not asking you to alter the plan; just throw them off the scent."

The man with the cane pondered the task with displeasure, but finally acquiesced. "Fine. I will see what we can do, but I make no promises." He looked the other man in the eyes. "We go back a long way, you and I. But do not take our friendship for granted. If you continue to modify our original agreement, there will be consequences."

The other man stiffened, not expecting such a riposte, then nodded. The man with the cane rapped on the window, and a stocky bodyguard opened the bulletproof door.

Two minutes later, the convoys sped off into the darkness, going in opposite directions.

CHAPTER 18

Tye ran like a heavily armed gazelle, bounding over desks, couches, and whatever else stood in his way. My parkour skills were respectable, but Tye leapt before he looked. It was suicide.

"Tye, hold up!" I panted.

"Keep pace," he commanded, speeding around a corner. I rounded it and saw the open elevator shaft.

"Tye!!" I shouted, skidding to a stop at the edge of the 1,100-foot drop. Peering over, I glimpsed only darkness, and listened for the crash of his body, 101 stories down. I would need to find a different route down.

"You think I'm that easy to kill?" said Tye over the headset.

"Where are you?"

"Floor ninety-seven. Beat feet!"

This is going to be sparky, I thought, as I backed up and then ran for the shaft. I timed it so my left foot pushed off the edge of the open elevator shaft while I spread my arms wide. My inner right arm caught the high-tension cables midflight, spinning me hard clockwise. I locked my legs around the cables, but I was not prepared for the speedy descent. My body zipped down the slick cables, and my stomach rose to my throat. Floor 97's door was propped open and I had only one chance, so I leapt. My body was weightless once more as I plunged through the darkness. My left hand caught the elevator's threshold while the rest of me dangled down the shaft. With a grunt, I heaved myself up and faced Tye, who was waiting for me.

"You have a thing for hurtling through space?" he asked. I could almost see the smirk through his black visor.

"Yeah, it makes me feel all tingly inside," I joked, but he simply turned and kept moving. So did I. The place looked like a high-end hedge fund office: ultramodern glass and steel design, exotic wood flooring, and whacko modern art. It smelled of cappuccino and rug cleaner, even though there were no rugs.

The hallway emptied into a two-story atrium, with a glass balcony and near-360-degree view of the city, as seen through the floor's glass walls and floor-to-ceiling windows. It was magnificent. Overlooking us from the balcony was artistic stupidity: an eight-foot marble statue of a man that looked like Michelangelo's *David* except his head was a gigantic chrome cloud. No doubt it was "priceless."

The team had moved all the furniture out of one corner and were now measuring distances from the walls with laser range finders. Another was taking the measurements and drawing a perfect circle on the Brazilian hardwood floor with indelible marker.

"Lava, we're here," said Tye.

"Roger. Tye, on me. Locke, on demo."

Demolitions. I liked demo. One of Lava's team was pulling out thick plastic tubes from his rucksack and screwing them together. As I approached, he didn't look up; he only held out a roll of 100 mph tape.

"Take it, rook," he said.

"Ain't no rookie," I responded, snatching the black duct tape from his hand. "I was leading an Apollo team when you were still a Bat Boy." It was a term for an army ranger. Rangers were my friends and I had gone through ranger school, but they were not known for subtlety, just like this guy.

"You watch yourself down there," he said coolly.

"Placement area ready," said the guy holding the marker in a deep bass. The ex-ranger and I carried over the tube, which was surprisingly heavy. On the floor, the trooper had drawn a four-foot diameter circle, noting distances and angles to various side walls.

"Ready the tape," said the ex-ranger, laying down the tube on the circle while I taped it to the floor. It fit perfectly. The tube looked like thick det cord, but it was something else.

"What is this stuff?" I asked.

"Been a while, eh, rook?" he said smugly while fastening the blasting caps. "It's Apollo proprietary: two parts CL-20 and one part HMX. Make big boom."

"Omega, we are preparing to breach," said Lava, and we scurried for cover.

"You are green," responded Omega.

"Fire in the hole!" cried the ex-ranger, and I muted my helmet's enhanced hearing. The explosion's shock wave walloped me in the chest, and shook the floor and windows. The marble man statue tottered and crashed to the floor with another loud boom, decapitating him. I sidestepped the chrome cloud head as it rolled by, adding a sense of surrealism. No alarms sounded, due to Apollo's building hack. But some security measures cannot be hacked, and my HUD indicated fire teams a few floors below us moving up the stairs.

"Valhalla, you are red. Security mobilized," said Omega. "Engaging countermeasures. You have sixty seconds before contact."

"Roger, Omega," said Lava, not surprised, as the team vanished down the newly made hole. In the background, I could hear automatic gunfire on the floors below, but not from small arms. They sounded heavier, like crew-served machine guns. But here? It could only mean one thing.

"Are those automated turrets?" I asked Tye.

"Affirmative. Retractable ceiling turrets on the floors above and below. They're controlled by the building's automated defense system, but Omega hacked them when we were in freefall.

Now Omega is using the turrets against the enemy's quick reaction force, but it won't take long for the QRF to take them out."

"Fifty-five seconds," said Lava as he disappeared down the hole. Tye dropped down and I followed, tucking my arms and weapon to my chest. The room below was dark and warm.

"Don't touch nothing," said Tye as he moved forward. It was a computer room. Actually, it was a computer floor. Rows of black computer racks the size of refrigerators lined a raised floor, presumably for cabling. The only entrance was a twenty-ton, circular bank vault door—sealed and locked—explaining why Lava chose to breach through the ceiling. The ex-ranger was already placing C4 charges in its guts.

"Find Alpha three-one-three-five," commanded Lava, and the team fanned out and searched the server rows.

I flipped on my point-to-point comms with Tye. "What are we looking for?"

"A specific node board, in a specific rack, in a specific server, in a specific quadrant. Alpha three-one-three-five," he said as I followed.

"This has gotta be the most expensive server farm on the planet, given the real estate prices around here," I quipped.

"Ain't no server farm, it's a supercomputer. And it ain't no ordinary supercomputer; it's a Frontier Super-AI, the fastest in the world. Even faster than its twin at Oak Ridge National Laboratory, and smarter too. It runs our enemy's everything."

Impressed, I asked: "And we're hacking it?"

"No," said Tye, stopping to face me. Multicolor computer lights reflected off his black visor, giving him a robotic look. "No one hacks Elektra, and she would fight back if they tried."

"Wait, it has a name?"

"Just watch your six in here," he said with impatience, and continued down the row. Looking, I noticed every other rack had an enormous but subdued letter on it in an ultramodern font spelling E-L-E-K-T-R-A across the entire row, with a silver lightning bolt through the A. I wondered if bullets would do any good against a foe like Elektra.

"Thirty seconds," said Lava. Tye and I were zigzagging, looking for the magic number.

"Valhalla, enemy on your floor," said Omega.

"Copy. Come on people, find me that rack!" yelled Lava.

My head was a volcano of questions, as I scanned for Alpha 3135. "Tye, if Elektra can't be hacked, then how did Apollo hack the building?"

"Because the building is not Elektra, and the enemy is not the only one with a Super AI."

"Wait, Apollo has an AI too?" I asked, flabbergasted. Apollo was many things, but not that.

Tye turned to me. "Who says it's ours? It's our client's. Now shut your pie hole and search."

Who was the client? Who was the enemy? What were we doing here? It reminded me why I left Apollo: ask a question and get two more in return.

"Omega, status?" asked Lava.

"Helicopter extraction on standby. Ground recovery team ready," replied Omega.

Lava paced. I had never seen him pace before. Perhaps he was nervous because he knew how Elektra would fight back. "Any new breach points?"

"Negative. Just the main entrance."

Lava turned to face that direction. "Is the vault door prepped and demoed?"

"Affirmative," said the ex-ranger over the comms. "Once the tangos touch it, the internal stanchions will blow and render it an unmovable hunk of junk. It will be impassable."

No sooner had he said that when a muffled explosion came from the enormous vault door, followed by a dull thud. We were sealed in, but not for long. The enemy would somehow find another way in; we sure would.

"Omega, update!" said Lava.

"Main entrance sabotaged. Tangos moving to points here and here," said Omega, and my HUD showed red dots massing at opposite ends of the floor. "They must be secret breach points, where the walls are thin, for contingencies like this. We estimate you have one minute before they breach, maybe less."

Silence as Lava weighed his options. Abort was one of them, but I've never known him to give up. Ever. Finally, he spoke: "Tye, Locke on breach point one. Hernandez, Kim on breach point two. The rest find me our node board!"

Tye and I sprinted to the other side of the floor and took up fighting positions, pointing our weapons at the breach point. At present, it was a wall. Soon it would be a hole with tangos swarming out. We each took cover behind a computer rack, laying in the prone position. By my side were two grenades, ready to throw, while Tye's weapon had an integrated 40 mm launcher. I could hear Tye controlling his breathing, readying for what came next.

"Found it. Cover down on me," said one of the commandos. Peering behind me, I saw two commandos far down the row pulling out a tray from the rack; inside were vertical rows of circuit boards, about twenty in all. Another unpacked a flat ballistic case he parachuted in with him.

"Omega, confirming node board Alpha three-one-three-five," said Lava.

"Good copy. You are green to proceed," said Omega.

"Careful now, we get only one shot at this," said the Israeli operator. One of the commandos inspected the contents of Alpha 3135, pulling out five large circuit boards and dumping them on the floor.

"Now hand me the replacements," he said. The other commando opened the ballistic case and took out five nearly identical boards.

"The swaps must be flawless," said the Israeli, "or Elektra will know."

"Preparing to insert new cards," said Lava.

"Copy, Valhalla. We are standing by for network penetration," replied Omega.

As I listened to the radio chatter, I grew confused. "Tye, you said it was impossible to hack Elektra. But it sounds like we're hacking her. What's going on?"

A pause. "Locke, you're a real burr in my ass, you know that?"

"I'm risking my life for this. You can at least tell me why."

Another pause. "It's true, you can't hack Elektra. We've tried. But there is another way, and it took months to figure out. People died."

"New compute cards inserted. Performing electrical tests on the PCBs," said the Israeli. Somewhere beyond the wall, I heard a loud clang. They were getting closer.

"Tye, what's the other way? What are we doing here?" I asked.

"Elektra can only be hacked from the *inside*. Someone has to physically swap out good circuit boards with bad ones inside the artificial neural network. But it can't be any circuit board; it has to be five specific boards within a critical control node."

"Alpha three-one-three-five," I said.

"Correct. We corrupted Alpha three-one-three-five with vulnerabilities our AI can exploit—"

"A back door," I interrupted again.

"Yeah, if you want to call it that. If all goes well, our AI will hack their AI and we win. If not . . . improvise."

Improvise. It was the Apollo way, and not my favorite strategy for dealing with mortality, even though I was good at it.

"Omega, swap complete. We are ready to integrate node

board back into the system. Proceed?" said Lava. I saw the team's collective heart rates spike on my HUD.

"Proceed."

Sirens blared and floodlights lit the entire floor.

"*Emergency.* Oxygen levels dropping," warned my onboard AI, although "AI" seemed a misnomer in the presence of Elektra. The comms channels went static. Even the polite female AI voice began distorting into a grotesque baritone as a massive electronic tidal wave jammed our systems. My head pounded, too.

"Guess it didn't go well," I shouted to Tye over the shriek of the sirens.

"Mission fail," confirmed Tye.

The wall in front of us blew inward, spraying our armor with concrete and steel. Elite mercenaries wearing advanced body armor and oxygen masks assaulted through the breach, shooting. Tye and I threw grenades into the hole, and the concussive blast threw them against the wall. But one got up, his body armor unbelievably strong. Then a second.

You gotta be kidding me, I thought, as a third sat upright. I had never seen grenade-proof armor, unless it was those turtled-up Explosive Ordnance Disposal guys who looked like a Kevlar Michelin Man.

Let's see how good your armor is, I thought. My SCAR fired high-velocity 7.62 mm cartridges with tungsten-carbide bullets, specifically designed to penetrate body armor. In rapid succession, I shot the three in the face, where body armor is weakest. They dropped instantly, but others swarmed in.

"There are too many. Let's go!" screamed Tye, but I knew he was wrong.

I have to thin the herd, or we won't make it five steps, I thought. Switching tactics, I shot three in the leg. They crumbled on impact, and their buddies swooped in and pulled them to safety, ridding me of nine enemies with three bullets in two seconds. The enemy had temporarily ceded the battlefield.

Tye yanked my boot. "E and E!" he shouted through his face mask, telling me to escape and evade. The enemy mercs were gathering on the other side of the breach, readying for another assault.

"Let's go-o-o!" yelled Tye. I pulled a grenade from my vest and threw it into the breach. The enemy mercs scattered instantly, but were too late. The explosion caught two in the chest, blowing them into the wall, killing them. The rest recovered, but they would not throw grenades back as we were in the guts of Elektra.

"Triple time!!" he shouted. I ran but grew dizzy from the depleted oxygen. We ditched our HALO oxygen bottles with the wingsuits on the 101st floor, but kept our reserve chutes and harnesses.

Tye staggered then collapsed, succumbing to the lack of oxygen. I grabbed him by the arms and lifted up, doing the fireman's carry, and stumbled toward the ceiling hole.

"We're surrounded," yelled Lava, as he grabbed Tye and lifted him up like a rag doll. Four hands reached down and pulled him up. I followed, then Lava. We were the last.

"Fire in the hole!" shouted Lava, pulling out a shiny steel cannister from his pack. He flipped open the control pad and armed it, then stuck his head down the hole and chucked the bomb into Elektra and the other mercs.

"Away! Away!" he screamed, as he stumbled backward from the hole. I turned to run and felt my ears compress like a skydive, then the shock wave blew me sideways through a glass wall. I heard and felt nothing, just blackness.

"Get up!"

Gunfire.

"Get up!!"

Explosions.

"Wake up!" It was Tye, crouching above me and firing, empty cartridges bouncing off my visor. I rolled over, disoriented from being knocked out by the blast. Flames licked up from the hole in the ground and black smoke filled the atrium. So much for Elektra.

Tye bolted away, but I felt too woozy to move. The rest of the team moved out, firing in short controlled bursts as they retrograded. Glass flew everywhere, as the firefight exploded the crystal office and modern art. Simultaneously, the sprinkler system rained on us, creating a surreal battlespace.

"Watch the left flank!" shouted Lava, followed by the buzz of a mini-Gatling gun and a waterfall of glass shards.

Get in the fight! I willed my legs to move, but they were kryptonite. As I lay sideways, I could see boots advancing along the floor, and they were not Apollo's.

Get. In. The. Fight. Shaking, my hands reached into my medpack and extracted an ampule. Opening my visor, I bit off the cap and stuck the ampule up a nostril, squeezed, and inhaled. Starbursts lit up behind my eyes as I felt my body power up. My heart turboed and each breath felt like a scuba tank of air. My senses buzzed and my limbs were itching to pounce. My brain turned predator.

The boots were approaching, but in slow motion now. I rolled to the prone position, SCAR up, and fired four shots. Three men tumbled to the ground, screaming as they clutched their blown-out ankles. Three more shots ended them.

I got up and saw I was alone, except for the enemy mercs twenty feet away. For a millisecond, we all paused, equally surprised. Then the gunfire erupted. I drew like lighting, capping one in the head as I dove sideways and slammed into the floor. A small, octagonal grenade bounced off a cubicle desk and rolled to a stop in front of me, and I sprint-rolled behind a steel filing cabinet. The explosion was deafening, even through my enclosed Apollo helmet, and propelled me into the next cubicle. But I felt nothing, other than the urge to kill. The chemical I snorted unlocked the primitive brain, and it was why everyone at Apollo called it "Mr. Hyde Dust."

Taking a grenade from my vest, I pulled the pin, cooked it for three seconds, and lobbed it for an airburst. The shock wave blew shrapnel through the cubicles like paper. The enemy screamed, and I liked the sound.

Brrrrrrrrrrr. I ducked and the cubicles around me exploded in splinters as a mini-gun shredded the area with six thousand rounds per minute. I could hear the multiple barrels spin to a stop, and a merc shouting at me in Russian. Poking my SCAR rifle around the corner, I could see the shooter from my muzzle camera. He was huge with a dense beard, and was so cocky that he stood straight up on a desk for all to see, like death itself.

Screw him, I thought. I knew I should keep moving and find Lava, but I wanted to rectify this faux grim reaper. Low-crawling, I slipped under two cubicles and peeked over the rim with my muzzle-cam. Fake reaper still there, like a statue in the sprinkler rain.

Good, I thought. With adrenaline-crazed fury, I popped up, obtained a perfect sight picture of his skull, and squeezed. One shot, one kill. A hailstorm of lead responded to my surprise attack, and I rushed ahead. The enemy ran down a parallel hallway, and we fired at each other through the glass walls on full automatic. Glass blew everywhere.

Find Lava and Tye, I thought. Through multiple glass walls, on the other side of the floor, I could see muzzle flashes and explosions. *Has to be them.*

As I sprinted, two mercs followed. Like Tye, I used parkour to leap over furniture, and shot my way through glass doors. A bullet clipped my left scapula, ricocheting off my armor and making me stumble.

Enough! I sprint-leapt onto the thirty-foot mahogany table and flipped so I was skidding backward on my stomach with my weapon up and aimed at the door. The merc charged in and I shot him in the chest. A second merc dove in as I skidded off the table. We unloaded at each other under the table, but hit only chairs and table legs, sending splinters everywhere.

Keep moving or die! screamed my intuition. I ran out a different exit, toward Lava and the skyscraper's windows.

"You are red," said Omega, the signal improving as I got closer to the windows.

Not helpful! I thought as I emptied a magazine and swapped it out for a new one.

Ahead of me, I could see the team pinned down in a swank corner office. They turned a massive brazilwood desk on its side for cover as a ring of mercs fired into the office space. The glass windows were shot out, and the enemy was trying to drive Lava's team over the edge. This was not a prisoners-of-war kind of war.

One of Lava's team was frantically waving me off.

Why the wave-off? I was trying to rescue them, I thought, then the glass walls around me exploded with the *brrrrrrrrrrrr* of another mini-gun. Bits of ceiling were still collapsing on me as I snuck my muzzle-cam above the remnants of a desk. To my right was the gunner, tucked behind a weightbearing wall, its dry wall shot away to reveal steel and concrete. To my left was the drone in a perfect hover ten meters outside the windows. Its weapon pods were retracted, showing an M134 Minigun and two missiles, in case I made a jump for it. As if that were even an option.

Well, that sucks, I thought, as I was thoroughly pinned down.

I didn't do surrender, and they didn't do POWs. Life just got simpler.

"Locke, is that you? Sitrep, over," said Lava over my earpiece. Being near the window restored some communications. The drone buzzed back and forth between us. It dared not open fire above Manhattan, unless we did something stupid.

"Affirmative. I'm pinned, over," I said.

"Roger. Keep your head down. We're about to exit, just be ready."

About to exit? Maybe shell shock had finally warped Lava's mind. I didn't blame the man; he was a battlefield legend. But there was no way out this time.

"Locke, pull out your reserve's pilot chute," instructed Tye.

"Say again?" I asked with incredulity.

"Ready your pilot chute!" yelled Lava.

No, no, no, no! my mind screamed as my hands snaked out my reserve parachute's pilot chute. Lava intended to BASE jump out the window, which was crazy. But I remember Lava once told me: it's not crazy if it works.

"Locke, on my command, shoot out the windows," said Lava.

"Copy," I said, leveling my weapon at one of the huge window panes.

Lava began the countdown as the enemy mercs crept forward. "Three, two, one, fire."

I unloaded half my magazine and the thick glass blew away, but not all at once. It was thick stuff. The rest of the team blew out their corner office, and the drone zoomed toward Lava's position. But he was ready.

"Fire in the hole!" cried Lava, as one of his commandos popped up with a stubby antitank missile on his shoulder and fired at the drone. It exploded, and the weapon's backblast knocked down the enemy mercs.

"Jump!" cried Lava, and the whole team leapt out the shattered windows, ninety-eight stories above the street. Without hesitating, I sprinted for the broken window in front of me, holding my pilot chute in my hand. I heard automatic gunfire behind me, and felt the zing of bullets around my head as I leapt into space and dropped like a stone. Far below, I could see a ball of fire falling, the dead drone. Seconds later it crashed through the roof of a nearby building in a flash of orange.

One thousand, I counted as I plummeted headfirst. I could see my dark silhouette against the skyline reflected in the mirror-like building. If I deployed my parachute too soon, I would be in range of the enemy. Too late and I would be splat.

Two thousand. The skyscraper was getting closer the farther I fell, as the wall tapered outward. If I didn't pull soon, I would smear the mirrored glass like a bug on a windshield.

Three thousand. I let go of the pilot chute and it caught wind, dragging the reserve parachute out of the pack. The opening G shock never felt better, but the crosswind blew me back toward the building, a dangerous situation.

"Damn you, riser," I said, pulling on my risers, but the parachute barely responded. Reserve parachutes are like doughnut spare tires; they get you where you need to go, but not with performance.

Uh-oh, I thought, as I drifted toward my reflection. The parachute would collapse if I collided with the building, and then I would fall. Looking up, I saw eleven other dark parachutes, all heading south. Somehow, they escaped the crosswind.

"Think!" I said, as I watched my reflection about to collide with me. I had maybe twenty feet before impact. Then I began rocking back and forth, like a kid on a swing set, a trick I learned as a paratrooper in the U.S. Army's Eighty-Second Airborne Division. I got higher. On my third swing, my boot tips nearly scraped the skyscraper's windows.

"Almost there," I said, swinging backward and then forward again. This time, I planted both feet on the window and pushed off. The next swing landed me on the window, and I was parallel to the ground. I pulled in my risers slightly, the parachute canopy partially collapsed, and my body begin to fall. At the same time, I twisted around so I faced straight down toward the street.

No fear, I commanded myself. I ran sideways along the windows at a forty-five-degree angle, the half-inflated canopy following me like a balloon. As I gained speed, air filled the parachute and yanked me off my feet. I swung out hard and felt the g-force against my harness, but now momentum was moving me away from the building. Working the risers, I sped away from the mirrored tower.

"Omega, this is Valhalla. Need immediate extraction. Lighting up LZ now," said Lava as we floated down. A light blue rectangle lit up in my HUD a few hundred feet in front of me. Our landing zone, or LZ, was a large warehouse roof. Two parachutes touched down in complete silence.

"Copy Valhalla. Choppers inbound, three mikes," replied Apollo command. As I floated down, I could see the warehouse was the length of the entire block and was actually a U.S. Post Office processing plant.

Four more chutes landed. Several stories down were late-night garbage trucks and street noise. But there were no sirens. No police. It seemed that I had stumbled into a secret war.

As I drifted in, I readied my body for a parachute landing fall. The ground came up faster than expected, and I landed on my feet, ass, and head, in that order. Not my best. But I was in grass! I looked around, and the top of the building was a converted meadow, almost custom made for renegade parachutists.

"Outstanding!" I cried, and heard others laughing and joking, too.

"Omega, this is Valhalla. We have twelve chutes, no injuries or casualties," said Lava, as I heard choppers approaching.

"Good copy, Valhalla."

Two black helicopters flying nap of the earth with no lights suddenly appeared above us. I flopped on my chute to prevent it from being sucked into the rotors, as they descended in perfect synchronization and hovered a foot above the roof.

"Get in! Get in!" yelled Lava. Abandoning my chute, I sprinted for the closest chopper and jumped in, next to the door gunner. Four Apollo drones hovered nearby, acting the armed sentry. As we pulled pitch, I saw black parachutes swirl beneath us before disappearing into the night.

A big paw clasped my shoulder. Turning around, I saw Tye with his helmet off. "Thanks for saving my ass back there. I would have suffocated for sure, and they would have capped me."

Lava removed his helmet, too, a big smile on his face. "You did good, Locke. You did good."

CHAPTER 19

The next morning Lin walked down Connecticut Avenue with her scarf up over her face. The FBI would be after her by now, but she knew they were too preoccupied to care. At least for now. A cold drizzle had blanketed the city, and people walked with their heads down. An umbrella almost poked her in the eye, and she swatted it away unconsciously. Her mind was elsewhere.

What cargo was the Lena *delivering?* She thought, assuming Dmitri could be trusted. As far as informants were concerned, he ranked toward the bottom. Lowest of the low. However, he was the only lead she had, and her future hung on it. *I need to deliver a big clue to get back into the FBI,* she thought grimly.

She'd spent the previous night lying in bed, trying to put the pieces together, but they didn't fit. The *Lena's* mystery cargo and the defunct Shulaya mob running it. The FBI was so distracted chasing terrorists that it was missing the Russian angle. *Or,* she thought with alarm, *perhaps there is no Russia angle.*

"Keep it together, girl," she told herself as she marched on. "Trust your gut."

When she got home from the bar last night, she texted Jason to call her, but he was already asleep. Then he texted her this morning saying he would call her as soon as he got into the office. That was about now.

She stopped at the Mayflower Hotel to get out of the weather. The place had a marble foyer and establishment Washington ambiance. The lobby had large TV monitors for a news-obsessed city, and they all showed the same thing: a partially burned roof of a Manhattan building where a drone crashed. According to reporters, it malfunctioned and the owner retrieved the wreckage before police could investigate, raising important issues about drone safety and regulations. Jen ignored the news as she took a seat in the foyer bistro and removed her wet jacket. A waiter promptly appeared.

"Green tea, please," she said, and the waiter nodded and left. Lin looked around the lobby but saw nothing suspicious. Just the usual: foreign diplomats, well-heeled lobbyists, and Midwestern tourists. She checked her personal phone again but still nothing from Jason.

Come on, Jason, she thought. Jason was her only inside contact, and the only person who could feed her FBI updates. It was times like this that she wished she could talk to her dad. He always knew what to do in a crisis of confidence. It seemed he had a Chinese saying for every contingency.

For a second, Lin thought about throwing the *I Ching,* asking the ancient oracle what she should do. She had three coins and could look up the *I Ching*'s text on her phone. All she needed was a hexagram or two. Then her tea arrived.

"Thank you," she said to the waiter, and inhaled the warm vapors with a smile. A crew of Chinese businessmen sat nearby, and she couldn't help overhearing their conversation. Sometimes the Chinese got lazy, assuming no one understood them in DC, so they could speak freely. Their mistake. However, in this case they were simply talking about the attractive young waitress from the previous night's steak dinner, albeit in colorful language.

Ugh. Men. They are all the same, Lin thought in Mandarin.

Then she felt it. A buzzing in her purse. She dug around her Glock and pulled out her personal phone. It was Jason.

"Jason!" she said, a bit too loudly. The Chinese men stopped talking and spotted her. They began ogling her while assessing her physical features in Mandarin, like a risqué beauty contest. She turned away and cupped her hand over her phone, so no one could hear her. "Jason, I need your help."

"Lin, where the hell are you?" said Jason. There was a brief silence, then he spoke in a low tone so others wouldn't hear him in the open-bay office. "Our boss went ballistic and said he fired you. Is that true?"

"Jason, be quiet and listen. This is important. Do you have a pen?"

"But Jen—"

"Jason," she interrupted again. "It doesn't matter. Here's what matters: the ship. Are you still working the Newark ship case?"

"No, the ADIC shut down the investigation shortly after you disappeared. Yesterday they had me tracking down hazmat licenses in New Mexico. Now I'm researching demolition vendors in Oakland. Super boring. Seems I'm just a computer monkey, backstopping whatever field office is most overwhelmed. I didn't join the FBI for this crap."

She ignored his rant. "The ship's name is *Lena*. It sailed from Novorossiysk in the Black Sea, and not Antwerp."

"Wait. Are you still chasing the ship—"

"Jason!" she yelled and the Chinese men froze and stared at her, then continued their conversation. Lin resumed her low voice. "Take notes. We don't have much time."

"OK, OK, fine." She heard him rummage around his desk for a pen. "How do you spell Novo-whatever it was?"

She spelled it. "The *Lena* made two trips, one in August and another nine days ago. It flew a Liberian flag and had a Russian crew. Owner is unknown. You can pull up the arrival manifests and port logs for details." She could hear him scribbling. "Each trip had one unregistered container, and the Shulaya secretly off-loaded it before the *Lena* went through CBP," she said, referring to Customs and Border Protection.

"What's a Shulaya?"

"Not what, but who. They are a particularly nasty branch of the Russian mafia in New York. We busted them over a year ago, and the FBI thinks they are defunct, but they're not. That gives them perfect cover for action, since the Shulaya are no longer on the FBI's radar."

"How do you know all this?" said Jason when he finished writing.

"Don't ask. It's better if you don't know."

Jason paused, comprehending the gravity of his situation. He could get fired, too, but he knew Jen wasn't bullshitting. "All right, go on."

"The Shulaya delivered each container to a transit warehouse in Secaucus, New Jersey."

"Do you know the address?"

"No, but it should be easy to find. They are probably linked to a warehouse. Check the databases."

"Will do. What was in the containers?"

Lin sighed. "No one knows. The Shulaya never opened them. Weren't allowed."

"Seems unusual."

"It is," said Lin. "Listen, Jason. You need to get a team to investigate the warehouse in Secaucus ASAP. That's where the trail goes cold."

She heard him guffaw on the other end. "Who do you think I am, the director?"

"Seriously, Jason, you need to find a way. Do whatever it takes." She could sense Jason's apprehension. It was a big ask.

Higher-ups would question him and there were no good answers. It could end badly for him.

"Why don't you call your old task force?" he said. "I'm a nobody to them, and they would remember you. Even if you did—" He was about to say *screw up their major bust* but obviously thought better of it.

"Because I'm toxic right now," she said reflexively, but then reconsidered it. *No, they would invite me in for an interview, then nab me.* She had to remain on the street where she could investigate the Russian angle and feed Jason information, who could work the inside. It was their only chance.

"Wait! Hold on," said Jason. Their boss was talking in the background, then his voice got muffled, replaced by a steady *thump-thump-thump* that quickened. Lin realized Jason was holding the phone to his chest and she could hear his heartbeat. Whatever her boss was saying was stressing Jason out.

A minute later, Jason returned.

"You OK?" she asked.

"No, not really. That was you-know-who, and he's asking about you again and now threatening my career. He wants your gun and badge." Jason paused. "I don't think I can cover for you much longer, Jen. He senses I'm holding out on him during a national emergency. This is career suicide." His voice was stressed.

Lin felt awful, but only for an instant. "Jason, this is bigger than either of us, or the boss. The terrorist attack was not done by terrorists, do you understand? It's a smoke screen, and the FBI is lost in it. We need to shift the Bureau's focus toward the real perpetrators before it's too late."

She waited for him to say something. Silence.

"Jason, I need you. I'll work the outside, and you work the inside. Together we can find enough evidence to reorient the

Bureau. We have a duty, remember? We swore an oath. It's not to our boss, it's to our country. Can I count on you?"

Silence.

"Jason, can I count on you?" she said with a tinge of desperation. Everything would be for naught without someone on the inside she could trust, and that left only one person.

"Jason?" she asked softly.

"Count me in."

CHAPTER 20

A caravan of black vans and an armored SWAT truck that looked like it came straight out of Afghanistan sped over a bridge and took a right on Seaview Drive, which had no view at all. Secaucus was an industrial park masquerading as a town. Vast warehouses lined the street and the traffic was mostly trucks. A trainyard was a central feature, surrounded by brownish water and interstates. In the distance was its client, the Manhattan skyline. The town was part of the logistical warren in north New Jersey that fed the great city and much of America's northeast.

The SWAT convoy traveled at speed, passing trucks with ease, but it did not use sirens or flashing blue lights. The element of surprise was essential.

"Approaching objective," said Sergeant Corelli, the SWAT commander, over the radio. He wore two sergeant's hats: one with the police and another with Army Special Forces in the reserves. He had completed three combat tours in Afghanistan and one in Iraq before seeking the quiet life of a New Jersey SWAT commando. Things had never been busier.

"Get ready," said Corelli as they took a left turn and snaked around a back street, crossing railroad tracks. Ahead of them was a warehouse, small by Secaucus standards. It was merely a gigantic building rather than a city block with a roof. It looked decrepit and unused. The parking lot was empty and weeds sprouted out of cracks in the asphalt. Beyond the building were marshes and the Hackensack River, a simmering toxic stew. A chain-link fence topped with concertina wire surrounded the facility, and the entry was locked by a heavy chain and meaty padlock.

"Breach team," said Corelli as they rolled to a stop. Two men in black fatigues jumped out of a van and popped the chain with bolt cutters. The armor vehicle rammed open the gate and the two men hopped back in the van.

"There," said Corelli, pointing to a front door made of steel with an iron outer gate. One van drove around the back, covering the rear exits. The other dropped off its team in front of the warehouse and then zoomed back to the main entrance, blocking the only vehicular escape route. The armored truck pulled up to the front door.

"Out, out, out!" yelled team leaders as SWAT ran out of the vehicles, all dressed in black. They had helmets with built-in radios, ballistic goggles, combat vests, Glock .40s strapped to their thighs, and M4 automatic assault rifles. Four-man teams ran stealthily with muzzles down to the warehouse exits. The lock on the front door was high-end, and not something any locksmith could pick. Small, high-tech cameras were tucked away in every corner of the lot. The place looked abandoned yet had impressive security. A red flag.

I don't like it, thought Corelli. He gestured to the armored truck and it backed up to the iron gate. A SWAT operator opened the back and yanked out a tow strap, attaching one end to the front door's iron gate and the other to the vehicle's tow hitch. Another team member took up position near the door with a shotgun, and two more had their M4s up and aimed at the door.

"Red in position," said the red team leader. Blue, green, and gold followed. From front gate to positions took less than twenty seconds.

"Copy all," replied Corelli. *Go time.* He walked up to the steel door and banged with his fist. "Police! Open up!" He nodded, not waiting for a response. The armored truck accelerated, ripping the iron gate off its hinges and dragging it across the parking lot.

The man with the shotgun chambered a shell and moved in, pointing its muzzle at the door lock. He aimed forty-five degrees in and forty-five degrees down, and squeezed the trigger. *Bang.* The cylinder lock blew inside. The breach man spun around, back-kicked the door open, and stepped out of the way so the stack could enter, Corelli in the lead.

"Go! Go! Go! Go!" he yelled as they entered. The building's alarm screeched in the background, but they ignored it as they worked the dark building.

The SWAT teams made their way through the warehouse, room by room and area by area. Each team had four individuals and shuffled like a centipede: the leader at the head followed by a man who kept his left hand on the shoulder of the guy in front of him and right hand clutching his weapon. When they entered a room, they fanned out, covering their assigned sectors and corners, until the room was clear. The golden rule of SWAT operations: Never enter a room alone. There is one right way and a hundred wrong ways to clear a room. Wrong means death.

"One clear!"

"Two clear!"

"Three clear!"

"Four clear!"

Corelli both loved and feared these missions most. It was a Russian mafia drug bust. You can always count on the Russians to be armed like the Taliban, think like the KGB, and fight like the devil. A tough foe.

"Stay tight, people!" said Corelli as they moved. *Hug the wall, spot the corners, scan your sector.* Corelli was known as a hardass, but the type of hard-ass you wanted next to you during a firefight. He had a simple philosophy: train, train, and train some more. They did this at Fort Dix, where they had access to a live shoot house. It's where his Afghanistan experience shown though, and where he earned the respect of the SWAT unit. Now he was its commander.

Where were all the Russians? thought Corelli. They were supposed to be armed, dangerous, and everywhere. The anonymous tip came in last night, and the command center thought it credible enough to wake his ass up at 2 A.M. By 6 A.M., his team was rolling down Seaview Drive.

One more room to clear, he thought as they shuffled down a lightless hall. Beams from their weapon-mounted tactical flashlights danced around the dark corridor, and the shadows were slightly disorienting. *Focus,* he thought. At the end of the hallway was a wooden door surrounded by unpainted cinderblock. It was locked.

"Shotgun on me," whispered Corelli.

"Shotgun up," muttered another SWAT. The back guy moved forward with a Mossberg and took up his position in front of the door. Corelli stood off at an angle, his M4 pointed at the door. Everyone awaited his nod.

Machine-gun fire ripped through the wooden door, and the guy with the shotgun collapsed, dead. The two other SWAT members returned fire, shielded from the bullet storm by their dead teammate. Corelli wasn't so lucky. He fell backward as if someone had taken a sledge hammer to his chest. He couldn't breathe.

Roll! Roll! he commanded himself, but his body was not taking orders. The gunfire continued through the door, splinters flying everywhere, and he saw another team member fall. *When in doubt, empty the magazine,* he thought and willed his M4 up. He switched to full-auto and emptied his magazine through the

door and the enemy gunfire withered. He heard Russians shouting on the other side.

"Go! Get him out of here," Corelli shouted hoarsely. The last
standing SWAT member dragged his injured comrade around
the corner to safety.

More Russian shouting, and Corelli could hear them cham-
bering fresh clips. It sounded like they were also handling ammo
belts. *Shit,* he thought.

Another SWAT squad was running down the hall to support
him, and Corelli furiously waved them back. Too late. A barrage
of lead shot through the door and two SWAT members fell,
catching it in the vest like him. *They'll be fine,* he reassured himself as he locked and loaded another magazine. The wood door
disintegrated, having absorbed a few hundred rounds too many.

Corelli yanked a flashbang grenade from his tactical vest and
tossed it into the room. It was a nonlethal grenade but could kill
you by heart attack. *Or one can hope,* thought Corelli as he threw
it. SWAT was not issued fragmentary grenades.

BOOOOM!! The sound was deafening and the gunfire
stopped. Corelli staggered to his feet, breathing heavily. Two
other SWAT threw flashbangs into the room. *BOOOOM!!*
BOOOOM!! Corelli smiled.

"On me," he commanded, and the three standing SWAT
shooters followed him into the dark room. Close-quarter automatic gunfire perforated the air, and muzzle flashes created a
strobe-light firefight. People shouted and some screamed. A minute later, only two men stumbled out.

"Clear," said Corelli, blood seeping from his vest, and collapsed.

CHAPTER 21

The sun was rising as Lava and Tye dropped me off at my safe house. Being on Lava's team again was a personal victory, and an important one, too. When I came back to the U.S., I assumed I would be operating alone. Now Lava had my back, and he was the cavalry.

Or so I hoped. Maybe I was Lava's pawn? I still needed to be cautious.

"Yow," I muttered as I removed my body armor and rubbed tender spots. My right flank was bruised purple and throbbed, now that the adrenaline had worn off. Worse, the Mr. Hyde Dust had left me with a pulsing migraine, making me sympathize with Dr. Jekyll. I gulped down three ibuprofens and a liter of water to help the Hyde hangover, but I doubted it would do much good.

"I need rack," I said as I lay down on my cot and zipped up the sleeping bag. Drained, I stared at the ceiling. Five minutes passed. Then ten. My mind and body were a combination of exhausted and exhilarated, and I knew I would never sleep. Twenty more minutes passed.

"Ah, screw it," I said, getting up and grabbing civvies. I had to walk it off, despite the risks. Minutes later I was on the street, not a smart move owing to street cameras, but I needed space to puzzle things out. I bundled up in a hooded parka, hat, jeans, and sunglasses to conceal my face. I looked like an everybody.

No one walked these empty streets but me. Still, I pulled up my scarf over my nose, and avoided cameras. My only companion was a long coal train lumbering toward the city power plant. In my younger days, I would have scaled the chain-link fence and hopped a ride.

Winters is alive. The news haunted me, despite the night's battle and many questions it produced. Winters was all that mattered. How was it possible? True, the guy could talk himself out of a sunburn, but could he talk himself out of a Saudi beheading? I shook my head. Somehow, he had.

I'm not safe, I realized with reflexive dread. If Winters was alive and knew I was here, he would come after me with everything he had. In other words, half of Apollo would try to kill me. I had better chances fighting the Eighty-Second Airborne Division.

In the ride back, Lava told me to stay hidden while he ran the traps. "I'll quietly ask around Apollo's headquarters. If they still think you are dead, then you're safe."

"If Apollo HQ doesn't know you are back, then the government surely wouldn't," added Tye. "And probably not Winters either."

Only if I'm lucky, I thought. The next hours would be like waiting for a verdict in a death penalty trial.

CHAPTER 22

Corelli sat upright in the parked ambulance, wrapped in a wool blanket. His top was stripped down to a black T-shirt, and his left arm hung in a sling with a heavily bandaged shoulder. The bullet went through a seam of his ballistic vest, in between the chest and shoulder Kevlar plates. Thankfully the bullet exited but he would still need surgery, plus months of physical therapy. It might even mean the end of his shooting days, depending on how it healed. Shoulders were tricky. But that wasn't what bothered him.

Three dead. Five wounded. Fuck, he thought. In all his combat missions and SWAT raids, he never lost a single person. It was a source of pride, and why people volunteered to join his team. Now three KIAs in one day, and five hurt. Six, if he included himself.

"You OK, champ?" asked a street cop. The parking lot was teeming with first responders. Police, fire trucks, ambulances, and unmarked FBI vehicles. There was even a van from a government agency he had never heard of before. Who knew what they'd found in the warehouse? He didn't care anymore.

"Yeah, fine," he lied.

"You guys did pretty well. Killed nine Russian mobsters. Wounded three," said the cop. Corelli eyed the three stretchers across the parking lot with police around them. The wounded were handcuffed to the stretchers. Two were smoking while the third lay unconscious. Corelli fantasized about taking the cop's 9 mm, walking over, and capping all three. They deserved it.

"Yeah, guess we did," he lied again.

The FBI had locked down the site for national security reasons but didn't explain what they were. Only those in critical condition were rushed to the hospital, and the rest were stabilized. They kept the dead in the warehouse, out of sight from the nosy news helicopter that buzzed overhead.

"When can I get out of here?" asked Corelli. The paramedics gave him painkillers and an icepack, but he could feel the ache in his shoulder.

"Dunno. The Bureau sealed the building, and I saw three guys in white hazmat suits enter."

"No shit?"

"No shit."

Corelli secretly worried that his team had been exposed to some toxic nerve agent or radiation. One more thing to stress about. *Purge it from your mind,* he thought. *It's too late now.*

Across the parking lot, an FBI agent who spoke Russian was interviewing the prisoners and getting impatient with their responses. One blew smoke in the Fed's face, and the agent took a thumb and gently pressed a bandage. The Russian screamed. Corelli smiled.

Two Feds exited a side door carrying an oddly shaped metal suitcase and deposited it in the mystery van. Some FBI gathered around the van door, watching whatever was going on, then looked upset. One agent, presumably the guy in charge, stepped away and made a call. At first he was placid, then began gesticulating wildly, and finally put his phone away with a worried expression. Both Corelli and the cop stared. They had never seen anything like it.

"What do you think they found in there?" asked Corelli. His team evacuated him after he was shot and then went back inside, where they remained. No one had back-briefed him since then.

"A whole lot of weapons but no drugs," said the cop.

"Then why all the hubbub?"

"I don't know," said the cop, also puzzled. "I spoke to a buddy who came out of the building. He said something about two empty containers."

"*Empty* containers?" said Corelli with a laugh.

"Yeah, can you believe it? All this fuss over empty containers."

Both men shook their heads as more FBI agents piled into the warehouse.

CHAPTER 23

Lin sat on a park bench cradling a green tea for warmth. Squirrels danced around her, expecting food, but she shook her head at them. The park across from the World Bank was historically a hotbed for protests against Third World debt. Now it was a small copse of trees among asphalt and cars. It also lacked people, which is why Lin liked it. She was done with people.

Her phone buzzed but she ignored it, focusing on the beautiful clear morning. It was her last moment of freedom. Dmitri was ultimately a bust. Now it was time to return to the FBI and surrender her badge and gun. Staying out longer would only make things worse. They might even charge her with something.

No, she thought, *they will* definitely *charge you with something.* Her boss's appetite for schadenfreude was limitless, the sign of a bitter old man with a dead-end career. Regardless of what he tried, she was done as an FBI agent, a truth she wasn't ready to admit. The pain, her disappointed father, her failed life—it was easier to ignore it. The birds chirped happily above her, over the din of the city.

The phone buzzed again, ruining her reverie with nature. *When my tea is done, I'll walk to the Hoover Building and turn myself in,* she thought, sipping very slowly. Maybe things weren't so bad. Perhaps they would give her a third chance, she rationalized. After all, they were short agents in a time of national crisis and her intentions were good. Mostly.

Bzzzzzzz. Bzzzzzzz. Bzzzzzzz.

Holy crap, she thought and reached for her phone. It was Jason.

"Jason, what is it?" she said, annoyed.

"You'll never believe it," he said with pride.

"Believe what?"

"Just take a guess."

"Just tell me. I'm not in the mood," sighed Lin, watching the birds fly away.

"We found the mystery containers!" he said triumphantly. She could hear him doing a victory dance at his desk and struggled to push the image out of her mind.

"What?!"

"Yeah! Your source was right. We found both containers this morning in a Secaucus warehouse."

Lin felt dizzy. Seconds ago, she was prepared to turn herself in, and maybe face arrest. Now, everything had flipped. "But . . . but, how?"

"I called it in last night, using the anonymous tip line on the internet. Said there was a huge drug and weapons shipment. I knew what key words would set off police alarm bells. It worked. They sent a SWAT team in this morning and found both mystery containers, sitting right there in the middle of the warehouse. It was glorious!"

Wow, Dmitri told the truth. She didn't see that coming.

"And there's more."

"More?"

"Yeah. Way more. The containers were empty, but they did a radiological sweep. One tested positive for traces of uranium."

"A nuclear bomb?"

"Even better: nuclear terrorism!" he said, genuinely gleeful. "The WMD Directorate is standing up a task force, and I've just been assigned to it. I'm graduating from dynamite to fissile material. It's like a promotion!"

"You must be so proud."

"This can launch my career," he said seriously, unaware of her sarcasm.

"What else did they find?"

"Not much. We're still trying to figure out who sent them, what was in them, and where the contents are now. All the essentials. Look, don't tell anyone because it's all hush-hush." He paused. "Uh-oh. The boss is on the prowl. Gotta run!" The phone went dead.

Lin sat astonished. This was a stay of career execution. She was still in play. Of all the disturbing things in the conversation, the worst was nuclear terrorism. *What the hell is going on?* The Russian mob didn't smuggle nukes because the Kremlin would never entrust them with WMD. Nor would the *bratva* work for radical Islamic terrorists; it wasn't their business model.

Yet what explained the trace uranium they found? It probably wasn't medical equipment. Also, the FBI must have found something linking it to the bridge or else Jason would not have used the term "nuclear terrorism."

She gulped the last of her green tea and stood up. Across the street was Washington's most empty tourist attraction: the World Bank gift shop, full of economic textbooks and cheap cuff links. Lin paused in the window, staring at the world map. Where would the mob obtain a nuke? Not from the Russian military. Not from anywhere.

"Impossible," she said softly. As a kid, she went through a Sherlock Holmes phase, reading every story. It was a reason she became an FBI agent. There was one line that always stuck with her: "When you have eliminated the impossible, whatever remains, however improbable, must be the truth."

If the mob has a nuclear weapon, it must have come from Moscow with orders. Lin reached into her purse and found her phone.

"Jason here," answered the voice.

"You know 'nuclear terrorism' is a dud, right, Jason? If terrorists had a nuke, they would have used it in the bridge attack, and
we'd already be incinerated."

"Jen, I'm super busy. Can we discuss later?"

Lin ignored him. "Nukes are way out of the terrorists' league.
Think about it, Jason: Where would they source a nuclear
weapon? The world was petrified of loose nukes after 9/11, but
it turned out to be a boogeyman. Why would Iran, Russia, Pakistan, North Korea, or anyone else trust a nuke to a terrorist
group? If they wanted to detonate a WMD in the United States,
they would use their own people."

Jason sighed and spoke. "Or-r-r-r, the terrorists are keeping
the nuke in reserve to instill maximum fear, using it when the
nation is most vulnerable. It could be in a van in Times Square
or buried in the pits of the Daytona 500. It could be a nuclear car
bomb near Arlington Cemetery, waiting to detonate at the vice
president's funeral. Think of it. All the cabinet secretaries, generals, foreign dignitaries . . . everyone will be there, and the world
will be watching. It'll create waves of panic globally and fill the
terrorist ranks with new recruits. A terrorist army."

Lin didn't like what she heard, not because it was wrong but
because it could be true.

CHAPTER 24

Jackson sat back in his chair, foot braced against the edge of his desk, and unconsciously twirled the phone cord in his hand.

"Um-hum . . . OK . . . That's disturbing," he said, then listened. A young woman knocked gently on the door and stuck her head in. He held up a finger, telling her to wait a minute, but she shook her head and pointed to her wrist, indicating he was late.

"OK, I'll pass that along to the president . . . Yes, I understand the urgency," he said into the phone. The young intern glared at him, reminding him of his mother. He reflexively spun his chair around so he couldn't see her.

"Got it . . . Keep me apprised," he said, and hung up.

"Sir, everyone is in the Oval Office and waiting on you. Including the president."

"Thank you, uh . . ."

"Anne."

"Anne," he said, putting on his suit jacket. Normally he wouldn't address an intern by name, but she was the daughter of one of their biggest campaign donors, and the president was going to press her parents to swipe another seven-figure check during reelection season. "Lead away," he said.

He followed her down the corridor. They turned left and walked past the Roosevelt Room. Then she motioned him into the Oval Office as if she were ground-guiding a 747. *I hate millennials,* he thought, entering the yellow room. It smelled slightly

of linseed oil and flowers. The National Security Council's principals were arrayed in chairs around the president, who was sitting behind the Resolute Desk.

"George, glad you could join us," said the president with a
tinge of bite. A few of the others looked away in awkwardness.
"Start us off, will you?"

Jackson took a seat and heard the door close behind him. Next
to him sat the secretaries of defense, state, and homeland security. There were also the director of national intelligence and the
chairman of the Joint Chiefs of Staff, the highest-ranking general
in the military. The only person absent was the vice president.

"I just got off the phone with the FBI director," said Jackson
in a smooth voice. "There's been a new development. A troubling one."

The director of national intelligence shifted uncomfortably in
his seat, probably because he already knew somehow.

"There's a possibility that a nuclear weapon was smuggled
into the U.S. through Newark, New Jersey." He briefed what
they knew so far. "The radiological test results could prove a false
positive. But until we know for sure, the WMD is our new main
effort."

The room sat stunned. President Anderson finally broke the
silence. "Are the two connected? Is there evidence linking this to
the bridge attack?"

"No, but we have to assume they are linked," said the director
of national intelligence. "Expect the worst and you'll never be
disappointed."

"It's been nine days since the ship docked in Newark. The
WMD could be anywhere by now," said the head of homeland
security, her voice quavering. "Mr. President, we may have to
consider evacuating key cities, like New York, Washington, Los
Angeles, Houston, Chicago—"

"There will be no evacuations," interrupted the president.

"We have credible evidence of a clear and present danger," she said. "We must act."

"The evidence is not credible until I say it is, and it's not. We don't want to start a panic. Period."

Her eyes narrowed, the only tell of her outrage.

"There will be no evacuations," repeated the president, sensing the tension. "We don't want to start something we can't control. That's how the terrorists win."

"We've already got the Bureau, Agency, and Department of Energy working the problem," said Jackson, turning to the secretary of homeland security. "We'll know more soon."

"Good, Jackson," said the president. "Keep me informed the second you learn something. I'm writing my speech for tonight, and a nuclear bomb changes everything. Let's have our next meeting in an hour by phone."

"Yes, sir," said everyone in chorus.

"And one more thing. Absolutely, positively, and under no circumstances can this leak to the press. The media cannot learn of this."

CHAPTER 25

NEWS ALERT: NUCLEAR TERROR flashed on televisions and in headlines around the world. Jackson watched the TV in disgust. Outside his window he could hear protestors chanting in Lafayette Square.

"Cities across the country are emptying out amid rumors of a terrorist nuclear bomb," said the news anchorwoman. The screen showed standstill traffic jams in major cities around the world.

"And who is responsible for spreading the rumor?" yelled Jackson to the TV. "Goddamn news cycle: create rumor, report rumor, repeat."

"Let's go live to New York City," said the anchorwoman.

"Thanks Cindy," said a reporter standing in the middle of the street amid an ocean of red taillights. "We're at Varick and Houston Streets, blocks away from the Holland Tunnel entrance, and as you can see, nothing is moving."

The reporter bent down next to a man who was leaning out of his car window.

"This is Donnie, from Bensonhurst," introduced the reporter. "How long have you been stuck here?"

"Six hours going on to eternity," he said in dense Brooklynese, dropping his *R*s.

"How did the day start for you?" asked the reporter, yelling over the din of honking horns and expletives.

"When the news came over the TV, I grabbed the kids from school and drove into the city to pick up my wife. She works on

Fulton. I thought we'd beat traffic, but will you look at this!" The man held out his hand, indicating the hoard of stationary vehicles.

"Have you considered another way out? The George Washington Bridge?"

"Yougottabekiddingme! It's backed up in every direction. The whole island is a mess! I can't even move," he said, throwing up a hand for effect. His kids were screaming behind him.

"It looks like we're all going to be here for a while. Back to you, Cindy."

"Stay safe," she said nonsensically. "There's been another attack on a mosque, this one in Houston." The news showed fire trucks around a large burning building. "Muslims and mosques are being targeted throughout the country, and police are asking people to remain calm."

The camera showed police trying to contain a crowd of people outside the White House, many holding signs with anti-Muslim slogans and images. Jackson heard the protest chants from outside his window and from the TV a millisecond later.

"Hey, hey! Ho, ho! Those Muslims got to go! Hey, hey! Ho, ho! Those Muslims got to go!" people yelled in unison.

The TV changed to live protests of people burning American flags in Cairo, Bagdad, Tehran, and Kabul.

"Anti-American protests are also occurring throughout the Middle East. It seems some people are celebrating the terrorist attack," said the anchorwoman. "Let's go live to Islamabad."

The scene cut to a reporter on the ground, where a sea of men draped in white-and-green Pakistani flags were yelling. One held up an effigy that looked like a scarecrow made of American flags, and lit it. Flames burst skyward followed by a plume of black smoke. The reporter looked terrified.

"Cindy, as you can see, demonstrators are chanting slogans

against the United States and burning American flags. There are protests just like this one across northwest Pakistan. The government here says—" A bottle flew through the air and hit the camera, and the screen went dark.

The camera went back to the news anchor, who sat frozen and pale. After a brief silence, she said, "We're having technical difficulties."

"Savages," said Jackson.

The screen changed to an empty White House press briefing room, showing an empty podium.

"We are still awaiting news from the White House," said the anchorwoman in a grave tone.

"Aw, come o-o-on!" Jackson yelled. "You bastards know the president will make an address within the hour. Stop rushing us!"

The camera zoomed in on the podium, jiggling slightly and somehow making it look ominous.

"Savages!" he said, turning off the TV.

CHAPTER 26

It was midday and I had still not heard from Lava or Tye, worrying me. Lava said he would be back in a few hours, and that was more than a few hours ago. Could I trust him? I didn't know.

Lava instructed me not to leave the warehouse or turn on any electronics that emitted a signal, regardless of what my fixer promised. To make the point, Tye grabbed my four laptops while whistling the "Heigh-Ho" song from *Snow White and the Seven Dwarfs*, then proceeded to smash them to bits with a fire ax. He took great pleasure in it. In exchange, Lava handed me a crappy burner phone.

"Take good care of this," said Lava. "Only call me in an emergency."

Since then, I had slept, cleaned my weapons twice, double-checked my surviving tech, and did a round of physical training. Now I was down to playing solitaire, and losing. A mouse scurried across the floor.

"Scram, mouse! I don't have food here," I said, and heard a small squeak as if in reply. *Defiant rodent,* I thought.

Tye left me the emergency weather radio. "Thing don't emit enough radio frequency to matter," he said. Luckily, it also pulled in FM radio, so I tuned in the news. NUCLEAR TERROR. TERRORIST NUKES. NUCLEAR BOMB OF ISLAM.

"No, no, no, no, no," I whispered as I listened to live coverage that interrupted normal programming. The radio announcer described a warehouse in northern New Jersey, its parking lot filled with fire trucks and police. Gridlock had frozen all major highways exiting New York City. People were panicked.

Next came the pundit brigade. Talking heads filled the airwaves with their yapping. One claimed the terrorists could have stashed multiple warheads in cities around the country. Another brushed it off as hokum. A third, a retired CIA director, said Iran was behind it but didn't explain why. Meanwhile, the U.S. government remained silent, confirming everyone's worst fears. I continued watching for ten minutes, absorbing the horror. New experts took to the airwaves but not with new facts. Ultimately it was just more palaver.

"What idiots," I said, turning them off. I scrolled to the classical music channel, which was playing a Chopin waltz called "L'Adieu." "How appropriate," I mumbled with a smirk, as I listened to the piano weep. Yet it was comforting.

My mind drifted back to Winters, now a nuclear threat. If the news reports were true, then he was surely behind it. A shiver took hold of me, and questions came fast. What was Winters's game? Where would Apollo obtain a nuclear warhead? A rebellion inside the company? It wasn't the Apollo I knew. Winters was capable of ghastly things, but half of Apollo joining him to kill the vice president and 230 Americans? Now a nuke? No. Something was off.

It can't be Winters, I thought, although it did not make me feel better. I opened up a can of tuna, my lunch. The mouse squeaked joy from somewhere beneath the kitchen cabinets, no doubt smelling the tuna. I tossed the empty can in the trash under the sink and heard mouse feet scamper around the cabinet. I felt like the mouse, except the trailer was my cabinet.

"OK, mouse, you win." I sighed and reached into a cabinet, unwrapped a cracker, and threw it under the sink. Happy scurrying. We were both pleased.

But the question that nagged me most: It seemed unlikely that Apollo would leave a clue for the FBI to find. That was the work of amateurs, not Apollo. Was somebody else behind the nuke? Definitely not terrorists; they weren't that sophisticated. Iran still didn't have the bomb and Pakistan wouldn't give one to a terrorist group, fearing their plan would literally backfire. China and North Korea didn't export WMD.

Maybe Russia did it, I thought. Russian mafia smuggled it in, so it made sense that Moscow could be involved. I had spent months in Ukraine dealing with Russia's shadow war there, which Russia won. The Kremlin could have used Russian mercenaries and mafia to facilitate the risky infiltration. They'd done it in other places, although not with a nuke.

Yeah, Russia could do it. But would they? Hard to know. If true, it would be a huge coup for the Kremlin, especially since Washington was convinced terrorists were behind it. Who knows how many warheads they had been secretly importing? Enough to worry.

Then it hit me like Hiroshima.

Winters does *have nukes!* I thought. A year ago, I was ensnared in Winters's scheme to steal ten nuclear bombs from Pakistan. I barely got out alive. I thought Winters was dead and the nukes lost, but I was wrong. *Winters lives, and now nukes are in play.* It was no coincidence.

Winters must have recovered some of the missing warheads, I realized in horror. The Chopin swelled into a crescendo, turning tragedy into triumph. *Not helpful, Chopin,* I thought. I opened the sink cabinet, but the mouse had vanished. I wish I could have, too. There were enemy nuclear weapons somewhere in America, and I prayed they were in the hands of the Kremlin and not Winters.

CHAPTER 27

Lin received Jason's text while in the mixed martial arts cage. She found that working out helped with stress, but pummeling strangers relieved it. Her sparring partner was a five-foot-five Hispanic man who was a flurry of hands and feet. The guy never stopped moving, making it hard to land a punch as well as see one coming. She stalled as long as she could, hoping his incessant acrobatics would wear him out, but he kept going.

Smack! He kicked her face hard, and she felt the sting through her protective headgear. Her opponent was a master of capoeira, an Afro-Brazilian martial art that is literally dance and death. It was developed by African slaves in Brazil in the sixteenth century, and—done well—was hard to beat. But Lin was a master, too.

Smack, smack, smack, oof! He landed two more punches, but she blocked the third and counterstruck with a punch that knocked him backward and sideways. In the millisecond of space, she delivered a perfect roundhouse kick to his chest like a baseball bat, sweeping him off his feet with 480 pounds of force. He lay on the floor, crunched over and sucking air, and she lurked over him like Muhammad Ali above the fallen George Foreman in Zaire. When he caught his breath, she extended a hand and helped him to his feet.

"Not bad, Little Sparrow," he said, using her gym nickname. She didn't care for it but couldn't stop it, so she'd finally accepted it.

"Not bad yourself. You almost got me with your disco moves," she said, rubbing her head with a padded glove. Lin had never met the guy before but had seen him practicing and challenged him to a match.

"Ow, that hurt," he said, still shaking off the roundhouse kick.

"Training should hurt. If there is no pain, there is no fear, and if there is no fear, then you are not training."

He gave a mock look of terror, and then smiled. "Another round?"

"Nah, gotta run. I just came in to loosen up. I got a lot going on right now."

"Ok, Sparrow. Maybe next time?"

"Yeah. Next time." She grabbed her towel and went to the locker room. Few women trained in mixed martial arts, so she had the showers mostly to herself. As she peeled off her clothes, she felt a little self-conscious that she was the only woman without tattoos. MMA fighters wore body art for the same reason soldiers displayed ribbons: to be admired. Their judging eyes on her inkless body always made her feel naked, even though she knew it was silly. More than a few times cage friends suggested she get an intricate Chinese dragon tattoo with flying sparrows on her back and ass. Her answer was always no, yet they would mention it again.

Lin loved long showers. She stood under the high-pressure nozzle for ten minutes, letting the heat and pressure work magic on her aching muscles. Stress was the culprit, not cage fighting. She moved side to side, getting her entire back and then her front.

Ahhhhhh, she thought, trying not to think about the FBI, Russia, nukes, and Armageddon. She was in a holding pattern until Jason got back to her with a follow-up lead, and she was growing impatient. It was why she'd come to the gym.

Where the hell is he? she thought, irritated. She performed deep breathing exercises to slow her heart rate, sucking in steam and exhaling loudly. Ten more minutes later, she reluctantly stepped out and dried off. After blow-drying her hair, she made her way to her locker, carrying only the lock key. Reflexively she grabbed her phone as soon as she opened the locker.

"Crap!" she said, seeing all of Jason's texts over the past thirty minutes. "CALL ME. NEW LEAD!" Immediately she dialed his number and paced nervously around the locker room in the nude.

"Jason here."

"Jason, it's me."

There was a pause, and she imagined Jason scanning the office for eavesdroppers before speaking. "Well, you're not going to believe it," he said in a hushed voice. "Actually, you probably will. *I* just don't believe it."

"Jason, just tell me."

"First, you're in big trouble. You've practically made the FBI's most wanted list, and you need to come in."

"If they want me, they can come get me," she said, equally defiant.

She heard Jason sigh. "I checked with Dan in counterintelligence," he whispered. "You remember him? A class ahead of us, my height, brown hair."

"Yes, I remember Dan. What did he say?"

"He said they've been tracking an uptick of Russian spooks in Northern Virginia, and not the ordinary kind."

"What kind then?"

"He got all cagey on me, not like him. He said they were close to moving in, when they got called off. Didn't say why. Now he's chasing bridge terrorists with the rest of us."

"That's too bad. Did he say anything else?"

"Yeah. I pressed him. Literally. We were in the gym. Three-two-oh-two Rockland Terrace in McLean," he said.

"What?" she said. A young woman with a scorpion-and-roses tattoo on her hip was drying off and looking at her curiously. Lin moved away. "Say again?"

"Three-two-oh-two Rockland Terrace, McLean, Virginia. That's the safe house they were monitoring."

Lin grabbed a pen from her locker, bit off the cap, and spit it out. *Crap, where's a piece of paper?* she thought, looking around, but they were in a locker room. She was naked and couldn't run out to the front desk for a sticky note. *Screw it.* "Repeat the address." Jason did and she wrote it on her left inner forearm. "Thanks, Jason. Are they still running surveillance?"

"Remote sensors only, but actually it sounds like no one is paying attention. The assistant director pulled them all for the bridge case. Everyone is working it, except me. I'm probably going to get fired, right along with you."

"Jason, you're a good man. A patriot," she said. "Did Dan say anything else? Like who was operating out of the safe house?"

"No, and he wouldn't give me anything more. It sounds heavy duty though, and not your typical Russian Federation bullshit."

She sat down on a changing bench, twirling the pen in her fingers as she thought. "But why aren't they investigating it? After Secaucus I assumed the Bureau would widen the scope of inquiry to include suspicious Russian activity in the Capital region."

"Yeah, they did *except* for this safe house. I asked around and the Bureau is looking into all the usual suspects, but this one address is getting a hard pass."

"Why?"

Jason was uncomfortable. "I don't know, and that's why I approached Dan when I learned he was on the team surveilling it. In fact, he specifically warned me not to ask about it. Didn't say why."

Lin sat quietly, puzzling over it but only one word came to mind. "Weird."

"I know. That's why I texted you."

She had deep knowledge of Russia, but it was mafia focused. This was different. *A Russian government safe house that's being*

protected by the FBI? she thought. Could it be a double agent? Unlikely. The FBI wouldn't harbor any safe house during a national
emergency, especially one involving WMD. There was only one
way to find out.

"I know that silence," said Jason. "It's the patented Lin-
Thinking-Something-Stupid. Whatever you're thinking, stop it."

"What am I thinking?"

"You are thinking about taking down a certain Russian safe
house all by yourself. That would be galactically stupid. And
certain death."

"I'm not going to take it down. I just want to see if it's there.
That's all," she protested, crossing her arms and legs. It was disturbing how well Jason knew her.

"Don't. Come in while you still can," he pleaded. "The Bureau
is now looking into Russia, thanks to the Secaucus bust. Mission
accomplished, Lin. You can come in now. We're shorthanded,
so they may overlook everything if you pitch in and work hard."

"You know it might be too late for me, even with the big bust.
That's why I need this. I can't show up empty-handed. I need
more than a lead; I need a victory."

A long silence followed. Lin could hear the dull chatter of
their office in the background and felt his patience fraying. Yet
he did not hang up.

"One more thing, Lin," said Jason reluctantly. "And I shouldn't
even be telling you this."

"What?"

"You may be more right than you know about the bridge," he
said, lowering his voice. "They found traces of some new, exotic
military explosive. Real state-of-the-art stuff."

"What is it?"

"Wait one second," he said, and she heard papers rustling
around his forever messy desk. "Here it is. I don't understand

it," he said, reading the report. "Something about the cocrystal-lization of two parts HMX to one part CL-20, both high-end military explosives. The new material, which they imaginatively labeled Explosive X, can produce a blast wave 225 miles per hour faster than pure HMX." He whistled in admiration, as if he knew what he was taking about. "And it's as stable and resistant to accidental detonation as HMX. Good safety tip."

"Custom-made?"

"Yup. This stuff was not cooked up in some terrorist's basement. There are only a few labs in the world capable of producing it at scale, and ATF and DIA monitor most of them. This development took the building completely by surprise. It's got everyone here on edge because no terrorist group in the world has it—"

"But Russia does," she said, finishing his sentence while doing a silent victory dance in the middle of the locker room.

"Just be careful," he said.

"Of course I will," said Lin, and hung up.

CHAPTER 28

Around 11 P.M., George Jackson snuck out the White House pedestrian gate and walked briskly across Lafayette Square, his two-man secret service detail following. He didn't want to be late. A winter gust assaulted his face, and he pulled up his scarf so that only his eyes showed. More important, he didn't want to be recognized. Even at this late hour, protestors stood on Pennsylvania Avenue, waving signs opposing police brutality, terrorism, and nuclear war. Forty people clustered together holding candle lanterns in an all-night vigil, despite the zero-degree weather.

"Hey, hey! Ho, ho! Police brutality has got to go!" chanted a smaller group weakly. The freezing temperature had taken a toll on their numbers, and only the most committed rallied on.

A twenty-foot banner read: WAR NEVER SOLVES ANYTHING. *Except for ending slavery, the Holocaust, fascism, and communism,* thought Jackson, rolling his eyes. The protestors were none too bright, yet he was sympathetic to their sentiment. They would accomplish nothing, of course. The president wasn't even in the White House tonight. Demonstrators were an irritant to men like Jackson, but he knew they were also necessary. America embraced dissent, and that was what separated it from the savage nations of the world.

Two protestors huddled together on a park bench with a large cardboard sign leaning against their knees. END FASCISM NOW! it read, scrawled with a Sharpie. Two portraits bookended the message, each with a Hitler moustache. It was expertly drawn, and

Jackson slowed to admire it. Then stopped. One of the portraits was of him.

Bastards! he thought, and quickened his step. Week-old ice and refrozen slush encrusted the sidewalks, and salt crunched under his shoes. They strode past the giant statue of Gen. Andrew Jackson atop his horse, doffing his hat at the White House. Sirens wailed in the background. If Washington had a soundtrack, it would be sirens, honks, and helicopters.

Jackson checked his watch again. "Let's pick up the pace," he whispered to the secret service agents flanking him.

"Yes, sir," replied one. Jackson knew these agents well, and he always requested them. Good men were hard to find. In battle this meant bravery, but in Washington it referred to discretion. There are acts of courage greater than taking a bullet for someone else, such as keeping another's dangerous secrets. And Jackson had many secrets.

They crossed H Street and walked up the stairs of St. John's Episcopal Church. The pastel yellow exterior and white colonnade stood in sharp opposition to the concrete landscape surrounding it. It was nicknamed "church of the presidents" because every sitting president had attended the church since it was built in 1816, starting with James Madison.

The agents pulled open the huge oak doors and Jackson glided through, stomping his feet in the narthex to get warm.

"Please wait here," he said, after they followed him inside. "I need to be alone."

Jackson walked down the nave toward the altar. St. John's was small by modern standards, with a wraparound balcony on three sides consistent with the eighteenth century. The floorboards creaked beneath his feet, and the smell of incense and wood polish lingered in the air. Somehow, it reminded him of boarding school in New England, a horrible period many lifetimes ago.

Fifty-eight, fifty-seven, fifty-six, fifty-five . . . ah, here we go, he thought, and slid into pew 54. A brass plaque on the armrest read THE PRESIDENT'S PEW in modest lettering. Jackson sat down, exhaling with relief.

God help us all, he thought, gazing at the cross on the altar. Even in the dim light, the empty church cast a glow of consolation. The United States was the world's superpower, but it was not omnipotent. During times of crisis, he needed succor.

No, he thought. *I need reassurance.*

The oak doors squeaked open behind him and clanked shut a moment later. Jackson smiled. Reassurance had arrived. Without turning around, he heard the *click-click* of a cane tapping its way up the nave, until a tall man stood beside him. The gentleman carefully leaned his antique cane against the pew's back, its ivory handle an exquisitely carved monkey's head. Then, with effort, he eased his large frame into the seat next to Jackson. Finally, he grabbed his left leg and stretched it out, wincing slightly.

"Good evening, George," he said in a raspy voice. His hoarseness came not from old age or too many cigarettes, but from injury.

"Thank you for coming on such short notice."

"Of course. Anything for a friend."

Jackson fidgeted with his glove, hesitating.

"What's on your mind, George?"

"The nuclear bomb. I need to know if it's real."

This time the tall man hesitated.

"I need to know if it's true or just rumor," repeated Jackson, both men staring straight ahead. Moments passed.

"I thought we agreed not to do this," said the older man.

"Do what?"

"Ask each other about details."

"WMD on American soil is not a 'detail,'" said Jackson in an unyielding whisper.

"You understand that it changes nothing," said the man.

Jackson stiffened, astonished by this response. Then spoke cautiously. "You *will* tell me, and I will judge what changes."

The man sighed, but Jackson didn't care.

"Very well, George. It's true. Nuclear weapons were smuggled into the country last Friday. They are in transit now."

Jackson paused, absorbing the barrage of implications. This was not what he expected. He thought the man would saunter into the church and laugh at the rumor, not confirm it. Jackson's mind felt adrift. Hundreds of questions exploded in his head, but he could only spit out two: "*Weapons*, plural? You brought nuclear weapons into the country?! Where are they now?"

"I cannot say."

"You can't? Or you won't?" asked Jackson, raising his voice in alarm.

"No more questions, George. We cooperate when we can, but do what we must. You have your duties, and I have mine. That was our arrangement, and nothing more," said the man.

"Give me the location of the nuclear weapons so my teams can intercept them."

"I cannot."

Jackson's face turned crimson and eyes bulged. His lips curled back, showing his teeth, and he whispered viciously: "So help me God, I will bring the full weight and might of the United States of America crashing down upon your head until you don't know your toes from your tonsils."

"You do that, we both burn."

"I don't care. You brought WMD into my country, on my watch. I will see us burn before I let a single American perish by your hand."

Both men hard-stared each other. Finally, the tall man broke the gaze.

"Fine, George. You win this round. I will give you something."

"What?"

"A name. A location. Something."

"Something?!"

"In time, George. In time," said the man, reaching for his cane.

"In time? Time is the one thing neither of us has. I need 'something' now. Immediately."

With a grunt, the tall man pulled himself upright and maneuvered into the nave with measured care. George sat perplexed by the man's indifference. Nuclear weapons changed the equation, and the law of unintended consequences could produce a mushroom cloud. This was never part of their deal. Never.

"I will get you actionable intelligence on the WMD soon. Very soon. I promise," said the man.

"But—"

"Have a good night, George," he interrupted, and hobbled out of the church with the *clickity-clack* of his cane. Jackson considered having his agents seize him, but that would only complicate matters, not solve them. Besides, he knew where to find the man and could grab him at any hour of any day. He was going nowhere. The heavy oak doors shut after the man exited, and Jackson slumped back into the president's pew.

God help us all, he thought.

CHAPTER 29

The next morning, Jackson sat in a corner of the press secretary's office, which was crammed with lesser staffers. Like every room in the West Wing, it was entirely too small for its purpose. Jackson's weekend cabin on the Chesapeake had larger rooms. Actually, it was a Georgian brick mansion named "Ridgely's Retreat," and it came with its own peninsula and former slave quarters. Still, it had larger rooms.

How can anyone run a superpower out of the dinky West Wing? Jackson often wondered. The press secretary, Kelsey Broderick, stood behind her L-shaped desk and shuffled through papers manically in preparation for her press briefing, which was in ten minutes. The White House press pool was hostile most days, but today was worse. Last night's televised presidential address was not the speech of destiny everyone had hoped for. In fact, it was a disaster, raising more questions than it answered, and now the media was frenzied. Hence the 10 A.M. press conference to lower the media fever.

"George, anything new?" she asked nervously.

"Not since yesterday. At least, nothing unclassified," he said. Jackson's only role during the meeting was to answer her national security questions before she faced the cameras.

"Good. Don't tell me anything classified. I might accidently repeat it," she said. "It's been that kind of morning." She turned to other staffers in the room for last-minute updates: homeland, FBI, intelligence, others.

Jackson tuned them out and watched the bank of TV monitors that lined her wall, each set to a different 24/7 news channel. He focused on one of the biggies, reading its closed captions.

NATIONWIDE MANHUNT CONTINUES FOR TERRORISTS, said the chyron. The screen showed militarized police going door-to-door in a wealthy suburb of Northern Virginia. An older man in a bathrobe was shown yelling at police, barring them from entering his home, and the police plowed by him. The man grabbed an urn and smashed it over a policeman's Kevlar helmet. Seconds later, he was on the ground in flex-cuffs, then two policemen in black fatigues dragged him across his lawn to a cruiser. An angry policeman yelled at the camera, which was then pointed down at the ground.

No, no, no! Jackson thought. *Dumb police.*

Kelsey saw it too. "What are they doing?!" she said, knowing the press pool would hold her accountable for the policemen's actions. They already looked more like soldiers than police, and now this. Civil rights groups were howling. The news anchor looked visibly shocked by the elderly bathrobed man's fate.

What a humiliating way to go, thought Jackson with a silent chuckle. *Hauled off across your lawn in nothing but a bathrobe and flex-cuffs as they dump you in a police car, and all broadcast live on international TV. The legacy of saps.* He thanked God that would never be him.

"Someone turn that off," said Kelsey. "I can't look at the news right now." A staffer diligently switched off all the monitors. "Good. Where were we?"

As others gave her last-minute updates, Jackson pulled out his phone and checked his social media feeds. He followed all the journalists who mattered in the national security space, and they were on fire with the government's door-to-door manhunt for the terrorists. "Gestapo," "desperate," "insane." Their descriptions got worse from there.

"Time to go," said one of the staffers.

"I'm not ready," protested Kelsey, still leafing through her binder.

"Ma'am, it's time. Being late only makes them worse," said the aide. "It eggs on conspiracy theory."

Really? Conspiracy theory?! read the expression on Kelsey's face, but she nodded. "Fine. I'm ready. Let's go."

They all stood up and followed the press secretary out of her office and into the overcrowded briefing room. It was slightly bigger than a double-wide trailer's living room. The chatter quieted as she took the podium.

"Good morning," she began, and then gave an elegant ten-minute statement that said absolutely nothing. When she was done, hands shot up. One by one, she took questions, and her answers sounded convincing yet revealed nothing.

God, she's good, Jackson thought as he stood on the side with her staffers.

The volley of questions and answers continued, while Jackson contemplated his conversation last night with the tall man. It infuriated him. How dare he bring WMD onto American soil? He promised actionable intelligence, but when? He needed it now.

"I have a question for the national security advisor," said one journalist, seeing Jackson, who looked up in alarm.

"Oh, he's not available for questions," said Kelsey, caught off guard.

"But he's right there!" protested the journalist, pointing to Jackson. All cameras swiveled toward him and zoomed in; he looked up at the monitor and saw himself, standing in the shadows and watching the monitor in shock. Not a good look.

Busted, Jackson thought, and instantly regretted following the press secretary into the vultures' lair. A dumb mistake, but it was too late now.

"Uh," said Kelsey, feeling herself losing control. "Dr. Jackson isn't available for comments."

"Dr. Jackson," said the journalist, ignoring the press secretary. "Is it true there's an American sleeper cell?"

"Where will the terrorists strike next?"

"Is there just one nuclear bomb or are there many?"

"Could they already be planted in cities across the nation?"

"What are you doing to stop it? The American people deserve to know."

"Can you stop it?"

The barrage continued as the chorus of camera shutters crescendoed and all eyes focused on him. Then the room fell silent, expecting an answer. Live TV abhors silence.

A pack of vultures! he thought and glanced at the press secretary, but her look offered no respite. He straightened up awkwardly, knowing he was in a no-win situation.

"The FBI and CIA are still working to ascertain any and all leads. Progress is being made. We are cautiously optimistic," assured Kelsey, but it was no use.

"Dr. Jackson," asked another journalist. "Is Russia behind this, making it look like terrorists? Is this an act of war?"

Silence hung in the air, making Jackson uncomfortable. The entire world was watching the press briefing live, and refusing to answer or walking out would only validate the conspiracy theorists. However, he had no gift for evading questions like the press secretary, and lying would make things worse later. It always did. There was only one thing to do.

Jackson approached the dais slowly, and Kelsey's eyes silently pleaded with him to stop.

You lie for a living, he thought, meeting her gaze. *I cannot. I'm the national security advisor.* She stepped aside as he took the podium.

"Are enemy nukes in the U.S. right now?" asked a journalist in the back.

Damn you, thought Jackson about the tall man as he stared down at the microphone. Then he spoke.

"There are some people who think they can get away with anything. They threaten our country and our homes. They think they are smarter than us, and they will never be caught. But I say to them—" Jackson leaned forward "—we will hunt you, find you, and finish you."

CHAPTER 30

The tall man shook his head in disdain as he watched the press conference unfold. He sat behind a large mahogany desk in a dark room that looked like a palatial Victorian study. It had dark oak paneling, Empire-style couches, and a palatial Persian carpet. An antique cane leaned against the desk. The monkey's face was a mixture of tortured grimace and laughing insanity. On TV, Jackson took to the podium and the cameras zoomed in; the tall man frowned.

"Fool," the tall man said when Jackson had finished. An aide turned off the TV, while another rushed into the room looking distressed. "What?" barked the man in a raspy voice.

"Sir, he's back."

"Who?"

"*Him,*" said the aide, handing a computer tablet across the desk. The tall man examined it, and his scowl turned into a grin. The aide stood by nervously, having never seen the tall man smile.

Brad Winters had not smiled in a year. Months in a Saudi torture prison had twisted him, like the carved monkey on his cane. It took all of his negotiating skills to buy back his life, and now the only evidence of his incarceration was a limp, a crushed larynx, and a massive vendetta. Tom Locke had put him in that torture cell, and he swore his vengeance daily the way other people said prayers. Now justice was at hand.

"Tom Locke," hissed Winters. "Alive."

"Yes sir."

Winters enlarged the picture. It showed Locke and two Apollo agents getting into a black Chevy Suburban near Eastern Market. He recognized one of the men as Lava, a reliable team leader who had chosen the wrong side in Winters's hostile takeover bid for Apollo Outcomes. The board had fired Winters as CEO because of unauthorized private military activity in Ukraine. Now he was back to reclaim what was rightfully his: the company he founded twenty years ago and the influence it wielded in Washington. It was to be his year of justice.

"When was this picture taken?" asked Winters, leaning back in his chesterfield leather desk chair.

"A little over forty-eight hours ago."

"Two days?! And I'm just seeing it now? Why did you take so long?"

The aide shuffled his feet, absorbing the tall man's ire. "Because we just figured out it was Locke."

"Explain."

"Locke wasn't the mark. We've been tracking one of the Apollo hunter-killer teams for the past four days. Our signals intelligence unit was able to place a transponder on their vehicle, and we've been two steps ahead of them ever since. Three nights ago, they were running agents in Langley and Meade, although the other night they went dark—"

"Get to the point," interrupted Winters.

The aide tensely cleared his throat. "Around nine A.M., they made a beeline for a coffee shop on Capitol Hill. It's an indicator because it's completely outside their normal operational profile, triggering us to slew and cue surveillance. We assigned a drone to get eyes on, and it captured this picture. At first, we had no idea who they were meeting. The facial recognition algorithms came up blank, as if someone had erased the individual's profile from the databases. It turns out someone did."

"Fascinating," said Winters, knowingly. "Who?"

"We did. A few years back, we won the IDIQ contract to manage the IC's persons of interest databases," said the aide. *IC* referred to the intelligence community: CIA, FBI, and fourteen other agencies.

"Ah, yes. I remember now. A handy little contract," Winters said of the billion-dollar deal. "We erased the identities of all our operatives without anyone knowing."

The aide gave a pro forma chortle, and then continued. "We got lucky, sir. One of our older techs recognized Locke. They used to work together."

Winters sighed and his frown returned as he placed the tablet on the desk. The aide stiffened reflexively, but Winters sat motionless.

"Help me understand something," said Winters. The aide swallowed hard. "I was led to believe that Locke was dead. Yet here is a picture of him alive, yesterday, in this city. Help me understand."

"We thought so too," said the aide with fear in his voice. Winters did not suffer bad news lightly. "He was reported killed in Syria by Jase Campbell's team."

The aide waited for a response, but none came.

"Campbell is the—" the aide began, but Winters held up a hand.

"Locke has more lives than an Afghan warlord," said Winters, eyeing Locke's photo on the tablet. "I'll deal with Campbell later. What concerns me is why Locke has returned. Why would he risk everything by coming out of hiding? And coming back here, my home turf? Help me understand. Why would a rogue like Locke do it?"

The aide remained silent, hoping it was a rhetorical question. It wasn't. Finally, he offered weakly: "We don't know, sir."

Winters glared. "How long has Locke been here?"

"We don't know."

"Where is Locke now?"

"We don't know."

"Dammit, what *do* you know?!" shouted Winters, who winced with pain and massaged his throat as he coughed. When he finished, his eyes turned to the aide, who was pale. "Why did you lose him?"

"We just fingered him five minutes ago. Had we known at the time, we would have abducted him. Now he's gone dark. But we're working up his digital signature. If Locke is working the Capitol region, we will find him."

Winters leaned back again, thinking. He was framed by floor-to-ceiling red velvet drapes and valanced windows that overlooked a private garden. A wrought iron balcony and elaborate cut stonework around the windows could have passed for a Haussmann apartment in Paris. After a few minutes, he sat forward.

"Could he have been involved in last night?" asked Winters.

The aide shifted uncomfortably. The destruction of Elektra was an unmitigated catastrophe for their contract, and Winters spent the morning on the phone sweet-talking the client and screaming at staff. Heads were rolling. "Possibly. We are still conducting the postop."

Winters stared at the picture of Locke. The aide's forehead glistened with sweat despite the room's cool temperature.

"Well, no matter. He's not our problem anymore," said Winters. He almost sounded happy.

"Yes sir," said the aide in astonished relief, not comprehending yet thankful.

"Get me a secure line to the national security advisor," Winters said. A moment later he was connected to the White House.

"Jackson speaking."

"Good morning, George. It's me. Nice performance today."

"Good morning, Brad. Thank you, I had someone specific in mind."

"Let's hope they were watching."

"Oh, don't worry. I have it on good authority he was," said Jackson with satisfaction. "Now, you are calling because you have a little something for me?"

"Indeed I do, as promised. I'm a man of my word," cooed Winters as if the world were unicorns and rainbows. He thought he deserved an Oscar.

"Thank you," said Jackson, and then paused. "I have to confess, Brad, this morning I expected you would sandbag me."

"George, we are both patriots," said Winters coaxingly. "We may have different methods, but we both want the same thing. We must trust each other, if we are to succeed."

"Agreed."

Winters picked up the tablet and stared at the picture on the screen.

"The man you're after is named Thomas Locke. He used to be one of mine, but he's gone rogue and taken a few colleagues with him. He's the one behind the WMD. I've committed every asset at my disposal to stopping them—"

"Wait, Winters!" interrupted Jackson, raising his voice in alarm. "Did you just say parts of Apollo Outcomes have gone rogue, and they have nuclear weapons *inside* the U.S.? Are you telling me you lost positive control of Apollo Outcomes?" Jackson's voice trailed off as he contemplated the horror. It was like a T-rex running loose on Noah's ark.

Winters had hoped the conversation would not veer in this direction, but perhaps it was for the best. "No George, I'm in control of Apollo. Locke is leading a splinter cell and we needed to know how large, which is why I couldn't speak about it last night. I had to be sure, and now I am. Locke is the man with the nukes. He is maniacal and has images of self-grandeur."

"Too much time in the field doing your dirty work, and now he's lost his ethical compass," said Jackson in a condescending tone.

"Doing *our* dirty work," corrected Winters. "I don't know what he wants, despite several overtures to talk reason to him. But Locke is not a reasonable man."

"How could you let this happen?" scolded Jackson. "This was never part of our deal. You were supposed to be better than this."

The words stung but Winters pushed ahead, feeling his trap closing around his prey. "What matters now is Locke has a nuclear weapon in the continental United States and the man is unhinged. He is a Tier One threat, George. Do you understand me? Tier One."

Jackson paused. "Where the hell did Locke obtain weapons of mass destruction?"

"Pakistan. Two years ago, Locke posed as Saudi secret service and bought a bomb, leaving Saudi a big bill and bigger embarrassment. They kept it a secret for obvious reasons, and now the Kingdom is after him too. We all thought he was dead, and the nukes lost somewhere in Yemen. Saudi launched a war in Yemen partly to recover the nukes before the Iranians could find them. But no one found them. It turns out Locke was hiding with the nukes, waiting for his opportunity to strike. The VP's death was Santa Claus for him."

"If what you're saying is true, Brad, then why didn't the CIA or NSA know about it?"

Winters chuckled. "There's much the CIA and NSA don't know, George." *Especially since they outsource much of their critical work to me,* he thought with a smug grin. Cooking intelligence to land more contracts was something of a specialty for him.

Winters could feel the tension over the phone. *Come on, Jackson, you old sentimental fool. Bite!* Winters had known him for thirty years, since Jackson was just a budding lobbyist for Boeing selling jet fighters to Congress. But the man was a true patriot, and that was what Winters was counting on. Perhaps he needed a sweetener to push him in the correct direction.

Winters cleared his throat. "George, I need your help. I can't stop Locke on my own," he said in a vulnerable tone. Now for the coup de grace. "And the country needs you too, George." Winters paused for effect. "The hour is desperate."

More silence. *Come on, Jackson!* thought Winters.

Jackson sighed. "Fine, I will clean up your mess. We cannot let this stand, and we are partners in this project until the end. *Alea iacta est,*" he said, quoting Caesar. He had a bevy of historical lines memorized for such occasions.

"'The die is cast,'" replied Winters without hesitation. "You are quite right, old friend. We crossed the Rubicon together months ago, and we are committed now. Let's work together and do what's best for America."

"Agreed. Where are the nukes now? Where's Locke?"

"No one knows. Find Locke and find the nukes," said Winters, eyeing Locke's photo on the computer tablet as he talked. *I got you,* he thought with satisfaction. *Checkmate Locke.*

"All I need is a description. We'll take it from there."

"Good. I'm sending over a man right now with Locke's file," said Winters, nodding to the aide, who left the room. "And George, one more thing. This Locke guy; don't underestimate him. You won't find him in any database because he's invisible. Worse, he's cunning. We originally recruited him for infiltration and assassination, but he proved—" Winters paused, searching for the right word "—artful. If you spot him, don't get creative, just take the shot."

"Understood, Brad, and don't worry. I have a Special Mission Unit at Bragg who will have Locke bagged and tagged by sundown, if the intel you give me is any good."

"Oh, it is," said Winters, beaming. "Happy hunting."

CHAPTER 31

It was the next day and I still had not heard from Lava or Tye. Even the tiny mouse had gone on sabbatical, free to roam the greater trash heaps of the I-695 underpass. *Lucky rodent,* I thought, nearly nodding off. Jet lag and solitaire do not mix.

Where are Tye and Lava? I thought about using the burner phone to call them, but opted against it. Boredom was not an emergency. Also, maybe they were setting me up. They could have been stalling, and it might be hours before they arrived. Even a day or two. Time was precious, and I was wasting it. Every hour in my safehouse was an hour lost finding evidence implicating Apollo in the terrorist attack. *This is bullshit,* I thought, grabbing my Mark 23s and holstering them.

"Who knows what side Lava is really on?" I said aloud, wanting to trust him but knowing Apollo was in the middle of a civil war. It was difficult to know where people's true loyalties lay in such circumstances.

Trust no one, and develop a contingency plan, I thought, *starting with my own intelligence sources.* Without good information, I was grounded.

"What I need is the ability to find people quickly, and track them. But how?" I said, pacing around the trailer. A good hacker could do it by scraping the web for mobile ad data. Who needs the NSA when you have large corporations spying on your every move, click, and preference through your smartphone? If I could recruit my own cyberagent, he or she could tap the online ad exchanges and track individuals for me in real time. *Bingo!* But it left a harder question.

"Now, where to find a talented hacker?" I mumbled as I absentmindedly twirled a 7.62 mm cartridge between my fingers. The University of Maryland was just outside the Capital Beltway and had one of the best computer science departments in the country. Not exactly the NSA but good enough.

"Should be easy. All I need is an underpaid and overtalented grad student who can code," I said, rummaging through one of my duffels and pulling out a cash roll. "A free meal and a thousand dollars will do the trick."

Wait! Is it worth the risk? screamed my intuition. Getting NSA-like surveillance was the vital next step. However, I had come all this way, spent all my money, and risked my life. Driving through DC in broad daylight was a rookie blunder. Or was it a rookie blunder to sit on my ass?

"'Who Dares Wins,'" I said, repeating the British SAS's motto as I grabbed the car keys.

The BMW purred as I drove it out of the garage and down the street, the sunlight blinding me for a moment. I took the side streets, away from the traffic cameras, congestion, and cops. Decades ago, during DC's crack epidemic, this area was gangster land, but now it was forgotten. One abandoned brick town house lay boarded up, with a gang of feral cats on the stoop. Progress.

My fixer had equipped the BMW with an illegal police scanner, and it chirped routine calls. Still, one had to be careful. DC is the most policed city in the country. I remember an instructor at the Ranch, Apollo's training facility in Texas, tell us there are fifty-seven cops for every ten thousand Washingtonians— almost twice the average for big cities and about four times the national average. And that's not even counting all the special

police, like Capitol, Park, and Metro. The nation's capital was a
nightmare for guys like me.

*Apollo at war with itself. Winters alive and leading the rebellion.
What are the stakes?* I mused as I drove. It seemed inconceivable.
The local classical radio station, WETA, was playing Gershwin's
"Lullaby," an orchestral lollipop that transported me into the
Great Gatsby's parlor before dawn.

I took a right, down a back street that would eventually dump
onto the Beltway, and then it was a straight shot to the campus. A
faint *wump-wump* of a chopper flew nearby. The music beckoned
to me, and I felt my jet lag weighing heavy upon my brain. The
chopper returned, getting in the way of the sweet tempos. DC
probably had the highest ratio of helicopters to people, too.

Then it struck me. I was in a deserted part of the city, and
no choppers should be circling above. They should not even be
transiting through this airspace; they used the rivers as highways.
I slowed and scanned the sky in a zigzag pattern but saw nothing.
The police scanner was quiet, too.

I must be getting tired, I thought, turning off the "Lullaby."
The *wump-wump* returned, but I could see nothing. Then no
chopper sound.

Am I going crazy? I rolled down the windows, cut the engine,
and coasted so I could hear better. At first nothing. Then the
ambient sounds of the city, a garbage truck emptying a dumpster, a fire truck racing toward an emergency, a jackhammer. A
helicopter.

The chopper was due east of my position, probably two klicks
out, and growing louder. I started the engine and raced forward.
When things don't make sense, move! Figure it out later.

Blue flashes flooded my peripheral vision, then I heard the
banshee of sirens. In every direction. Before my mind registered
the threat, adrenaline shot through my arteries and rocked my

brain. *Ambush!* I floored the accelerator, and seven hundred horses stampeded under the hood, pressing me hard into my seat. A police car nosed out a hundred meters ahead; I swerved and clipped his bumper, nearly spinning out. I counted three cruisers and two black SUVs behind me. No doubt there were more vehicles flanking me on the parallel roads, blocking my escape. But my real worry was the spotter helicopter. No car was faster than eyeballs in the sky with a radio.

My intuition was pinging: something was awry. All these vehicles behind me, but none in front? It was a trap. They were flushing me forward, into an ambush zone with tire spikes and SWAT. I had to find a way out.

I dropped to 30 mph, allowing the chase vehicles to catch up, then found my impossible corner: an alley that ran behind rotting row houses. I jerked the wheel one quarter to the right and slammed the brakes. The car drifted right, into the alley, with the piercing squeal of tires and smell of rubber. The left rims hit the alley's curb so hard that the BMW lifted up on two wheels, then bounced down, jerking my head. I warped from 0 to 60 mph in 2.9 seconds, which sucked the breath out of me, and I heard the crash behind me. The lead cruiser had attempted the tight turn but smashed into a row house instead, blocking the alley for follow-on police.

Now to get out of here, I thought. Too late. A police Harley turned into the alley two blocks ahead and sped for me. *Gutsy sucker,* I thought, then I saw his play. All he had to do was close the gap between me and the next street exit. If he could seal it off, I would be trapped in the alley between him and the crashed cruiser. I floored it.

"Come on!" I shouted, as I raced for the next street and the cop for me, in a twisted game of chicken. We made the street simultaneously. I pitched left, skidded, and felt the lateral g-force pull my body against the seat belt. The tires clung to the pavement, but what I would have given for thirty minutes on a skid pad a day ago. The motorcycle went down and smashed through a derelict storefront, its rider expertly rolling across the pavement.

The police chopper was waiting for me, flying fifteen feet above my head, its blades just clearing rooftops. The rotor wash kicked up dust and trash, so I couldn't see, but I punched through and emerged onto a main thoroughfare. The BMW swayed violently as I slalomed through traffic at speed.

I could hear the sirens now. A battalion of them. I flashed my lights and honked, trying to get people out of my way. RFK Stadium was ahead, then the freeway. *Avoid the highway.* It's the first rule of motorized escape and evasion because the police box you in and cut you down.

"Find an exit," I commanded myself, as I sped around the stadium at 90 mph. I veered through the traffic but could not lose the nimble police Harleys.

"Bollocks!" I shouted as a black SUV appeared in front of me, its blue lights flashing through its grill. It was headed for me, as if to ram me off the road. I swung right so violently that the car nearly flipped, and I shot three lanes over and launched onto the highway. The motorcycles and SUV were jammed in the maelstrom of traffic I left in my wake.

"*Bollocks!*" I yelled again, as I accelerated up the highway. It was the one place I didn't want to be. Hugging the left shoulder to avoid congestion and oncoming cars, the BMW vibrated unnaturally as I ran through a debris field. A flat at this speed was lethal.

Another police car and the black SUV materialized behind me, and the chopper's shadow crossed overhead. Then a second. I glanced up and saw the police helicopter had picked up a pal, a news chopper. *There goes my cover,* I thought. *I should have listened to Lava.*

Ahead was a large iron bridge that spanned the Anacostia River, and I topped 120 mph going across it. I felt the car shimmy beneath me. The police helicopter flew at eye level, and the pilot and I regarded one another, each wearing sunglasses despite the cloudy day.

A police car was waiting for me as soon as I got off the bridge. I slammed the brakes and heard the screech of tires as I decelerated from 120 to 60 mph. I thought I would rear-end the police cruiser but it sped up, then slowed down to block me. The second cruiser rode my tail, boxing me in. I skewed left, then right, but the police matched my every move. Our bumpers mashed as they slowed down, taking me with them. I was trapped.

Grrr, I grunted, as I slammed on the brakes and knocked the cruiser behind me. More important, it cleared a few precious inches between me and the lead vehicle. Enough to get free. In that space I swerved right, escaping the cruisers, then rammed the lead car's rear right panel. The impact was visceral, as I lifted the cruiser's back tires off the pavement. When they reengaged the road, the police car turned violently sideways at 40 mph. I tapped my brake, allowing the cruiser to spin around my nose in a graceful arc before smashing into the Jersey barriers. I dodged the wreckage, but the trail vehicle hit it head on.

I veered across the lanes and took the first exit too fast, heading back into DC. The black SUV followed me with unexpected grace. Once I hit the city streets, I blew through lights and snaked around traffic, hoping to lose the heavier SUV. It wasn't working. A turning dump truck caused me to nearly skid out, and the SUV almost rear-ended me. I could see the woman driving it, wearing a dark suit and sunglasses, too. I accelerated, taking a series of sharp lefts through intersections, hoping the oncoming traffic would ensnarl her. It didn't.

She's good, I thought. Maybe she was one of Winters's people.

Two miles ahead was the Capitol dome. I needed to disappear before I hit that warren of cops. First, I had to ditch the SUV, and then outsmart the choppers. I reached for my Mark 23 and rolled down the windows. I could tell the SUV was uparmored by the way it listed heavily around turns. The driver's skill was the only thing keeping it upright. But armored vehicles have a weakness. They can't roll down their windows, which meant they couldn't shoot back. I readied one of my HK Mark 23 handguns.

I took a side street with thin traffic, allowing me space. She followed. I timed an upcoming four-way intersection and jerked the wheel a quarter turn right then hit the brakes, sending the car's back end skidding. The BMW careened into a J-turn and stopped, so that I sat perpendicular to the oncoming SUV. The driver gave a toothy smile and accelerated, intent on ramming me.

I lifted my Mark 23 and unloaded the clip through my open window and into the SUV's front tires, then accelerated before the beast could T-bone me. The SUV tried to make the turn but flipped on its shredded tires. Run flats don't perform high speed turns, regardless of what manufacturers promise.

Both choppers climbed after witnessing the gunshots. Fine by me. I lurched around cars, both my bumpers half dragging on the ground from the collision with the police cruisers. I headed toward the bridges and tunnels of I-395 and the train tracks near the waterfront. Maybe I could lose the chopper in that scrum of concrete and steel. It was my only chance before the next wave of police arrived.

The police helicopter anticipated my plan and zoomed ahead to keep an eye on me as I approached. I heard sirens approaching. A lot. *Change of plan,* I thought. I skidded right, taking advantage of ten-story buildings to break the chopper's line of sight with me. DC has few tall buildings owing to a law prohibiting anything taller than the Capitol building. This gave the helicopter an advantage, but not always. I glanced at my mirrors, but I didn't see the chopper. Still, that didn't mean it couldn't see me.

Must find an underground garage or get to a safe house before being spotted again, or I'm finished, I thought grimly as I wound through traffic, drove on empty sidewalks, and fishtailed through a small park. It was all drivable terrain. Minutes later, I rolled into the empty part of Southeast, home to feral cats and my safe house. In the distance I could see the police helicopter circling around the spot where it lost me, the ten-story buildings. The news chopper hovered above it. No doubt an army of police were sealing the buildings' underground garages and exits.

Satisfied, I crept toward my safe house using trash alleys to avoid other vehicles until I pulled into my dilapidated ex-taxi home. Once inside, the warehouse doors shut automatically behind me, and I killed the engine. The roofing was thick enough to conceal the hot engine from a police chopper's thermal imaging lens, but I was taking no chances.

I rested my forehead on the BMW's steering wheel, breathing deeply in the dark. Only one question remained: *How did they find me so fast?*

CHAPTER 32

Jackson stared in disbelief at the TV, his mouth agape. The high-speed car chase was being covered live on international news, showing smashed police vehicles and the black BMW driving like a maniac through the streets of Washington, with the Washington Monument as backdrop. Pillars of black smoke beset the landscape as if it were Yemen and fire engines screamed throughout the city.

In the nation's capital! he thought, as if it were a personal affront. *The gall!*

The news reported the terrorist escaped, which his sources confirmed minutes earlier. But the damage was done. The city began panicking like New York and people started evacuating en masse. Highways grew into parking lots and gas stations went dry. The president was not a patient man and would demand answers. So would Jackson.

It was supposed to be a simple snatch and grab, he thought. *What went wrong?* Winters warned him about Locke, but his intuition screamed there was more to Tom Locke than Winters was divulging. In fact, there was more to everything than Winters was revealing, a pattern he could now see clearly from the start.

Winters has been playing me the entire time. The realization made him woozy. Jackson did not esteem himself a fool, yet it was embarrassingly obvious that their secret partnership was a sham. It was a one-way street, and he was facing the wrong way.

But what game was Winters playing, and what did it mean for national security? Nothing good. *No more games,* he thought.

"Get me Winters," yelled Jackson to his executive assistant. "*Now!*"

Ten minutes later, Jackson and Winters met at the lowest level of a downtown garage, their respective black SUV convoys filling up much of the space. All the exits were sealed, and the depth of the garage guaranteed no electronic eavesdropping. The wall-to-wall concrete and dim fluorescent lighting were a stark contrast to the Cosmos Club. The two men faced off in the middle of a circle of bodyguards wearing dark suits, earpieces, and shoulder holsters. It looked like a geriatric fight club.

"Get them out of here!" yelled Jackson, and Winters waved his bodyguard away. Jackson followed suit, and both security details returned to their vehicles, waiting out the confrontation. Only Jackson and Winters remained.

"Who the hell is Locke?! He's no ordinary operator, but a worst-case scenario. Just like everything else you've been feeding me, it's all bullshit!" Jackson fumed. "You've been a huckster from the start, Winters, getting me to clean up your myriad in-house problems while you fall short on your end of the deal. I am no longer your corporate janitor. This ends here! Now!"

"Balderdash," Winters croaked. "I've been holding up my end of our agreement, but you keep manifestly failing and then blame me for your ineptitudes. You can't even eliminate a single man! If anything, I warned you: Locke is crafty. Worse, he's lucky. The only failure here is yours, because *you* let him get away."

"Me?!" yelled Jackson, eyes bulging. "This is not about Locke."

"It is *all* about Locke!" snarled Winters, jabbing his cane in the air at the national security advisor. "You came to me for a favor; you wanted a lead on the nuclear bomb. I didn't have to, but I gave you one. In fact, I gave you more. I lined up the man responsible for the headshot and you missed. Now he's gone to ground, and you won't get another shot. You're an imbecile!"

"This isn't about Locke, you fossilized moron, it's about you!" shouted Jackson, stabbing his index finger at Winters. "Locke is part of a wider pattern of your vast incompetence. Remember, Locke is *your* guy. How did he get loose in the bullpen in the first place? Because *you* lost control of him. Then *you* called me in to clean up your fiasco. Don't fuck with me, Winters. I've been at this longer than you, and I will put you down."

Winters laughed. "Don't threaten me. We've both been at this a long time. You wish to discuss patterns of incompetence? The mark was the president and not the vice president. How could you screw *that* up? I upheld my end of the deal, now uphold yours! All the residual problems are yours to rectify."

"It's not my fault POTUS got sick that day and the VP took his place," said Jackson defensively. "They don't announce last-second changes like that for security reasons."

"POTUS was *your* responsibility. And if the president wants your scalp for the Locke debacle, so be it. I'll find a new partner."

Jackson took a step back, aghast at the concept. "Ridiculous! I could shut you down in hours, Winters. *Remember that.*"

"You perfidious swindler," rasped Winters, his face contorting with rage. He knew it was true, but somehow he expected Jackson would never stoop so low. It was a bullet in the corporate head.

"One phone call. That's all it would take, Winters. That's all you're worth to me."

Winters's anger gave way to a hoarse belly chuckle, surprising Jackson. "You're just a swamp creature. *Remember that.* You came to *me.* You asked for *my* help eliminating a spineless president, rallying the nation around the flag, and galvanizing a complacent country against foreign enemies. You said . . . how did you put it? 'Killing three birds with one stone.' You told me a massive terrorist attack at home was the only way to unite a bitterly divided nation. We even negotiated the acceptable casualty rate for collaterals," he said. "I said six thousand minimum to make it look plausible, but you insisted on less than five hundred. I said you were squeamish and you told me my estimate was overkill. Remember that?"

"Yes. That was the plan, and it is in jeopardy now thanks to your rogue agent, Locke. You were supposed to stage a fake terrorist attack to scare people, but instead you produced an actual nuclear terrorist who might blow up a city. Locke is your guy, Winters, and he's off the leash. That's on you, Winters. Your stupidity created this nuclear Frankenstein!"

Winters ignored him. "The plan was I take out POTUS, you blame terrorists, and then you give me big contracts to go after them in faraway lands. Forever wars are my business model, something you accepted. You would play the hero, I would get rich, and America would come together against common enemies. That was our arrangement, Jackson."

"Then why is my interagency spun up about Russia?" asked Jackson in anger. "I blame you, Winters. Your guy Locke smuggled in a nuke through New Jersey using the Russian mob. Half the intelligence community is implicating the Kremlin, and Moscow is getting twitchy. Once again, your incompetence has become my emergency. Now I have to avert World War Three in addition to cleaning up your mess."

Winters grinned wide, showing scraggly teeth. "And who says the Russians are not a part of *my* plan?"

Jackson stammered but no words came out. He felt woozy again.

"Don't fuck with me, George. You're out of your depth," warned Winters.

Jackson recovered. "You commit high treason, and then seek to dictate terms to me, the national security advisor? You are soft in the head, Brad. I can pin *everything* on you. I can connect you to the bridge, Locke, and the nuke. It will be done before the morning news cycle is over, and there are no favors or tricks you can pull that will save you this time. I'll have your ass in manacles and finish what the Saudis started. Consider it a promise, and you know I'm a man of my word."

"The only person here who will hang for high treason is you! Because that's where the evidence will lead. I can dust my tracks and disappear, but you leave a paper trail."

"You really believe that?" sneered Jackson. "I can manipulate the government, you cannot. I can direct investigators, influence findings, and steer presidential decisions. What do you have, Winters? A board meeting?" Jackson laughed. "You will burn, and I will light the fire."

Winters's bad leg nearly buckled, and he wavered on his cane. *Damn Locke!* he thought. Locke's ill-timed resurrection made him susceptible to Jackson, putting his grand plan at risk. As long as Jackson could plausibly frame him for everything, the man had leverage. There was only one way to rebalance the equation. *I must remove Locke,* he thought.

Jackson sensed Winters's vulnerability and went for the kill. "You fix Locke, or I fix you! He's your man and that makes him your nuclear terrorist. You think eliminating one man is nothing? Good, then Locke should be easy for you to kill. I want proof of death. And get me that nuke!"

"Fine, I will kill Locke. I will clean up your mess," said Winters with a smile. He couldn't resist adding the last bit.

"*Your* mess, Winters! Your man, your mess," corrected Jackson as he moved in close. "And don't *ever* threaten me again. Remember that I feed you and remain your master, not the other way around." Jackson was pointing to the floor in front of him, as if commanding a dog to sit. "I have dealt with detritus like you my entire career. Never forget that I have the power to send you to hell and keep you there."

Winters chuckled, which was not the reaction Jackson expected. "You are a swamp creature, and that makes you predictable. It's why I took out an insurance policy. Three, to be precise."

Jackson's expression changed from wrath to bewilderment.

"Locke doesn't have the nukes. *I do.*"

"Bullshit," said Jackson, but Winters stood motionless like a tripod, waiting for him to think it through. "Impossible. I don't believe it," muttered Jackson, but his apprehensive tone betrayed his strong words.

"Three," taunted Winters, with the joy of a cat playing with its prey. "Not one. *Three.*"

"Three?" replied Jackson weakly. He expected Winters was lying again, but could he really take chances if it were remotely true?

"Correct. The nukes are already hidden in America's largest cities. You will never locate them, so don't try. I will not hesitate to pull the trigger if I feel threatened. If anything should happen to me, three American cities will evaporate—and on your watch, Mr. National Security Advisor." Then Winters bayoneted Jackson's weak spot. "Think of your legacy. How will American history remember you?"

Jackson turned noticeably paler, even under the garage's dim fluorescent light. His mouth moved but nothing came out. Finally, just a whisper: "You wouldn't dare. Is this another bluff?"

"And you thought the president was your biggest problem. What a fool!" cackled Winters.

"This better not be more lies, Winters, or so help me God I will string you up in Lafayette Square like Mussolini. Do not gamble with American cities!" bellowed Jackson, spittle flying from his mouth. "WMD was deliberately precluded from our arrangement."

"The arrangement has changed."

Jackson clenched his fists, and Winters feared the man would strike him.

"There is no place you can run, hide, or slither, Winters, that I cannot find you. Nukes or no nukes. And if not me, then someone like me. You can't outrun the government."

"The people I work for are far less forgiving than me," said Winters in a severe tone. "They will destroy you, someone like you, or the entire government, if they must."

"People? What people?" retorted Jackson, doubt on his face. "You're a bottom feeder, Winters. All you crave is power, but there are things more important, like country."

"'Country'?! Listen to yourself, old man. You are stuck in the twentieth century, while the rest of the world has moved on. Today's superpowers are no longer countries but something else. They operate in the shadows and manipulate the rest."

"That torture cell warped your brain worse than I thought."

Winters squeezed the ivory monkey head but held his temper. "There's a war going on, Jackson, an invisible one, and it's not being fought by nations. Its weapons are not militaries, but deception and manipulation. Its pawns are countries and corporations. Nothing else matters. Don't you see it? The U.S. invades faraway places that pose no existential threat, like Iraq and Afghanistan, and stays there forever regardless of who sits in the Oval Office. It makes no sense, yet Americans wave their flags and support the troops, and for what? It's all for naught. The U.S. is no longer a superpower—it's a tool. We've been manipulated into fighting other people's wars. Sometimes the more obvious a thing is, the harder it is to see."

"When did you become a conspiracy theorist?" mocked Jackson, and Winters's face darkened.

"Talent is hitting targets no one else can hit, but genius is hitting targets no one else can see. I made a choice, George, and so should you. You're a pawn in a global war you don't see or comprehend. If you care about your country, then you should choose not to become a tool."

Winters started walking away.

"Hey, where are you going? I'm not done," yelled Jackson.

"But I am," rasped Winters without stopping. "You've been warned. I'm just the messenger."

"What does that mean?"

Winters spun around. "It means you're expendable."

CHAPTER 33

Lin waited until nightfall before driving to the mystery safe house in McLean, Virginia. Dan's counterintelligence team monitored Russian agents from this house and saw them meeting with Apollo Outcomes teams covertly. No one knew why. When his boss ran it up the chain, he was ordered to shut down his operation. When he refused, he was exiled to Omaha and his team dispersed with prejudice.

Someone high up is protecting this safe house, and I want to know why, thought Lin as she drove a little too fast. Even if she wasn't fired by the FBI, she would always choose her own car, a zippy Mini Cooper, over the FBI's joke of an unmarked car, the conspicuous Ford Crown Vic. Twenty minutes later, she found Dan's mystery safe house in a cul-de-sac of McMansions deep in suburban Virginia, ironically not far from CIA headquarters.

"There you are," she whispered as she cut the engine. Parking well up the street, she observed the surreptitious safe house. Nothing stood out. Trees surrounded the property and swayed in the winter gusts. Lights were on but she saw no movement. Nearby homes were equally quiet, but she saw people inside.

It's go time, Lin thought as she zipped up her black jacket and pulled her wool cap low. Casually, she walked down Rockland Terrace, as if she were there visiting relatives. The houses were spaced well apart, marking it as an affluent suburb, and no one looked out their windows at this late hour. Somewhere in the distance, a dog barked.

Lin's heart beat faster as she approached the McMansion. Its front double doors were framed by a two-story colonnade and unpruned shrubbery. Sheer curtains hung in the windows, obscuring the house's interior. However, she could see the outline of a humongous but cheap chandelier hanging in the atrium; several of its bulbs were dead. Up close, the place looked inert and run down. Then she saw silhouettes in a second-story window.

Someone's definitely home, she thought, and unconsciously felt her Glock beneath her coat. Lin moved into the tree line, and the frozen snow crunched beneath her sneakers. The driveway was shoveled and salted, another clue that people lived here. She crept to the backyard and found a wooden deck and rusty barbeque. The backyard was even more unkept than the front.

An outside light flicked on. *Crap!* she thought, then realized it was a motion sensor light, the kind you can get at any hardware store. She froze, blending into the night's shadows. Seconds later, the light turned off and she moved.

Calm. Be calm, she told herself, gliding furtively up the deck stairs. Kneeling in front of the back door, she pulled out a screwdriver and a ring of bump keys, each with a small O-ring around its base. Working rapidly, she tried each key until she found one that fit the lock. She turned it slightly to the right and tapped on the back of the key with the screwdriver's handle. Two taps later, the lock turned, and she was inside.

Eeeeeee. The house alarm buzzed, but it was not the siren that called in reinforcements. She had about thirty seconds to find the alarm panel and disable it before the real alarm blared. Alarms give owners a grace period to deactivate the alarm, even safe houses, and she was operating within that grace period.

Thirty, twenty-nine, twenty-eight, she counted as she entered the house, Glock drawn. Alarm panels were usually in a basement utility closet. Bounding across the supersized kitchen, she started opening closets. Pantry. Coats. Junk. It was the utility closet, and up near the ceiling was the alarm panel, an unassuming gray steel box. Too high for a circuit breaker.

That's it, she thought as she closed the door behind her and turned on her Maglite. Upstairs, footsteps were moving down a hallway and then down the stairs. *Fifteen, fourteen, thirteen.*

Slow is smooth, and smooth is fast, she told herself. Climbing up on a washing machine, Lin bump-keyed the steel box open. *Ten, nine, eight.* Inside lay a tangle of wires, lights, and circuit boards. Holding the Maglite in her mouth, she located the power supply and yanked it lose. *Five, four, three.* Then she found the battery backup and pried it out with the screwdriver. The alarm died.

Lin didn't move and just listened over the pounding of her heart. Someone—a man, by the weight of the footsteps—sped past the closet door and into the kitchen. Slowly, she slid off the washing machine and aimed her weapon at the utility closet's door. No sound. The man stopped in the kitchen, or did he? She wasn't sure. She could feel her pulse throbbing in her head.

Click, click. She heard him unlock and lock the back door's deadbolt. Then silence again. *Keep moving. Nothing to see here,* she thought. Finally, the footsteps crossed the kitchen and opened the refrigerator door. She heard a plate clink on the stone countertop, and she thought he was probably loading up some snacks. Then he headed back upstairs at a leisurely pace. Lin lowered her weapon and breathed deeply to tame her heart rate.

Let's see who you are, she thought as she slipped out the closet door. *If you're nobody, I'll leave and you'll never know I was here.*

Lin padded through the dining room and living room, each with a vaulted ceiling. The place was sparsely furnished in the anodyne style of a hotel lobby. There were no magazines, personal pictures on the walls, or any other artifacts of life. The

McMansion had a home office/library, but the shelves were vacant and the desk drawers empty. There was not even pen and paper.

I've seen motel rooms with more soul, she thought and continued her security sweep. Stealthily, she crept up the large double staircase in the atrium, Glock pointing forward, until she reached the top floor. Bedrooms with male clothing, mostly active sportswear. A grand bathroom with no female accoutrements. Closets, mostly empty.

She heard voices. Humans. Lin stopped. Someone was watching a movie behind a closed door, an action thriller by the sound of it.

OK, time to leave, she told herself, turning around and feeling awkward. *Jason was right, I should never have come here.*

Two young men laughed in unison, then spoke in Russian. Lin froze and felt adrenaline shoot through her veins. She strained to hear them but couldn't make out the conversation, only the language. It was definitely Russian. She had to get closer.

This could be my big break, but I need to be sure, she thought, inching toward the door. Her heart thumped against her rib cage, making her Glock shake. *Steady,* she commanded as she got closer. They were talking about the movie.

"She is a sexy chick but has miserable tits," judged a young man in Russian.

Pigs! she thought, and her Glock went steady.

"Yeah, I've seen ironing boards more fuckable," said the other, laughing.

So rude, she thought as she carefully extended a hand for the doorknob while the other held the Glock. Slowly she turned it and cracked open the door so she could peak inside.

Two young men leaned back in desk chairs with their feet on makeshift desks. An array of large computer monitors hung

off a steel frame, and one showed the movie. Old boxes of mi-
crowaved junk food littered their desks, and the place reeked
of sweat socks and pizza. It could have been a frat house, save
the multiple computer screens with high-end spy programs in
Cyrillic.

Russian hackers, all right, she thought. Probably on loan from
the Troll Factory in St. Petersburg, the nickname for the Russian government's notorious hacker unit. Normally they operated
from the motherland. *What are they doing here?*

"I bet he screws like a squirrel," said one of the Russians about
the movie star, who was busy shooting bad guys.

"And she's his nut," said the other and laughed.

"Women need to be crushed like nuts in sex. A man must
show her who is fucking who."

"As in sex, so too in life. The woman is under the man, as
it's meant to be." Both young men nodded in their perceived
wisdom.

"Then what does that make me?" said Lin in Russian. The
men jerked upright in shock and spun around to face her, only to
see her gun pointing at them. "On the ground, boys!"

"Who are . . ." stammered one, unable to finish his sentence.

"I'll tell you what. Since you're the weaker sex, I'll put my
gun away." Carefully she slid the Glock back into her holster and
both men eyed their own 9 mm pistols sitting on the computer
console. She saw the weapons, too. "There, now it's a fair fight.
Two dicks versus one woman. Let's see how it ends."

The two men reached for their pistols, but the hackers were
no match for Lin. Seconds later they were flex-cuffed to furniture, each breathing heavily through the pain. One man's nose
was smashed and bled all over his T-shirt and the floor. He instinctively held his nose up in the air, as if that would slow the
bleeding, but it made no difference. The other was balled up in

a fetal position, clutching broken ribs and taking shallow sips of air. Each breath caused sharp pain to shoot up his side. Lin stood over them, dominant.

"Looks like you're the bitches now," she said, then dug her toe gently into the second man's injured side. He shrieked and she smiled. "That's on behalf of the other fifty percent of the human race."

Lin wheeled up one of the office chairs and sat down, legs crossed and arms on the armrests, like a queen in judgment. "Now that introductions are over, I wish to have a friendly conversation. If you refuse to reciprocate, our discussion will become progressively unfriendly."

"Piss off," said the one with the broken nose, in bad English. "You have no idea who you're dealing with, bitch. We will fuck you up!"

"Not friendly," replied Lin calmly in Russian. "And do not worry. I will fuck you hard, but not in the way you think. I will crush you like a nut. I may even pulverize all four nuts," she said, holding the Glock by its barrel and swinging it like a hammer. Both men closed their legs unconsciously and turned away from her glare. "Last chance, and try to use your brains before you answer this time. Who are you? Who do you work for? What are you doing here? When did you arrive?"

Neither man spoke.

"Talk to me!" shouted Lin, and both men jumped in alarm. But they remained silent, and the man with the broken nose spat blood at her. Lin walked over to him and hammered his nose again with the butt of her weapon. His scream was horrific, and the other man grimaced with fear.

"I don't have all goddamned night," she said, and it was true. They could have tripped a silent alarm, and heavies could be on the way.

"Go to hell," wheezed the man with broken ribs, each word a stabbing pain. "You're a dead woman. Dead!" He started coughing in agony.

Lin knelt beside the man huddled on the floor and nuzzled her gun gently into his broken ribs. He screeched. "Talk to me, Ribs, or I will blow Nosebleed's head off. Talk to me or I kill your friend. Five seconds, you decide." She stood up and aimed the gun at Nosebleed's head, cocking the hammer; the man looked away. "Five, four . . ."

"Do it Yuri! Tell her!" shouted the man with the broken nose. Yuri didn't speak.

". . . three . . ."

"Stop! Stop!" screamed the man with the broken nose. Lin steadied her aim.

". . . two . . ."

"I will tell you! I will tell you!!"

Lin lowered her weapon. "Tell me what, Nosebleed?"

"The room," said the man with the broken nose.

"You traitor!" yelled the man on the floor, and contorted in pain.

"Screw you, Yuri! I'm not dying for this. Besides, she's dead anyway."

"Do I look dead to you?" asked Lin, amused.

"You will be. Now untie me, and I will show you."

"Show me what?"

"Untie me." No one moved. Growing impatient, Lin raised her Glock to his head. "Stop, stop, stop!" he said, blood still trickling down his mouth and chin. "What you want is in the basement. I promise. Untie me, and I will show you."

It could be a ploy, she thought. *But I can take him, especially in his beat-ass state.* "OK, Nosebleed," she said, drawing a small boot knife and holding it to his jugular. "But fuck with me and I will gut you." With that she sliced the flex-cuff, and he fell away, rubbing his wrists. "Up! Show me."

"Andrei. My name is Andrei."

"Whatever, Nosebleed. Walk." They moved down the hall, and she kept her gun at his back. They walked downstairs and into the basement. It was empty, save a laundry area.

"Are you lying to me, Nosebleed?" asked Lin in disbelief, holding her Glock to his head.

"No, no! Please. Secret room," he said, pointing to a dark corner. She followed at a distance and aimed her pistol at his torso as he opened up a large fuse box. Then he opened the front panel, a fake. Behind it was a handprint scanner. Andrei pressed his right hand on the scanner, and she heard a heavy bolt inside the wall release. With a grunt, he pushed and the entire wall rotated inward and to the right, revealing a spacious hidden room.

"Impressive," Lin heard herself say out loud.

"They will come for me," said the hacker, smiling. "They will kill you. After their fun."

"Who? FSB? Spetznatz? Who?"

He smiled, blood dibbling down his chin. "Worse."

Worse? She thought. *Who's worse than Russian special forces? You have to be a qualified psychopath to make their ranks.* What the civilized world considered human rights abuse, they considered training. New recruits had to survive *dedovshchina,* or the "Rule of the Grandfathers," that left many maimed or dead. Those that made it were ethically unhinged. Even the Russian mob feared them.

"Don't bluff me, asshole," said Lin, and flex-cuffed him to a pipe in the safe room. He continued smiling, feeding off her fear. She found the light switch and flipped it. The place was an armory: racks of assault rifles, pistols with silencers, .50-cal snipers with Forward Looking InfraRed (FLIR) thermal imaging scopes, munitions crates, high-end surveillance kits, communications gear, laptops, and a large street map of Washington, DC, taped to the wall. Everything needed to start a world war, except . . .

"Where's the demo?" demanded Lin.

"I do not understand," he said with a puzzled expression.

"The demolitions! How did you blow the bridge, Nosebleed?" she repeated, but the man was perplexed. Then she heard the garage door open above, and a large vehicle drive in and park.

"They're here!" said Andrei with bloody glee.

CHAPTER 34

Tye stood with his arms folded and Lava gave a low whistle as they inspected my wrecked BMW. Both its front and rear ends were smashed in, with a lake of neon-green radiator fluid under the chassis. I wondered how I made it back to my safe house at all. As soon as I did, I called Lava on the burner phone. What else could I do? I was ambushed and he was my only lifeline. He said he would come as soon as possible; that was hours ago and now it was midnight.

"Not exactly the 'quiet professional,' are you, Locke?" teased Tye, referring to a maxim of special operators everywhere. "Every cop in the city is looking for you."

"The country," corrected Lava. "Every cop in the country. And Interpol, too. Your name, picture, and physical description are on every blotter and news website in the world. They're saying you're the terrorist that assassinated the vice president." Lava gave a mock expression of admiration.

"Me?!" I exclaimed, breathless.

"Correct. Also, Winters probably knows you are here, in the city. He will be coming for you," said Lava, and I felt the blood drain from my face. Lava nodded, as if reading my mind and affirming my dread.

"Pretty impressive for a guy who's only been on the ground for seventy-two hours," said Tye with a smirk. "That's gotta be a record. We should create a new category for you called the FUMTU Awards."

"FUMTU?" I asked.

"Fucked Up More Than Usual."

I ignored his grin and turned to Lava. "How did they find me so fast? How could they possibly get my file? Know where I would be? I've gone over it a million times in my mind, Lava, and I don't get it."

"You should have stayed put, Tom, and let me run the traps at Apollo first," said Lava, kicking my dead bumper. It fell off.

"Yeah, I know. But I—"

Lava held up a hand to silence my excuses. Tye rolled his eyes. I felt like a butter bar again.

"Let's go inside," said Lava, and we followed him into the trailer.

"Real shithole of a place you got here, Locke," said Tye as he entered.

"Yeah, Lava said the same exact thing two nights ago."

"The man ain't wrong."

"Suit up, Locke. We need to get you out of here," said Lava.

I was already packed to go, hoping he would say that. Nonetheless, I went over my equipment one last time. Old habit.

"Learn anything at Apollo?" I asked, as I put on my Apollo armor.

"Nada. They think you're off the board."

"KIA," added Tye. "In Syria, a year ago by Jase Campbell's team. Curiously, he's MIA as of today. Go figure."

Winters had sent Campbell's team after me in Iraq. He was good, too. "If Apollo didn't ambush me, then maybe it was Winters," I said.

"Negative," said Tye. "You'd be dead if it was Winters's guys."

"Agreed," said Lava. "Unless they're framing terrorists, they don't operate in daylight. Neither do we, for that matter. You were definitely hit by govvies." *Govvies* referred to government actors such as the military, intelligence, and law enforcement. It was a term of derision at Apollo.

"How is that possible?" I asked, slipping my Mark 23s into thigh holsters. Now wasn't the time for subtlety. "I just landed and no one knows I'm here but you. The CIA is good, but not that good. I have no digital signature, so the NSA can't track me. Anyway, they're not even looking for me. Everyone thinks I'm dead." I assumed Lava and Tye didn't give up my position to the govvies, although I was beginning to wonder. Trust no one.

"I don't understand it either, Tom. Until I do, we're all at risk," said Lava in an unsettling voice, looking at Tye, who nodded. His smirk had vanished. "I got a place in Virginia, in the Shenandoah. It's real primitive but you'll get used to it. I'm taking you there until I figure this out." Lava turned to me, holding up an index finger in my face. "And *stay put* this time!"

"Yes sir," I said automatically. We began loading my equipment into the back of Lava's armored SUV. "How goes the war with Winters?"

"It's a draw at the moment. It seems the turncoats are always one step ahead of us," said Tye as we carried a ballistic chest to the vehicle. "For now."

"Maybe you have a leak in your organization. Someone with divided loyalties," I said as we heaved the chest into the vehicle's back.

"A few months back, we launched a mole hunt and it almost tore the organization apart," said Lava, tossing the grenade launcher on the backseat. "It led nowhere. I believe our opsec is tight." Opsec, or operational security, is a religion at Apollo. It meant keeping a secret.

"I don't know how they're tailing us, but they are," said Tye.

The time had come to ask the most important question. If

I couldn't trust Lava now, then I was already a dead man. "Do you think Winters blew the bridge?"

Both stopped what they were doing and turned to me. Before Lava could answer, he received a text. "We need to leave now! A renegade Apollo assault team is inbound."

Tye sprinted to the driver's seat and cranked the engine.

"Leave the rest!" commanded Lava, and I dove into the back, SCAR in hand.

"Go, go, go!" shouted Lava as we crashed down the garage door and fishtailed around the corner, accelerating down the abandoned street. In seconds, we cleared six blocks.

"Wait! Slow down," said Lava, and Tye looked at him quizzically. "We need to observe this. Maybe it will tell us how they're tracking us."

"That's suicide," warned Tye. "They'll nab us for sure."

Lava didn't speak but shot him a command glance. I knew that look, and it always made me feel lower than whale shit.

"Wilco," responded Tye, soldier speak for *I understand and will comply*. We donned our full-face Apollo helmets with night vision, and Tye switched to blackout drive. The street became day in the vehicle's infrared headlights. Lava pointed two fingers to the left, and we drove down a side alley.

"This should be good," he said over the earpiece. "Pull in here."

Tye took a right and we bumbled over rotting train tracks to a decrepit brick warehouse, much bigger than my safe house. It looked 1890s, with smashed-out windowpanes and a multistory coal smokestack. A rusty corrugated-steel sheet covered an antiquated truck entrance.

"Hold on," said Tye. He put the SUV in reverse and rammed through the corrugated-steel sheet. Tye was about to turn off the engine when Lava's hand blocked him.

"Leave it running," said Lava. "Grab your shit."

Tye grabbed his sniper rifle, a highly modified Finnish SAKO TRG 42. "They can run, but they'll just die tired," he joked, sort of.

I flipped on my night vision gunsight and could see everything my barrel saw, plus what was behind and ahead of me. Apollo fabricated custom equipment for its operatives, no expense spared, and it was always better than what the SEALs or Delta had. Always. It was a great recruitment tool, too.

We climbed up flights of broken stairs and then a rusty iron ladder to the roof. The place smelled like rotting machines. Once on the roof, I could see the Washington Monument, the Capitol building, and the National Airport across the Potomac River. A chilling winter breeze cut across us.

"Hear them?" asked Lava. Tye nodded, but I heard nothing.

"There," said Tye, pointing down the river. I strained my eyes and then saw them. Four black helicopters flew in perfect formation and stealth, skimming the Potomac. They were unlike any aircraft I had seen before: double rotors on top and a pusher propeller in the back. There were weapons pods on each flank and a 20 mm chain gun.

"Here they come," said Lava. "Move!" We slid down the rusty ladder, evading the choppers' thermal cameras. They flew directly over us, as quiet as golf carts and no *thwop-thwop-thwop* sound. I always thought "stealth helicopter" was an oxymoron, but apparently not.

"Follow me," commanded Lava, and we walked to the edge of the roof. Through my night vision, I saw the four helicopters hovering above my safe house. Ropes dropped from their sides and men fast-roped down. Sixteen in all. The choppers disappeared into the night while the men breached the roof and dropped into the warehouse, followed by flashes and loud explosions from within the building. The attack was withering, even from our distance, and took less than a minute.

There was no way I could have survived that, I realized.

"Show's over, let's go," said Lava. A powerful spotlight shown down on us, and then another and another and another. Rotor downdraft beat the air around us, but all I could hear was a steady whine, like a high-speed train engine, and not chopper blades. The stealth helicopters' 20 mm antitank cannons were leveled at our chests.

"Move and die," came a voice over a loudspeaker. We were surrounded. Lava and Tye slowly put their weapons down and raised their hands. I followed their lead; we had no options beyond death. Armed men wearing the same body armor as those in the skyscraper streamed up the ladder and pushed us hard to the ground. In seconds, we were flex-cuffed and searched, removing all weapons. They even found my handcuff keys, both handcuff shims (belt buckle and rear beltloop), and the ceramic razor blade sewn into my tactical pants. In the distance, I saw the sixteen commandos evacuate my former safe house, now ablaze with a fire plume fifty feet high. Fire trucks wailed in the distance.

They yanked us to our knees and the leader removed our helmets one by one. Lava stared straight ahead, face revealing nothing. However, Tye's faced revealed everything: rage, murder, death. When they got to me, I heard the leader snort in contempt, then look up and wave.

A cable lowered from one of the black helicopters, and two men wound it around my chest and under the armpits. The leader looked up at the pilot and gave him a thumbs-up. The helicopter shot straight up, yanking me off my feet and sucking the air out of my lungs. I began rotating clockwise in midair but could see men putting hoods over Lava and Tye. They were not nice about it, either.

"Lava! Tye!" I shouted, but my voice was drowned out by

distance. Ten-story buildings passed beneath my boots as we zoomed over the waterfront and then descended to the river, where they dunked me at high speed, which was like being waterboarded by a hydrofoil. My body skimmed the surface, each body blow knocking the wind out of me.

Dicks, I thought, knowing the pilots were having fun. I was still coughing water out of my lungs when we climbed sharply, and the Potomac looked black in the moonless night. I spun in wild arcs as the chopper banked, all the while attempting to loosen my wrists behind my back, but it was no use. We crossed the far bank, passing over Route 50, and I could see the lights of the Pentagon.

The helicopter slowed to a hover above six black Chevy Suburbans, arranged in a circle with their headlights on and facing inward, making a perfect LZ. The pilots lowered me down into the middle of the circle, lined with more commandos in black, all guns on me. The towline went slack, and I hit the ground hard. The chopper accelerated back into the night. The commandos slowly walked toward me in unison as I struggled to stand up, my hands tied behind my back.

"Go ahead, assholes! It's the only chance you'll get!" I shouted, but they came to a halt, weapons trained on my head. A vehicle door opened, and an ornate cane emerged, followed by a tall man with a limp.

I couldn't believe what I was seeing.

"Winters," I hissed as he hobbled toward me. He looked different. Meaner, ghastlier, more evil.

"Did you really think I would let you get away a second time, Locke?" he rasped.

"I'm going to strangle you with my own hands!" I screamed, and two commandos rushed to restrain me, forcing me to my knees before him. "I'll beat you to death with that cane!"

Winters laughed as they placed the hood over my head.

CHAPTER 35

Lin was trapped. She heard men speaking Russian on the floor above her, but the accents were strange. A few spoke like it was their second language. It sounded like there were six of them, and they were definitely military, and not FSB. *I need backup,* she thought, and tried her mobile phone, but her signal was dead inside the hidden bunker. The hacker smiled despite his broken nose. He knew she was trapped, too.

She looked around, desperately. The secret room took up half the McMansion's basement and was part armory and part electronics workbench. It had its own filtrated ventilation system and was lined with paneling that blocked electronic signals. Ballistic chests were stacked against the walls, alongside homemade weapons racks and shelves full of spy equipment. Everything except a landline.

"Do you have a phone down here?" she whispered in Russian to her prisoner, but he laughed through his duct tape gag. Furiously she scoured the armory for a way to communicate to the outside world. There were satellite phones and military-grade radios, but nothing usable. Then she found a stack of laptops under a ballistic jacket, flipped one open. It whirred to life but had a lock screen. *Maybe I can make a call using the laptop,* she thought. Although it was electronically locked, it did have a camera and fingerprint reader.

"Can you unlock this?" she asked the imprisoned hacker. He looked blank, as if he had never seen a computer before. She grabbed his right hand and he fought her, yelping through his gag. Both his hands were flex-cuffed around a vertical pipe, giving him little room to resist.

"Mmmmmm!! Mmmmmm!!!!!" he grunted in protest as she pried open his right index finger with pliers and pressed it against the finger pad. The screen went blue with acceptance and then prompted a face shot. She held up the computer camera up to his face, hoping it would see him and unlock itself. The hacker dodged and looked away, as she chased him around the pipe.

Screw this, she thought, and gut-punched him. The hacker slumped over, facing the floor, coughing through the gag. She grabbed the back of his head and yanked up while holding the computer in the other hand, so it could see him. The screen came alive. *Bingo!* she thought, and he groaned with defeat.

"How do I make a call out with this thing?" she said, working the keyboard. Everything was in Cyrillic, slowing her down. Upstairs, the Russians started shouting and running around. *They must have discovered the other hacker,* she thought. *I don't have much time.*

A metallic crash hit the floor next to her, causing her to jump in alarm. A utility shelf full of loaded magazines and equipment lay on the floor, with a smiling hacker lying next to it. He had kicked it over, so his comrades above would hear it. Then he started screaming through his gag.

"Shut up!" she commanded, holding her hand against his gag. The man yelped louder, and she heard heavy footsteps above, moving toward the basement stairs. *No time for a phone call. I gotta get ready!* she thought, and ripped the place apart for anything useful. Shedding her coat, she grabbed the ballistic vest that covered the laptops and put it on, even though it was two sizes too large. Next, she found night-vision goggles in a foot locker and slipped them over her head. The dim room became bright gray with good three-dimensionality. The muffled footsteps above grew louder, as did the Russian expletives. Lin resumed her mad search.

"That'll do nicely," she says, discovering a steel box of hand grenades secured in cut-out foam. She grabbed four and stuffed them into her vest pockets, praying no bullets hit them. Not smart, she knew, but in her mind grenades were like condoms: better to have them and not need them than need them and not have them. And when it came to crazed Russians, she preferred grenades over condoms.

The basement door slammed open above her, and footsteps started down the stairs. The hacker screamed louder.

"Faster!" she told herself, opening a wall locker and finding MP5s leaning upright. "Good," she said, picking one up and cycling the charging handle. Then she dropped the MP5, spotting her weapon of choice.

"Sweetness," she whispered, picking up the Saiga-12 fully automatic shotgun with folding stock and collimator sight. Next to it were six banana clips, each holding twelve rounds of twelve-gauge shells, enough to obliterate a flock of ducks. Lin had only heard of this mythical weapon from her mafia informants. The thing looked like a black and bloated AK-47, and it was the wet dream of every Russian mobster to possess one. However, only Spetznatz had the military-grade version, and now so did Lin. "Sweetness," she repeated.

Lin heard the man on the other side of the wall, and she fumbled to get the clip into the Saiga. The bound hacker began shouting ecstatically. The deadbolt inside the door released and a man heaved it against the wall, swinging it open. Lin's hands shook, and she couldn't get the ammo clip to sit properly in the weapon. She crouched in a corner, behind a footlocker, so she was not visible to the gigantic Russian across the room.

Slow is smooth, and smooth is fast, she reminded herself again, focusing on the clip and ignoring the man across the room. It clicked into place, and the man spun around. Lin charged the bolt and they both heard the round slide into the chamber. He raised his pistol and she the Saiga, followed by a pistol shot and an explosion of shotgun rounds. The man blew backward off his feet, and the hacker shit himself.

Lin turned off the lights and used her night vision as she prowled through the basement, covering her corners as she moved. The Russian voices above her were frenetic now, and two heavy men came charging down the stairs. Lin was waiting and pulled the trigger, full auto. A *ruuurrrppp* sound shook the room, as the weapon walked upward and knocked her back. Gunsmoke clung to the air and two dead men lay facedown on the stairs, their bodies shredded by the wall of lead pellets. Hundreds of small holes peppered the dry wall in the stairwell, except for where the men had stood.

Lin loaded a fresh magazine and leapt up the stairs to the main hallway on the ground floor. No use sneaking around at this point. To the left was the kitchen and back door, but the passageway had two blind corners. When she worked on the FBI Special Weapons and Tactics (SWAT) teams, the shoot house taught her never to trust blind corners, especially when heavily armed Russians were lurking about. Lin glanced right, seeing the open atrium and front door. It was her best chance, even though she could take fire from the second-floor balcony.

All footsteps stopped and the house fell silent. *Bad sign,* she thought, not knowing where the enemy was. Slowly, she crept toward the atrium until she got to a bend in the hallway. Using a compact mirror, she peered around the corner. Nothing. She leapt up and the space around her exploded in automatic gunfire. Lin screamed involuntarily as she dove under a narrow hallway table, its marble top adding the minimum of protection.

"Come out and we won't hurt you!" yelled a man in bad English.

"Fuck off, dickless!" she yelled back, in Russian. One thing her time on the Slavic mafia beat taught her: *never* trust a Rusky with a gun. Another burst of rounds blew into the tabletop, splintering wood and marble around her. She was trapped.

"No need for such foul talk, little lady," said the man gently from around a corner. "Put down the gun and I promise not to hurt you."

Lin heard stealthy footsteps coming from the living room. Two pairs. *He's distracting me while his buddies flank me,* she realized. *I can play at that too.* "Who are you? Spetnatz?"

The man laughed. "No, little lady. We eat Spetnatz for happy hour."

"Then who are you?"

"OK, I will tell you since you ask nicely. We are Wagner Group."

"Russian mercenaries?!" exclaimed Lin, knowing he would only admit this if he intended to kill her.

"*Da,* little lady. Now come out, and I won't hurt you. I promise. I'm sure it's a misunderstanding, and no more people need to die tonight."

The two men in the living room were closing in and would soon block her exit to the front door. But she needed more information. "Wagner only works for the GRU. You're nothing but Spetznatz little green men," she said.

The man laughed. "Is that what they think here? No, we do not always work for Moscow and, no, we are not all Russian or Spetznatz. We are what Spetznatz should be." Then his tone got sterner. "We work for ourselves."

Lin heard the footsteps sneaking around the atrium's far corner, near the front door. It was down the hall about twenty feet, and they would annihilate her in a cross fire if she tried to escape.

All of this truly scared Lin. The Wagner Group did the Kremlin's nasty work around the globe: Ukraine, Syria, Venezuela, central Africa, and now the United States. They were potent and almost wiped out Delta force and Rangers in eastern Syria in 2018. When Russia wanted to fight a shadow war, they deployed the Wagner Group. When the Kremlin wanted to assassinate a leader, like the president, they used the Wagner Group because it offered maximum effectiveness and plausible deniability. Mercenaries operated without constraint, even compared to Spetznatz. Lin's pulse raced.

I must warn the FBI, she thought. *But first I need to get out of here.* She breathed deeply to focus her spirit, as her father taught her at Golden Gate Park while they practiced tai chi. Trust your training, he would counsel, and let the Tao flow through you like water going downhill. You will survive. A lifetime of training came down to moments like this. *Focuuuuus,* she thought and exhaled.

"Little lady, are you OK? Please come out."

She heard the men around the corner. "How do I know I can trust you?" she asked in a high-pitched whine, feigning panic.

"Please, I won't harm you. Just lay down your weapon and slide it forward, so I can see it."

Lin shoved the Saiga in front of her, but still within reach.

"Good," said the voice. "Now, come on out slowly."

"Is it only you?" she whimpered while she pulled out two grenades.

"Yes, it's just me. You killed my friends, but I promise I won't hurt you. I know you are scared. Come out."

"OK, OK. I think I'm ready to come out, if you put your gun down too," she said, pulling the grenades' pins but keeping their spring levers depressed.

"Here's my gun," said the man, sliding an MP5 into the hallway. She still couldn't see him, which meant he couldn't see her, either.

"Just give me a few seconds. I'm scared," she said with frailty as she let fly the two grenades' spring levers. *One-one thousand,* she counted.

"Take your time," he said.

Two-one thousand.

"I'm scared," she pleaded.

Three-one thousand. She shot the first grenade like a pool ball across the wooden atrium floor, banking it off a wall and into the living room.

Four-one thousand. Lin tossed the second grenade toward the voice, bouncing it off the back wall and into the voice. Then she ducked, plugging her ears.

The explosions concussed the room, shattering windows. Men screamed. Lin picked up the Saiga and moved toward the voice's corner. There wasn't much left of the man, and the hallway was blown out and on fire. Without stopping, she moved around the corner through the living room's back entry and saw two bodies at the far end, near the front door. As she approached, muzzle first, it was clear they were actually dead and not faking it. The living room was on fire, too.

Lin heard sirens in the distance. *I can't be caught here,* she realized. There would be too many questions, and it would end badly. She needed to find whoever was behind this, and she couldn't do it locked inside an FBI holding cell.

One more thing! Lin thought, and sprinted back into the burning house. Minutes later, she emerged with a laptop. When the fire trucks arrived, she was gone. The firefighters found two survivors in flex-cuffs, six bodies, and a secret room full of Russian spy gear and heavy weapons. First responders scattered as live ammunition popped off in the fire, which consumed the house and most of the useful intelligence. Then the news trucks showed up.

Six black Suburbans snaked through the sparse night traffic, only feet from one another's bumpers despite their high speed. They shuffled their order as they passed through tunnels, and aggressively blocked other vehicles that got too close. Above them flew the four black Sikorsky S-97 helicopters, escorting them in stealth mode. The roads were generally clear at this hour, and the air-land convoy drove in a wide circling pattern, as Winters awaited a phone call. They stuck to the Virginia side of the river, where the roads were wider, allowing them more freedom to maneuver should a problem occur. Still, Winters didn't like traveling in the open. It wasn't the govvies he worried about; it was Apollo Outcomes. He was at war with them, and they both stalked the night. Operating in the open made him a target.

"Give me a secure line to the national security advisor," commanded Winters from the backseat of one of the armored Suburbans.

"Yes sir," said the aide. Moments later he handed Winters a handset. "It's secure."

"It's me. I have Locke, tied and trussed," said Winters.

"Excellent. I knew you would come through for me," said Jackson on the other end. "I think we can solve many problems with this guy."

"Wait, I'm not done, Jackson. If you want to use Locke as your fall guy, you must do something for me first."

"What?" answered Jackson, angry.

"Kill the president."

Silence. Then, "Say again?"

"Kill the president, Jackson."

"Are you mad?! Have you lost all sanity, Winters? What did they do to you in that prison cell?"

Winters did not react to the swipe but checked his watch, then interrupted Jackson's tirade. "Kill the president, per our original agreement."

"We're well beyond that, Winters."

"You know it's the only way. He will eventually find out that you had a hand in everything. When he does, he will come for you. It's cleaner this way, George. You know it is, and it will solve my problems too."

More silence. Winters could feel Jackson thinking it over. Both men knew they were in a standoff: Jackson could link all the terrorist events to Winters, and Winters could help enlighten the president to Jackson's treason. Both men also knew the standoff served no one's interests, and they needed a way forward. Winters was offering a path.

"Jackson, this is a onetime offer. I give you Locke right now, and your men kill the president. You can blame Locke for everything. We will both achieve our goals. Take the deal."

Jackson said nothing, still mulling it over, so Winters continued the assault. "When it's over, you can 'catch' Locke, link him to the Russians, and take full credit. I will even help you, if you wish. Think about it, George. The country is galvanized once more and hardened. Isn't that want you wanted? To do a little evil in order to achieve a greater good? To inoculate America against national security threats and unite the country? To awaken the sleepwalkers, as you put it?"

"Yes, but—"

"Then make a choice," interrupted Winters. "We don't have

much time. It's a onetime offer, and the best you will get. You must finish what you started, and that means POTUS. If you refuse, then I will find a new partner. Remember our last conversation; you're expendable."

Winters could hear Jackson breathing into the phone, no doubt furious, but the man had to learn his place. There were authorities greater than the White House, and they weren't divine.

"OK, fine," whispered Jackson.

"Speak up. I didn't hear that."

"I'll do it. I'll make the arrangements for POTUS. But we have to use your men."

"Done. We will stage another terrorist attack, but you need to line him up. No mistakes this time, and it will be harder now," said Winters. President Anderson had disappeared since the first terrorist attack and attempt on his life. The Secret Service kept the man essentially under house arrest for his own safety, and few knew where. Not even Winters.

"President Anderson is at Camp David," said Jackson quietly. "The place has been turned into a fortress. You're going to have trouble getting in there."

"No, I won't," assured Winters. "Just tell me where he is, exactly, and I will take care of the rest." Jackson didn't respond, perhaps regretting his decision. "I knew you would come through for me, George. This is the right thing to do, and you know it."

"Brad, there must be another way. Killing the president of the United States. Well, it's—"

"Don't soften on me now, Jackson!" interrupted Winters, angry. "There is only one way this ends. You know it; I know it. As long as POTUS is alive, we're both at risk."

Jackson knew it was true but didn't want to admit it to himself. The plan seemed simple enough but killing the president—regardless of who sat in the chair—was twisting his soul in unexpected ways. It would harm the country and embolden enemies. Ultimately, all he could muster was: "I'm a patriot, Brad."

"Then uphold your end of the bargain, George," said Winters, detecting Jackson's wavering resolve. "I'll be watching your moves closely, and if I sense you might double-cross me . . . don't. I have three nukes in three American cities. Call my bluff, and watch one incinerate."

"No need to get nasty, Winters," said Jackson, steel back in his voice. "I said I would take care of it, and I will. Deliver Locke to me directly. Meet me in the same garage as before. Give me fifteen minutes."

"Don't be late," said Winters, and Jackson hung up.

CHAPTER 37

Lin's hands were still shaking as she drove down the George Washington Memorial Parkway. Adrenaline still raged through her veins, and she was driving to calm down. Now she was driving to calm down. She didn't know where she was going nor cared; she just needed to drive. In the front seat sat her Saiga automatic shotgun, next to a bag of grenades and ammo. It would be impossible to explain if she got pulled over, but her mind wasn't there.

Should I have stayed at the scene? she kept asking herself, but there was no right answer. If she stayed, she would have been arrested, and who knew if the FBI would have believed her. Probably not. But running made her look guilty. Running always does.

The FBI will think I'm a criminal now, she thought, tears of frustration welling up in her eyes. She wiped her eyes with her sleeve, then her nose. *But I'm a good agent! I know I am.*

"Crap, crap, crap!" she yelled at the windshield, pounding the steering wheel. She pulled over into one of the scenic overlooks on the Potomac River, and got out of the car. Then screamed. No one was around, so she screamed again. Cars whizzed by and took no notice. She slumped on the hood, gazing at the lights of Georgetown across the river. In the distance were the bell towers of the National Cathedral, with a blinking red warning light on one for aircraft. The only sound was the occasional passing car and airliners on approach to the airport.

Lin fetched the Russian hacker's laptop from the car and sat down at a picnic table. Maybe it would reveal a clue. She opened it and tried several random passwords, in Russian, but it was no use. The thing was locked. She had contemplated kidnapping the hacker but had no time. Fire trucks were pulling into the burning house's driveway when she was still downstairs in the hidden armory, stuffing grenades into a rucksack. She had to leave immediately.

Another dead end, she thought, holding her head in her hands. She wanted to talk to someone but didn't know whom to call. All her friends were in the FBI, and she wasn't on speaking terms with her dad, even though she wanted to talk to him most. He would know what to do, but she couldn't face his judgment. She took out her phone and called the only person she could.

"Hello, Lin? Is that you?" asked Jason, waking up from sleep.

"Jason," she said, her voice breaking.

"What's the matter?"

"I can't . . ." She stopped and resisted the urge to sob, especially to Jason.

"Just slow down. Breathe," he said, and Lin took multiple deep breaths. "I'm guessing you went out to the safe house and found something?"

"Yeah," she said, getting control of herself. It was all she could say.

"Well, what?"

Lin put a hand over her eyes and looked down at the ground to help focus. *Get it together, girl,* she kept telling herself. *Don't let Jason hear you like this.*

"Lin? Are you there?"

"Yeah."

"What did you find?" asked Jason, and Lin told him. "Holy shit," was all he could say when she finished. "Holy. Fucking. Shit."

Neither spoke for several minutes.

"What's the Wagner Group doing running around Washington, DC?" asked Jason at last.

"I think they're the ones who are behind the bridge attack," said Lin. "But the guy said they weren't working for Moscow."

"Then who hired them?"

"I don't know. I don't even know if he's even telling a half truth."

"Well, it makes more sense than any other theory I've heard so far at headquarters," said Jason. They sat in silence, mulling over the implications. No one would believe them. Finally, he asked the only question that mattered: "What are you going to do now?"

"I need to find out what's going on. I need to finish my investigation. If not me, then who?" She paused, waiting for an encouraging response, but Jason said nothing. "Also, it's the only way to clear my name." His silence confirmed her suspicions that it was too late for that. *I don't care,* she thought and then spoke with fire. "What do I have to lose at this point?"

"Be careful what you wish for," said Jason, and Lin balled up a fist. It was exactly the kind of irritating thing her father would say.

"Are you going to help me or not, Jason?"

"Yes," he said, voice wavering. He would hang now, too. "Although I don't know why, Jen."

"Because you want to do the right thing."

"Yes, I suppose," he said unconvincingly.

"Because you like me?"

"Yes, that too."

"You're the only friend I have right now, Jason," said Lin, her vulnerable tone surprising them both.

After another pause, Jason changed the subject. "I talked to

Dan in counterintelligence again. We went out for drinks and he got a little tipsy. He's super stressed. It turns out that safe house was under some sort of surveillance embargo."

"Surveillance embargo? I've never heard of such a thing."

"Neither had his boss, who ignored it. Seems like you're not the only rebel in the Bureau."

Lin chuckled, her mood lifting.

"It turns out the men in the safe house would frequently make late-evening runs."

"Yeah, they came home late tonight too. Did Dan say what they were doing?"

"This is when drunk Dan got all weird on me. He said the Russians would meet up with another party. At first, they thought it was CIA Ground Division because they were all huge dudes that dressed like Secret Service agents, drove black SUVs, and met with scumbags late at night in strange locations."

"But that's illegal. The CIA is not allowed to operate domestically."

"Yeah, agreed, which is why his boss ran it by some friends at Langley, totally deep background, but they told him it wasn't their guys. It's not us either."

"Then who was it? DIA? DOD? DHS? Who?"

"None of the above. You'll never guess, Jen. They were meeting with a company."

"A company?" asked Lin incredulously. "Like Booz Allen?"

Jason laughed. "Nope. Ever heard of Apollo Outcomes?"

"Who are they?"

"Heavy hitters. They run paramilitary ops for the government, strictly off the books. It's like the CIA and JSOC combined, but Apollo Outcomes can do things those guys can't. That's why they're hired."

"*American* mercenaries? Like Wagner Group, but working for

us?" said Lin, not believing it, but cognitive dissonance had become the theme of her evening.

"Yeah, but even more hardcore."

"Let me guess. When you say Apollo Outcomes can do things the CIA and DOD can't, you're talking about domestic missions," she said. The CIA and DOD were absolutely forbidden from working inside the United States. From the Posse Comitatus Act of 1878 to the Church Committee of 1976, the one thing every intelligence, military, and law enforcement officer learns is no domestic spying or military operations. Not only was it illegal, it was considered a threat to democracy. However, outsourcing it to a private company would neatly circumnavigate the issue.

"Exactly. Dan's boss feared these guys were running some sort of modern COINTELPRO operation, so he started watching them too."

Lin stiffened when she heard COINTELPRO, the Bureau's low point. Starting in the late '50s, FBI director J. Edgar Hoover ran a covert and illegal program aimed at surveilling, infiltrating, discrediting, and disrupting left-wing political organizations. He thought the USSR was behind the antiwar riots and cultural war that seized America, and he took Machiavellian steps to stem the imagined threat. Some even blamed COINTELPRO for the assassinations of Martin Luther King Jr. and Malcolm X. The CIA launched its own domestic espionage project in 1967 called Operation CHAOS. All recruits at the FBI Academy were made to learn it so they would know what sin looked like.

"And is Apollo running a private sector COINTELPRO with Wagner Group's help?" asked Lin with anxiety. "It sounds like we have American mercenaries working with Russian ones to assassinate U.S. political leadership and frame terrorists. If so, we don't know who hired them, or why."

Jason let out a stressed sigh. "We may never know. The next

day, Dan's boss was transferred to the Omaha office, and everyone was forbidden to communicate with him. They shut down the operation and were told never to speak about it again, or have their security clearance yanked. It's why Dan got so cagey before."

"Geez."

"Yeah. I had no idea. Nobody does. I didn't know the FBI could keep secrets like that."

Lin was thinking. As if he could hear her think, Jason said, "Wait, stop, Lin! Just stop. You're in enough trouble as it is. Whatever you're thinking, do not do it! Every time you do this, things get worse for both of us!"

"Where can I find these Apollo Outcomes guys?" she asked, starting up the car.

"Jen, don't even think about it. They're heavy hitters and work for pay grades way above ours."

"But you just told me they're doing some COINTELPRO thing, are collaborating with the Wagner Group, and the FBI is prohibited from investigating it. It's treason, pure and simple. If we don't stop them, who will? It's obviously an inside job, Jason, and the insider has the Bureau tail-chasing on purpose."

"And that's why you need to quit, right now," pleaded Jason. "It's too dangerous. Leak it to the *Times* or *Post*, I don't care. Just stop chasing leads!"

She scoffed and buckled up. "You know me. You know I can't do that."

"Yes, I do," he sighed. "I wish I wasn't in love with you."

Lin didn't know how to respond. She had not heard anyone tell her that in a long time, and she preferred it that way. All her past boyfriend experiences were humiliating catastrophes, and now this, and at this moment. She needed to focus, but Jason's impromptu admission jolted her.

Focus, she thought. *Compartmentalize.* "Give me a location, and I don't mean Apollo's corporate headquarters. I want the CEO's house or something like that."

Jason sighed again, and she could hear him work a keyboard. "I got one better. Something major just went down in South East DC. I would bet my monthly salary it's Apollo. Your best bet is to follow them."

"There's no time to follow. It's time to intercept."

"It's my ass if this goes badly. And it will." He gave her the convoy's last coordinates, captured by a traffic camera minutes earlier. She left tread marks at the scenic overlook and sped toward the capital, passing cars as if they were standing still. Lin no longer cared about police.

"Thank you, Jason. Really," she said over a headset as she swerved around traffic. "As a thank-you gift, I saved one of the Russian hacker's laptops for you. It's the only one that survived."

"Sweetness! I've always wanted one of those," he joked, knowing it would catapult their unofficial investigation and his career, if he found a way to "discover" it as evidence and get it unlocked. He would.

She told him the location of the scenic overlook. "It's sitting on a picnic table, so you should get there before it rains, or people show up."

"Thanks, Jen."

"And one more thing," said Lin. "When this is all over, dinner's on me."

CHAPTER 38

Jackson hung up the phone with Winters and poured himself a tall scotch, neat. It was nearly 2 A.M. and he stood in a silken bathrobe with his initials, GJJ, inscribed on its left breast pocket. His private study looked like old Beacon Hill, Boston. It was adorned in dark oak and brass fittings, with hunter green walls. A small marble fireplace with two leather chesterfield chairs sitting on an ornate Persian carpet with a tree-of-life motif. By the window, on a side table, stood an exquisite model of the clipper ship *Cutty Sark*, its rigging lovingly tied by tweezer. An authentic Tiffany desk lamp was the only light in the room, casting a multicolor glow on the room.

Jackson leaned back and put his pajamaed legs on the desktop, sipping the single malt with exquisite care. One does not gulp twenty-five-year-old Macallan. Pictures of his children and grandchildren crowded his desk. One showed a hoard of laughing grandkids piling on him at Ridgely's Retreat, their mansion off the Chesapeake. It was the best day he could remember in ten years, and he wanted more like it.

Winters had been working him over from the beginning, and Jackson had let him. He had a country to secure and did not have time for Winters's puerile mind games. The man was more conniving than Iago and more foolish than Oedipus. But that time was drawing to a close, and Winters had finally earned Jackson's full attention. Winters would regret it.

Kill the president? Impossible. Laughable, he thought, rubbing his head. It was clear now: Winters had gone insane in his Saudi prison cell. He was not the same man he used to know. Even if Jackson could orchestrate the president's death, he wouldn't dare. He now deplored his partnership with Winters and needed to make repair.

Christ. Henry and Martha are dead, he thought. They were family friends long before Henry became vice president, and they vacationed together on Martha's Vineyard one summer. It was divine. *I'm sorry, old friends,* he thought and took another and sip of scotch.

Jackson leaned back, weighing his options. He understood predators like Winters, and what to do about them. He had been dealing with them his entire career. They mistook his niceness for weakness, and learned too late of their errors. Jackson had left a trail of gutted rivals as he climbed his way into the White House. Winters was no different.

"Damn Winters," Jackson muttered, angry that he had to expend power—real power—on the idiot. But he knew it was necessary: the man required a firm reminder of who was the alpha in their partnership. He had to bring the man to heel.

I have no choice. He's pushed me too far. Jackson picked up his secure government phone. Being the national security advisor afforded him great power.

"Give me Joint Task Force National Capital Region, special operations division."

The operator put him through.

"This is National Security Advisor George Jackson. This is a Code One NSC emergency. Terrorist attack in progress. Activate Sierra Mike Uniform One Niner."

"Copy all. Authentication?" replied an alert military voice.

"Authentication code is . . ." Jackson authenticated.

"Authentication is confirmed."

"Target is linked to the following mobile phone," Jackson added, giving Winters's last used number. Winters thought he was calling from a concealed number, but Jackson had the NSA crack it long ago. The NSA had cracked all his known phones, which helped Jackson keep abreast of the man's many nefarious intentions.

"Copy."

"One more thing," added Jackson. "Capture, do not kill. I want the leader alive, but I don't care about the rest."

"Roger."

It's done, Jackson thought, hanging up the phone. Perhaps it was extreme, but breaking Winters required extreme measures.

CHAPTER 39

Helicopter rotors began turning at Andrews Air Force Base, just south of Washington, DC. Special Mission Unit 19 had been scrambled, and men in black tactical gear ran to the choppers sitting on the tarmac. SMU 19 was the government's secret counterterrorism assault force for the capital region, and comparable to SEAL Team 6 and Delta Force. Their mission: defeat terrorists who threaten the nation's capital. Their motto: "Life, Liberty and the Pursuit of Anyone Who Threatens It."

"Go, go, go!" shouted the team leader, as shooters climbed aboard two MH-60M Black Hawks. These birds were unlike normal Black Hawks, and were customized for special operations forces. Next to them, two AH-6 Little Birds were already hovering, each equipped with Hellfire and Stinger missiles, and two multibarrel miniguns that shot six thousand rounds per minute—accuracy by volume. Seconds later the helicopters lifted off in blackout flight. Four up-armored SUVs dashed out the base's main gate, sirens raging.

CHAPTER 40

Winters checked his watch again, and then looked up. His body swerved with the SUV, as they made turns at twice the speed limit. Traffic was light at this hour, as the tourists were still asleep in their hotels. Winters's convoy was a black flash in a dark night: six armored Chevy Suburbans escorted by four Sikorsky S-97 helicopters, all black and traveling in blackout mode. The police, if they could catch them, were the least of Winters's worries.

That snake Jackson better not double-cross me, thought Winters. He was taking a risk, but one worth taking. However, he had contingencies for Jackson, should he betray his trust. Winters always had such plans.

"ETA seven minutes, sir," said the convoy commander from the front seat. Winters nodded. They turned onto Memorial Bridge and headed for the Lincoln Memorial, which was lit up in splendor. If all went according to plan, it would be the last time he would ever meet with Jackson. The truth was, he didn't need Jackson to kill the president; he could do that anytime. Rather, he agreed to it just to torment the moron, with his morality of convenience and hypocrisy of necessity. Men like Jackson were lice, and Washington suffered an infestation.

Seven minutes until I'm rid of this troublesome office seeker, thought Winters with satisfaction.

The hood and gag were suffocating, and I felt nauseous as the vehicle veered and lurched around traffic. I estimated we were traveling around 90 mph but I had no idea where we were going; I assumed Winters's lair. My hands and feet were each flex-cuffed, and I was belted into the backseat, stuffed between two brawny men. Their elbows jabbed my ribs every time we took a turn. I worked at the wrist cuffs, but they weren't budging. I was stuck.

I could only imagine what horror show Winters had ready for me at his makeshift Apollo dungeon. He had changed, no doubt. Torture does that to a man. Knowing Winters, he would exact his revenge on me, one torture instrument at a time, each with expert precision and medieval tenacity. I would become his new hobby, and he would nurse me along for months just so he could see me scream again. Winters was always a twisted person, but torture unleashed his inner Lucifer. And I would pay.

I had been physically tortured before, once by a warlord in the Congo and another time by police in West Africa. They were equally awful. Everything they teach you about endurance at SERE School is mostly worthless. There is no mental "happy place" to go to when someone is electrocuting your junk. You could pray, but God doesn't answer men like me, and why should he? Ultimately, it's just a long night. I had many long nights ahead of me.

The four helicopters of Special Mission Unit 19 skimmed the Potomac so fast they left a wake. They were locked onto the digital signature of Winters's phone, and Memorial Bridge was in the distance. The plan was standard operating procedure: the aviation would draw first blood and hold down the terrorists until the ground units caught up, who would go in for the capture and kill. They had practiced this endlessly, but this was their first live mission.

"Joker One, this is Joker Three," said a Little Bird pilot to the lead Black Hawk and pilot in command. "Are you seeing this?"

"Affirmative, Joker Three. I see four rotary-wing bogies, flying dark and moving east with the target over the bridge toward the Mall. Control, confirm?"

"Negative, Joker. We see nothing. Scopes are clean," replied Mission Control.

Terrorists with their own stealth rotary-wing escorts? thought Joker 1 with concern. No one had ever heard of such a thing. It was a clear and present danger, which meant there was only one course of action.

"Control, permission to engage?" asked Joker 1.

There was a pause on the radio net, as the mission commander sweated. The consequences of being wrong were extreme, but he was trained for this. In moments of extreme decision, always choose prudence.

"Joker, you are weapons free," said Control.

"Copy. We are weapons free. Engage," commanded Joker 1. The Little Birds fanned out.

"Arming Stingers. Acquiring targets," said Jokers 3 and 4, the Little Bird pilots. An *EEEEEEEEEE* sounded over their headsets as the stingers locked onto the heat signatures of the enemy choppers. "Got tone. Firing."

Four missiles launched from pods on the side of the AH-6s and flew toward the Memorial Bridge. The same instant, the four Sikorsky S-97s scattered and dropped flares. The bridge shimmered in the twilight glow of burning magnesium, creating a surreal scene.

"Negative hits," said Joker 3.

Who are these guys? thought Joker 1.

"Incoming! Incoming!" squawked the command net. Winters peered out the window and saw his Sikorsky S-97s jerk left and right while dropping flares. They looked like starlit snowflakes as they drove through them. Cars swerved to avoid the descending goblets of white fire, not knowing what they were, and hit other vehicles. The convoy deftly maneuvered through the debris field as the Stingers rocketed overhead.

"Those were Stingers! Who's got eyes on? Where's the bogie?" shouted the convoy commander into the radio. Winters looked out over the river but saw nothing. *Jackson, is that you?* he thought.

"This is Bandit," said the pilot in command. "We got four bogies in our FLIR, south of the bridge six klicks and closing fast."

"Annihilate them," ordered Winters, sitting back again.

"Weapons free," ordered the convoy commander.

"Copy."

Above them, they heard the launch of heavier rockets designed to kill aircraft and tanks. The enemy choppers down river immediately dumped flares, lighting up the river near the National Airport. A 737 airliner on approach banked upward in an emergency procedure and accelerated back into the sky. Winters smiled. *Take that, Jackson.*

"Go to guns," commanded Bandit. "Engage." The attack helicopters flew past the convoy, heading toward the oncoming bogies. They were too close for missiles and would have to fight in an air duel of skill and nerve.

"Give 'em hell, boys," said Winters. Jackson had betrayed him, but he would leave a stinking turd on the White House's front lawn for him to clean up in the morning. "No prisoners."

"Holy crap!" said Lin, skidding around a three-car accident on the Memorial Bridge as flares dropped all around them. The white light lit up the sky and what she glimpsed made her heart stop. Meters above the bridge, four black helicopters flew in tight formation. She had never seen anything like them: dual rotor, one on top of the other, and a rear pusher propeller. Missiles were launched off side pylons and they headed south, toward the airport.

Then her eye caught the convoy that Jason told her about. Six black, armored Chevy Suburbans weaved through the wreckage on the bridge, driving almost bumper to bumper. They drove like NASCAR.

There goes my lead! she thought as she floored the accelerator to catch up and slalomed through the traffic. *I've come too far to lose them now.*

"Incoming! Incoming!" shouted Joker 1 as a warning alarm squawked in the cockpit. He yanked the cyclic and stick, and the Black Hawk banked hard right, its rotor almost splashing the water. The shooters inside held on as loose stuff in the cabin flew everywhere. The Black Hawk's flares showered the river but extinguished in the water before the incoming missiles could lock onto them.

Shit, thought Joker 1, watching all his flares go out. They were exposed.

The other Black Hawk exploded in an orange fireball that illuminated the early-morning sky. The impact was so intense that a million pieces rained down, making little splashes in the water several hundred meters in diameter. There was nothing left of the chopper, or the ten souls on board.

"Joker Two is down! Repeat, Joker Two is down!" It was the nightmare scenario they had drilled for over and over, but the reality was no less shocking.

"Copy, Joker Two down. Scrambling the Falcons," said Mission Control, referring to the F-16s of the 121st Fighter Squadron at Andrews Air Force Base. However, the firefight would be over by the time the F-16s arrived on station, something Joker 1 and Mission Control knew.

"Signal now moving down Independence Avenue. Jokers, give me covering fire. I'm tracking the signal," said Joker 1 to the Little Birds. Even secure phones emitted electrical signals, and they could be tracked with the right equipment.

There was a pause as they moved into position, then Joker 4 said, "I spot six black SUVs in blackout drive moving at high speed." The vehicles were traveling fast down the broad lanes of Independence Avenue, which lined the National Mall. They were in the open and vulnerable to fire, but not for long. In a minute they would come upon buildings, making a clean hit with a Hellfire missile risky.

"Signal is coming from either the lead vehicle or the second," said Mission Control. "Mission requires capture the leader and eliminate the rest."

"Take out the rear four vehicles," ordered Joker 1.

"Roger, switching to Hellfires," said Joker 3 and 4. "Got tone."

"Take the shot!" said Mission Control.

Hellfire missiles launched off the rails of the Little Birds toward the convoy.

Winters turned around as he heard the explosions. The trailing three Suburbans were hit and a civilian car disintegrated, probably killed by a Hellfire missile. There would be no survivors. "Leave them. Continue mission," he said.

"Roger," said the convoy commander, and then ordered "Charlie Mike," for "continue mission," over the radio.

"Was Locke in one of those vehicles?" asked Winters.

"Yes sir," said the convoy commander. "The rear one."

Damn you, Jackson! thought Winters. You will pay for denying me my vengeance.

· · ·

I sensed the explosion before I felt it. The air pressure quadrupled in the cabin as the armored Suburban lifted off the ground and spun through space, flat like a frisbee. I felt the g-force pull my face away from my skull. The noise was deafening, like being inside a lightning strike. Actually, it felt like I was a shell being fired out of a howitzer. We impacted a second later, bounced twice, and rolled violently for what seemed a minute. I heard the heads of the men next to me smash repeatedly against the bulletproof windows, and I stiffened my neck to avoid whiplash. When the vehicle stopped, I hung upside down, suspended in place by my seat belt.

Whatever hit us had struck our ass and ripped off the rear end of the vehicle. Armored SUVs have blast glass and bullet-proof steel between the passenger compartment and the trunk area. That, and being sandwiched between thick guys, was the only reason I was alive. And from the sound of it, I was the lone survivor.

The vehicle was on fire, and I struggled against my flex-cuffs, but no joy. I was trapped, dangling upside down in a lit gas can. My fun meter was pegged.

Lin followed the black SUV convoy as it circled around the Lincoln Memorial and blew through red lights. Independence Avenue was a tree-lined boulevard, and the SUVs accelerated to 100 mph on the straightaway, with no headlights or lights of any kind. Lin struggled to keep up, dodging cars. They were approaching the bridge over the Tidal Basin when three Sub-urbans and a car blew sideways off the road and into the trees. They vanished like a golf ball hit by a driver. The concussive wave hit her car.

"Holy crap!" screamed Lin, as she skidded sideways and bounced off the median's curb, spinning uncontrollably to a complete stop. Cars screeched behind her, also stopping, and she could hear the crunch of steel and glass as vehicles collided. Lin looked up and saw the surviving Suburbans speed away.

Dammit! she thought, as she watched them vanish into the dark night. She turned to the Mall and saw the three burning hulks that were once armored SUVs, now blown hundreds of feet off the road. *All may not be lost.*

Lin grabbed the Saiga shotgun and backpack full of grenades and jumped out of the car. Victims of the car pile-up behind her were tending to one another, and she could hear the sirens of emergency vehicles in the distance. She didn't have much time to scour the wrecks for clues.

There was nothing left of the civilian car, save a burning chassis blown two hundred meters away. It looked like a Toyota Camry, judging by the body parts in the trees, sixty feet up. One of the SUV wrecks exploded, causing her to jump. A millisecond later, she felt the hot, forceful wave impact her face. She ran to the second SUV, also on fire. No survivors. Lin had to turn back, so intense was the heat from the fire, and it would yield no clues. The last SUV's rear was blown clean off, and lay upside down among the trees.

There could be survivors, she thought, and approached with caution. Crouching as she walked, she could see people inside, hanging upside down, and lifeless. Then she heard a muffled scream.

"Anyone there?" she yelled and heard the mumbling increase with urgency. The vehicle was on fire, and she knew she should leave immediately. However, she couldn't. She needed information and this was her one chance, before the police showed up and locked the place down.

This is insane, she thought. *No piece of information is worth my life*. Nonetheless, she tried one of the doors but it was jammed. The explosion and rolling had bent the vehicle's frame, and the door was wedged shut. She tried two more doors, but they were stuck, too. The last one opened, and a man's body rolled out, clutching a Heckler and Koch SDMR assault rifle. Lin stepped over the body and looked inside. A man hung upside down in the darkness with a hood over his head and hands tied. He rocked back and forth, trying to free himself.

"Are you OK?" she asked, knowing full well the answer: the vehicle was on fire and could explode at any moment. He scream-mumbled in assent.

Lin reached in and released the hanged man's seat belt, and he plopped to the ceiling and crawled out. She pulled a combat knife from the dead man's equipment vest and cut his flex-cuffs. The man quickly yanked off the hood, removed the gag, and took deep breaths. Then he looked up and said, calmly, "Thank you. Now we should get out of here before the police arrive."

"Let's go," she said, turning to escape. She looked back but the man was not following her, as expected. Instead he was stripping the dead guy's weapons and ammo.

"What are you doing? The truck's going to blow! Get out of there!" she shouted from a distance, and the man sprinted toward her. They took cover behind a forgotten granite memorial in the trees and expected the SUV to explode, but it didn't. It just burned. The howl of fire trucks grew louder.

The strange man smelled faintly of wet dog and rubbed his sore wrists. He looked like one of them but was their prisoner. *Odd*, she thought. Hopefully it meant he would cooperate with her. Either that, or he might try to kill her.

"Thank you," he said again, then perked up when he saw what she was carrying. "Nice Saiga. Is that the 040 Taktika model? Only Spetznatz has those. You're not Spetznatz, are you?"

"Do I look like Spetznatz?" she replied in a defiant tone.

"No, I don't suppose you do," he said, cycling the bolt of the H&K. "Do you have a car? We need to get out of here."

"Follow me."

"Three KIA, and one collateral," said Joker 3.

"Roger, BDA is three tango ground vehicles and one civilian," said Mission Control. *BDA* referred to "battle damage assessment."

"Keep the bogies off me. I'm tracking the remaining vehicles until ground support arrives," said Joker 1. "What's their ETA?"

"Joker One, this is Zebra One. ETA three mikes," responded the ground convoy commander.

"Roger, Zebra 1. I'll keep him lit, you box him in," said Joker 1, skimming the Tidal Basin. The shooters' legs dangled over the side and the crew sat behind six-barrel rotary-door guns. They were operating in urban terrain, which was a high risk for collateral damage. However, their orders were clear: prevent another terrorist attack at all costs, especially since they reportedly had WMD.

"There! Eleven o'clock," said the copilot. The remaining three SUVs sprinted across the Tidal Basin bridge in complete darkness.

"Gotcha," said Joker 1.

"Light them up?" asked one of the door gunners.

"Negative," replied Joker 1. "Orders are capture the leader, and we don't know which vehicle is emitting the leader's digital signature. It could be any one of the three."

"We could disable all three vehicles," said the door gunner.

"Negative. Can't risk killing the leader."

The Black Hawk settled low behind the vehicles, captured in its powerful spotlight. All Zebra had to do was follow the light, and it would be checkmate.

No escaping now, thought Joker 1.

• • •

"Aauurgh!!" yelled Winters's driver as the Black Hawk's spotlight lit them up. He ripped off his night vision goggles and blinked several times, adjusting to the brightness. "Switching to head-lights," he said.

The convoy commander was nervous, too. They would be trapped if ground vehicles caught them. Their only chance was for the Sikorsky S-97s to take out the Black Hawk and Little Birds before the ground vehicles arrived. *It's inevitable, but will it happen in time?* he wondered. *I have to lose the spotlight.*

"Take Maine Avenue, here," ordered the convoy commander, pointing right, and the Suburbans turned hard right. They sped under interstate and railroad bridges and through a nest of power lines, but still the spotlight would not go away. They raced down side streets and a main road, lined with eight-story buildings. Yet the Black Hawk skillfully followed them, flying expertly between the buildings and leaping over seemingly invisible power lines.

"He's good," said the driver.

"We should have hired him," replied Winters.

"Hard left on South Capitol Street," said the convoy com-mander, tracking their movements on a dash-mounted screen.

"Hard left," repeated the driver, and attacked the turn at 60 mph. The rear end drifted and the lateral g-force pulled them all to the right. Winters sat calmly, hands on his cane. The two other Suburbans followed, and civilian cars scurried out of the way.

"Catch I-395 and make the tunnel. It has multiple exits and is our best chance of losing the Black Hawk before ground units arrive," said the convoy commander.

"Copy," said the driver. The three vehicles sped around cars at 90 mph as they entered the highway. Traffic was thin at o-dark-thirty. They took the first exit and descended into a tunnel that goes underneath the National Mall. No more spotlight.

"Good. Now pull onto the shoulder, and back out in black-out drive," said the commander. Using the side of the road, the three SUVs reversed at full speed until they reached I-395 again. The spotlight was elsewhere. When they made the highway, they disappeared.

The two Little Birds took up ambush positions on the Mall, waiting for their prey. Joker 3 hovered at the center of the World War II monument, its massive granite colonnade providing some concealment against the Sikorsky S-97s' infrared thermal sights, which could target pigeons in the dark a thousand feet out. Joker 4 hovered behind the Washington Monument, halfway up. It would remain invisible to the bogies, but no less deadly. The two Little Birds shared a collective targeting system; what one could see, the other could shoot.

"Joker Three, in position."

"Joker Four, in position. Stingers ready."

"Nothing on our scopes," said Mission Control.

Wait for it. Waaaait for it, thought Joker 3, monitoring his FLIR. He'd done tours in Iraq, Afghanistan, and Syria, but he'd never faced an equal. It was what he'd trained for his entire life, and it was intoxicating and terrifying.

Biiiing, sounded an alarm. "Bogey's got tone on me! Bogey's got tone!" shouted Joker 3, as he jerked the stick and cyclic. The nimble Little Bird darted between the Stonehenge-like slabs of the monument, breaking the line of sight of the enemy's laser targeting system.

"I have eyes on," said Joker 4 calmly. "Two bogies, due south-west, hovering low in the trees. Switching to Hellfires. Got tone. Firing." Two Hellfires screamed toward the tree line, and the Sikorsky S-97s jumped, dropping flares. The first made a clean break, and the missile obliterated an ancient oak. The second's rotor clipped a branch, causing it to shudder. In that instant, the Hellfire found its target and blew the chopper into the ground, making a crater.

Biiiing. Joker 4 heard the alarm and immediately spiral-dove around the Washington Monument, trying to elude the missile's guidance system. Then there was an orange flash and thunder-clap, and the Little Bird vanished.

Motherfucker, thought Joker 3, as he skimmed the tree line. "Control, Joker Four is down."

"Copy, Joker Three. Falcons' ETA four mikes. Stand fast. Repeat, stand fast."

Joker 3 heard nothing. Three bogeys were hunting him and he was blind. He would be dead in four minutes unless he took charge of the situation. Taking a chance, he zoomed across the National Mall, flying so low he had to pull up to cross the Re-flecting Pool. He made a copse of trees near Constitution Ave-nue, expertly gauging the diameter of his rotors. Only a few pilots in the world had the skill to fly their choppers through trees.

"Where are you?" he whispered, looking out the canopy through his FLIR. He'd grown up in the woods of northern Georgia, and his hunting instincts told him this was the spot to ambush his quarry. He had large fields of fire, and the trees offered some cover and concealment. Plus, the car traffic at his tail would create hash for the enemy's FLIR.

"There you are!" he said, as a shadow dashed through the World War II monument, his previous position. Missiles proved futile against these bogies because their reflexes were too fast. He would need to get close.

"Switching to guns," he said, and picked up the shadow in his FLIR as it banked toward him, unwittingly. "Gotcha!" He flew out of the trees and rolled to optimize the angle of attack. The

Little Bird rocked as his mini-gun sent three thousand rounds of lead into the bogey. The Sikorsky S-97 turned left then right, trying to get away as it bled black smoke.

No escape for you, he thought as he matched his prey's every feint until it crashed on the Mall.

Biiiiing, sounded the alarm, and his reflexes sprung to action. He ducked around the Smithsonian Castle, and then over and into the Hirshhorn Museum's donut hole. The alarm went quiet. The art museum was shaped like a gigantic "O," making its center a perfect helicopter foxhole.

"Falcons ETA two mikes," said Mission Control. Joker ignored it, knowing the enemy would soon discover him.

Move or die, he thought, and cautiously hovered out of the Hirshhorn. He peeped over the roof and saw empty skies. The flashing lights of ground emergency vehicles were distracting and interfered with his FLIR, but it would do the same to his enemy. Fine by him. He had been flying attack helicopters for twenty-three years, and he was one of the best pilots in Task Force 160 SOAR, the Army's special operations aviation regiment, also known as the Night Stalkers. Any environmental challenge would harm the enemy more than him.

Joker 3 nearly flew on the sidewalk and then floated up to a position behind the Smithsonian's 1870s tower, using it as cover. When it comes to helicopter battles, whoever sees the other first survives.

"Where are you?" he muttered again. He scanned the Mall, its trees, the museums that lined it. His instincts knew where a chopper would hide, would avoid, would stand ground. Then he saw it: a Sikorsky S-97 stalking through trees across from him, near the Smithsonian American History Museum. The pilot was hunting him, but Joker 3 was better.

You're mine, he thought, and pitched forward to line up the shot when his peripheral vision caught the other Sikorsky S-97, one hundred meters to his left. It hovered in perfect ambush, waiting for him at the far end of the Smithsonian Castle's roof. Muzzle flashes burst from its twenty-millimeter chain gun, shredding the Little Bird.

"Where did they go?!" asked Joker 1 after the convoy entered the tunnel but did not exit. "Anyone have eyes on?"

"Negative," replied the shooters who sat on the edge of the open doorway.

"Control, we lost them. Last seen vicinity of the Third Street tunnel," said Joker 1, as they searched the area.

"Roger, Joker One. Zebra One on site, and we have alerted local law enforcement. Falcons on station," said Mission Control.

"Copy all," replied Joker 1. "Status Joker Three, Joker Four?"

Silence.

"How copy Joker Three, Joker Four?"

"Joker Three and Four presumed KIA," said Mission Control. "Return to base. Falcons will handle the bogies."

Joker 1's hands squeezed the controls in silent fury, his face contorting with rage. Then, in a placid tone, he said. "Roger, returning to base."

Beneath the Black Hawk, an orchestra of sirens and flashing lights converged on the National Mall in the predawn light. The F-16s screeched above, waking up the city, but found no targets.

CHAPTER 41

"Who the hell are they?!" Lin shouted as she sped away from the firefight. "And who the hell are you?!"

The man didn't answer. Instead, he rolled down the window and stuck out his head, scanning the skies. He held the Heckler and Koch SDMR like a pro.

"Hey, I'm talking to you!" she yelled, and the man turned to face her.

"My name is Tom. Pleasure to meet you," he said with a smile. "What's your name?"

"Not important right now."

"Agreed," he said, and stuck his head back out the window, looking for helicopters. Two explosions shocked the night air, and a plume of fire shot up from the Mall. Lin could see the orange glare in her rearview mirror.

"They must have taken out a chopper, but I wonder whose," he shouted over the wind.

"Who's 'they'?" asked Lin.

"I'll tell you when we're safe. Can you go faster?"

"We're going seventy," she said, tires squealing around turns. Rock Creek Parkway runs alongside the Potomac and follows its curves. Ahead was the Kennedy Center for the Arts, an all-in-one performance palace that looked like a giant Kleenex box.

"They're doing *Traviata* later this month. I was really hoping to catch a performance," said Locke, slumping back into his seat with the H&K muzzle pointing out the window.

"What?"

"It's an opera. You'd love it. It features a noble heroine," he said.

"Don't make me punch you."

She slowed down as multiple police cars sped by in the opposite direction. Their flashing lights temporarily blinded them, and Locke reflexively closed his shooting eye to preserve his night vision.

"Hey, dumbass. Hide the weapon," she said, and Locke quickly lowered the H&K as the last police cruiser passed in a flash of blue. In the background, the buzz of a mini-gun echoed through the city, accompanied by sirens in every direction.

Locke whistled in amazement. "They've really done it this time."

"*Who's* done *what* this time?" demanded Lin, frustrated by his lack of specificity. She needed answers.

"Get us out of here, and I'll tell you."

"Tell me now."

"It's not safe on the roads. They're looking for me."

She glanced at him. It was dark, but he looked vaguely familiar.

"Fine," she decided, and violently jerked the car left, cut across oncoming traffic, and made a hairpin turn onto an exit intended for the opposite lane. It dumped them underneath an elevated freeway in Georgetown that ran a mile. There was no traffic, just parked cars and massive steel girders and highway above. Lin floored it, and Locke braced himself.

"What's the matter? Scared I'm going too fast?" she said with a smirk.

"Nope. We're all good here," he lied, reaching for the seat belt.

Where have I seen him before? she thought as they topped 100 mph. The road narrowed and got dark, until it came to an abrupt end. Lin stomped the breaks and Locke braced himself as the Mini Cooper screeched sideways to a stop.

They were under an enormous stone trestle bridge, the type constructed by the great works programs of the 1930s. Above was a multilane highway that spanned the river and connected Georgetown to Interstate 66. Lin cut the engine. No one was down here at this hour, and the huge trestle hid them from helicopters and street cameras.

"Nice spot," said Locke, impressed, getting out of the car.

"Hey! Stay in the car!" shouted Lin, but he walked into the darkness. "Where are you going? Get back in here!" Locke continued to ignore her. *Damn him!* she thought, unbuckling and grabbing her Saiga. When she stepped out, he was gone. She looked back at the car and saw his H&K had disappeared, too. She had chosen this spot because of its seclusion. It never occurred to her that it was also the perfect place for a psycho to murder her.

This is bad, she thought. The only sound was highway traffic above, and the stranger had disappeared. He was her last, best clue. *I've come too far to turn around now,* she thought, furtively moving into the boatyard. *He could be anywhere, watching me.* Her heart raced, and she paused to breathe and calm down. Her father used to say: *If you face just one opponent, and you doubt yourself, you're out-numbered.*

You got this, girl, she told herself as she breathed through her fear. Ahead stood the boathouse, a green barn with white trim. Beyond was the river. Lin snuck forward, maximizing the shadows.

"Over here," came a whisper from around the corner, on the dock. It was Tom, but she didn't want to answer and give away her position. It could be a trap.

"Over here," he whispered again. Lin froze and listened, trying to discern his exact location, but heard nothing.

"Hey! Are you coming?" he shouted. Lin wheeled around the boathouse's corner, Saiga at the ready. Before her was a wooden dock the size of a small parking lot. It was painted red with a big white star in the middle. There stood Locke, the H&K dangling by his side as he stared across the river.

"What are you doing?" she asked, lowering the Saiga slightly.

"I missed this. Seeing this. Smelling the air. America."

Where have I seen him before? The thought nagged her. She scrutinized his figure, but it was dark out. "Who are you?"

"I told you. My name is Tom—"

"That's not what I meant," she interrupted.

"Ah. Well," he paused. "That's more complicated."

"There was a helicopter battle on the National Mall, a whole bunch of SUVs got blown away by missiles, and I find you bound and gagged upside down in one of them. Who were they? Why was there combat on the National Mall? How is that even possible?! Answers, now!" she demanded.

Locke sighed and walked over to the edge of the water. Lin followed cautiously, Saiga up.

Suddenly Lin realized where she had seen him before, and felt faint. His face was all over the news. He was the one everyone was looking for, the mastermind behind the death of the vice president and 230 Americans. He was extremely dangerous.

"Stop! Don't move. You're the nuclear terrorist, Tom Locke," she said, stepping rearward and aiming the Saiga at his back, but the muzzle shook nervously.

"Don't believe everything in the news," he said quietly.

"Lose the weapon. *Lose it!*" she commanded, and he let it slip off his shoulder and clank to the ground. "Kick it into the water!" He only kicked it four feet down the dock.

Damn him, she thought, knowing it was out of reach yet too close. However, she dared not interrupt the cuffing procedure. It was the most dangerous part of an arrest, and mistakes get cops killed.

"Get your hands up! Higher!" she said as he slowly raised both hands. "Get on one knee!" He did. "Now the other. Place both hands on the ground! Now lie down, on your stomach, and cross your ankles!"

Locke complied, still looking at the far shoreline.

Lin felt giddy inside. If she bagged Tom Locke, the FBI would have to reinstate her. She couldn't believe her luck. "Put your arms out to the side, and face right." He did, laying prone in a T position. Cautiously she moved around to his left side, where he could not see her, pointing her weapon.

"You have the right to remain silent," she began while pulling out the handcuffs. "Anything you say can and will be used against you in a court of law." She knelt down by his left arm and slung the Saiga over her back. "You have the right to an attorney." She grabbed his wrist and twisted it in a joint lock, making him grunt in pain. "If you cannot afford an attorney, one will be provided for you."

Lin knelt on his scapula while moving his wrist behind his back with both hands, the Saiga slung across her back. As soon as the metal touched Locke's skin, his body snapped into a crescent moon on his right side like a sprung trap. The force threw Lin backward, and the cuffs slipped from her hands and bounced into the river.

Crap! she thought, then spotted the H&K assault rifle a few feet from him. *CRAP! He's going for it!* But he didn't. As she pulled the Saiga over her head and into a firing position, Locke stepped forward, grabbed her arm, spun around her front and catapulted her into a rack of life preservers. The Saiga flew through the air, landing in the middle of the dock not far from the H&K. Lin was buried in a mound of orange, gasping for breath.

You like to play rough. So do I. Lin rocked on her back, then kicked forward, landing on her feet. Locke was moving for the weapons. She grabbed a paddle and threw it like a javelin, hitting him in the head.

"Ow!" he yelped, staggering sideways while clasping his skull. She sprinted toward him and executed a perfect flying kick, five feet above the ground, and impacted his chest. Locke hurtled backward into a rack of upright metal canoes, which then collapsed on him.

"*OW!*" she heard from beneath the mound of metal. Lin smiled. The canoes started rustling, and Locke emerged both angry and bewildered.

"You want to dance? Let's dance," he sputtered, clambering to his feet and assuming a fight stance.

"I doubt you have the skills to be my dance partner," she taunted back, settling into her own stance. "I expect your moves won't satisfy me."

"They will take your breath away, guaranteed," he said, as they circled around the weapons in the middle of the dock.

Lin attacked first and fast, landing critical hits despite his blocks. Locke tried to keep up, but she was a tornado of speed, anticipating his every reaction. In a four-move combo, she delivered a devastating reverse roundhouse kick to his torso, taking him by surprise and flipping him on his ass.

Coughing, Locke stumbled up as she stood, arms crossed, smiling. "OK, that was a pretty good move," he admitted. "But I got stamina."

Locke launched into her, using elbows and knees like a prison fighter. Locke and Lin were a blur of limbs and grunts. She was quick but he was solid, absorbing massive damage and recovering quickly. He landed fewer blows, but each one made her body whither. Locke was slowly driving her to the water's edge.

Crap, he's good, she realized. *Time to end this before I get wet.*

In a fiery combo, she blocked a punch and threw a palm heel to his nose. But Locke was quick, ducking her hand and smashing his left forearm into her abdomen, buckling her, and did a double leg takedown. They landed with a mutual gasp inches from the dock's edge, her long hair in the water and Locke on top between her legs, inches from her face.

Locke smiled. She grimaced. Both were breathing heavily. Lin looked like she might kiss him but headbutted him instead, then rolled on top of him as he cringed in pain. Sitting back on his abdomen, she smiled with triumph.

"Ow!" he muttered, rubbing his nose. "That hurt."

"Had enough?" she gasped between breaths, still sitting on him. They were spent.

"We could go on like this all night, nonstop," said Locke hoarsely, in between gulps of air.

Lin's pulse was still racing, and she struggled to slow her breathing. She tried to speak but could only manage: "Uh-huh."

Moments later, he said, "That was . . . incredible."

"Uh-huh."

"You're really amazing, you know that?"

"Uh-huh." A few seconds passed. "You're not bad yourself, Tom Locke."

He smiled. "I told you I had moves."

"Yeah, I bet you would make a good dance partner," she said and they both chuckled awkwardly as she slid off of him. She wanted to arrest him, but she was too exhausted and had lost her handcuffs in the river. She would have to figure out another way.

"What's your name?" he asked.

"Jennifer Lin. People call me Jen."

Locke turned his head to see her. Lin's body lay still, except her breasts, which moved up and down with each breath. Even in the dark, her profile was undeniably alluring, even though she had kicked his ass.

Locke eyed the H&K and Saiga, somehow untouched during the fight. "You're not going to arrest me now, are you?" he asked half-jokingly.

"Not sure yet," she replied half-seriously.

Locke rolled on his side to face her and was taken aback by her physical splendor. She lay with her arms and legs sprawled out, and her long black hair cast to the right, as if blown. Her face was luminous against the night environs and her dark cloths. She was a Rembrandt.

"Are you gawking at me?" she asked.

"Only a little."

She rolled to face him and smiled.

CHAPTER 42

Jackson sat in his office, hands clasped under his nose as we watched the news. The TV was muted to block the news anchor's ravings, but the pictures were devastating. A Little Bird burned in front of the Vietnam Memorial, like an apocalyptic shrine. Another lay at the foot of the Smithsonian Castle. A Sikorsky S-97 helicopter was in an impact crater near the Reflecting Pool. The carcasses of three armored SUVs with armed men—"Terrorists," as the press dubbed them—were scattered in the tree line off the Mall, and shreds of a civilian car hung in the trees. The body count was twenty-four and rising. Jackson also knew a Blackhawk full of Tier One operators was missing and presumably at the bottom of the Potomac.

"What a clusterfuck," uttered Jackson, his hands trembling. It was beyond an official Charlie Foxtrot; it was worst case. Hysteria had set in, and I-95 was backed up as people fled the city for fear of follow-on terrorist attacks. Black smoke wafted through downtown Washington like a warzone.

The news dubbed it the "Battle on the Mall" and compared it to the 1812 British invasion, except the enemy was nuclear terrorists. At least the media was framing it as a win for America: the military had foiled the biggest terrorist attack in American history. But the world still lay in shock and disbelief. If this could happen to the U.S.'s capital, then where was safe?

Christ, Jackson thought. *What the hell happened?* It was a simple show of force. Winters wasn't supposed to fight back. Now what? Jackson was still processing the implications. He got the call from the Situation Room around 2 A.M., when the battle was taking place. At first, he didn't believe it, and then rushed to the White House. Things got worse from there.

How can I use this disaster for good? he thought, crossing his arms and legs. *Think, think, THINK!* If this attack galvanized the American people against its enemies, it could be harnessed for good. But it would have to start with the president. *I need to make him think it's his idea.* He imagined the president giving the Churchillian speech of his career, something akin to Sir Winston's rousing "We Shall Fight on the Beaches" address, which he'd given to the House of Commons at the outbreak of World War II.

Yes, it could work, he thought, sitting back with a partial smile. America focuses on external threats rather than internal bickering, the president sets his legacy, and Jackson shepherds the United States into a new era of vigilance.

But there was still one big problem. At the moment, no one knew of Apollo Outcomes' involvement, but they would. When they did, the trail might lead to him. Jackson turned pale and felt woozy. Clever people would figure it out in hours, if not sooner. The dead Sikorsky S-97 guaranteed that. Where did Winters get one of those? Jackson didn't know the helicopter was in production, much less illegally sold to a corporation. *Deal with that later,* he thought. In the meantime, he needed to find a way to distance himself from Apollo Outcomes and tie Winters to all the terrorist attacks, present one included.

All is not lost. I can still salvage the situation, he mused. He could downplay his connections to everything. After all, he had taken extraordinary care not to ever be seen with the man, and everything Winters might accuse him of could be denied.

What did the old CIA used to say? thought Jackson with a

grin. Admit nothing, deny everything, and make counteraccusations.

Winters, you are going down.

Jackson resolved to blame it all on Winters, and why not? For if there was anyone to blame, it was that perfidious cretin. The evidence was overwhelming, but it needed marshaling for investigators to reach the appropriate conclusions. Manipulating bureaucratic agendas was Jackson's forte.

Smiling, Jackson picked up his phone. "Give me the FBI Director."

"Yes sir," said the voice on the other end, as he was placed on hold.

I'll turn this misfortune into a fortune, he thought. The original scheme of framing terrorists for the bridge assassination was unraveling, as the FBI began questioning the ability of any group to organize such a sophisticated attack. Worse, someone in the FBI was leaking this conclusion to the press, and now everyone was focusing on Russia. Jackson now needed everyone's attention to shift one last time to Winters. The evidence would be overwhelming were it nudged into the light.

I need a new fall guy, and Winters is perfect, thought Jackson. The solution had both elegance and rectitude, giving Winters what he opulently deserved. And it would be easy. In the Japanese martial art of aikido, you use the enemy's weight against him. Jackson would aikido Winters. He would put the FBI on the scent of the Sikorsky S-97, and that would lead them to Apollo and then, ultimately, Winters. If the Bureau veered down the wrong path, Jackson would lay breadcrumbs to get them back on the trail, and burn any investigator who got too close to him. *Child's play,* he thought.

"Where's the FBI director?" asked Jackson.

"Still waiting."

"Try his other numbers."

"I'm doing that, sir."

Jackson's mind drifted back to his escape plan. After the call, he would initiate a whisper campaign against Winters. A few leaked fake documents and accompanying deep background conversations with key journalists should do the trick. He would "accidentally" let slip something about a rogue mercenary company that attempted a shadow coup d'etat in the United States, and how he'd squashed it in the night. Unthinkable! Outrageous! Shocking! It was just the sort of claptrap the press ate up. Told enough times, it would eventually become reality in the minds of many.

But will it be enough to convince the president? thought Jackson with a frown. His own role with Winters was complicated, even though he'd covered his tracks expertly. Still, there were tracks. Jackson exhaled a worried sigh. POTUS possessed the worst sort of mind to influence—stubborn—and the man had a legendary temper that got in the way of, well, everything. Much of Jackson's job was anger management.

"Sir, I've located the FBI director."

"Excellent. Patch him through," said Jackson with a grin. He was going to get ahead of the problem.

"Sir, he's in the Oval," said the assistant over the phone. Jackson's smile disintegrated. "And the president wants to see you, too. He's angry."

CHAPTER 43

"Hey buddy, get up!"

Pain in my ribs woke me from a deep sleep. I was disoriented, having no idea where I was.

"Get up and get out of here. Now!"

Opening my eyes, I saw wooden rafters on the ceiling above, and smelled timber and varnish. Crew shells were stacked from floor to ceiling in steel frames, and small day sailers sat on trailers in the back. My back ached, as if I had slept on rope. A sail was my blanket, covering me from head to toe. The sun was high, and I must have fallen asleep in the boat house.

Pain shot through my ribs again, as another pain stabbed me in the side. "Ow," I muttered for compliance's sake.

"You and your girlfriend need to leave. I called the police. This isn't a motel," said a guy holding a canoe paddle. He was in his twenties and built like a lacrosse player but looked like a stoner.

Where's Lin?! I thought, panicked. I turned my face into a mound of black hair. Lin was asleep next to me, also under the sail. I had no recollection of entering the boathouse, making a bed, or falling asleep. Exhaustion must have overtaken us.

"Hey, are you listening to me? You need to leave. The police are coming," said the man, jabbing at my side with the paddle again, but I blocked him. I wanted to whip out my H&K assault rifle and stick it under the jerk's chin to see if he would soil his preppy boxers, but I knew better. I couldn't attract any attention during a nationwide manhunt for me, so instead I played the fool. Hopefully the guy was an NPR listener.

"Sorry, dude. So sorry. Chill. We're moving," I said, trying to act the wimp. I needed to convince him that I was a nobody with a no-one girlfriend.

"Hurry up. Out."

"Come on, my honeysuckle," I said softly to Lin, keeping up the act. Cautiously, my hands traveled beneath the sail-blanket and found her side. I held my breath, fearing she might awake disoriented, panic, and blow my head off. Yet I had to play the nobody for the canoe tyrant. Slowly, my hands made contact with her side; she was warm and firm.

"Come on, darling," I whispered as I gently shook her awake, ready to defend myself. "Come on, my tulip, time to go."

"Get on with it! I don't have all day," he said, waving the canoe paddle menacingly.

"Come on, love," I said tenderly as the guy stood over my shoulder. Lin's eyes opened and then her hand shot up for my throat. Anticipating it, I grabbed her wrist and tried to make it look normal, but it just looked weird. I glanced back at the guy with a smile, hoping it would defuse the situation, but he looked horrified and curious, like a rubbernecker slowing down to view a gruesome traffic accident.

"She always does this when I wake her up unexpectedly," I whispered as Lin expertly broke my grip and grabbed my larynx with a Krav Maga hold. My whole body stiffened in pain, and both my hands clung to her wrist. "Easy, my darling," I rasped, and tried to smile though the pain. She looked pissed.

"You two are a pair of sex freaks. Is that what you've been doing in my boathouse? Heavy bondage and S&M? Let me guess. She's the dominatrix and you're the slave?"

Lin looked at him in revulsion and let go of me, blushing.

I lay rubbing my throat and whispered hoarsely, "Y-y-yes." The pain was enormous, but I could not drop the act. Under no circumstances could I let him become suspicious. It was far better to be thought of as perverts than terrorists.

"I never understood the whole S&M thing," he said, folding his arms in disapproval. The man turned to Lin and said, "Take your gimp and get out of my boathouse."

Lin grinned slightly. "Come on, gimp. Up with you!"

"We're leaving," I said, sounding like a frog. Then I realized we couldn't stand up with the guy watching since our weapons were hidden beneath the sail. If paddle boy saw our artillery, he would flip out. Lin saw the problem, too.

"Could you, uh . . ." she said, pulling the sail up to her chin and spinning an index finger in the air, indicating she wanted him to turn around. "We're not decent and I need to get dressed."

The man dutifully turned his back, and we stood up, fully clothed. Our weapons lay at our sides, and we looked at each other, trying to figure out how to carry them away without the man glimpsing them.

"Um, do you have a spare beach towel or something lying around?" coaxed Lin.

"What do you need a beach towel for?" he asked suspiciously, and Lin looked at me for help.

Before I could say anything, he said, "Don't tell me. I'd rather not know. You'll find a pile of towels we lend to customers on the shelf by the door."

"Thanks," she said and walked across the boathouse, fetching towels. Minutes later, our weapons were wrapped in aquamarine blue. The guy eyed the odd package curiously.

"Like you said, you don't want to know," said Lin, then she added in a malevolent whisper: "Not unless you want to feel the whip and chain."

He involuntarily cringed, and she blew him a kiss. Then he began squinting at me. "Hey, aren't you—"

"Aren't I what?" I interrupted, a little too defiantly.

"You look like the guy on TV. The guy everyone is looking for. The guy who . . ." His voice trailed off in fright and recognition.

Lin stepped in. "Do you really think the world's number one terrorist mastermind would spend last night *here*?" She laughed. "I had him tied up four ways to Friday last night on your davenports. He's just a slave, trust me," she giggled and slapped my ass hard. It stung.

The guy looked at me, then her, then me again. "Just get out of here."

We walked to the car holding hands, keeping up the act, and it felt good. It had been a long time since I felt a woman's touch, and I missed it. I liked her. It was always my fate to find the right woman at the wrong place and worse time.

"You were pretty convincing back there," I said as we got in the car, and she flashed a knowing smile but said nothing. She started the Mini Cooper as I put the weapons in the tiny backseat, ensuring the towels covered them. As we drove away, a police cruiser passed us, heading to the boathouse.

"Honeysuckle?" she giggled. "Did you actually call me honeysuckle?"

CHAPTER 44

The Kremlin's smaller press room was adorned in eighteenth-century artifice. Pillars painted to look like precious green chrysocolla stone stood beside deep red walls. White wainscoting and crown molding with gold leaf trim gave the room a wedding-cake feel. On the walls hung menacing oil paintings of uniformed leaders from past centuries staring down at the gathered journalists. A single podium sat at the front of the room, on a dais. The low rumble of conversation gave way to silence as Russia's president, Vladimir Putin, took the tiny stage and greeted the room with a politician's smile. After pleasantries, Putin got to his message.

"Everyone knows the United States is being attacked by terrorists. We strongly condemn this brutal and cynical crime against civilians. What has happened once again emphasizes the need for the global community to join efforts to fight against the forces of terror. Russia stands ready to help the United States," said Putin with a grin.

Hands shot up around the press pool. Most were state-owned media, but some international outlets were present. Putin nodded at the front row and a reporter from Russia 24, a domestic network, spoke up. "Mr. President, America's media is reporting that Russian agents and not terrorists are behind the assassination of their vice president. I know you have denied all involvement, but why do you think Americans continue to blame us?"

"Russia has no involvement in the United States' problems.

None. Some in America think they can blame others for their problems, but this is wrong. Terrorism in America's homeland is the result of their actions abroad. They have inflamed the Middle East and are now surprised they are on fire too. Sometimes it's easier to blame others than face the truth."

Hands went up again. Putin paused and then called on a Western reporter.

"I'm with Bloomberg News," said a young man in Russian. "You say Russia is not involved in the terror attacks. However, sources tell us that the FBI raided a Russian safe house outside of Washington last night and found evidence pointing to Russian collusion in the vice president's . . . death." The reporter was careful not to use the word "assassination."

"The FBI did not raid a Russian safe house last night. Check your facts."

"But sir—" said the Bloomberg reporter.

"Check your facts," interrupted Putin. "Next question."

"I'm Niles with the *Guardian*. Mr. Putin, it's well known that Moscow tries to interfere in the internal affairs of other countries. Examples include Ukraine, American elections, and the Brexit vote. Do you really expect the world to believe you when you say Russia is not involved with the chaos in Washington right now?"

"Yes. Russia has nothing to do with it. For twenty-five years, the United States has antagonized the world with its wars, and now it has come back to America's motherland," Putin said, and leaned forward casually, putting an elbow on the lectern while gesticulating with the other hand. "It's strange, even amazing. It's a typical mistake of any empire, when people think that nothing will have any effect. They think they're so sustainable, there can be no negative consequences, but those come sooner or later."

"Just to be clear," said the reporter, "you are saying Russia has

260 ·   SEAN McFATE

absolutely no involvement in anything going on inside Washington right now?"

"That's what I said," replied Putin with condescension. "Did you know last night there was a helicopter battle in front of the White House? Yes, in front of the *White House*. Such a thing would never happen at the Kremlin." He chuckled.

"Yes. The entire world knows."

"Do you know what kind of helicopters they were?" asked Putin.

The reporter looked stunned, not expecting the president of Russia to interview him on live TV. "Uh, no."

"They were all U.S. military aircraft. Not Russian. Not any other country. *All* were American," said Putin, enjoying himself.

"What are you saying?" asked a reporter from a different Kremlin-owned media outlet.

Putin smiled and shrugged.

"I'm with the BBC," said another reporter. "Mr. Putin, could you please elaborate on your last point? If true, it doesn't sound like terrorism. What do you believe is actually happening in Washington?"

The Russian president looked down and smirked as he composed his answer. "It's the curse of empire. When a country gets the sense of impunity, that it can do anything, then it will turn inward and destroy itself. History shows this to be true. This has arisen from a dangerous American monopoly on power, from a unipolar world. Soon it will come to an end and we will all be safer."

"Do you think the U.S. is fighting some sort of civil war?" continued the BBC reporter, barely able to contain his skepticism.

"Who can say?" said Putin unconvincingly. "But thank God this situation of a unipolar world, of a monopoly, is coming to an end. It's practically already over."

The BBC man was about to ask a third question when he was cut off.

"Will Russia's policy toward the U.S. change now?" asked another state-owned reporter.

"Russia is prepared to assist America in its troubled times," said Putin. "We understand. After the collapse of the Soviet Union—the worst calamity of the last century—chaos ensued. Russia became a lawless and tyrannical country, on its way down. It was not until 1999, when I was first elected president, that we reversed course. Now we are a great power once again. Russia is prepared to help the United States in its moment of need, even though the U.S. did not help us."

"This is CNN. What kind of assistance are you offering? What does 'help' mean?"

"Building up tension and hysteria is not our way. We are not creating problems for anyone," Putin said. "I hope we can build dialogue."

One of Putin's staffers gave a subtle nod, and Putin stepped away from the podium. Everyone waited quietly as he walked toward the exit. Then suddenly he turned around to face the room again.

"I just want to help," said Putin with a big smile and open arms. Then he disappeared.

CHAPTER 45

"Listen, you need me. We want the same thing. We should work together, combine forces," I said as Jen drove. She had told me about her fall from the FBI, and how I could be her ticket back inside.

But she had yet to arrest me.

"Why shouldn't I haul your ass into the Hoover Building right now?" she asked, steel in her voice.

"Because you need me. You're alone and the FBI is hunting you, along with everyone else. You walk us into the Hoover Building and we *both* get arrested. It only helps the bad guys."

"Aren't *you* the bad guy?"

Somehow it hurt, coming from her. "Maybe you should slow down," I said gently as she took another turn too fast.

"Driving helps me think."

"Speeding gets us noticed, and that would burn us both."

Jen let the car coast until we resumed the speed limit. It was rush hour, but the inner city was almost deserted as everyone had either left town or shuddered themselves at home. The radio said highways to Baltimore and Richmond were a crawl and I-66 was stopped up. The last time I had seen the city this empty was September 11, 2001. Police had enforced an armed curfew, but no one wanted to be outside anyway. At the time, I was staying at the Army Navy Club on Farragut Square, and vets sat around the bar talking about Pearl Harbor while getting drunk before noon. It was a horrible Tuesday.

"What's the plan?" I asked, concealing my impatience. There was an international manhunt for me, and we were driving to nowhere. I had risked everything coming back to stop Apollo Outcomes—Winters, really—from conducting another terrorist attack on American soil for profit. But so far, my mission was a complete bust, and time was running out before the next attack.

And they have a nuke, maybe more than one, I shuddered to think. *I must find Winters and take him down.*

"I'm still thinking," she said, unconsciously speeding up again. Her interrogation of me started shortly after we got in the car. I figured I owed her, and she was the only potential ally I had left, so I gave her a little background. However, the more I shared the less she believed. Now she was in full denial and speeding.

"Do you have a plan?" I repeated. "Because—"

"I don't believe you," she interrupted. "There's no way a company could do what happened last night. Take out an elite special forces unit on the Mall? No way. Russia could *maybe* do it, but wouldn't dare. And you're telling me a corporation did? One that normally works for the government?! I don't buy it."

"Mercenary companies like Apollo Outcomes, Wagner Group, and others are how dirty foreign policy is done today. When you need something absolutely, positively, done in a shadow war, you outsource it. That way Washington or Moscow has maximum plausible deniability, and in the information age that's worth more than firepower."

Jen shot me a skeptical look. "Yeah, that's why we have the CIA and SEALs, for that kind of wet work."

"We are *all* former SEALs, Delta, CIA, and more. Where do you think Apollo recruits? Washington secretly likes mercs because if things go badly—and they do—then the client disavows the whole thing. The White House cannot abandon SEALs or CIA in the field, but mercenaries are expendable."

"But isn't that their job?"

"Sort of," I said, uncomfortably. "Also, mercenaries can do things special operations forces and the CIA cannot."

"Like what?"

"Like break the law: domestic military operations, spying on citizens, shaping operations abroad, political assassinations . . . lethality without the red tape. In the industry, we call it 'Zero Footprint' operations because mercenaries operate like ghosts."

"Bullshit. I'm an FBI agent and I've never heard of it. You think I would have," she said with sarcasm.

I sighed. "Apollo works above the FBI. You just don't know it because it happens waaaay above your pay grade. For example, the safe house you blew up last night. You said the FBI put it under a surveillance embargo. Ever heard of that before?"

"No, never," she admitted uncomfortably.

"That's what I'm talking about. Someone at Apollo called it into the FBI."

"How is that even a thing?"

"Not how, but why. 'Why' is the only question that matters," I said, and Jen took a hard left in anger, lifting the car up on two wheels. I clung to the armrest. Jen slowed down as she spotted a police cruiser around the corner. We exhaled as soon as it was out of sight.

"OK, smart guy, let me ask you a question. Washington uses Apollo for its dirty work and Moscow uses Wagner. Washington and Moscow are enemies. Then why are Apollo and Wagner working together? Wouldn't their big clients disapprove?"

"I don't know," I said, disturbed. The question was the supernova that blew my mind apart, and my fixation since she first brought up the Wagner Group.

Jen laughed. "It's obvious. They are in business together to overthrow the United States government!"

"Now wait a minute, Jen. Apollo would never—"

She cut me off. "Don't be an idiot. You're the operator but I'm the detective. You said ask only the 'why' question, and now you're afraid of the answer."

Maybe I was, I realized. My mission was failing. Since arriving, I discovered more questions than answers and I was nearly killed twice in twenty-four hours. If I were smart, I would leave while I still could. But I'm not smart that way. I never was.

"Tom, who is Apollo's real client?" asked Jen, using my name for the first time. I wanted to scream *Brad Winters*, but up till now I had omitted his name and the civil war within Apollo. It was dangerous information. Yet her tone was confident, as if she knew the answer. Did she know something I did not? *Unlikely,* I thought, so I gave the stock answer.

"Apollo works for the U.S. government. Sometimes they work for an ally or an American company sanctioned by the White House, usually in the extractives or financial services industries," I said. It was true, aside from Winters's rebellion.

Jen giggled. "You might be a top-tier knuckle dragger, but you make a lousy detective."

"Then tell me, Ms. Detective, who is Apollo really working for?"

"Russia."

My mind staggered. The National Security Council hired Apollo to wage shadow wars against Russia in Ukraine, Syria, the Baltics, Libya, and central Africa. I lost my team in Ukraine to Russian special forces and the Wagner Group. Only one word came to mind: "Impossible."

"Impossible? Think about it. Why else would Apollo be working with Wagner?"

I knew the answer was somehow connected to Winters, but I couldn't tell her. Not yet, at least. Then the bomb hit me: *Could Winters be working for Russia?*

"Well?" she pressed, speeding down an ally strewn with litter.

It made sense but it was too frightening to contemplate. My mind felt like a satellite spinning out of orbit and heading for earth. She was more right than she knew: The Kremlin must have bought Winters. If true, we were all screwed.

"Well?!"

I gave her the honest truth. "I don't know. Why?"

"Not to service safe houses. There's only one reason why anyone would hire Apollo Outcomes: to do their dirty work. You said it yourself. Things that no FSB agent or mafioso or Spetznatz could do."

"And what dirty work, exactly?"

"To stage a palace coup inside the White House."

I guffawed, not ready to accept the implications. "Unlikely. It's the White House that keeps Apollo in business."

"Not if they cut a better deal with Moscow. They're mercenaries, Tom," said Jen with a twinge of stigma she extended to me.

"In a former life, maybe," I said defensively. "I'm a patriot, Jen, first and foremost. I came back to stop Apollo and I'm risking everything doing it. That's what our country means to me."

Jen nodded. "Well, your former employer ain't. If Russia wanted to leverage the U.S., how would they do it? During the Cold War they threatened us with nuclear annihilation. Now they hire Russian mobsters to smuggle in nukes and employ mercenaries to bury them in American cities. Moscow could secretly blackmail whoever sat in the White House because no politician would ever break the bad news to the American people. Who cares about threatening World War III when you can turn the president into your own sock puppet?"

She could be right, I thought with a chill. My obsession with Winters had gotten in the way of my judgment. Earlier I assumed Apollo staged the terrorist attack to extort the government into more ten-figure contracts. It never occurred to me that they would go full-on traitor, Winters or not.

But the facts lined up. Could killing the president be part of the plan, if only a small part? Blaming terrorists was the ruse to distract law enforcement from the bigger mission of smuggling in the nukes and pre-positioning them around the country. There would be no one better than Apollo, with Wagner providing on-the-ground oversight for the Kremlin.

"America would be fucked," I concluded with a whisper.

"Correct, which is why we need to get inside Apollo headquarters and find some evidence. It's the only way we can turn the FBI and rest of the country around before it's too late."

"So, then . . . you're not arresting me? We're working together?" I asked.

She paused. "Yes."

We both sat back, realizing the gravity of her decision. She wanted to save the country, even if it destroyed her career and labeled her a forever terrorist. I liked her.

"You're doing the right thing," I said, but she turned away in anguish. It's not easy walking away from family, career, a life.

"Let's go get the motherfuckers," she said softly, her voice cracking and her eyes moist.

"Oh, we'll get them. We will damn them to the inferno," I said. *I'm coming for you, Winters!*

"We need information. How do we get inside Apollo HQ?"

It made good sense, but there was a catch. "It would be easier to break into the CIA than Apollo HQ."

"Figure it out, Apollo boy," she said with a teasing smile. "Isn't that what you said their motto was?"

"Unofficial motto."

"What is their actual motto?"

"No clue."

We drove for a while in silence, both of us thinking. Traffic came to a standstill by the colossal National Basilica, the largest Catholic church in North America. People were praying.

"Well, we have one advantage," I said at last.

"What's that?"

"Everyone thinks I'm dead. Again."

"Time for a resurrection," said Jen with a smile.

CHAPTER 46

"I just fired the national security advisor," said the president, seated at the center of the large table in the Cabinet Room inside the West Wing. Sitting around the table were the principals of the National Security Council and select cabinet members. "I spent last night in a tiny safe room beneath the White House, holed up by the Secret Service. You know why?"

The room was quiet.

"Because there was a *battle* a few hundred yards from my bedroom last night." The president paused to let the silence do its work. "*A battle!*" Silence. "And Jackson was *surprised!* Ignorant advisors have no purpose, and things that have no purpose are replaced." Silence again. "So, I'm asking you. What happened?"

They all looked down, avoiding the president's gaze as he scanned the room.

"I want answers *now*!!" shouted the president, pounding the table with both fists, making a few cabinet members wince. "Who did this?!"

More silence.

"CIA, who did this?" President Anderson shouted, turning to CIA Director Nancy Holt. She faintly shook her head, knowing better than to engage the president during a rant. "How about FBI, any clue? Homeland Security? DOD? Secret Service? Does anyone have a *freakin'* clue?!"

Finally, an aide in the back spoke up. "Uh, sir. We have no idea who did this."

President Anderson's eyes widened, and his mouth pursed as

he balled his hands into fists. Holt reflexively looked away, the same way one looks away when a dog is about to run through an airplane propeller. The president unloaded a verbal barrage with spittle flying from his mouth, and the aide withered with each wave of invective. When it was done, the man stood there but his soul had departed.

"Does anyone else have wisdom to proffer?" asked the president, oozing derision.

"Yes sir, I do," Holt said, leaning forward in her chair. Her voice was firm, and this alone got the president's attention. "The downed enemy chopper . . . I know where it was made and who bought it."

"You do?"

"Yes sir. We haven't run all the details to ground yet, so it's premature to conjecture—"

"Out with it!" demanded the president.

"Apollo Outcomes," she blurted. Whispers crescendoed around the table as people reacted.

"The private military company?" asked the president, not believing it, either. "*Our* private military company?! We use them in the Middle East, Africa, Asia. Everywhere. If this is true, then why would they bite the hand that feeds them?"

"I'm not surprised," huffed Secretary of State Novak. "Apollo is not a private military company—they're mercenaries on the scale of a big global corporation. And this is what happens when you hire mercenaries, as we have increasingly done for the past quarter century. They got greedy, stupid, and dangerous."

Some nodded in agreement while others remained placid. President Anderson turned back to Holt and gestured for her to continue.

"We don't have all the details yet," said Holt, "and we need to be careful about drawing early conclusions."

"Concur. Let's follow the facts and then make decisions," said FBI director Romero.

"We're at war and don't have time for a committee," said the president. "We need to make decisions today. What do we know right now?"

"We know that one of the burning helo wrecks out there is not ours," said Holt. "It's an S-97, a next-generation attack helicopter made by Sikorsky in Stratford, Connecticut."

"Made in America?" asked the president, his voice high-pitched with incredulity. "You're telling me our military aviation was shot down by an American-made helicopter?"

"I didn't believe it either, until I saw the wreckage," said General Butler. "The S-97 is not even in production. How could a company buy one? And right under our nose?"

"Not one. *Four*," said Holt. More whispers as people turned to one another in astonishment.

"Four?" asked the president. "Explain."

"Multiple reports from witnesses," said Holt. "We're still running it to ground, as I said, and the CIA and FBI are working jointly on the investigation."

"We will find the answers. It's only a matter of time," added Romero.

"Good, good," muttered the president.

The room fell silent again, in a group ponder.

"What I don't understand," said General Butler, breaking the quiet, "is how Apollo obtained four S-97s without us knowing. The national security implications are severe."

"It's not wise to speculate—" cautioned Holt.

"Speculate!" interrupted the president. "No more wishy-washiness. I need to know. How did a corporation buy the most advanced attack helicopters in the world before we could, even though we commissioned them? And then use them to blow our helicopters out of the sky a few hundred yards from the White House?"

"Uh, sir. Well . . ." fumbled Holt, hesitant to offer a hypothesis that might prejudice the investigation. They needed to be careful because it was possible a foreign power was manipulating them, causing the U.S. to go to war against itself. Their best weapon at the moment was information, and this depended on a deliberative investigation.

"It's possible the S-97s are off-the-books copies made by the manufacturer. Sikorsky is double-dipping," said one of the president's political pollsters, who had no background in national security. *She shouldn't even be in the room,* thought Holt, except she was a presidential favorite. Holt glared at her, and the woman turned away.

"Unlikely," said Romero. "The U.S. government is Sikorsky's major client, and Sikorsky is owned by Lockheed Martin, one of the biggest defense contractors in the country. I doubt either would risk alienating their primary customer, no matter how much money Apollo shovels at them. No one is richer than the United States of America or buys more military aviation."

"Then how?" asked the president, leaning back in his chair.

"We have agents at Sikorsky and Lockheed right now," said Romero, holding up his phone. "Their executives are as shocked as we are and deny selling S-97s to anyone. In fact, according to my agents, the executives also didn't know S-97s were in the field."

"Maybe Apollo stole them?" asked the deputy national security advisor.

"A good question," replied Romero. "However, our agents confirmed all known S-97s are accounted for and in their hangars. All of them."

People all started speaking at once, offering theories. However,

Holt sat very still. President Anderson noticed her silence and gestured for the room to quiet down.

"Nancy, what do you think?" asked the president.

"It's possible Apollo stole the plans and sold them to a hostile foreign power, who then fabricated the aircraft for Apollo offshore," said Holt. "They probably modified them to outperform our best aviation. Maybe they even anticipated battling Task Force 160." The Special Mission Unit helicopters last night were part of Task Force 160.

The room was quiet again. The more everyone thought, the worse the implications became. Finally, General Butler broke the spell. "I might be a dumb old grunt at the end of the day, but there are only two things I want to know. Why the hell is Apollo Outcomes killin' our boys? And when can I take them out?" He leaned over to the president. "It'll all be over by COB, I promise. Just give the word."

The president nodded, his expression darkening. Others in the room nodded too.

The attorney general raised his hand and spoke. "Sir, I would counsel holding off on the military option until the investigation is complete. Apollo Outcomes is a U.S. company and undoubtedly has citizens in it. Killing them without a trial would be illegal. Remember the siege at Waco, Texas in 1993. We must observe their rights."

President Anderson's hands formed fists again, and the General's expression looked like he had smelled something rancid.

"The people at Apollo Outcomes forfeited their rights when they declared *war* on the United States of America," said the president, suppressing his rage. "I swore an oath to protect the Constitution, and that means against enemies foreign and *domestic*. I will do what is required to uphold my oath. Do you understand me?"

"Sir, you are considering the extrajudicial killing of American citizens. Even if they are domestic terrorists, we must respect their rights because we are a rule-of-law society," said the attorney general with delicacy.

"What do you want me to do? Sit back and let them get away with war as they tie everything up in court for years, all to be dismissed on some technicality? Is this what our society has come to: endless legal proceedings while corporations murder our troops and get away with it? You think Americans will stand for it? You think I will?" President Anderson leaned forward so he could look the attorney general in the eye, and spoke in a hiss. "Understand me. I will risk impeachment before I let our country travel down that perverse road."

General Butler nodded, and so did Novak. Romero looked pale.

"It's called 'lawfare,'" said Holt. "Enemies both foreign and domestic attempt to tie us up in our own legal system while they exploit us. Russia and China do it. So do many others."

"So might Apollo Outcomes," said Butler. He looked angry, not only because he had lost troops but because they were killed by a Frankenstein corporation that the Pentagon helped create.

"Sometimes you got to break the law to achieve justice," said the president.

"Breaking the law to enforce the law is not justice, Mr. President. It's tyranny. The time for military action has not yet come," argued the attorney general. President Anderson's eyes grew wide with impatience, and General Butler looked like he wanted to stuff the lawyer into the room's fireplace and light a match.

"There is another reason to slow-go the military response," intervened Holt. President Anderson whipped around to face her, surprised. "We don't know how deep this goes yet, sir. We don't know if Apollo is holding some sort of bargaining collateral—"

"'Bargaining collateral'?" interrupted the president. "What's that mean exactly?"

"Blackmail," said Romero. "They could have something locked away so that if they are attacked, we get hurt. If they had the gumption to attack our choppers on the Mall last night, then they were probably prepared for the blowback."

The president leaned forward, both elbows on the table, and looked vexed.

"What could they possibly do?" asked General Butler. "I mean, really, we are a superpower and they are just a corporation. We can squash them like an Alabama fire ant."

"They could dump classified information on the internet, like WikiLeaks. Or release politically compromising footage like sex tapes to foment a debilitating scandal. They may have a trove of government secrets that they can sell to our enemies. Goodness knows we read them into enough secrets," said Romero.

"Don't forget, General, we used them to do our dirtiest work for years. What they know and could release to the worldwide media . . ." Holt sucked in a breath. "Well, let's just say that not all weapons fire bullets."

"It would be goddamned devasting!" said the president, pounding the table with his fist. A few cabinet members jumped. Some began wondering if Apollo had dirt on POTUS.

"It's a negotiation insurance policy, in case we come after them," concluded Romero.

The general laughed. "Who cares? We are the U-S of A. Ultimately, what's a corporation going to do to us? File a lawsuit?" He turned toward the attorney general with a mocking grin. "We're at war. Who. Cares."

"We should," said Romero.

"And why is that?" said the general.

President Anderson was watching the conversation like a tennis match.

"Because they may have nukes," said Holt, chilling the room. "A few days ago, we received intelligence about loose nukes on U.S.

soil and we assumed it was a phony or a terrorist group. We're still chasing down leads, but the trail is suspiciously well concealed."

"It's true," said Romero. "It might not be a terrorist group after all, but a false flag operation run by someone very sophisticated, we think Apollo. If so, those nukes are probably hidden in several U.S. cities by now. That would give Apollo substantial bargaining collateral."

The general's nostrils flared. "What are you implying?" he asked, leaning forward in his chair. "That Apollo also tried to assassinate the president and got the vice president instead? That they're prepared to nuke American cities? Connect the dots for me."

"Yes, be specific," said the president. His earlier bravado had transformed into genuine concern.

Holt cleared her throat. "All I'm saying is this: We move against them, then they could move against us, and it could involve mushroom clouds. We need to get smart about Apollo first, and then make our move. If my theory is correct, Apollo has spent a great deal of time planning this and has anticipated our responses. Few outsiders know our systems and playbooks better than Apollo. Hell, we've all hired them. This makes us extremely vulnerable, and it's not the time to shoot from the hip. Instead, we need to take careful aim, like a sniper. One shot, one kill."

The general nodded. Everyone else in the room was frozen.

President Anderson turned to Holt. "Out with it, Nancy. I know that look. You're holding something back." All eyes turned to her.

"There is an additional possibility, Mr. President, and one we cannot ignore," she said. "Apollo may have a new client."

"Who?" asked Romero.

"Russia."

The room let out a collective gasp.

"The Russians?" exclaimed the general, shifting in his seat uncomfortably.

"Follow the facts," said Holt. "Radiological teams have confirmed trace amounts of weapons-grade material were smuggled through New York Container Terminal on Staten Island. The Russian mafia facilitated the smuggling. Last night, someone hit a safe house used by the Wagner Group, a Russian mercenary company, in McLean, Virginia."

"But we used to hire Apollo to kill Wagner in Ukraine and Syria," said the general, perplexed.

"They're mercenaries, general. They'll work for anyone," said Novak with disdain.

"We cannot ignore the possibility that Apollo, Wagner, and the Russian mob may have all been hired by the Kremlin to preposition WMD in our major cities."

President Anderson turned white. No one spoke.

"That's why we need to proceed with care, Mr. President," said Holt.

"Buuuuuullshit!" said the general, nearly leaping out of his chair. "We need to move against Apollo now, before the situation gets worse. What are the Russians going to do to us if we take out an American company? Declare war?" He scoffed. "No, of course not. And let's take out Wagner, while we're at it. Russian mercenaries operating on American soil? In the nation's capital?!" The general calmed himself down and spoke slowly in his Southern drawl. "Mr. President, this is a clear and present danger, if there ever was one."

All eyes turned toward the president, awaiting a decision. The man slumped forward, his eyes narrowed, then looked up at Holt.

"I'm declaring a national emergency. I want to know everything earthly possible about Apollo Outcomes and the Wagner

Group. Everyone connected to them, where they operate, their financials. *Everything.* Treat it as a counterterrorism operation, and not a legal case." President Anderson turned to the attorney general, who remained stoic. "Make arrests, disregard civil rights—I don't care, just find those nukes. When they're all accounted for, we move against Apollo and Wagner. Moscow be damned! You have seventy-two hours," he said to Holt, and then turned to General Butler. "And I want options. One shot, one kill."

Holt nodded, and Butler smiled.

CHAPTER 47

Three black Chevy Suburbans sped around the outer rim road that encircled Dulles Airport. A rusty chain-link fence was the only thing separating the potholed road from the runways where 747s took off. There was no traffic since only utility vehicles used the road, and rarely even then.

Inside the middle vehicle, Winters checked his watch and frowned. Every second on the ground was a second too long. The battle last night left clues that would lead to his identity, and at some point this morning, he expected all of American law enforcement to crash down upon his head. Even he could not escape that nightmare. He was surprised they were not on him already.

I need to be in the air, thought Winters, *before it's too late.*

"Driver, how much longer?" he asked, leaning forward from the backseat.

"Five minutes, sir."

Winters slumped back and twirled his antique cane. The morning sun spread warmth across the yellowed grass patches in between the runways. Winters scowled at the sun for being so bright. It was irritating.

Your move, Jackson, he thought. Last night was a surprise. He did not expect Jackson to make the mistake of attacking him in the open. For that, Jackson was punished. The Apollo forces had done devastating work. However, it left Winters exposed, and that was nearly as bad. Apollo had won the battle but muddled the war. Now he had to flee the country and manage his clients, who would soon ask difficult questions.

What will I tell them? thought Winters. His clients were even less patient than he was. *How can I turn this fiasco into a win?* Nervously, Winters checked his watch again.

"Driver, how long?"

"Less than two minutes."

Too long, he thought, twirling his cane faster. The small convoy came to a stop in front of a gate in the chain-link fence. A man from the lead vehicle got out with a large pair of bolt cutters and snipped the padlock, then swung open the gates. The convoy passed through. Normally they would have driven through the front gate to Dulles's corporate executive jet terminal, but these were not normal times. Precautions were vital.

"Sir, the pilots say they are ready to go."

"Excellent," mumbled Winters absentmindedly. His thoughts shifted from managing his clients' expectations to exploiting the situation. Unexpected turns of events always produced opportunities, but he could not see any good ones now. The battle on the Mall would surely expose him.

I'll frame the other half of Apollo for the battle, he thought with satisfaction. A few phone calls with media executives should do the trick, but he knew it would not be enough. The spotlight of the federal government would fall on all of Apollo, including him, and it was the last place he wanted to be. Like all creatures of the dark, Winters abhorred the light.

Damn you, Jackson! he thought bitterly. He reviled being cornered, especially on the cusp of his plan's fulmination. Now everything was in jeopardy. *What a fool Jackson is. Or was.* There was a good chance the man would be cashiered. However, Winters preferred dealing with the devil he knew rather than what could follow.

Maybe, if I'm lucky, the president will appoint an academic to replace Jackson. They were the easiest to fool since they thought they knew everything but, in reality, comprehended nothing. Winters smiled at the prospect.

"We're almost there, sir."

"Good. Confirm with the crew that the package is already on the plane," said Winters. The driver radioed the plane.

"The crew confirms the package is on the plane."

Excellent, thought Winters. *It will be my day of days yet!* But first, he had to get airborne and out of the country. It was his most vulnerable moment of the operation, and it made him neurotic.

The convoy raced down the tarmac, passing lines of parked private jets, and pulled up to one sitting alone. It wore Apollo's corporate colors: black underbelly and gray top. It had no other markings. Winters had commandeered one of Apollo's Gulfstream Vs and a faithful crew; he found money went a long way toward inspiring loyalty.

"Sir, we're arriving," said the driver as he stopped in front of the aircraft's stairs. A man rushed to the passenger door and pulled it open with a grunt. It was laden with several hundred pounds of bulletproof armor. Winters carefully extracted himself from the vehicle and hobbled his way up the stairs. In the distance, a car with flashing blue lights accelerated toward them.

"Take care of it," said Winters as he climbed the stairs. The convoy commander nodded and gave a sharp whistle to his men. They jumped back into the SUVs and sped off to intercept the airport security vehicle. Winters smirked, knowing how it would end. The aircraft stairs retracted the moment Winters was inside the fuselage, as he was its only passenger.

"Care for coffee or tea, sir?" asked the steward.

"Show me the package," demanded Winters. The steward

pulled out an aluminum briefcase. It was slightly bigger and
thicker than a standard case, and it was badly scuffed and dented,
in contrast to the faultless interior of the Gulfstream jet. Winters
smiled.

"Good. Now give it to me, and get us off the ground," he said,
as he belted himself into the nearest seat.

The steward turned and gestured to the pilots, and tucked
the case next to Winters's feet. The turbines roared and the
plane lurched forward, making the steward stumble. Winters
could hear the airport radio chatter emerge from the cockpit,
which still had its door open, and watched as they taxied for
the runway. Out the window, he saw the three large SUVs block
in the airport security vehicle and his men get out. They were
not armed, a smart move. However, Winters had no doubt they
would get the job done.

Good men are hard to find, he thought. The plane swung onto
the runway without slowing and immediately went full throttle.
As it nosed up, he could see his men get back into their vehicles
and drive away. The jet climbed at a steep angle and hit some
turbulence passing through a cloud bank. The blue sky shimmered in the beyond, and they banked east, toward the Atlantic
and international airspace.

Free at last, thought Winters, his hand affixed to the aluminum brief case.

CHAPTER 48

"It's mission impossible," I declared, and tossed my pen at the pad. "There's absolutely no way we can get inside Apollo's headquarters. No way!"

Jen was taking a shower. "What?" She insisted on leaving the bathroom door open so we could converse, but so far it wasn't working well. And it was distracting. Very, very distracting. I tried to be a gentleman and not look. A Fort Benning obstacle course would have been easier.

"I said: no way in!" I repeated, louder. Her shower was going on ten minutes, and steam perforated the minuscule hotel room. Even my pad of paper felt damp.

"Not a winner's attitude," she scolded. I peeked around the door and saw her feline silhouette moving behind the shower curtain, her long black hair falling to one side. She made shadows and vinyl curtains sexy.

We rented a cheap room off Highway 50 on the outskirts of DC. It was all we could afford with our shared cash on hand. When we checked in, the Indian guy at the counter asked if we wanted the room by the hour. Jen blushed and I said no. The place was a fleabag brothel, but it eschewed surveillance cameras and cops, making it a perfect safe house for one night.

The water turned off, replaced by a drip-drip. Next came the rustling of towels, not the fluffy, gigantic ones at the Four Seasons but the skimpy, puny ones.

Focus, Locke. Focus! I know I shouldn't have, but I did. I could see her vague reflection in a fogged-up wall mirror attached to the bathroom door, the kind that's four feet tall. Long, jet-black hair tumbled down her naked back as she dried off. Fog could not conceal her toned body. Jen could have been a swimsuit model.

"Tom? Did you hear me?"

I snapped out of my trance, not knowing what I missed. "Uh, yeah, sure."

Jen emerged wearing nothing but two towels: one for the hair, and the other for everything else. In street clothes, she was attractive; now she was molten hot. However, she was also inscrutable. I was always awkward around women I was truly attracted to, and I was never sure how to proceed. To be a gentleman in this day and age is a quandary. If she was interested, she would let me know. At least I hoped that was how it worked.

She grinned slightly. "Everything OK with you, Tom?"

"Oh, yeah, yeah. No problem."

She discarded the towel around her head, and wet hair billowed out. Strands fell to her waistline. I tried not to gaze at her glistening legs or anything higher. It was frustrating.

"You seem . . . off," she said.

"No, I'm fine. Just frustrated."

"Frustrated?" she asked coquettishly, as she sat next to me on the bed's edge, crossing her legs. She was still wet, and the remaining towel was waterlogged and semitransparent.

"*Very* frustrated," I muttered, starring at her naked thighs. *Focus, Locke! Snap to.* I looked away, and collected my thoughts. "I can't figure out a weak point in Apollo's defenses. It's *very* frustrating."

Jen giggled. "Oh, is *that* what's bothering you?"

"Yes," I lied. I thought she could tell.

"Maybe there's something I can do to help?" she smiled

devilishly. Jen reached across me and I leaned back to make room. Her towel slackened as she stretched over my lap for the pad of paper, her wet hair cascading on my legs. I wanted to rip off the thin towel, but couldn't. *Look away!* I told myself. Once she grabbed the pad, she sat back up, leaving my pulse sprinting.

"Tell me what you know," she said professionally, preparing to take notes as she saddled up next to me, hip to hip. The towel was meagre, like a miniskirt.

"Uh, OK," I said, trying not to seem distracted.

"From the top."

"All right." I told her what I knew. In a past life, I had spent countless hours at Apollo's corporate headquarters at Tysons Corner in northern Virginia. It looked like any other banal people warehouse, but inside it was an electronic and physical fortress. Its security was tighter than the CIA. I ended with: "I don't see a way in."

Jen stared at the floor layouts I had sketched out, to the best of my memory. "Could we pose as building inspectors or something? I still have one friend at the FBI who might be able to arrange a legal reason for us to be there."

"Don't bet on it. Apollo's lawyer will meet us at the front door. Then they will recognize me, and nab us both." I groaned. "I'm telling you, the place is worse than Fort Meade meets Terre Haute."

Somewhere in the background, a headboard was banging furiously, which we tried to ignore.

"There's always a way in, Tom, we're just not seeing it," she sighed, tossing aside the pen and paper. She leaned back on her arms. "I need you to help me clear my head."

"Sure," I mumbled.

Holding the remaining towel with one hand, she slunk across

the bed. There wasn't much towel to go around as she maneuvered herself against the headboard. It was revealing. She patted the spot next to her, and I lay back, too.

The headboard banging got louder.

"Real classy place you found us," she said coyly, poking a toe into my calf.

"They don't ask questions at establishments like this," I replied, fixated on her toe. "Or have cameras. Drives off business . . ." My sentence trailed off as she squirmed to get into a more comfortable position, her towel relaxing along the way. It seemed to shrink across her body.

The headboard banging stopped. Someone must have gotten their money's worth. Jen and I looked at each other; her expression exuded raw power, like during a dock fight. My body tensed reflexively, but she ran her fingers through my hair tenderly. Then she kissed me, a peck at first and then vigorously. I reached around her waist and ejected the towel, my enemy. My hands traced up and down her smooth body as we kissed.

Jen was as passionate a lover as she was a fighter, and as physical, too. An hour later, we lay together entwined. She was perfectly asleep on me, while I felt I had gained a bruise or two. Best bruises of my life. I lay in reverie with Jen's naked body against my side, her head on my shoulder and my hand on her ass.

Riiinnnggggg. Riiinnnggggg. The hotel telephone jolted us awake. *Riiinnnggggg. Riiinnnggggg.* Under a pillow on the floor lay a decades-old phone with push buttons and annoyingly loud bells.

I felt Jen's body tighten and her hands grip my sides with each ring. "Should we answer it?" she whispered.

"No one knows we're here. Wrong number," I said, reaching down and hanging up.

Jen started giggling and nuzzled her face into my shoulder. "Gosh, I can't believe how jittery I am!"

"I know a cure for that," I offered, but she was already on top of me. I felt her thighs wrap around my waist, as she reached down.

Riiinnnggggg. Riiinnnggggg.

Argh!! I thought, scanning the room for a club, bat, bazooka, or anything else that would silence the phone.

"Hello?" It was Jen, the phone's receiver to her ear as she lay flat on my chest.

What are you doing?! I thought.

"It's for you," she said in a stunned tone. I shook my head no, while she nodded yes. Then she put the receiver to my ear, and started kissing the other. It was very persuasive.

"Hello," I said. Lin's kissing swelled in intensity and her hot breath in my ear hijacked my brain. The enchantress was distracting me for her pleasure.

"Dr. Locke?" said a garbled voice on the other end, its sound digitally altered to conceal someone's identity. My hand grabbed her hips to cease their mischievous wiggling, but she put my hand in a joint lock, paralyzing me while still kissing.

"Aaahhh!" I cried in pain.

"Is this Tom Locke?" asked the voice again.

"Who is this?" I managed in a hoarse whisper.

"We wish to meet with you."

"Who *is* this?"

"We have much to discuss—"

Jen surprised me, and I gasped.

"—much in common."

With focused concentration, I mustered: "W-w-why should I?"

"All will be revealed when you arrive."

It could be a trap. Must ask one more question, I commanded myself as Jen became electrified. I summoned all my strength to form the words: "How can I trust you?"

There was silence. "You cannot. But we want Winters, too, and we know where he is. Do you want a piece of him?"

Jen collapsed on me, her hair covering my face and phone. She lay motionless, and I could feel her heartbeat race against mine. But my next words took no effort. "Absolutely."

CHAPTER 49

Jackson sat in his living room, watching the news unfold in his bathrobe and drinking twenty-five-year-old scotch from the bottle. It was 10 A.M., he was drunk, and it felt good. His plan to enmesh the president in his cover-up had failed spectacularly. Now he watched the news with a vacuous expression, like a German soldier after D-Day. He gulped another swig of whiskey.

News choppers circled the Mall, showing the burning wrecks of aircraft and vehicles. It was Yemen with a reflecting pool. The news anchor was recalling what was known: the bridge explosion, the unsolved VP assassination, the mysterious battle on the Mall, a White House in pandemonium, loose nukes, and a country under attack. He stopped talking midsentence, listening to something coming in through his earpiece.

"We have breaking news," it began, but the news banner said it all: NATIONAL SECURITY ADVISOR FIRED! B-roll footage of Jackson took over the screen.

"Ah, come *on!*" yelled Jackson and switched channels.

". . . sources say National Security Advisor George Jackson was fired . . ." said another newscaster.

"Shut up!" said Jackson, changing the channel again.

". . . breaking news, the president has fired Jackson . . ."

"No, no, no!" screamed Jackson as he flipped through the news channels.

". . . Jackson fired . . ."

". . . fired . . ."

"... terminated ..."

"... blamed ..."

"... his fault ..."

"... treason?"

"No, no, no, no, no-o-o-o!" yelled Jackson. He stood up on the couch and threw a cushion at the monitor.

Then the news changed again, under a different BREAKING NEWS banner. It showed a SWAT truck and police cars pulling up to an elegant Georgetown mansion. The truck's back doors swung open and SWAT poured out, turtled up in paramilitary gear. The cameraman shook the lens as he tailed the SWAT team toward the house's front door. A trailing SWAT member turned around and waved him to stop following, which the cameraman did.

Jackson froze and stared at the screen in a drunken haze. That house. It was—

"No, no, no, no, no, no, no, no, no, no!!!!" Jackson screamed and tripped off the couch and smashed his head into the coffee table, scotch spilling everywhere. A crash of wood and steel came through his front door.

"FBI! FBI! HANDS UP! GET ON THE FLOOR!"

The SWAT team surrounded him, some aiming tasers while others held MP5 submachine guns. Jackson held up trembling hands and blood trickled down his forehead, where he hit the coffee table. Jackson's eyes darted around the room like a caged animal, and he began hyperventilating.

"You are under arrest!" shouted a policeman, then read him his Miranda rights as two other men roughly threw him face-first on the coffee table and cuffed him.

"Wa-wait! There must be some mistake," pleaded Jackson. The anger, scotch, head injury, and arrest had him drowning in cognitive dissonance.

"No mistake," said the arresting officer in a commanding tone. The two other SWAT lifted him to his feet but he could not stand.

"What am I being charged with?" Jackson said in a wispy voice.

"Treason."

Jackson let out an involuntary whimper as the men dragged him down his grand hallway, his bare feet dragging on the floor. The great room with twin wraparound staircases was lined with pictures of him meeting world leaders, advising presidents, international awards, American flags—all meant to impress and even intimidate guests. Blood dripped from Jackson's head, smearing a trail on the polished oak floor.

"There must be a mistake, there must be a mistake. I'm George Jackson, the national security advisor. There must be a mistake," he kept repeating softly.

The blast of winter air through his bathrobe coupled with the dozen cameras sobered him up as the FBI hauled him across the lawn. Jackson stared blankly at the news cameras, seeing the reporters' mouths move but hearing nothing.

In a brief moment of self-awareness, he knew. His legacy could have been ending terrorism in America, negotiating a peace in the Middle East, putting China in its place. He was destined for greatness, something he had known since childhood. But it was not to be. This moment, on his front lawn, was to be his everlasting legacy: a scotch-soaked drunk in a bathrobe with blood running down his face, being perp-walked by the FBI for treason. Jackson wanted to float away but was instead thrown into the back of a SWAT vehicle.

CHAPTER 50

The Mercedes-Maybach made its way up the steep country road that was barely two cars wide. Dusk's shadows darkened the forest, giving it a haunted feel, and Winters half expected Hansel and Gretel to emerge. Like the car, the forest seemed prolifically manicured. But that was Austria: cleanliness, order, and child-eating witches.

The aluminum briefcase sat next to Winters, and he kept a hand planted on it at all times. He checked his watch out of nervousness now rather than necessity. Winters disliked meeting his client, but especially since the operation had drifted so far off track.

What went wrong? he thought as the car took a tight turn. He had turned it over in his mind ever since boarding the jet in Dulles. Winters gazed out the window and twirled his cane in annoyance. The sun was disappearing, and the forest shadows grew opaque and creepy. How did it happen?

Locke, he thought with malice. He was the X factor, the independent variable, the free radical. Everything went awry when he appeared, an absolute surprise. No one could have foreseen it. *You should have stayed dead!* Winters did not even have the privilege of revenge. Jackson also took that away from him, and Winters squeezed the cane's ivory monkey head in silent rage. *Eternal shame is too good for you, Jackson,* he thought as they rounded the last turn on the switchback. *Crucifixion is better.*

The car reached the top of the ridgeline, where a medieval castle stood, dominating the valley below. The lights of Vienna twinkled in the distance, and the Danube River meandered through the far plain. For most, it would have been an idyllic sight, but Winters was inured to its glory, unless it came with raw power.

The castle was lit up and well maintained, rare for an eight-hundred-year-old building. Like all citadels of the Middle Ages, it was not large compared to those of later centuries. But unlike eighteenth-century palaces, it was a true stronghold and not just a symbol. A central keep with banqueting hall was surrounded by high walls, each with a mixture of square and circular towers. Walls ten feet thick protected those inside, and battlements lined the ramparts that overlooked a dry moat. Perhaps it once had a drawbridge, too, but the Mercedes-Maybach drove up a ramp and fixed bridge. Immense wooden doors opened to swallow the vehicle, and the gate's raised portcullis looked like teeth. After the Mercedes-Maybach passed, the portcullis came down.

Winters stiffened as the car came to a halt on the cobble-stoned inner courtyard. Staff dressed as if they were plucked from a Habsburgian docudrama opened the car door and assisted Winters out. He shook them off, hating being touched. A valet reached in and retrieved the beat-up aluminum briefcase.

"Be careful with that," snapped Winters, startling the man. Winters was far too jet-lagged and strained for pleasantries. "Take me to the master of the house."

"He awaits you in the library," said the head butler. Winters followed him into the keep, as did the valet carrying the steel case. The interior was fully updated with modern amenities yet retained its old-world personality: racks of antlers lined the plastered walls, suits of armor and weapons adorned the passages, and hefty wood furniture filled each chamber, along with rich tapestries and silks. With the exception of the lights, nothing looked younger than three hundred years old.

Looks like the goddamned Wizard of Oz *in here,* thought Winters. He didn't care for the Old World. A man like him would have been hindered in the ancient régime owing to his low birth station while ingrate nobles raped the people, generation after generation. *God bless America,* he thought while passing through a hall of shields, each with an aristocratic coat of arms. Winters had always identified with Robespierre—a misunderstood revolutionary, in his mind.

"Herr Winters, the library," said the manservant while heaving open large double doors. Winters hobbled in without acknowledging the butler. The medieval library was a three-story atrium lined with bookcases from floor to ceiling. Narrow steel balconies lined the walls, affording access to its leather-bound tomes, some dating back to the Gutenberg press. On the ceiling was a magnificent rococo mural depicting the heavens above, with an eight-pointed star at its zenith. Reading tables stacked with oversized books made the place look almost scholarly.

Winters walked into the middle of the library and heard the door clink shut behind him. At the far end of the room sat a gargantuan marble fireplace, ten feet wide, with an intricate carving of a forgotten battle, and an eight-pointed star at the center. Leather wingback chairs were arrayed around the blazing fire, all facing away from Winters and the entrance. Four Rottweilers lay sleeping at the blaze's edge, weighing about 170 pounds each. A hand extended from one of the wingbacks and placed an empty cordial glass on the side table, next to a silver platter of raw meat.

All the money and connections in the world and the fool shuts himself up a library. What a failure of imagination, thought Winters with disdain as he limped over the oriental carpets. The four dogs lifted their heads in unison as he approached, and he froze. Winters hated dogs, especially these four.

"Mr. Winters, thank you for coming before I had to beckon you," came an old man's voice from the wingback, facing away from Winters. He was the library's only occupant besides the dogs. His gravelly baritone spoke in Queen's English with no trace of his Germanic heritage.

"You would never need to beckon me, Chevalier. A good servant always knows when he is needed before his master does," coaxed Winters, flipping his bitterness into delighted sycophancy. Winters waited. After a pause, a hand emerged from the wingback and waved him forward. Winters tottered forth and the Rottweilers put their heads down.

"Are you here to deliver good news or the other type?" asked the man, still staring at the fire. He was in his eighties and had a long face, square jaw, puffiness under his eyes, and a receding line of formerly blond hair. The wrinkles on his face made him look rugged rather than old. On each hand he wore a large ring as old as the castle, one a family signet and the other an eight-pointed star.

"Good news," responded Winters with a smile, standing in front of a man he knew only as the Chevalier, or "knight" in French, which puzzled him because the man was Austrian. In fact, he was more than Austrian; he was a true Habsburg, one of the last.

"Are you certain?"

His skepticism was an affront to Winters. "Absolutely. We have achieved all of our objectives. Per your commission, I have sewn seeds of chaos and distrust at the highest levels of the U.S. government. I have generated paranoia among the American people against terrorists. Some think Russia is behind it, but they are a small minority." Winters coughed nervously, hoping it would not upset his patron. "The United States overwhelmingly believes terrorists are behind everything, and not Moscow."

"And what of the instrument?"

The library's double doors swung open and the valet carrying the aluminum briefcase appeared, as if summoned. The valet carefully laid down the case on an ottoman next to the Chevalier's feet, and promptly disappeared. The old man looked slightly pleased to see the battered metal case.

"Voilà," said Winters, beaming with pride. "A nuclear briefcase. The fate of three cities and whoever sits in the Oval Office rests at your feet."

"Open it," commanded the Chevalier, leaning forward with anticipation. Winters entered a combination in the ten-digit tumbler lock, which unlocked the side latches. Flipping them up revealed two small fingerprint readers. Simultaneously, he pressed both index fingers on the pads and heard an internal click. Winters opened the case and rotated it to face his client. The internal workings looked like a customized laptop with a handset, biometric authentication, and more buttons.

"Turn it on," ordered the Chevalier.

"I can send for a technician—"

"Turn it on," interrupted the old man.

Winters paused.

"Activate it, Mr. Winters," repeated the Chevalier. "I must have absolute confidence in the genuineness of the instrument before I deliver it to the people I represent."

Was the medieval fossil going to nuke a city? thought Winters, then wondered whether he would be horrified or impressed. "May I please sit to do this?" The Chevalier always made his servants stand. Only peers were allowed to sit.

How I loathe this antiquated turd, thought Winters behind his amicable smile.

The man nodded. Winters sat down in a wingback and pulled the ottoman closer so he could work the nuclear trigger.

He fished out a necklace from inside his shirt and removed the control key from its end. It resembled a thumb drive, but only fit this unique nuclear briefcase. Winters inserted the key into the control panel, and the laptop lit up. It scanned his face, iris, all fingerprints, and accepted a pass-code sentence that Winters typed. The screen changed from sky blue to a world map. A few keystrokes later, three bombs with eleven-digit numbers appeared on the map.

Winters smiled and spun the metal briefcase to face the Chevalier. "There you are. New York City, Los Angeles, and Washington, DC. Their fate is in your hands. You can blackmail presidents, auction off a mushroom cloud, or blow up one just to create mayhem."

"I want proof of concept."

"Excuse me?"

"You heard me, Mr. Winters. I want proof concept. Destroy a city."

Winters was speechless. You don't shoot hostages just to prove they can die, otherwise you lose your leverage. "Did you have a particular city in mind?"

"No. Any one will do."

Winters's throat went dry and he could feel his palms get sweaty. Despite what some believed, he was a businessman and not a mass murderer. Yet his client demanded it, and the client was always right. Winters looked at the map with the nukes. Which city would he end today? Los Angeles was smug and always took national security for granted, making them an ideal candidate. Or maybe New York, where he was mugged once as a kid. Nuking Washington would eliminate a few personal enemies, a nice perk.

"How about DC?" offered Winters.

"Fine."

Winters worked the keyboard, and the Chevalier leaned closer
to observe. Using the track pad, Winters selected the bomb located in Washington and clicked it. The screen zoomed to a satellite image of Sixteenth and O Streets, just five blocks from the
White House. Winters had his teams hide all three nuclear weapons; he knew the noisome inhabitants of this building, and he
grinned.

Gotcha, he thought with contentment. Winters right-clicked
the target indicator on the map, and a menu appeared. He
scrolled down to "Detonate." Click. A safety screen appeared:

Do you wish to detonate K-class weapon 0124?
Latitude: 38.909140 Longitude:-77.037150
Confirm   **Cancel**

"Sir?" asked Winters, turning to the Chevalier, who continued to stare at the screen. The "Cancel" button was blinking but
the cursor stood over "Confirm."

"Remarkable," said the Chevalier at last.

"Would you like me to confirm?" asked Winters, holding his
finger over the "Enter" key.

"No, no, not necessary, Mr. Winters. I am satisfied," said the
Chevalier as he leaned back into his seat once more. "Shut it down."

Winters exhaled more loudly than he wished as he pressed
"Cancel" and shut down the system. The valet appeared again,
as if summoned, to take the aluminum case away.

"My client will be pleased," said the Chevalier, who was a cut-
out for an end client. They never spoke of it, but Winters knew
it was the Kremlin.

"You will need a technician to reset the pass codes so your client can operate the controller," said Winters, watching his greatest achievement disappear into a side room of crossbows.

"We already have such a technician on-site," said the Chevalier. "He will inspect the equipment now."

You were testing me, you bastard! thought Winters with spite.

"You have done well, Mr. Winters," said the Chevalier, and Winters nodded sagaciously. "Everything went nearly according to plan. *Nearly.*"

Winters looked up, confused. "I delivered on all your objectives, did I not?"

The Chevalier shook his head. "All except the most important of all: anonymity. We cannot abide the battle on the Mall last evening. It was too public. Secrecy is our safety and strength, and you have exposed us," said the Chevalier, using the royal *we*. "As they say in medicine: 'Doctor, the operation was a success, but the patient is dead.' You delivered our objectives but made a pig's breakfast of the entire affair."

"With respect, Chevalier, let me explain—"

The Chevalier interrupted him before Winters could continue. "No. Your actions speak for you." The man's voice was firm, and one of the dogs lifted his head in concern. "You disappoint me, Winters."

"I can assure you, Chevalier, none of this will blow back on you or your client," soothed Winters. "Terrorists and their collaborators will ultimately take the blame, as you instructed. I've fabricated an 'insider threat' terrorist scenario within Washington circles, so that everything will fall on the heads of two individuals. The first is George Jackson, the national security advisor who regrettably went insane. The second is Tom Locke, a lowlife mercenary turned nuclear terrorist. The evidence trail will lead to them; I have arranged it."

"And where are they now?"

Winters smiled, feeling the Chevalier coming around. "Jackson has been arrested for treason, and I will manufacture the necessary proof to see him convicted. Locke was killed last night." Winters shifted uneasily, as his men had yet to find Locke's body.

However, how could he survive a direct hit from a Hellfire missile? Locke had to be dead. "It's easy to blame a dead man with a suspicious past."

"Dead?" asked the Chevalier in a tone that unsettled Winters. "Are you certain?"

"Absolutely, my Chevalier," said Winters, concealing alarm that the Chevalier might know something he did not. "Locke was killed by missile fire on the Mall, and a good thing too. He was in a convoy leading a group of renegade mercenaries. They were hired by a rich Middle Eastern monarchy, or at least that is how it will play out. Thankfully, the American military learned of Locke's plans and took him out on the Mall last night. That was the true impetus for the battle: to stop Locke and his terrorist plot."

"Is that so?" asked the Chevalier in mild surprise.

Winters grinned internally, believing he had successfully circumnavigated the Locke affair. Now to seize the initiative.

"Who do you think tipped off the Americans? It was *me*," said Winters. "It was the only reason they caught Locke so quickly. I saved you too, Chevalier. Locke was a dangerous man. He was a greater threat to you than you realize. It was worth the risk."

The Chevalier's expression soured. "I will judge threats and risks, not you. Do you understand me, Winters? I can use capable men regardless if they are good or evil. All men are governable, for those with the acumen to do it. My family has been doing it for a very long time. Now, which do you think you are, Mr. Winters: governor or governed?"

The geriatric reprobate! thought Winters, and was tempted to withdraw the hidden sword inside his cane and slice the dunce's throat open. Then he eyed the sleeping Rottweilers. *Time for that later,* he thought.

"Your quiet is confirmation enough," continued the Chevalier, and Winters hand tightened around the ivory monkey head. "We have doubts about you, Mr. Winters. We even question whether you comprehend the task we commissioned you to perform. Your brusque methods may have imperiled us." The Chevalier paused, allowing the implications to fester in Winters's mind. The Rottweilers lifted their heads, as if on cue, to glare at Winters. "That is unforgivable."

"Sir, I think there may be a misunderstanding," said Winters coolly.

"Locke is alive!" bellowed the octogenarian, the dogs looking up in alarm.

"Alive?" stammered Winters, his face pale. "Impossible!"

"What is impossible is your dim grasp of reality, Mr. Winters." The old man flung a piece of meat at one of the Rottweilers. It ripped the meat with its mandibles before swallowing it with an audible gulp. Winters stood and unconsciously took a step backward.

"No. Locke has to be dead," muttered Winters.

"You have disappointed me for the last time, Mr. Winters," said the old man, his tone imperious. "Locke undid your fragile work in four nights. You are an incompetent."

Winters's scowled. "But Chevalier—"

The old man cut him off. "You will return to the United States and make repair. You will finish what I commissioned you to start." He tossed three more hunks of meat at the dogs, who swallowed them without chewing.

"But I—"

"And eliminate Locke this time," interrupted the Chevalier again. "Everywhere he goes, calamity follows. No more mistakes, Mr. Winters." He paused to throw a handful of meat, and the animals inahled it midair. The old man threw larger, boned morsels. "On pain of death."

Winters's jaw went slack as he watched the Rottweilers rip

apart their food. The valet mysteriously appeared again, followed by two armed men in body armor wielding cattle prods.

The Chevalier faced Winters at last. "Never forget Mr. Winters; you're expendable."

Winters face went ashen as the valet and guards escorted him out.

CHAPTER 51

Putin sat in Stalin's old office in the Kremlin, cradling a gilded teacup. The room was smaller and less ornate than his official chambers, but he felt the great man's presence here. The Soviet Union began its slow decline after the Man of Steel's death in 1953. The fall of the Soviet Union remained a personal injury for Putin. If he could restore just an iota of the glory that Stalin had imbued in the USSR, then his reign would be a success. Working in the great man's office reminded him of his charge.

Putin sat behind Stalin's smallish wooden desk, overlooking a large U-shape of chairs rimming an oriental rug before him, a court audience before a throne. The walls were deep red fabric with oil paintings of the great man on all sides, peering down on the occupants. Beside the desk sat the old couch where Uncle Joe would sleep during World War II. Putin tried it once but it was absurdly lumpy and he got no sleep.

However, today Putin and his aides were doing something Stalin never did: watching TV. All the international news networks streamed live coverage of America's turmoil. An aerial view of the smoking National Mall was shocking, even to the Kremlin apparatchiks, who smiled. Next came the pundits who agreed loose nukes may be covertly hidden in American cities by unknown foes, although many suspected Russia was behind it. The apparatchiks' smiles grew. Lastly, live footage of National Security Advisor George Jackson being dragged out of his home wearing only a bathrobe and handcuffs and arrested for treason. The apparatchiks beamed.

"What an idiot!" laughed one of the aides, and the rest joined in the ridicule chorus.

"And to think," said Putin while stirring his tea, "I barely lifted a finger."

Everyone chuckled in smug glee, a stark reversal from a few hours ago. Operation Zapad-20 (West-20) was launched in 2016 to sow chaos in America's capital, but declared a failure earlier this morning after one of their safe houses was mysteriously taken out. Everyone assumed it was a CIA hit, but their sources in the Agency denied it. Putin didn't care much because it was only mercenary casualties. The Wagner Group served many purposes, including dying.

But now this? thought Putin as he sipped his tea, smiling. The chaos yield surpassed even his optimal hopes. This was no accident; it was the work of a master.

"I wonder who did this," said one of the aides.

"Who knows. Who cares. How did Shakespeare put it?" said Putin, then spoke in heavily accented English. "'All's vell that ends vell.'"

Everyone chuckled.

CHAPTER 52

"Who was that?" asked Lin after I hung up. Only her mouth moved. The rest of her lay immobile on top of me.

"Dunno," I replied, equally spent. *How did they track me?* I wondered. "We should leave."

After a pause, she said, "Yeah."

Neither of us moved.

"We need to bounce," I said in a tender whisper. With a sigh, she rolled off and I sat up, ruing our predicament. My head was puzzling through the mysterious call.

"What did they want?" she asked, as I put on my pants and checked the time. It was 1900.

"They said they know where Winters is, and invited me to the party," I said from the bathroom.

"It's a trap," she offered.

"I know," I agreed, lacing up my boots. "That's why we need to scoot."

"Crap," she uttered, putting the back of a hand over her eyes. Neither of us wanted to go; instead we wanted to make the evening last all night. Now we were on the run again, from people we did not know. Real life was intruding once more. "Crap," she repeated.

Jen got vertical and started putting on her pantsuit.

"We need to find you something more practical to wear," I said.

"Practical to wear?" she guffawed.

"Yeah. You can't go running backstreets in a pantsuit," I said. At least she wore tasteful running shoes; presumably her heels were still under her desk at work.

"What?!" she retorted, offended. "As an FBI agent, I chased and arrested Russian mobsters all over New York City dressed in Ferragamo. Turns out Italian wool works just fine for roundhouse kicks and judo throws." Her eyes bore into me. "What do you know about women's clothes, anyway? When I want your fashion advice, I'll give it to you."

Yikes! I thought, chastised, while doing a functions check on my H&K. Then I did her Saiga and handed it to her.

"Thanks," she said coolly, taking the weapon while brushing knots out of her hair.

Catching myself in the mirror, I realized it was me who needed civilian clothes. I looked like a lost SWAT team member.

Knocking at the door.

We both froze, looked at each other, and then at the door. The knocking continued. Thinking the same thing, we swapped weapons. She took up a protected position from the bathroom, aiming the H&K at the door. The Saiga's wide shot pattern would have obliterated the enemy and me.

The rapping got louder. I stood with my back to the wall that was flush with the door, Saiga pointed at whoever walked through it. Jen nodded at me and I nodded back.

"Who is it?" I asked in a normal voice. The knock's rhythm changed to something out of a Bugs Bunny cartoon. Jen and I exchanged quizzical looks, and then fixed on the door again.

"Who *is* it?" I repeated in a stern voice.

"Open up," said the voice, exacerbated.

Tye?! I thought. *How is that possible?*

"Let me in, lover boy," whispered Tye. Jen looked revolted, as I waved an all clear sign, and opened the door. There was Tye, dressed in sport hiking clothes. The guy probably never wore a tie in his life.

"Tye!" I said in shock after the door closed. He bear-hugged me and, I think, cracked a rib. Jen looked bewildered, lowering her weapon.

"Introduce me to your lady," said Tye before I could ask a single question.

"Tye, Jen," I said, motioning one to the other. "Jen, Tye."

Jen looked equal parts polite and appalled.

"Nice weapon, Jen," he said admiringly. "Sounds like you're C4 in the sack, too. A real *heat* round," he joked.

Jen's face turned crimson, and she unconsciously pointed the H&K at Tye's chest.

"Whoa, whoa, whoa!" I said, lowering the assault weapon with my hand. "Tye's a friend."

"You know this jerkwad?" she asked me, astonished.

"Yeah. He's a battle buddy," I replied.

Her expression read: *Are you serious?* My expression replied: *Hells yeah.*

"Come on, lovebirds, we gotta go, now!" said Tye. "If we can track you, so can they."

"Wait," I interrupted, my head spinning. "How did you find us? I thought you were captured. How are you here?"

"I'll explain in the van. We need to evac now," he said. Hastily we wrapped our weapons in bedsheets and followed Tye down the hall. Clients were busy behind the thin walls, and Jen avoided touching surfaces, doorknobs, everything.

We exited down a second-story fire escape with a defunct alarm. In the ally, a beat-up white van idled ready. I noticed it had new high-performance tires and was probably not your average plumber's ride, despite appearances. Tye opened the rear doors and gestured for us to enter as if he were a butler. Jen shook her head at his puerile behavior despite the gravity of the situation, while I grinned. We clambered inside and sat on a few wooden crates that probably concealed weapons and ammo.

"Let's go," Tye told the driver, and we sped out.

My mind reeled in confusion, I had so many questions. *Is he saving or abducting us?* That Apollo was divided was clear; however, which side Tye and Lava fought for was not. Maybe they worked for Winters? My mind didn't want to accept it, but I could not ignore it.

"Where are we going?" I asked.

"Someplace safe," said Tye, watching the road ahead. Jen looked concerned.

Exhaling deeply, I sat back. Tye was right about one thing: if he could find us, others could, too. The hotel was not safe. Probably no place was, except maybe with Tye and Lava. They were our least bad option. I regretted dragging Jen into Apollo's civil war, and needed to find out more.

"How did you find us so quickly?" I asked.

"You never were lost, buddy. Remember when Lava came to your safe house and he gave you a thermos of special energy drink?"

"Yeah, it tasted like fruit punch. I'm guessing now it had some sort of tracing agent."

"Correct, it was laced with nanotech. It lasts for a few days, and we've been tracking your every move."

I wondered who else could track me. The thought chilled me, but I needed to move on to the next question. "Tye, how is it possible you are here? I saw you and Lava get captured next to me on a rooftop by Winters's men." Then I realized the truth. "Have you both turned? Are you working for Winters now?"

Tye laughed, as did the driver. "No, Tom. It was a setup. Winters's men captured us, but not everyone on his team is working for him. We have guys on the inside feeding us intel and releasing captives, including Lava and me. We escaped. It was all part of the plan, and you were the bait."

"The bait?" asked Jen, shocked.

"Correct. I'm sorry, Tom, but we had no choice," said Tye, turning to face me with sincerity in his voice.

"No choice?!" responded Jen defensively. She seemed more irate than me.

"The public doesn't know it, but there's a secret war going on in the United States and the stakes are existential, just like during the Cold War," said Tye. "Our client wants Winters's foreign client identified and neutralized, 'off the books' in ways the CIA can't do anymore. That's our contract. We've been running a mole hunt to smoke Winters out, but he doesn't make mistakes. Our mission in New York was to hack Elektra and reveal Winters's client, but the mission failed. They now have nuclear weapons on U.S. soil, waiting to detonate." Tye turned to me. "We are *losing* and need an edge. That edge is you."

I heard but did not comprehend. "Say again?"

"We needed to flush out Winters but we didn't know how, then you came back from the dead. We used you as bait, Tom, knowing you were the only thing that could lure Winters out of the shadows. But to set Winters in play, we had to get you captured, and fake our own capture. Then it was simply following the body trail, which led us here."

"Where is 'here'?" asked Jen.

"'Here' is the imminent demise of Brad Winters and his mysterious client," said Tye, turning to face us again. "Are you still fit to fight, Locke?"

"Always."

"How about your girlfriend?" he asked, looking at Jen.

"Always," she said, with less enthusiasm.

"Good. Because we're going to need every swinging muzzle we can find for this one."

"One what, exactly?" asked Jen distrustfully.

"For this operation," said Tye with resolve. "We are going to take down Winters once and for all. And we need your help. Both of you."

CHAPTER 53

Winters slumped in the leather chair as the plane hit turbulence. His steak went untouched; it reminded him of the Rottweilers. He sat alone in the corporate jet, save the steward, who avoided him, and checked his watch again.

Eight hours, he thought. He had eight hours to formulate a new plan, because that was when the plane would land outside of Washington. So far, his plan was rudimentary: kill Locke. Everything else was already in place: the nukes, the controller, and the extortion. Why could the old man not see his victory? But Winters knew the answer.

"Inbred nitwit," he muttered. Generations of intermarriage had dimmed aristocratic IQs over the centuries the same way a fine oil painting fades when left in sunlight. The old man was timid, like a serf. But the Chevalier's treating him like a dog was unforgivable.

"When I am done with Locke, I am coming for you, Chevalier," he swore under his breath. Settling scores gave him purpose. Only now did Winters comprehend that he always possessed the tools he needed and had never required the Chevalier's assistance. Experience is something you get only after you need it.

It's now my *time,* he thought. Once Locke and the Chevalier were disappeared, Winters would locate and reclaim the nuclear briefcase. Then he would bring the U.S. and Russia to the brink of war, exploiting the ensuing chaos for wealth and power. Iago was his favorite Shakespeare character, and Winters never understood why Iago was vilified rather than admired.

Yes, it would be easy enough, he mused, inspired by the Chevalier's near detonation of Washington, DC. Two crazed countries with a history of enmity; simply vaporize an American city and frame Russia. The rest would take care of itself. He didn't give a damn about either anymore. The Americans were hunting him, owing to his connection to Jackson, and the Russians soon would be. The Chevalier would undoubtedly tip off Moscow once Winters had outlived his usefulness.

Faithless black knight, Winters thought as his hand squeezed his cane. He was happy to see them all burn. Revenge is justice in an unjust world, he believed. But first, there was a personal matter begging his attention.

"Locke, Locke, Locke," hissed Winters. "Where are you?" Locke was a bad-luck charm that needed killing. Until he was off the gameboard, nothing was certain. More important, watching Locke tortured to death slowly would give Winters peace. After all, it was Locke who'd set him up in Saudi Arabia, where he spent a year in a torture gulag awaiting beheading. He escaped, but his larynx was crushed and his right knee smashed. Locke owed him, and he intended to collect with payday-loan interest.

"Now that you have earned my full attention, Locke, there is no place you can slither to this time," said Winters with the zeal of a trophy hunter. He had already activated every stringer at his disposal to search for the miscreant, although it would be instantaneous if Elektra was still online. *What a waste,* he thought with pity.

Winters flipped through the news channels to get his mind off of Locke. They all replayed footage of Jackson being hauled out of his house drunk, in a bathrobe at ten that morning. Winters belly-laughed, and it made him feel better. *Old fool. I warned you, didn't I?*

The news prattled on about stock market jitters, politicians blaming one another, urban flight, domestic terrorism, Brad Winters.

What?! Winters lurched out of his seat. There was a picture of him on the TV, an older photo taken from before his Riyadh internment. Winters turned up the volume.

"Brad Winters . . . conspiracy . . . Winters . . . domestic terrorism . . ." The newscaster was remarkably well informed about Winters's background. No journalist knew this much about his life.

Impossible! he thought, feeling lightheaded and sweaty. Flipping channels, he saw every major news outlet carried a similar story. A foreign-language news crawl even had his name: BRAD WINTERS. In a panic, he checked internet news sites; his name, picture, and biography were plastered everywhere.

"Shit!" exclaimed Winters as he shut off the monitor, cringing. "Shit, shit!" Winters was always five steps of everyone else, and ten ahead of his foes. How had he been so spectacularly blindsided? It was a bullet in the head for a man like Winters.

Who did this to me? His mind raced. Maybe it was the Chevalier? *No, he has too much to lose by exposing me now.* Jackson? *No, I dusted my trail. All Jackson's raving will lead the FBI in circles.* Locke? *No, the media would not find him a credible source.* Apollo? *No, they would never risk the blowback.* A foreign power? Terrorists? Others? No. He had many enemies but none with this level of information.

Whoever leaked my identity to the press has power, real power. The kind that Winters sought, and that was what scared him. It had been a long time since he tasted fear. Even in the Riyadh prison cell, he somehow knew he would negotiate a way out. But now, who would he bargain with?

Damn you, whoever you are! he thought with venom. With

shaky hands, he picked up a water glass and drank. *I will outlast this, find you, and kill you.*

"I'll need a new plan," said Winters to himself. "Bold. Creative. Unexpected." His fingers absentmindedly tapped the burl wood table. Gazing out the window, his brow furled in concentration as he puzzled out the angles. He considered turning the plane around to seek safe harbor; he had multiple secret bank accounts and a private island halfway around the world just for such a day. But he shook his head.

"Nothing changes, except the timeline," he concluded. "The sooner I control the WMD, the sooner I become a superpower, and then game on." There would be no shortcuts. He still had to start with Locke, then the Chevalier, then the nuclear briefcase. All within days. Then find and fix whoever leaked his identity to the media. It was mission impossible for most, but not Winters.

"I will survive this," he resolved. He sat immobile with a grave expression, his fingers interlaced under his nose. Ten minutes passed. Twenty. Thirty. At last he smiled, then laughed. *It was so obvious!* he thought.

"Hammersmith Hall," murmured Winters with a proud grin. It was the Chevalier's estate on Long Island's Gold Coast, managed under layers of shell companies, and where he first met the Chevalier. No one would think to look for him there. Even better, it was defendable. The 1904 mansion sat on a private peninsula, surrounded by water and hundreds of acres of patrolled land with an Israeli-style border fence. Nothing got in or out without the guards' knowledge. It was an ideal location to regroup and prepare for an attack he knew would be coming.

"Overkill is underrated," he said, picking up the phone. Within ten minutes, all his key assets were mobilizing for Hammersmith Hall, and most would arrive before he did. He instructed the estate to receive his visitors, but neglected to say they would be extremely armed and dangerous. Once his Apollo teams locked down the estate, they would prepare for the next phase: attack. Later, Winters would solicit the Chevalier's forgiveness, after his victory. *In fact, that meeting could be the perfect opportunity to capture the Chevalier,* Winters thought with a grin.

"Pilots, divert to Westchester, New York, and lay on a chopper. A fast one."

"Yes sir," said the voice over the intercom.

Just one more call to make, the most important one of all, he thought as the plane banked slightly right. After he was finished, he placed the phone back in its holder and stared at the dark clouds below. *Not only will I kill Locke, I will destroy all my enemies in a single blow.*

"The die is cast," he declared, reminded of Julius Caesar crossing the Rubicon to invade Rome.

CHAPTER 54

After driving an hour on country roads, we pulled into a community airport in The Middle of Nowhere, Virginia. The tarmac's residents were single-engine planes, two crop dusters, and one Stearman biplane. At the end was an uncharacteristically large hangar, our destination. The massive doors shut behind the van as we coasted to a stop.

"We're here," said Tye, stepping out. We were not alone. The place was teeming with people and vehicles of all types. Crammed in the hanger was a Bombardier corporate jet and four turboprop, twin-engine cargo planes, like the aircraft Lava used over Manhattan. A work crew was heaving a space-age hunk of machinery up the tailgate of the nearest one.

"Is that a drone?" asked Jen as we passed. It looked like an armed rotary-wing drone with its boom and blades folded up. Attached was a cargo chute.

"Yes," I said, thinking that would have been handy in Manhattan. Mechanics were sliding air-to-air missiles on the rails of two fixed-wing jet drones, presumably our escorts. They were twenty feet of black sleekness, and looked like half-size fighter jets rather than the wide-wing variants used by the U.S. government.

"What are those?" asked Jen, amazed. She was pointing to the two fighter jet drones.

"Apollo proprietary tech," said one of the mechanics, overhearing her. "We call them Hunters because they can search and destroy targets autonomously. No humans in the kill loop."

"But isn't that dangerous?" she asked, as I tried to pull her along. We had a lot to do. The mechanic looked confused, as if saying, *All war is dangerous.*

"She's new here," I told him as we left.

"Hey, Locke, grab gear. You'll know it when you see it," shouted Tye over the din as he walked away. Parked against the wall was a box van of HALO equipment and oxygen bottles. Another was loaded with body armor and weapons. A third was filled with ammunition and demo. An assembly line of technicians equipped male and female warriors. Apollo was getting ready for battle; except I had never seen a full-court press before.

"What is this place?" asked Jen as we ducked under the wing of the corporate jet. People shuffled around us, moving with a purpose, but there was a jitteriness in the air. Several were wheeling matte-black dirt bikes onto one cargo plane. Jen cocked her head in surprise, noticing they had no license plates, lights of any kind, or mufflers. They were unique.

"Apollo Outcomes, my old company," I said. *Or what's left of it*, I thought. Apollo's civil war had taken a toll, and the hangar had a Rebel-Alliance-on-planet-Hoth vibe.

"What are we doing here?" whispered Jen, troubled.

"It's not your fight, Jen. You don't need to be here," I said, hoping she would say it was her fight, too. But she said nothing. "Let's find Lava, my old commander. We both have questions and he has answers."

Two people passed us wearing head-to-toe battle armor that made them look like black cyborgs, and with futuristic assault rifles slung over their shoulders. Jen stood still, gaping.

"What is that?" she asked, pointing to their weapons.

"Precision-guided firearms. One shot, one kill, guaranteed by AI. Shoots around corners, from choppers, and through Kevlar like margarine, even when sprinting. Standard issue at Apollo."

"Holy crap," she murmured.

"Our military could have the same equipment if the government's procurement system wasn't so FUBAR."

"I'm starting to understand what you were saying about Apollo. I just didn't . . . believe it," she said.

"Few do. I didn't either, until I was recruited. They don't hire; they only recruit," I said, scanning the hangar for Lava, but no luck. Along the back wall were four thirty-foot satellite trucks, like the kind TV networks use, except these were different: NSA-level command and control nodes with cyber warriors and drone pilots for mobile operations. In the past, one truck would support a high-intensity mission. I had never seen four deployed simultaneously. In fact, I had never seen four at all.

It looks like a final stand, I thought.

"Tom, who's that?" asked Jen. In a corner, a burly tall man surrounded by people waved at us.

"That's Lava," I said. "Let's go."

We clasped forearms and he pounded my back in greeting. "Nice to see you back, Tom. We need your gun on this one. It's big. It's everything."

"Lava, about using me to get Winters . . ." I said with anger, but he cut me off.

"And who is this?" he asked warmly, extending a hand to Jen.

"Um," Jen looked at me, wondering if she should give her real name.

"You must be Ms. Jennifer P. Lin, former FBI agent," said Lava. "You know the Bureau has issued an arrest warrant for you." Jen's face went white. "Makes no difference to us, of course. We're outside the law."

"Jen's one of the good guys . . . er, gals," I said.

"So I've heard," said Lava with genuine admiration. "Good work last night, taking down one of Wagner's safe houses, and solo no less. I'm impressed." Her mouth dropped. "Even Tye was impressed, and that's rare," Lava chuckled. "I don't know what you did this morning, but he called you a thermonuclear tigress." Lava gave me a knowing smile.

Jen's expression transformed from astonishment to wrath, and her fists balled up.

"More later. But first . . ." Lava clambered onto the top of a truck so all could see him. "Gather around, everyone! Gather around!" People dropped what they were doing and assembled in front of Lava. They numbered about seventy in all, the last of Apollo Outcomes. It was once six hundred.

"It's been a long campaign. We've all lost friends, but the time has come to strike back and end this war in a single, decisive attack. Our client leaked Winters's identity to the media, hoping it would force him to make a mistake we can exploit. It did."

The group murmured in speculation, and Lava continued.

"We have actionable intelligence on where and when Winters *and his entire team* will be in three hours. We must hit them *now,* while they are regrouping and not when they have regrouped. Surprise is on our side, making this our one, best, and last chance to eliminate the threat. If we fail, Winters and his foreign enemy client may destroy three American cities and dictate terms to the White House. We can never allow that to happen."

Murmurs of alarm in a variety of languages escalated. Lava then gave the mission brief, making an impromptu "sand table" on the hangar floor using airplane chocks as buildings, rope for terrain features, and coffee cups as units, both friendly and enemy. He walked around with a broomstick, pointing at units as he explained the plan.

"This is crazy!" whispered Jen in my ear as the plan became evident.

"We specialize in crazy," I replied with no irony. She grabbed my hand, perhaps unconsciously, but her expression remained impassive for the rest of the brief. At the end, the team let out a battle cry, and everyone hurried back to their tasks. Wheels up in three-zero mikes.

"We need to talk," said Jen in her business voice. I followed her into a tool cage toward the back of the maintenance annex.

"Who are you fighting?" she asked.

"Wagner Group mercenaries and Apollo renegades," I answered, and explained Winters. She absorbed it.

"Let me get this straight," she said. "Your old boss, Winters, finds a foreign client. In exchange for power, money, whatever, he recovers three nuclear bombs that he previously stole from Pakistan—"

"I tried to stop him in Iraq and Syria," I added.

"—then he goes into business with the Wagner Group, Russian mercenaries—"

"They wiped out my team in Ukraine. Winters sold me out," I interrupted again, bitter.

Jen ignored me. "—and Wagner hires the Shulaya mafia to smuggle nukes into New Jersey. At the same time, Winters returns to Apollo and creates a schism within the company, hijacking half of it. They bury the three nukes in American cities, and give the trigger to a foreign, unknown client. Is that correct?"

I nodded.

"You have some fucked-up colleagues," she opined.

I nodded again. "No longer colleagues, and about to become extinct. Winters's whole team is massing as we speak, and we can take them out in one assault. It's gutsy, but Lava is right. It's our one and only chance."

"And who is your client?" Jen asked, ever the investigator. I honestly did not know, and she shook her head in disapproval.

"I trust Lava," I blurted, surprising myself. But my gut knew him to be true.

Jen glared at me. "Are you really dumb enough to do this, Tom?"

I was taken aback. "Yes. Absolutely. Why do you think I came out of hiding from halfway around the world? If we don't stop this here and now, we might as well auction off the Oval Office to any foreign power willing to pay third parties."

Jen crossed her arms and shot me a look of enraged disappointment, as I stood resolute.

"Hey!" It was Tye's voice, as he poked his head into the tool cage. "I've been looking for you everywhere. We got fifteen minutes before wheels up. You need to suit up, Locke." Then he noticed our body language. "Lovers' quarrel?"

Jen spun around and scowled at him. I had never seen Tye slink away so fast. I grabbed her hands and we hugged, then kissed. I could taste her salty tears. Curiously, I never thought about death before an operation, no matter how risky. Death is what happens to other people, I irrationally believed.

"You don't need to do this. It's not your fight," I said again.

"Yes, it is. You came out of hiding and I left the FBI for the same reason. We've risked everything for this opportunity." We kissed again.

"Let's go, yous!" bellowed Tye's voice from the hangar. A minute later, we emerged. The hangar was frantic, and the main doors were open. Vehicles were departing and ground crews were towing out the aircraft. The night air refreshed the hangar.

"Locke, you're on me again. We're on bird alpha," said Tye, pointing to one of the cargo aircraft. "You know the drill."

"Roger," I said, looking at the tech assembly line by the three box vans. They were waving to me to hurry up.

Then Tye turned to Jen. "Are you in the fight?"

Jen paused and looked at me then the aircraft. One of the turboprops spun to life, followed by others. She nodded.

"Is that a yes?" asked Tye with care.

"Yes, yes. Count me in. I speak Russian. It might come in handy."

"I know it will," said Tye. "Everyone is glad you're on the team." He pointed to the corporate jet being towed onto the tarmac. "You're riding in that. When it lands, you will be on the ground team. Jinx will brief you inflight. Locke can help with your equipment." He slapped me on the shoulder twice, put on his black helmet, and jogged over to our cargo plane.

Jen and I suited up at the vans, and I taught her how to operate the tactical cuff with its AI. She opted to keep her Saiga automatic shotgun and grabbed four more grenades, "for old times' sake," she said nervously.

"Hey Locke, hurry your ass up!" I heard Tye yell from the aircraft. The hunter drones taxied to the airstrip and screeched into the sky. One of the cargo planes started rolling. It was time.

"Come back to me," I said.

"Kick ass, my darling," she whispered in my ear, then slapped my butt and sauntered to the Bombardier jet, her long hair billowing in the prop blast.

I smiled, locking the image of her in my memory, then double-timed to the lead cargo plane. Minutes later, we were all airborne and flying north.

CHAPTER 55

The business helicopter touched down on the manicured lawn after dark, the rotor wash blowing leaves and dirt into the empty marble swimming pool. The backdrop was a faux Normandy castle, complete with ivy-covered turrets and hypergothic architecture, like Neuschwanstein's baby cousin.

Staff members rushed out to greet the chopper; some wore butler black tie while others looked like SWAT. Winters lumbered out of the aircraft, his overcoat flapping in the down wash. As soon as the door closed, the engines whined as the pilots pulled pitch, sending the Sikorski S-76 up in a graceful swoop toward Long Island Sound.

"Where are the commanders?" yelped Winters to no one in particular. "I want a sitrep ASAP!"

A man dressed in black body armor with a bullpup assault rifle nodded to the others, who returned to the mansion.

"Who are you?" demanded Winters.

"I've been assigned as your aide-de-camp for this phase of the operation, sir," said the commando, clearly not a job he volunteered for. "The commanders are assembling in the library, waiting for you, sir."

Winters's chin bobbed, a faint nod of approval.

Hammersmith House sat on its own peninsula, which jutted out into the sound. It was built during the Gilded Age by a robber baron of industry, its stones meant to rival the nobility of Blenheim Palace in England. Exquisite gardens sloped downward from the grand portico to the shoreline and offered superlative views of Connecticut on the horizon. The surrounding grounds were mostly wooded, lending a pastoral beauty at odds with the asphalt of Manhattan, thirty miles away. However, Winters took no notice of it.

"What are our troop levels?" asked Winters as he walked across the lawn to the mansion. He moved with vigor, despite his infirmity. The scent of battle animated him, giving him inexplicable strength. Whatever monster he had mutated into, he began as a soldier at West Point, and he was a good one, too.

"About ninety percent assembled, sir. We expect stragglers over the next twenty-four hours."

Winters shook his head and the aide felt the scorn. "Show me the rest of the defenses," he said as he marched forward.

Heavily armed men dressed in black scurried about, turning the Gold Coast mansion into an Afghanistan firebase. The estate's staff scampered about, mortified. The decorative eighteenth-century porcelain collections were a particular worry, and a footman sprawled his body across a display case as two paramilitaries eyed the hand-painted figurines with curiosity.

Winters and the aide reached the expansive stone patio facing the sound. It was built for outdoor parties of four hundred during the Gatsby era, but now it entertained missile launchers and auto-turrets, covering every conceivable avenue of approach.

Winters surveyed the battleground: a one-thousand-foot lawn and garden from the mansion to the sea. Men were laying anti-personnel mines, and two Boston Whaler speedboats were pressed into service patrolling the banks with machine guns and automatic grenade launchers. Then he looked skyward.

"Where's the air defenses? I ordered this kitsch shrine transformed into a fortress. Nothing in or out. And that means the goddamn heavens too!" he shouted, jabbing his cane at the stars.

The aide gestured to the roof. Winters leaned back and squinted into the moonless sky. "Give me those," he said, removing the aide's night vision. Donning it, he could see men patrolling the imitation battlements. Some were snipers while others had surface-to-air missiles on their shoulders. "Where is our radar? What kind of early warning do we have?"

"We have tapped all ground radar from local airports," said the aide. "It's not Patriot missile quality, but it should work."

"Not good enough," Winters grumped. "Drones. Show me."

"Follow me, sir," replied the aide.

They entered the mansion, a temple of antiques and art. They passed a squad of Russian-speaking mercenaries, then Spanish speakers. Then a group of English speakers unpacking crates of Claymore mines and blasting caps. The only things they all had in common were heavy weapons and a penchant for black.

It's like the Tower of Babel in here, thought Winters. There were two command languages, Russian and English, increasing the chances of fratricide. To date, the Wagner Group and Apollo mercenaries had never fought together, only against each other.

Winters hobbled across the harlequin tile of the grand foyer, commandos stepping out of his way in respect. He walked like MacArthur returning to the Philippines. The aide gestured toward the front door, a monstrosity of wood and iron. Beyond it, on the other great lawn, were rows of armed rotary and fixed-wing drones.

"The fixed wings are capable of vertical takeoff. Another six are patrolling the skies right now. What you see is the airborne quick reaction force that can deploy within twenty seconds. Main armaments include 7.62 miniguns, Hellfires, and Stingers," said the aide like a salesman.

"OK," mumbled Winters, and the aide smiled. It was as close to a compliment as anyone would receive from the boss.

"Do you want me to show you the forward firing positions?" asked the aide. "We have minefields, mortars, and obstacles to channel a ground assault into an ambush kill zone. We requisitioned"— meaning *stole*—"and outfitted speedboats. Two are patrolling the shoreline as we speak, using acoustic detection for a waterborne assault. The Russians made improvised depth charges."

"What about an air assault?" asked Winters, listening closely as they walked the grounds.

"The Wagner Group has next-generation Verba surface-to-air missiles scanning the sky, better than the ones the Russian army uses. They are positioned across the peninsula, giving us defense in depth and interlocking fires. Anyone foolish enough to attack us by land, sea, or air will be sent to their maker, and fast."

Winters liked the man's spirit, and paused to consider if he would be his next protégé or cannon fodder. He judged the latter, and hobbled away. Both men snaked through the firing line, as mercenaries filled sandbags and converted marbled architecture into fighting positions. The library reminded Winters of the Chevalier, with his exquisite carpets, the smell of old leather books, and eight-pointed stars on the ceiling.

"Atten-HUN!" yelled a former Marine as Winters entered the spacious room. Everyone stood at attention, their battle dress a collage of origin and technology. Winters took the seat at the head of a long oaken table. The magnificent library now served as a tactical operations center, with map boards, laptops, and large monitors. The background noise was a polyglot of radio chatter.

The staff was bifurcated. At Winters's right sat English-speaking ex-Apollo warriors with next-generation battle gear. On his left were the Russian commanders of the Wagner Group. What they lacked in tech they made up for in attitude. There was neither enmity nor love between them, just a common mission.

"Skip the brief. I just walked the line, and do you know what I saw?" said Winters, pausing for an answer from the group. None came. "Weak defenses. We're not ready."

"Sir, with all due respect," said one of the ex-Apollo commanders. "We've only been on the ground a few hours and have secured the AO. Give us a day and it will be Fort Knox."

"We don't have a day," rasped Winters. "Make no mistake about it. What's left of Apollo is a desperate, cornered wild animal. They will attack tonight. *Tonight!*" Winters grasped his throat in pain, as alarm was expressed in numerous languages.

"But how is that possible?" asked a Wagner Group commander with a heavy Russian accent. "Even we didn't know where we would be eight hours ago."

"Because *I* leaked them our position," responded Winters coolly.

Silence. Then the Russian spoke again, with care, voicing what everyone was thinking. "But why would you do such a thing? Why not wait a day? In twenty-four hours we will be at one hundred percent strength and dug in."

"Because it's a trap. Waiting a day would not bait them because they know we have numerical superiority. It must be tonight! If they thought we were still collecting our forces and vulnerable—and they had the element of surprise—they would attack us with everything they have. When they do attack, we will obliterate them in a single battle!" Winters leaned forward, fist clenched and spittle flying from his mouth.

The commanders pumped their fists in the air, whooping their support in a babel of tongues. Winters continued, and they quieted down.

"We have more troops, more firepower, and the advantage of a prepared defensive position. They think we are weak and regrouping, but that is a ruse. Their attack will be our opportunity to wipe them out cleanly, once and for all!"

Cheers resounded and butt stocks banged on antique tables.

"And when the last of old Apollo is gone, there will be nothing to stop us. Our moment of victory is at hand!"

Multicultural battle cries filled the library in a roar of warfare. Winters sat back, pleased. With any luck, Locke would come, too—and when he did, Winters would have a special surprise waiting for him.

CHAPTER 56

The cargo airplane's rear ramp lowered, and night air blasted us. The lights of Manhattan were far below, and two more cargo planes flew behind us. Somewhere beyond were the Hunters escorting us. The Bombardier corporate jet and the other cargo airplane had flown ahead and were already on the ground. Jen would be among them, but doing what I didn't know.

"Five minutes," came the pilot's voice over my headset. The door light flicked on to red, meaning it was not time to jump. We were not the only thing HALOing in; two rotary-wing drones were packaged up and ready to free-fall. The loadmaster came aft to triple-check their cargo chutes as we inspected our own. With a voice command, my HUD came alive.

"OK, team, this it," came Lava's voice over the command net. Tye turned to me. "You a go?"

I nodded, and he slapped the side of my arm in support.

"Check equipment!" shouted Lava, and we all sounded off. I was slinging the newest precision-guided firearm with tag-and-shoot technology. It looked like a regular 7.62 mm assault rifle with a built-in sound suppressor, except it had a larger scope with a convex bug-eye. No need to zero it, either; its onboard computer did everything. The weapon also produced enough chamber pressure to shoot through any kind of body armor. Strapped to my thigh was a tactical bullpup shotgun less than two feet long that held nine shells. Good for tight firefights.

"Ground team on the move," said Lava, and we cheered. Lava was the mission commander and monitored all Apollo command nets, while I heard just my team's. Like horse blinders, sometimes it's better to focus on what's in front of you rather than the whole world.

"One minute," said the pilot. The loadmaster made a final adjustment to the drones' rigs and then scooched forward, away from the tail ramp.

"I want a nice, clean exit," said Lava, standing on the edge of the ramp with the ground thirty-five thousand feet below. Lava always led by example.

"Ten seconds," said the pilot.

"Clear the deck," commanded Lava, and we all got behind the drones, ready to push.

"Five, four, three, two, one." The light switched to green, and the two drones were sucked out the fuselage by a drogue chute, making an audible *zing*. We followed, diving en masse off the ramp headfirst. The other two planes zoomed overhead, and I felt their prop blast.

Looking around, I saw thirty-five jumpers and six drones hurtling to Earth. Each drone was packaged up in a ball of aluminum and firepower. In the southwest, the lights of Manhattan contrasted to the inkiness of the sound to the north and Connecticut in the distance. At this altitude, our planes were out of range of all but the best surface-to-air missiles and in any case would be profiled like commercial flights. In the distance, my HUD tracked the two Hunters circling us protectively, but they were invisible to most radar and the naked eye in the moonless night. We were also mostly invisible. Skydivers are difficult to spot on radar, making HALO a good ingress for covert missions.

"Chase the drones!" commanded Lava, and we all dove ahead. My HUD lit up one of the drones in green, five hundred feet below; the machine's small drogue parachute slowed and stabilized it as it fell. Its twin side rotors and tail boom were folded in, making it more streamlined. I assumed the flat-track position in my wingsuit and sped toward it.

"Locke, give me a hand," said Tye, who had already met the drone and was now kneeling on top of it and working a loose cargo strap. But I was coming in too fast. "Watch your speed! Watch your speed!" he said as I nearly collided into him.

"Quit screwing around, Locke," he jibed as I circled around for another pass. His armed reach out and snagged me, pulling me in, while his other was anchored to the drone.

"Thanks, man," I said. Because he was my designated battle buddy, we could communicate directly without anyone hearing us.

"Don't mention it."

"Positions," commanded Tye as four more jumpers arrived. We gathered on one side of the drone. "Control it! Control it! It's rotating clockwise!" said Tye, floating above us. With precision, he dropped and rammed against the direction of spin. We all fought it, gaining control.

"Now fly it!" shouted Tye. The drone had no wingsuit, like us. To get it over the drop zone required "flying" it, but that was an understatement. Lining up on the same side, we spread our legs in the delta position, pushing the drone toward the estate twenty-four thousand feet below.

"That's it! Keep it up," said Tye.

The Bombardier and the other cargo plane touched down at a community airport about twenty miles from the objective. The ground commander, call sign Jinx, went over the mission inflight. Lin couldn't believe what she was hearing. It was suicide. Even crazier than the time her FBI SWAT team was ambushed by two dozen mafia foot soldiers in a Brooklyn warehouse. She took a bullet that day, saved by her body armor. But it felt like a truck hit her.

No one else on the plane seemed too concerned about the plan's insanity quotient, so she kept her mouth shut. The last seventy-two hours had been a string of life-stunning events, so why question things now?

The Apollo tactical armor felt strange, almost flimsy. As soon as she deplaned, she did a series of high kicks on the tarmac that landed in a split. Incredibly, the armor moved with her like a leotard. While still in a split, she held up her armored hands and waved them around in the dark, her HUD revealing colors, allies, objective, her vitals, everything. *Unbelievable,* she thought.

"Hey Princess, gonna stop playing with yourself and get back in the war?" It was her assigned battle buddy. She went by the name Valkyrie and was one of the few women to serve in Delta before jumping the fence for Apollo. Lin did not care for her, and the feeling was obviously mutual.

"On me, Princess," said Valkyrie as they double-timed to the cargo plane, where the rest of the team was wheeling out motorbikes. Only the field surgeon remained in the Bombardier. Lin followed Valkyrie into the cargo plane and helped unstrap a large dirt bike. Before Valkyrie could walk it out, Lin blocked her.

"Listen, Valkyrie, if you want this night to go well, stop calling me Princess. Do you understand?" said Lin in her command voice.

"Anything you say, Tinkerbell. Now help or get out of the way."

Lin let her pass. Now was not the time to pick a fight. Valkyrie started the bike in perfect silence; it was electric.

"Come on, get on," said Valkyrie. Lin swung her leg over the back and mounted. "Strap in, Dimples." Lin's fists balled up, and she fantasized about twisting this jackass's neck.

Be cool, Jen. Be cool, she thought, calming herself down. She looked around for a strap or seat belt but saw none. Valkyrie twisted around and reached down, extracting two thin nylon straps from each side of the seat.

"Clip these to your belt," said Valkyrie. Lin snapped them to the body armor's D-ring belt buckle. Conveniently, they had quick-release levers in case she needed to ditch.

What the crap am I getting into? she thought.

"Keep that Saiga up. Don't shoot until I tell you. And do not blow our surprise," cautioned Valkyrie in a tone suggesting she disdained babysitting newbies.

"Got it," said Lin.

The crew wheeled out an armed rotary-wing drone from the cargo plane, and unfolded its dual, traverse rotors. It looked like a miniature V-22 Osprey with a rotorless tail boom. Its chin was a mini-gun turret, and missile pods were its flanks. A minute later it was hovering, controlled by remote pilots.

"Our guardian angel," said Valkyrie over the headset.

The municipal airport was closed after dark, but it did not stop a beat-up, compact car from speeding toward them, an amber strobe pulsing on top.

"Ye gads, local airport security. Pathetic," spat Valkyrie. The two aircraft powered up and started taxiing toward the runway.

"Let's ride!" yelled Jinx, a woman. Apollo's ranks had a lot of female warriors, Lin realized. She liked it.

The drone vanished into the darkness, scouting the route ahead. Sixteen riders mounted twelve bikes. None of the vehicles had lights because the HUD showed everything like daytime. Lin found it a little freaky.

"Keep the Saiga pointed forward, but do not shoot my arm, baby doll," said Valkyrie. She accelerated so hard that Lin almost dropped her weapon. The only thing that held her in place were the safety straps.

Crap! thought Lin as she struggled to right herself. The

shadow bike gang swooshed around the security vehicle in black silence, making it skid sideways as the driver panicked. Then they ghosted into the night.

"Sir, we've got activity. Looks like you were right," said the aide, although it was unnecessary.

Of course I was right, thought Winters. The library-cum–tactical operations center had been buzzing since they'd electronically eavesdropped on a call to the police. The local airport security guard reported seeing a corporate jet and military cargo plane land and its crew start unloading motorcycles. The police thought nothing of it, but Winters knew it was Apollo.

"High alert," commanded Winters as he stirred a cup of tea. Like Napoleon, he liked to fast before battles. It honed his strategic thinking.

"*High alert!*" yelled the battle captain, and a siren blared outside. Men ran to position. The battle captain had the body of an operator and the face of a cowboy. In a past life, he commanded at every level in U.S. Army Special Forces, up to general. Now he quarterbacked operations for Winters and was exceedingly good at it.

"Get the fixed wings in the air. Find them. Kill them," said Winters calmly. All was going as planned. *They are easy to bait because they are stupid,* he thought as he sipped his tea.

The battle captain gave a nod, and pilots in the library wearing virtual reality goggles worked joysticks. In the background, the jet drones whirred to life. A second later they were gone.

"Fixed-wing drones deployed," confirmed the battle captain. Silence, save the background radio chatter. The long, oak library table was crowded with specialists wearing headphones and working laptops. Monitors displayed what the drones saw, which was nothing out of the ordinary as they skimmed the roads and trees, scanning for prey.

Winters checked the time and estimated they had four minutes before the Apollo motorcycles would cross the estate fence.
Plenty of time to kill them, he knew.

"How many tangos?" he asked. "Do we have an estimate?"

"Ground surveillance radar?" said the battle captain.

"Scopes are clean," replied a technician.

Something nagged at Winters. With a corporate jet and cargo
plane, he calculated a motorcycle ground attack could range
from ten to sixteen riders, and probably a drone. A threat, if they
had the element of surprise, but they didn't. But could this small
force really be Apollo's main effort? It didn't completely scan, yet
all the other sensors showed zero activity.

"Chatter on local 5G spectrum in ops box," said a tech.
"Could be something."

"What are they saying?" asked the battle captain, who walked
up behind him and looked over his shoulder.

"Uh . . . hard to discern. One guy is telling another he thinks
he just witnessed wild horses running in the night. Other guy
thinks he's high again."

"That's them," said Winters.

"But sir, it could be anything," said the battle captain with
caution. He did not want to tie up precious assets chasing down
every hunch. They had one minute to find the threat.

"That's them," repeated Winters. "Deploy the drone QRF."

The battle captain nodded, and the rest of the drones took off.

"Annihilate them," said Winters, sipping tea. Main effort or
not, he saw no reason why they needed to live.

"Incoming!" yelled Jinx over the radio net, and Lin's heart
jumped. Four red dots blinked on her HUD, indicating the
enemy drones. A missile arced across the sky and blew up their
drone, sending it crashing into the trees where it exploded.

"Follow me," said Jinx, and the lead bike peeled off the back road and into the wood line.

Did she just drive into the trees? thought Lin in horror. Then all the bikes raced into the woods, going for cover. Trees and speed afforded some protection against missiles.

"Hang on!" yelled Valkyrie, as they bounced through the woods at 40 mph. It was a mature forest with minimal underbrush, making it dangerous but navigable. Missiles exploded tree trunks around them, blowing shards of wood everywhere. Lin was too stunned to be scared, as Valkyrie dodged trees.

"Contact! Request backup," radioed Jinx. "Backup twenty seconds," Jinx relayed to the team.

"Jinx, you have three more fast movers inbound," warned Mission Control, and Lin's HUD showed two additional red dots in the distance, although she could see nothing.

"Ah shit," said Valkyrie.

Before Lin understood why, she felt her weight press into the seat as they raced up a sharp slope and became airborne, jumping thirty feet in the air. They were exposed.

Eeeeeeeeeeeeee! sounded an alarm in Lin's earpiece.

"Tone!" yelled Valkyrie as they flew through branches. Missiles burst trees around them as they fell back to earth. They landed hard and Valkyrie fought for control, showing great skill as they recovered.

Three drone jets screamed over them, skimming the treetops. Then they exploded; Lin felt the concussion wave as they fireballed through the night sky. A second later, one of Apollo's larger Hunter drones shrieked above.

"Yeah!!" shouted Valkyrie.

"We just lost three drones," said the battle captain in shock. "What happened? Surface-to-air missiles?"

"Negative. The thermal trails came from the air, and low altitude," said a tech, monitoring a laptop.

"An enemy drone?" said the battle captain, contemplating the implications. If true, it was new stealth technology and could tip the battle.

We're not prepared for this, thought Winters.

"We lost two more!" shouted the tech.

"Where is it? Somebody get me a bead on the enemy drone!" commanded the battle captain. "We can't kill what we can't see."

Hunter drones, thought Winters uneasily. They were next generation, and he realized they possessed no radar that would see them. Apollo had only two prototypes, but he had assumed them defunct due to technological challenges. Apparently not. He wondered if one or both were flying.

Both, he reasoned. *But no matter.* He had numbers on his side.

"Approaching phase line Zulu at speed," said Jinx, referring to the estate's border fence. "Requesting zero one, cleared hot."

"Roger. Stand by, Jinx," said Control.

Lin heard a jet engine rev up somewhere behind her, then felt the noise as a Hunter screeched overhead at high decibels. Moments later the ground shook and the sky was on fire. A hundred-foot-high wall of fire and white phosphorus shot up into the night, cutting a highway of flame through the perimeter's double steel fence and antitank ditch.

"I love the smell of napalm in the evening!" shouted Valkyrie.

Holy crap! thought Lin. They were the only two words her mind could conjure as the motorcycles drove into flame highway.

"Good hit, Control," said Jinx.

"Hang on, Princess," said Valkyrie. "YEEEEEEEE-HAAAAAW!!!" she screamed as they hit the ditch hard and flew up the backside, making a twenty-foot jump over the remains of the security fence.

"We're in," confirmed Jinx to Mission Control.

"They're in, all of them," radioed Lava, and the HALO team whooped.

"Looks like I lost a case of scotch, Locke!" teased Tye over our closed battle buddy net. "I bet Jinx your honeypot wouldn't make it to the fence."

"Tye, don't be jealous. I still have feelings for you too," I jabbed back. Six packaged drones were being pushed by six warriors each, in free fall. Below us I could see the dark outline of woods and the paler loam of meadow, despite the moonless night. Far below was the mansion, and somewhere was Jen.

Focus, Tom, I told myself. Thinking about Jen now would get me killed.

"Prep drones," ordered Lava. We had less than two minutes to unfold our drone and make it operational, otherwise it would crater into the earth. Unfolded, the drone looked more like a miniature Osprey tilt-rotor aircraft than a standard helicopter. It had two arms, each with a rotor that could swivel for steering, and a tail boom with stabilizer fins. For armaments, it had two side pods that held four missiles each, capable of destroying air or ground targets, and a chin turret with a six-barrel 5.56 mm mini-gun. The pilot was in a mobile command truck driving someplace in Virginia. The drone would be our close air support on the ground, but unfolding it in freefall required aerial ballet.

"Let's do it!" said Tye, our fire team leader. Tye pulled a quick-release strap, and the cargo netting and aluminum pallet flew away. Next, in a choreography of precision, we simultaneously unfolded the drone's left and right rotor booms, then the tail boom. The machine began to wobble dangerously.

"Careful, careful!" said Tye as we frantically sought to steady it. Once stabilized, we worked like a floating pit crew, fastening bolts on the rotor booms and locking them in place. Tye rechecked the drone's parachute straddled across its back, in between the rotors. A ringlike blade guard surrounded the propellers, preventing them from accidentally slicing the parachute chords.

"Five thousand feet," said Lava. Tye crawled around the drone upside down, inspecting our work. When done, he said: "Drone Six, ready,"

"Copy. Systems check," said the pilot over the network.

"Three thousand feet," said Lava.

"All systems green. Ready for chute deployment," reported the pilot. "Thanks, guys."

"Happy hunting," said Tye. "And cover our asses."

"Wilco," said the pilot, ground-pounder-speak for *Understand and will comply.* At 750 feet above ground level, the pilot would deploy the parachute and start the rotors. At one hundred feet, the drone would drop free of the parachute and fly on its own, and kill something.

"Fifteen hundred feet. Positions!" said Lava. We banked away from the drone and toward the lit-up mansion among dark woods, a superlative drop zone. Below, I could see paramilitaries on the grounds. There were significantly more than Lava briefed. It felt like a trap.

"Tye, there's a lot of tangos down there," I said, speaking just to him.

A second later, he replied: "Roger, things are going to get sporty."

"One thousand feet," said Lava. "Check your DZ."

My HUD lit up a blue patch of gabled roof on one of the east wings. We each had a patch. I steered with my body, adjusting my heading.

Lava switched to a countdown. "Five."

The roof came alive like a Christmas tree, as my HUD identified all the enemies in red.

"Four."

"Marking targets," said Control. Apollo's computer system conducted collective targeting that racked and stacked threats, assigning each of us multiple targets. Three red dots blinked on the roof: my prey.

"Three."

I was speeding at 140 mph, and the ground was coming up uncomfortably fast. Timing would be everything.

"Two."

I breathed deeply, readying my body for what followed.

"One."

My parachute deployed automatically, and my body jerked upright. The HUD displayed a negative-three-second countdown clock. When it got to zero, we would all shoot simultaneously in perfect ambush.

So it begins, I told myself as I unzipped my arm wings and pulled out my weapon. The precision-guided rifle locked onto my three targets; all I needed do was aim, pull the trigger, and the computer would fire at the optimal time. Other black parachutes descended on my sides. We surrounded the entire mansion.

Three, two, one, I counted as I aimed and squeezed. The weapon fired three shots, its built-in sound suppressor muffling the noise. It sounded like three taps on a door. One of the targets fell over the side. The three blinking red dots turned gray: targets down. The whole roof went gray, as I reached up for the toggles and steered for a landing.

"All targets down," confirmed Mission Control. "Congratulations."

My boots skidded across the steeply angled gable roof, then I was jerked backward, hard.

What the—? I thought, looking up. My parachute was snagged on an ornamental roof spike. Decorative iron spikes lined the roof's spine, and I was caught. I yanked my riser's quick-releases, and I slid down the slate roof, crashing into a dead mercenary with a .50-cal sniper rifle. My bullet had penetrated his steel-plated body armor, center of mass.

Six stories below me, men in black combat gear patrolled the estate's grounds. There seemed to be hundreds, but we were undetected. Surprise and stealth were still ours.

"Phase one complete," said Lava. "Move to phase two."

"They're in, sir," reported one of the intel techs. The battle captain watched the monitors in alarm as the dozen motorcycles penetrated the perimeter fence and sped through the woods toward the mansion. They were effectively skirting all his defenses, avoiding roads and security checkpoints. His plan to channel a ground assault into an ambush zone was now defunct, since it assumed the enemy would use roads and not motorcycle through woods.

"This can't be happening," muttered the battle captain.

Winters was also concerned, although he dared not reveal it. Twelve loose Apollo operatives on the grounds was bad. Twelve plus two Hunters was a disaster. But Winters knew how to even the odds.

"Deploy everything," said Winters.

"Deploy everything," instructed the battle captain over the command net.

"Ground teams," said Winters. "Annihilate them."

The Wagner Group commander smiled and gave orders in Russian. He looked like a bodybuilder in fatigues who only shaved twice a month. People called him Colonel Yuri, but that was not his real name. At his disposal were 120 high-end mercenaries drawn from around the world, and all were lethal. Outside, men scurried into vehicles, shouting in different languages. Twelve armored SUVs sped to confront the intruders, with a ten-to-one advantage in terms of combatants.

"Battle Captain, make sure the ground team also has air support," instructed Winters, and the other man nodded. Winters wanted the battle over fast. *If it's a fair fight, you're not trying hard enough,* he thought.

"Two more drones downed by the enemy," said one of the techs.

"We still can't see their UAV," said another.

"Somebody ID that enemy drone!" shouted the battle captain. The Hunters were picking apart their air force, gaining air supremacy. The threat was mounting.

"We can't. It's invisible to our sensors," said an aggravated tech.

The battle captain turned to one of the Russians. "I want your snipers on the roof to stop looking at the ground and start looking at the sky. Do you understand me? We need eyeballs in the sky looking for the enemy drone!"

The Russian nodded and worked his radios, then gave a puzzled look as if something were wrong. He tried again, and his expression transformed to terror.

"Sir, sir," he said in a thick Russian accent, trying to flag the battle captain's attention, but he was interrupted.

"I'm tracking the lead motorcycle!" shouted one of the drone pilots.

"On screen," commanded the battle captain, and one of the large monitors showed the infrared profile of a dirt biker speeding through the trees. "Take him out."

"Firing," said the pilot and automatic gunfire sounded outside, in the distance.

"Missed," said the battle captain, disappointed. The speed of the bike and tree branches prevented a clean shot.

"Flush them toward this area," said Yuri, pointing to a spot on the map.

"What's there?" asked the battle captain, examining the spot on the topographical map.

"Our ambush zone. We're already in position. *All* of us," he said. "Just have your drones flush them toward us. The terrain features will channel them into the ambush zone. Then we will destroy them."

The battle captain nodded, and ordered the drones to drive the enemy toward Yuri's grid coordinate.

Winter was impressed. "Excellent plan, Colonel Yuri," he said. "But what happens when they don't go through your ambush zone?"

The Russians shrugged. "Then we will run them down and kill them. As Stalin said, there is a quality about quantity."

Winters smiled approval and decided he liked Yuri.

"Sir, sir!" It was the Russian radio operator. Yuri and the battle captain turned to face him, and then a loud thud outside, as if someone dropped a bag of cement mix. Then another.

"What's that?" asked the battle captain.

"Check it out," ordered Winters, and two fighters ran out of the room.

"That's what I've been trying to tell you," said the Russian. "Parachutes! A lot of them!"

A second later, one of the fighters radioed in. "Two bodies," he said in an Armenian accent. "Both snipers, probably from the roof."

"The roof!" said the battle captain. The Russian tech looked worried. "Shooters to the roof, now!"

"*Pull back everything!*" shouted Winters. "*The motorcycles are a ruse!*"

· · ·

Sirens blasted around the mansion followed by shouting in Russian over outside speakers. Last time I heard something like it, I was in Ukraine being ambushed by Russian Spetsnaz special forces, and it did not end well. My HUD showed the sky dotted with red enemy drones speeding toward us. Men below started shooting at the roof.

"We're compromised, proceed to Phase Three. Seize the objectives!" said Lava as a stream of bullets erupted the slate roof around me. I dove behind the faux battlements as an enemy drone stalked me. A dead Wagner mercenary lay twenty-five feet in front of me with an SA-18 surface-to-air missile by his side.

Go for it! I told myself, sprinting for the weapon. The roof blew up around me again in a stream of mini-gun fire, and my back felt like I was being pounded by a jackhammer. I was knocked off my feet as bullets hit my body armor. Coughing, I willed myself to roll over despite the pain.

The enemy rotary-wing drone swerved to a hover, its mini-gun trained on me. I raised my rifle at it and heard the buzz of the mini-gun, then watched it explode. Its flaming body crashed into a battlement and tipped over the side. Behind it was Drone 6, its mini-gun whirring to a stop. I mustered a thumbs-up, and it flew away, in search of new prey.

God, I hate getting shot, I thought as I sat up. The Apollo tactical suit stopped the three bullets, but it still hurt like hell.

"Locke, where are you?" It was Tye. "Stop your lollygagging and get down here, we need an assist!" My HUD registered three green dots in the floor beneath me; the dots were blinking, indicating request for backup.

"Copy," I wheezed and got to my feet. Bullets zinged through the air as a full-on drone dogfight was occurring before me. A black streak screeched overhead, and an enemy drone was blown to pieces. My HUD tracked the Hunter do a six-G turn and return to smoke another enemy UAV. Two kills in four seconds.

"Glad that thing is on our side," I muttered as it screeched by.

"Locke, say again?" said Tye. "Get down here!"

"Good copy," I said, and hopped across dormers. Below I saw multiple black armored SUVs crash out of the woods and plow through the baroque gardens, then fishtail to a stop at the base of the mansion directly beneath me. About forty heavily armed men in combat armor got out and ran into the mansion.

"Uh, Valhalla," I said, using Lava's call sign. "Spot report: thirty tangos just entered the building, south side, first floor."

"Good copy," replied Mission Control. Valhalla must have been busy.

"Locke, where are you?" asked Tye, angry.

I turned to run and saw Jinx fly out of the wood line, followed by more Apollo bikes. But not all of them. Chasing them was a fleet of enemy SUVs, armed dune buggies, and dirt bikes. It was a running firefight, and two of the Apollo fighters were hit; one of the passengers was slumped over, shot.

"*Jen!*" I screamed. They were driving into a death trap. Gauging the ground six stories below, I took out my 550 parachute cord. *I can repel down, if I double up the strand,* I thought. Not ideal, but I would land without breaking my legs.

"Get in here, Locke! We're pinned down and about to get wasted!" shouted Tye. I had never heard him panic, ever. It was an evil choice: Tye versus Jen.

"Control, we're getting chewed up. We need backup!" yelled Jinx as she sped through the woods. Their plan worked, sort of. They drew the enemy out of the mansion long enough for the main effort to HALO safely to the roof. But it failed because there were ten times more enemy than expected. Winters had laid a trap to lure them in and kill them.

"Control?" she repeated.

"Deploying a Hunter your way," said Control. Automatic gunfire ripped through them and she saw one of her teammates fall.

NO! thought Jinx. *They will pay,* she promised, as she twisted around and returned fire. She was down to nine riders. Then she noticed her own bike losing power. She looked down; it had somehow taken a hit and was grinding metal.

"Control, my bike has taken damage and slowing. If I fall, Valkyrie is my second. Confirm," she said.

"Confirmed," said Valkyrie.

"Confirmed," said Control. "You are four hundred meters from the objective. Make it!"

The Hunter shrieked overhead, then four seconds later passed above again. Two enemy drones dropped out of the sky on fire. Jinx dodged one as it smashed into the ground and rolled toward her.

"Jinx, heads up!" warned Control.

But it was too late. Jinx's bike shot into the air as the sloping downhill turned into a twenty-foot drop, sending her across the great lawn of the estate. The whole team was airborne as they followed her blindly over the edge, and she heard Valkyrie's trademark *yee-haw!* The team landed rough, but not as hard as the enemy. The bikes made it, like Jinx, but the armed speed buggies and SUV flipped end over end. One exploded. It was hard to imagine anyone survived.

"Jinx, get to mansion ASAP and assist Valhalla," ordered control. "Urgent!"

Bullets sprayed everywhere as they were caught in the open, and one hit her in the back, pitching her forward. She fought through the pain to keep control. An enemy bike was on her tail, and no matter what she did, it was getting closer.

I need to kill my tail fast, or it will kill me, she realized.

Jinx hammered the back brake, locking the wheel up. The enemy bike zoomed past. As her bike started to slide, Jinx laid it down on its left side, pulling up her left leg up so it didn't get crushed. She let go. The bike continued to skid as she lifted up her precision-guided rifle, locked onto the enemy rider, and squeezed the trigger. He went down.

Jinx slid to a stop, her body armor making the ride feel like snow. Other vehicles swerved around her, shooting at each other, but Jinx ignored them. She pushed the rider's immobile body over with her foot, put the muzzle at his neck where the body armor was weakest. The man jerked up a concealed 9 mm pistol, and she fired. He died.

"Jinx, how copy, over?" said Control.

Jinx looked up and saw five SUVs barreling down on her. They had no shooters sticking out of the windows because bulletproof glass does not lower, so the drivers intended to run her down.

Move! she thought and sprinted for the fallen rider's bike, mounted it, and accelerated forward, kicking up dirt.

"Jinx?" asked Control.

"Negative, Control," she said. "We need an assist. Outnumbered."

The SUVs fanned out across the gigantic lawn, running over antipersonnel mines while trying to catch and crush her between two vehicles. Jinx scanned the terrain. There was nowhere to run.

"Roger," said Control after a pause. "We have no reinforcements."

Ahead, Jinx saw the last of her bikes disappear into an eight-foot-high hedgerow. *Where did they go?* she wondered, and opened the throttle. The SUVs followed.

"Copy, Control," she said, speeding for the hedge row, and saw the entrance. Then she understood; it was a garden maze, the kind made of hedges that occupied an entire acre. She entered the maze and skid-turned around the corners. The lead SUV followed and crashed into the ancient hedges, stuck. Jinx smiled.

"Valkyrie, status over?" said Jinx, muscling the bike around ninety-degree turns. She heard shooting a few hedges over.

"We're eight, I think. Lost in this goddamned maze with the enemy!"

"Me too."

The library was a hive of intensity as techs worked their stations. Outside was a hurricane of explosions and automatic gunfire, with the occasional shriek of a Hunter drone. The mansion's interior had become a battle zone, and more of Winters's reinforcements streamed in by the minute.

"Everyone, to the mansion!" ordered Winters, smiling. It was a war of attrition now, guaranteeing his victory. The battle captain nodded in affirmation while speaking into two different headsets. Yuri was last seen slinging his AKM rifle and GP-25 grenade launcher over his shoulder and leaving the room with two other Wagner mercenaries. The battle got louder, and closer.

Yuri's got a point, thought Winters, admiring the Russian's leadership. *Time to get in the fight.* Pulling out an ampule, he stuck it up his nose and snorted the Mr. Hyde Dust. Instantly his body tensed up, and his cane dropped to the ground. His heart pounded in pain, like it might burst, but he ignored it. He exhaled loudly but no one noticed in the fervor of battle.

"Yeeessss!" he roared, standing up. The ache in his leg faded as he limped over to a large weapons case in the corner. He flipped open the lid and removed a precision-guided grenade launcher. It looked like a revolver for 40 mm grenades, and it could sniper-fire six of them in five seconds. Winters held it, admiring its weight as he aimed through the reflex sight. Next to it sat a field bag of medium-velocity, high-explosive rounds. He slung the whole bag over his shoulder.

"Tom Locke," he said, lumbering out of the room.

"Tye, where are you?" I panted, bounding down the stone stairs two at a time. Jen would be OK, I reasoned, because she was . . . Jen. Also, Valkyrie was her battle buddy, who I only knew by reputation: she was bulletproof.

"Here! Over here," said Tye, and a green dot blinked on my HUD. The stairs dumped into a vaulted hall that overlooked an elegant four-story atrium with multiple rooms off balconied hallways. Four large chandeliers hung from the coffered ceiling, with bullets zooming through them. Wagner and Apollo were in a three-dimensional firefight, shooting across the atrium from different levels.

"Incoming!" shouted Tye.

I reflexively hit the floor. An RPG rocketed over my head, blowing out a wall at the far end of the hall.

"Are you OK?"

"Roger," I said, spotting Tye pinned down in a vestibule closet. Enemy were swarming the opposite side, and several IR laser dots danced around the vestibule entrance, ready to kill whatever stepped out. But that wasn't the biggest problem.

"Take out the RPG!" said Tye.

I high-crawled to the marble railing and used my weapon's scope to scan for the RPG. I saw two Wagner mercenaries running across the ground floor and get whacked by an Apollo sniper in the rafters. I scanned right and spotted a Wagner fire team assault into a room, blowing it up.

No one could survive that, I thought sadly. Then I located Lava one floor below. He was firing his pistol into a room, until it ran dry. He threw it at the target, and ran inside, knife drawn.

It's Stalingrad down there, I realized, *except there's a lot more of them than us.* I continued to scan. On the third floor, I spotted two Wagner commandos running from room to room; one carried an RPG.

That's my target, I thought, as I picked up and sprinted toward a staircase, using speed as my cover. Bullets ricocheted around me as I skidded across the marble floor and down the stairwell, my weapon facing forward.

Turning the corner, I ran down the third-floor balcony hallway, bullets everywhere, and slid to a stop by the door where I last saw the RPG. Holding my rifle parallel to my chest, I stuck it into the room and saw one of the Wagner troops in my HUD. I locked on and fired; he fell. The other spun and shot at me. I tossed in a grenade, and took cover. Where there was once a room was now a pile of bricks covering antique furniture and two Wagner bodies.

"Thanks, Locke," said Tye.

"Hold fast. I'm coming to you."

"Negative. I can take care of myself. Find Lava, he needs backup," said Tye. I could hear him shoot and move as we talked.

"Copy," I said, sneaking around the atrium perimeter with my weapon at the ready. I slipped into the room I saw Lava enter, but it was empty. There were signs of an intense firefight: bullet holes, spent cartridges, bodies. I followed the blood trail through a Versailles-like bedroom and down an interior hallway.

"Lava?" I asked. "Find Lava," I commanded my HUD, and it enlarged a green dot next to two red ones. He was in close combat. I ran down the hall, rounded a corner of another palatial

HIGH TREASON   · 351

bedroom, and then felt myself picked up and thrown through a
standing mirror.

What . . . ?! My mind raced as my body got to its feet and
raised my rifle. Powerful hands yanked it away and threw it
across the room, then slammed me into the floor so hard my
helmet busted through the plaster. Looking up, I saw a colossus
of a Russian with a week-old beard and gray peppered hair.

"My mercenaries have killed many of you," he said in a thick
Russian accent. "You will die, like your friends."

"Not today," I said, pulling my knife. But the Russian colossus anticipated it, grabbed my forearm and tossed me across the
room and into an armoire.

Ow, I thought, writhing on my back. Heavy footsteps approached, and the man appeared above me, brandishing a fire
poker like an iron stake.

"Wagner better than Apollo. Let me show you," he said, raising it to impale me. Another hulking figure tackled him, and
both crashed through a Chippendale letter desk. I got to my feet
and recovered my weapon as Lava picked the Russian up and
rammed him through the bathroom door.

"Lava, stand back!" I cried, aiming my rifle at the Russian
behind him.

"No, Yuri's mine!" he commanded. "Blood debt. Now go!"
He waved at an open door that blended into the wall. It was the
secret passage he'd entered through. "Find Winters. Kill him!"

The Russian howled and tackled Lava from behind, but Lava
tossed Yuri with a judo throw. Last I saw, both colossuses were
punching it out as I disappeared down the secret passage to find
Winters.

Lin fired her Saiga from the back of the dirt bike like a rear turret gunner, as Valkyrie bounced around corners. They had been

352 ·

SEAN McFATE

playing deadly hide-and-seek for five eternal minutes, and ammo was getting low.

"He's still on us," cried Valkyrie as they sped toward a dead end.

"I know," replied Lin, slamming the last magazine in the Saiga.

The enemy dirt bike made the corner as Valkyrie slammed the brakes. Like so much of the garden maze, the dead end revealed a 180-degree turn, and she skidded around it, planting her right foot like a pivot. Dirt and stone kicked up as she accelerated down the opposite side the hedge wall.

Lin was ready with her Saiga, and she aimed it at the hedges. As soon as the enemy passed the other side, she squeezed, and automatic shotgun fire blew a lateral gash through the hedge wall. Then came the thud of a body hitting dirt.

"Nice job, Princess," said Valkyrie. It was their fourth kill in five minutes. To Lin's amazement, they made a good team.

"Thanks," said Lin.

"Now to get out of this infernal maze," she said, zooming up and down the corridors. The hedges were impossible to walk through, their little branches deceptively strong.

"Valkyrie, this is Jinx. How copy?"

"Charlie miking," she said. All was OK.

"Get to the mansion. They need help badly."

"Good copy," said Valkyrie. By now the mansion was burning, casting a red glow in the sky. No fire trucks could save it because Winters had sealed the estate.

"Head toward the glow," said Lin.

Valkyrie nodded. "Seems your boyfriend needs saving."

"Don't they all?" joked Lin, and they both chuckled.

Minutes later they were out. The fight had left the great lawn and moved to the mansion's interior. Only the occasional burning hulks of ex-drones littered the otherwise pristine grounds. The building fire was impressive in a terrifying way. The century-old structure made of wood and stone was engulfed in flame.

Valkyrie drove through the garden and up the stairs, to the wedding-sized patio overlooking the sound, and skidded to a stop. Lin leapt off.

"Hey, wait!" shouted Valkyrie. "Where are you going?! The building is falling down."

"No time. Boyfriend needs saving."

"Locke! Locke! *Locke!*" It was Winters, his voice wafting through the secret passage, as if he knew where to find me. "Locke, I know you are nearby. I see you on my monitor."

I froze, realizing he must have locked onto the nanotech streaming through my veins just as Tye did when he found me at the hotel. *I hate technology,* I thought.

"What's the matter Locke, scared? Show yourself!" taunted Winters.

I continued to move. Winters wasn't the only one craving this moment; I had come out of hiding and risked everything for it. I followed the voice's echo through the secret passages, despite the ongoing noise of battle.

Dead end.

"Locke, I know you are close by," shouted Winters from the other side of the wall. Examining the passage, I noticed a faint breeze emanating from the corners. On the floor were century-old scuff marks.

Another secret door, I realized. Searching around, I discovered a handle and pulled at the door. It opened onto a covered wooden balcony at the rear of a magnificent banqueting hall, the kind you might see at Oxford, except it was lined with suits of medieval armor, part of the estate's gilded charm.

"Locke, where are you?" shouted Winters from below, louder. I crept forward onto the balcony, probably where the musicians played for the lord's dining delight. Using the rifle's scope, I peered over the balcony's edge. The three-story walls were blanketed in colorful murals of kings, knights, princesses, cities, battles, and Jerusalem. Every mural contained eight-pointed stars, some overt and others hidden. Even the coffered ceiling was covered in eight-pointed star ornamentations.

At the far end of the hall was a hearth the size of a horse with a roaring bonfire casting shadows around the great hall. Above it was a painting of an enthroned king in full eight-star regalia, holding court over all who dined in the hall. To his left and right were murals of full-sized jousters, also in star regalia, tilting their lances toward each other.

"Locke, don't be a coward!" goaded Winters.

Then I spotted him pacing atop the massive banquet table, almost inviting a headshot. He wore advanced tactical goggles and carried a weapon that looked like a cross between a grenade launcher and a .45 revolver.

Finally, I can end this nightmare, I thought as I lay on my back and held my weapon up to get a target lock on his torso. *Steady,* I told myself, as the site picture jiggled as I zoomed. It was like shooting around a corner, and I could not get a clean target lock.

"Locke?" asked Winters, stopping but not facing me. "Locke, is that you?" He placed the weapon on his shoulder, rocked it back toward me, and fired.

Incoming! My mind panicked as I rolled sideways, and the balcony was blown to smithereens. The concussion threw me down the servants' narrow stairwell to the first floor. Looking up dazed, I saw an eight-pointed star painted on the ceiling. I was in the banquet hall's antechamber on the floor below, but hidden from Winters.

"I know you're still here," cried Winters.

I heard a *thunk* and rolled for cover. The banquet hall's main doors exploded into wooden shards, and the blast wave concussed me. The body armor offered protection, but I would not survive a direct hit.

"Locke, come out and fight. You were a fool, but never a coward."

Pointing my weapon around the corner, I saw Winters scanning for me. He wore no visible body armor, just a Jermyn Street bespoke suit, Hermes tie, and grenade launcher. Classic Winters.

Thunk. I spun away from the wall but too late. The grenade impacted the other side of the stone wall, throwing it and me to the other side of the antechamber. I bounced off the back wall, breathing through the pain. Through the new hole, I saw Winters and he saw me.

"Locke!" he said, aiming the grenade launcher at me. But I was quicker. I snapped off a round and he fell backward, off his feet and onto the floor. *Thunk.* His weapon fired up as he fell, and the ceiling exploded. Chunks of concrete, brick, and timber crashed into the hall.

Warily, I got up, ignoring the pain, and approached the pile of rubble where Winters once stood, weapon pointed forward. *Dead, finally!* I thought with a smile.

Thunk. I dropped and felt the *zing* of a round pass above my head and explode the wall behind me. Then coughing from under the rubble.

Winters is still alive! Impossible, I thought, not understanding. He must have had some new reactive chest armor under his shirt. The coughing came from under the oak banquet table, shielding him from the ceiling's demise.

"Come on Locke, show yourself. Tell me the gods have been merciful and granted me revenge," he said in a rational tone.

"Revenge is mine, old man," I said.

"Lo-o-o-o-o-ocke," hissed Winters. I heard bricks move, and

suddenly Winters was standing ten feet before me, aiming his grenade launcher at me. I leapt sideways as I heard the *thunk*. Another portion of the wall blew out, and the roof timbers began to creek as the structure weakened. Flames licked the hall's wooden paneling.

"You're out of ammo, old man," I said, noting the grenade launcher's six-shell cylinder.

"No matter, Locke," he said, tossing it away and holding up his fists. "Why should a guy like you be afraid of an old man like me?"

My weapon was trained on his chest. *Do it,* I told myself. *Do it!* But I couldn't. Winters did not deserve a clean death, not after killing 230 Americans, assassinating the vice president, and threatening to nuke three U.S. cities. It was why I came back.

"You stand guilty of high treason," I said, taking off my helmet. "A bullet in the head would be too good for you." I dropped my rifle. "I have returned to render justice." I tossed my mini-shotgun. "My way."

Winters smiled as I took up a fighting stance. We circled. The banquet hall was on fire and coming down around us, giving a hellish appearance, but neither of us noticed.

He jabbed with shocking speed, and sucker-punched my throat, followed by a cross elbow to the jaw, knocking me sideways and off my feet. *Where did that come from?* I thought, surprised and seeing stars. Winters grunted as he kicked me hard in the stomach. I felt it through the body armor, paralyzing my diaphragm so I could not breathe. Turning red, I rolled over and sipped air.

Winters snorted as he bent down and picked up my shotgun. "You were my biggest disappointment, Locke," he said, aiming the shotgun at my face. "So much wasted potential."

I raised my forearms to my face, arms clasped tightly together, as I heard the shot. The pellets deflected off my body armor, pushing my forearms into my head. Winters unloaded the shotgun, pumping its action in rapid succession. Each shot was a body blow, but none of the pellets penetrated the armor.

"Damn you, Locke!" he screamed, throwing the shotgun at me as I stood up.

"I condemn you to death for high treason," I said, walking slowly toward him. With every step I took, he limped backward one, bumping into wood-hewn chairs and a drinks cart. Finally, he stopped, sandwiched between me and the massive stone hearth, its fires blazing. He turned to face it, then me. He was cornered.

Winters's expression softened. "There is no honor in killing an old man, Tom. Take me into custody. Let the law decide. It's the honorable thing to do."

"We are past honor," I said, and roundhouse-kicked him into the fire. The man screamed and thrashed as the inferno consumed him. I grabbed a dusty bottle of brandy off the drinks cart and sprayed it on him; it caught fire midair, like unholy water. Flames shot up from his clothes and face, blinding him. Hoping to escape hell but unable to see, he bolted into the back wall of the ten-foot fireplace and smacked his skull on the stone, then fell backward onto the fire again. The shrieks were gruesome.

Only now did I feel pity for the man who tried to murder me three times. I walked to a suit of armor and jerked away a large Zweihänder sword, leaving the suit to collapse in a jarring clang as I walked back to the screaming fire, where the burning man tried to stand. Stepping halfway into the flames, I thrust the sword through Winters's chest, pinning him to the back wall. A moment later, I withdrew it and his body collapsed onto the fire. I watched it burn, ignoring the stench.

The hall started collapsing around me, on fire itself. However,

I could not break my gaze; I needed proof the flames would claim this devil. The body lay motionless, consumed by flame. Satisfied, I walked through the burning hall, as timber beams groaned above, having suffered too much destruction. Picking up my helmet and rifle, I walked out of the great hall, down a passage, and into the library. It had been converted into a tactical operations center, but its occupants had fled. The battle must be over. I paused to admire the temple to books before it perished. Flames were already licking at the bottom rows.

"Locke!" cried Jen. "Tom, what are you doing? We got to get out of here, now!"

"No, wait. Let's take a second to admire this, before it's gone. All of it," I said, sadness in my voice. It was an Armageddon of books, knowledge, culture.

"Seriously?!" Bits of flaming ceiling rained down.

"Yeah."

She gut-punched me, and I gasped. Then she picked me up and took me in a fireman's carry to the window, which her Saiga obliterated. Then she tossed me out headfirst. Next, she landed on me.

"Ow!" I said as she rolled off.

"Serves you right, you dunderhead," she said, grabbing my arm and yanking me to my feet. The entire mansion was ablaze with no firefighters because all roads to the estate were blocked. We ran into the baroque garden and flopped in a concealed flower bed. There we lay on our backs, staring at the moonless sky and its soft, flame-red glow. Automatic gunfire occasionally echoed in the distance, as did the wail of sirens. Soon the police would arrive and we would need to vanish again.

"I need a vacation," she said.

"Me too."

CHAPTER 57

The Chevalier descended the narrow spiral stairs to the castle vault. The medieval stairway was encased in rough-hewn stone and was barely a man's width, allowing a single defender to hold off a group of invaders. The air was moist and stank of mildew as he approached the bottom. Once a mighty athlete, the Chevalier was still nimble despite his age.

To think that Winters believed I served the Russians, he thought. Earlier, he had downgraded Winters from "useful idiot" to "brazen knave," a more dangerous species of moron. Now he was demoted to full dead, an improvement but not without costs to the organization.

At the bottom of the stairs, he felt around and found the light switch. Dim fluorescent lights flickered to life, and he continued through tunnels dating back to the castle's founding in the thirteenth century, if not earlier. Before it was a stone castle, it had been a wooden fortress. No one knew how old the passages were, and some speculated they dated back to the Roman era.

At last the Chevalier came to a heavy wooden door with black iron rivets and an ornate hinge that looked like ivy covering the door. He pulled out a key made of titanium, inserted it in a secret hole hidden in the metal ivy, and opened the door. Beyond was the vault. Lights automatically turned on. The air was climate controlled and fresh.

The space was cavernous and two stories tall, with no windows. The vaulted ceiling was painted night blue with eight-pointed stars crafted in silver leaf. Inscribed around the rim of the ceiling was: *Monstrant regibus astra viam* ("The stars show the way to kings"). The walls and columns were painted red with gold leaf trim. As a boy, he remembered how the secret room would shimmer under torchlight. Now it looked comatose with modern electrical lighting.

Not everything new is better, he lamented as he entered. Lining the walls were treasures that the Louvre would salivate over. But his greatest prize was the tomb of Sir Geoffroy de Charny, who fell defending the king of France at the disastrous Battle of Poitiers in 1356. De Charny was one of Europe's most admired chevaliers during his lifetime, a true and perfect knight. Now he rested here, in the family vault, after centuries of aristocratic intermarriage that took his remains across Europe.

"How are you today, old friend?" asked the Chevalier, patting the sarcophagus.

De Charny and the French king founded the Order of the Star in 1351, and the group went underground after the battle, where it had remained and thrived ever since. Once a secret society dedicated to good, it had devolved into a for-profit conglomerate controlled by a dozen intermarried families.

Mon Dieu! How we have fallen, he thought. Only he took the Order's original vows seriously, and was hence dubbed "Chevalier" by his cousins. It was not a compliment.

"I wonder what counsel you would give us now. It is a desperate hour," he said to the sarcophagus. With a sigh, he approached a mammoth wooden desk with stars carved into it, and took a seat. A bank of large-screen monitors lit up and looked wholly out of place in the ancient vault. Eleven faces stared back at him, some old and others merely middle-aged.

Oh dear, I'm late again, he thought.

"The Order of the Star is now convened," an elderly woman said, her voice sharp and alert.

"Let us not waste time. Chevalier, please provide us with an update," said a man in his forties on a private jet. Its ceiling was a light corporate gray with a subtle pattern of eight-pointed stars.

"It is a setback, cousins. Our headquarters in Manhattan and Long Island estate were destroyed in one week. Elektra was demolished, as you know, and our agent is dead—"

"Are we exposed?" interrupted a man, about as old as the Chevalier. A few others nodded their mutual concern. The rules of the Order did not permit interruption, but these were exceptional times.

"No, cousin. As of now, we are not exposed," replied the Chevalier. "I am working to contain the problem. There is no link between us and our field agent, Winters. Ultimately, others shall be blamed, and we will remain anonymous, as always."

"Blowback could destroy the Order," spoke a woman in her fifties. "It's not 1351 anymore. News travels fast now." The Chevalier dismissed her swipe.

Another member spoke up. "As I said from the beginning, it was madness to stoke an arms race between the U.S. and Russia for profit's sake. Even with our substantial holdings in the cyber, aerospace, and defense sectors, such a scheme was hubris."

"Not so," countered the Chevalier. "Our predecessors did well in the 1930s, backing Franco and the Communists."

"But it midwifed World War II and the Holocaust," said the youngish woman.

"We did not create Hitler—" said the Chevalier.

"Nor did we stop him," she interrupted.

The Chevalier nodded acquiescence. "Not our finest hour, cousins. But let us not be hypocritical. We have always done well by war. The Order's vast wealth was not made in the cool forges of agriculture but in the furnace of conflict."

"Perhaps, but you risk too much," added a hoary voice. "For

670 years our families have worked together to achieve greatness, and now we gamble everything?"

"We are great *because* they gambled," said the Chevalier, pounding his fist on the medieval table. "We plan our enterprises cautiously and carry them out boldly. It has been our way since Chevalier Geoffroy, but we have grown flaccid in our success and decadence."

The Council erupted in raucous argument.

"Silence! Silence!" gaveled the elderly woman who convened the meeting. Everyone fell quiet.

"All is not lost, brothers and sisters. We still have this," said the Chevalier, pulling out the aluminum briefcase. "Inside is the fate of three American cities. Shall we proceed with a new plan?"

Heads nodded and knuckles rapped.

CHAPTER 58

President Hugh Anderson sat behind the Resolute Desk, his forehead resting in his hands as if he were praying. He was alone. The situation was far worse than most knew.

Lord, you know I've never been much of a churchgoer. But if you're listening, I could sure use some help, he prayed. He glanced around the empty Oval and saw oil paintings of dead presidents staring down at him. Judging him.

"Yeah, and what would you do?" he asked defiantly, but Washington, Jefferson, Jackson, Lincoln, and Teddy Roosevelt remained mute. "Didn't think so."

Anderson sighed and looked out the window at the Rose Garden. It was just shrubbery and the yellow grass of March. Dozens of pictures were displayed on the small credenza behind his chair, and he grabbed the one of the vice president, himself, and their wives deep-sea-fishing off Key West ten years ago. He had caught an eight-foot-long sailfish, and all four of them sat at the back of the boat, holding it on their laps for the camera with big grins. He could still smell the engine fumes, fish guts, and salt spray. *Happier times,* he thought with a smile, and his eyes glistened.

"I'm sorry, Henry and Martha. Please forgive me, wherever you are," he said, and a tear streamed down his face as he delicately put the picture back in its spot. *Good grief, I haven't cried in forty years,* he thought as he struggled to hold it in.

Henry and Martha were not supposed to die. *What was I*

supposed to do? he thought, choking back tears. *Don't blame your-self. Blame Brad Winters.*

"Winters," he whispered with loathing, prolonging the name like a curse. Somehow Winters had corrupted George, another old friend. He picked up a second picture, this one of Jackson and himself at a rodeo in Dallas while on the campaign trail. They were both holding plastic mugs of cheap beer and wearing cowboy hats. Ever the Boston Brahmin, Jackson looked uncomfortably out of place in a button-down oxford shirt and blue blazer amid cows.

"You old codger," he said. Anderson wanted to give his friend a pardon but knew he couldn't. Treason is treason, and his was high treason. "We all make our choices."

And I made mine, he thought. Forty-five years paddling around the DC swamp bestowed a sixth, seventh, and eighth sense for bullshit. He smelled the reek of feces from Jackson and Winters shortly after his inaugural address, two years ago. But how to rein them in? Both men were powerful and shrewd, and they could manipulate the system for their protection just as easily as he could order their arrest.

That was when he had turned to Apollo Outcomes. Sometimes you needed an outside-the-system solution to fix an inside-the-system problem. In this case, he needed someone to bring Jackson and Winters to heel—by any means necessary—while keeping his name out of it. Apollo did its job perfectly.

Thirty minutes earlier, Apollo had confirmed that all three nuclear weapons in the three cities were recovered and disarmed. Jackson was contained, Winters had disappeared, and the Wagner Group was destroyed, at least on American soil. None of it would make the news.

Only Winters's client remained a mystery, but Apollo was on their scent now. Soon they would be neutralized, one way or another. Unlike the CIA, Apollo could liquidate America's enemies where they hid. The company was not constrained by Executive Order 12333, which prohibited assassination. All it took was a phone call and a phrase—"Search and destroy"—and it would be done, off the books of course. National security without the red tape.

A knock on the door. "Mr. President? Are you ready, Mr. President? We're running late," came a woman's voice on the other side. It was his press secretary.

"Give me another minute, please," he replied, as he removed a handkerchief and dried his eyes. Then he straightened himself and checked his looks in a vanity mirror kept in the top drawer.

Focus. Insight. Hope, he thought. He closed his eyes and took three deep breaths. Holding in the last breath, he opened his eyes and gave a long exhale. Refreshed, he said, "Send them in."

The door swung open and journalists streamed in, crowding the Oval. People murmured in anticipation. Half an hour ago, the White House press office shocked the media world and announced the president would deliver a speech. In it, he would explain who was behind the VP's assassination, the terrorist attack on the bridge, and the battle on the Mall. All would be made clear. The press release simply said "new evidence had come to light" and the "responsible party will surprise you." Lastly, "these incidences prove the world is facing a new breed of threat."

The global news cycle went berserk.

All his life, the president wanted to deliver a speech that would change the destiny of the world. As a boy, he kept a copy of *100 Greatest Speeches in History* on his nightstand, and would pen overwrought monologues the way artists doodled on scraps of paper. Such is the legacy of every great statesman, from Pericles to Churchill, and *his* moment had finally arrived. But he was about to do something previously unthinkable: ad lib it. Not even an outline. Somehow it felt true.

Anderson beamed as everyone got situated, with the staccato of camera shutters punctuating the air. Under the desk and against his legs were a dozen blown-up photographs. Each photo was a secret shot of Winters meeting Jackson: deep in a garage, in a pew of an empty church, lunch at an elite members-only club, parked at the end of a runway, and other obscure venues. Each photo would make a dramatically timed appearance during his speech, and all were courtesy of Apollo Outcomes, which would go unnamed.

Once the reporters were packed in, the president opened his mouth and delivered his perfect Churchillian speech.

EPILOGUE

We lay together under the cabin roof, our minds and bodies contented. A warm ocean breeze gently blew chimes made of seashells, making a peaceful clacking sound. The surf sang us a lullaby. Our cabin sat on a rocky outcrop with its own deck and pool overlooking the aquamarine Pacific, with a petite stairway to the sand. The bungalow had no walls because it had no neighbors, other than sea turtles that occasionally dug nests in the beach below. Polynesia is where you go to escape the world.

"Are you awake, my darling?" cooed Jen, stirring slightly. We had been doing this for two weeks or more, and it had become our new lifestyle.

"Barely," I murmured, pressing her naked body into mine. She giggled.

"What do you want to do this afternoon?"

We had spent our days talking about life's mysteries, hiking the volcanic ridgeline, sparring on the beach, scuba diving the atoll, and playing in our bungalow. Of our list, we favored playing the most.

"I have an idea," I whispered, as she inhaled sharply and closed her eyes.

Before we left, Lava and Tye were heading for Austria. New mission, they said, inviting us along. But we demurred. In the course of one week, our individual lives exploded and then miraculously reassembled as one. We wanted to explore it together, away from the din of the world.

"No one deserves a break more than you," Lava had said, nodding. "I've asked our client to clear your names, so you can travel normally again. Your names have been purged from every government watchlist and Interpol database. Think of it as a parting thank-you."

"Wait, how's that possible? Who's your client?!" asked Jen, ever the FBI agent. But I knew better than to ask such things, and I also had a hunch.

"When you get bored—and you will—call me," said Lava. "We need quality people. Also . . ." He pulled out two slim phones slightly larger than a credit card. "If you ever need our help, give us a call."

"For anything," added Tye.

"We take care of our own," said Lava, putting his hands on our shoulders. We exchanged man hugs and departed.

That was more than two weeks ago.

Now, Jen crumpled on me, breathless. We were both sweaty.

Bzzzzzz. Bzzzzzz.

"What's that?" asked Jen, alarmed. We'd packed no electronics.

Bzzzzzz. Bzzzzzz.

I got up, trying to locate the source of the electronic noise.

Bzzzzzz. Bzzzzzz.

Jen reached into her backpack and started rummaging around.

"I think it's coming from here," I said, digging through my backpack.

"No, I'm pretty sure it's here," she said, holding up a travel purse.

I held up my passport pouch, also buzzing, and we exchanged quizzical glances. Opening them, we pulled out the slim phones Lava had given us. We had forgotten they were there.

"Hello?" "Hello?" we answered simultaneously, hearing each other as if we were on a conference call.

"Voice match indicates Tom Locke and Jennifer Lin," said a serious voice.

Jen paused, thinking about whether to respond. Not me.

"Affirmative," I said.

Jen shot me a glance saying: *What the heck are you doing?*

My expression read: *Hey, Lava gave us this phone. It's probably OK.* But she shook her head in dumbfounded amazement.

"This is a secure line," said the voice. "Lava, Tye, and their entire team went missing outside of Vienna twenty-six hours ago. We need help investigating what happened, and a possible rescue mission. We are critically low on available personnel right now. Are you available to assist? It's urgent."

Jen's face screamed: *Wait! Let's think this through like rational adults and arrive at consensual decision.*

"Absolutely! When can you extract us?" I blurted.

Jen glowered at me, her expression saying: *You are totally untrainable, Locke.*

"We already have a seaplane inbound to your location, ETA ninety minutes. It will take you to Fakarava airport, where a jet is on standby."

"Roger," I said, and the phone went dead.

"Tom Locke, don't make me punch you," said Jen, joking. I think.

"Look, honeysuckle, we're built for action and Lava needs our help. He'd do it for us," I added. "Besides, he was right. We'll soon get bored here, all this paradise. Yuck!" I teased. Jen punched me.

"Ow!" I said, although she didn't hit hard. Then she pounced.

"We only have ninety minutes," she said.